EIGHTH EDITION

EDUCATIONAL TESTING AND MEASUREMENT:
Classroom Application and Practice

TOM KUBISZYN
University of Houston

GARY BORICH
The University of Texas at Austin

JOHN WILEY & SONS, INC.

PUBLISHER	Jay O'Callaghan
EXECUTIVE EDITOR	Christopher Johnson
SENIOR PRODUCTION EDITOR	Valerie A. Vargas
MARKETING MANAGER	Jeffrey Rucker
SENIOR DESIGN ASSISTANT	Hope Miller
EDITORIAL ASSISTANT	Katie Melega
MEDIA EDITOR	Alexander Sasha Giacoppo
PRODUCTION SERVICES	Ingrao Associates, Inc.
COVER PHOTO	© PhotoDisc, Inc./Getty Images

This book was set in 10/12 Times Roman by Wiley/Australia and printed and bound by R.R. Donnelley. The cover was printed by Phoenix Color, Inc.

This book is printed on acid free paper. ∞

To order books or for customer service, please call 1-800-CALL WILEY (225-5945).

ISBN-13   978- 0-471-70005-0
ISBN-10   0-471-70005-3

Printed in the United States of America

10 9 8 7 6 5 4 3 2 1

PREFACE

Welcome to the eighth edition of *Educational Testing and Measurement: Classroom Application and Practice*, an up-to-date, practical, reader-friendly resource that will help you navigate today's evolving and complex world of educational testing, assessment, and measurement. When the last edition of this text was published we mentioned that the federal No Child Left Behind Act (NCLB) was passed in 2002. We stated that the many testing and assessment related features of the NCLB would likely have significant impact on education, and we were not mistaken.

With the passage of NCLB, the stakes associated with testing and assessment have never been higher; the focus on required annual academic assessments, related benchmark tests (see Chapter 1), and the monitoring of Adequate Yearly Progress (AYP) has never been more intense; and controversy and confusion about NCLB abounds. Performance of *all* students in schools on annual academic assessments is now under an increasingly powerful microscope at local, state, and national levels. For everyone to survive and thrive in this new accountability-driven environment, we believe that accurate, understandable, up-to-date, balanced, and relevant information must be made accessible to those on the NCLB/high-stakes testing front lines: classroom teachers and other educators.

Our primary goals for this revision are to (a) provide you with relevant information about the testing and assessment-related aspects of NCLB, (b) help you see how the educational measurement concepts and practices we present in the text apply to NCLB and other accountability requirements, and (c) seamlessly integrate this information throughout the text to help reduce confusion about this complex, far-reaching federal law. To ensure integrated treatment of the measurement implications of NCLB and state high-stakes testing requirements throughout the text, we revised several of the chapters. We also completed a number of updates and additions, which are not specific to NCLB, that were suggested by users of the text. To facilitate the transition to the eighth edition for previous users of the text (and to introduce the text to new users!) we will describe the changes to this edition later in this preface.

As with previous editions of *Educational Testing and Measurement,* we present complex test and measurement content in a reader-friendly, nonintimidating, and unique manner, and relate this content in meaningful ways to important developments in educational measurement and assessment. In this revision we keep our primary audience—classroom teachers—fully in mind. We strive to present often abstract and sometimes difficult concepts and procedures in an up-to-date and accurate, but accessible manner. Rather than overwhelm students with jargon and statistical theory, we use a friendly, conversational style to enhance our emphasis on the application of theory. At the same time, we provide sufficient theoretical background to ensure that students will understand the foundations of measurement and avoid an oversimplified approach to measurement. Thus, we expect that both new and long-time users of the text should feel comfortable with the text.

As though NCLB and state high-stakes testing complexities weren't enough to digest, the Individuals with Disabilities Improvement Act of 2004 (IDEA–04) was passed in November 2004. Although final federal regulations for IDEA–04 were not yet released when this text went to press, IDEA–04 appears to continue the trend that began with IDEA–97 toward emphasizing the education and assessment of children with disabilities within the regular curriculum and with regular assessment instruments. IDEA–04 includes an optional, very controversial change to the traditional method of determining Specific Learning Disabilities (SLD), the most common type of disability. This change, known as the response to intervention/instruction (RTI) model, can have substantial impact on the regular classroom teacher (see Chapter 20), if adopted. Because both IDEA–04 and NCLB require annual academic assessment for *all* students with disabilities, and because they are intertwined in complex ways, the implementation of these acts will prove challenging and controversial for years to come.

Given the intensity of the controversy that surrounds NCLB, high-stakes testing, and IDEA–04 it was tempting to take sides and advocate for one position or another in preparing this edition. However, we felt that this would be a disservice to you. Rather than take sides or advocate, our goal was to address NCLB, high-stakes testing, and IDEA–04 complexities and controversies in a thoughtful and balanced way to inform you about the issues, so that you can then decide the merits of these policies yourself.

THE ORGANIZATION OF THE TEXT

Past users of the text should have no difficulty recognizing and adapting to this revision. The chapter sequence remains the same as in the 7th edition, and the flexible organization of the text continues to enable instructors either to follow the chapter sequence as is or to modify it to meet their particular needs. In response to requests, two new appendices help students prepare for the Praxis II measurement section and provide a more accurate way to determine the median when there are multiple tied scores in the middle of a distribution. The other major changes to the eighth edition are described in more detail next.

Chapter 1 has a number of additions. We continue our emphasis on "tests as tools that can be used or misused," and expand our treatment of the potential effects on test usefulness and validity evidence when the same test is used for different purposes, or with individuals from diverse backgrounds. The increasingly important distinction between testing or assessment and the assessment *process* has also been expanded. New information is included about a variety of contemporary trends, including NCLB, state high-stakes testing programs, and the implications of IDEA–04 for regular education teachers. Chapter 1 also introduces a new initiative cosponsored by the Joint Committee on Testing Practices (JCTP), the National Council on Measurement in Education (NCME), and John Wiley and Sons that provides purchasers of this text with free access to an informative video entitled *The ABCs of School Testing* produced by JCTP and NCME, and a JCTP policy statement entitled *The Code of Fair Testing Practices in Education* on the Wiley website.

Chapter 2 begins by clarifying the similarities and differences between NCLB and state high-stakes testing programs. It also provides updated information regarding the history of high-stakes testing, describes both sides of the controversy surrounding NCLB and high-stakes testing, continues to consider the position taken by national measurement associations regarding the use of high-stakes tests, and provides future teachers with concrete recommendations they can use to prepare themselves and their students for high-stakes tests.

Chapters 3 and 4 are revised to clarify the linkage between classroom objectives and state academic standards, and to clarify the relationships between NCLB requirements and procedures and classroom-based assessment practice. Throughout Chapter 4 and in several later chapters we substituted "validity evidence" for "validity" when appropriate to ensure continuity with language included in the most recent edition of the *Standards for Educational and Psychological Tests* (AERA, APA, NCME, 1999). Chapters 5 through 11 remain largely the same as in the last edition, with only minor wording changes and additions. In response to reader requests for exercises that will help students prepare for the measurement section of the Praxis, we added a new appendix (Appendix B), entitled "Preparing for the Praxis II: Principles of Learning and Teaching Assessment." The appendix may be most appropriate to assign to students after they have completed Chapters 6 through 9, since it integrates information from those chapters. It introduces the Praxis series and then presents case studies followed by sample short answers and scoring criteria that familiarize students with how short answer items on the Praxis are scored. Finally, a sample of multiple-choice items similar to those included on the Praxis is provided.

To be consistent with the latest version of the *Publication Manual of the American Psychological Association* (APA, 2004) we replace the $\overline{X}$ symbol for arithmetic mean or average with M in Chapters 12 and 13. Reviewers also requested additional explanation and procedural guidance regarding the determination of the median when there are multiple tied scores in the middle of a score distribution. Part of this is provided in Chapter 12, and a second new appendix (Appendix C) includes additional information and a computational example. Chapter 14 is updated.

Chapter 15 is now entitled "Validity Evidence" to make it consistent with the approach to the establishment of validity evidence described in the latest edition of the *Standards for Educational and Psychological Tests* (AERA, APA, NCME, 1999). This chapter reinforces the importance of considering the potential limiting effects on test usefulness and validity evidence that can emerge when one test is used for multiple purposes or with diverse populations. Chapters 15, 16, and 17 are also updated to help ensure their integration with NCLB.

Chapter 18 includes information regarding the new IDEA–04 option to use a response to intervention/instruction (RTI) model instead of the traditional discrepancy model to determine special education eligibility under the Specific Learning Disability (SLD) category. Integration of various aspects of the chapter with NCLB, high-stakes testing, and other aspects of IDEA–04 is also new. Chapter 19 is updated to include the latest revisions of several standardized tests and now has updated information relevant to cognitive assessment research and theory.

Chapters 20 and 21 are significantly revised and updated to better inform regular education teachers about NCLB, state high-stakes testing programs, and IDEA–04 as they apply to all children, including children with disabilities. NCLB requires that *all* students participate in the annual academic assessments required of regular education students, but allows appropriate accommodations and alternate assessments for students with disabilities, if so designated in the student's Individual Educational Plan (IEP). Regardless, the performance of students with disabilities must also be reported annually, with *penalties applied to the whole school if students with disabilities fail to make Adequate Yearly Progress* (AYP) toward state academic proficiency standards. Chapter 20 also provides an update on the legislative requirements of IDEA–04 and provides expanded treatment of the new, very controversial, option that IDEA–04 makes available for Specific Learning Disability (SLD) identification. States and districts can now adopt this model, known as the response to intervention/instruction (RTI) model, as an alternative to the traditional aptitude–achievement discrepancy SLD eligibility model. Finally, Chapter 22 also reflects the impact of NCLB, state high-stakes testing programs, and IDEA–04 on educational testing and measurement.

Throughout the text we reference a variety of contemporary measurement trends, tying these to day-to-day decision making for the classroom teacher. We include updated references, suggested readings, list of supplemental statistics and measurement texts, and we cite recent articles, chapters, and books that reinforce and expand the changing face of educational measurement in today's classroom.

As with earlier editions, readers will find at the conclusion of each chapter a step-by-step summary in which all important concepts in the chapter are identified for review, and a section of practice items and discussion questions. The summaries are updated for most of the chapters, incorporating information relevant to NCLB, state high-stakes testing programs, and IDEA–04. The discussion questions and exercises should help students learn how to apply the concepts presented and, along with the newly revised *Instructor's Manual*, should help instructors identify organized activities and assignments that can be integrated into class presentations. Discussion questions and exercises marked with an asterisk have answers listed in Appendix F.

We have tried to select traditional and contemporary topics and provide examples that help the teacher, especially the beginning teacher, deal with practical, day-to-day issues related to the testing and assessment of students and measuring their behavior, in the context of NCLB, state high-stakes testing programs, and IDEA–04. The topics we have chosen, their natural sequences and linkage to the real-life tasks of teachers, the step-by-step summaries of major concepts, and our discussion questions and exercises all work, we believe, to make this text a valuable tool and an important resource for meeting the accountability requirements of today's educators.

ACKNOWLEDGMENTS

We express our appreciation to the following instructors for constructive comments regarding this text: W. Robert Houston, University of Houston, Alice Corkill, University of Nevada–Las Vegas; Robert Paugh, University of Central Florida; Priscilla J. Hambrick, City University of New York; and Pam Fernstrom, University of North Alabama. Thanks also to Bill Fisk, Clemson University; David E. Tanner, California State University at Fresno; Gregory J. Cizek, University of North Carolina–Chapel Hill; Thomas J. Sheeran, Niagara University; Jonathan A. Plucker, Indiana University; Aimin Wang, Miami University; William M. Bechtol, late of Southwest Texas State University; Deborah E. Bennett, Purdue University; Jason Millman, Cornell University; David Payne, University of Georgia; Glen Nicholson, University of Arizona; Carol Mardell-Czudnowski, Northern Illinois University; and James Collins, University of Wyoming, for constructive comments on earlier revisions. Also, thanks to Marty Tombari for contributions to Chapters 8 and 9 and other examples, illustrations, and test items in this volume, and to Ann Schulte for contributions to Chapter 17.

Tom Kubiszyn
Gary Borich

CONTENTS

AN INTRODUCTION TO CONTEMPORARY EDUCATIONAL TESTING AND MEASUREMENT

CHANCES ARE that some of your strongest childhood and adolescent memories include taking tests in school. More recently, you probably remember taking a great number of tests in college. If your experiences are like those of most who come through our educational system, you probably have very strong or mixed feelings about tests and testing. Indeed, some of you may swear that you will never test your students when you become teachers. If so, you may think that test results add little to the educational process and fail to reflect learning, or that testing may turn off students. Others may believe that tests are necessary and vital to the educational process. For you, they may represent irrefutable evidence that learning has occurred. Rather than viewing tests as deterrents that turn off students, you may see them as motivators that stimulate students to study and provide them with feedback about their achievement.

TESTS ARE ONLY TOOLS

Between those who feel positively about tests and those who feel negatively about them lies a third group. Within this group, which includes the authors, are those who see tests as tools that can contribute importantly to the process of evaluating pupils, curriculum, and teaching methods, but who question the status and power often given to tests and test scores. We are concerned that test users often uncritically accept test scores. This concerns us for four reasons. First, tests are only tools, and tools can be appropriately used, unintentionally misused, and intentionally abused. Second, tests, like other tools, can be well designed or poorly designed. Third, both poorly designed tools and well-designed tools in the hands of ill-trained or inexperienced users can be dangerous. Fourth, the usefulness of even well-designed tools can be affected by the purpose the test is used for and the population it is used with. In other words there is no "one size fits all" test that is appropriate for every purpose and every person.

The four concerns we mentioned above motivated us to write this text. By helping you learn to design and to use tests and test results appropriately we hope you will be less likely to misuse tests and their results, be better able to recognize and avoid using poorly designed tests, and be always mindful of how the purpose of testing and the population to be tested can affect a test's usefulness. This last point will be discussed in more detail next.

TESTS ARE NOT INFALLIBLE: USEFULNESS CAN VARY ACROSS PURPOSES AND PERSONS

Test misuse and abuse can occur when users of test results are unaware of the factors that can influence the usefulness of test scores. The most important factor that influences a test's usefulness is a test's technical adequacy. The technical adequacy of a test includes several factors. Two that are of primary importance are the evidence of its validity (see Chapter 15) and its score reliability (see Chapter 16), for its intended use(s), and for the persons it is used with, because the evidence for a test's validity and score reliability can change when the test is used for different purposes or when it is used with different populations of people (see Chapter 18).

As we said before, there is no test that is a "one size fits all" test. Thus it is inappropriate to speak of the "validity of a test" or the "reliability of a test," as though validity and reliability are permanent, unchanging characteristics of the test. Nevertheless, we seem to do that all the time! Instead, it is most appropriate to speak of the evidence of a test's validity and score reliability for a particular use and with a particular population. The need to clarify a test's intended use and the intended population when discussing the test's usefulness emerged from deliberations among measurement experts from the American Educational Research Association (AERA), the American Psychological Association (APA), and the National Council on Measurement in Education (NCME) over several years when they developed the latest edition of *Standards for Educational and Psychological Testing* (AERA, APA, and NCME, 1999). The Standards are widely regarded as one of the most authoritative and influential guidelines in the testing, measurement, and assessment arena. Beginning with the last edition of this text we attempted to conform what we said in our text to the latest edition of the Standards, but we digress .... Let's consider a couple of examples that should help you understand why it is so important to consider a test's validity and reliability evidence within the context of a test's intended use and the intended population.

Different Purposes: Effects on Test Usefulness

Tests are commonly used for more than one purpose, like other tools are. For example, a screwdriver is intended to be used to drive screws. Nonetheless, who hasn't used a screwdriver as an ice pick, a lever or pry bar, a chisel, a paint mixing stick, to poke an older sibling in the eye, or for some other purpose? Did it work? Probably. Did it work as well as an ice pick, a lever or pry bar, a chisel, or a sharp stick would have? Probably not. In short, the screwdriver's usefulness (i.e., its validity, if you will) depends on the purpose you are using it for.

Similarly, a test's usefulness (i.e., the evidence of its validity and reliability) can vary, depending on the purpose of testing. For example, the evidence for a test's validity and score reliability may be strong when it is used to predict a potential employee's ability to quickly and accurately recognize typographical errors in a book manuscript. This would make the test quite useful when used for this purpose. On the other hand, the validity and the reliability evidence for the same test may be substantially lower if the test is used to predict a person's ability to actually write a book. In this case, the test's usefulness is more limited. This does not mean it is useless for this purpose, but there are probably better tools . . . oops, we mean tests, that would be more useful.

So, a test's usefulness, or validity, can be high for one purpose and low for another. Let's be careful here though. This does not mean that a test should never be used for multiple purposes, or for a purpose for which the test is less useful than for some other purpose. Instead, always try to select the test that is most useful for the purpose of testing, and be especially thoughtful and careful in interpreting test results that are less useful, or less valid, than they would be if the test were used for a different purpose.

Different Populations: Effects on Test Usefulness

The evidence of a test's validity and reliability can also vary depending on the characteristics of the people the test is used with. Similarly, the usefulness of other tools can also vary, depending on the characteristics of the people that use the tools. An electric drill (the corded type, not the battery-powered ones that always seem to need recharging) can be very useful in the hands of an experienced electrician who needs to carefully drill holes in a wall while avoiding electrical and water lines behind the wall. The same drill may be far less useful, and even dangerous, in the hands of a child or in the hands of an adult who acts like a child. Could a child use the drill to drill holes in the wall? Probably. Could the child avoid all the electrical and water lines behind the wall? And could the child avoid drilling a hole in his hands, or electrocuting himself? We can only hope! In short, the electric drill's usefulness varies depending on the characteristics (e.g., experiences) of the person using it.

Tests are no different. For example, let's consider a multiple-choice test used to assess achievement in a 10th grade American History class. The class is composed largely of two groups: native English-speaking American children who have taken many multiple-choice tests and recent immigrants from Nicaragua who speak little English and have had little formal schooling. Excellent evidence may exist for the test's reliability and validity when it is used to assess achievement for the American students. However, evidence for the same test's validity may be less impressive (or even nonexistent!) when used to assess achievement for the limited English proficient (LEP), recently emigrated males from Nicaragua. In this case, linguistic (lack of familiarity with the English language) and cultural (lack of experience with multiple-choice tests in Nicaragua) factors may seriously limit the usefulness of the test. Again, this does not necessarily mean the test should not be used at all with this population. It does mean we should always be thoughtful and try to select the test that is most useful for the population we are testing—if there is one available and to be very careful in interpreting results.

You may be wondering why we said that limited evidence of validity for a particular purpose or population did not necessarily mean we should not use a test. This is a matter of practicality. We simply lack tests that have strong evidence for their validity and usefulness with all populations and for all purposes for which tests are used. For example, almost 200 different languages are spoken by schoolchildren in the Houston, Texas, metropolitan area, with a similarly wide range of cultural backgrounds. Because the linguistic and cultural backgrounds of the students in the Houston area are so diverse, it follows that there will be variation in the validity evidence of the limited number of tests that are used to evaluate children.

What to do? Depending on whom you ask you will get a variety of suggestions. Here are ours. When evidence of a test's validity and reliability is limited for the population being tested, test results should be interpreted very cautiously. And, in such situations, the results of a single test should never be used independently to make important decisions. Instead, we recommend that important decisions should be based on a thoughtful, multifaceted assessment, rather than a single test.

That said, with the rapid spread of the high-stakes testing movement (which we will discus in detail in Chapter 2) a disturbing number of promotion, graduation, and other high-stakes educational decisions are being made based entirely, or primarily, on test scores. Instead of relying on such a limited "snapshot" of student achievement for important decision making, we recommend that test results should be considered to be part of a broader "movie" or process called assessment. It should be the findings of the broad assessment process, not just test results, that should be the basis for important educational decision making. We will describe this process in the next section and distinguish between testing and assessment. See the sidebar about the Waco, Texas, public schools for an example of the controversial use of test results alone to make important educational decisions (Box 1-1).

TESTING: ONLY A PART OF THE ASSESSMENT PROCESS

Unfortunately, the situation described in the sidebar is not unusual. Well-intended educators continue to rely solely or primarily on test results to make important educational decisions. At times, they may have little choice because federal, state, or district one size fits all mandates or policies dictate that their decisions must be based on scores from a specific, "approved" test, without regard for the extent to which the validity and reliability of the scores may vary for different populations of students.

Educators, and others, may unintentionally misuse test results because they have come to regard test results as the end point rather than an early or midpoint in the much broader process of assessment. Or they may mistakenly believe that testing and assessment are synonymous, because today the terms are often used interchangeably. Indeed, some seem to have eliminated the word "test" from their vocabularies and replaced it with the term "assessment" because they believe that use of the word assessment is less evaluative, threatening, or negative than use of the word "testing". For purposes of this text, however, it is critical that you understand that there is a clear difference between a test or an assessment, which typically occurs on a specific day, and an assessment *process*, which may span an entire semester or even the entire school year.

BOX *1-1*

WACO, TEXAS, SCHOOLS USE STANDARDIZED TEST SCORES ALONE TO MAKE PROMOTIONS DECISIONS

Concerned with possible negative effects of social promotion, the Waco, Texas, public schools decided to utilize standardized test scores as the basis for promotion decisions beginning with first graders in 1998. As a result, the number of students retained increased from 2% in 1997 to 20% in 1998 (*Austin American-Statesman*, June 12, 1998). The Waco schools are not alone in curtailing social promotion. The Chicago public schools, in the midst of a wide-ranging series of educational reform initiatives, retained 22,000 students in 1994, with 175,000 retained in 1998 (*Newsweek*, June 22, 1998). Social promotion is a practice that purports to protect student self-esteem by promoting students to the next grade so that they may stay with their classmates even when students are not academically ready for promotion.

Educational, psychological, political, fiscal, cultural, and other controversies are all associated with social promotion. What has come to be known by some as the "Waco Experiment" also raised a number of measurement-related issues.

While the Waco schools' decision was doubtless well intended, their policy may have overlooked the fact that the utility of test scores varies with age, with test results for young children being less stable and more prone to error than those for older children. A relatively poor score on a test may disappear in a few days, weeks, or months after additional development has occurred, irrespective of achievement. In addition, older children are less susceptible to distractions and, with years of test-taking experience under their belts, are less likely to be confused by the tests or have difficulty completing tests properly. All these factors can negatively affect a student's score and result in a score that under-represents the student's true level of knowledge.

Furthermore, a single standardized test score provides only a portion of a child's achievement over the school year, regardless of the grade level. As we will see when we consider the interpretation of standardized test results in Chapter 18, there are a number of student-related factors (e.g., illness, emotional upset) and administrative factors (e.g., allowing too little time, failing to read instructions verbatim) that can negatively affect a student's performance on the day the test was taken. Thus, making a decision that so substantially affects a child's education based on a single measure obtained on a single day rather than relying on a compilation of measures (tests, ratings, observations, grades on assessments and portfolios, homework, etc.) obtained over the course of the school year seems ill-advised.

On the other hand, using data collected on a single day and from a single test to make what otherwise would be complex, time-consuming, and difficult decisions has obvious attraction. It appears to be expedient, accurate, and cost-effective, and appears to be addressing concerns about the social promotion issue. However, it also may be simplistic and short-sighted if no plan exists to remediate those who are retained. As noted in a June 12, 1998, editorial in the *Austin American-Statesman*, "Failing students who don't meet a minimum average score, without a good plan to help them improve, is the fast track to calamity." Nevertheless, this trend has not diminished since we first reported on it in our sixth edition. Indeed, the use of test scores to make high-stakes promotion decisions has increased across the nation. We will explore this phenomenon in depth in Chapter 2.

We define the assessment process as a comprehensive evaluation made up of many components. A comprehensive assessment process will include test results but also may include results from a variety of other measurement procedures (e.g., performance and portfolio assessments, observations, checklists, rating scales—all covered later in the text), as appropriate. All these findings are then integrated with relevant background and contextual information (e.g., reading level, language proficiency, cultural considerations—also covered later in the text), to help ensure that educational decisions are appropriate. So, you can see that from our perspective testing is one part of the process of assessment, but that the assessment process encompasses much more than just testing. Figure 1.1 further clarifies the distinction between testing and the assessment process.

Throughout the text we will refer to testing or assessment, and the assessment process. To avoid confusion later, be sure to understand the distinction we make between testing or assessment and the assessment process, as illustrated in Fig. 1.1. Let's review where we have been. We have covered some of the basics. Now we know that testing is only part of an assessment, tests are only tools that can be well or poorly designed, even well-designed tests can be misused, the usefulness of tests or assessments varies depending on persons and purposes, and, as a result, best practice dictates that important educational decisions should not be made based only on test results. That's the ideal world. Let's see what the reality is like for educational testing. To understand current testing practice it will be helpful to briefly trace testing history since the 1960s.

RECENT HISTORY OF EDUCATIONAL MEASUREMENT

Beginning in the late 1960s, a fairly strong antitest sentiment began to develop in our country. Over the next two decades many scholarly papers and popular articles questioned or denounced testing, and even the assignment of grades in school, for a variety of reasons. Some decried tests as weapons willfully used to suppress minorities. To others, tests represented simplistic attempts to measure complex traits or attributes. Still others questioned whether the traits or attributes tested could or should be measured, or whether these traits or attributes even existed! From the classroom to the Supreme Court, testing and measurement practice came under close scrutiny. It seemed to some that tests were largely responsible for many of our society's ills.

Initially it looked as though the antitest movement might succeed in abolishing testing in education—and there was professional and lay support for such a move. Today, it appears that this movement was part of a swinging pendulum. Calls for the abolition of

---

Testing

1. Tests (or assessments) are developed or selected (if standardized, see Chapter 18), administered to the class, and scored.
2. Test results are then used to make decisions about a pupil (assign a grade, recommend for an advanced program), instruction (repeat, review, move on), curriculum (replace, revise), or other educational factors.

An Assessment Process

1. Information is collected from tests and *other measurement instruments* (portfolios and performance assessments, rating scales, checklists, and observations).
2. This information is critically evaluated and integrated with relevant background and contextual information.
3. The integration of critically analyzed test results and other information results in a decision about a pupil (assign a grade, recommend for an advanced program), instruction (repeat, review, move on), curriculum (replace, revise), or other educational factors.

FIGURE 1.1 The distinction between testing and assessment, and the assessment process.

testing and grading gradually subsided, and by the late 1980s more tests than ever were being administered.

In large part, this shift toward more and more testing was driven by the release of the report *A Nation at Risk* by the National Commission on Excellence in Education in 1983. This report documented shortcomings of the U.S. public education system and led to increased calls for education reform and accountability. Tests and assessments have been the cornerstones of the accountability aspects of the education reform movement that has been increasingly prominent in education for the last 20 years. Today, all 50 states and the District of Columbia have some sort of test and assessment–based accountability program in place. Test and assessment–based accountability became a national priority and requirement with the passage of the No Child Left Behind Act (NCLB) in 2002, landmark legislation intended to raise overall achievement, but especially for economically disadvantaged youth. To be eligible for federal education dollars states must now adhere to the many accountability requirements of NCLB. The test and assessment–related requirements of this complex and controversial law will be described later in this chapter.

Although there are still voices calling for the abolition of testing, they have been over-shadowed by the test and assessment–based accountability juggernaut and its primary or entire reliance on test scores to make important educational decisions that affect students, educators, property owners, policy makers, and the general public. When tests are used to make such important decisions they are called "high-stakes" tests. The high-stakes testing movement, which has also been controversial, will be discussed in detail in Chapter 2.

Measurement experts applaud efforts to raise student achievement, especially for the economically disadvantaged. However, measurement experts continue to emphasize that all test scores are at best estimates that are subject to greater or lesser margins of error, and thus test scores should never be the sole basis for high-stakes decision–making. In short, much like we described in the previous section, measurement experts advocate that important educational decisions should only be made based on the integrated findings from a process of assessment that includes test scores, rather than from test scores alone. This position has also been taken in policy documents issued by major national professional associations with interest and expertise in educational testing and assessment, such as the American Educational Research Association (AERA), the American Psychological Association (APA), and the National Council on Measurement in Education (NCME). We will discuss in more detail the positions taken by the AERA, APA, and NCME in Chapter 2.

So what has happened to the critics of testing over the last 20 years? Have they just disappeared? No, but most have come to realize that abolishing testing will not be a panacea for the problems of education and contemporary society. Even the most outspoken critics of testing would have to agree that in our everyday world decisions must be made. If tests were eliminated, these decisions would still be made but would be based on nontest data that might be subjective, opinionated, and biased. For example, you may have dreaded taking the Scholastic Assessment Test (SAT) during your junior or senior year in high school. You may have had some preconceived, stereotyped notions about the test. However, the SAT had no preconceived, stereotyped, or prejudiced notions about you! Advocates and many critics of testing would now agree that it is not appropriately developed and used tests that are biased, but rather the people who misuse or abuse them.

While education reform and the high-stakes testing movement has swept the nation, there has been a related shift from the historical emphasis on multiple-choice, true–false, and matching item formats for tests to the use of more flexible measurement formats. More and more calls are being heard and heeded for tests and procedures that assess higher level thought processes than are typically measured by such item formats. Essay tests, knowledge organization assessments, portfolios, and various performance tests (all discussed in detail in Chapters 7, 8, and 9) are increasingly being utilized in addition to traditional multiple-choice tests (discussed in detail in Chapter 6) in contemporary educational measurement efforts. Advocates refer to performance and portfolio assessments as authentic assessments, a term which suggests that these measures may be more accurate and valid than traditional tests.

Advocates argue that authentic assessments represent the most objective, valid, and reliable information that can be gathered about individuals. However, the performance and portfolio measures do have their disadvantages as well. They are costly and time-consuming to administer and score, and are hampered by questions about the evidence for their validity and score reliability. Finally, by calling these measures assessments, advocates often attempt to distance these techniques from traditional tests, confusing these measures with the assessment process we described earlier. Be sure to keep in mind that when you hear someone talk about assessment, they may be talking about a specific test or measurement instrument, or they may be talking about the process of assessment we described earlier. Sorry for the confusion, but we didn't start it!

Next, we will describe recent federal and state accountability requirements and several recent developments have also generated much confusion and controversy. Taken together, the developments we are about to describe have led us to conclude that today it is more vital than ever for all educators to obtain a firm grounding in educational testing and assessment practice. For the foreseeable future, use of testing and assessment in education will at least remain at today's elevated levels, and may even increase. Competency in educational testing and assessment practice will enable informed educators (like you will become!) to recognize and engage in "best practices" in the measurement area. Best practice includes not only avoiding test misuse yourself, but also recognizing and calling attention to test misuse when it is evident from others, whether intentional or not.

CURRENT DEVELOPMENTS AND TRENDS

Next, we will describe briefly several recent, interrelated developments and trends that have led us to conclude that today's classroom teachers will be required to engage in more testing and assessment than ever before. And, because the decisions that will be made based on tests and assessments may be of greater importance than has been the case in the past, we believe that a firm grounding for teachers in testing and assessment is not only important, it is vital!

The No Child Left Behind Act (NCLB)

President George W. Bush signed into law the reauthorization of the Elementary and Secondary Education Act (ESEA) in January 2002. The reauthorization renamed ESEA to become the No Child Left Behind Act (NCLB). Since then the act has come to be referred to commonly as "Nickel-B," after the act's acronym, NCLB.

According to the U.S. Department of Education, which is charged with implementing the law, the intent of the law is to "improve educational opportunities for every American child—regardless of ethnicity, income, or background." The law specifically intends to raise the academic achievement of traditionally low performing, economically disadvantaged students. To accomplish its objectives, the law was built on what the Department calls "four common-sense pillars":

- Accountability for results;
- An emphasis on doing what works based on scientific research;
- Expanded parental options; and
- Expanded local control and flexibility.

Although it is difficult to object to the intent of the law or the four pillars, NCLB has gathered many detractors and many advocates. As you might imagine (or have already heard!) implementation of the law has been controversial. Comprehensive coverage of this important law is beyond the scope of this text. Instead we will address briefly the aspects of the law that have an impact on testing and assessment and touch on some of the controversy.

NCLB is a wide-ranging act, with several important federal education programs included within it. These include Education for the Disadvantaged, Reading First/Early Reading First, 21st Century Community Learning Centers, Safe and Drug-free Schools, Bilingual and Migrant Education, Education Technology, Teacher Quality, Rural Education, and Impact Aid. While none of these program titles is specific to assessment, federal funding for these programs is closely linked to state, district, and school compliance with at least four of several key features of NCLB. These key features are

- Standards and Annual Assessments
- Accountability/Proficiency
- Adequate Yearly Progress (AYP), and
- Disaggregated Data/Reporting

Although these features are intertwined with one another, we will briefly discuss each in turn to provide you with an idea of how they will affect educational testing and assessment, pupils, teachers, and schools in coming years. Then we will briefly describe some of the controversy that surrounds NCLB.

Standards and Annual Assessments   Annual academic assessment for accountability purposes (i.e., high-stakes testing), which will be discussed in detail in Chapter 2, is a fundamental requirement of NCLB. In general, the new law requires that all annual assessments under NCLB be

Tied to state standards,

Applicable to all students (including students with disabilities), and

Technically reliable.

Furthermore, NCLB requires that all students in all schools must be assessed, regardless of race, ethnicity, gender, disability, English proficiency, or economic status. Previously, assessment was mandatory only for those schools that received Title I federal funding (intended for impoverished and struggling students), and students with disabilities could be excluded from annual district-wide assessments. Several chapters in this text discuss the thorny issues that complicate efforts to validly include students with language and cultural differences (Chapters 4 and 18) and disabilities (Chapters 20 and 21) in annual district-wide assessments.

NCLB reaffirmed previous ESEA requirements of reading and math tests at least once in each of three grade spans (grades 3–5, 6–9, and 10–12). However, it also stipulated that by the 2005–2006 school year, annual testing in at least math and reading will be required for all students in grades 3–8, and at least once in grades 10–12. Starting in 2007–2008 annual science assessment at least once in elementary, middle and high school will also be required. In addition, a sample of fourth and eighth graders in each state must also participate in the National Assessment of Educational Progress (NAEP) program in reading and math every other year.

Accountability/Proficiency The Accountability/Proficiency feature of NCLB is linked to the concept of Adequate Yearly Progress, or AYP (to be discussed in the next section), and requires all 50 states and the District of Columbia to submit accountability plans clarifying state standards and the methods that will be used to assess them to the U.S. Department of Education for Department approval. In June 2003 President George W. Bush announced that all state and District plans were approved by the Department. However, various reports indicate that only some of these accountability plans received full approval, whereas others received merely tentative approval (Laitsch, 2003; Goldstein, 2004). NCLB also requires states to set ever increasing annual proficiency goals (e.g., passing scores), with the requirement that 100% of students who take the test must achieve the state's standard of proficiency by the 2013–2014 school year.

Adequate Yearly Progress (AYP) Adequate yearly progress, or AYP, is a new requirement under NCLB. It requires that sufficient yearly progress must be made overall for the school and for economically disadvantaged students, students from major racial and ethnic minority groups, students with disabilities, and limited English proficient students enrolled in a school since the beginning of a school year. Schools will also be monitored to see whether at least 95% of their enrolled students participate in annual assessments and whether high school graduation rates are improving as part of AYP.

Schools must also report AYP for each of the groups described above. If any group within a school fails to make "AYP" the entire school fails to make AYP. After two years of failing to make AYP schools are subject to a variety of sanctions, including a requirement that the school provide supplemental services (e.g., tutoring) to students in need (at school expense), enabling students to transfer to other schools (i.e., school choice), and the development of a school improvement plan. After four years of failing to make AYP, the school district must take corrective action, and after five years of failure to make AYP the school may be restructured (see Chapter 2).

By the 2013–1014 school year 100% of students enrolled in a school at the beginning of a school year must meet state proficiency standards in reading, math, and science.

Between now and 2013 states must set increasingly higher proficiency standards, initially after two years and then at least every third year.

Disaggregated Data/Reporting Under NCLB schools will have to issue annual "report cards" that describe student achievement, the percentage of students participating in annual assessments, changes in achievement from previous years, and graduation rates. In these reports, data must be disaggregated. This means that results must be reported for the overall school but also broken down, or disaggregated, for economically disadvantaged students, students from major racial and ethnic minority groups, students with disabilities, and limited English proficient students.

What is the controversy about? Even though NCLB has not been fully implemented or funded, it has been extremely controversial. Space limitations preclude an effective examination of the complex positions detractors and advocates have taken regarding the multifaceted law. However, most of the objection and resistance to NCLB has come from within the education community, including state education agencies. For example, the Texas Education Agency recently found its federal funds allotment reduced by 4% (about $444,000) for failing to comply with NCLB requirements (Hoff, 2005). Public support outside education is fairly strong (News from the Committee on Education and the Workforce, 2004), although there are signs this may be changing somewhat (Robelen, 2004a). The news media may also be fanning the flames since NCLB has apparently captured the interest of the general public, and controversy sells (Robelen, 2004b). As schools come under sanctions for failing to make AYP in future years the controversy may even intensify, so stay tuned!

The Rapid Spread of State High-Stakes Testing Mandates

In addition to the federal accountability requirements of NCLB, there now exist in all 50 states and the District of Columbia a wide variety of state regulations that require the use of test results entirely, or primarily, to make annual "high-stakes" decisions about students (e.g., promotion, graduation), school personnel (e.g., pay increases and continued employment), and even control of schools (e.g., state takeover of low performing schools). State high-stakes testing initiatives predate the passage of NCLB. As we mentioned in the last edition of this text, high-stakes testing grew out of the standards-based reform movement (see Chapter 2) and expanded rapidly during the 1990s and the first part of the 21st century. Spirited and vocal protests and complaints from teachers and other educators, attorneys and other advocates, and some parents and students failed to slow the spread of high-stakes testing.

We will discuss the issues and controversies attendant to high-stakes testing more fully in Chapter 2. In case you were wondering whether the required NCLB annual assessment and the state high-stakes test overlap, the answer is that they often do. Under NCLB states can determine the test they use for the NCLB annual assessment, so the states often "kill two birds with one stone," using the state high-stakes test as the NCLB annual assessment. In any case, teachers can expect continued or increased expectations to frequently monitor and assess their pupils to determine whether their students are prepared to do well on high-stakes tests.

2004 Reauthorization of the Individuals with Disabilities Education Improvement Act (IDEIA–04)

The *Individuals with Disabilities Education Improvement Act* reauthorization (IDEIA–04), passed in November 2004, appears to continue the special education reforms initiated by the previous version of this law, IDEA–97. The reason we say it "appears to" is because at the time of publication of this text final federal regulations issued by the U.S. Department of Education were not available. Because these regulations may change the meaning or implications of ambiguous or vague legislative language, we will limit our comments here to the test and assessment–related language of the law that is not likely to be altered significantly by the regulations when they are released.

The intent of Congress in passing IDEIA–04 was to reaffirm that children with disabilities are entitled to a free and appropriate public education (FAPE) and to ensure that special education students have access to all the potential benefits that regular education students have from the general curriculum and education reform, including the reforms initiated by NCLB in 2002. As we described in the sixth and seventh editions of this text, IDEA–97 raised expectations for students with disabilities by requiring schools to meaningfully include students with disabilities in the regular classroom, curriculum, and assessment. IDEIA–04 requires that the instruction of students with disabilities follows the general education curriculum and takes place in the regular classroom, except for the most severe cases. In addition, IDEIA–04 requires that students with disabilities should be assessed with the same measures used to assess regular education students, with extreme cases to be assessed with appropriate accommodations or alternate assessments.

Under IDEIA–04 regular education teachers are required to be members of the Individual Educational Plan (IEP) teams for each child with a disability. The IEP teams must determine how the performance and progress of special learners in the general curriculum will be assessed, and must collect the data necessary to make such determinations, including behavioral data when the behavior of a child with a disability impedes progress in the general curriculum. It is the IEP team that also decides whether a student with a disability will be evaluated using the standard annual state-wide assessment, whether the assessment will be administered with accommodations, or whether a state-approved alternate assessment should be used.

The implications of IDEIA–04 for the testing and assessment skills of teachers will be discussed more thoroughly in Chapters 20 and 21, including a controversial change in the way students with specific learning disabilities (SLD) may be identified. For now, suffice it to say that full implementation of the law will require more, rather than less, testing and assessment involvement from regular education teachers. Testing of children with disabilities within the regular classroom by the classroom teacher will be required to help determine whether a student is in need of special education, to adhere to each student's IEP, to evaluate the progress of each child with a disability toward the annual objectives established in the IEP, to help determine whether behavior is impeding progress in the general curriculum, and to meet the accountability requirements of IDEIA–04, and NCLB. This may seem to place an additional burden on regular classroom teachers, and it does. In Chapters 20 and 21 we will explain how the testing and assessment skills you will develop in this course, coupled with the use of existing standardized tests, checklists, and rating scales, can enable you to meet these new requirements with a minimum of additional effort.

The Need to Identify Pupils at-Risk for Low Performance on Accountability Measures

In addition to preparing students for the annual NCLB assessment or state high-stakes test, teachers today must also prepare all their students for one or more state, district, or school-wide benchmark tests. Benchmark tests are used to identify students at risk for failure on the annual assessment. Benchmark tests are usually developed by the states, may be administered one or more times per year on a school-wide or grade-wide basis, and are designed to resemble the state's annual high-stakes test. Results of benchmark tests are generally not made public, but they can be disaggregated for the school or district, to help identify low performing students, or groups of students, who may be at risk of later failure on the annual high-stakes test. Want to guess who has to administer the benchmark tests? (Hint: It's not the principal or counselor!)

To identify students who may be at risk to be low performers on the benchmark tests and the annual high-stakes test, teachers may increasingly be encouraged to use standardized (see Chapter 18) and formal teacher-made measures. In addition to traditional paper and pencil tests (see Chapters 6, 7, and 10), teacher-made measures may include performance and portfolio assessments, observations, checklists, and rating scales (see Chapters 8, 9, and 21) to assess academic progress and support day-to-day instructional decisions. The same applies to students with disabilities who must, whenever possible, be evaluated with the same annual assessments used for regular education students. Instead of simply waiting for high-stakes test results and risking federal and state penalties in April, schools now may encourage more frequent measurement of achievement throughout the year to identify students or groups of students—including students with disabilities—in need of additional, specialized instruction.

The Lake Wobegon Effect and High-Stakes Testing

In author Garrison Keillor's (1985) fictional town at Lake Wobegon, all students score above the national average. How can this happen? At first, it seems a statistical impossibility. If the average is the sum of all the test scores divided by the number of students who took the test, then about half must score below average. Right? Right! Well, then, what is the explanation? We could simply remind you that the novel is fiction and let it go at that, but by now you know we would not do that. Here goes.

First, a standardized norm-referenced test uses a norms table to determine score rankings. The table is compiled from the scores of students who took the test earlier when the test was being developed or revised. In reality, none of the scores of the students who take a standardized test after it is distributed will affect the norms table. In theory, it is possible for all students who take a test to score above average, or even above the 90th percentile. Indeed, as teachers and district administrators become more familiar with a particular test it becomes increasingly enticing to "teach to the test," a practice that should be condemned but too frequently is condoned either directly or indirectly. This is most likely to occur when standardized test scores become the only basis for high-stakes decisions involving promotion; graduation; financial incentives for schools, administrators, and teachers; teacher evaluations; allocation of tax dollars; local real estate development; or when political rather than pedagogical considerations are allowed to become of paramount concern. The important point is that scoring above the average on a standardized test may not necessarily mean a student is doing well. It may mean the teacher has been teaching to the test rather than teaching the critical thinking, independent judgment, and decision-making skills that are more closely related to performance in the real world. This is one of the reasons why the performance and portfolio assessment trends we describe in Chapters 8 and 9 have become as popular as they have.

Will We See a National Test?

Where is all this interest in statewide high-stakes testing headed? Calls for the creation of a single, national set of tests for the various academic subjects came from former Republican President George H. W. Bush in 1991 and former Democratic President William J. Clinton in 1996. NCLB, signed into law by Republican President George W. Bush in 2002, requires annual academic assessments but stopped short of calling for a national test. Instead, states are free to decide on the type of annual test or assessment to administer, rather than being compelled under NCLB to use a single, national test. Because each state can use its own test under NCLB there is no way to compare "apples to apples" across the states, which interferes with the accountability intention of the NCLB. So why did the second President Bush, and Congress, not require all states to use a common, national test?

Perhaps it is because the concept of a uniform national test that would be required of all students in all states has proved to be a political hot potato. Advocates emphasize the need for a single test to uniformly evaluate education reform initiatives and to facilitate accountability among states, districts, and schools. Detractors argue that a national test is the first step toward a federal "takeover" of local and state-determined educational curricula, or that the results of such a national test will be used to reinforce biases against low performing students, schools, and states. In spite of the fact that both Republican and Democratic presidents and others have argued for national tests, the issue remains a highly emotional and politicized one that may prove difficult to resolve.

Currently, the closest thing we have to a single, national test or assessment is the National Assessment of Educational Progress (NAEP). The NAEP is an independent and comprehensive assessment system used to evaluate progress toward the six National Education Goals established by the first President Bush and the nation's governors in 1989. The National Education Goals were renamed "Goals 2000" when the Educate America Act was passed in 1994, and they are listed in the sidebar (Box 1-2).

The NAEP is administered by the National Education Goals Panel, an independent bipartisan panel charged with reporting annually on progress toward the National Education Goals. While the NAEP potentially enables "apples to apples" comparisons across students, schools, districts, and states, this potential has yet to be realized because it is not uniformly accepted or administered across states and localities. In contrast, there now exist a wide variety of state-required tests and dozens of standardized tests in various subjects that states and districts are free to choose from in order to evaluate their educational programs. If you were a district administrator, would you choose a test that might make your district look bad, one that would make it look good, or one that accurately reflects student achievement, regardless of how the district looks? If you make the last choice, are you prepared to find a job elsewhere next year if your district doesn't look good?

BOX *1-2*

THE NATIONAL EDUCATION GOALS (GOALS 2000)

1. By the year 2000, all children in America will start school ready to learn.
2. By the year 2000, the high school graduation rate will increase to at least 90%.
3. By the year 2000, American students will leave grades four, eight, and twelve having demonstrated competency in challenging subject matter, including English, mathematics, science, history, and geography; and every school in America will ensure that all students learn to use their minds well, so they may be prepared for responsible citizenship, further learning, and productive employment in our modern economy.
4. By the year 2000, U.S. students will be first in the world in science and mathematics achievement.

5. By the year 2000, every adult American will be literate and will possess the knowledge and skills necessary to compete in a global economy and exercise the rights and responsibilities of citizenship.
6. By the year 2000, every school in America will be free of drugs and violence and will offer a disciplined environment conducive to learning.

For more information contact:

National Education Goals Panel
1850 M Street NW, Suite 270
Washington, DC 20036
Or visit the website at
http://govinfo.library.unt.Edu/neap/

Performance and Portfolio Assessment

Performance and portfolio assessment, sometimes referred to as authentic assessment, began to gain popularity in the 1990s for different reasons. To some, these approaches represent a small revolution in the way testing is defined and implemented. No longer do test scholars cling to the notion that accurate assessments of behavior can be derived only from formal tests, such as multiple-choice, true–false, matching, short answer, and essay examinations. Recently added to this list of testing formats are performance and portfolio examinations that ask the learner to carry out the activities actually used in the real world (such as measuring the tensile strength of a building material, estimating the effects of pollutants on aquatic life, designing circuitry for a microprocessor, or assembling a folder or portfolio of "works in progress" to reflect growth in critical or integrative thinking or other skills over the course of a semester or school year).

Performance and portfolio assessment techniques might include having students videotape portions of their own projects, conducting interviews with the student in order to probe for understanding and thinking abilities, or making a visual inspection of the product in order to determine whether it has the required characteristics for successful operation. These forms of assessment are intended to reduce pressures to test solely for facts and skills, and to provide a stimulus to introduce more extended thinking and reasoning activities in the curriculum (Resnick & Resnick, 1989; Tombari & Borich, 1999). We will have more to say about performance and portfolio assessment in Chapters 8 and 9.

Under IDEIA, children with disabilities must be evaluated regularly to assess their ongoing progress in the general education curriculum. The purposes of these evaluations are twofold: (a) to provide parents with regular reports of progress and (b) to determine whether children with disabilities as a group are progressing in the general curriculum as indicated by their performance on annual assessments, as required by state mandates and NCLB.

Yet, the same disabilities that qualify some pupils as children with disabilities may also hamper or preclude their ability to participate appropriately in testing that is required for nondisabled pupils. Performance and portfolio assessment may offer general and special education teachers alternative means by which to annually evaluate the progress of children with disabilities in the general education curriculum and on a day-to-day basis in the classroom.

Education Reform and the Global Economy

Two other trends, educational reform and the emergence of the global economy, or global competition, have been the impetus for much change in education. Increased use of tests and other assessments is ensured because they will be used to evaluate the effectiveness of these reforms and changes, at least in part.

The education reform movement arose in response to the National Commission on Excellence in Education's release of *A Nation at Risk: The Imperative for Educational Reform* in 1983, which documented shortcomings of the U.S. public education system at that time. Since then a number of reforms have been widely adopted in public education. These include raising expectations, establishing academic and performance standards, high-stakes testing, greater accountability, incentives for improved performance, improved teacher salaries, local or site-based management and decision making, and innovations in teacher training. Nevertheless, the results of more than 20 years of education reform have been mixed, and decision makers continue to rely on test results to evaluate the effectiveness of various reforms.

With advances in telecommunications and technology it is now clear that our students will have to compete in an international or global marketplace for jobs that will require strong skills in mathematics and science. But are our students able to hold their own in an international competition? A recent study indicated that U.S. fourth and eighth graders scored above the international average in science and math on the Fourth International Mathematics and Science Study (TIMSS), with eighth graders showing relative improvement in international standing between the 1995 and the 2003 TIMSS studies (Cavanagh, 2004). However, fourth graders' relative performance on the TIMSS declined between 1995 and 2004. In addition, the Program for International Student Assessment (PISA), conducted in 2003, which evaluates the mathematics competence of 15-year-olds, found that U.S. students performed below the average for industrialized nations in the areas of mathematics literacy and problem-solving skills (Cavanagh & Robelen, 2004). In both areas, the United States ranked 24th out of 29 countries, indicating that U.S. students are not internationally competitive in these areas.

Since public education is supported by taxpayers, educators must be responsive to the demands of taxpayers. With education reform's results mixed, and with continued concern about global competition, increasingly high-tech job requirements, grade inflation, and decreasing confidence in public education, school boards and the general public are becoming more and more concerned that they "get what they pay for." Yearly, high-stakes tests and NCLB report cards have become the mechanism through which these accountability demands are currently being met. Often these results are combined with other ratings (e.g., attendance, drop-out rates) and linked to complex formulas that are used to evaluate the performance of districts, schools, principals, and teachers, with financial and other incentives, or penalties, tied to improvements or declines in ratings.

Competency Testing for Teachers

Another current trend in our educational system is toward competency testing for teachers. In the early 1980s a number of states passed legislation requiring teachers to pass paper and pencil competency tests of teaching. Concurrent with these trends were the development of professional teaching standards. The National Board for Professional Teaching Standards (NBPTS) for advanced certification was formed in 1987 with three major goals:

1. To establish high and rigorous standards for what effective teachers should know and be able to do;

2. To develop and operate a national, voluntary system to assess and certify teachers who meet these standards; and

3. To advance related education reforms for the purpose of improving student learning in American schools.

During the same year, the Interstate New Teacher Assessment and Support Consortium (INTASC) was formed to create "board-compatible" standards that could be reviewed by professional organizations and state agencies as a basis for licensing beginning teachers (Miller, 1992). Much controversy still surrounds the use of tests aligned with these standards. No one wants to see poorly trained teachers in the classroom. However, the development of a cost-effective, valid, and reliable paper and pencil method of measuring the complex set of skills and traits that go into being an effective classroom teacher remains elusive. Currently, such tests are not ordinarily used to prohibit a teacher from teaching or to terminate an experienced teacher. Instead, they often are used on a pre-employment basis to document minimum levels of competency in various content areas (Miller, 1992; Holmes Group, 1986). But with the increase in emphasis on performance and portfolio assessment of students (several types of which will be described in Chapters 8 and 9), development of standardized performance and portfolio assessment methods for teachers are on the horizon. If such procedures are developed, they may provide for a more valid assessment of teaching competency than paper-and-pencil measures alone for both pre-service and in-service teachers.

Nevertheless, interest in the use of paper and pencil tests to evaluate teacher competency has continued to increase. In 1998 the Higher Education Act required teacher training programs in colleges and universities to report their students' scores on teacher licensing tests. By 2001 42 states and the federal government relied heavily on test scores to judge teacher quality and the quality of teacher preparation programs (Blair, 2001). Yet, a report from the National Research Council (2000) cautioned that there are many limitations in reliance on tests as a sole measure of teacher competence.

Increased Interest from Professional Groups

A variety of contemporary issues have drawn the attention of professional organizations, researchers, and policy makers in recent years. Individually and in collaboration, professional organizations have established high-level committees to study a variety of test and assessment-related issues. These include the implications of NCLB, increased use of high-stakes tests, performance and portfolio assessment, concerns about equity issues in testing, modification of tests for students with disabilities, the required participation of students with disabilities in annual achievement assessments under IDEIA–04, new assessment options for students with specific learning disabilities (SLD) under IDEIA–04, culturally sensitive and language appropriate assessment, and concerns related to increased use of computer-based tests and interpretations. There is also increased interest in the development of competency standards for all test users and others involved in the assessment process (American Psychological Association, 2001) and the *Standards for Educational and Psychological Testing* have recently been revised (American Educational Research Association, 1999) as has the Code of Fair Testing Practices in Education (Joint Committee on Testing Practices, 2004). Taken together, all these activities reflect a growing emphasis among professional organizations on appropriate educational test and assessment use. If these professional organizations are able to influence policy as they historically have, educational testing and assessment may become even more prominent in the future.

In summary, the antitest sentiment that once seemed to pervade education has passed. By all indications, demand for testing has increased over the last two decades. Over the last decade the high-stakes testing movement has spread to all 50 states and the District of Columbia, and the passage of NCLB in 2002 now makes annual academic assessments mandatory for all students, including students with disabilities. Educators are devising new approaches to testing and assessment, and, more than ever, test users may understand that test data, fallible as they sometimes may be, are more objective when used properly than any of the alternatives.

Educators realize that they must make decisions and that properly used test data can enhance their ability to make sound decisions. Increasing demands for accountability are also being made by the general public. By and large, the public tends to respect and accept test data to judge accountability. Remember, the taxpaying public, through school boards and voting behavior, controls educational programs and the purse strings of these programs. The accountability movement grew in reaction to the public's increasing disenchantment with education. As long as the public continues to be disenchanted with education, calls for accountability and testing will be heard. Since the public's disenchantment with current education is not likely to subside quickly, we are likely to see continuing demands for accountability and testing in the future. Next, we describe a novel partnership between two national professional associations and a book publisher that reflects growing public and private interest in testing and assessment.

A Professional Association–Book Publisher Information Initiative

In this chapter we mentioned that the rapid expansion of interest in testing and assessment has captured the attention of a wide variety of individuals and organizations. Recognizing that consumers can be easily overwhelmed by the complex, technical nature of testing and assessment information, John Wiley & Sons, the private publisher of this textbook, and two public national organizations, the Joint Committee on Testing Practices (JCTP) and the National Council on Measurement in Education (NCME), have collaborated to make available to purchasers of this textbook a "plain English" video entitled *The ABCs of School Testing*. The video provides a lively and informative introduction to parents' most frequently asked questions about school testing. Various types of tests and their appropriate uses in the school setting are illustrated, and aptitude and achievement tests are also discussed. Although the video was originally designed for lay audiences it has proved helpful to professional educators as well.

The video previously was available for purchase only from JCTP and NCME. Now, the video has been made available for free in streaming video format on the Wiley website http://www.wiley.com/college/kubiszyn.

In addition, the JCTP and Wiley have also agreed to make the *Code of Fair Testing Practices in Education* available for downloading at the Wiley website. The Code was initially developed by JCTP in 1988 to clarify the primary obligations that professionals who develop or use educational tests have toward test takers. It was revised in 2004. Although designed primarily for professionals who develop and use tests, it provides information helpful to consumers as well and is appropriate for both lay and professional audiences.

About JCTP   The Joint Committee on Testing Practices (JCTP) was established in 1985 by the American Educational Research Association (AERA), the American Psychological Association (APA), and the National Council on Measurement in Education (NCME). Other national organizations interested in testing and assessment joined in later years. These organizations include the American Counseling Association (ACA), American Speech and Hearing Association (ASHA), National Association of School Psychologists (NASP), and the National Association of Test Directors (NATD). According to the JCTP bylaws, this interorganizational body "provides a means by which professional organizations can work together to improve the use of tests in assessment and appraisal. The goal is to work cooperatively to advance, in the public interest, the quality of testing practices." The JCTP has developed a number of other testing and assessment resources in addition to *The ABCs of School Testing* video and the *Code of Fair Testing Practices in Education*. JCTP resources may be found at its website (click on http://www.apa.org/science/jctpweb.html).

About NCME   The National Council on Measurement in Education (NCME) is a professional organization for individuals involved in assessment, evaluation, testing, and other aspects of educational measurement. NCME members include university faculty; test developers; state and federal testing and research directors; professional evaluators; testing specialists in business, industry, education, community programs, and other professions; licensure, certification, and credentialing professionals; graduate students from educational, psychological, and other measurement programs; and others involved in testing issues and practices. During the past 20 years, NCME membership has become more diverse, broadening the scope of the organization's vision. Service to communities and ensuring that assessment is fair and equitable for all students have become essential elements of NCME's mission and purposes. Resources and other information about NCME may be found at the NCME website (click on http://www.ncme.org/).

EFFECTS ON THE CLASSROOM TEACHER

As we said earlier, we believe that a firm grounding in testing and assessment practice is vital to today's classroom teacher. However, teachers traditionally have not been well trained in test construction and use or in assessment. Many teachers see no need for training in testing and assessment because they believe these activities are supplemental or peripheral to the instructional process. Indeed, many prospective teachers have been heard to say things like, "If I need to know about tests I'll go to the counselor!" Perhaps the trend toward seemingly ever-increasing "specialists" in education has fostered or reinforced such beliefs. Nevertheless, regardless of how a teacher feels about the relationship of tests and assessments to instruction, it is frequently the classroom teacher who must administer and then organize and interpret state-mandated high-stakes and teacher-constructed test and assessment data, including performance and portfolio data, to curious and sometimes hostile parents and other concerned parties. Under IDEIA–04, regular classroom teachers will now interpret these kinds of data to the parents of children with disabilities, and their advocates. Figure 1.2 illustrates many sources of pressure influencing a teacher's use of tests. It is intended to convince you of the seriousness with which you should consider your knowledge or lack of knowledge of testing and assessment.

After years of consulting and teaching experience in the public schools, we have concluded that discussing test results with parents is frequently an anxiety provoking experience for teachers. Lacking appropriate training, some teachers are tempted to try to avoid interpretation entirely by dismissing test data as unimportant or inaccurate, not realizing that such data are often very important and thought to be quite accurate by parents. The following dialogue occurred when one of the authors had a conference with his son's second-grade teacher.

TEACHER: Hi, I'm Jeff's second-grade teacher. What can I do for you so early in the year?

AUTHOR: Jeff says he's in the low reading group, and I am curious about why he is. Could you explain that to me?

TEACHER: Oh, don't worry—we don't label kids at this school. I think that would be a terrible injustice.

AUTHOR: I see, but could you explain why Jeff is in the "Walkers" instead of the "Runners"?

TEACHER: Oh, those are just names, that's all.

AUTHOR: Are both groups at the same level in reading?

TEACHER: They're both at the first-grade level, yes.

AUTHOR: I'm beginning to catch on. Are they reading in the same level books in the same reading series?

TEACHER: Of course not! Some children are further along than others—that's all—but the kids don't know.

AUTHOR: Let me guess, the "Runners" are further ahead?

TEACHER: Yes, they're in Book 9.

AUTHOR: And the "Walkers" are in . . . .

TEACHER: Book 5. But they are only grouped for instructional purposes—I have 25 students, you know!

AUTHOR: I'm confused. Jeff's reading scores on the California Achievement Test last May were above the 90th percentile.

TEACHER: (*Chuckles to herself*) I can understand your confusion. Those test scores are so hard to understand. Why, even we professionals can't understand them.

AUTHOR: A score at the 90th percentile means the score was higher than the scores of 90% of the students who took the test all across the country.

TEACHER: Oh, really? (*Blushing*) It is very complicated. As I said, even professional educators don't understand testing.

AUTHOR: Some do, Mrs. B.

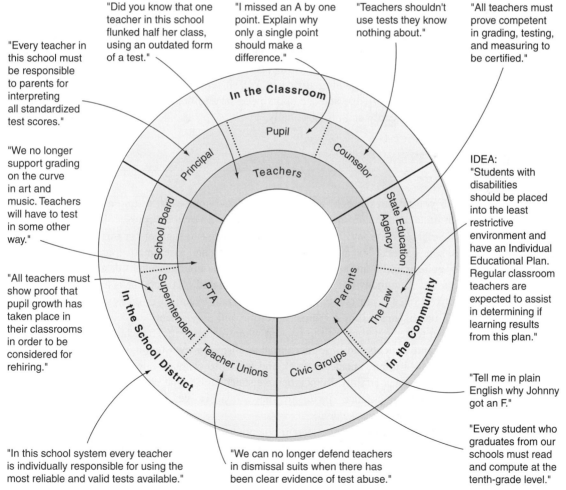

FIGURE 1.2 Some of the many forces influencing the teacher's use of tests.

Had the teacher understood the data she was dealing with, an embarrassing situation might have been avoided. Unfortunately, many classroom teachers have similar experiences.

Another often overheard statement is, "I don't even have time to teach; how can I learn about test construction and interpretation?" We are well aware that paperwork and bureaucratic requirements increasingly burden teachers and most other professionals. However, the trends discussed earlier point toward increased levels of test and assessment use in the future. The public will be keeping an increasingly watchful eye on the collectors and users of test data! Thus it appears that, more than ever, teachers of the future will need adequate training in testing and assessment practice. Ignoring or denying the need for proper training in this area will make neither this need nor the watchful eye of the public go away. Given the time constraints under which the average teacher must operate, it appears wiser to seek such training now, before you begin teaching. The alternative may be to attend what might seem like an endless series of workshops later on, while you also have to attend to your class of students and all the related responsibilities.

In short, it looks like tomorrow's teachers will be increasingly exposed to test and assessment data. With increasing public pressure for accountability, it does not appear likely that the average teacher will be able to get ahead or even get by without a good working knowledge of test and assessment practice. With practicing teachers getting more and more involved with paperwork, prospective teachers should acquire this working knowledge before beginning to teach. We sincerely hope that this text will help you acquire such knowledge and the skills necessary to construct good tests and to use test data knowledgeably and professionally.

ABOUT THE TEXT

When you talk to teachers who have completed courses in testing and assessment, you often find that they are somewhat less than inspired by their courses. In fact, talking with such veterans may have made you a little reluctant to register for this course. Nevertheless, here you are! The authors have taught testing and assessment courses for many years and, quite frankly, are accustomed to hearing the course content described as "dry, but necessary." Too many times, however, we have heard, "The course is dry, but necessary— I think!" Since a fair amount of straightforward, technical information is presented, we could understand calling a course in testing and assessment "dry." Indeed, this is almost how we feel about some of the content when we teach it! Thus, hearing "dry, but necessary" from students did little more than confirm our own feelings. But, to hear "dry, but necessary—I think!" made us think and led us to evaluate our courses to determine the cause for this uncertainty. Remember, we stated earlier that we think knowledge of testing and assessment practice is vital to today's teacher, yet somehow this was not coming across to some of our students.

We considered many different potential problems and each of us came to the same conclusion: Although each of us has used several different textbooks, we were never really satisfied with them. The introductory testing and measurement texts we used all did a fine job of relating information and explaining concepts, but they seemed to fall short in relating both traditional and innovative test and assessment practices and concepts to real-world situations. We found that we were supplementing the texts with anecdotes and suggestions based on our own experiences in the public schools. Our conclusion was that what is needed is a text that emphasizes the relationship of traditional and innovative test and assessment practices and concepts to real-world situations. With this aim in mind we wrote, and recently revised, this text. Only you can tell whether we have succeeded. We invite your comments and suggestions.

WHAT IF YOU'RE "NO GOOD IN MATH"?

Since tests yield numerical scores and test theory is based on statistical principles, it is no surprise that many who feel weak in math have great reservations about being able to succeed in a course in testing and assessment. If you fall into this category, rest assured that many of your fears are groundless or exaggerated. In our experience, fewer than 1% of the students who have completed the testing and assessment courses we have taught have done poorly solely because of a weak math background.

Naturally, knowledge of the basic mathematical functions—addition, subtraction, multiplication, and division—is a necessity. Mix these with fractions, decimals, and a sprinkling of algebra and you are all set! If you are still doubtful, work your way through the review of math skills provided in Appendix A. That review and accompanying self-check test should also prove useful to you if you feel a little rusty in math—a fairly common experience in this age of calculators and personal computers. All operations necessary to complete the calculations in this text are covered in the review. We think you will agree that our review of math skills in Appendix A will be all that's needed.

SUMMARY

In this chapter we have introduced you to issues related to educational testing and measurement and have described the orientation of the text. Its major points are as follows:

1. Tests are only tools, and like all tools, poor design, unintentional misuse, and intentional abuse can impair their usefulness.

2. Like other tools, tests and assessments are not equally useful for all purposes and all people.

3. Linguistic and cultural factors, for example, can affect the usefulness and the validity evidence for a test.

4. Testing, or assessment, is the administration and use of test or assessment results to make educational decisions. Testing and assessment are only a part of an assessment *process* that includes testing and the use of other measurement techniques (e.g., performance and portfolio assessments, rating scales, checklists, and observations) along with relevant background and contextual information in a critical, integrated way to make educational decisions.

5. Tests, because they have no preconceived or biased notions about test takers, can provide objective data that can be helpful in educational decision making and can minimize bias and subjectivity that may characterize decisions based on subjective data.

6. Test use is more likely to increase than decrease in the foreseeable future, in part because annual academic assessments are now required under the No Child Left Behind Act (NCLB).

7. The No Child Left Behind Act (NCLB), also know as "Nickel-B," became federal law in 2002 and has important implications for testing and assessment. Its key assessment features include requirements for Standards and Annual Assessment, Accountability/Proficiency, Adequate Yearly Progress (AYP), and Disaggregated Data/Reporting. NCLB also requires that all NCLB-required annual assessments must be tied to state standards, applicable to all students (including students with disabilities), and technically reliable.

8. NCLB requires annual assessments in math and reading in grades 3–8 and at least once in grades 10–12; annual science assessment at least once in elementary, middle, and high school beginning in the 2007–2008 school year; and participation of a sample of fourth and eighth graders in each state in the National Assessment of Educational Progress (NAEP).

9. Under NCLB states may choose the test they will use for the annual academic assessment (typically this is the state's high-stakes test) and the states must choose ever-increasing proficiency goals (i.e., passing scores) each year, culminating with 100% of test takers achieving proficieny by 2013–1014.

10. Under NCLB, annual reports of a school's Adequate Yearly Progress (AYP) must be made public, including disaggregated scores for all students as well as those in four groups: economically disadvantaged, limited English proficient (LEP), minority group membership, and students with disabilities.

11. An outgrowth of education reform, high-stakes testing, or the use of test data to make decisions that have significant educational, financial, and social impact, has spread rapidly across the nation.

12. The public continues to clamor for evidence that schools and teachers are in fact educating children, and the federal government, through NCLB, and all 50 states now use some form of high-stakes testing for such evidence.

13. The 2004 reauthorization of the Individuals with Disabilities Education Improvement Act (IDEIA–04) requires involvement of regular education teachers not only in the instruction and assessment of progress in the general education curriculum of special education students, but also in participation on IEP teams.

14. Annual academic assessments of students with disabilities under NCLB also is now required, with appropriate accommodations or through alternate assessments, as dictated by the students' Individual Educational Plan (IEP).

15. Under IDEIA–04, regular education teachers will also be involved in the development and assessment of behavior plans for children with disabilities whose behavior impedes progress in the general curriculum.

16. Since test use is likely to increase, and since the emphasis of special education has shifted to instruction and evaluation of progress of children with disabilities in the general curriculum, the burden of interpreting test results will fall more and more on the classroom teacher.

17. As test use has increased national organizations have also become more involved in educational testing and assessment.

18. The trend in testing has been away from the traditional multiple-choice type test and toward more open-ended performance and portfolio assessments, sometimes referred to as authentic assessments.

19. The classroom teacher who is trained in educational testing procedures will be able to use test results more efficiently and effectively and will be less likely to misuse or abuse test results.

20. This text is oriented toward the sound application of measurement principles to real-world situations.

FOR DISCUSSION

1. Thinking back to your own high school days, what were some of the factors that turned you off about tests?

2. Were these factors connected with the tests themselves, or were they the result of how the tests were used?

3. Point out some societal trends (e.g., changing demographics, increased population, or global competition for jobs) occurring in your city, state, or region that will likely make testing and measurement in our schools more complicated and important in the future.

4. In the teachers' lounge you hear a colleague mention "Nickel-B," annual academic assessments, AYP, and disaggregated data reporting. Define what each of these terms means in no more than one sentence.

5. You have just learned that your principal will receive a financial incentive if test scores at your school increase for the next three years, and will be reassigned if they do not. How do you, as (a) a teacher in the school, (b) a parent of a student in the school, or (c) a school board member feel about this example of high-stakes testing? What do you consider to be the pros and cons from each of the perspectives identified?

6. Critics of high-stakes testing say that it results in teaching to the test and that this is what is responsible for test score increases rather than real learning improvement. Keeping this in mind, argue for and against the use of high-stakes tests to measure learning.

7. Imagine the modern American high school 20 years from now. Identify several ways in which testing and measurement will have changed since the time you were attending high school.

8. You notice that one student is "different" from the rest of the class. The student behavior is disruptive, and you think he or she needs special attention. You say so to your principal, expecting the principal to transfer the student to a special education class. However, the principal says, "We have to collect the data first—get started." What kind of data do you believe the principal would want you to collect? How likely is it that the child will actually be taken out of your class? If the child is found to be eligible for special education, what role will you continue to have with this student?

9. Review the National Education Goals (see Box 1-2). Which of these have the greatest impact on classroom measurement practice? Why?

CHAPTER 2

HIGH-STAKES TESTING

OUR PRIMARY intent when we added this chapter to the seventh edition of this text was to inform readers about the complex and controversial topic of "high-stakes" testing (HST). Because the topic is very controversial we also wanted to ensure that our presentation gives more or less equal weight to the proponents and opponents of HST. This remains our primary intent for this edition.

However, before we address HST and its accompanying controversies in detail we feel it is important to at least briefly distinguish between key assessment-related provisions of state HST programs and the No Child Left Behind Act (NCLB), passed in 2002 (see Chapter 1). While there are similarities between state HST programs and NCLB, there also are important differences. There are times where discussions with colleagues (not to mention between the authors!) have made it clear to us that at least some of the controversy that surrounds NCLB and HST stems from confusion about similarities, differences, and overlap between NCLB requirements and state HST requirements, which differ from state to state. With 50 different state HST programs in place, comprehensive treatment of this topic is well beyond the scope of this text. Thus, we decided to compare and contrast some key assessment-related features of NCLB and state HST programs to reduce at least some of the confusion.

COMPARING AND CONTRASTING NCLB AND STATE HIGH-STAKES TESTING PROGRAMS

Let's start with some history. State HST programs began with a minimum competency testing program in Florida in the 1970s, but it was the 1990 appearance of the Texas Assessment of Academic Skills (TAAS) that heralded today's HST movement (Amrein & Berliner, 2002). By 2002 HST programs had spread to all 50 states and the District of Columbia (Doherty, 2002). By contrast, NCLB did not exist until 2002. Because HST existed before NCLB, the architects of NCLB, for both practical and political reasons, gave states the authority to select the tests and assessments that would be used to meet federal NCLB accountability requirements. In many cases, states opted to use the same measures they were already using for their HST programs to meet NCLB accountability requirements, effectively "killing two birds with one stone." As a result, when annual assessments are discussed, they may be referred to in the context of NCLB requirements, state requirements, or both. See why things can get confusing?

How results are reported can also be confusing. Both NCLB and many state HST programs require that public "report cards" be issued annually that describe the performance of students on the annual assessment. For NCLB, these reports must include overall performance by grade level. The results must also be disaggregated, or broken down, to show performance differences among economically disadvantaged students, ethnic minorities, limited English proficient (LEP) students, and students with disabilities. State HST programs may or may not report their scores this way. These report cards also are used to rank schools under NCLB, and under most state HST programs, into categories that range from "low performing" to "exceptional" based on whether student achievement meets specified proficiency levels.

States are allowed to set their own academic proficiency criteria under NCLB, but all state criteria must specify that 100% of students who take the annual assessment will be academically proficient by the 2013–2014 school year. Thus, the criteria set by the states must increase each year to reach the NCLB goal of 100% proficiency by 2013–2014. Under NCLB, if a school fails to meet the state proficiency criteria two or more years in a row, states must impose increasingly serious consequences on the school (see Chapter 1).

Beyond the NCLB proficiency criteria, states may establish additional proficiency criteria that drive other decisions not directly related to NCLB. For example, state HST programs may require that certain levels of proficiency are necessary for students to be promoted to the next grade (see the sidebar, Box 1-1, of Chapter 1), for students to graduate from high school (18 states in 2002, with 9 more being developed; Amrein & Berliner, 2002), for educators to receive salary increases or bonuses, or, if criteria are not met, for authorities to take over schools or reassign school staff to other schools. Although controversy regarding the use of tests to make decisions about promotion, retention, and financial incentives or penalties for school staff is often attributed to NCLB, these are not NCLB requirements—they arise from state HST program requirements.

We hope these examples help clarify that there are important similarities and differences between NCLB and state HST programs. Sorting them out can be frustrating and complex. Why is it the way it is? It may help to keep in mind that when NCLB was passed in 2002 states were faced with the challenge of quickly meeting the law's accountability requirements. Since all states already had HST programs in place, most states adopted their state assessments and adapted their school report cards to meet both NCLB and state HST requirements rather than start from scratch. However, as we will discuss in this chapter, not all state HST assessments and programs are of equivalent quality. So the extent to which state HST programs will fulfill the intent of NCLB and meet their own state requirements remains to be seen. We hope that by clarifying some of the similarities and differences between NCLB and state HST programs your understanding of this chapter will be enhanced.

HIGH-STAKES TESTING: A NATIONWIDE PHENOMENON

With the possible exception of NCLB, there is no development during the last decade that has generated more controversy among educators than the high-stakes testing (HST) movement, which spread to every state in the nation by 2002 (Doherty, 2002). And the controversy is not limited to educators. Parents, state and local school boards, the media, realtors, businesspersons, and politicians have all joined the fray. Depending on the source, you may hear that high-stakes tests are the greatest thing since sliced bread or that high-stakes tests are the work of the devil. Because HST has spread so rapidly and broadly we have dedicated an entire chapter to helping you understand and cope with the demands and controversies that surround this timely and important topic. To familiarize you with some of the controversy, consider the following dialogue between two teachers.

(Hearing raised voices from the teachers' lounge you peek in to see what's happening. You see Ms. Caldwell and Ms. Cantu engaged in a rather heated exchange with one another. This surprises you because both teachers are normally calm, professional, and rational).

"I'm telling you again, Ms. Cantu, high-stakes testing is the worst thing that ever happened to education," said Ms. Caldwell, glaring at Ms. Cantu.

"Either you can't be serious or you are seriously misinformed! High-stakes testing is the best thing that ever happened to education" said Ms. Cantu haughtily. "You probably don't know it but high-stakes testing is helping to bridge the gap between Caucasian and ethnic minority achievement in schools," asserted Ms. Cantu.

"What?" said Ms. Caldwell. "That's not true at all! High-stakes testing is only increasing the gap between Caucasian and ethnic minority achievement in the schools. Furthermore, because of high-stakes tests I can't teach my students the critical thinking and problem-solving skills they need to compete. The weeks we spend going over practice tests and filling out test-related worksheets is narrowing instruction. I don't have time now help students learn to think! And then we have to lose more instructional time attending pep rallies and assemblies to get us motivated to do well on the high-stakes test. All we seem to care about is test scores! Well I care about whether my students can think, not just how they score on a simple-minded test!" said Ms. Caldwell, struggling to contain her frustration.

"Maybe you should be a little less critical, Ms. Caldwell," snapped Ms. Cantu. "High-stakes testing is helping students to develop the building blocks they need to develop critical thinking skills!" said Ms. Cantu emphatically. "Without the test results we won't know whether our kids are learning and we won't know what we need to focus our instruction on. What you don't seem to understand, Ms. Caldwell, is that high-stakes tests are helping to improve school quality and student learning," Ms. Cantu concluded icily.

"I don't have any problem understanding anything, Ms. Cantu. What you don't understand is that high-stakes testing is narrowing the curriculum and undermining school quality, teacher morale, and student learning," said a now red-faced Ms. Caldwell.

Who is right? Who should you believe? Can two reasonable teachers really have such sharply discrepant perceptions about high-stakes tests? Or is this exchange an exaggeration we made up to make some point? We can assure you this exchange is no exaggeration. Strong differences of opinion exist about the appropriateness and utility of HST, and its effects on students, teachers, and others. We will review several of the issues and arguments on both sides of the HST debate later in this chapter.

But just what is a high-stakes test? How did this phenomenon, almost unheard of a decade ago, spread so rapidly? Are high-stakes tests good or bad? How are results used or misused? How does HST affect teachers and students? What can teachers do to help students prepare for and cope with high-stakes tests? All these questions are now vital for teachers to be informed about because teachers today are increasingly affected by this phenomenon. High-stakes test results can potentially affect their careers as well as the futures of their students.

To help you understand how the HST phenomenon evolved and why it is so controversial we will review briefly some of the history, growth, and issues related to HST in this chapter. We will then share with you the guidance provided by national professional associations to help you evaluate how well your state's HST program measures up. Finally, we will provide you with suggestions to help your pupils cope with and perform at their best on high-stakes tests. Many of these suggestions can also help teachers cope with the added stress that often accompanies HST programs.

HIGH-STAKES TESTS ARE ONLY TOOLS

Since the topic is so controversial, you may wonder where we stand on the issue of HST. If you read Chapter 1 you know that our position is that tests can provide objective information that can be useful for educational decision making. We certainly have nothing against tests, as long as they are properly developed and used. Like any other test, a high-stakes test is only a tool, and the way a tool is constructed can limit its usefulness.

A poorly constructed tool may not only be useless, but dangerous. But certainly high-stakes test are carefully constructed, administered, and scored, you may think. However, Katzman and Hodas (2001) reported that lapses in the construction, administration, and scoring of high-stakes tests affected student scores in more than 20 states. Furthermore, even well-constructed tools can be used effectively, ineffectively, or abused. Swiss Army knives, for example, are well-constructed tools but cannot be equally effective for all potential uses. We don't think high-stakes tests are any different. We could use a Swiss Army knife to cut down trees, sharpen sticks, and dig trenches, if we had to. However, there certainly are other tools that are far better suited for cutting down trees and digging trenches than a Swiss Army knife.

Similarly, we believe that some high-stakes tests or tools may be better planned, developed, and implemented than others. In other words, we believe that some high-stakes tests may be better than others, and some may be used more appropriately than others. Remember what we discussed in Chapter 1? A test's usefulness can vary depending on the purpose of testing and the characteristics of the persons the test is administered to. No test can be a "one size fits all" test that is equally suitable for all purposes (e.g., assessing academic proficiency of regular and special education students, and evaluating teachers and curricula) and for all students. The rapid growth of HST since the early 1990s may have created political and legislative pressure to develop and implement high-stakes test programs so quickly that leaders may have overlooked or compromised important technical and practical considerations to meet unrealistic deadlines. When such compromises occur, the risk of potential high-stakes test misuse or abuse increases.

To sum up, we believe high-stakes tests are potentially useful. But we also have concerns about the way some high-stakes tests have been developed and the way some of these tools have been used. Next, we will define HST, describe its history and expansion, and address several issues commonly raised by HST supporters and detractors.

WHAT IS HIGH-STAKES TESTING AND WHY DOES IT MATTER?

We define high-stakes testing as "the use of a test or an assessment to make decisions that are of prominent educational, financial, or social impact." Some examples of important decisions that are made based on high-stakes tests include whether

- A student will be promoted to the next grade,
- A student will receive a high school diploma,
- Schools are classified as unacceptable, acceptable, or exemplary in terms of their educational performance,
- Schools, principals, or teachers receive financial or other incentives, or penalties, based on student performance on a high-stakes test,
- A state educational agency or a private corporation takes over the administrative control of local schools, and
- Principals, teachers, or other school staff are reassigned to other schools or are offered employment contract renewal.

To make these high-stakes decisions states rely on a variety of state-constructed and off-the-shelf standardized tests produced by commercial test publishers. What do these tests look like? According to Doherty (2002), 49 states include multiple-choice items (see Chapter 6) and 38 include short answer essay items (see Chapter 7) on their annual tests. Seven states use performance assessments (see Chapter 8) and two require portfolio assessments (see Chapter 9). Doherty (2002) also reported that by 2003 seven states would use these tests to determine whether students will be promoted to the next grade and 18 states now require students to pass a test to graduate from high school, although only half of these states provide funds for remediation for students who fail.

Promotion and Graduation Decisions Affect Students

Obviously, the impact of promotion and graduation decisions on students and their families is both significant and controversial. Using test data to inform these decisions is usually not controversial in and of itself. What is controversial is that (a) in many HST programs these decisions are based entirely, or in large part, on the results of a single test and (b) many people question whether high-stakes tests are valid measures of learning.

For example, let's consider the use of a high-stakes test instead of a report card for promotion decisions. The use of high-stakes tests for promotion decisions has been recommended to combat social promotion. Social promotion is the tendency to promote students with academic skills deficits to the next grade to keep them with same-aged peers to offset presumed damage to self-esteem and social development. When high-stakes tests are used, the promotion decision is determined by an objective "snapshot" of the student's achievement obtained from the test (i.e., a test score) rather than on a more comprehensive but potentially more subjective series of grades and ratings on a report card. This high-stakes promotion model greatly simplifies the decision-making process—those who score high enough are promoted, those who do not are retained. Figure 2.1 compares the promotion decision-making process based on a high-stakes test with the traditional decision-making process based on a report card.

From Figure 2.1 we can see why basing promotions on high-stakes test scores has appeal. It is simple and it is objective. So what's the problem? Test scores are fallible. As we will learn later, all test scores are surrounded by a margin of error, a concept we will address in depth in Chapter 17. As you know from your own test-taking experiences, your performance on a test on any given day may vary, depending on a number of student-related factors (e.g., illness, fatigue, emotional state), and on factors such as timing or other errors made by the test administrator. In addition, a student's language facility, the appropriateness of the opportunities the student has had to learn the material the high-stakes test measures, the test's validity evidence, and potential errors in the test itself and in its scoring are other factors that can affect a student's score. We will address these important issues in Chapter 18 when we help you learn to interpret standardized test scores.

With these factors in mind, do you think it is more appropriate to base an important promotion or graduation decision on a single high-stakes test snapshot? When you take a snapshot, does it always turn out the way you expected? Of course not. So what do professional photographers do? They take a series of snapshots. No professional photographer would ever rely on a single snapshot to record an important moment.

Recognizing the potential for misuse of high-stakes tests alone for promotion and graduation decisions, a National Research Council (1999) report on HST recommended that promotion and graduation decisions "should not automatically be made on the basis of a single test score, but should be buttressed by other relevant information about the student's knowledge and skills, such as grades, teacher recommendations, and extenuating circumstances." Similarly, the *Standards for Educational and Psychological Tests* (AERA, 1999), which were developed by the American Educational Research

	High-Stakes Test Model	Report Card Model
Source(s) of data	A high-stakes test	Multiple teacher constructed tests, projects, homework and seatwork, observations, attendance, and other data
Basis for the promotion decision	Score on the high-stakes test	Scores and ratings on tests, projects, homework and seatwork, observation of social and emotional development, maturity, citizenship, attendance, and other data
Objectivity of the decision	High—based solely on the score	Variable—grades and ratings may require judgments and may be influenced by a variety of nonachievement factors

FIGURE 2.1 The decision to promote or retain based on a high-stakes test versus a traditional report card.

Association, the American Psychological Association, and the National Council on Measurement in Education to "promote the sound and ethical use of tests and to provide a basis for evaluating the quality of testing practices" (p. 1), states that "a decision or characterization that will have major impact on a student should not be made on the basis of a single test score" (p. 146). We agree. We believe that promotion and graduation decisions should be based on a "movie" that illustrates the complexities of achievement over time rather than a single frame or "snapshot" from that movie.

Principal and Teacher Incentives Are Linked to Performance

So far, we have been talking about the effects of high-stakes tests on students. Incentives (i.e., rewards and penalties) for principals, teachers, schools, and school districts have also been attached to high-stakes test results to motivate school staff to encourage and prepare students to do well on high-stakes tests. As we discussed earlier, school and school district performance is reported by the state via school "report cards," with financial and other incentives provided for schools, educators, and districts that do well on the high-stakes test. School performance is also reported to the public through the media, so that high or low performing schools are either applauded or chastised in the court of public opinion. Where unacceptable performance continues from year to year the school staff may be "reconstituted." This means the principal and all or part of the existing school staff are reassigned, or their contracts are not renewed, and the school is then restaffed. The principle of reconstitution is based on the controversial belief that such massive restructuring will break the cycle of low expectations and low achievement for the school's pupils.

Effects on Property Values, Business Decisions, and Politics

The impact of HST has been felt outside the schools, and it has also become a popular political issue. High-stakes test results are now widely anticipated by the public and are reported regularly in the media. As a result of this widespread media coverage, HST results now influence real estate values and even business decisions. For example, real estate values tend to increase in areas where high-stakes tests indicate that students are performing well, as a result of increased demand for housing in these areas by parents with school-aged children, and vice versa. High-stakes test results are also considered by business executives when they decide to relocate or expand their operations. Business executives realize that it will be easier for them to attract qualified employees if the local schools have records of high achievement on high-stakes tests.

HST has also become a part of state and national political campaigns. HST was a prominent part of President George W. Bush's election campaign in 2000. HST became a cornerstone of the No Child Left Behind (NCLB) Act (see Chapter 1) that was signed into law in January 2002 following significant advocacy by President Bush. NCLB assessment requirements were modeled closely after the Texas Assessment of Academic Skills (TAAS) HST program that President George W. Bush promoted when he was governor of Texas. The TAAS was the cornerstone of student, teacher, and school accountability in Texas from 1994 to 2003, when it was replaced by a more difficult high-stakes test, the Texas Assessment of Knowledge and Skills (TAKS).

So, we can see that the HST phenomenon has had broad impact across many facets of society. Next let's briefly review the history of HST to see how this phenomenon developed.

THE HISTORY OF HIGH-STAKES TESTING

We will describe how the educational reform movement led to widespread calls for educational accountability. Then we will discuss what has come to be known as standards-based reform and see how high-stakes tests came to be used as measures of accountability under standards-based educational reform programs.

Education Reform

The impetus for HST can be traced to the broader issue of education reform. We mentioned in Chapter 1 that the education reform movement is generally considered to have begun with the release of *A Nation at Risk* by the National Commission on Excellence in Education in 1983. This report documented shortcomings of the U.S. public education system and led to increased calls for educational reform and accountability. In response to *A Nation at Risk*, educators, public policy makers, business people, and the public clamored for improvements in public education and increased accountability to ensure that student learning improved.

Standards-Based Reform

Academic Standards   As part of the education reform movement several states began to identify the objectives of instruction for pupils in each of their academic subjects across the elementary, middle, and high school years. We will discuss instructional objectives at length in later chapters, but for now suffice it to say that these statewide objectives are specific, measurable outcomes of learning that have been accepted by committees of educators and others. Over time, these instructional objectives came to be known as academic standards and formed the basis of what came to be known as standards-based reform. In general, there has been limited disagreement and controversy about what should be included in a state's academic standards. Nevertheless, development of state academic standards in all core subjects that are clear, measurable, hierarchical, coherently organized, and based on research findings has proved challenging for many states, as the following reports indicate.

In 2001, according to *Making Standards Matter 2001, the Annual Report of the American Federation of Teachers* (AFT, 2001), all states and the District of Columbia had in place some form of academic standards in 2001. However, only 29 states and the District had clear and specific standards in all the core subjects (math, English, science, and social studies) at the elementary, middle, and high school levels. Four years later, a report from the Fordham Foundation compared current state standards to those in existence in 2000. The report found that most states had strengthened their reading or English standards, with 20 states receiving grades of A or B for their reading or English standards, and 8 states receiving grades of D or F, with deficiencies particularly noted at the high school level. On the other hand, the report found that math standards in most states remained problematic across all grade levels. The report found that 40 states replaced or revised their math standards since 2000, but only 6 states received an A or B rating, with 29 states receiving a D or F (Thomas B. Fordham Foundation, 2005).

Performance Standards   Once a state's academic standards were established, committees then identified appropriate levels of performance for each standard that would indicate that the objective, or academic standard, had been met. Generally, whether a student passed a test section (e.g., reading, math, writing or the entire test depended on whether the student met or surpassed the performance standard on a majority of the objectives or standards. In turn, schools and districts were also given "report cards" and rated as "exceptional, proficient, acceptable, or unacceptable" depending on the proportion of students who passed various sections of the test. This aspect of standards-based reform became known as performance standards.

Unlike academic standards, performance standards often are controversial, with definitions of accomplishment sometimes very different for educators and for non-educators (e.g., parents, businesspersons, and others). Performance standards can vary considerably from state to state, and even within states over time. Thus, what separates "acceptable, unacceptable, proficient, and exceptional" performance may vary both across states and within states with the passage of time, and may vary from the perspective of educators and non-educators. The intention of performance standards is to raise expectations enough to raise achievement but not to raise expectations so high that students, teachers, and others fail to take them seriously because they are unattainable.

An assumption that underlies standards-based reform is that all children can meet high expectations. Whether all children can meet high expectations or not, standards-based reform has arisen from the realization that achievement expectations for economically disadvantaged and minority students have generally been lower than for other students. Thus, many believe that setting high standards for all students will especially enhance achievement for low income and minority students. Indeed, increasing achievement in economically disadvantaged youth is a primary intent of NCLB.

Alignment of High-Stakes Tests with Academic Standards   After establishing academic and performance standards states had to decide on ways to measure whether students were achieving these standards. In the late 1990s some states (e.g., New York, California, Tennessee) chose off-the-shelf tests published by standardized test developers to measure state standards. In other states (e.g., Texas, Massachusetts, Florida) state education agencies, with assistance from standardized test developers, developed state-specific tests to measure state academic standards. Not all these high-stakes tests measured the states' standards or objectives equally well. In other words, some high-stakes tests (both commercial and state developed) may have failed to measure the very standards they were intended to measure. In other cases high-stakes tests have been criticized because they fail to measure a broad enough sample of the state's academic standards. The term alignment has come to refer to the degree to which a high-stakes test measures a state's academic standards.

Alignment is what measurement specialists consider to be evidence of an achievement test's content validity. When evaluating the appropriateness of an achievement test for a particular use, the strength of the evidence for a test's content validity is the single most important technical criterion an achievement test must fulfill. The importance of content validity evidence, or alignment, and how this is determined will be addressed in more detail in later chapters.

According to *Making Standards Matter 2001* (AFT, 2001) the alignment of high-stakes tests with state standards is very much a work in progress. AFT (2001) reported that while 38 states began to align their tests with state standards only 9 states met the AFT criteria for aligned tests in the four core areas at the elementary, middle, and high school levels. Figure 2.2 illustrates the relationships between academic standards, performance standards, and test items.

Criterion-Referenced High-Stakes Tests   In Texas, the high-stakes Texas Assessment of Academic Skills (TAAS) test was designed specifically to measure achievement against the state's academic standards, the Texas Essential Knowledge and Skills (TEKS). Because the TAAS only measured a portion of the TEKS standards it was replaced for the 2003–2004 school year in an effort to better align that state's high-stakes test with its state standards, and to address other criticisms of the TAAS. Texas' new high-stakes test is called the Texas Assessment of Knowledge and Skills (TAKS). Both the TAAS and its replacement, the TAKS (note that TEKS refers to the state standards, TAKS refers to the new test of those standards), are examples of a criterion-referenced test, a type of test you will learn more about in Chapter 4. To give you an idea of what a high-stakes test looks like, Figure 2.3 includes sample math and reading items from the spring 2001 third-grade TAAS test.

Criterion-referenced tests are primarily intended to measure student performance against a criterion for mastery so they are well-suited for measuring state standards, all

Academic Standards	Performance Standards	Test Items
Determined by state appointed experts. Reflects the learning outcomes and content the state decides is important for its students to learn.	Determined by educators and other stakeholders (businesspersons, parents, politicians). Reflects the level of performance necessary for a student to be judged as having mastered a component of the state standards. Can also refer to the percentage of components that must be mastered for a student to pass the test, pass with proficiency, pass with honors, or fail.	Developed to measure the content and process specified in the state academic standards. May be objective, essay, or performance in form (see Chapters 6, 7, 8, and 9). One or more items may measure each of the academic standards and it is the percentage of items the student answers correctly that is used to rate the student according to the state performance standards.

FIGURE 2.2   The relationships among academic standards, performance standards, and test items.

other factors being equal. Where states have developed clear academic standards and where their high-stakes tests are well aligned (or have good content validity evidence) high-stakes test results probably provide the most useful information for educational decision-making. This is because the score reports provide specific information about what students have mastered, and this enables remedial instruction to be targeted specifically to areas of weakness. However, compared with the time-consuming, expensive, and often meticulous process involved in developing a norm-referenced test (see Chapter 18) criterion-referenced high-stakes tests may be developed under restrictive time constraints and limited budgets as a result of legislative deadlines and political pressures, potentially limiting their usefulness.

Norm-Referenced High-Stakes Tests   Not all states' HST systems utilize criterion-referenced tests that are closely aligned with the state standards (Olson, 2001). In some states, norm-referenced tests developed for national rather than specific state use by commercial test publishers were selected for state HST programs. You will learn about norm-referenced tests in Chapter 4. National norm-referenced tests are designed to focus on broad national goals and objectives, which may differ considerably from state academic standards. In addition to compromising their validity as measures of progress toward state standards (i.e., their alignment with state standards) such tests may also fail to give teachers much in the way of specific help in identifying which aspects of their instruction may need revision to enhance attainment of state standards.

For example, during the 2001–2002 school year in Tennessee students in grades 3–8 took the multiple-choice component of the Terra-Nova, Second Edition, published by CTB-McGraw-Hill. However, this test is designed to compare students to their peers on a national basis. Tests like this were originally designed to enable us to compare how students in one part of the country compare with those in another. They were not initially designed to align with state standards. Thus, they may lack validity as measures of achievement of state standards. California rated schools in 2001–2002 primarily based on performance in grades 2–11 on the Stanford Achievement Test, Ninth Edition, produced by Harcourt Educational Measurement. However, because this test too is a norm-referenced national test it may not align well with California's state standards. Therefore, it may be a flawed, or at least limited, measure of achievement of California's standards.

In recognition of criticisms regarding alignment, standardized norm-referenced test publishers are attempting to improve their tests' alignment with state standards and increase the usefulness of their score reports to classroom teachers. How successful these efforts will be compared to state tests designed specifically to measure state standards remains to be seen.

When states are interested in determining how students compare to others across the nation and whether they have achieved state standards, both norm-referenced, off-the-shelf commercial tests and state-developed criterion-referenced tests can be employed. In 2001 Florida began to administer both types of tests to its students. Of course this increases the time students spend preparing for and taking tests and may reduce instructional time. Now that we have a better understanding of HST let's consider some of the controversy.

2 Which shows 2 lines of symmetry on a figure? Mark your answer.

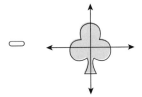

3 What is the perimeter of the rectangular rug? Mark your answer.

8 feet

6 feet

○ 14 ft

○ 16 ft

○ 28 ft

○ 48 ft

4 What does the 3 in the number 273,049 represent? Mark your answer.

○ 3 tens

○ 3 hundreds

○ 3 thousands

○ 3 ten thousands

Page 7

GO ON ▶

FIGURE 2.3 Questions from the spring 2001 third-grade TAAS math and reading tests.

5 Which two figures are congruent? Mark your answer.

1   2   3   4

⚬ 1 and 3

⚬ 2 and 4

⚬ 1 and 4

⚬ 3 and 4

6 Which number sentence is in the same fact family as $4 \times 3 = 12$? Mark your answer.

⚬ $12 \div 2 = 6$

⚬ $3 \div 9 = 12$

⚬ $6 \times 2 = 12$

⚬ $12 \div 4 = 3$

Page 8

7 Which temperature is shown on the thermometer? Mark your answer.

⚬ 73°F

⚬ 74°F

⚬ 76°F

⚬ 78°F

GO ON ▶

FIGURE 2.3   *continued.*

Gathering Things on the Moon

In the U.S. astronauts traveled to the moon. One of the first things they did when they stepped on the moon was gather some rocks and dirt. By studying the surface of the moon, scientists can learn how the moon formed and how it is changing. If rocks and dirt from the moon are compared to rocks and dirt on Earth, scientists can tell if they match.

Gathering rocks and dirt on the moon was not easy. The astronauts had to wear big, bulky space suits that made it hard to bend over. Since they could not pick up things in the usual way, they had to use special tools.

Moon Tools

Astronauts used four kinds of tools to pick up rocks and dirt on the moon. These were the scoop, rake, grabber, and hammer. The scoop looked like a shovel hooked to the end of a long pole. It gathered bits of moondust and dirt. The rake looked like a large comb at the end of a long pole. It scratched the ground to dig up tiny pieces of rock. Larger rocks were gathered with a grabber. This tool opened and closed around a rock. It was on a long pole and lifted one rock at a time. Sometimes a rock was too big and heavy to lift. Then a hammer was used to break off small chips. Like the other tools, the hammer was at the end of a long pole.

Storing Moon Rocks and Dirt

As rocks and dirt were gathered, they were put into bags. The bags were put into strong metal boxes that were airtight. Then each box was wrapped in another bag and stored in the spaceship. Back on Earth the rocks and dirt were carefully taken off the spaceship. They were kept in special places where they would not be harmed.

Scientists have learned much about the moon and the Earth from the rocks and dirt gathered by the astronauts. They would have learned much less if the astronauts hadn't had the right tools to use.

Scoop   Rake   Grabber   Hammer

Page 42   GO ON

FIGURE 2.3   *continued.*

30 The reader can tell that scientists have probably —

- ⬭ found a way to live on the moon

- ⬭ decided that moon rocks are boring

- ⬭ discovered many things about the moon

- ⬭ forgotten about traveling to space

31 In this story, the word <u>bulky</u> means —

- ⬭ fun

- ⬭ hot

- ⬭ dry

- ⬭ thick

32 After the rocks and dirt were taken back to Earth, they were —

- ⬭ broken into small chips

- ⬭ kept in special places

- ⬭ returned to the moon

- ⬭ gathered with a scoop

33 Large rocks were gathered with a —

- ⬭ rake

- ⬭ hammer

- ⬭ scoop

- ⬭ grabber

Page 43

34 What is the main idea of this story?

- ⬭ U.S. astronauts traveled to the moon in 1969.

- ⬭ Special tools were needed to gather rocks and dirt on the moon.

- ⬭ Astronauts wear space suits and travel in spaceships.

- ⬭ Some rocks on the moon are big and heavy.

35 In this story, things are compared to see if they are —

- ⬭ strong

- ⬭ alike and different

- ⬭ dangerous

- ⬭ big and heavy

36 When the astronauts returned to Earth, they were probably —

- ⬭ proud

- ⬭ mad

- ⬭ amused

- ⬭ sad

STOP

FIGURE 2.3 *continued.*

THE HIGH-STAKES TESTING BACKLASH

Not everyone has jumped on the HST bandwagon. Those who decry the high-stakes movement include FairTest, a national organization that advocates for alternatives to standardized tests as measures of learning. In a January 7, 2002, response to the passage of the No Child Left Behind Act, FairTest criticized high-stakes tests as failing "to produce evidence of sustained learning improvement for all students or to close the academic achievement gap between minority group and low-income students and their more advantaged peers" (p. 1) and as yielding scores that are "both too narrow and unreliable" (p. 1). They also object to reconstitution of low performing schools, stating that reconstitution has "failed to produce positive changes in schools" (p. 2) (FairTest, 2002).

Resistance to NCLB has also been evident at the state and district level. For example, in 2005 Connecticut filed suit against the U.S. Department of Education over NCLB assessment requirements (Archer, 2005), and two school districts in Illinois also filed suits alleging that NCLB conflicts with the Individuals with Disabilities Education Act (IDEA–97) in requiring alterations to the Individual Educational Plans (IEPs) for students with disabilities (Samuels, 2005). Several states have either refused to comply with NCLB or have prohibited the use of state funds to meet NCLB requirements (The State of NCLB, 2004).

In an article entitled "High-Stakes Tests Are for Tomatoes" in the August 2000 edition of the *Atlantic Monthly*, Peter Schrag describes a boycott of a high-stakes graduation test, the Massachusetts Comprehensive Assessment System (MCAS), by 300 students, supported by parents, teachers, and community activists. He also reported that in Wisconsin in 1999 the state legislature refused to fund a graduation examination that the legislature had approved only two years earlier. Pressure from middle-class parents was cited by Schrag as the reason. High-stakes graduation tests in Virginia and New York were reportedly also under fire because of concerns about a large number of seniors who would be denied diplomas. In Ohio, parent and teacher groups were reportedly circulating petitions calling for repeal of that state's HST laws. While acknowledging that the high-stakes backlash had not yet reached majority status, Schrag pointed out that the anti-test coalitions were broad based, including liberals and conservatives and teachers and parents alike.

And criticism of HST also has come from academicians too. Popham (2000) in a paper entitled "Educational Mismeasurement: How High-Stakes Testing Can Harm Our Children," alleges that high-stakes tests are causing a decline in instructional quality and teacher morale, as well as a decline in citizens' regard for public education, and that the results for students are "devastating" (p. 1). Indeed, says Popham "When it comes to high-stakes testing programs these days, devastation abounds" (p. 1).

A sampling of articles from a popular weekly educator's magazine, *Education Week*, included the following titles that suggest widespread sentiment against HST:

"NEA Hopes to Derail High Stakes Testing" (July 11, 2001)

"Citing Instructional Time, New York City Scraps 3 Assessments" (June 13, 2001)

"California Considering Assessment Role Reversal" (June 13, 2001)

"The Trouble with Testing" (October 24, 2001)

"Protest Over State Testing Widespread" (May 16, 2001)

An *Education Week* survey in 2000 showed that 66% of teachers think state tests are forcing them to concentrate too much on what's tested to the detriment of other important topics. About one-half said they spend a great deal of time helping students prepare for the tests (Doherty, 2002). Doherty (2002) also reported that there are concerns that high-stakes tests are culturally biased because they primarily reflect the experiences of Caucasian middle-class students. Alaska and Arizona have delayed attaching consequences to their graduation tests as a result of protests about the fairness of the tests. And other critics say that schools are not providing students with what they need to perform well on high-stakes tests—high quality teachers, strong curricula, and enough time to master the content and process contained in the state's standards that the test hopefully measures.

The news media have also brought significant attention to the HST concerns, in large part because of the scandals that have been associated with it. In a June 6, 2001, broadcast on *Nightline* entitled "Cheating Teachers," Ted Koppel chronicled a series of incidents that illustrated the lengths to which some teachers and administrators will go to improve high-stakes test scores. The episode documented the resignation of a school principal in Bethesda, Maryland, an upper middle class suburb of Washington, D.C., after she was caught telling five students to change their incorrect answers on a high-stakes test. Interestingly, it was the students themselves who brought the principal's actions to the attention of their parents. A number of other incidents of teacher or administrator abuses intended to increase high-stakes test scores also were reported during the episode (Koppel, 2001).

Even the courts have been involved. In January 2002, the Austin, Texas, school district became the first district in the nation to face criminal charges and to be convicted and fined for tampering with high-stakes test scores. The Travis County Attorney charged administrators and data processing staff with tampering with the high-stakes test scores from three Austin schools to raise school ratings above the low performing/unacceptable range. The incentive for doing so was to avoid negative publicity and other potential penalties for the district and the schools when the test results were released. The district pleaded no contest to the charges and was fined after a two year court battle (Martinez, 2002). Nevertheless, since the *Nightline* "Cheating Teachers" episode aired in 2001 there has been a steady stream of teacher cheating incidents in Texas, Florida, California, Massachusetts, Arizona, Mississippi, Illinois, Kentucky, South Carolina, and other states (Axtman, 2005).

IS THERE REALLY A HIGH-STAKES TESTING BACKLASH?

The outcry against HST and the abuses associated with it we just reviewed may seem to suggest that HST will soon wither on the vine. When we consider arguments advanced by proponents of HST, however, a more balanced picture emerges.

For example, public opinion polls suggest that the majority of the general public supports NCLB, high-stakes tests, and standards-based education reform. A poll of over 1,000 registered voters conducted by the Winston Group for the Americans for Better

Education in October 2004 found that parents of public school children were in favor of NCLB by a 62–28 margin, with comparable results for ethnic minority and Caucasian parents. In the same poll 72% said they believe the federal government should hold states and schools accountable, while 25% disagreed (Americans for Better Education, 2004). These findings parallel those from earlier public opinion polls reported in a National Council on Measurement in Education (NCME) newsletter (Driesler, 2001). A spring 2000 poll conducted by the American Association of Publishers (AAP) found that 83% of parents surveyed said standardized tests provide very important information, 90% wanted comparative data about their children and their schools, and 74% said test scores informed them about their children's progress. This survey also found that African-American and Hispanic parents support HST even more strongly than their Caucasian counterparts, and that lower income parents supported HST more than middle income parents. A September 2000 poll conducted by Public Agenda reported that about 80% said statewide tests are useful in evaluating performance of teachers, students, and schools, 79% support tougher academic standards and oppose social promotion (promoting a child to maintain the child with same aged peers even if the child's achievement lags the others' achievement), even if significantly more students are held back, 69% said students should have to pass a test to graduate from high school, and 51% wanted to tie teacher salaries and bonuses to test scores. Respondents called for greater educational accountability in conjunction with increased resources to support educational reforms. The respondents also supported testing, but in conjunction with other information about student performance for high-stakes decision making. Finally, a survey of parents, educators, and educational policy makers commissioned by Educational Testing Service (ETS), a test publisher, found that 68% of respondents wanted standardized testing to be part of a broader education initiative and 77% of the public, 61% of educational policy makers, and 47% of educators supported measures to strengthen accountability, including testing student achievement and holding teachers and schools responsible for achievement.

After reviewing these and other data, Driesler (2001) concluded that intense media coverage of HST was at least in part responsible for the perception that there is a public backlash against HST. He said "there is no evidence of a widespread public 'backlash' against testing. ... The truth is these anti-testing protests only reflect the views of a small, vocal minority of parents and not those of the much larger, assessment-supporting public" (p. 5).

In our society, controversy often finds resolution in the courtroom. Given what you have just read, it will be no surprise to hear that HST has come under legal challenge. In Texas and Indiana the use of high-stakes tests for graduation was challenged as racially biased, and the use of the Louisiana HST system for promotion was challenged because the plaintiffs alleged that students did not have a chance to learn the material they needed to pass the test (Robelen, 2001).

And HST has increasingly found its way into the political arena of our nation's capital. In addition to President Bush's advocacy for the annual assessments in the No Child Left Behind Act, U.S. Secretary of Education Rod Paige labeled those who argue against high-stakes tests defenders of "a broken system of education that dismisses certain children and classes of children as unteachable" (Ehrenfeld, 2001). Several statements from the U.S. Department of Education website also reflect how strongly the current administration believes in annual HST. "To get truly useful information that allows teachers to identify individual students who need help, we must test every child every year" (http://www.ed.gov/inits/backtoschool/teachers/part4.html). "Another benefit of annual testing is that it allows us to identify successful schools … and we can identify and reward schools that are helping their students make the most progress" (http://www.ed.gov/inits/backtoschool/teachers/part5.html). "Test score data allow schools to make decisions based on facts rather than guesses" (http://www.ed.gov/inits/backtoschool/teachers/part6.html).

Obviously, our limited review shows there are both strong opponents and proponents of HST and NCLB, and neither side has been shy about voicing their opinions. So what are you to do? We asked at the beginning of the chapter, "Who should you believe?" Our suggestion is that you consider both sides of the issue, but that you also consider the perspective of experts in the measurement field before you take a position on HST. Let's find out what they have to say, as reflected in the position taken about HST by national associations interested in educational testing and measurement. To date, none of the national professional associations has taken a position regarding NCLB.

WHAT DO NATIONAL ORGANIZATIONS SAY ABOUT HIGH-STAKES TESTS?

National organizations have memberships that are typically broad, diverse, and often opinionated. Thus, it is common within such organizations for the many and varied beliefs, philosophies, and backgrounds of the membership to be at odds with one another. This can limit the degree to which these organizations can "speak with one voice" and still represent their diverse members. National organizations of measurement experts are no different. Thus, you might expect that these national organizations would not be able to arrive at a consensus about a topic as controversial as HST. If so, you are mistaken.

Prominent national measurement organizations such as the American Educational Research Association (AERA), the American Psychological Association (APA), and the National Council on Measurement in Education (NCME) have individually developed policy or position statements about HST that are remarkably consistent. They all acknowledge the potential benefits that can accrue from HST programs when they are properly used. Yet, they also express concerns about the potential misuse of high-stakes tests.

The policy and position statements issued by organizations are similar, so we have chosen to focus on the policy statement released by the AERA as an exemplar of what national measurement organizations have to say about high-stakes tests. In case you are wondering, we also agree with what the AERA policy says. We also believe that many of our colleagues in the educational measurement arena support most, if not all, of the AERA recommendations as well. Let's see what it says.

The *AERA Position Statement Concerning High-Stakes Testing* in prek-12 Education (AERA, 2000) "is based on the 1999 *Standards for Educational and Psychological Testing* (AERA, APA, NCME, 1999)." The AERA statement clarifies that the 1999 Standards, which were developed in collaboration with the APA and NCME, "remain the most comprehensive and authoritative statement by the AERA concerning appropriate test use and interpretation." (p. 1). The AERA statement goes on to identify 12 conditions that "every high-stakes achievement testing program in education should meet" (p. 2). These 12 conditions are described briefly next.

AERA's Twelve Conditions That High-Stakes Testing Programs Should Meet

1. Protection against High-Stakes Decisions Based on a Single Test. Consistent with the position taken by many critics, the AERA recommends that when promotion and graduation decisions are based on a high-stakes test students should be given multiple opportunities to pass the test. When the test score is not a valid representation of a student's achievement the student should be provided with alternative, acceptable means to demonstrate achievement.

2. Adequate Resources and Opportunity to Learn. AERA recognizes that not all students have equal access to learning and resources. Thus, AERA recommends that when students are required to complete high-stakes tests the curriculum, materials, and instruction the students receive should reflect the content and processes measured by the high-stakes test, which in turn should reflect the state's academic standards.

3. Validation for Each Intended Separate Use. The same tests may be used for several different purposes and the validity evidence may differ for each intended use. AERA recommends that a separate evaluation of the test and testing program's strengths and limitations for each use should be completed. This is a critical point, because the same test may be used for promotion, for graduation, for school and district evaluation, and for comparisons with other schools, districts, and states or with past performance on the same test. Since tests are tools they may be better at one task than another. Some tests may be used as multipurpose tools, like Swiss Army knives; however, just as Swiss Army knives are better for some tasks than others, so too are tests.

4. Full Disclosure of Likely Negative Consequences of HST Programs. While it may not always be possible to fully identify all potential negative outcomes of a HST program, AERA reminds us that test developers and publishers should make an effort to appraise consumers about as many of these as they can identify. For example, estimates of the percentage of students expected to fail a high-stakes promotion test should be made available before the test is administered so that adequate planning for remedial instruction can be undertaken.

5. Alignment between the Test and the Curriculum. The content and the cognitive or mental processes called for by the test should be the same as called for by the curriculum or the state's academic standards. And when the test is used to evaluate the school or state curriculum it is important that the test reflect the state's academic standards. This relates to the important issues of content validity that we addressed earlier in this chapter and that we will address extensively in later chapters. However, AERA also recognized that close alignment of a test with state standards may result in a narrowing of the curriculum and recommended development of

multiple forms of a test and the development of new tests on a regular basis to decrease the likelihood that teachers simply teach to the test.

6. Validity of Passing Scores and Achievement Levels. AERA recommends that the purpose and meaning of passing scores (e.g., pass–fail) and ratings of achievement levels (e.g., unacceptable, acceptable, proficient, excellent) should be clearly stated. The validity of the test in identifying and classifying students within these different levels should be established. Similar to what we discussed earlier regarding state performance standards, there often is confusion between educators and non-educators regarding the meaning of such scores and ratings.

7. Opportunities for Meaningful Remediation for Examinees Who Fail High-Stakes Tests. AERA recommends that remedial efforts focus on the content and cognitive or mental processes necessary for success on the test and not simply on increasing test performance. Adequate time for students to master the content and processes also should be provided before the student retakes the test.

8. Appropriate Attention to Language Differences between Examinees. Obviously, those who are not proficient in the English language will not be able to perform to their potential on high-stakes tests administered in English. Thus, accommodations for students not proficient in English should be provided.

9. Appropriate Attention to Students with Disabilities. Similarly, we would not expect a child whose visual impairment hampers the ability to read the test items to do as well as a non-visually impaired student, all other factors being equal. Thus, accommodations should be given to students with disabilities so that score differences on a high-stakes test reflect differences in achievement rather than the child's disability. We will discuss a variety of assessment issues as they relate to students with disabilities in Chapters 20 and 21.

10. Careful Adherence to Explicit Rules for Determining Which Students Are to Be Tested. There are youth sports coaches who "forget" to tell weak players about games or encourage their parents to leave the players at home for important matches, so "they won't get stressed if they lose the game." Unfortunately, there have been allegations of teachers and administrators doing the same with children who are likely to perform poorly on high-stakes tests. To combat this abuse, AERA recommends that explicit policies be developed that specify which students will be excluded and under what circumstances, and that these policies be strictly adhered to over time. This is especially important where high-stakes test performance is compared over time, to ensure a stable basis for comparison.

11. Sufficient Reliability for Each Intended Use. You will learn more about reliability and its closely related cousin, accuracy, in Chapters 16 and 17. AERA recommends that separate reliability studies be performed for all intended uses of a high-stakes test for every group (e.g., ethnic minorities) or subgroup (e.g., ethnic minorities from several different income brackets) that may be considered.

12. Ongoing Evaluation of Intended and Unintended Effects of HST. Similar to condition 4, AERA recommends that state education agencies engage in an ongoing program of research designed to identify and disseminate the positive and negative effects of HST programs.

How Can a Teacher Use the Twelve Conditions?

We have included these conditions, and indeed this entire chapter, to empower you to speak out in an informed way about HST. As you know from our earlier discussions there is no shortage of opinion being offered, often forcefully and in seeming authoritative fashion, by the proponents and opponents of HST. Some of this is informed and helpful, some is naïve, misinformed, or intended to advance a personal or business agenda.

As a classroom teacher you may have the opportunity to provide input into local, district, or state level committees or other groups that can inform your state's HST program. We wish we could say that all state testing programs are aware of and follow the AERA conditions that summarize our own position so nicely. Unfortunately, this is not the case. If it were the case, there would be no need for the AERA to issue its position statement!

So, what you can do is use the checklist contained in Table 2.1 to help you inform others about the 12 conditions that all HST programs should meet. We know this may be intimidating or difficult, but we strongly encourage you to do so. Now that all 50 states have adopted it, and because HST is a component of NCLB, HST will be with us for many years to come, if not permanently. But we must remember that, compared to other aspects of educational reform, the movement is in its infancy, or toddler years at best. By questioning whether your state's program meets the 12 conditions you are helping inform decision makers and you are focusing the debate. If you don't, we fear that the debate will continue to be driven by the media, political considerations, financial interests, and

TABLE 2.1 A Checklist to Help Determine Whether Your State's High-Stakes Testing Program is Being Implemented According to the AERA Conditions

Condition	Yes	No	?
1. Protection against high-stakes decisions based on a single test	—	—	—
2. Adequate resources and opportunity to learn	—	—	—
3. Validation for each intended separate use	—	—	—
4. Full disclosure of likely negative consequences of HST programs	—	—	—
5. Alignment Between the Test and the Curriculum	—	—	—
6. Validity of passing scores and achievement levels	—	—	—
7. Opportunities for meaningful remediation for examinees who fail high-stakes tests	—	—	—
8. Appropriate attention to language differences between examinees	—	—	—
9. Appropriate attention to students with disabilities	—	—	—
10. Careful adherence to explicit rules for determining which students are to be tested	—	—	—
11. Sufficient reliability for each intended use	—	—	—
12. Ongoing evaluation of intended and unintended effects of HST	—	—	—

This checklist lists the 12 conditions that characterize a sound HST program, as identified by the American Educational Research Association (AERA). By visiting your state education agency's website or by asking questions of your state's HST program staff, you can determine whether your state's program meets these conditions.

emotion rather than by reason. If reason prevails we believe we will eventually reach the point where high-stakes tests and their use assume a respected, but limited, place in the educational reform movement.

Now that we have informed you about the complex, controversial world of high-stakes tests, and encouraged you to advocate for reform, if needed, in your state, we can turn to our last topic for this chapter. We will conclude this chapter with suggestions to help your students (and yourself) prepare for and complete high-stakes tests.

HELPING STUDENTS (AND YOURSELF) PREPARE FOR HIGH-STAKES TESTS

Some things are clear about high-stakes tests. They are in use in all 50 states, are part of federal law, and will be around for some time to come. Thus, getting frustrated and annoyed with them, dreading high-stakes day, or wishing the test would just go away will do nothing but increase your stress level, and possibly that of your students. Too much stress can interfere with your performance as a teacher, and with the performance of your students on a high-stakes test. And, the more you focus on your frustrations and wishes the less effective you are likely to be as a teacher. What to do? We suggest you keep yourself focused on the task, be sure students and parents have accurate information about the test, incorporate test-taking skills and strategies into your daily lessons, respond to student questions about the test honestly and appropriately, and utilize whatever test preparation materials are made available to you.

Focus on the Task, Not Your Feelings about It

Since promotion and graduation of your students, and your teaching position, can be affected by your state's HST program it makes sense to focus less on your feelings about the test and more on the demands of the task before you. What exactly are those demands? Well, because the content and the cognitive processes identified by state academic standards are very detailed and differ across states, we can't tell you exactly what you need to focus your instruction on. However, it is critical that you obtain your state's standards. If your state's test is aligned (i.e., has content validity) with those standards you will have a good idea about what content and processes will need to be mastered by your students to ensure good performance on the high-stakes test. In many cases, this information will be provided to you by your school or district. If it isn't, visit your district's curriculum director or your state's website and it should be available there.

If you have become accustomed to teaching the same topics the same way over the years you may have to modify your instructional methods a little, somewhat, or a lot to match the content and processes identified in the state standards. We can't say how much modification will be necessary. We can say that ensuring that you target your state standards in your instruction is probably the single most important thing you can do to prepare your students to perform well on the tests. Of course, to the degree that they do well you improve your chances of obtaining recognition and other incentives and minimize the likelihood that you will face embarrassment, reconstitution, or other penalties.

Inform Students and Parents about the Importance of the Test

Providing accurate, developmentally appropriate information to students and their parents can enhance motivation, preparation, and performance.

Keep Students Focused on the Facts   While some students will already under-stand the purpose and relevance of the test, there will always be several who do not. To get students to try their best some advocate scare tactics or use of rewards. Others say these strategies will only increase the stress and pressure students feel and impair their performance, or that we are sending students the wrong message. Our position is that neither of these approaches is as effective as taking the time to explain the reason the test is being administered, how the results will be used, and how the test is relevant to their learning. We believe that if you approach the test in a rational, informed way and inform your students in a rational way you will be more likely to engage and motivate your students to do well and they will be more likely to take the test seriously and carefully.

Keep Your Discussion Developmentally Appropriate   In talking with your students keep their developmental level in mind. You may feel negatively about the tests or the way they are used. You may also be a strong advocate for tests or the way they are used. Indeed, you may see the tests as both beneficial and harmful. As an adult you are capable of discerning the "shades of gray" that always accompany important issues and policies like accountability and educational reform. However, cognitive and develop-mental psychologists have long demonstrated that children are not capable of this kind of multidimensional, complex thought until their adolescent years (Steinberg, 2002). And even when they are capable of this type of complex thought they are not skilled in its application. Why do we mention this?

Too often as adults we view children as small versions of adults instead of recog-nizing there are qualitative differences in the way children and adults think. So, instead of presenting long, complex lectures about the tests, or the pros or cons of the tests, keep it simple. Let your students know they have learned what will be necessary to do well, and that you expect them to do well. Frame the testing as an opportunity to demonstrate their knowledge and mastery. Resist the temptation to get on the soapbox or engage the class in discussions that involve pedagogical, political, financial, and other elements that are well beyond their capacity to comprehend, especially in the elementary grades.

Be Sure Parents Are "in the Loop"   Keep in mind that your pupils' parents are also key to appropriately motivating the students to do well. But do not assume that because of increased media attention to HST that all parents have adequate and accurate information about the purpose of the test and the uses to which results will be put. Check with your principal to see whether you can circulate a brief letter or newsletter to parents informing them about the relevant issues, describing what you are doing to help their students do their best, and asking them to support your efforts. Be sure parents know the purpose, relevance, and uses of the test and important details like the test dates and times. If you are supplying the child with assignments to help prepare for the high-stakes test be sure the parents know about this and monitor the child's completion of these assignments with at least the same degree of attention afforded to regular assignments. You can also encourage parents to avoid scheduling appointments on test days (because partial test results are sometimes disallowed) and to be sure the child gets to bed on time, has a good breakfast, and arrives at school on time on the day of the tests, and that the child is encouraged to do his or her best.

Teach Test-Taking Skills as Part of Regular Instruction

Some students seem to perform better on tests than other students. This may seem to be because of luck, aptitude, confidence, or some other factor. However, there also is an element of skill in test taking that affects student performance. If all students in your class are at least aware of various test-taking skills, overall performance on the high-stakes test should increase. We realize that with everything else a busy teacher has to do it may be difficult to find time to include instruction in test-taking strategies. However, you should be able to teach most of the following test-taking skills as part of your regular instruction on an ongoing basis without greatly increasing your burden. For example, you can teach your students to do the following.

Follow Directions Carefully   Some students, especially those who tend to be impulsive or who have difficulty reading, may neglect to read directions at all. In some cases, these students may not format their answers correctly and may lose much or all credit for an entire section, and not because of a lack of mastery! To minimize this emphasize the importance of not just reading but understanding directions in your classroom before the test. You can address this critical point frequently during your daily classroom routine and remind students about it during your regular classroom tests rather than devoting additional time to it.

Read Test Items, Passages, and Related Information Carefully   Who hasn't rushed through a test item only to find out you missed or misread a word and lost credit as a result? You may reduce the likelihood your pupils will do this on the high-stakes test by providing practice during in-class and homework assignment and during your regular tests in highlighting key words, re-reading items, double-checking answers if time allows, etc. For multiple-choice questions, remind students to read each option before selecting their answer. Sometimes students answer multiple-choice items incorrectly because they answer the first option that sounds right when a later option is more correct. Again, some of your pupils will already be doing this, but as we mentioned above there can be a wide variation in test-taking experience, and this may be especially true for pupils raised in cultures where standardized tests are nonexistent or not employed as much as they are within our culture.

Manage Test-Taking Time   While students must work quickly to complete high-stakes tests, they must also work accurately. This too is a skill that can be improved with practice in the classroom before the test. Because it may not be possible to spend valuable instructional time on this skill, you may be able to incorporate it into your lessons. Instead of giving students "as much time as they need" to answer a question or complete a project, impose a time limit. For complex tasks you can also ask students to plan out the number of minutes they will allocate to each phase of the performance or project. You may also consider awarding two marks or grades, one for accuracy and one for speed, to enable pupils to get a sense of how their performance in each domain compares with that of their peers.

Attempt Easier Items First   Many teacher-made tests begin with easy items and then end with the most difficult items. High-stakes tests typically have a more random order to their difficulty level. Unprepared students may encounter a difficult item or set of items early in the test and spend inordinate amounts of time on the difficult items, items that even the best students may miss the great majority of the time! As a result they may allocate too little time to the moderately difficult items that they have a better chance of answering correctly. When you administer your own tests encourage the students to answer as many items as they know initially, before they attempt the more difficult items. This will help ensure they do not miss credit for easier items at the end of the test because time has run out. And instead of making your test progress from easy to difficult, mix up the order to enhance transfer of this skill to the HST setting.

Eliminate Options before Answering   Test-wise students will know that they can increase their chances of answering correctly if they can eliminate one or two multiple-choice or matching options. Other students will need to be instructed in this strategy. Again, this can be incorporated into your typical classroom assignments and exercises and in preparation for classroom tests; it does not have to be something you add on to your other responsibilities.

Teach Students to Check Their Answers after They Complete the Test
Some pupils have such an aversion to tests or take tests so lightly that they do not check their answers after they finish a test, even if time remains. While there may not be any way to be sure that all your pupils will check their answers, you can help them learn a strategy for doing so by modeling this as you review the scoring rubrics you will learn to develop later in this text for various teacher-made tests, experiments, projects, term papers, etc., or by providing checklists, "to do" lists, etc., that may be posted on the board or kept on the pupils' desks as they take tests and complete projects.

As the Test Day Approaches Respond to Student Questions Openly and Directly

When we have unanswered questions about important events we develop an air of uncertainty. Before a high-stakes test we can expect that some children will begin to wonder or worry about various things. (For example, What will the test look like? Will I be the last one finished? What if I get a bad grade? What can I do if I have a question?) This sense of uncertainty is a common cause of anxiety, too much of which can also interfere with test performance. To minimize this anxiety (which may peak the day before the test day) provide your pupils with as much information about the test's format and administration procedures as you have. This may include basic information such as days, times, subjects, format or style of responding, and how their questions will be addressed during the test. It may be useful to role play various scenarios with the class to ensure they are clear on various procedures.

Take Advantage of Whatever Preparation Materials Are Available

In many states the state education agency, your district, or some other entity may also provide you with helpful practice tests and exercises designed to familiarize students with the style, format, and other aspects of the high-stakes test. While these exercises will likely take away from instructional time, they may also help with test-taking efficiency and stress management, by minimizing students' uncertainty and thereby increasing the proportion of time students spend focusing on the test items rather than wondering or worrying about how they fill in the answer sheets. In any case, we encourage you to take full advantage of preparation materials that are provided to you to supplement the other suggestions we have offered. Remember, by doing so you are not only helping your students, you are also helping yourself. Good luck!

SUMMARY

This chapter has introduced you to high-stakes testing (HST). Its major points are as follows:

1. The No Child Left Behind Act (NCLB) was passed in 2002, after all 50 states and the District of Columbia developed state HST programs.

2. Although there are similarities between NCLB and state HST programs there also are important differences. NCLB is about much more than HST, but HST is a part of NCLB.

3. HST is controversial but is now widespread.

4. High-stakes tests, like other tests, are only tools and their usefulness depends on how well constructed they are and whether they are used and interpreted appropriately.

5. HST is the use of test and assessment results to make decisions that are of prominent educational, social, or financial impact.

6. The impact of HST may be felt by pupils, teachers, administrators, homeowners, the business community, politicians, and others.

7. HST affects students by determining or influencing strongly promotion and graduation decisions.

8. HST affects incentives for teachers and administrators, including financial rewards and reconstitution.

9. HST affects homeowners and business decisions because of its effects on real estate values.

10. HST has also become a prominent part of state and national political campaigns.

11. All states now have some form of academic standards that are the objectives of instruction, with the development of reading or English standards being more advanced than those for math or science.

12. Performance standards refer to the level of performance necessary for a student to demonstrate mastery of academic standards.

13. Alignment refers to the extent to which a high-stakes test actually measures, or has evidence of content validity with, a state's academic standards.

14. The extent of alignment varies from state to state and may be better with well-constructed, state-designed criterion-referenced high-stakes tests than with national, norm-referenced high-stakes tests.

15. While protests over the use of high-stakes tests have been prominent, they have arisen mainly from within the education community. The majority of the public seems to support the use of high-stakes tests.

16. National measurement associations have taken similar positions regarding HST and these are summarized in the American Educational Research Association (AERA) Position Statement entitled "12 Conditions That HST Programs Should Meet."

17. Teachers can utilize the checklist provided in Table 2.1 to determine whether their state's high-stakes test meets the 12 conditions offered by the AERA.

18. To help students (and teachers) prepare for high-stakes tests we recommend these strategies:
    a. Focusing on the task, not your feelings about it,
    b. Informing students and parents about the importance of the test,
    c. Teaching test-taking skills from the first day of school as part of regular instruction,
    d. Responding openly and directly to student questions especially as the test day approaches, and
    e. Taking advantage of whatever preparation materials are made available.

FOR DISCUSSION

1. One of the criticisms of HST is that preparations for the test focus on rote memory at the expense of higher level thinking. Describe some ways that higher level thinking may be encouraged by high-stakes tests. How could the preparation process be modified to encourage higher level thinking? (Note: If you are not already familiar with it, you may find it helpful to review Bloom's taxonomy in Chapter 5 to help you understand what higher level thinking is like before you attempt this task.)

2. Speculate about why HST remains popular with the majority of the public and yet generates so much criticism from teachers and other educators. Be sure to consider education reform and accountability and other contemporary issues addressed in this chapter.

*3. Alignment of a high-stakes test with state academic standards is critical for a test to demonstrate evidence of its content validity—the most important technical consideration of an achievement test. NCLB also requires that annual academic assessments should be based on state standards. When would a state test developed to measure the state's standards be more likely to be aligned with state standards than an off-the-shelf, nationally standardized test?

*4. If a state-developed test is more likely to be aligned with state standards, why do you think some states use a nationally standardized test that may not be so well aligned?

5. Imagine that you have used the AERA's 12 conditions to evaluate your state's HST program and you have found it to be lacking in several dimensions. How could you as a classroom teacher draw attention to the test's limitations? What might the implications be of drawing such attention to your state's test?

6. After reviewing the suggestions we have provided to help your students and yourselves prepare for high-stakes tests consider how those suggestions may need to be modified based on your knowledge of yourself and a hypothetical class of high-achieving students. How might the strategies need to be modified for low-achieving students?

*Answers to Questions 3 and 4 appear in Appendix F.

CHAPTER 3

THE PURPOSE OF TESTING

IN THE classroom, decisions are constantly being made. As a teacher you may decide:

John, Don, Marie, and Jeri are ready to advance to level 7 in reading, but Chris and Linda are not.

Keisha receives an A; Mary receives a C.

Ed has difficulty discriminating between long and short vowel sounds.

My teaching method is not effective for this group of students.

Arthur is a social isolate.

Mike's attitude toward school has improved.

Pablo should be moved to a higher reading group.

Mrs. Morrison's class is better at math concepts than my class.

Donna is a "slow learner."

On what basis do teachers make decisions such as these? In some cases the teacher relies solely on personal judgment. In other cases the teacher relies solely on measurement data. In still other cases the teacher combines measurement data with judgment or subjective data. Which approach is best?

Anti-test advocates suggest that testing should be done away with. Unfortunately, decisions will still have to be made. Teachers, as human beings, are subject to good and bad days, biases, student and parent pressures, faulty perceptions, and a variety of other influences. In other words, relying solely on a teacher's judgment means relying on a subjective decision-making process. Naturally, no teacher would intentionally make a "wrong" decision about a student. However, all of us make mistakes.

Tests represent an attempt to provide objective data that can be used with subjective impressions to make better, more defensible decisions. This is the purpose of testing, or why we test. Tests are not subject to the ups and downs or other influences that affect teachers. Subjective impressions can often place in perspective important aspects of a decision-making problem for which no objective data exist. Thus, it seems likely that a combination of subjective judgments and objective data will result in more appropriate rather than less appropriate decisions. Reliance on measurement data alone can even prove to be detrimental to decision making. Although such data are objective, we must remember that they are only estimates of a student's behavior. Test data are never 100% accurate!

In summary, we test to provide objective information, which we combine with our subjective, commonsense impressions to make better educational decisions. However, suggesting that combining objective measurement data and subjective impressions results in better educational decisions assumes that:

- Measurement data are valid; and
- The teacher or individual interpreting such data understands the uses and limitations of such data.

Unfortunately, too often one or both of these assumptions are violated in the decision-making process. Obviously, when this happens, the resultant educational decisions may be invalid.

TESTING, ACCOUNTABILITY, AND THE CLASSROOM TEACHER

It is no longer surprising to say that the American public has become disenchanted with education. Reduced school budgets, defeated bond issues, and the elimination of special programs are common occurrences. The reasons for this disenchantment are many and complex, but at least some can be traced to poor decision making in our schools—decision making not just at the classroom level, but at the grade, school, district, and national levels as well. Nevertheless, the most frequently made decisions are the everyday decisions of the classroom teacher, which also form the cornerstone for other decisions at higher levels of the educational structure. If the cornerstone is weak, the structure itself cannot be sound.

At the classroom level, the extent to which unsound educational decision making occurs is not yet known. However, the everyday decisions of classroom teachers are coming under closer and closer scrutiny. Classroom teachers are increasingly being asked questions like:

PARENT: On what grounds was Jane moved to the slower reading group?

PRINCIPAL: Are your students well prepared for the annual academic assessment next week?

COUNSELOR: How is it that you've determined Tom has a behavior problem?

PARENT: Is Billie performing at a level in math that will help us make AYP?

In Chapter 1 we described some of the new responsibilities that classroom teachers will have to assume under the 2002 No Child Left Behind Act (NCLB) and the 2004 Individuals with Disabilities Education Improvement Act (IDEIA–04). Regular education teachers are now expected to help both regular and special education students make Adequate Yearly Progress (AYP) under NCLB. Regular education teachers also are required to be members of the Individual Educational Plan (IEP) teams: Teachers will now have to include and assess students with disabilities in the general curriculum to help the IEP team determine performance and progress and to provide parents with regular reports of progress. While special education staff may assist in this task, it is regular, not special education, teachers who are experts in the general curriculum. As a result, regular education teachers may now expect to hear questions like:

SPECIAL ED TEACHER: We need objective data about Billie's progress in the general curriculum for the IEP team meeting next week. What do you have?

PRINCIPAL: The annual CTBS [i.e., a standardized test battery] testing is next month. Based on what you know from testing Billie in the regular classroom, will he need any special accommodations to take it?

IDEIA–04 also extends the teacher's involvement with students with disabilities to require participation in behavior plan development, implementation, and evaluation when behavior impedes progress in the general curriculum. As a result, classroom teachers can now expect to hear questions like these:

PARENT: What evidence do you have that Billie's behavior plan is working?

SCHOOL PSYCHOLOGIST: Is Billie's behavior plan working in the regular classroom? What about his attitude? Attitudes can affect behavior, so it would be nice to know whether his attitude toward being in the regular class has changed.

To respond to questions about behavior, teachers will need more than data about achievement. In Chapter 21 we describe a number of measures, both teacher-made and standardized, that classroom teachers can use to collect classroom-based achievement, behavioral, social, and attitudinal information that can be invaluable to the IEP team (including the regular education teacher!) in developing and evaluating progress in the general curriculum and behavior plans.

Clearly, the requirements of IDEIA–04 will place increased demands on the regular education teacher's time and skill. What does the teacher do? Give up? Complain? Yearn for the "good old days"? We hope not! Yet, the answers to these and many other questions need to be provided if education of all learners is to improve.

Fortunately, in passing IDEIA–04 Congress recognized that regular education teachers must be given support to achieve the goals of the new law. IDEIA–04 requires increased staff development resources and support for regular education teachers to meet these demands. And the task may not be as overwhelming as it may appear at first glance. Many of the techniques that regular education teachers currently use to assess regular education students are readily applicable to the assessment of special learners. A good working knowledge and understanding of testing and measurement—what you will have on successful completion of this course—will help you meet the requirements of both IDEIA–04 and NCLB.

The successful teacher of tomorrow not only will have to report test data to parents, principals, counselors, academic review committees, and even the courts, but will have to interpret test data and be fully aware of the uses and limitations of such data to more closely monitor progress toward state proficiency standards under NCLB. One of the first steps toward acquiring the ability to interpret test data is to understand the different types of educational decisions that are made from measurement data.

Types of Educational Decisions

Measurement data enter into decisions at all levels of education, from those made by the individual classroom teacher to those made by the state Commissioner of Education. There are several ways of categorizing these decisions. We have found the following classification approach, suggested by Thorndike, Cunningham, Thorndike, and Hagen (1991), useful for understanding the various types of decisions that can be made in schools. The categories range from specific everyday in-class decision making to much less frequent administrative decisions. The categories of decisions discussed here are instructional, grading, diagnostic, selection, placement, counseling and guidance, program or curriculum, and administrative policy.

Instructional Decisions   Instructional decisions are the nuts-and-bolts types of decisions made by all classroom teachers. In fact, these are the most frequently made decisions in education. Examples of such decisions include the following:

> Spending more time in math class on addition with regrouping,
>
> Skipping the review you planned before the test, and
>
> Sticking to your instructional plan.

Since educational decisions at classroom levels have a way of affecting decisions at higher levels, it is important that these types of decisions be sound ones. Deciding more time should be spent on addition with regrouping when it doesn't need to be wastes valuable instructional time and may have very noticeable effects on achievement in other areas, or classroom behavior. Students may get turned off, tune you out, or act up.

You may expect similar detrimental effects when you present material too quickly. Moving too quickly almost invariably results in skill deficiencies in some students. You can be sure that many currently illiterate people were unable to master various reading skills in school because their teachers moved through the curricula too quickly for them to acquire the needed skills.

Today, instructional decisions are also linked to NCLB accountability requirements. If students do not do well on valid classroom tests, they are likely to do poorly on benchmark and annual academic assessments. This can potentially have negative effects on the school and the student (see Chapter 1).

Grading Decisions   Educational decisions based on grades are also made by the classroom teacher, but much less frequently than instructional decisions. Grades, or marks, are usually assigned about every six to nine weeks, and the teacher often considers test scores and other data in making decisions about who gets A's, B's, and so on. If test data are used, naturally it is important that such data be acquired from appropriate tests, including performance and portfolio assessments, which will be described in detail in Chapters 8 and 9. Teacher-made tests are usually the most appropriate for grading decisions.

Other factors such as attendance, ability, attitude, behavior, and effort are sometimes graded also. A common mistake is to combine one or more of these with achievement data to decide on grades. Although each of these factors represents an area of legitimate concern to classroom teachers, and although assigning grades for one or more of these factors is perfectly acceptable, these grades should be kept separate from grades for achievement. These issues will be discussed at length in Chapter 11. Methods used to measure nonachievement factors will be presented in Chapter 21.

Grade inflation—or the tendency for teachers to assign higher grades today than in the past for the same level of performance—has become a matter of considerable public concern. Annual academic assessments under NCLB and state high-stakes testing programs to make decisions about student promotion and graduation have helped bring grading concerns to the public's attention. Consequently, it will be no surprise if grading decisions and policies come under increasing public scrutiny and accountability in the future.

For most students, grading decisions are probably the most influential decisions made about them during their school years. All students are familiar with the effects grades have on them, their peers, and their parents. Given all the attention and seriousness afforded to grades today, it is advisable for teachers to invest extra care and time in these important decisions, since they may be called on to defend their decisions more frequently in the future. The teacher who is most likely to be able to defend the grades that are assigned will be the teacher who (1) adheres to an acceptable grading policy, (2) uses data obtained through multiple, appropriate measurement instruments, and (3) knows the uses and limitations of such data.

Diagnostic Decisions Diagnostic decisions are those made about a student's strengths and weaknesses and the reason or reasons for them. For example, a teacher may notice in test results that Ryan can successfully subtract four-digit numbers from four-digit numbers, but not if carrying is involved. Given this information, the teacher decides that Ryan does not fully understand the carrying process. The teacher has made a diagnostic decision based, at least in part, on information yielded by an informal, teacher-made test. Such decisions can also be made with the help of a standardized test.

Because these decisions are of considerable importance, we believe that objective test data should always be used along with the teacher's subjective judgment to make such decisions. In the past, diagnostic decisions often have been delegated to specialists. Under IDEIA–04, however, inclusion of students with disabilities in the regular classroom is now the norm and the regular classroom teacher can increasingly be expected to make diagnostic decisions to facilitate their progress in the general curriculum. We will discuss the role of the regular classroom teacher in making decisions about students with disabilities in Chapter 20, and we address the appropriate development, use, and interpretation of teacher-made and standardized assessment data to make better diagnostic decisions about students with disabilities in Chapter 21.

The three types of decisions listed—instructional, grading, and diagnostic—are types of educational decisions every classroom teacher must make. The five remaining types of decisions are made by specialists, administrators, or committees composed of teachers, specialists, and administrators. Their decisions are typically based on standardized rather than teacher-made tests. Although teachers are not directly involved in the decisions based on standardized test data, it is a fact that teachers are often called on to interpret the results of standardized tests for parents and students since parents often turn to teachers to explain standardized test results, and since the tests are part of a student's cumulative work record. Standardized testing will be discussed in detail in Chapters 18 and 19. For now, let's get familiar with the types of decisions in which standardized tests play a role.

Selection Decisions Selection decisions involve test data used in part for accepting or rejecting applicants for admission into a group, program, or institution. The SAT that you probably took before being admitted to college and the Graduate Record Examination (GRE) that you will be required to take if you intend to go to graduate school are examples of standardized tests that are used to help make selection decisions. At the elementary and secondary school level, teachers are often asked to assist with testing pupils for selection into remedial programs that are designed to improve educational opportunities for economically disadvantaged students.

Placement Decisions   Placement decisions are made after an individual has been accepted into a program. They involve determining where in a program someone is best suited to begin work. For example, you may have had to take an English test prior to freshman college registration to determine whether you were ready for first-year college English courses, needed remedial work, or were ready for intermediate or advanced courses. Standardized achievement test data are often used in elementary and secondary schools for placing students in courses that are at their current level of functioning.

Counseling and Guidance Decisions   Counseling and guidance decisions involve the use of test data to help recommend programs of study that are likely to be appropriate for a student. For example, in your junior or senior year in high school you probably took the Differential Aptitude Test (DAT) or some similar aptitude test battery. Partly on the basis of your scores, your guidance counselor may have recommended that you consider one or more career paths or apply to a particular set of colleges.

Program or Curriculum Decisions   Program or curriculum decisions are usually made at the school district level after an evaluation study comparing two or more programs has been completed. Your district's decision to abandon a traditional math program in favor of a new math program is an example of a program or curriculum decision. Teachers are often required to participate in these studies and even to help collect test data for them.

Administrative Policy Decisions   Administrative policy decisions may be made at the school, district, state, or national level. Based at least in part on measurement data, these decisions may determine the amount of money to be channeled into a school or district, whether a school or district is entitled to special funding, or what needs to be done to improve a school, district, or the nation's achievement scores. In Chapters 1 and 2 we discussed NCLB and high-stakes testing and the types of decisions they are now associated with. Typically these decisions have the most impact on students or on school staff. The decisions that have impact most directly on students are

> Promotion decisions—whether a student's score is at or above the cut-off established to allow the student to be promoted to the next grade, whether the student will be offered an opportunity for remedial instruction, or whether the student is retained and must repeat the year, and
>
> Graduation decisions—whether a student's score is at or above the cut-off established to allow the student to obtain a high school diploma, or whether the student must retake the test.

The decisions that have impact most directly on school staff include

Reconstitution—if a class, school, or district's performance on a high-stakes test is unacceptably low, or fails to make Adequate Yearly Progress (AYP) a teacher, principal, or an entire school staff may be replaced or "reconstituted" in an effort to break a pattern of low achievement.

Recognition—if a class, school, or district's performance on a high-stakes test is high enough the class, teacher, school, principal, district, or superintendent may qualify for financial or other incentives, including recognition at local, state, and national gatherings designed to recognize exemplary or high-performing classes, school, and districts.

Thus far we have considered the purposes of testing, or why we test. Next, let's consider two other aspects of educational measurement: how we measure and what we measure.

A Pinch of Salt

Jean-Pierre, the master French chef, was watching Marcel, who was Jean-Pierre's best student, do a flawless job of preparing the master's hollandaise sauce. Suddenly, Jean-Pierre began pummeling Marcel with his fists. "Fool!" he shouted. "I said a pinch of salt, not a pound!" Jean-Pierre was furious. He threatened to pour the sauce over Marcel's head, but before he could, Marcel indignantly emptied the whole salt container into the pot.

"There, you old goat, I only added a pinch to begin with, but now there is a pound of salt in the sauce—and I'm going to make you eat it!"

Startled by his student's response, Jean-Pierre regained his composure. "All right, all right. So you didn't add a pound, but you certainly added more than a pinch!"

Still upset, Marcel shouted, "Are you senile? You were watching me all the time and you saw me add only one pinch!" Marcel pressed his right thumb and index finger together an inch from the master's nose to emphasize his point.

"Aha! You see! There you have it!" Jean-Pierre said. "That is not the way to measure a pinch. Only the tips of the thumb and index finger make contact when you measure a pinch!"

Marcel looked at the difference between his idea of a "pinch" of salt and the master's. Indeed, there was quite a difference. Marcel's finger and thumb made contact not just at the fingertips, but all the way down to the knuckle. At Jean-Pierre's request, they both deposited a "pinch" of salt on the table. Marcel's pinch contained four or five times as much salt as Jean-Pierre's.

Who is correct? Is Marcel's pinch too much? Is Jean-Pierre's pinch too little? Whose method would you use to measure a pinch of salt? Perhaps relying on an established standard will help. *Webster's New Collegiate Dictionary* defines a pinch this way: "As much as may be taken between the finger and the thumb." If *Webster's* is our standard of comparison, we may conclude that both Jean-Pierre and Marcel are correct. Yet, we see that Marcel's pinch contains a lot more salt than Jean-Pierre's. It seems we have a problem. Until Marcel and Jean-Pierre decide on who is correct and adopt a more specific or standard definition of a "pinch," they may never resolve their argument. Furthermore, if we were to try to match the recipes they develop for their culinary masterpieces, we might never succeed unless we know which measuring method to use.

This measurement problem resulted from the lack of a clear, unambiguous method of measurement. Who is to say Jean-Pierre's method is better than Marcel's or vice versa? In Jean-Pierre's eyes, his method is correct and Marcel's is not. In Marcel's eyes, his method is correct and Jean-Pierre's is not. According to *Webster's*, both are correct. A clear and unambiguous method of measuring a "pinch" would resolve the problem. It seems reasonable to suggest that any time measurement procedures—that is, how we measure—are somewhat subjective and lack specificity, similar interpretive problems may arise.

"Pinching" in the Classroom

Mr. Walsh assigns his history grades based entirely on his monthly tests and a comprehensive final examination. He takes attendance, comments on homework assignments, encourages classroom participation, and tries to help his students develop positive attitudes toward history, but none of these is considered in assigning grades. Mr. Carter, another history teacher, assigns grades in the following manner:

Monthly tests 20%

Comprehensive final 20%

Homework 10%

Attendance 20%

Class participation 15%

Attitude 15%

Both teachers assign roughly the same numbers of A's, B's, C's, D's, and F's each semester. Does an A in Mr. Walsh's class mean the same thing as an A in Mr. Carter's class? Obviously, Mr. Walsh "pinches" more heavily when it comes to test data than does Mr. Carter (100% versus 40%). On the other hand, Mr. Carter "pinches" more heavily on attendance and participation in assigning grades than does Mr. Walsh (35% versus 0%).

Which method is correct? In interpreting grades earned in each class, would you say that students who earn A's in either class are likely to do equally well on history tests constructed by a third teacher? Should Mr. Walsh "pinch," that is, assign grades, more like Mr. Carter, or should Mr. Carter assign grades more like Mr. Walsh? Obviously, there are no easy answers to these questions. The differences in how chefs Jean-Pierre and Marcel measure a pinch of salt result from the lack of a clear, unambiguous definition of a pinch. Similarly, the differences in how Mr. Walsh and Mr. Carter measure learning in history result from the lack of a clear, unambiguous definition of what constitutes a grade. As a result, their grades represent somewhat different aspects of their student's performance. The way they "pinch" or how they measure differs.

For Jean-Pierre and Marcel, there is a relatively easy way out of the disagreement. Only their method of measurement or how they measure is in question, not what they are measuring. It would be easy to develop a small container, a common standard, that could then be used to uniformly measure pinches of salt. In the classroom, the task is more difficult for Mr. Walsh and Mr. Carter. What is in question is not only their measurement method, or how they weigh components of a grade, but what they are measuring.

Much of what we measure or attempt to measure in the classroom is not clearly defined. For example, think of how many different ways you have heard learning, intelligence, or adjustment defined. Yet, we constantly attempt to assess or measure these traits. Furthermore, the methods we use to measure these often ill-defined traits are not very precise. But even good methods cannot accurately measure ill-defined or undefined traits.

Only when both what to measure and how to measure have been considered, specified, and clearly defined can we hope to eliminate the problems involved in measuring and interpreting classroom information. The task is formidable. We cannot hope to solve it entirely, but we can minimize the subjectivity, the inaccuracy, and the more common interpretative errors often inherent in classroom measurement. Achieving these goals will go far toward helping us "pinch" properly. Sound measurement practice will benefit you professionally. Moreover, it will benefit most those unwitting and captive receptors of measurement practice, your students.

The examples presented are intended to alert you to two general problems encountered in classroom measurement:

1. Defining what it is that you want to measure, and

2. Determining how to measure whatever it is that you are measuring.

WHAT TO MEASURE

Defining what to measure may, at first glance, not appear like much of a problem, but consider the following example:

> *Mrs. Norton taught first-year math in a small private high school with high-achieving students. She prided herself on her tests, which stressed the ability to apply math concepts to real-life situations. She did this by constructing fairly elaborate word problems. When she moved to another part of the state, she went to work in an inner city high school teaching an introductory math skills course. Realizing that her new students were not nearly as "sharp" as her private-school students, she "toned down" her tests by substituting simpler computations in her word problems. Even with this substitution, 29 of her 31 students failed the "easier" test. Dejected, she substituted even simpler computations into her next test, only to have 30 out of 31 fail. She concluded that her students "totally lack even basic math skills," and applied for a transfer.*

Think about these questions:

Do you agree with Mrs. Norton's conclusion? If so, why? If not, why not?

Are there any possible alternative conclusions?

What might she have done differently?

We disagree with Mrs. Norton. While it may be that some of her students lack or are weak in basic math skills, there seems to be little conclusive evidence that all, or even most, lack these skills. There may be another explanation for her students' poor performance.

Her tests were originally designed to measure the ability of her high-achieving private-school students to apply their skills to real-life situations. This is what she wanted to measure.

In her public-school skills class, what Mrs. Norton wanted to measure was a bit different. What she wanted to measure was not the ability to apply skills (at least not at first) but whether the skills were ever acquired. How she measured must also be considered. Her tests consisted of fairly elaborate word problems. They may have been tests of reading ability as much as tests of math applications. Their reading level may have been appropriate for her "bright" students but too advanced for her new students. Since her tests measured skill application and reading ability rather than skill acquisition, how Mrs. Norton measured also was not appropriate. Assuming you are convinced it is important to define what you are measuring, let's look in more detail at what we mean by determining how to measure.

HOW TO MEASURE

Mrs. Norton got into trouble mainly because she wasn't sure what she was measuring. At least by giving a written test she had the right idea about one aspect of how to measure basic math skills . . . . Or did she? How else could basic math skills be measured? An oral test, you say? But in a class of 31 students? Any other ideas? What about a questionnaire without any math problems, just questions about math skills to which students respond yes or no to indicate whether they believe they have acquired a certain skill? How about simply observing your students in the process of completing a math problem? Or how about requiring your students to complete a practical project requiring math skills?

The techniques mentioned are all possible measurement methods, some for measuring basic math skills, others for measuring attitudes toward math. Questionnaires, oral responses, observation, and projects are common methods of measurement. These and a variety of performance assessment techniques, including portfolios, will be discussed later in this text. For now, simply be aware that there are alternatives to written tests and that how we measure is often determined by what we measure. Let's return to Mrs. Norton and the most commonly used form of measurement, the written test.

Written Tests

The test Mrs. Norton used was heavily verbal, which suggests that it relied almost exclusively on words to ask questions. Although the answers to her questions may have been numerical, the questions themselves were word problems. While there is probably no better way to measure basic math skills than through a written test, was the written test that Mrs. Norton used the best type of written test? We would say no and suggest that her test should have looked more like the following instead of consisting of only word problems:

$$(1)\ \begin{array}{r} 1431 \\ +\ 467 \end{array} \qquad (2)\ \begin{array}{r} 798 \\ -581 \end{array} \qquad (3)\ \begin{array}{r} 125 \\ \times\ 7 \end{array} \qquad (4)\ 21 \div 11 =$$

The advantages of a basic math skills test with items similar in format to those here include the following:

- They do not rely on reading ability.

- Basic skills are measured directly.

- More items can be included in the same amount of test time.

All these points are important. The first two help ensure that the test measures what it is supposed to measure (i.e., the test's validity). The last improves the test's score reliability, or the consistency of the scores it yields over time. Furthermore, inspecting a student's written work on such a test can help you diagnose errors in the process used by students to arrive at an answer.

So, you see, there can be different types of written tests. The point of our discussion about Mrs. Norton is simply that how you measure must always match what you measure. Whether you give word problems, use number formats, or provide real-world examples depends on whether you are measuring problem-solving ability, knowledge of facts or processes, application, and so on. Table 3.1 defines some common types of written tests.

In this section we have considered the importance of knowing what we want to measure and how we want to measure. We also saw that determining what and how may not be as simple as it appears. However, both considerations are vitally important in classroom measurement, since failing to be clear about them is likely to result in invalid measurement.

TABLE 3.1 Types of Written Tests

Type of Written Test	Description
Verbal	Emphasizes reading, writing, or speaking. Most tests in education are verbal tests.
Nonverbal	Does not require reading, writing, or speaking ability. Tests composed of numerals or drawings are examples.
Objective	Refers to the scoring of tests. When two or more scorers can easily agree on whether an answer is correct or incorrect, the test is an objective one. True–false, multiple-choice, and matching tests are the best examples.
Subjective	Also refers to scoring. When it is difficult for two scorers to agree on whether an item is correct or incorrect, the test is a subjective one. Essay tests are examples.
Teacher-made	Tests constructed entirely by teachers for use in the teachers' classrooms.
Standardized	Tests constructed by measurement experts over a period of years. They are designed to measure broad, national objectives and have a uniform set of instructions that are adhered to during each administration. Most also have tables of norms, to which a student's performance may be compared to determine where the student stands in relation to a national sample of students at the same grade or age level.
Power	Tests with liberal time limits that allow each student to attempt each item. Items tend to be difficult.
Speed	Tests with time limits so strict that no one is expected to complete all items. Items tend to be easy.

SUMMARY

This chapter has introduced you to why we test, what we test, and how we test. Its major points are as follows:

1. The purpose of testing is to collect objective information that may be used in conjunction with subjective information to make better educational decisions.

2. In our age of increasing demands for accountability, it has become imperative that teachers be able to understand and demonstrate the role that objective test data can play in educational decision making.

3. Classroom teachers are responsible for the bulk of educational decision making, such as everyday instructional decisions, grading decisions, and diagnostic decisions. Such decisions are often based, or ought to be based, on information obtained from teacher-made tests. With the passage of NCLB and IDEIA–04, regular education teachers increasingly will be required to extend these skills to students with disabilities as well.

4. Other, less frequent kinds of educational decisions are usually made by administrators or specialists other than the classroom teacher. These include decisions about selection, placement, counseling and guidance, programs and curriculum, and administration. Such decisions are usually based on information obtained from annual standardized tests.

5. Measurement problems may be expected any time testing procedures lack definition or specificity, or when we fail to clearly specify the trait we are measuring.

6. Specifying or defining what we want to measure often determines how the trait should be measured.

FOR DISCUSSION

1. Identify some of the ways we measure "pinches" of achievement, intelligence, and classroom conduct.

2. Make a list of all the different kinds of behaviors you will need to measure, formally or informally, during your first month of teaching. Identify two different ways of measuring each of these behaviors.

3. List some of the instructional, grading, and diagnostic decisions you will be expected to make during your first month of teaching. Identify which category each decision represents.

4. Using Mrs. Norton's problem as a guide, make up some examples in your own subject area that illustrate mismatches between what is being tested and how it is being tested.

5. Think about our discussion about the effects of different populations on a test's usefulness in Chapter 1. How does this apply to Mrs. Norton's problem?

CHAPTER 4

NORM- AND CRITERION-REFERENCED TESTS AND CONTENT VALIDITY EVIDENCE

IN CHAPTER 3 we stated that the purpose of testing is to provide objective data that can be used along with subjective impressions to make better educational decisions. In this chapter we begin by discussing norm-referenced and criterion-referenced tests. These types of tests give us different types of information. Both inform us about how well students are performing, but they are based on different approaches to testing (i.e., "how" we measure). We will then discuss how our ability to clarify "what" we want to measure can help us decide "how" we measure to ensure that our test measures what we intend it to (i.e., that the test has evidence of its content validity).

DEFINING NORM-REFERENCED AND CRITERION-REFERENCED TESTS

One type of information tells us where a student stands compared to other students. In other words, certain kinds of test data help us determine a student's "place" or "rank." This is accomplished by comparing the student's performance to a norm or average of performances by other, similar students. A test that yields this kind of information is called a norm-referenced test (NRT). Such information is useful only for certain types of decisions, which we will discuss later in this chapter.

A second type of information provided by tests tells us about a student's level of proficiency in or mastery of some skill or set of skills. This is accomplished by comparing a student's performance to a standard of mastery called a criterion. A test that yields this kind of information is called a criterion-referenced test (CRT) because the information it conveys refers to a comparison with a criterion or absolute standard. Such information helps us decide whether a student needs more or less work on some skill or set of skills. It says nothing about the student's place or rank compared to other students and, hence, it too is useful only for certain types of decisions. Figure 4.1 illustrates the relationship of NRTs and CRTs to the purpose of testing.

As you may have guessed, it is important to identify the type of information you need before you administer a test. If you fail to do so, you may have test data but be

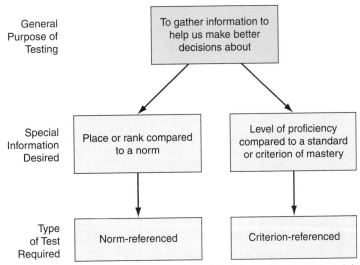

FIGURE 4.1   Relationships among the purpose of testing, information desired, and the type of test required.

unable to use the data to make necessary decisions. Too often teachers, parents, and others report that they know little or nothing more about students after testing than before. This can result when decision makers fail to clearly identify the purpose of testing before selecting and administering a test. In such cases teachers, parents, and others may be quick to denounce or blame the test, not recognizing that this frustrating outcome may be the result of a failure to identify the purpose of testing prior to testing. Attempts to use existing test data may be equally frustrating if test users are not clear about the kinds of information NRTs and CRTs yield. Consider the following:

> *Pat, the counselor, was checking her records when she heard a knock at the door.*
> *It was Mary, a sixth-grade teacher.*

PAT: Come in. What can I do for you?

MARY: I just stopped by to get the latest test information you have on Danny. As you know, he's going to be in my class this year after being in remedial classes for the last five years. Mrs. French, his teacher last year, said you have all the test information on him.

PAT: Well, I'd be glad to help out. In fact, I was just reviewing his folder.

MARY: Great! Can I see it?

PAT: Well, his Math Cluster score on the Woodcock-Johnson is at the sixth percentile, and his Reading Cluster is at the first percentile. Good luck with him.

MARY: Boy, he sure is low. I guess that's why he's been in the remedial classroom for so long.

PAT: You're right.

MARY: Okay. That's about what I was expecting. Now what about his skill levels?

PAT: What do you mean?

MARY: You know, his academic skill levels.

PAT: Oh, his grade levels! Now let's see, his math grade equivalent is 2.6, and his reading grade equivalent is even lower, 1.7.

MARY: That's not really what I need to know. I know he's way below grade level, but I'm wondering about his skills—specific skills, that is. You know, like what words he can read, what phonetic skills he has, whether he can subtract two-digit numbers with regrouping ... things like that.

PAT: (*Becoming a bit irritated*) Mary, what more do you need than what I've given you? Don't you know how to interpret these scores? Perhaps you should have taken a tests and measurements course in college.

MARY: (*Beginning to get frustrated*) Pat, I have taken a tests and measurements course and I do know what those scores mean, but they only compare Danny to other students. I'm not interested in that. I want to know what he can and can't do, so I can begin teaching him at the proper skill level.

PAT: (*Shaking her head*) Look, he's at a first-grade level in reading and second-grade level in math. Isn't that enough?

MARY: But what level of mastery has he demonstrated?

PAT: Mastery? He's years behind! He has mastered very little of anything.

MARY: This has been a very enlightening conversation. Thank you for your time.

It appears there is a communication gap between Mary and Pat. Pat has provided a lot of test data to Mary, yet Mary doesn't seem to care about it. Pat is frustrated, Mary is frustrated, and little that may be of help to Danny has resulted. Why? Just what is the problem? Is it Pat or is it Mary? Or is it something else?

Take another look at the situation. Do you think Mary was being unreasonable? Why did Pat seem satisfied that she had provided the necessary data? Should Mary's course in tests and measurements have helped her "understand" the test data better? What if Danny's mother were asking the questions instead of Mary—would the outcome have been different? Finding answers to these questions may help us. Let's consider each of these in turn.

Was Mary being unreasonable? Mary's questions were specific: Does he have phonetic skills? Can he subtract two-digit numbers with regrouping? Certainly these are not unreasonable questions. She was probably expecting answers that were fairly specific. Maybe something like "yes" or "no" or maybe something like "about 80% of the time" or "about 20% of the time." Responses like these would have helped her plan instruction for Danny. She would know which skills he had mastered, which he was a little deficient in, and which would require a lot of work. However, the grade-equivalent and percentile scores that Pat reported provided her with none of this information. No wonder she was frustrated.

Then why was Pat reporting these scores? Obviously, they were close at hand, and she probably thought she was conveying useful information. Actually, she was conveying useful information; it just wasn't very useful in this particular case. She may have thought she was answering Mary's questions by relaying this information.

Does Mary need another course in tests and measurements? Maybe, but we don't really know. Mary seems to have a perfectly adequate understanding of the information that grade-equivalent scores convey. If we agree that her questions were reasonable, is it necessarily a lack of understanding of test scores that prevented her from making use of the data Pat provided? Or could it be that the information provided failed to answer her questions? The latter explanation appears most satisfactory. Indeed, as you will discover shortly, it seems that it is Pat, not Mary, who would benefit most from a tests and measurements course.

Would things be different if a parent questioned? Maybe. Teachers may respond differently to other teachers than to parents. In some cases inquisitive parents can be intimidated by authoritative-sounding test scores and jargon. But is a parent–teacher conference supposed to cloud or sidestep issues, rather than deal with them directly? We think not. If a parent were as concerned as Mary was about certain skills, that parent would probably end up feeling as frustrated as Mary. While Mary might go home and complain to a friend or husband, a parent might complain to a principal or a superintendent!

Mary's questions, whether raised by her or a parent, are legitimate. Pat probably could answer these questions if she thought about them. However, she seems to think that the test scores she reported are acceptable substitutes for direct answers to questions about specific skills.

Then what is the problem? The problem appears to be Pat's, not Mary's. Mary's questions refer to competencies or mastery of skills. Referring back to Fig. 4.1, we can conclude that she was interested in information about Danny's level of proficiency. Pat's answers refer to test performance compared to other students, which, according to Fig. 4.1, means information about Danny's place or rank compared to others. Answers to Mary's questions can come only from a test designed to indicate whether Danny exceeded some standard of performance taken to indicate mastery of some skill. If a test indicated that Danny could subtract two-digit numbers with regrouping, he would probably be considered to have "mastered" this skill, at least if, say, 80% or more correct was the standard for having attained mastery. In other words, he would have exceeded the standard or criterion of "80% mastery of subtraction of two-digit numbers with regrouping." Recall that a criterion-referenced test is a test designed to measure whether a student has mastered a skill, where the definition of mastery depends on the level or criterion of performance set.

The information Pat was providing was normative or comparative rather than mastery information. Grade-equivalent scores only allow you to make decisions involving comparisons between a child's performance and that of the typical or average performance of a child in a "norm" group. Danny's grade-equivalent score of 1.7 in reading indicates that his reading ability is equivalent to that of the average first grader after seven months in the first grade. It says nothing about which words he knows, gives no information about the process he uses to read new words, and does not indicate how long it takes Danny to comprehend what he reads or to learn the meaning of new words. All this score indicates is that his ability to read is below that of the average fifth grader and equivalent to that of an average first grader after seven months of school. In short, grade-equivalent scores, and a variety of other scores obtained from standardized, norm-referenced tests, allow one to make only general, comparative decisions, not decisions about mastery of specific skills. Unfortunately, situations like the one described occur every day. Only by becoming knowledgeable about the information yielded by CRTs and NRTs can we avoid these situations.

Recall that in the previous chapter we talked about eight types of decisions for which test data are used. Of these eight we decided that for instructional and grading decisions a teacher-made test was most appropriate. We said that both teacher-made and standardized tests are useful in diagnostic decisions and that standardized tests are most appropriate for selection, placement, counseling and guidance, program or curriculum evaluation, and administrative policy decisions. Most teacher-made tests should be of the mastery type, since these are most useful for instructional decisions—the type of decision most frequently made.

Mary's questions were related to instructional decisions. She was interested in Danny's skill levels. The information Pat was providing came from a norm-referenced, standardized test. If Mary had been interested in where Danny stands compared to national norms, then Pat's information would have been perfectly appropriate. However, she was apparently not all that interested in his position relative to others; she was interested in what he knew or what he had mastered. Most often in the classroom we are concerned with mastery of information. Although we are constantly reminded of where our class, school, or district stands in comparison to national norms, these reminders are usually of secondary importance to the classroom teacher. Of prime importance in the classroom is whether our students are mastering what we teach—whether they are reaching the goals and objectives set for them. Daily decisions to reteach, review, or push ahead depend on whether mastery is occurring. What better way to measure whether our students have mastered an objective than to test them to see if they can perform the learning outcome specified, under the conditions or with the materials specified, and at or above the standard of performance specified for them.

COMPARING NORM-REFERENCED AND CRITERION-REFERENCED TESTS

As you may have guessed, criterion-referenced tests must be very specific if they are to yield information about individual skills. This is both an advantage and a disadvantage. Using a very specific test enables you to be relatively certain that your students have mastered or failed to master the skill in question. The major disadvantage of criterion-referenced tests is that many such tests would be necessary to make decisions about the multitude of skills typically taught in the average classroom.

The norm-referenced test, in contrast, tends to be general. It measures a variety of specific and general skills at once, but fails to measure them thoroughly. Thus you are not as sure as you would be with a criterion-referenced test that your students have mastered the individual skills in question. On the other hand, you get an estimate of ability in a variety of skills in a much shorter time than you could through a battery of criterion-referenced tests. Since there is a trade-off in the uses of criterion- and norm-referenced measures, there are situations in which each is appropriate. Determining the appropriateness of a given type of test depends on the purpose of testing.

Finally, the difficulty of items in NRTs and CRTs also differs. In the NRT, items vary in level of difficulty from those that almost no one answers correctly to those that almost everyone answers correctly. In the CRT, the items tend to be equivalent to each other in difficulty. Following a period of instruction, students tend to find CRT items easy and answer most correctly. In a CRT, about 80% of the students completing a unit of instruction are expected to answer each item correctly, while in an NRT about 50% are expected to do so. Table 4.1 illustrates differences between NRTs and CRTs.

DIFFERENCES IN THE CONSTRUCTION OF NORM-REFERENCED AND CRITERION-REFERENCED TESTS

In the following chapters we will describe in detail test planning, construction, and evaluation procedures. The procedures outlined in the test planning and test construction phases are, for the most part, equally appropriate whether you are using a norm-referenced test or a criterion-referenced test. However, because of differences in the difficulty level of the items and the amount of variability in student scores, different evaluation procedures must

TABLE 4.1   Comparing Norm-Referenced and Criterion-Referenced Tests

Dimension	NRT	CRT
Average number of students who get an item right	50%	80%
Compares a student's performance to	The performance of other students.	Standards indicative of mastery.
Breadth of content sampled	Broad, covers many objectives.	Narrow, covers a few objectives.
Comprehensiveness of content sampled	Shallow, usually one or two items per objective.	Comprehensive, usually three or more items per objective.
Variability	Since the meaningfulness of a norm-referenced score basically depends on the relative position of the score in comparison with other scores, the more variability or spread of scores, the better.	The meaning of the score does not depend on comparison with other scores: It flows directly from the connection between the items and the criterion. Variability may be minimal.
Item construction	Items are chosen to promote variance or spread. Items that are "too easy" or "too hard" are avoided. One aim is to produce good "distractor options."	Items are chosen to reflect the criterion behavior. Emphasis is placed on identifying the domain of relevant responses.
Reporting and interpreting considerations	Percentile rank and standard scores used (relative rankings).*	Number succeeding or failing or range of acceptable performance used (e.g., 90% proficiency achieved, or 80% of class reached 90% proficiency).

*For a further discussion of percentile rank and standard scores, see Chapters 12 and 13.

be used in selecting test items. These will be described further in Chapter 10. At this point, we will simply describe some of the general differences in the construction of these two items, which are designed to measure a student's knowledge about the Gulf War in 2003:

> *Item 1.* During the 2003 Gulf War against Iraq, which of the following were employed against American soldiers?
>
> **a.** Biological weapons
> **b.** Nuclear weapons
> **c.** Roadside bombs
> **d.** Naval bombardment
>
> *Item 2.* During the 2003 Gulf War more Iraqi tanks were destroyed by this aircraft than by all other aircraft combined.
>
> **a.** F14 Tomcat
> **b.** F16 Hornet
> **c.** A6 Intruder
> **d.** A10 Thunderbolt

What are the correct answers? Most would answer Item 1 correctly (i.e., Roadside bombs), and probably only military buffs would answer Item 2 correctly (i.e., A10 Thunderbolt). The second item involves a subtle point that is probably of interest only to military professionals and historians. Such an item might prove useful in discriminating among individuals who have mastery of specific details of the second Gulf War, such as in a class in military history. For a high school or junior high unit on American history, however, this level of specificity would be unnecessary. Item 1, which assesses common knowledge about the second Gulf War, would be most appropriate for a criterion-referenced test, since it measures a common fact about the war. Item 2 would be most appropriate for a norm-referenced test or a more advanced course, since it attempts to make more subtle distinctions among the facts. Owing to the difficulty and specificity of Item 2, few junior or senior high students would answer Item 2 correctly, even if they showed mastery of other aspects of the unit.

Let's complicate matters, however: Item 2 might be included in a criterion-referenced test in a military history class. Students of military history might be expected to be familiar with the intricacies and specifics of weaponry employed during the second Gulf War. In such a class we would expect the content of the item to represent basic knowledge extensively addressed in text and lecture. In other words, test items are not norm-referenced or criterion-referenced by nature. They need to be considered in terms of the audience for whom they are being prepared.

NORM- AND CRITERION-REFERENCED TESTS AND LINGUISTIC, CULTURAL, AND CONTEXTUAL SENSITIVITY

NRTs compare a student's performance to a norms table based on a nationally representative sample, called a norm group or normative sample, of students in the same grade and of a similar age. The resultant scores or rankings tell us how a student compares to this national sample. Such comparisons are appropriate when the student's cultural, language, economic, family, and other characteristics are comparable to those of the students in the normative sample.

The appropriateness of norm-referenced test results can be compromised when comparisons are made for children whose language, cultural, socioeconomic, or other important characteristics differ importantly from those of the norm group. For example, let's consider the case of Svetlana, a recent Russian immigrant, and Diana, a recent immigrant from England. Which student would you expect to score higher on the verbal portion of the Scholastic Assessment Test (SAT)? Of course, Diana would most likely outscore Svetlana, assuming Svetlana's English language skills are weak and all other factors are equal. Does this mean that Diana is brighter than Svetlana, or that Diana will necessarily fare better in college over the next four to five years than Svetlana? You probably answered "Not necessarily" to these last two questions, illustrating your sensitivity to the effect language proficiency can have on test performance. Similarly, other factors such as poverty, the importance placed on achievement in the family, and various differences across cultures (e.g., assertiveness, competitiveness, and compliance with authority figures) can affect performance on tests that reflect primarily the majority culture in our country.

Ideally, test publishers would include in their large, nationally representative norm groups sufficient numbers of pupils representative of our nation's diversity to enhance NRT comparability for all students, or develop separate norms tables representative of the nation's language, cultural, and socioeconomic diversity. There is movement in these directions. Test publishers have been sensitive to our nation's growing diversity, and increased norm group diversity is being sought as tests are periodically restandardized or as new tests are developed. And although it is expensive for test publishers to develop them, we are now beginning to see specialized norms tables for students for whom English is a second language, for students in low-achieving schools, and for students from low socioeconomic backgrounds. Other specialized norms tables likely will follow, although their sizes will be smaller than the nationally representative sample. Therefore we must not be overconfident about the accuracy of scores obtained from comparisons with such specialized norm groups. So what should we do when interpreting NRT performance for diverse minority groups?

There is no single or simple answer to that question, and any answer is likely to be controversial. Our suggestion is that a two-pronged approach be adopted. First, where a student's background is not comparable to a test's norm group, the weight given to the score obtained by comparing the student to the norm group should be reduced, or even eliminated in some cases. Second, where a student is not from the majority culture, additional attention should be given to the effects of the student's cultural and socioeconomic context when interpreting NRT scores. The factors to consider in interpreting NRT scores are many and complex, even for students from the majority culture. We will review these in Chapter 18 when we consider standardized tests in more depth.

What about CRTs? Do the same considerations apply? Because CRTs do not utilize comparisons to norm groups to obtain scores, differences between a pupil's background and that of the students in the norm group are not relevant. Use of CRTs with pupils from diverse backgrounds may be more appropriate—but only if a CRT is appropriate for the purpose of testing! Nevertheless, language, cultural, and socioeconomic contextual variability can also affect performance on CRTs and should always be considered in administering and interpreting CRTs. Some students cannot read English, have been acculturated not to ask authority figures questions, have never seen or been expected to complete an essay question before, or have not eaten breakfast. These, and a variety of other factors, will negatively affect test performance, regardless of whether it is a NRT or a CRT.

NORM- AND CRITERION-REFERENCED TESTS AND VALIDITY EVIDENCE

Thus far in this chapter we have discussed some important aspects of how we measure. We have distinguished between NRTs and CRTs and have discussed the importance of sensitivity to language, culture and social diversity issues for both NRTs and CRTs. In the remainder of this chapter and in the next we will consider how we determine whether how we intend to measure (i.e., an NRT or CRT) taps into what we want to measure. If we can demonstrate that a test measures what it is intended to measure we have accumulated evidence of the test's validity. As we will learn in Chapter 15 the validity evidence supporting a test's use is the single most important characteristic that determines whether a test's use is appropriate or not.

To help us determine whether a test does what we intend it to we will present a model for classroom measurement that links instructional objectives, instructional methods, and test items. We will help you learn to write specific, measurable instructional objectives in Chapter 5, but for now let's simply keep in mind that all teachers have some objectives in mind (or on paper!) when they teach. Increasingly, as noted in Chapter 2, state standards are included in these objectives as a result of the passage of NCLB and the growth of high-stakes testing.

For now, we will not be concerned with the differences between educational goals, standards, and objectives, or even the differences among different kinds of objectives. What we will be concerned with is the fact that all teachers have some objectives in mind when they teach. Usually these are both long- and short-term objectives. An example of a long-term objective is

The student will master all phases of addition.

With this long-term objective come several short-term objectives, which might include such goals as

The student will correctly add one-, two-, three-, and four-digit numbers without regrouping.

The student will correctly add two-digit numbers with regrouping.

The student will correctly add three-digit numbers with regrouping.

Regardless of whether we are talking about long- or short-term objectives, it is important to know when your students have mastered your objectives. Remember Mrs. Norton? One of her objectives was probably "The student will master basic math skills." Like any good teacher, she tried to determine through a test whether her students mastered this objective. The problem was that her test did not measure mastery of basic math skills. It measured the ability to apply math skills and to read and to comprehend word problems.

In short, she knew what she wanted to measure, but her test did not actually measure it. This is another way of saying that her test lacked validity evidence as a measure of her students' mastery of basic math skills. More specifically, it lacked evidence of content validity. In the classroom, evidence of content validity is of utmost importance. Simply stated, content validity evidence is the extent to which a test actually measures the teacher's instructional objectives. Later in this chapter we will introduce procedures for examining a test to determine whether it has evidence of its content validity. Since most educational decisions are based on classroom achievement tests, we cannot overemphasize the importance of constructing tests that have adequate evidence of content validity. If the tests you construct have evidence that they are content valid, you will be on your way to making sound instructional decisions and having valid evidence to support your decisions should they ever be questioned.

A THREE-STAGE MODEL OF CLASSROOM MEASUREMENT

Most classroom instruction takes place with some objective in mind. One way to determine whether the objective has been reached is through a test. The three-stage classroom measurement model in Fig. 4.2 depicts these relationships. We will illustrate this model by describing how a criterion-referenced test is constructed.

The first stage in the model is the first step in constructing a criterion-referenced test. It is also the first step in sound instructional planning. For our purposes we will use as examples only a few of the many possible objectives in a unit on writing instructional objectives. Some of these objectives might be as follows:

The student will discriminate learning activities from learning outcomes.

The student will discriminate observable learning outcomes from unobservable learning outcomes.

The student will construct well-written instructional objectives.

Each of these objectives would fit in Stage 1 of the model.

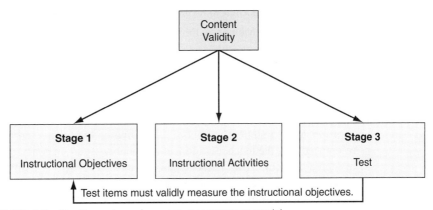

FIGURE 4.2   The three-stage classroom measurement model.

In Stage 2, instructional activities designed to develop student mastery of these objectives would be implemented. For example,

> Objective: The student will discriminate learning activities from learning outcomes.

> Instructional Activity: Define and provide examples of learning activities and learning outcomes. Point out similarities and differences between the two.

Naturally, the instructional procedures will vary depending on the content and type of learning outcomes desired. Courses in teaching methods are most concerned with the structure of the procedures in Stage 2 of this model. For our purposes, however, we are more concerned with determining the effectiveness of the procedures, not necessarily the nature of the procedures themselves. Thus it is Stages 1 and 3 that will be of most interest to us.

In constructing a criterion-referenced test, our task is made easier if we develop clear and measurable instructional objectives. In Chapter 5 we will learn how to do this. Once we have measurable instructional objectives, our task is to construct several items to validly measure each objective. Typically this means about three to ten items per objective. Furthermore, we normally define mastery not as perfect performance but as 70, 80, or 90% correct performance. A student who answers four of five or eight of ten items that validly measure an objective generally is considered to have mastered the objective. The following is an example of a five-part test item to measure the first objective.

> OBJECTIVE: The student will discriminate learning activities from learning outcomes.

> TEST ITEM: Indicate which terms in the following list are learning activities by placing an A in the space to the left of the term, and indicate which are learning outcomes by placing an O in the space.

> _____ **1.** Practice multiplication tables.

> _____ **2.** List the parts of a carburetor.

> _____ **3.** Recall the main events in a story.

> _____ **4.** Listen to a foreign language tape.

> _____ **5.** Memorize the names of the first five U.S. presidents.

> Answers: 1. A;   2. O;   3. O;   4. A;   5. A.

These response alternatives are content-valid measures of the objective because they ask the student to do exactly what the objective requires. There are certainly other equally valid ways of measuring this objective, but the response alternatives listed are appropriate. If a student answers four of five or five of five correctly on this criterion-referenced test, the teacher could feel reasonably secure in concluding that the student has mastered the objective. These types of tests are called criterion-referenced because a specific level of acceptable performance called the criterion is established directly from the instructional objectives. As we shall see, we are less confident of the mastery of specific objectives when a norm-referenced test is employed.

Regardless of the type of achievement test you select, the issue of content validity evidence is of paramount concern. Keep the three-stage model in mind when you select or develop an achievement test, and you are likely to be aware of the issue of content validity.

Now that we have an overall framework for thinking about classroom measurement, let's get into test construction itself. Keep in mind that any good classroom test begins with your objectives, Stage 1 of our three-stage measurement model. Much of the remainder of this chapter and the next will be devoted to considering instructional objectives and ways of ensuring the content validity of items intended to measure instructional objectives.

WHY OBJECTIVES? WHY NOT JUST WRITE TEST ITEMS?

What if you don't believe that instructional objectives are necessary? What if you feel that they are a waste of time? What if you don't think you will need to use or construct instructional objectives in your teaching career? Many believe that objectives for classroom instruction are unnecessary, limiting, too time-consuming, and mechanistic. If you agree, then learning to write instructional objectives may be a frustrating, difficult task. If we told you they're necessary and you're better off learning to write them, you probably would not believe us. We do think it is important for teachers to be able to write measurable instructional objectives, but we also understand and respect your right to hold another opinion. You should, however, take the time to consider the place of instructional objectives in the overall instructional process. Consider the situation described next and then decide whether it's worthwhile to take the time to learn to write instructional objectives to guide your teaching.

Two Schools: Their Objectives

As Maude got off the bus, she was immediately taken by the name of the first of the two schools she was about to visit: the Center for Self-Actualization and Humanistic Experiences. Maude was awestruck. At last she would see what education really should be about—free from dry, mechanical methods and curricula, and characterized by the teachers' loving acceptance and excitement and the students' sense of freedom. To her surprise, the door was open, so Maude walked in and was greeted with a warm smile and hug from the "facilitator."

"Is that another name for teacher?" Maude asked.

"Heavens, no!" said the facilitator. "I only facilitate learning, I don't teach. For your information, use of the words teacher and educator are forbidden here at the Center; we are all facilitators." Maude was confused, but decided not to press the issue.

The students were engaged in a variety of activities or lack of activities. One was reading a book; another worked with an abacus; a third was asleep on a couch; others were talking, playing, and generally having what appeared to Maude to be a pretty good time. Maude was encouraged by the facilitator to "experience" the students. Almost unanimously the students felt the Center was "fun." One said, "You never have to do nuthin' around here."

Concerned, Maude questioned the facilitator about this comment. The facilitator's reply was that freedom of choice is strongly encouraged at the Center. All students are free to choose what to do or not to do. "After all, reality is only a construct!" he said.

"But are they learning anything?" Maude asked.

"They are learning that they are free and independent human beings, capable of personally or socially constructing their own realities" said the facilitator. "When they are ready, they will choose to learn on their own. Now, if you'll excuse me, I have an appointment with my aroma therapist." At a loss for words and feeling troubled, Maude said goodbye and left the Center for Self-Actualization and Humanistic Experiences.

The Center for Accelerated Education was Maude's next stop. After knocking on the door she was greeted by a rather stern-faced, middle-aged man who was wearing a "Better Living Through Behaviorism" button on his lapel. He called himself a "behavioral engineer." He said hello and handed Maude a list of "behaviors" that the students would be engaging in for the next 30 minutes or so and told her to feel free to "collect data." He then picked up a box of plastic strips—"tokens," he called them— muttered something about a "reinforcement schedule" and "consequating appropriate behaviors," and walked off toward his "subjects."

The students at the Center for Accelerated Education sat in individual cubicles or carrels. Each student had a contract specifying what was expected of him or her. Privileges, such as free time, and rewards from the "reinforcement menu" were earned by performing on-task behavior (like sitting quietly in a cubicle, working on a worksheet, or reading). The behavioral engineer circulated around the room, periodically "reinforcing" on-task behaviors he referred to as "operants" with tokens and also providing tokens for each completed worksheet. Students demonstrating off-task and disruptive behavior relinquished tokens or, in extreme cases, were required to spend several minutes in the time-out room. The time-out room was "devoid of all potential reinforcers," according to the behavioral engineer. In other words, it was a barren room—no windows, tables, or anything interesting.

When Maude asked whether the pupils were learning, the behavioral engineer pointed to the stacks of completed worksheets almost filling a large storeroom.

"Let's see you get that much learning from the kids at the Center for Self-Actualization and Humanistic Experiences," chuckled the behavioral engineer.

More confused and concerned than she had been before she entered, Maude decided not to press the issue and instead to engage in some exiting behaviors.

As you probably guessed, both the Center for Self-Actualization and Humanistic Experiences and the Center for Accelerated Education are, we hope, exaggerations. They represent extremes in educational theory. On the one hand, the "hands-off" approach is characteristic of nondirective, discovery approaches to learning. On the other hand, the regimented approach is characteristic of a directive, guided approach to learning. Which approach is better for every student? We don't know, and probably no one knows. Fortunately, most educational institutions operate with some combination of directive and nondirective approaches.

Instruction is not a rigid, easily defined procedure. It tends to be different things to different people. No one will ever be completely happy with any one approach to instruction since no one approach is really a single method but a combination of methods. As a result, specific educational goals and objectives are unlikely to be approved or supported by everyone. So where do the goals and objectives come from, and who decides on the goals and objectives or standards for education? The answer is that society, government, school boards, school administration, teachers, students, and parents all, to some extent, set educational goals and objectives.

Where Do Goals Come From?

Educators must be responsive to societal needs and pressures. This is especially true for public-school educators, since the purse strings that make public education a reality are controlled by all who make up our society. If a superintendent or school board implements educational policies or procedures that are too far removed from what the community wants and needs, the superintendent may find himself or herself looking for work elsewhere, and board members may not be re-elected.

We frequently make the mistake of thinking that it is the administration that is completely responsible for the curriculum implemented in a given school or district. This is only partially true. Ultimately, the general public, or society, sets the goals for education. With the passage of NCLB in 2002 and the explosion of interest in high-stakes testing over the last decade this has become increasingly evident. In Chapter 2 we discussed how the establishment of academic standards has now spread to all 50 states and the District of Columbia as part of the standards-based reform movement. These standards will eventually define for each grade and each subject area what pupils are expected to master to qualify for promotion to the next grade or to graduate, and the annual academic assessments required by NCLB are to be linked to these standards. Figure 4.3 uses a specific example to illustrate the flow from goals to objectives in education. This illustration shows how public pressure for a back-to-basics movement can reach the classroom.

We may also view this process as a funneling or narrowing of focus, with the often ambiguous wants and needs of society gradually translated into manageable "bits" called instructional objectives, as shown in Fig. 4.4. State academic standards, because they still represent a "work in progress" in many states, may at times resemble broad goals or more specific objectives.

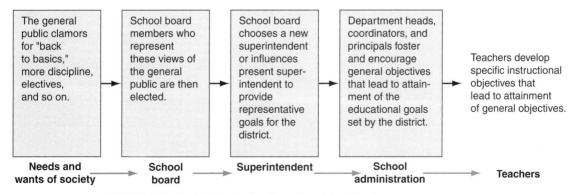

FIGURE 4.3 Back to basics: the flow of goals to objectives.

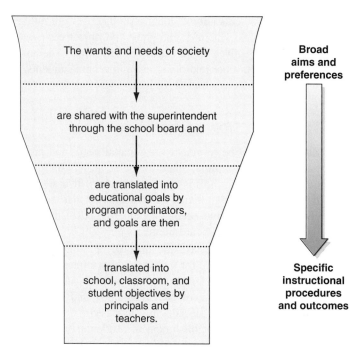

The wants and needs of society

are shared with the superintendent
through the school board and

are translated into
educational goals by
program coordinators,
and goals are then

translated into
school, classroom, and
student objectives by
principals and
teachers.

**Broad
aims and
preferences**

**Specific
instructional
procedures
and outcomes**

FIGURE 4.4   The funneling of societal wants into objectives.

Are There Different Kinds of Goals and Objectives?

What do you think are the instructional goals and objectives of the schools Maude visited? Well, you probably can't say precisely, but you could probably look at a list of objectives and decide which would be accepted by the Center for Self-Actualization and Humanistic Experiences or which by the behaviorist Center for Accelerated Education. Look at the objectives in the following exercise and indicate the school with which they would most likely be associated.

Exercise: *Write H for humanistic or B for behavioristic in the blank to the left of each objective to indicate which school they would probably go with.*

_____**1.** With 80% accuracy, subtract two-digit numbers from three-digit numbers without borrowing.

_____**2.** Identify initial consonant sounds correctly 90% of the time when listening to an audiocassette.

_____**3.** Enjoy the beauty of nature.

_____**4.** Interpret *The Lion, the Witch, and the Wardrobe.*

_____**5.** Type at least 25 words per minute with no more than two errors, using a manual typewriter.

_____**6.** Visit the zoo and discuss what was of interest.

_____**7.** Be creative.

_____**8.** Be spontaneous.

_____**9.** List the days of the week in proper order, from memory, with 100% accuracy.

This exercise points out the difference between two types of educational objectives: behavioral (specific) and expressive (general). A behavioral objective is a precise statement of behavior to be exhibited; the criterion by which mastery of the objective will be judged; and a statement of the conditions under which the behavior must be demonstrated. Objectives 1, 2, 5, and 9 are examples. As you can see, they are specific statements or "bits" of observable behavior with specific conditions under which the behavior is to be observed and the level of performance attained. Using these objectives, two or more observers would likely agree about whether a student was, for example, able to list the days of the week in proper order, from memory, with 100% accuracy.

An expressive objective is somewhat different. Behaviors are not usually specified, and a criterion performance level is generally not stated. What is stated in an expressive objective is the experience or educational activity to be undertaken. The outcome of the activity is not detailed in specific terms, but in general terms such as interpret or analyze. Examples of expressive objectives include items 4 and 6 from the list. They specify an activity or experience and a broad educational outcome.

Now you might ask, "What about items 3, 7, and 8?" They do not describe a specific observable behavior, conditions, or criterion level of performance, and they do not describe an educational activity or experience. What do they describe? They describe broad, hard-to-define entities. We would have little agreement among individuals trying to define enjoyment, creativity, and spontaneity. These may be best classified as broad goals rather than objectives because they are the end result of perhaps a complete educational program.

Educational goals reflect the general needs of society. As a result, most goals, if stated in general terms, tend to be accepted or adopted by most educators and educational institutions. Regardless of whether a program is directive or nondirective, behavioral or humanistic, rigid or flexible, various general goals will be held in common. When we get more specific, often at the local school level, disagreements over methods used to reach these goals arise. For example, the two schools described would probably agree that creativity is an important goal for education but disagree as to how creativity should be fostered or developed. One school may say creativity is best developed through structured experiences. Another school may say creativity is best developed in an open, unstructured environment.

As a result, sometimes different methods are employed to reach the same goal. But it is important to realize that, in addition to having a goal, any method must also have some implicit or explicit steps thought necessary to achieve the goal. Such steps may vary in specificity but are present in any logically constructed instructional program. For example, in the Center for Self-Actualization and Humanistic Experiences the facilitators most certainly had some steps in mind in trying to foster creativity. It is unlikely that they expected creativity to develop without any guidance. If they did, why would they see a need for their Center? The expressive objectives mentioned might be one of the steps they would use. Others might include:

Welcome students each morning.

Encourage students to try out new activities and methods of expression.

Encourage students to express all ideas, regardless of how inappropriate they may seem.

Statements such as these help define the atmosphere or philosophy of the Center, but are they instructional objectives? Some would say yes, and some would say no. We would say no, since they do not meet our criteria for instructional objectives. That is, they do not (1) specify student behaviors and do not (2) specify observable, measurable behaviors. This is not to say that they are unimportant, but for our purposes instructional objectives must specify observable, overt student behavior. The test of this is whether two independent observers would agree as to the presence or absence of the student behavior in question. Would two or more observers agree that "expression of student ideas is always encouraged, regardless of how inappropriate they may seem"? Some probably would agree and some would not. This statement would not qualify as an instructional objective according to our criteria. But consider this statement: "During each period the students will write an alternative ending to each assigned short story." Here it seems more likely that observers would agree as to whether students displayed this behavior. It is student oriented, and it is easily observed.

Thus far, we have discussed the difference between specific instructional objectives and general expressive objectives. These tend to reflect a school's educational philosophy. We have also mentioned general goals that tend to reflect the overall needs of society. From this point on, we will focus on specific instructional objectives, but we will also consider another type of objective called a general or program objective. Although these are usually formulated at the state education agency or school district level, they are sometimes confused with classroom instructional objectives. Table 4.2 illustrates the differences among educational goals, program objectives, and instructional objectives.

Since the average classroom teacher will have little input into the formulation of either educational goals or general educational program objectives, we will not concern ourselves further with these. For the remainder of this chapter and in the next we will focus on those objectives that classroom teachers must formulate themselves. In other words, we will concentrate on instructional objectives. Instructional objectives can make a teacher's day-to-day job easier, save time, and result in more effective instruction.

HOW CAN INSTRUCTIONAL OBJECTIVES MAKE A TEACHER'S JOB EASIER?

When we were first learning about goals and objectives, we also wondered how instructional objectives could make a teacher's job easier. How can something that takes time to prepare actually save time, and how does that make a teacher's job easier?

You've probably heard the old saying that it takes money to make money. It's true. An equally relevant but far less popular expression is that it takes time to save time. In other words, taking time to plan and to organize will save you time in the long run. Planning your lessons, getting organized, and being efficient all take time but can save time later.

Nevertheless, writing good instructional objectives does take time and skill. We will help you develop the skill in Chapter 5, but we can't do much about time! Fortunately, personal computers (PCs) are now so common in schools that they can help. Beginning

TABLE 4.2 **Goals, Program Objectives, and Instructional Objectives**

Category	Description	Examples

Goals	Broad statements of very general educational outcomes that:
	  do not include specific levels of performance.
	  tend to change infrequently and in response to societal pressure.
		Become a good citizen.
		Be competent in the basic skills areas.
		Be creative.
		Learn problem solving.
		Appreciate art.
		Develop high-level thinking skills.

General educational program objectives	More narrowly defined statements of educational outcomes that:
	  apply to specific educational programs.
	  may be formulated on an annual basis.
	  are developed by program coordinators, principals, and other high school administrators.
		By the end of the academic year, students receiving remedial reading program services will realize achievement gains of at least 0.8 of a grade level, as measured by the Iowa Test of Basic Skills.

Instructional objectives	Specific statements of learner behavior or outcomes that are expected to be exhibited by students after completing a unit of instruction. A unit of instruction may, for example, mean:
	  a six-week lesson on foreign culture.
	  a one-week lesson on deciduous trees.
	  a class period on "Subtracting with Borrowing."
	  a five-minute lesson on "Cursive Letters: Lowercase b."
	These objectives are often included in teacher manuals, and more and more frequently instructional objectives are also being included for specific lessons. Unfortunately, they are not always well written and do not always fit a particular class or style. Instructional objectives often have to be formulated by classroom teachers to fit their individual classrooms.
		By Friday, the students will be able to recite the names of the months in order.
		The student will be able to take apart and correctly reassemble a disk drive with the tools provided, within 45 minutes.

with this chapter we will include sidebars that will show how computers can help with a variety of measurement tasks. Visit the sidebar for this chapter titled PCs and Instructional Objectives to learn how PCs can help with this important task (Box 4-1). Your state legislature and state education agency may also help. If you teach in a state where the state education agency has developed academic standards for each grade level and for each subject as part of its high-stakes testing and accountability program, you may find that some of the state standards can be adopted as is or modified to provide you with your instructional objectives.

Research has identified several factors that are associated with effective, successful teaching. Among these are organization and clarity, which typically go hand in hand. While it is possible to be clear without being organized, and vice versa, it is unlikely. Unfortunately, we spend a lot of time "spinning our wheels" because we do not have clear objectives for our students. In other words, we often don't know where we're going so we don't know when we get there. Using instructional objectives helps minimize this floundering by clearing the way. The result is increased efficiency and effectiveness in teaching and learning.

BOX *4-1*

PCS AND INSTRUCTIONAL OBJECTIVES

One of the measurement tasks teachers find to be time-consuming is writing instructional objectives. Educational software will not diminish the necessary skills and time initially needed to construct good instructional objectives. However, a word processing program (a program that allows you to add, delete, shift, or revise written information quickly and efficiently) enables teachers to retain and modify their objectives from year to year to reflect changing state academic standards, educational trends, and goals. A file of instructional objectives on a PC's hard drive or on CDs can enable teachers to develop a "bank" of instructional objectives that may be drawn on as educational needs change over time. Such a file also can minimize the amount of time a teacher spends writing and rewriting instructional objectives each year. As a result, teachers may find they have increased amounts of time available for instructional or other measurement tasks. Saving instructional objectives on recordable media or on your hard drive also facilitates analysis of objectives and sharing of well-written objectives among teachers at the same grade level, thus saving still more time and leading to better written objectives, thereby improving measurement practice. Finally, printing the objectives and distributing them to your students, especially in the secondary grades, will help students focus on the most relevant content areas.

SUMMARY

This chapter introduced you to norm-referenced and criterion-referenced tests, content validity evidence considerations, and educational goals and objectives. Its major points are as follows:

1. A norm-referenced test (NRT) indicates how a pupil's performance compares to that of other pupils.

2. A criterion-referenced test (CRT) indicates how a pupil's performance compares to an established standard or criterion thought to indicate mastery of a skill.

3. What type of test you use depends on the purpose of the testing, which should be determined before you administer the test.

4. Information from NRTs is usually not as useful for classroom decision making as information from CRTs.

5. In addition to differing in regard to what a pupil's performance is compared to, NRTs and CRTs differ in the following dimensions:
   - Item difficulty,
   - Content sampling (breadth and depth),
   - Variability of scores,
   - Item construction, and
   - Reporting and interpreting considerations.

6. Because NRTs compare a student's performance to the norm group to establish a student's score, language, culture, and socioeconomic differences between the student and the norm group can affect the student's score.

7. For this reason it may be appropriate in such cases to reduce the weight given an NRT score and to give additional attention to the factors that influence NRT scores when interpreting NRT scores.

8. Although CRT scores do not require a comparison to a norm group, performance on CRTs also can be negatively affected by language, cultural, and socioeconomic factors.

9. Content validity evidence describes the extent to which a test measures or matches the teacher's instructional objectives, or aligns with state academic standards.

10. There are three stages involved in classroom measurement:
    - Constructing instructional objectives,
    - Implementing instructional activities, and
    - Testing to measure the attainment of the instructional objectives.

    Each of these must match with the others for measurement to be valid.

11. Instructional activities tend to vary across educational institutions, and they range from flexible to rigid.

12. These instructional activities tend to be determined by instructional objectives, which tend to be derived from educational goals and state academic standards, which tend to reflect societal attitudes and values.

13. One type of instructional objective is the behavioral objective. It specifies an observable, measurable behavior to be exhibited, the conditions under which it is to be exhibited, and the criterion for mastery.

14. Another type of instructional objective is the expressive objective. It specifies an educational activity but does not specify the particular outcome of the activity.

15. Instructional objectives help the teacher clarify and organize instruction, enabling the teacher to save time in the long run.

16. State academic standards have now been developed across the nation but vary from state to state both in terms of their academic content and in terms of their specificity.

FOR DISCUSSION

1. Identify five characteristics that distinguish a norm-referenced from a criterion-referenced test.

2. Describe several testing decisions for which you would want to use a norm-referenced test and several situations in which you would want to use a criterion-referenced test.

3. A parent calls you and wants to set up a conference to discuss Johnny's potential for getting into the college of his choice. Which type of test score, NRT or CRT, should you be prepared to discuss first? Why?

4. Another parent calls and wants to discuss why Brittany received a D in math this grading period. Which type of test score, NRT or CRT, should you be prepared to discuss first? Why?

5. Imagine that you have been randomly chosen to be evaluated by your school district's Office of Evaluation. They ask you for your students' scores on an achievement test. What type of test scores, NRT or CRT, would be most indicative of your success as a teacher?

6. Think back to the last NRT and CRT that you took. Describe how your performance on each test would have been affected if
    - You were not fluent in English.
    - This was the first time you were asked to take this kind of test.
    - You came from a culture that seldom used tests to make important decisions.
    - You and your parents believed that your future success depended on your performance on this test.

7. Now, try to imagine that the conditions described in Item 6 apply to you. Describe your thoughts and feelings related to taking a NRT and a CRT.

8. Compare and contrast the following:
- Behavioral and expressive objectives
- Program objectives and instructional objectives
- Educational goals and instructional objectives

9. A teacher is complaining about having to write instructional objectives. He just cannot see any benefit they may have and thinks they are too time-consuming. Role-play with another student and describe how well-written objectives can make teaching more effective.

*10. Identify which of the following are expressive (E) and which are behavioral (B) objectives.

_____ **a.** Properly use and adjust a microscope without a checklist.

_____ **b.** Develop an appreciation for the nature of plant growth.

_____ **c.** Enjoy driving a car.

_____ **d.** Appreciate the role of physics in everyday life.

_____ **e.** Be able to divide fractions with 80% accuracy.

_____ **f.** Be able to dissect a starfish using only a scalpel.

_____ **g.** Value the importance of eating the right foods.

_____ **h.** List the parts of the abdomen from memory with 100% accuracy.

*Answers to Questions 10 and 12 appear in Appendix F.

11. Convert the following goals to general objectives:
- Become a good citizen.
- Be creative.
- Appreciate art.
- Know math.
- Develop musical ability.

*12. Match the following general objectives to the most content-valid method of testing.

OBJECTIVES

1. From memory, describe the main figures in classical music.

2. Match the classical composers with their compositions.

3. Identify the titles and composers of the classical pieces discussed in class, after listening to no more than two minutes of each piece.

4. Play two classical compositions on the piano by the end of the semester.

TESTING METHOD

a. Copy by hand at least two classical compositions.

b. Associate the composers listed with their compositions.

c. Chronicle the lives of three European composers who lived between 1500 and 1875.

d. After listening to this tape, identify the composer.

e. Play two classical selections of your choice.

MEASURING LEARNING OUTCOMES

IN **CHAPTER 4** we considered the differences between norm-referenced and criterion-referenced tests, the important concept of content validity, various types of goals and objectives, and some reasons instructional objectives are helpful to the teacher. Next we will describe methods for writing instructional objectives, matching test items to objectives, and using a test blueprint to ensure balanced classroom tests that include items that measure higher-level thinking.

WRITING INSTRUCTIONAL OBJECTIVES

An instructional objective should be a clear and concise statement of the skill or skills that your students will be expected to perform after a unit of instruction. It should include the level of proficiency to be demonstrated and the special conditions under which the skill must be demonstrated. Furthermore, an instructional objective should be stated in observable, behavioral terms, in order for two or more individuals to agree that a student has or has not displayed the learning outcome in question. In short, a complete instructional objective includes:

- An observable behavior (action verb specifying the learning outcome).
- Any special conditions under which the behavior must be displayed.
- The performance level considered sufficient to demonstrate mastery.

The following series of exercises should help you become familiar with each of these components. With practice, they should lead to your mastery in writing instructional objectives.

Identifying Learning Outcomes

An instructional objective must include an action verb that specifies a learning outcome. However, not all action verbs specify learning outcomes. Learning outcomes are often confused with learning activities. Try to determine which of the following examples represent learning outcomes and which represent learning activities:

1. By the end of the semester the child will identify pictures of words that sound alike.
2. The child will demonstrate an appreciation of poetry.

3. The student will subtract one-digit numbers with 80% accuracy.

4. The student will show a knowledge of correct punctuation.

5. The student will practice the multiplication tables.

6. The student will sing "The Star-Spangled Banner."

In the first four objectives the action words identify, demonstrate, subtract, and show all point to outcomes, or end products of units of instruction. However, practice, the action word in objective 5, only implies an activity that will lead to a learning outcome. Thus objective 5 has no learning outcome; it is a learning activity. The means rather than the end is identified.

Objective 6 is a little troublesome, too. Is sing an outcome or an activity? It's hard to say without more information. If your goal is to have a stage-frightened pupil sing in public, this may be a learning outcome. If singing is only practice for a later performance, however, it is a learning activity. The following exercise should help you discriminate between learning outcomes and learning activities. Look at the examples of outcomes and activities, then work through the exercise and check your answers.

Learning Outcomes (Ends)	*Learning Activities (Means)*
identify	study
recall	watch
list	listen
write	read

EXERCISE: *Distinguish learning outcomes from learning activities by marking an O next to outcomes and an A next to activities.*

_____**1.** Fixing a car radio.
_____**2.** Reciting the four components of a good essay.
_____**3.** Adding signed numbers correctly.
_____**4.** Practicing the violin.
_____**5.** Recalling the parts of speech.
_____**6.** Outlining the main theme in *House of Seven Gables*.
_____**7.** Reciting the alphabet.
_____**8.** Punctuating an essay correctly.

Answers: 1. O; 2. O; 3. O; 4. A; 5. O; 6. O; 7. A; 8. O.

If an activity implies a specific product or result, we have considered it an outcome. What we want our instructional objective to include is the end product of the instructional procedure. It is on this end product that we will base our test item. If you find your objective includes a learning activity (means) and not an outcome (end), rewrite it so that the product of the intended activity is stated. Next, let's consider two types of learning outcomes: those that are observable and directly measurable, and those that are not.

Identifying Observable and Directly Measurable Learning Outcomes

At this stage, your task is to determine whether the outcome is stated as a measurable, observable behavior or an unmeasurable, unobservable behavior. That is, would two or more individuals observing a student agree that the student had demonstrated the learning outcome? Sometimes we need to replace the unobservable behavior with an observable indicator of the learning outcome. For example, if our objective is

The student will show a knowledge of punctuation.

then the learning outcome, "show a knowledge of punctuation," is unmeasurable. How would we know whether knowledge was shown? Ask the student? Would we assume that if a student was present for a lecture or read the appropriate section of a text, knowledge followed? Probably not. Instead we would need some indication that would demonstrate evidence of knowledge. For example, to indicate knowledge of punctuation, a student would have to "insert commas where appropriate" in sentences, "list the rules governing the use of colons or semi-colons," and so on. Instructional objectives are specific, measurable statements of the outcomes of instruction that indicate whether instructional intents have been achieved (add two-digit numbers with regrouping, independently pick up a musical instrument and play it, and so on).

Let's practice identifying observable learning outcomes. Study the following examples of observable and unobservable outcomes, work through the exercise, then check your answers.

Observables	*Unobservables*
list	value
recite	appreciate
build	know
draw	understand

EXERCISE: *Distinguish observable learning outcomes from unobservable outcomes by marking O next to observables and U next to unobservables.*

_____ **1.** Circle the initial sound of words.
_____ **2.** Be familiar with the law.
_____ **3.** Add two-digit numbers on paper.
_____ **4.** Understand the process of osmosis.
_____ **5.** Enjoy speaking French.
_____ **6.** Change the spark plugs on an engine.
_____ **7.** Recite the names of the characters in *Tom Sawyer*.
_____ **8.** Really understand set theory.
_____ **9.** Appreciate art deco.
_____**10.** Recite a short poem from memory.
Answers: 1. O; 2. U; 3. O; 4. U; 5. U; 6. O; 7. O; 8. U; 9. U; 10. O.

Stating Conditions

An instructional objective describes any special conditions in which the learning will take place. If the observable learning outcome is to take place at a particular time, in a particular place, with particular materials, equipment, tools, or other resources, then the conditions must be stated explicitly in the objective, as the following examples show:

Given a calculator, multiply two-digit numbers, correct to the nearest whole number.

Given a typed list, correct any typographical errors.

Given a list of six scrambled words, arrange the words to form a sentence.

EXERCISE: *Write conditions for the following learning outcomes:*

_____**1.** Given _____, change the oil and oil filter.
_____**2.** Given _____, identify the correct temperature.
_____**3.** Given _____, add three-digit numbers.

Possible answers: 1. a foreign automobile; 2. a thermometer; 3. an electronic calculator.

Stating Criterion Levels

An instructional objective indicates how well the behavior is to be performed. For any given objective a number of test items will be written. The criterion level of acceptable performance specifies how many of these items the student must get correct for him or her to have attained the objective. The following are examples of objectives with criterion stated:

> Given 20 two-digit addition problems, the student will compute all answers correctly.

> Given 20 two-digit addition problems, the student will compute 90% correctly.

EXERCISE: *Write criterion levels of acceptable performance for the following objectives.*

_____**1.** Given 10 words, circle those that contain a silent "e" with _____ percent accuracy.
_____**2.** The student will swim freestyle for 100 yards in less than _____ .
_____**3.** The good student must be able to leap tall buildings _____ .

Possible answers: 1. 80; 2. 60 seconds; 3. in a single bound.

Remember, criterion levels need not always be specified in terms of percentages of items answered correctly. They may also be stated as follows:

- number of items correct,
- number of consecutive items correct (or consecutive errorless performances),
- essential features included (as in an essay question or paper),
- completion within a prescribed time limit (where speed of performance is important), or
- completion with a certain degree of accuracy.

Now that you have worked through the exercises, you have some idea of what is necessary for a complete instructional objective. The following are examples of complete instructional objectives:

> With a ballpoint pen, write your name, address, birthdate, telephone number, and grade with 100%accuracy.

> Without reference to class notes, correctly describe four out of five alternative sources of energy discussed in class.

> The student will reply in grammatically correct French to 95% of the French questions spoken orally during an examination.

> Given a human skeleton, the student will identify at least 40 of the bones correctly.

To this point we have shown you how to

> discriminate learning outcomes from learning activities,
>
> discriminate observable/measurable learning outcomes from unobservable/unmeasurable learning outcomes,
>
> state conditions, and
>
> state criterion levels.

Before moving on to our next topic, let's consider one more issue related to the construction of instructional objectives.

Keeping It Simple and Straightforward

We often make the mistake of being too sophisticated in measuring learning outcomes. As a result, we often resort to indirect or unnecessarily complex methods to measure learning outcomes. If you want to know whether students can write their name, ask them to write their name—but not blindfolded! Resist the temptation to be tricky. Consider the following examples:

> The student will show his or her ability to recall characters of the book *Tom Sawyer* by painting a picture of each.
>
> Discriminate between a telephone and a television by drawing an electrical diagram of each.
>
> Demonstrate that you understand how to use an encyclopedia index by listing the page a given subject can be found on in the *Encyclopaedia Britannica*.

In the first example, painting a picture would likely allow us to determine whether the pupils could recall the characters in *Tom Sawyer*, but isn't there an easier (and less time-consuming) way to measure recall? How about asking the students to simply list the characters? If your objective is to determine recall, listing is sufficient.

For the second example, another unnecessarily complex task is suggested. Instead, how about presenting students with two illustrations, one of a telephone, the other of a television, and simply ask them to tell you (orally or in writing) which is which?

Finally, the third example is on target. The task required is a simple and efficient way of measuring whether someone can use an encyclopedia index.

The next step is to practice writing objectives on your own. Return to the exercises when you have trouble, and be sure you include the three components in each objective. Remember, the three components are:

- observable learning outcome,
- conditions, and
- criterion level.

Once you have written an instructional objective, it is always a good idea to analyze it to make sure that the necessary components are included. Determining whether an observable learning outcome has been stated is usually the initial step. The checklist for written objectives in Fig. 5.1 addresses this point and provides you with a step-by-step method to analyze and improve written objectives. We are now ready to consider the third stage of the classroom measurement model introduced in Chapter 4—matching a test item to the instructional objective.

	Yes	No

1. Are the objectives composed of only learning outcomes, and not learning activities?
  a. If yes, go to Step 2.
  b. If no, eliminate the learning activities or replace them with the learning outcomes.
	____	____

2. Are the learning outcomes stated in overt observable terms?
  a. If yes, go to Step 3.
  b. If no, replace the unobservable outcomes with indicators of the outcomes. Remember, because this almost always results in more specific objectives, you may have to write several overt objectives to adequately "sample" the covert learning outcome.
	____	____

3. Now that you have all overt learning outcomes listed, are they the simplest and most direct ways to measure the learning outcomes?
  a. If yes, you now have a useful list of instructional objectives that will serve as a asis for a content-valid test.
  b. If no, rewrite the indirect or complicated means of measurement so that they are as simple and direct as possible. Once you have done so, you have the basis for a content-valid test.
	____	____

FIGURE 5.1 Checklist for written objectives.

MATCHING TEST ITEMS TO INSTRUCTIONAL OBJECTIVES

There is one basic rule to keep in mind when matching test items to instructional objectives: The learning outcome and conditions specified in the test question must match the learning outcome and conditions described in the objective. This rule will ensure that the test you are developing will have content validity. Because content validity is so important, let's go through some exercises to be sure we can actually match correctly.

The following exercises illustrate the two steps involved in matching items to objectives.

Step 1: Identify the learning outcome called for by the objective. Check to determine if your item requires the same learning outcome.

EXERCISE: *For the following, employ Step 1 and decide whether the learning outcomes match.*

	Match?	
	Yes	No
1. *Objective:* Recall the names of the capitals of all 50 states.	____	____

    Test item: List the capitals of Texas, New York, California, and Rhode Island.

2.   *Objective:* Discriminate fact from opinion in the President's most   ——   ——
recent state of the union address.

   Test item: Given a text of the state of the union address, list three
examples of facts and three examples of opinion.

3.   *Objective:* The student will write complete instructional   ——   ——
objectives, including behavior, conditions, and criteria.

   Test item: Describe why instructional objectives must contain an
observable behavior, conditions, and criteria.

4.   *Objective:* Using your text as a reference, recognize the names of   ——   ——
the various components of the central nervous system.

   Test item: From memory, list the various components of the
central nervous system.

5.   *Objective:* Given a written story, list the main events in   ——   ——
chronological order.

   Test item: From the story provided, list the main events in
chronological order.

Answers: Items 1, 2, and 5 have learning outcomes that match; items 3 and 4 do not have learning
outcomes that match.

Step 2:   Identify the learning conditions that are called for by the objective. Check to
determine if your item requires the same learning conditions.

EXERCISE: *For the following, assume Step 1 has been performed.
Employ Step 2.*

	Match?	
	Yes	*No*

1.   *Objective:* Using your map as a guide, make a freehand drawing   ——   ——
of Australia.

   Test item: Without using your map, draw the continent of
Australia.

2.   *Objective:* Given a complete instructional objective, write a test   ——   ——
item that matches the objective's learning outcome and conditions.

   Test item: Write an item that matches the learning outcome and
conditions of the following objective: "The student will add on paper
10 two-digit numbers without regrouping within one minute with
80% accuracy."

3.   *Objective:* Given a list of words, the student will circle the nouns   ——   ——
with 90% accuracy.

   Test item: Give 10 examples of nouns and 10 examples of verbs.

4.   *Objective:* Using their own nondigital watches, the students will   ——   ——
tell time to the quarter hour with 90% accuracy.

   Test item: Look at the digital clock on my desk and write down
the correct time when I ask.

5. *Objective:* The student will sing "The Star-Spangled Banner" —— ——
in front of the class with the aid of a record.

Test item: Sing "The Star-Spangled Banner" in front of
the class.

Answers: Item 2 has matching conditions; items 1, 3, 4, and 5 do not have matching conditions.

In summary, ensuring content validity is as simple as making sure that both the learning outcomes and conditions called for by your test items match the learning outcomes and conditions called for by your instructional objectives. Remember, your goal is to measure achievement, not to trick your students or to have them guess what kind of answer you are looking for. The best way to measure achievement is to ask your students to demonstrate mastery of a skill under the conditions you specify in your instructional objectives. With time, Steps 1 and 2 will become second nature. Until then, subject your items to these steps to ensure their content validity.

TAXONOMY OF EDUCATIONAL OBJECTIVES

We've now considered methods not only to analyze objectives already written, but to write instructional objectives and to match test items to instructional objectives. In the rest of this chapter we will consider different levels of complexity at which objectives and test items may be written and a method for test construction that will help us write items at these levels to ensure that our classroom tests measure higher-level thinking skills.

Cognitive Domain

The level of an objective refers to the cognitive, mental, or thought complexity called for by the objective. For example, the objective "The student will list from memory the names of at least three of the last four U.S. presidents" is a relatively straightforward cognitive task. It involves only recall of the information. Such an objective would be considered lower level. On the other hand, an objective such as "Given an eyewitness account of an event, separate fact from opinion with at least 75% accuracy" is a relatively complex cognitive task. It requires the ability to analyze an eyewitness account and to apply some criteria in determining whether statements are observable and objective or subjective and based on inference. Such an objective would be considered higher level.

One method of categorizing objectives according to cognitive complexity was devised by Bloom, Englehart, Hill, Furst, and Krathwohl 1984. It is a taxonomy of educational objectives for the cognitive domain and delineates six levels of cognitive complexity ranging from the knowledge level (simplest) to the evaluation level (most complex). As illustrated in Fig. 5.2, the levels are presumed to be hierarchical. That is, higher level objectives are assumed to include, and be dependent on, lower level cognitive skills. Each level of the taxonomy has different characteristics. Each of these is described next with examples of action verbs usually indicative of the different levels.

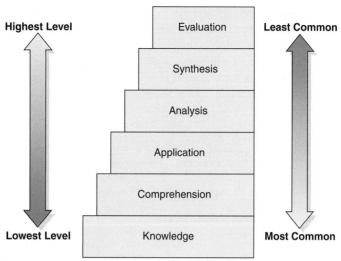

FIGURE 5.2   Taxonomy of educational objectives: cognitive domain.

Knowledge   Objectives at the knowledge level require the students to remember. Test items ask the student to recall or recognize facts, terminology, problem-solving strategies, or rules. Some action verbs that describe learning outcomes at the knowledge level are

define	list	recall
describe	match	recite
identify	name	select
label	outline	state

Some example objectives are

> The student will recall the four major food groups without error, by Friday.

> From memory, the student will match each U.S. general with his most famous battle, with 80% accuracy.

Comprehension   Objectives at the comprehension level require some level of understanding. Test items require the student to change the form of a communication (translation), to restate what has been read, to see connections or relationships among parts of a communication (interpretation), or to draw conclusions or consequences from information (inference). Some action verbs that describe learning outcomes at the comprehension level are

convert	explain	infer
defend	extend	paraphrase
discriminate	estimate	predict
distinguish	generalize	summarize

Some example objectives are

> By the end of the semester, the student will summarize the main events of a story in grammatically correct English.

> The student will discriminate between the "realists" and the "naturalists," citing examples from the readings with 80% accuracy.

Application Objectives written at the application level require the student to use previously acquired information in a setting other than that in which it was learned. Application differs from comprehension in that questions requiring application present the problem in a different and often applied context. Thus the student can rely on neither the question nor the context to decide what prior learning information must be used to solve the problem. Some action verbs that describe learning outcomes at the application level are:

change	modify	relate
compute	operate	solve
demonstrate	organize	transfer
develop	prepare	use
employ	produce	

Some example objectives are

On Monday, the student will tell the class what he or she did over the holiday, without using notes.

Given fractions not covered in class, the student will multiply them on paper with 85% accuracy.

Analysis Objectives written at the analysis level require the student to identify logical errors (e.g., point out a contradiction or an erroneous inference) or to differentiate among facts, opinions, assumptions, hypotheses, or conclusions. Questions at the analysis level often require the student to draw relationships among ideas or to compare and contrast. Some action verbs that describe learning outcomes at the analysis level are

break down	distinguish	point out
deduce	illustrate	relate
diagram	infer	separate out
differentiate	outline	subdivide

Some example objectives are

Given a presidential speech, the student will be able to point out the positions that attack an individual rather than his or her program, with at least 90% accuracy.

Given absurd statements (e.g., "A man had flu twice. The first time it killed him. The second time he got well quickly."), the student will be able to point out the contradiction more than 60% of the time.

Synthesis Objectives written at the synthesis level require the student to produce something unique or original. Questions at the synthesis level require students to solve some unfamiliar problem in a unique way, or to combine parts to form a unique or novel whole. Some action verbs that describe learning outcomes at the synthesis level are

categorize	create	formulate
compile	design	rewrite
compose	devise	summarize

Some example objectives at the synthesis level are

> Given a short story, the student will write a different but plausible ending within 15 minutes.

> Given a problem to be solved, the student will design on paper a scientific experiment to address the problem, without using any reference materials.

Evaluation Instructional objectives written at the evaluation level require the student to form judgments about the value or worth of methods, ideas, people, or products that have a specific purpose. Questions require the student to state the basis for his or her judgments (e.g., what external criteria or principles were drawn upon to reach a conclusion). Some action verbs that describe learning outcomes at the evaluation level are

appraise	criticize	support
compare	defend	validate
contrast	justify	
conclude	interpret	

Some example objectives at the evaluation level are

> Given a previously unread paragraph, the student will judge its value according to the five criteria discussed in class.

> Given a description of a country's economic system, the student will defend it, basing arguments on principles of socialism, described in your text.

Affective Domain

The affective taxonomy, which describes objectives that reflect underlying emotions, feelings, or values rather than cognitive or thought complexity, has been developed by Krathwohl, Bloom, and Masia (1964). This taxonomy describes a process by which another person's, group's, or society's ideas, beliefs, customs, philosophies, attitudes, etc., are gradually accepted and internalized by a different person, group, or society. This process usually begins with a minimal, partial, or incomplete acceptance of an alternative point of view and culminates with the complete integration of this point of view into an individual's personal belief system.

For example, an individual who naively believed in early 1985 that the return of Halley's Comet in 1986 would cause the end of life on Earth may at first have found it difficult even to listen to, *receive*, or *attend* to information that indicated that the comet's return would have no significant or lasting effect on life on Earth. Instead, the individual may have ignored such information, attempting instead to convince others of Earth's impending doom. However, with the passage of time throughout the year, and with increased media and educational reports about the event, the individual may have increasingly listened to such information and even considered, discussed, or *responded* to explanations regarding Earth's safety due to the comet's distance from Earth, its lack of mass, the protection afforded by Earth's atmosphere, etc. Eventually the individual likely began to *value* the argument that the comet would have little or no effect on life on Earth and ceased preaching Earth's demise. Finally, after trying unsuccessfully even to see the comet on numerous occasions during its closest approach to Earth, the individual may have accepted and *organized* the arguments against the total destruction of the human race to the extent that these have come to be internalized and now *characterize* the individual's *value complex*. This would be evident by the individual's calm acceptance of near approaches by celestial bodies in the future and efforts to reassure others of their safety in the face of such events.

The preceding italicized words indicate the five categories or levels of the affective domain. Each of these is described further under the following heads, and sublevels within each of these levels are italicized also. As with the cognitive taxonomy, the levels and sublevels are generally considered to be hierarchical.

Receiving (Attending)   Progressing through the receiving level requires that a student have at least an *awareness* of some stimulus. Once this has occurred, a *willingness* at least to listen or attend to the stimulus must be present (i.e., tolerance). A student will next be able to *attend selectively* to various aspects of the context within which the stimulus exists, differentiating those that are relevant to the stimulus from those that are not.

Responding   Student responses at the responding level indicate more than passive listening or attending; they require active participation. In the most basic form of responding, a student will at least *acquiesce* to a teacher's or other's request, although given a choice the student might choose some other activity. More complete responding would be indicated by a student's *willingness* to engage in an activity, even when allowed a choice. The highest level within this category is indicated by *satisfaction* after engaging in a response. Not only does the student participate, but it is evident that the student enjoys the activity.

Valuing   At the valuing level students judge an activity as to its worthiness and tend to do so consistently enough that the pattern is recognizable to others. The most basic sublevel involves the *acceptance* of a belief, idea, attitude, etc. The individual may not be willing to publicly defend the idea but has internalized it. When a student actively pursues an idea, he or she is demonstrating a *preference* for it, the next sublevel of valuing. Finally, after becoming convinced of the validity of an idea, a student expresses *commitment* to the idea. At this point the student demonstrates conviction by pursuing the goal or idea diligently.

Organization   As ideas are internalized they become increasingly interrelated and prioritized. That is, they become organized into a value system. This requires first that a student *conceptualize* a value by analyzing interrelationships and drawing generalizations that reflect the valued idea. It may be noted that such an activity is cognitive. However, it is classified here because such conceptualizing would only be undertaken after an idea or philosophy was valued. Next, values that have been conceptualized are subject to the *organization of a value system*. That is, the valued ideas are arranged to foster their consistency and compatibility with one another.

Characterization by a Value or Value Complex   Students operating at the value complex level behave in a way that is consistent with their value system, avoiding hypocrisy and behaving consistently with an underlying philosophy "automatically." The first sublevel is characterized by a *generalized set*. This means the individual is predisposed to perceive, process, and react to a situation in accordance with an internalized value system. The next level, *characterization*, is evident in the consistency between an individual's thoughts and behaviors. Such individuals would never say "Do as I say, not as I do."

Now that you are familiar with the affective taxonomy you may ask, "What do I do with it in the classroom?" First of all, it is probably unrealistic to expect a classroom teacher to structure experiences over a one-year period that would lead a student through all five levels. Indeed, there are many who would argue that few human beings ever reach a point in their lives where they function at the fifth, or even the fourth, level. Nonetheless, this taxonomy has important implications for instructional activities and for methods to evaluate instructional activities.

Let's look at an example. Suppose most of the children in your class say they hate history and avoid all stimuli related to history. Asking those students to write a paper describing the importance of history courses in the public-school curriculum would likely be a frustrating experience for them and for you, since those students are not even at the receiving or attending level when it comes to history. You might spend a good deal of time developing a reliable scoring scheme for such a paper and grading the papers only to find that the students failed to see any value in history courses in general or in the topic of the paper. It would be more appropriate, given this example, to develop activities and ways to evaluate those activities that are aimed initially at the receiving or attending level; progressing to the responding level only after the students have demonstrated their willingness to consider history as an important part of the curriculum and after they have demonstrated the ability to attend selectively to history when distracting stimuli are present; and progressing to the valuing level only after the students have demonstrated their willingness to deal objectively with history and/or their satisfaction with history as a subject. While individualizing instruction in this way may not always be completely practical, the affective taxonomy will at least provide you with a framework to allow you to better assess "where they are" regarding various topics. This should help you keep your expectations for the class realistic and keep you from pushing for too much too soon, perhaps frustrating yourself and the class in the process. Practically speaking, it is probably unrealistic to expect students to progress much beyond the valuing level as a result of their elementary and secondary school experiences.

The Psychomotor Domain

In addition to the cognitive and affective taxonomies, a taxonomy of psychomotor behaviors has been developed by Harrow (1972). This domain includes virtually all behaviors: speaking, writing, eating, jumping, throwing, catching, running, walking, driving a car, opening a door, dancing, flying an airplane, etc. The psychomotor domain has proved most difficult to classify into taxonomic levels since all but the simplest reflex actions involve cognitive, and often affective, components. Nonetheless, Harrow's taxonomy is presented because it does again provide a framework within which to consider the design of instructional activities and methods to evaluate the activities. This taxonomy may prove especially useful to teachers in the lower elementary grades and teachers of physical education, dance, theater, and other courses that require considerable movement.

The psychomotor taxonomy listed under the following headings ranges from the lowest level of observable reflexive behavior to the highest level, representing the most complex forms of nonverbal communication.

Reflex Movements Reflex movements are involuntary movements that either are evident at birth or develop with maturation. Sublevels include *segmental reflexes*, *intersegmental reflexes*, and *suprasegmental reflexes*.

Basic-Fundamental Movements Basic-fundamental movements are inherent in more complex or skilled motor movements. Sublevels include *locomotor movements*, *nonlocomotor movements*, and *manipulative movements*.

Perceptual Abilities Perceptual abilities refer to all the abilities of an individual that send input to the brain for interpretation, which in turn affects motor movements. Sublevels include *kinesthetic*, *visual*, *auditory*, *tactile discrimination*, and *coordinated abilities*.

Physical Abilities Physical abilities are the characteristics of an individual's physical self which, when developed properly, enable smooth and efficient movement. Sublevels include *endurance*, *strength*, *flexibility*, and *agility*.

Skilled Movements Skilled movements are the result of learning, often complex learning. They result in efficiency in carrying out a complex movement or task. Sublevels include *simple*, *compound*, and *complex adaptive skills*.

Nondiscursive Communication Nondiscursive communication is a form of communication through movement. Such nonverbal communication as facial expressions, postures, and expressive dance routines are examples. Sublevels include *expressive movement* and *interpretive movement*.

THE TEST BLUEPRINT

Thus far we've devoted a good deal of time to writing and analyzing objectives and showing you how to match test items to objectives. We also need to spend some time discussing a technique to help you remember to write objectives and test items at different levels to ensure our tests include items that measure higher-level thinking. This technique is referred to as a *test blueprint*. Much like a blueprint used by a builder to guide building construction, the test blueprint used by a teacher guides test construction. The test blueprint is also called a *table of specifications*.

The blueprint for a building ensures that the builder will not overlook details considered essential. Similarly, the test blueprint ensures that the teacher will not overlook details considered essential to a good test. More specifically, it ensures that a test will sample whether learning has taken place across the range of (1) content areas covered in class and readings and (2) cognitive processes considered important. It ensures that your test will include a variety of items that tap different levels of cognitive complexity. To get an idea of what a test blueprint helps you avoid, consider the following:

> *Joan was nervous. She knew she had to do very well on the comprehensive final in order to pass American History: 1945–2005. To make matters worse, her teacher was new and no one knew what his final exams were like.*
>
> *"Well," she told herself. "There's really no point in worrying. Even if I don't do well on this test, I have learned to analyze information and think critically—the discussions were great. I've studied the text and lessons very hard and managed to cover every topic very thoroughly beginning with the end of World War II in 1945 through the re-election of President George W. Bush. I realize I missed the class dealing with the late 1960s and early 1970s, but that stuff only covered a few pages in the text anyway, and we only spent one class on it!"*
>
> *Feeling more relaxed and confident, Joan felt even better when she saw that the entire final was only one page long. After receiving her copy, however, Joan began shaking. Her test is reproduced here.*

American History: 1945–2005

Name: _____   Date: _____

It has been a long year and you have been good students. This short test is your reward.

1. *On what date did American soldiers first begin to fight in Vietnam? _____*
2. *How many years did Americans fight in Vietnam? _____*
3. *What was the capital of South Vietnam? _____*
4. *On what date did Richard Nixon become president? _____*
5. *Who was Richard Nixon's vice president during his second administration?*
   _____
6. *What is Vietnam's largest seaport? _____*
7. *Who was the president of South Vietnam? _____*
8. *On what date did Americans begin to leave Vietnam? _____*

   Have a good summer!

We wish we could safely say that things like this never happen, but they do! Chances are you have had a similar experience—perhaps not as extreme, but similar. This test is not a comprehensive assessment of American History: 1945–2005. It is not comprehensive; it focuses on events that occurred during the Vietnam War. It fails to representatively sample content presented in the text and omits content presented in class, except for one class. Finally, it fails to tap any higher level thinking processes. Each question requires rote memorization at the knowledge level. A test blueprint, as shown in Table 5.1, helps us avoid falling into this or similar traps in test construction.

A test blueprint is essential to good test construction. It not only ensures that your test will sample all important content areas and processes (levels of cognitive complexity), but is also useful in planning and organizing instruction. The blueprint should be assembled before you actually begin a unit. Table 5.1 illustrates a test blueprint appropriate for a unit on instructional objectives being taught in an education course.

Let's consider each component of the blueprint. Once we understand how the components are interrelated, the significance of a test blueprint will become more clear.

TABLE 5.1   **Test Blueprint for a Unit on Instructional Objectives**

Content outline	Knowledge	Comprehension	Application	Analysis	Total	Percentage
			(Number of Items)			
1. Role of Objectives						
a. The student can state purposes for objectives in education.	4			4		12%
b. The student can describe a classroom system model and the role of objectives in it.		1			1	3%
2. Writing Objectives						
a. Given a general educational goal, the student will write an instructional objective that specifies that goal.			5		5	14%
b. The students can match instructional objectives with their appropriate level in the cognitive domain.		5			5	14%
c. The student can identify the three parts of an objective: behavior, conditions, criteria.		5			5	14%
d. The student can distinguish learning activities from learning outcomes when given examples of each.		10			10	29%
3. Decoding Ready-Made Objectives						
a. Given instructional objectives in need of modification, the student will rewrite the objective so that it is a suitable instructional objective.				5	5	14%
Total	4	21	5	5	35	
Percentage	12%	60%	14%	14%	100%	

Content Outline

The content outline lists the topic and the important objectives included under the topic. It is for these objectives that you will write test items. Try to keep the total number of objectives to a manageable number, certainly no more than are needed for any one unit.

Categories

The categories serve as a reminder or a check on the "cognitive complexity" of the test. Obviously many units over which you want to test will contain objectives that do not go beyond the comprehension level. However, the outline can suggest that you try to incorporate higher levels of learning into your instruction and evaluations. In the cells under these categories, report the number of items in your tests that are included in that level for a particular objective. For example, five items are to be constructed to measure comprehension level objective 2b in Table 5.1.

Number of Items

Fill in the cells in Table 5.1 using the following procedure:

1. Determine the classification of each instructional objective.
2. Record the number of items that are to be constructed for the objective in the cell corresponding to the category for that objective.
3. Repeat Steps 1 and 2 for every objective in the outline.
4. Total the number of items for the instructional objective and record the number in the Total column.
5. Repeat Steps 1 through 4 for each topic.
6. Total the number of items falling into each category and record the number at the bottom of the table.
7. Compute the column and row percentages by dividing each total by the number of items in the test.

Functions

The information in Table 5.1 is intended to convey to the teacher the following:

- How many items are to be constructed for which objectives and content topics.
- Whether the test will reflect a balanced picture of what was taught.
- Whether all topics and objectives will be assessed and their level of cognitive complexity.

Seldom can such "balance" be so easily attained. The little extra time required to construct such a blueprint for your test (and your instruction!) will quickly repay itself. You will not only avoid constructing a bad test, but you will have to make fewer and less extensive revisions of your test. You'll also have a sense of satisfaction from realizing you've constructed a representative test.

Since test blueprints are so important to test construction (not to mention instructional planning), we have included a second example of a test blueprint in Table 5.2. This table illustrates a test blueprint appropriate for an elementary unit on subtraction without borrowing.

Clearly, constructing test blueprints requires considerable time and effort. This will be time and effort well spent, we believe, because it will serve you and your students well by improving the appropriateness of your test. Nevertheless, we realize that time is of the essence. For some tips on how a PC can help save time in revising test blueprints see the sidebar (Box 5-1).

TABLE 5.2 **Test Blueprint for a Unit on Subtraction without Borrowing**

Content outline	Knowledge	Comprehension	Application	Total	Percentage
				Categories	
			(Number of Items)		
1. The student will discriminate the subtraction sign from the addition sign.	1			1	4%
2. The student will discriminate addition problems from subtraction problems.	2			2	8%
3. The student will discriminate correctly solved subtraction problems from incorrectly solved subtraction problems.		4		4	16%
4. The student will correctly solve single-digit subtraction problems.			6	6	24%
5. The student will correctly solve subtraction problems with double-digit numerators and single-digit denominators.			6	6	24%
6. The student will correctly solve double- digit subtraction problems.			6	6	24%
Total	3	4	18	25	
Percentage	12%	16%	72%		100%

This concludes our introduction to test planning and instructional objectives. In the next two chapters we'll consider the actual process by which objective and essay test items are constructed. Soon you'll be able to construct not just a representative test, but a good representative test!

BOX 5-1

PCS AND TEST BLUEPRINTS

If instructional objectives have been saved in a PC word processing file it is relatively simple to use your word processing program's cut and paste functions to transfer the objectives to the content outline section of a test blueprint outline in a separate word processing file. A spreadsheet file can be established that will automatically sum and convert to percentages the cell totals for the rows and columns. If the word processing program is compatible with a spreadsheet program, or is part of an integrated "suite" of related programs, you can also use the cut and paste functions to transfer the spreadsheet file into the cell space in the word processing file. Once you have done so, you can make modifications to the combined word processing and spreadsheet file as needed for future revisions of the test.

SUMMARY

Chapter 5 introduced you to the first two steps in test construction, writing instructional objectives and preparing a test blueprint. Its major points are as follows:

1. A complete instructional objective includes
   a. an observable learning outcome,
   b. any special conditions under which the behavior must be displayed, and
   c. a performance level considered to be indicative of mastery.

2. Learning outcomes are ends (products); learning activities are the means (processes) to the ends.

3. Objectives may be analyzed to determine their adequacy by
   a. determining whether a learning outcome or learning activity is stated in the objective,
   b. rewriting the objective if a learning outcome is not stated,
   c. determining whether the learning outcomes are stated in measurable or unmeasurable terms, and
   d. determining whether the objective states the simplest and most direct way of measuring the learning outcome.

4. Learning outcomes and conditions stated in a test item must match the outcomes and conditions stated in the objective if the item is to be considered a valid measure of or match for the objective.

5. The taxonomy of educational objectives for the cognitive domain helps categorize objectives at different levels of cognitive complexity. There are six levels: knowledge, comprehension, application, analysis, synthesis, and evaluation.

6. A test blueprint, including instructional objectives covering the content areas to be covered and the relevant cognitive processes, should be constructed to guide item writing and test construction.

7. The test blueprint conveys to the teacher the number of items to be constructed per objective, their level of cognitive complexity in the taxonomy, and whether the test represents a balanced picture based on what was taught.

FOR PRACTICE

1. For the same content area, make up two objectives each at the knowledge, comprehension, application, analysis, synthesis, and evaluation levels of the taxonomy of cognitive objectives. Select verbs for each level from the lists provided. Try to make your objectives cover the same subject.

2. Exchange the objectives you have just written with a classmate. Have him or her check each objective for (1) an observable behavior, (2) any special conditions under which the behavior must be displayed, and (3) a performance level considered sufficient to demonstrate mastery. Revise your objectives if necessary.

3. Now take your list of objectives and arrange them into the format of a test blueprint (see Table 5.1). To construct a test blueprint, determine some general content headings under which your specific objectives can be placed. List these with your objectives vertically down the left side of the page. Next, across the top of the page, indicate the levels of behavior at which you have written your objectives. In the cells of the table, place the number of items you would write for each objective if you were to prepare a 100-item test over this content. Total the items and compute percentages as indicated in Table 5.1.

*4. Column A contains instructional objectives. Column B contains levels of cognitive learning outcomes. Match the levels in Column B with the most appropriate objective in Column A. Write the letter that indicates the highest level of cognitive outcome implied in the space next to the numbers in Column A. Column B levels can be used more than once.

Column A

_____1. Given a two-page essay, the student can distinguish the assumptions basic to the author's position.

_____2. The student will correctly spell the word mountain.

_____3. The student will convert the following English passage into Spanish.

_____4. The student will compose new pieces of prose and poetry according to the classification system emphasized in lecture.

_____5. Given a sinking passenger ship with 19 of its 20 lifeboats destroyed, the captain will decide who is to be on the last lifeboat on the basis of perceptions of their potential worth to society.

Column B

a. Knowledge
b. Comprehension
c. Application
d. Analysis
e. Synthesis
f. Evaluation

5. Using the following test blueprint or table of specifications for a unit on mathematics, answer the following questions:

a. How many questions will deal with long division at the comprehension, application, and analysis levels?

b. What percentage of the test questions will deal with multiplication and division?

Major Area	Minor Area	Knowledge	Comprehension	Application	Analysis	Synthesis	Evaluation	Total	Percentage
Addition	Whole numbers	2	1	2				5	
	Fractions		1	1	2	1		5	20%
Subtraction	Whole numbers	1	1	2	1			5	
	Fractions		1	1	2	1		4	20%
Multiplication	Tables	2	2					4	
	Whole numbers			2	2	1		5	
	Fractions	1	1	2	1	1		6	30%
Division	Long division	1	2	1				4	
	Whole numbers	1	1	2	1			5	
	Fractions	1	2	2	1			6	30%

*Answers to Questions 4 and 5 appear in Appendix F.

CHAPTER 6

WRITING OBJECTIVE TEST ITEMS

THUS FAR we have discussed how to establish general goals for instruction and how to develop instructional objectives derived from those goals. We have also discussed using the test blueprint to ensure an adequate sampling of the content area, accurate matching of test items to instructional objectives, and that our test measures higher-level thinking skills. We are now ready to put some "meat" on this test "skeleton." In this chapter we will discuss objective test items and how to construct them. Objective test items include items with the following formats: true–false, matching, multiple choice, and completion or short answer. The essay item, because of its special characteristics and scoring considerations, will be treated in Chapter 7, along with methods to measure the way students organize knowledge and suggestions for open-book exams.

WHICH FORMAT?

Once you have reached the item writing stage of test construction, you will have to choose a format or combination of formats to use for your test. Although your choice can be somewhat arbitrary at times, this is not always the case. Often your decision has already been made for you, or, more correctly, you may have at least partially made the decision when you wrote the objective or objectives. In many instances, however, you will have a choice among several item formats. For example, consider the following objectives and item formats.

> OBJECTIVE 1: Given a story, the student can recognize the meaning of all new words.

> TEST ITEMS: Circle the letter that represents the correct meaning of the following words:

1. intention
   a. desire
   b. need
   c. direction
   d. command

2. crisis

   a. feeling

   b. message

   c. pending

   d. critical

OBJECTIVE 2: The student can associate the characteristics of leading characters with their names.

TEST ITEM: The first column is a list of the names of the main characters in *Huckleberry Finn*. Descriptions of the main characters are listed in the second column. In the space provided, write the letter of the description that matches each character.

Character	*Description*
_____ **1.** Tom	**a.** Cruel
_____ **2.** Becky	**b.** Always by himself, a loner
_____ **3.** Jim	**c.** Popular, outgoing, fun loving
_____ **4.** Huck	**d.** Always critical
_____ **5.** Mrs. Watson	**e.** Sneaky, lying, scheming
	f. Kind, gentle, loving
	g. Dull, slow moving

OBJECTIVE 3: The student can write a plausible alternative ending to a story.

TEST ITEM: You have just read the story *Huckleberry Finn*. In 40 words, write a different ending to the story that would be believable.

OBJECTIVE 4: The students will recognize whether certain events occurred.

TEST ITEM: Here is a list of incidents in *Huckleberry Finn*. Circle T if it happened in the story and F if it did not.

1. The thieves were killed in the storm on the river.	T		F
2. Jim gained his freedom.	T		F
3. Tom broke his leg.	T		F

Objective 1 was measured using a multiple-choice format. We might also have tested this objective using a true–false or matching format. Similarly, objective 2 lends itself to a multiple-choice as well as a matching format. Since in many circumstances alternative item formats may be appropriate, the choice between them will be made on the basis of other considerations. For example, time constraints or your preference for, or skill in, writing different types of items will undoubtedly influence your choice of item format.

Objective 3, however, requires an essay item. There is no way this objective can be measured with an objective item. Similarly, objective 4 lends itself almost exclusively to a single format. Perhaps other formats would work, but the true–false format certainly does the job. In short, there are times our objectives tell us which format to use. At other times we must consider other factors. Let's look more closely at the different item formats.

TRUE–FALSE ITEMS

True–false items are popular probably because they are quick and easy to write, or at least they seem to be. Actually, true–false items do take less time to write than good objective items of any other format, but good true–false items are not that easy to write. Consider the following true–false items. Use your common sense to help you determine which are good items and which are poor.

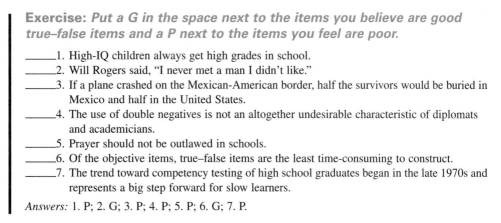

Exercise: *Put a G in the space next to the items you believe are good true–false items and a P next to the items you feel are poor.*

_____1. High-IQ children always get high grades in school.

_____2. Will Rogers said, "I never met a man I didn't like."

_____3. If a plane crashed on the Mexican-American border, half the survivors would be buried in Mexico and half in the United States.

_____4. The use of double negatives is not an altogether undesirable characteristic of diplomats and academicians.

_____5. Prayer should not be outlawed in schools.

_____6. Of the objective items, true–false items are the least time-consuming to construct.

_____7. The trend toward competency testing of high school graduates began in the late 1970s and represents a big step forward for slow learners.

Answers: 1. P; 2. G; 3. P; 4. P; 5. P; 6. G; 7. P.

In item 1, the word always is an absolute. To some extent, true–false items depend on absolute judgments. However, statements or facts are seldom completely true or completely false. Thus, an alert student will usually answer "false" to items that include always, all, never, or only.

To avoid this problem, avoid using terms like all, always, never, or only. Item 1 could be improved by replacing always with a less absolute term, perhaps tend. Thus item 1 might read:

High-IQ children tend to get high grades in school.

Item 2 is a good one. To answer the item correctly, the students would have to know whether Will Rogers made the statement. Or do they? Consider the following situation:

Mrs. Allen, a history teacher and crusader against grade inflation, couldn't wait to spring her latest creation on her students. She had spent weeks inserting trick words, phrases, and complicated grammatical constructions into her 100 item true–false test. In order to ensure low grades on the test, she allowed only 30 minutes for the test. Although her harried students worked as quickly as they could, no one completed more than half the items, and no one answered more than 40 items correctly. No one, that is, except Tina. When Tina handed her test back to Mrs. Allen after two minutes, Mrs. Allen announced, "Class, Tina has handed in her test! Obviously, she hasn't read the questions and will earn a zero!" When she scored the test, however, Mrs. Allen was shocked to see that in fact Tina had answered 50 items correctly. She earned the highest score on the test without even reading Mrs. Allen's tricky questions. Confused and embarrassed, Mrs. Allen told the class they would have no more true–false tests and would have essay tests in the future.

This points to the most serious shortcoming of true–false items: With every true–false item, regardless of how well or poorly written, the student has a 50% chance of guessing correctly even without reading the item! In other words, on a 50-item true–false test, we would expect individuals who were totally unfamiliar with the content being tested to answer about 25 items correctly. However, this doesn't mean you should avoid true–false items entirely, since they are appropriate at times. Fortunately, there are ways of reducing the effects of guessing. Some of these are described next and another will be presented in Chapter 10.

1. Encourage all students to guess when they do not know the correct answer. Since it is virtually impossible to prevent certain students from guessing, encouraging all students to guess should equalize the effects of guessing. The test scores will then reflect a more or less equal "guessing factor" plus the actual level of each student's knowledge. This will also prevent test-wise students from having an unfair advantage over non-test-wise students.

2. Require revision of statements that are false. With this approach, space is provided for students to alter false items to make them true. Usually the student also underlines or circles the false part of the item. Item 1 is revised here along with other examples.

> T   F   High-IQ children *always* get high grades in school. *tend to*
>
> T   F   Panama is *north* of Cuba. *south*
>
> T   F   *September* has an extra day during leap year. *February*

With such a strategy full credit is awarded only if the revision is correct. The disadvantage of such an approach is that more test time is required for the same number of items and scoring time is increased.

Item 3 is a poor item, but Mrs. Allen would probably like it because it is a trick question. "Survivors" of a plane crash are not buried! Chances are that you never even noticed the word survivors and probably assumed the item referred to fatalities. Trick items may have a place in tests of critical reading or visual discrimination (in which case they would no longer be trick questions), but seldom are they appropriate in the average classroom test. Rewritten, item 3 might read:

> If a plane crashes on the Mexican-American border, half the fatalities would be buried in Mexico and half in the United States.

Item 4 is also poor. First of all, it includes a double negative—*not* and *undesirable*. Items with a single negative are confusing enough. Negating the first negative with a second wastes space and test-taking time and also confuses most students. If you want to say something, say it positively. The following revision makes this item slightly more palatable.

> The use of double negatives is an altogether desirable trait of diplomats and academicians.

We said slightly more palatable because the item is still troublesome. The word altogether is an absolute, and we now know we should avoid absolutes, since there usually are exceptions to the rules they imply. When we eliminate altogether the item reads:

> The use of double negatives is a desirable trait of diplomats and academicians.

However, the item is still flawed because it states an opinion, not a fact. Is the item true or false? The answer depends on whom you ask. To most of us, the use of double negatives is probably undesirable, for the reasons already stated. To some diplomats, the use of double negatives may seem highly desirable. In short, true–false statements should normally be used to measure knowledge of factual information. If you must use a true–false item to measure knowledge of an opinionated position or statement, state the referent (the person or group that made the statement or took the position), as illustrated in the following revision:

> According to the National Institute of Diplomacy, the use of double negatives is a desirable trait of diplomats and academicians.

Item 5 further illustrates this point. It is deficient because it states an opinion. It is neither obviously true nor obviously false. This revision includes a referent that makes it acceptable.

> The American Civil Liberties Union (ACLU) has taken the position that prayer should *not* be outlawed in schools.

Notice the word *not* in Item 5. When you include a negative in a test item, highlight it in italics, underlining, or uppercase letters so the reader will not overlook it. Remember that, unlike Mrs. Allen, you intend to determine whether your students have mastered your objective, not to ensure low test scores.

Item 6 represents a good item. It measures factual information, and the phrase "Of the objective items" qualifies the item and limits it to a specific frame of reference.

The last item is deficient because it is double barreled. It is actually two items in one. When do you mark true for a double barreled item? When both parts of the item are true? When one part is true? Or only when the most important part is true? The point is that items should measure a single idea. Double-barreled items take too much time to read and comprehend. To avoid this problem, simply construct two items, as we have done here:

> The trend toward competency testing of high school graduates began in the late 1970s.

> The trend toward competency testing represents a big step forward for slow learners.

Better? Yes. Acceptable? Not quite. The second item is opinionated. According to whom is this statement true or false? Let's include a referent.

> According to the Office of Education, the trend toward competency testing of high school graduates is a big step forward for slow learners.

Whose position is being represented is now clear, and the item is straightforward.

Suggestions for Writing True–False Items

1. The desired method of marking true or false should be clearly explained before students begin the test.

2. Construct statements that are definitely true or definitely false, without additional qualifications. If opinion is used, attribute it to some source.

3. Use relatively short statements and eliminate extraneous material.

4. Keep true and false statements at approximately the same length, and be sure that there are approximately equal numbers of true and false items.

5. Avoid using double-negative statements. They take extra time to decipher and are difficult to interpret.

6. Avoid the following:
   a. verbal clues, absolutes, and complex sentences.
   b. broad general statements that are usually not true or false without further qualifications;
   c. terms denoting indefinite degree (e.g., large, long time, regularly), or absolutes (e.g., never, only, always);
   d. placing items in a systematic order (e.g., TTFF, TFTF, and so on); and
   e. taking statements directly from the text and presenting them out of context.

MATCHING ITEMS

Like true–false items, matching items represent a popular and convenient testing format. Just like good true–false items, though, good matching items are not as easy to write as you might think. Imagine you are back in your tenth-grade American History class and the following matching item shows up on your test. Is it a good matching exercise or not? If not, what is wrong with it?

Directions: Match A and B.

A	*B*
1. Lincoln	a. President during the 20th century
2. Nixon	b. Invented the telephone
3. Whitney	c. Delivered the Emancipation Proclamation
4. Ford	d. Recent president to resign from office
5. Bell	e. Civil rights leader
6. King	f. Invented the cotton gin
7. Washington	g. Our first president
8. Roosevelt	h. Only president elected for more than two terms

See any problems? Compare the problems you have identified with the list of faults and explanations below.

Homogeneity   The lists are not homogeneous. Column A contains names of presidents, inventors, and a civil rights leader. Unless specifically taught as a set of related public figures or ideas, this example represents too wide a variety for a matching exercise. To prevent this from happening you might title your lists (e.g., "U.S. Presidents"). This will help keep irrelevant or filler items from creeping in. If you really want to measure student knowledge of presidents, inventors, and civil rights leaders, then build three separate matching exercises. Doing so will prevent implausible options from being eliminated by the student. When students can eliminate implausible options they are more likely to guess correctly. For example, the student may not know a president who resigned from office but may know that Washington and Lincoln were presidents, and that neither was recent. Thus the student could eliminate two options, increasing the chance of guessing correctly from one out of eight to one out of six.

Order of Lists   The lists should be reversed; that is, Column A should be Column B, and Column B should be Column A. This is a consideration that will save time for the test taker. We are trained to read from left to right. When the longer description is in the left-hand column the student only reads the description once and glances down the list of names to find the answer. As the exercise is now written, the student reads a name and then has to read through all or many of the more lengthy descriptions to find the answer, a much more time-consuming process.

Easy Guessing   There are equal numbers of options and descriptions in each column. Again, this increases the chances of guessing correctly through elimination. In the preceding exercise, if a student did not know who invented the cotton gin but knew which of the names went with the other seven descriptions, the student would arrive at the correct answer through elimination. If there are at least three more options than descriptions, the chances of guessing correctly in such a situation are reduced to one chance in four. Alternatively, the instructions for the exercise may be written to indicate that each option may be used more than once.

Poor Directions   Speaking of directions, those included were much too brief. Matching directions should specify the basis for matching. For example,

> DIRECTIONS: Column A contains brief descriptions of historical events. Column B contains the names of presidents. Indicate which man was president when the historical event took place by placing the appropriate letter to the left of the number in Column A.

The original directions also do not indicate how the matches should be shown. Should lines be drawn? Should letters be written next to numbers, or numbers next to letters? Failure to indicate how matches should be marked can greatly increase your scoring time.

Too Many Correct Responses   The description "President during the 20th century" has three defensible answers: Nixon, Ford, and Roosevelt. You say you meant Henry Ford, inventor of the Model T, not Gerald Ford! Well, that brings us to our final criticism of this matching exercise.

Ambiguous Lists The list of names is ambiguous. Franklin Roosevelt or Teddy Roosevelt? Henry Ford or Gerald Ford? When using names, always include first and last names to avoid such ambiguities.

Now that we have completed our analysis of this test item, we can easily conclude that it needs revision. Let's revise it, starting by breaking the exercise into homogeneous groupings.

> DIRECTIONS: Column A describes events associated with U.S. presidents. Indicate which name in Column B matches each event by placing the appropriate letter to the left of the number of Column A. Each name may be used only once.

Column A	*Column B*
_____1. A president not elected to office	**a.** Abraham Lincoln
_____2. Delivered the Emancipation Proclamation	**b.** Richard Nixon
_____3. Only president to resign from office	**c.** Gerald Ford
_____4. Only president elected for more than two terms	**d.** George Washington
_____5. Our first president	**e.** Franklin Roosevelt
	f. Theodore Roosevelt
	g. Thomas Jefferson
	h. Woodrow Wilson

We can make one more clarification. It is a good idea to introduce some sort of order—chronological, numerical, or alphabetical—to your list of options. This saves the reader time. Students usually go through the list several times in answering a matching exercise, and it is easier to remember a name's or date's location in a list if it is in some sort of order. We can arrange the list of names in alphabetical order to look like this:

Column A	*Column B*
_____1. A president not elected to office	**a.** Gerald Ford
_____2. Delivered the Emancipation Proclamation	**b.** Thomas Jefferson
_____3. Only president to resign from office	**c.** Abraham Lincoln
_____4. Only president elected for more than two terms	**d.** Richard Nixon
_____5. Our first president	**e.** Franklin Roosevelt
	f. Theodore Roosevelt
	g. George Washington
	h. Woodrow Wilson

Our original exercise contained two items relating to invention. If we were determined to measure only knowledge of inventors through a matching exercise, we would want to add at least one more item. Normally, at least three items are used for matching exercises. Such an exercise might look like the following:

DIRECTIONS: Column A lists famous inventions and Column B famous inventors. Match the inventor with the invention by placing the appropriate letter in the space to the left of the number in Column A. Each name may be used only once.

Column A	*Column B*
_____1. Invented the cotton gin	**a.** Alexander Graham Bell
_____2. One of his inventions was the telephone	**b.** Henry Bessemer
_____3. Famous for inventing the wireless	**c.** Thomas Edison
	d. Guglielmo Marconi
	e. Eli Whitney
	f. Orville Wright

Notice we have complete directions, there are three more options than descriptions, the lists are homogeneous, and the list of names is alphabetically ordered. But what about the final item remaining from our original exercise? Let's say we want to determine whether our students know that Martin Luther King, Jr., was a civil rights leader. We can construct another matching exercise with one column listing the names of civil rights leaders and another listing civil rights accomplishments. However, an alternative would be simply to switch item formats. Usually, single items that are removed from matching exercises because of nonhomogeneity are easily converted into true–false, completion, or, with a little more difficulty, multiple-choice items. For example,

True–False

T   F   Martin Luther King, Jr., was a civil rights leader.

Completion

The name of the black civil rights leader assassinated in 1968 is _____ .

Multiple Choice

Which of the following was a civil rights leader?
a. Jefferson Davis
b. Martin Luther King, Jr.
c. John Quincy Adams
d. John Wilkes Booth

Suggestions for Writing Matching Items

1. Keep both the list of descriptions and the list of options fairly short and homogeneous—they should both fit on the same page. Title the lists to ensure homogeneity and arrange the descriptions and options in some logical order. If this is impossible you're probably including too wide a variety in the exercise. Try two or more exercises.

2. Make sure that all the options are plausible distractors for each description to ensure homogeneity of lists.

3. The list of descriptions should contain the longer phrases or statements, while the options should consist of short phrases, words, or symbols.

4. Each description in the list should be numbered (each is an item), and the list of options should be identified by letter.

5. Include more options than descriptions. If the option list is longer than the description list, it is harder for students to eliminate options. If the option list is shorter, some options must be used more than once. Always include some options that do not match any of the descriptions, or some that match more than one, or both.

6. In the directions, specify the basis for matching and whether options can be used more than once.

MULTIPLE-CHOICE ITEMS

Another popular item format is the multiple-choice question. Practically everyone has taken multiple-choice tests at one time or another, but probably more often in high school and college than in elementary school. This doesn't mean that multiple-choice items are not appropriate in the elementary years; it suggests only that one needs to be cautious about using them with younger children.

Multiple-choice items are unique among objective test items because, contrary to popular opinion, they enable you to measure at the higher levels of the taxonomy of educational objectives. Our discussion of multiple-choice items will be in two parts. The first part will consider the mechanics of multiple-choice item construction applied to knowledge level questions. The second part will deal with the construction of higher level multiple-choice items. As before, let's start by using common sense to identify good and poor multiple-choice items in the following exercise.

Exercise: *Place a G in the space next to a good item and a P next to a poor item.*

_____1. U.S. Grant was an
    a. president.
    b. man.
    c. alcoholic.
    d. general.

_____2. In what year did humans first set foot on the moon?
    a. 1975
    b. 1957
    c. 1969
    d. 1963

_____3. The free-floating structures within the cell that synthesize protein are called
    a. chromosomes.
    b. lysosomes.
    c. mitochondria.
    d. free ribosomes.

_____**4.** The principal value of a balanced diet is that it
   a. increases your intelligence.
   b. gives you something to talk about with friends.
   c. promotes mental health.
   d. promotes physical health.
   e. improves self-discipline.

_____**5.** Some test items
   a. are too difficult.
   b. are objective.
   c. are poorly constructed.
   d. have multiple defensible answers.

_____**6.** Which of the following are not associated with pneumonia?
   a. quiet breathing
   b. fever
   c. clear chest x-ray
   d. a and c
   e. b and c

_____**7.** When 53 Americans were held hostage in Iran,
   a. the United States did nothing to try to free them.
   b. the United States declared war on Iran.
   c. the United States first attempted to free them by diplomatic means and later attempted a rescue.
   d. the United States expelled all Iranian students.

_____**8.** The square root of 256 is
   a. 14.
   b. 16.
   c. 4×4
   d. both a and c.
   e. both b and c.
   f. all of the above.
   g. none of the above.

_____**9.** When a test item and the objective it is intended to measure match in learning outcome and conditions, the item
   a. is called an objective item.
   b. has content validity.
   c. is too easy.
   d. should be discarded.

Go over the exercise again. Chances are you'll find a few more problems the second time. Here's the answer key, and a breakdown of the faults found in each item follows in the text.

Answers: 1. P; 2. G; 3. P; 4. P; 5. P; 6. P; 7. P; 8. P; 9. G.

Most students would probably pick up on the grammatical clue in the first item. The article "an" eliminates options a, b, and d immediately, since "U.S. Grant was an man," "an president," or "an general" are not grammatically correct statements. Thus option c is the only option that forms a grammatically correct sentence. Inadvertently providing students with grammatical clues to the correct answer is very common in multiple-choice items. The result is decreased test validity. Students can answer items correctly because of knowledge of grammar, not content.

Replacing "an" with "a/an" would be one way to eliminate grammatical clues in your own writing. Other examples would be "is/are," "was/were," "his/her," and so on. As an alternative, the article, verb, or pronoun may be included in the list of options, as the following example illustrates:

Poor: Christopher Columbus came to America in a

    a. car.
    b. boat.
    c. airplane.
    d. balloon.

Better: Christopher Columbus came to America in

    a. a car.
    b. a boat.
    c. an airplane.
    d. a balloon.

Let's return to the first item and replace "an" with "a/an":

U.S. Grant was a/an

    a. president.
    b. man.
    c. alcoholic.
    d. general.

There! We've removed the grammatical clue, and we now have an acceptable item, right? Not quite. We now have an item free of grammatical clues, but it is still seriously deficient. What is the correct answer?

This item still has a serious flaw: multiple defensible answers. In fact, all four options are defensible answers! U.S. Grant was a president, a man, a general, and, as historians tell us, an alcoholic. Including such an item on a test would contribute nothing to your understanding of student knowledge. But what can you do when you have an item with more than one defensible answer? The answer, of course, is to eliminate the incorrect but defensible option or options.

Let's assume item 1 was written to measure the following objective:

The student will discriminate among the U.S. presidents immediately before, during, and immediately after the U.S. Civil War.

We could modify item 1 to look like this:

U.S. Grant was a

    a. general.
    b. slave.
    c. pirate.
    d. trader.

This item is fine, from a technical standpoint. The grammatical clue has been eliminated and there is but one defensible answer. However, it does not match the instructional objective; it is not very valuable as a measure of student achievement of the objective.

We could also modify the item to look like this:

Of the following, who was elected president after the Civil War?

    a. U.S. Grant
    b. Andrew Johnson
    c. Abraham Lincoln
    d. Andrew Jackson

This item is technically sound, and all response alternatives are relevant to the instructional objective. It meets the two main criteria for inclusion in a test: The item is technically well constructed and it matches the instructional objectives.

We said item 2 was good, but it can still stand some improvement. Remember when we recommended arranging lists for matching items in alphabetical or chronological order? The same holds true for multiple-choice items. To make a good item even better, arrange the options in chronological order. Revised, the item should look like this:

In what year did humans first set foot on the moon?

    a. 1957
    b. 1963
    c. 1969
    d. 1975

The major deficiency in item 3 is referred to as a "stem clue." The statement portion of a multiple-choice item is called the stem, and the correct answer and incorrect choices are called options or response alternatives. A stem clue occurs when the same word or a close derivative occurs in both the stem and options, thereby clueing the test taker to the correct answer. In item 3 the word free in the option is identical to free in the stem. Thus the wise test taker has a good chance of answering the item correctly without mastery of the content being measured. This fault can be eliminated by simply rewording the item without the word free.

The structures within the cell that synthesize protein are called

    a. chromosomes.
    b. lysosomes.
    c. mitochondria.
    d. ribosomes.

Item 4 is related to the "opinionated" items we considered when we discussed true–false items. Depending on the source, or referent, different answers may be the "right" answer. To Person X, the principal value may be to promote physical health; to Person Y, the principal value may be to improve self-discipline. As stated earlier, when you are measuring a viewpoint or opinion, be sure to state the referent or source. To be acceptable the item should be rewritten to include the name of an authority:

The USDA says the principal value of a balanced diet is that it

    a. increases your intelligence.
    b. gives you something to talk about.
    c. promotes mental health.
    d. promotes physical health.
    e. improves self-discipline.

Item 5 is, of course, meaningless. It has at least two serious faults. To begin with, the stem fails to present a problem, and it fails to focus the item. What is the item getting at? The test taker has no idea what to look for in trying to discriminate among the options. The only way to approach such an item is to look at each option as an individual true–false item. This is very time-consuming and frustrating for the test taker. Be sure to focus your multiple-choice items by presenting a problem or situation in the stem.

Like item 1, item 5 also has more than one defensible answer. However, option d seems to control this problem. But if more than a single option is defensible, how can you mark as incorrect someone who chooses a, b, or c and not d? Sometimes, however, you may wish to construct items that have two defensible answers. Is there any way to avoid the problem just mentioned? Fortunately, there is a way to avoid the problem, as illustrated in item 6:

Which of the following are not associated with pneumonia?

   a. quiet breathing
   b. fever
   c. clear chest x-ray
   d. a and c
   e. b and c

Where the possibility of more than one answer is desirable, use an option format like that just shown. This approach avoids the wording problems we ran into in item 5. We would caution, however, that "a and b," "b and c," and so on should be used sparingly.

Now, how about the rest of item 6; is it okay? No; again a grammatical clue is present. The word *are* indicates a plural response is appropriate. Options a, b, and c can automatically be eliminated, leaving the test taker with a 50% chance of guessing correctly. This fault can be corrected by using the same approach we used with item 1, where we substituted "a/an" for "an." Of course, in this instance we would substitute "is/are" for "are." Rewritten, the item looks like this:

Which of the following is/are not associated with pneumonia?

   a. quiet breathing
   b. fever
   c. clear chest x-ray
   d. a and c
   e. b and c

All set? Not yet! Remember what we said about negatives? Let's highlight the "not" with uppercase letters, italics, or underlining to minimize the likelihood of someone misreading the item. After this revision we have an acceptable multiple-choice item.

Two very common faults in multiple-choice construction are illustrated by item 7. First, the phrase "the United States" is included in each option. To save space and time, add it to the stem. Second, the length of options could be a giveaway. Multiple-choice item writers have a tendency to include more information in the correct option than in the incorrect options. Test-wise students take advantage of this tendency, since past experience tells them that longer options are more often than not the correct answer. Naturally, it is impossible to make all options exactly the same length, but try to avoid situations where correct answers are more than one-and-a-half times the length of incorrect options. After eliminating the redundancies in the options and condensing the correct option, we have:

When 53 Americans were held hostage in Iran, the United States

    a. did nothing to try to free them.
    b. declared war on Iran.
    c. undertook diplomatic and military efforts to free them.
    d. expelled all Iranian students.

Item 8 has some problems, too. First, let's consider the use of "all of the above" and "none of the above." In general, "none of the above" should be used sparingly. Some item writers tend to use "none of the above" only when there is no clearly correct option presented. Students, however, can quickly catch on to such a practice and guess that "none of the above" is the correct answer without knowledge of the content being measured.

As far as "all of the above" goes, we cannot think of any circumstances in which its use may be justified. We recommend avoiding this option entirely.

The use of "both a and c" and "both b and c" was already discussed in relation to item 6. In that item, their use was appropriate and justifiable, but here it is questionable.

Again, let us see just what it takes to arrive at the correct choice, option e. Presumably, the item is intended to measure knowledge of square roots. However, the correct answer can be arrived at without considering square roots at all! A logical approach to this item, which would pay off with the right answer for someone who doesn't know the answer, might go something like this:

> *Sure wish I'd studied the square root table. Oh well, there's more than one way to get to the root of the problem. Let's see, 14 might be right, 16 might be right, and 4×4 might be right. Hmmm, both a and c? No, that can't be it because I know that $4 \times 4 = 16$ and not 14. Well, both b and c have to be it! I know it's not "none of the above" because the teacher never uses "none of the above" as the right answer when she uses "both a and c" and "both b and c" as options.*

When using "both a and c" and "both b and c," be on the alert for logical inconsistencies that can be used to eliminate options. Naturally, this problem can be minimized by using such options sparingly. Also try to monitor your item construction patterns to make sure you're not overusing certain types of options.

Finally, we come to a good item. Item 9 is free of the flaws and faults we've pointed out in this section. There are a lot of things to consider when you write test items, and keeping them all in mind will help you write better multiple-choice questions. But it's virtually impossible for anyone to write good items all the time. So, when you've written a poor item, don't be too critical of yourself. Analyze it, revise or replace it, and learn from your mistakes.

Higher Level Multiple-Choice Questions

Good multiple-choice items are the most time-consuming kind of objective test items to write. Unfortunately, most multiple-choice items are also written at the knowledge level of the taxonomy of educational objectives. As a new item writer (and, if you're not careful, as an experienced item writer) you will have a tendency to write items at this level. In this section we will provide you with suggestions for writing multiple-choice items to measure higher level thinking.

The first step is to write at least some objectives that measure comprehension, application, analysis, synthesis, or evaluation to ensure that your items will be at the higher than knowledge level—if your items match your objectives! The following objectives measure behavior at the knowledge level:

> The student will name, from memory, the first three presidents of the United States by next Friday.
>
> Given a color chart, the students will identify each of the primary colors.

Objectives such as those will generate multiple-choice items that will measure only memorization. By contrast, the following objectives measure at higher than the knowledge level:

> Given a copy of the President's state of the union address, the student will be able to identify one example of a simile and one of a metaphor.
>
> The student will be able to correctly solve three-digit addition problems without regrouping.

With objectives such as those, higher level multiple-choice items would have to be constructed to match the objectives. Some suggestions for other approaches to measuring at higher than the knowledge level follow.

Use Pictorial, Graphical, or Tabular Stimuli Pictures, drawings, graphs, tables, and so on require the student to think at the application level of the taxonomy of educational objectives and may involve even higher levels of cognitive processes. Also, the use of such stimuli can often generate several higher level multiple-choice items rather than a single higher level multiple-choice item, as Fig. 6.1 illustrates.

Other items based on the map in Fig. 6.1 could be as follows:

1. Approximately how many miles is it from Dube to Rog?
   a. 100 miles
   b. 150 miles
   c. 200 miles
   d. 250 miles

2. In what direction would someone have to travel to get from Wog to Um?
   a. northwest
   b. northeast
   c. southwest
   d. southeast

In the following questions you are asked to make inferences from the data which are given you on the map of the imaginary country, Serendip. The answers in most instances must be probabilities rather than certainties. The relative size of towns and cities is not shown. To assist you in the location of the places mentioned in the questions, the map is divided into squares lettered vertically from A to E and numbered horizontally from 1 to 5.

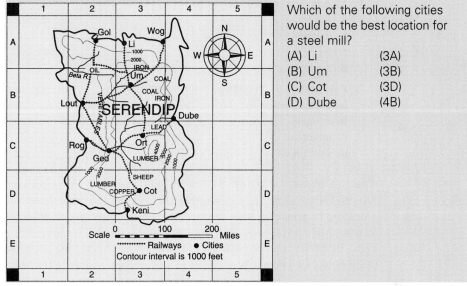

Which of the following cities would be the best location for a steel mill?

(A) Li   (3A)
(B) Um   (3B)
(C) Cot   (3D)
(D) Dube   (4B)

FIGURE 6.1   Use of pictorial stimulus to measure high-level cognitive processes.

A variation on the same theme is to include several pictorial stimuli to represent options and build several stems around them. The following items would be appropriate for a plane geometry class:

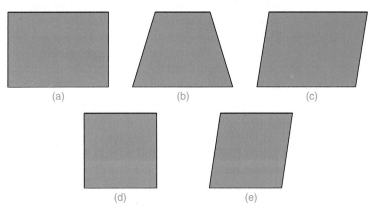

1. Which of the figures is a rhombus?
2. Which of the figures is a square?
3. Which of the figures is a trapezoid?

Naturally, it is important to include several more stimulus pictures than items in order to minimize guessing.

Use Analogies That Demonstrate Relationships among Terms To answer analogies correctly students must not only be familiar with the terms, but be able to understand how the terms relate to one another, as the following examples show.

1. Man is to woman as boy is to
   a. father.
   b. mother.
   c. girl.
   d. boy.
2. Physician is to humans as veterinarian is to
   a. fruits.
   b. animals.
   c. minerals.
   d. vegetables.

Require the application of Previously Learned Principles or Procedures to Novel Situations To test whether students really comprehend the implications of a procedure or principle, have the students use the principle or procedure with new information or in a novel way. This requires that the student do more than simply "follow the steps" in solving a problem. It asks the student to demonstrate an ability to go beyond the confines within which a principle or procedure was originally learned.

1. In class we discussed at length Darwin's notion of the "survival of the fittest" within the animal world. Which of the following best describes how this principle applies to the current competitive residential construction industry?
   a. Those builders in existence today are those who have formed alliances with powerful financial institutions.
   b. Only those builders who emphasize matching their homes to the changing structure of the family will survive in the future.
   c. The intense competition for a limited number of qualified home buyers will eventually "weed out" poorly managed construction firms.
   d. Only those home builders who construct the strongest and most durable homes will survive in the long term.
2. (*Follows a lesson on division that relied on computation of grade point averages as examples.*) After filling up his tank with 18 gallons of gasoline, Mr. Watts said to his son, "We've come 450 miles since the last fillup. What kind of gas mileage are we getting?" Which of the following is the best answer?
   a. 4 miles per gallon.
   b. 25 miles per gallon.
   c. Between 30 and 35 miles per gallon.
   d. It can't be determined from the information given.

These examples are intended to stimulate your creativity—they are by no means exhaustive of the many approaches to measuring higher level cognitive skills with multiple-choice items. Rather than limit yourself to pictorial items and analogies, use them where appropriate and also develop your own approaches. Remember the main point: Be sure your items match your objectives. Do not write higher level items if your objectives are at the knowledge level. Doing so will impair your test's content validity. In Chapter 8 we will consider another way you can measure higher level thinking skills, called performance-based assessment, and we cover yet another, called portfolio assessment, in Chapter 9.

Suggestions for Writing Multiple-Choice Items

Here are some guidelines for writing multiple-choice tests:

1. The stem of the item should clearly formulate a problem. Include as much of the item as possible, keeping the response options as short as possible. However, include only the material needed to make the problem clear and specific. Be concise—don't add extraneous information.

2. Be sure that there is one and only one correct or clearly best answer.

3. Be sure wrong answer choices (distractors) are plausible. Eliminate unintentional grammatical clues, and keep the length and form of all the answer choices equal. Rotate the position of the correct answer from item to item randomly.

4. Use negative questions or statements only if the knowledge being tested requires it. In most cases it is more important for the student to know what a specific item of information is rather than what it is not.

5. Include from three to five options (two to four distractors plus one correct answer) to optimize testing for knowledge rather than encouraging guessing. It is not necessary to provide additional distractors for an item simply to maintain the same number of distractors for each item. This usually leads to poorly constructed distractors that add nothing to test validity and reliability.

6. To increase the difficulty of a multiple-choice item, increase the similarity of content among the options.

7. Use the option "none of the above" sparingly and only when the keyed answer can be classified unequivocally as right or wrong. Don't use this option when asking for a best answer.

8. Avoid using "all of the above." It is usually the correct answer and makes the item too easy for students with partial information.

Thus far we have considered true–false, matching, and multiple-choice items. We have called these items objective items, but they are also referred to as recognition items. They are recognition items because the test taker needs only to "recognize" the correct answer. Contrast this with "recall" or "supply" formats such as essays and completion items. With essays and completion items it is much more difficult to guess the right answer than with true–false, matching, or multiple-choice items.

Nevertheless, we will classify completion items with true–false, matching, and multiple-choice items. We call items written in these formats objective items because of the way they are scored, which tends to be fairly straightforward and reliable. This is in contrast to essays, which we will call subjective, because their somewhat less reliable scoring makes them more prone to bias.

COMPLETION ITEMS

Like true–false items, completion items are relatively easy to write. Perhaps the first tests classroom teachers construct and students take are completion tests. Like items of all other formats, though, there are good and poor completion items. Work through the following exercise, again relying on your common sense to identify good and poor items. After having worked through the three previous exercises, you are probably now adept at recognizing common item-writing flaws.

Exercise: *Put a G in the space next to the items you feel are good, and a P next to the items you feel are poor.*

_____**1.** The evolutionary theory of [Darwin] is based on the principle of [survival of the fittest].
_____**2.** Columbus discovered America in [1492].
_____**3.** The capital of Mexico is [Mexico City].
_____**4.** In what year did William J. Clinton become president of the United States? [1992]
_____**5.** [Too many] blanks cause much frustration in [both test takers and test scorers].
_____**6.** [Armstrong] was the first American to [walk on the moon].

Answers: 1. P; 2. P; 3. P; 4. G; 5. P; 6. P.

The first item probably reminds you of many you have seen. It is a good rule of thumb to avoid using more than one blank per item. The item writer had a specific evolutionary theorist in mind when writing this item, but the final form of the item is not at all focused toward one single theorist. There are a variety of possible correct answers to this item. Not only are such items disturbing and confusing to test takers, they are very time-consuming and frustrating to score. An acceptable revision might look like this:

The evolutionary theory of Darwin is based on the principle of [survival of the fittest].

If you marked item 2 with a G, you were probably in the majority. This is a standard type of completion item that is frequently used. It is also the kind of item that can generate student–teacher conflict. Granted, "1492" is probably the answer most students who studied their lesson would write. But how would you score a response like "a boat" or "the 15th century" or "a search for India?" These may not be the answers you wanted, but they are correct answers.

This illustrates the major disadvantage of completion items and gives you some idea on a much smaller scale of the kinds of difficulties encountered in scoring essay items as well. Unless you take pains to be very specific when you word completion items, you will come across similar situations frequently. In general, it's better to be very specific in writing completion items. Item 2 could be made specific by adding the words "the year," as illustrated here:

Columbus discovered America in the year [1492].

In this form the item leaves little to be interpreted subjectively by the student. The test taker doesn't spend time thinking about what the question is "really" asking, and the test scorer doesn't spend time trying to decide how to score a variety of different, but correct, answers. For once everybody's happy.

Item 3 is a similar case. Consider the following dialogue as heard by one of the authors in a teachers' lounge at an elementary school:

MISS RIGIDITY: (*To no one in particular*) Smart-aleck kids nowadays! Ask them a simple question and you get a smart-aleck answer. Kids today don't give you any respect.

Miss Feelings: I hear some frustration in what you're saying. Anything I can do?

Miss Rigidity: No, there's nothing you can do, but listen to this. On the last test one of the questions was "The largest city in Puerto Rico is _____." Simple enough, right? Well, not for Mitch! Instead of answering "San Juan," he answered "the capital city." Smart-aleck kid. We'll see how smart he feels when he gets no credit for that ridiculous answer.

Miss Feelings: What I hear you saying is that you feel Mitch may not have known that San Juan is the largest city in Puerto Rico.

Miss Rigidity: Of course he doesn't know—otherwise he would have given the correct answer. That's the whole point!

Author: (*Never known for his tactfulness*) He did give a correct answer. Your question wasn't specific enough.

Miss Rigidity: I've been using this same test for years, and there are always one or two kids who give me the same answer Mitch did! And they are always kids who lack respect!

Author: How do you know they lack respect?

Miss Rigidity: Because they always argue with me when they get their tests back. In fact, they say the same thing you did! You're as bad as they are!

MISS FEELINGS: I'm hearing some frustration from both of you.

How could this have been avoided? Let's look at Miss Rigidity's item again.

The largest city in Puerto Rico is _____.

Since San Juan is the largest city in Puerto Rico and is the capital city of Puerto Rico as well, then "the largest city in Puerto Rico is the capital city." There are at least two defensible answers. Just as in true–false, matching, and multiple-choice items, we should strive to avoid multiple defensible answers in completion items. But how can this be avoided? Again, be specific. Made more specific, Miss Rigidity's item looks like this:

The name of the largest city in Puerto Rico is [San Juan].

Of course, you could have students who carry things to an extreme. For example, some might claim the following is a defensible answer:

The name of the largest city in Puerto Rico is [familiar to many people].

Only you, as the classroom teacher, can determine which answers are defensible and which are not. Your job will be to determine which responses are logical derivations of your test item and which responses are creative attempts to cover up for lack of mastery of content. Keep an open mind, and good luck! Don't be like Miss Rigidity!

We can clean up item 3 in much the same fashion as we did Miss Rigidity's item. Revised in this way, item 3 looks like this:

The name of the capital city of Mexico is [Mexico City].

Adding "name of the" to the original item minimizes your chances of students responding that the capital of Mexico is "a city," "very pretty," "huge," "near central Mexico," and so forth.

Item 4 is an example of a well-written completion item. It is specific, and it would be difficult to think of defensible answers other than "1992."

Both the fifth and sixth items illustrate a case of having too many blanks, which prevent the item from taking on any single theme. Blanks are contagious—avoid using more than one.

Suggestions for Writing Completion or Supply Items

1. If at all possible, items should require a single-word answer, or a brief and definite statement. Avoid statements that are so indefinite that they may be logically answered by several terms.

   a. Poor item: World War II ended in _____.

   b. Better item: World War II ended in the year _____.

2. Be sure the question or statement poses a problem to the examinee. A direct question is often more desirable than an incomplete statement (it provides more structure).

3. Be sure the answer that the student is required to produce is factually correct. Be sure the language used in the question is precise and accurate in relation to the subject matter area being tested.

4. Omit only key words; don't eliminate so many elements that the sense of the content is impaired.

   a. Poor item: The _____ type of test item is usually more _____ than the _____ type.

   b. Better item: The supply type of test item is usually graded less objectively than the _____ type.

5. Word the statement such that the blank is near the end of the sentence rather than near the beginning. This will prevent awkward sentences.

6. If the problem requires a numerical answer, indicate the units in which it is to be expressed.

You've now used common sense and an increased level of "test-wiseness" to analyze and think about different types of objective test items. In Chapter 7 we will extend our discussion to essay items. Before we move on to essays, however, let's consider one more topic related to item writing, one that applies equally to objective and essay items. This topic is gender and racial bias in test items.

GENDER AND RACIAL BIAS IN TEST ITEMS

An important but often overlooked aspect of item writing involves gender or racial bias. Over the last decades many have become increasingly aware of, and sensitive to, such issues. Professional item writers take great care to eliminate or minimize the extent to which such biases are present in their test items. The classroom teacher would be wise to follow their lead.

One example of gender bias is the exclusive use of the male pronoun he in test items. Since the item writer may use it unconsciously, it does not necessarily follow that the item writer has a sexist attitude. However, this does not prevent the practice from offending a proportion of the population. Similarly, referring exclusively in our items only to members of a single ethnic group will likely be offensive to individuals of different ethnicity. Again, such a practice may be almost unconscious and may not reflect an ethnic bias, but this will not prevent others from taking offense to it.

To avoid such bias, you should carefully balance your references in items. That is, always check your items to be sure that fairly equal numbers of references to males and females are made. Obviously, equal care and time should be devoted to ensure that ethnic groups are appropriately represented in your items. Such considerations are especially relevant when items are being written at higher than the knowledge level. Since such items often are word problems involving people, gender and racial bias can easily creep in. The test assembly checklist in Chapter 10 (Figure 10.1) will help remind you to be on the watch for such bias.

Remember, our goal is to measure learning in as valid and reliable a fashion as possible. When emotions are stimulated by gender-biased or racially biased items, these emotions can interfere with valid measurement, leaving us with results that are less useful than they would be otherwise. Given all the care and time we have taken to learn to develop good tests, it makes good sense to take just a bit more to avoid racial and gender bias in our items.

GUIDELINES FOR WRITING TEST ITEMS

In this chapter we have provided you with a good deal of information related to item writing. Much of this information is condensed in the summary, and some general guidelines for item writing are also included. Following these guidelines you will find a summary of the advantages and disadvantages of various item formats. This section should help you make decisions about the type of format to use for your test items. Remember, you will write poor items until the recommendations we have provided become second nature, which comes only with practice. Finally, review the sidebar (Box 6-1) for some suggestions on how a PC can save item-writing time and—with appropriate item-writing software—actually help improve the quality of the items you write.

1. Begin writing items far enough in advance that you will have time to revise them.
2. Match items to intended outcomes at the proper difficulty level to provide a valid measure of instructional objectives. Limit the question to the skill being assessed.

BOX 6-1

PCS AND TEST ITEMS

PCs can help save item-writing time through word processing functions and item-writing software. With a word processing program, you can easily make minor or major modifications to test items or even whole tests. You also can reorder the items or change the order of distractors for multiple-choice items much more quickly than you or a typist could make such changes with a typewriter. This could be a major time saver when it is important to develop alternate forms of a test. Sharing of well-written items is facilitated if they are stored on a diskette or hard drive and available to all teachers, either by sharing diskettes and hard drives or through a local area network (LAN) or over the World Wide Web or Internet.

Commercial software is also available that can assist the teacher in constructing test items. By indicating common faults of a test item, these programs minimize the chances that you will construct and use poor items. Programs are also available that will generate alternate forms of tests according to instructional objectives and difficulty levels. Given a pool of test items and their difficulty levels, the computer could be instructed to make a number of shorter tests based on common objectives and at prespecified difficulty levels, thereby ensuring that different tests would be comparable.

With the passage of NCLB and IDEIA–04, regular classroom teachers will play a greater role in the evaluation of the progress of special learners in the general education curriculum. Because the range of achievement of special learners may vary considerably, and because a variety of accommodations may be needed because of their disabilities, a wider range of item difficulties and formats may be required for special learners than for regular education pupils. The PC may be helpful in this regard, allowing easier and more accurate item storage, modification, and incorporation into tests and assessments of varying lengths and difficulties. Being able to use a PC to efficiently "customize" tests designed for a classroom of regular education students to fit the needs of the special learners will enable you to devote more time to instructional activities. This may minimize the frustration of having to "start from scratch" with each new addition to your class, and may also reduce frustration in special learners and enhance the validity of your assessments of their progress in the general education curriculum.

3. Be sure each item deals with an important aspect of the content area and not with trivia.

4. Be sure that the problem posed is clear and unambiguous.

5. Be sure that each item is independent of all other items. The answer to one item should not be required as a condition for answering the next item. A hint to one answer should not be embedded in another item.

6. Be sure the item has one correct or best answer on which experts would agree.

7. Prevent unintended clues to the answer in the statement or question. Grammatical inconsistencies such as *a* or *an* give clues to the correct answer to those students who are not well prepared for the test.

8. Avoid replication of the textbook in writing test items; don't quote directly from textual materials. You're usually not interested in how well the student memorized the text. Besides, taken out of context, direct quotes from the text are often ambiguous.

9. Avoid trick or catch questions in an achievement test. Don't waste time testing how well the students can interpret your intentions.

10. Try to write items that require higher level thinking.

ADVANTAGES AND DISADVANTAGES OF DIFFERENT OBJECTIVE ITEM FORMATS

True–False Tests

Advantages

Because true–false questions tend to be short, more material can be covered than with any other item format. Thus true–false items tend to be used when a great deal of content has been covered.

True–false questions take less time to construct, but avoid taking statements directly from the text and modifying them slightly to create an item.

Scoring is easier with true–false questions, but avoid having students write "true" or "false" or a "T" or "F." Instead, have them circle "T" or "F" provided for each item.

Disadvantages

True–false questions tend to emphasize rote memorization of knowledge, although sometimes complex questions can be asked using true–false items.

True–false questions presume that the answer to the question or issue is unequivocally true or false. It would be unfair to ask the student to guess at the teacher's criteria for evaluating the truth of a statement.

True–false questions allow for and sometimes encourage a high degree of guessing. Generally, longer examinations are needed to compensate for this.

Matching Tests

Advantages

Matching questions are usually simple to construct and to score.

Matching items are ideally suited to measure associations between facts.

Matching questions can be more efficient than multiple-choice questions because they avoid repetition of options in measuring associations.

Matching questions reduce the effects of guessing.

Disadvantages

Matching questions sometimes tend to ask students trivial information.

They emphasize memorization.

Most commercial answer sheets can accommodate no more than five options, thus limiting the size of any particular matching item.

Multiple-Choice Tests

Advantages

Multiple-choice questions have considerable versatility in measuring objectives from the knowledge to the evaluation level.

Since writing is minimized, a substantial amount of course material can be sampled in a relatively short time.

Scoring is highly objective, requiring only a count of the number of correct responses.

Multiple-choice items can be written so that students must discriminate among options that vary in degree of correctness. This allows students to select the best alternative and avoids the absolute judgments found in true–false tests.

Since there are multiple options, effects of guessing are reduced.

Multiple-choice items are amenable to item analysis (see Chapter 10), which permits a determination of which items are ambiguous or too difficult.

Disadvantages

Multiple-choice questions can be time-consuming to write.

If not carefully written, multiple-choice questions can sometimes have more than one defensible correct answer.

Completion Tests

Advantages

Construction of a completion question is relatively easy.

Guessing is eliminated since the question requires recall.

Completion questions take less time to complete than multiple-choice items, so greater amounts of content can be covered.

Disadvantages

Completion questions usually encourage a relatively low level of response complexity.

The responses can be difficult to score since the stem must be general enough so as not to communicate the correct answer. This can unintentionally lead to more than one defensible answer.

The restriction of an answer to a few words tends to measure the recall of specific facts, names, places, and events as opposed to more complex behaviors.

SUMMARY

This chapter introduced you to four types of objective test items: true–false, matching, multiple choice, and completion. The major points are as follows:

1. Choice of item format is sometimes determined by your instructional objectives. At other times the advantages and disadvantages of the different formats should influence your choice.

2. True–false items require less time to construct than other objective items, but they are most prone to guessing, as well as a variety of other faults. These include absolutes in wording, double negatives, opinionated and double-barreled statements, excessive wordiness, and a tendency to reflect statements taken verbatim from readings.

3. Matching items are fairly easy to construct but tend to be subject to the following faults: lack of clarity and specificity in directions, dissimilar and nonordered lists, and reversal of options and descriptions.

4. Multiple-choice items are the most difficult of the objective items to construct. However, higher order multiple-choice items lend themselves well to measuring higher level thinking skills. They are subject to several faults, including grammatical cues or specific determiners, multiple defensible answers, unordered option lists, stem clues, opinionated statements, failure to state a problem in the stem, redundant wording, wordiness in the correct option, use of "all of the above," and indiscriminate use of "none of the above."

5. Completion items rival true–false items in ease of construction. Since answers must be supplied, they are least subject to guessing. On the other hand, they require more scoring time than other objective formats. Common faults include too many blanks, lack of specificity (too many potential responses), and failure to state a problem.

6. To avoid gender and/or racial biases in test items, avoid using stereotypes and be sure to make equal reference to both males and females and to various ethnic groups.

FOR PRACTICE

1. Write a behavioral objective in some area with which you are familiar. Using this objective as your guide, write a test item using each of the four test item formats (true–false, matching, multiple-choice, and completion) discussed in this chapter.

2. Exchange your test items with a classmate. Have him or her check the appropriateness of each of your items for a match with the appropriate objective and against the criteria and guidelines given in this chapter for each test item format. List and correct any deficiencies.

*3. Each of the following items is defective in some way(s). Identify the principal fault or faults in each item and rewrite the item so that it is fault-free.

    1. "The Time Machine" is considered to be a
      a. adventure story.
      b. science fiction story.
      c. historical novel.
      d. autobiography.

    2. Thaddeus Kosciusko and Casimer Pulaski were heroes in the Revolutionary War. What was their country of origin?
      a. Great Britain
      b. Poland
      c. France
      d. Italy

3. The use of force to attain political goals is never justifiable. (T   F)

4. The personal computer was invented in _____ .

5. _____ spent his life trying to demonstrate that _____ .

6.
1. Discovered the Zambezi River	**a.** Webb
2. First female governor	**b.** Armstrong
	c. Minuit
3. Invented the cotton gin	**d.** Livingstone
	e. Whitney
4. First to swim the English Channel	**f.** Edison
	g. Cortez
5. Purchased Manhattan Island	**h.** Keller
	i. Rhodes
6. First to walk on the moon	

*Answers to Question 3 appear in Appendix F.

WRITING ESSAY TEST ITEMS

9 a.m., Tuesday, October 20

"I can't believe it! I just can't believe it!" Donna thought to herself. "How can he do this to us?" Donna was becoming more and more upset by the second, as were many of the other students in Mr. Smith's government class. They were taking the midterm exam, on which 50% of their grade would be based. Before the exam, the students spent two classes discussing this issue. All other classes that semester dealt with a rather mechanical review of the federal government. The exam consisted of a single essay item:

Why should presidents be limited or not be limited to two consecutive terms in office? (100 points)

DOES THIS ring a bell? Test questions that do not reflect classroom emphasis can frustrate test takers. "How could he do it?" Well, there are probably several answers to this question, but we can only speculate about Mr. Smith's reasons. Just as we could generate a variety of explanations for Mr. Smith's test item, students could generate a variety of answers to his question! Let's look at his question again.

Why should presidents be limited or not be limited to two consecutive terms in office? (100 points)

What answer is he looking for? Again, only Mr. Smith knows for sure. "Come on," some of you may say. "He's not looking for any specific answer—he wants you to take a position and defend it, to test your knowledge and writing ability, that's all!" Well, if that's the case, why didn't he phrase the test item something like this:

In class and in your assigned readings, arguments both for and against giving presidents the opportunity to complete more than two consecutive terms in office were presented. Take a stand either for or against two consecutive terms in office. Use at least three points made in class or in your readings to support your position. Both the content and organization of your argument will be considered in assigning your final grade. Use no more than one page for your answer. (28 points)

This item focuses the task for the student—he or she has a clearer idea of what is expected, and, therefore, how he or she will be evaluated. Remember, your goal is not to see whether students can correctly guess what you are expecting as an answer. Your goal is to measure learning—to determine whether your instructional objectives have been met.

In the remainder of this chapter we will discuss various aspects of essay item construction. While this will go far in helping you avoid writing poor essay items, we will also discuss several other equally important issues related to essay items. We will begin with a general discussion of what an essay item is, describe the two major types of essay items and their relationships to instructional objectives, identify the major advantages and disadvantages of essay items, provide you with suggestions for writing essay items, and discuss various approaches to scoring essays.

Then, we will show how you can apply your knowledge of essay item writing to several other types of measures, including the open book exam and dialectical and interpretative questions. By appropriately using these measures you can ensure that your tests challenge your learners to engage in higher levels of critical thinking, problem solving and decision-making. With this comprehensive treatment, we hope to increase your awareness of classroom assessment techniques beyond just objective test items.

WHAT IS AN ESSAY ITEM?

An essay item is one for which the student supplies, rather than selects, the correct answer. The student must compose a response, often extensive, to a question for which no single response or pattern of responses can be cited as correct to the exclusion of all other answers. The accuracy and quality of such a response can often be judged only by a person skilled and informed in the subject area being tested.

Essay Items Should Measure Complex Cognitive Skills or Processes

Like objective test items, essay items may be well constructed or poorly constructed. The well-constructed essay item aims to test complex cognitive skills by requiring the student to organize, integrate, and synthesize knowledge, to use information to solve novel problems, or to be original and innovative in problem solving. The poorly constructed essay item may require the student to do no more than recall information as it was presented in the textbook or lecture. Worse, the poorly constructed essay may not even let the student know what is required for a satisfactory response, like our initial example in this chapter.

The potential of the essay item as an evaluation device depends not only on writing appropriate questions that elicit complex cognitive skills, but also on being able to structure the student's response so that other factors do not obscure your ability to evaluate whether the student is applying the complex cognitive skills you are trying to measure. For example, differences in knowledge of factual material can be hidden by differences in ability to use and organize those facts. The time pressures of a test situation, student anxiety, and deficiencies in writing ability (which does not necessarily mean there are corresponding cognitive deficits!) can all interfere with a student's ability to demonstrate mastery of complex cognitive skills. A well-constructed essay item will clearly indicate the cognitive skills or process that should be employed to formulate the answer, clarify ambiguous details, and set appropriate page or time limits. A well-constructed essay makes it easier for you to evaluate accurately the student's response.

Consider the following essay item:

QUESTION 1. What methods have been used in the United States to prevent industrial accidents?

What learning outcomes are being tested? To provide an acceptable answer, a student need only recall information. The item is at the knowledge level; no higher level mental processes are tapped. It would be easy and much less time-consuming to score a series of objective items covering this same topic. This is not abuse of the essay item, but it is a misuse. Now consider a second question:

QUESTION 2. Examine the data provided in the table on causes of accidents. Explain how the introduction of occupational health and safety standards in the United States accounts for changes in the number of industrial accidents shown in the following table. Be sure to consider at least three specific occupational health and safety standards in your response. Limit your response to one-half page.

Causes of Accidents and Rate for Each in 1980 and 2000

	Accident Rate per 100,000 Employees	
Cause of Accident	1980	2000
1. Defective equipment	135.1	16.7
2. Failure to use safety-related equipment	222.8	36.1
3. Failure to heed instructions	422.1	128.6
4. Improperly trained for job	598.7	26.4
5. Medical or health-related impairment	41.0	13.5

This question requires that the student recall something about the occupational health and safety standards. Then, the student must relate these standards to such things as occupational training programs, plant safety inspections, the display of warning or danger signs, equipment manufacturing, codes related to safety, and so forth, which may have been incorporated in industrial settings between 1980 and 2000.

The second question clarifies considerably what you are expecting from the student. In short, the student must use higher level mental processes to answer the question successfully. The student must be able to analyze, infer, organize, apply, and so on. No objective item or series of items would suffice. This is an appropriate use of the essay item. However, not all essays are alike. We will consider two types of essay items: extended response and restricted response items.

Essay Items: Extended or Restricted Response

Essay items can vary from lengthy, open-ended end-of-semester term papers or take-home tests that have flexible page limits (e.g., 10–12 pages or no more than 20 pages) to essays with responses limited or restricted to one page or less. The former are referred to as extended response essay items and the latter are referred to as restricted response essay items. Essays may be used to measure general or specific outcomes of instruction. The restricted response item is most likely to be used to assess knowledge, comprehension, and application types of learning outcomes. An extended response essay is more appropriate to assess the ability to evaluate, to synthesize, to analyze, to organize, and to select viewpoints.

Extended Response Essays   An essay item that allows the student to determine the length and complexity of response is called an extended response essay item. This type of essay is most useful at the synthesis or evaluation levels of the cognitive taxonomy. When we are interested in determining whether students can organize, integrate, express, and evaluate information, ideas, or knowledge, the extended response essay may be the best option. The extended response item also is useful for assessing written communication ability. The following is an example of an extended response essay.

> **EXAMPLE:** Identify as many different ways to generate electricity as you can. Give the advantages and disadvantages of each and how each might be used to provide the electrical power requirements of a medium-sized city. Your response will be graded on its accuracy and your evaluation of how practical each source of electricity would be, if implemented. Your response should be 12–15 pages in length and will be evaluated based on the scoring criteria distributed in class. For maximum credit be sure that your response addresses each of the scoring criteria components.

To respond to this essay the students must be able to assemble relevant information, critically analyze the information and apply the information to a novel situation, and synthesize and evaluate potential outcomes. Obviously, responding to this complex task is not something you would expect students to be able to do in a class period, or without access to suitable reference materials. Nevertheless, this may be an important set of skills that you need to evaluate. If so, the extended range essay can work well.

Keep in mind, however, that a complex item like this will take time to develop and will be even more time-consuming to score. It is also difficult to score extended response essays objectively. For both these reasons it is important to use extended range essays only in those situations where you have adequate time to develop the extended response item and specific scoring criteria for it and when your students have adequate time and resources to devote to their responses. Later in this chapter we will provide you with a variety of suggestions that you can use to develop and score both extended and restricted response items.

Restricted Response Essays   An essay item that poses a specific problem for which the student must recall proper information, organize it in a suitable manner, derive a defensible conclusion, and express it within the limits of the posed problem, or within page or time limits, is called a restricted response essay item. The statement of the problem specifies response limitations that guide the student in responding and provide evaluation criteria for scoring.

> **EXAMPLE:** List the major political similarities and differences between U.S. participation in the Korean War and in World War II. Limit your answer to one page. Your score will depend on accuracy, organization, and brevity.

Typically, a restricted response essay item may supplement a test that is otherwise objective, or there may be several (e.g., 5–7) restricted response items in an essay test designed to be completed during a class period. When several essay items are used students may be expected to respond to them with or without various resources, depending on your instructional objectives. The classroom teacher will use restricted response essays far more often than extended response essays. Thus, in the next section we will focus primarily on suggestions to help you develop and score restricted range essays. Nevertheless, you will find that almost all these suggestions will also be applicable should you choose to use extended range essays. We will consider several examples of restricted range essays next.

Examples of Restricted Response Essays

EXAMPLE: The Learning to Like It Company is proposing profit sharing for its employees. For each one percent increase in production compared to the average production figures over the last 10 years, workers will get a one percent increase in pay. In no more than one page;

1. List the advantages and disadvantages to the workers of this plan.
2. List the advantages and disadvantages to the corporation of this plan.

EXAMPLE: Now that we've studied about the Gold Rush, imagine you are on a wagon train going to California. Write a one page letter to your relatives back home telling them of some of the (a) hardships you have suffered, and (b) dangers you have experienced.

To demonstrate that they know the advantages and disadvantages of profit sharing and the hardships and dangers of traveling West by wagon train during the Gold Rush, your learners must do two things: They must respond in their own words and not simply recall what their text said--or what they copied from an overhead, and they must give original examples. If they can do this, then you can correctly say that your learners have acquired the concept of profit sharing and understood the difficulties of traveling West during the Gold Rush.

When Should Restricted Response Essays Be Considered?   The following describes some of the conditions for which restricted-response questions are best suited.

- The instructional objectives require supplying information rather than simply recognizing information. These processes often cannot be measured with objective items.

- Relatively few areas of content need to be tested. If you have thirty students and design a test with six restricted-response questions, you will spend a great deal of time scoring. Use restricted responses when class size is small, or use them in conjunction with objective items.

- Test security is a consideration. If you are afraid multiple-choice test questions will be passed on or told to other students, it is better to use a restricted-response question. In general, a good restricted response essay test takes less time to construct than a good objective test.

Some learning outcomes and example content for which restricted response questions may be used include the following:

- Analyze relationships.

  EXAMPLE: The colors blue and gray are related to cool temperatures. What are some other colors related to? What effect would these colors have on a picture you might draw?

- Compare and contrast positions.

  EXAMPLE: Compare and contrast two characters from stories you have read to understand how the characters responded differently to conditions in the stories.

- State necessary assumptions.

  EXAMPLE: When Columbus landed on San Salvador, what did he assume about the land he had discovered? Were his assumptions correct?

- Identify appropriate conclusions.

  EXAMPLE: What are some of the reasons for and against building a landfill near homes?

- Explain cause-and-effect relations.

  EXAMPLE: What might have caused early Americans to travel west in the 1780s? Choose one of the pioneers we have studied (like Daniel Boone) and give some of the reasons they traveled west.

- Formulate hypotheses.

  EXAMPLE: What can you predict about a coming storm by observing clouds? Explain what it is about the clouds that helps you predict rain.

- Organize data to support a viewpoint.

  EXAMPLE: On the board you will find the numbers of new homes built and autos purchased for each month over the past year. Use these data to support the viewpoint that our economy is either growing larger or smaller.

- Point out strengths and weaknesses.

  EXAMPLE: What is either a strength or a limitation of the following musical instruments for a marching band: oboe, trumpet, tuba, violin?

- Integrate data from several sources.

  EXAMPLE: Imagine you are celebrating your birthday with nine of your friends. Two pizzas arrive but each is cut into four pieces. What problem do you have? What method would you choose for seeing that everyone gets a piece of the pizza?

- Evaluate the quality or worth of an item, product, or action.

  EXAMPLE: What should be considered in choosing a balanced meal from the basic food groups?

PROS AND CONS OF ESSAY ITEMS

We've already mentioned some of the benefits of using essay items, and the following list summarizes the advantages of essays over objective items.

Advantages of the Essay Item

Most Effective in Assessing Complex Learning Outcomes To the extent that instructional objectives require the student to organize information constructively to solve a problem, analyze and evaluate information, or perform other high-level cognitive skills, the essay test is an appropriate assessment tool.

Relatively Easy to Construct Although essay tests are relatively easy to construct, the items should not be constructed haphazardly; consult the table of specifications, identify only the topics and objectives that can best be assessed by essays, and build items around those and only those.

Emphasize Essential Communication Skills in Complex Academic Disciplines If developing communication skills is an instructional objective, it can be tested with an essay item. However, this assumes that the teacher has spent time teaching communication skills pertinent to the course area, including special vocabulary and writing styles, as well as providing practice with relevant arguments for and against controversial points.

Guessing Is Eliminated Since no options are provided, the student must supply rather than select the proper response.

Naturally, there is another side to the essay coin. These items also have limitations and disadvantages.

Disadvantages of the Essay Item

Difficult to Score It is tedious to wade through pages and pages of student handwriting. Also, it is difficult not to let spelling and grammatical mistakes influence grading or to let superior abilities in communication cover up for incomplete comprehension of facts.

Scores Are Unreliable It is difficult to maintain a common set of criteria for all students. Two persons may disagree on the correct answer for any essay item; even the same person will disagree on the correctness of one answer read on two separate occasions.

Limited Sample of Total Instructional Content Fewer essay items can be attempted than any objective type of item; it takes more time to complete an essay item than any other type of item. Students become fatigued faster with these items than with objective items.

Bluffing   It is no secret that longer essays tend to be graded higher than short essays, regardless of content! As a result, students may bluff.

The first two limitations are serious disadvantages. Fortunately, we do have some suggestions that have been shown to make the task of scoring essays more manageable and reliable. These will be discussed shortly. First, however, we will consider several suggestions to help you write good essay items.

SUGGESTIONS FOR WRITING ESSAY ITEMS

Here are some suggestions to keep in mind when preparing essay questions:

1. Have clearly in mind what mental processes you want the student to use before starting to write the question. Refer to the mental processes we have discussed previously and the various levels of the Bloom et al. taxonomy of educational objectives for the cognitive domain described in Chapter 5 (e.g., comprehension, application, analysis, synthesis, evaluation). For example, if you want students to apply what they have learned, determine what mental processes would be needed in the application process.

   Poor item: Describe the escape routes considered by Mark and Alisha in the story "Hawaiian Mystery."

   Better item: Consider the story about Mark and Alisha. Remember the part where they had to escape over the volcanic ridge? Compare the advantages of Mark's plan of escape with that of Alisha's. Which provided the least risk to their safety and which plan of escape would get them home the quickest? Which would you have chosen, and why?

   Poor item: Criticize the following speech by our President.

   Better item: Consider the following presidential speech. Focus on the section dealing with economic policy and discriminate between factual statements and opinions. List these statements separately, label them, and indicate whether each statement is or is not consistent with the President's overall economic policy.

2. Write the question to clearly and unambiguously define the task to the student. Tasks should be explained (a) orally, (b) in the overall instructions preceding the questions, and/or (c) in the test items themselves. Indicate whether spelling and grammar will be counted, and whether organization of the response will be an important scoring element. Also, indicate the level of detail and supporting data required.

   Poor item: Discuss the choices Mark and Alisha had to make in the story "Hawaiian Mystery".

   Better item: Mark and Alisha had to make three decisions on their journey home. Identify each of them and indicate if you disagree with any of these decisions and why you disagree. Organize your response into 3 or 4 paragraphs and check your spelling.

   Poor item: What were the forces that led to the outbreak of the Civil War?

Better item: Compare and contrast the positions of the North and South at the outbreak of the Civil War. Include in your discussion economic conditions, foreign policies, political sentiments, and social conditions.

3. Start essay questions with such words or phrases as compare, contrast, give reasons for, give original examples of, predict what would happen if, and so on. Do not begin with such words as what, who, when, and list, because those words generally lead to tasks that require only recall of information.

Poor item: In the story "Hawaiian Mystery," who made the decision to take the path by the sea?

Better item: Give three reasons why, in the story "Hawaiian Mystery," Alisha decided to take the path by the sea and predict what would have happened if they had stayed on the mountain for another night.

Poor item: List three reasons behind America's withdrawal from Vietnam.

Better item: After more than ten years of involvement, the United States withdrew from Vietnam in 1975. Predict what would have happened if America had not withdrawn at that time and had not increased significantly its military presence-above 1972 levels.

4. A question dealing with a controversial issue should ask for and be evaluated in terms of the presentation of evidence for a position rather than the position taken. It is not defensible to demand that a student accept a specific conclusion or solution, but it is reasonable to assess how well the student has learned to use the evidence on which a specific conclusion is based.

Poor item: What laws should Congress pass to improve the medical care of all citizens in the United States?

Better item: Some feel that the cost of all medical care should be borne by the federal government. Do you agree or disagree? Support your position with at least three reasons.

Poor item: Provide arguments for the support of laws to speed up the economic development of a community.

Better item: Some local laws work to slow the economic development of a community while others are intended to speed it up. Discuss the advantages and limitations of each point of view for (a) the home owner and (b) the business community and decide which you would support if you were on the City Council.

5. Establish reasonable time and/or page limits for each essay question to help the student complete the question and to indicate the level of detail for the response you have in mind. Indicate such limits orally and in the statement of the question.

6. Use essay questions with content and objectives that cannot be satisfactorily measured by objective items.

7. Avoid using optional items. That is, require all students to complete the same items. Allowing students to select three of five, four of seven, and so forth decreases test validity and decreases your basis for comparison among students.

8. Be sure each question relates to an instructional objective.

Not all of the suggestions may be relevant for each item you write. However, the suggestions are worth going over even after you've written items, as a means of checking and, when necessary, modifying your items. With time you will get better and more efficient at writing essay items.

SCORING ESSAY QUESTIONS

Restricted response questions are difficult to score consistently across individuals. That is, the same answer may be given an A by one scorer and a B or C by another scorer. The same answer may even be graded A on one occasion but B or C on another occasion by the same scorer! As disturbing and surprising as this may seem, these conclusions are supported by research findings (Coffman, 1971).

To understand the difficulties involved in scoring essays reliably, it is necessary to consider the difficulty involved in constructing good essay items. As you saw earlier, the clearer your instructional objective, the easier the essay item is to construct. Similarly, the clearer the essay item in terms of task specification, the easier it is to score reliably. Make sense? If you're not sure, look at the next two examples of essay items and decide which would likely be more reliably scored.

> **EXAMPLE 1:** Some economists recommend massive tax cuts as a means of controlling inflation. Identify at least two assumptions on which such a position is based, and indicate the effect that violating each assumption might have on inflation. Limit your response to one-half page. Organize your answer according to the criteria discussed in class. Spelling, punctuation, and grammar will be counted in your grade. (8 points)

> **EXAMPLE 2:** What effect would massive tax cuts have on inflation? (100 points)

Which did you select? If you chose the first one, you are catching on. Example 2 is a poor question. It is unstructured and unfocused; it fails to define response limits; and it fails to establish a policy for grammar, spelling, and punctuation. Thus, depending on the scorer, a lengthy answer with poor grammar and good content might get a high grade, a low grade, or an intermediate grade. Different scorers would probably all have a different idea of what a "good" answer to the question looks like. Questions like this trouble and confuse scorers and invite scorer unreliability. They do so for the same reasons that they trouble and confuse test takers. Poorly written essay items hurt both students and scorers.

But the first example is different. The task is spelled out for the student; limits are defined; and the policy on spelling, punctuation, and grammar is indicated. The task for the scorer is to determine whether the student has included (1) at least two assumptions underlying the proposition and (2) the likely effect on inflation if each assumption is violated. Granted, there may be some difficulty agreeing how adequate the statements of the assumptions and effects of violating the assumptions may be, but there is little else to quibble over. Thus, there are fewer potential sources of scorer error or variability (i.e., unreliability) in this question than in the second. Remember, essay scoring can never be as reliable as scoring an objective test, but it doesn't have to be little better than chance.

What can you do to avoid such scoring problems?

1. Write good essay questions. Poorly written questions are one source of scorer inconsistency. Questions that do not specify response length are another. Depending on the grade, long (e.g., three-page) responses generally are more difficult to score consistently than shorter responses (say, one page). This is due to student fatigue and subsequent clerical errors as well as to a tendency for grading criteria to vary from response to response, or for that matter from page to page or paragraph to paragraph within the same response.

2. Use several restricted response questions. Instead of using a single comprehensive extended response question, use several shorter, more specific and detailed restricted response questions. This will provide a greater variety of criteria to respond to and thus give students a greater opportunity to show off their skills.

3. Prepare a rubric (i.e., a scoring plan or scheme) that identifies the criteria for a correct or acceptable response to each of your questions. All too often, questions are graded without the scorer having specified in advance the criteria for a "good" answer. If you do not specify the criteria beforehand, your scoring consistency will be greatly reduced. If these criteria are not readily available (written down) for scoring each question, the criteria themselves may change (you may grade harder or easier after scoring several papers, even if the answers do not change). Or your ability to keep the criteria in mind will be influenced by fatigue, distractions, frame of mind, and so on.

What do such criteria look like? Scoring criteria, or rubrics, may vary from fairly simple checklists to elaborate combinations of checklists and rating scales. How elaborate your scoring scheme is depends on what you are trying to measure. If your essay item is a restricted response item simply assessing mastery of factual content, a fairly simple listing of essential points would suffice. Table 7.1 illustrates this type of scoring scheme. For many restricted response items a similar scoring scheme would probably suffice. However, when items are measuring higher level cognitive skills such as synthesis and evaluation, more complex schemes are necessary. This is true whether the item is a restricted or an extended range essay. Tuckman (1975) has identified three components that we feel are useful in scoring high-level essay items: content, organization, and process. We will consider this approach and another method called the rating method in the next section.

Scoring Extended Response and Higher Level Questions

Remember that an extended range essay item is best employed when we are measuring at the synthesis or evaluation levels of the cognitive taxonomy. Thus extended response essays often take the form of a term paper or a take-home assignment. As you might imagine, the breadth and depth of material extended response essays can cover poses a real challenge to scoring reliability. Using a checklist or similar simple scoring rubric is not likely to work well for these measures. Fortunately, this daunting task is made manageable if we use Tuckman's recommendations. Let's consider his approach, which essentially assigns ratings for content, organization, and process. Table 7.2 illustrates the application of these three criteria to an extended response essay item.

TABLE 7.1   An Essay Item Appropriate for a Tenth-Grade American Government Course, Its Objective, and a Simple Scoring Scheme

Scoring Scheme	Description
Objective	The student will be able to name and describe at least five important conditions that contributed to the Industrial Revolution, drawn from among the following: Breakdown of feudal ideas and social boundaries (rise of ordinary people) Legitimization of individualism and competition Transportation revolution, which allowed for massive transport of goods (first national roads, canals, steamboats, railroads, etc.) New forms of energy (e.g., coal) that brought about factory system Slow decline of death rates due to improved hygiene and continuation of high birth rates resulted in rise in population Media revolution (printing press, newspapers, telegraph, etc.) Migration to urban areas
Test item	Name and describe five of the most important conditions that made the Industrial Revolution possible. (10 points)
Scoring criteria	1 point for each of the seven factors named, to a maximum of 5 points 1 point for each appropriate description of the factors named, to a maximum of 5 points No penalty for spelling, punctuation, or grammatical error No extra credit for more than five factors named or described Extraneous information will be ignored

Content   Although essays often are not used to measure factual knowledge as much as thinking processes, the information included in an essay—its content—can and should be scored specifically for its presence and accuracy. In other words, in addition to grading for application, analysis, synthesis, etc., your assessment should include whether the student has acquired the prerequisite knowledge and content needed to demonstrate any higher level behaviors that may be required by your question. A scoring rubric for content similar to those illustrated in Tables 7.1 and 7.2 would improve scoring reliability for the presence and accuracy of content. Alternatively, a rating scale similar to the one portrayed in Figure 7.1 may be used, depending on the type of content called for by the item.

Organization   Does the essay have an introduction, body, and conclusion? Let the students know that you will be scoring for organization to minimize rambling. Beyond the three general organizational criteria mentioned, you may want to develop specific criteria for your class. For example, are recommendations, inferences, and hypotheses supported? Is it apparent which supporting statements go with which recommendation? Do progressions and sequences follow a logical or chronological development? You should also decide on a spelling and grammar policy and develop these criteria, alerting the students before they take the test. Table 7.2 illustrates how organization will be scored in the sample essay.

TABLE 7.2 **An Essay Item Appropriate for a High School American History Course, Its Objectives, and a Detailed Scoring Scheme**

Objectives	The student will be able to explain the forces that operated to weaken Southern regional self-consciousness between the Civil War and 1900. The student will consider these forces and draw an overall conclusion as to the condition of Southern self-consciousness at the beginning of the 20th century.
Test item	The Civil War left the South with a heritage of intense regional self-consciousness. In what respects and to what extent was this feeling weakened during the next half century, and in what respects and to what extent was it intensified? Your answer will be graded on content and organization; on the accuracy, consistency, and originality of your conclusion; and on the quality of your argument in support of your conclusion. Be sure to identify at least seven weakening factors and seven strengthening factors. Although spelling, punctuation, and grammar will not be considered in grading, do your best to consider them in your writing. Limit your answer to two (2) pages. (32 points)
Detailed scoring criteria	(A) *Content*

       1 point for each weakening factor mentioned, to a maximum of 7 points
       1 point for each strengthening factor mentioned, to a maximum of 7 points—all factors must come from the following lists:

       Forces weakening Southern regional self-consciousness:
       Growth of railroads and desire for federal subsidies
       Old Whigs join Northern businessmen in Compromise of 1877
       Desire for Northern capital to industrialize the South
       Efforts of magazines and writers to interpret the South
       The vision of the New South
       Aid to Negro education by Northern philanthropists
       New state constitutions stressing public education
       Supreme Court decisions affecting Negro rights
       Tom Watson's early Populist efforts
       Booker T. Washington's "submissiveness"
       The Spanish–American War
       The "white man's burden"
       After 1890, new issues did not conform to a North–South political alignment
       World War I

       Forces strengthening Southern regional self-consciousness:
       Destruction caused by the war and its long-range effects
       Reconstruction policy of Congress
       One-crop economy, crop-lien system, and sharecropping
       Carpetbaggers, Ku Klux Klan, Redshirts
       Waving the bloody shirt
       Memories of the lost cause
       Glorifying the prewar tradition
       Continuing weakness of Southern education compared with the rest of the Union
       Populism
       Jim Crow laws after 1890
       Solid South
     14 points possible

   (B) *Organization*
      0 to 6 points assigned, depending on whether the essay has an introduction, body, and conclusion.
      6 points possible

TABLE 7.2 *(Continued)*

(C) *Process*

    1. Solution: 0 to 6 points depending on whether the solution is
        a. Accurate (0 to 2 points)
           Does the solution or conclusion fit?
        b. Internally consistent (0 to 2 points)
           Does the solution or conclusion flow logically?
        c. Originality and creativity (0 to 2 points)
           Is the solution or conclusion novel or creative?
    2. Argument: 0 to 6 points, depending on whether the argument is
        a. Accurate (0 to 2 points)
           Does the argument fit the situation?
        b. Internally consistent (0 to 2 points)
           Is the argument logical?
        c. Original and creative (0 to 2 points)
           Is the argument unique or novel in its approach?
    12 points possible
  Maximum score of 32 points possible for this item overall

Process If your essay item tests at the application level or above, the most important criteria for scoring are those that reflect the extent to which these processes have been carried out. Each process (application, analysis, synthesis, and evaluation) results in a solution, recommendation, or decision and some reasons for justifying or supporting the final decision, and so on. Thus, the process criteria should attempt to assess both the adequacy of the solution or decision and the reasons behind it. In Table 7.2 the process component is broken down into two components, solution and argument, and each of those in turn is broken down into three subparts, accuracy, internal consistency, and originality/creativity. Whenever you require your students to develop or synthesize a

Scale	Description
5	Firm command of basic concepts Uses terminology correctly Identifies important principles
4	Shows nearly complete understanding of basics Most terms used correctly Has identified most important principles
3	Has only tentative grasp of concepts Some terms used incorrectly Some inference evident
2	Lacks command of most of the important concepts Uses little relevant terminology Little evidence of ability to abstract principles
1	Shows no understanding of basic concepts No attempt to use relevant terminology No evidence of abstraction or inference

Points _____

FIGURE 7.1 Rating scale for scoring an essay for knowledge of basic concepts.

solution or conclusion as part of the assessment we recommend that you evaluate the solution or conclusion according to those criteria to enhance scoring reliability. Some additional clarification of the criteria follows.

Accuracy and Reasonableness   Will the solution or conclusion work? Have the correct analytical dimensions been identified? Scorers must ultimately decide for themselves what is accurate but should be prepared for unexpected, but accurate, responses.

Completeness and Internal Consistency   To what extent does the solution or conclusion sufficiently deal with the problem presented? Again, the scorer's judgment will weigh heavily, but points should be logically related and cover the topics as fully as required by the essay item.

Originality and Creativity   Again, it is up to the scorer to recognize the unexpected and give credit for it. That is, the scorer should expect that some students will develop new ways of conceptualizing questions, and credit should be awarded for such conceptualizations when appropriate.

As the scorer reads through each response, points are assigned for each of the three major criteria of the scoring scheme. As you can probably guess, there are some disadvantages to this approach. It is likely to be quite laborious and time-consuming. Furthermore, undue attention may be given to superficial aspects of the answer. When used properly, however, such a scoring scheme can yield reliable scores for extended range essay answers. Another advantage of this approach is that constructing such a detailed scoring scheme before administering the test can often alert the teacher to such problems in the item as unrealistic expectations for the students or poor wording. A third advantage is that discussion of a student's grade on such an item is greatly facilitated. The student can see what aspects of his or her response were considered deficient.

Keep in mind that Table 7.2 represents a scoring scheme for an extended response essay item. When reliability is crucial, such a detailed scheme is vital. Scoring schemes for restricted response items would be less complex, depending on what components of the answer the teacher felt were most critical. The point we have been making is that using some kind of scoring scheme is helpful in improving the reliability of essay scoring.

Your criteria should be made known to students. This will maximize their learning experience. Knowing how you are going to score the test, students will be able to develop better and more defensible responses. In addition, we would also like to refer you to the item development and scoring rubric (i.e., scoring criteria) suggestions provided in Chapter 8, Performance-Based Assessment, for additional help with extended response items. The suggestions provided in Chapter 8 have direct applicability because extended response essays actually represent one form of performance assessment. Next, we will consider another essay scoring method called the rating method.

The Rating Method   With the rating method, the teacher generally is more interested in the overall quality of the answer than in specific points. Rating is done by simply sorting papers into piles, usually five, if letter grades are given. After sorting, the answers in each pile are scanned and an attempt is made to ensure that all the A papers are of comparable quality (i.e., that they do not include B and C papers) and so forth. This step is important, since the problem of the criteria changing during grading is always present in rating answers. It helps minimize the likelihood, for example, that an A paper gets sorted into the C pile because it was graded early while the teacher was maintaining "strict" criteria.

This method is an improvement over simply reading each answer and assigning a grade based on some nebulous, undefined rationale. However, this method is still subject to the problem of unintentionally changing the criteria, if they have not been written beforehand.

General Essay Scoring Suggestions

In addition to the specific suggestions we have offered for restricted and extended response essays there are several other suggestions that apply regardless of the type of essay that is used. Some of these we have already mentioned. Do you remember our first three suggestions?

1. Write good essay items.
2. Use mostly restricted response rather than extended response items, for in-classroom assessments.
3. Use a predetermined scoring scheme.

Now let's consider several other suggestions to improve essay scoring reliability.

4. Use the scoring scheme consistently. In other words, don't favor one student over another or get stricter or more lax over time. How can you do this?
5. Remove or cover the names on the papers before beginning scoring (e.g., with sticky notes). In this way you are more likely to rate papers on their merits, rather than on your overall impression of the student.
6. Score each student's answer to the same question before going on to the next answer. In other words, do all of the answers to the first question before looking at the answers to the second. Why? First, you want to avoid having a student's score on an earlier question influence your evaluation of his or her later questions; and second, it is much easier to keep scoring criteria for one question in mind than it is to keep scoring criteria for all the questions in mind.
7. Try to keep scores for previous items hidden when scoring subsequent items, for the same reason already mentioned.
8. Try to re-evaluate your papers before returning them. When you come across discrepant ratings, average them.

Well, there you have it! Eight suggestions for improving the reliability of essay scoring. If you use essay items, try to incorporate as many of these suggestions as possible. Next we will turn to our final topic for this chapter, essay items you can use to assess student ability to organize knowledge or information and open-book exams.

ASSESSING KNOWLEDGE ORGANIZATION

The mind spontaneously organizes information as it is learned. As students attend and listen to your presentations and discussions, or read from their books, they link this new information with prior learning, and this linking helps them to learn concepts, principles, and generalizations. Over time, as their knowledge base grows, it becomes increasingly organized in a hierarchical fashion. Even though learners construct this organization on their own, teachers can facilitate it in these ways.

1. At the start of a lesson, you can ask questions that get learners to recall previous learning.

2. During the lesson you can ask questions and provide activities that help learners see similarities and differences and to detect patterns and relationships among the pieces of information that they are hearing or reading.

3. You can also construct outlines or other schematics that visually remind learners of how new information is organized and relates to previously learned information.

Figure 7.2 represents a visual plan constructed by a teacher for an interdisciplinary thematic unit. This important tool helped the teacher organize knowledge for instruction and assess it in ways that emphasize the interrelationships that build to more important themes and concepts.

FIGURE 7.2 Teacher's visual representation of the interdisciplinary unit theme "Gold Rush."
(*Source:* Developed by Cynthia Kiel, teacher, Glendora, California.)

Thus, knowledge organization is an important goal of instruction because an organized knowledge base helps students acquire new information, learn it in a meaningful way, remember it, and better solve problems that require it. Assuming that knowledge organization is a goal for your learners, what are some of the ways you can assess it?

First of all, assessing knowledge organization and concepts are not the same. The assessment procedures previously discussed let you determine understanding of terms and expressions like photosynthesis, plants, and chlorophyll. But they don't tell you much about how well the student understands the relationships among the concepts. It is these connections that you will want to assess when you evaluate your learners' knowledge organization.

The connections between and among concepts represent the student's knowledge and understanding of rules, principles, and generalizations. Now the learner has moved from simple knowledge (recall and recognition) to simple understanding (the learner can give examples, tell how a term is different from and similar to other terms and expressions, and explain what it means in their own words) to the organization of knowledge (not only does the learner know the pieces, but the pieces are connected to one another and ordered hierarchically). For example, the learner not only knows about the California Gold Rush but also its connections to the food the pioneers ate, the songs they sang, how they calculated the amount they traveled each day, the diaries they kept, and how they weighed and measured the gold. In other words, they constructed concepts, principles, and generalizations that connected the gold rush experience to larger concepts found in everyday life, representing knowledge organization.

Learners construct these concepts, principles, and generalizations as a result of your instruction that allows them to explore similarities and differences, and to establish relationships and connections. Learners of all ages spontaneously organize information and form orderly knowledge bases in this way.

Thus, assessing for knowledge organization requires identifying the connections among concepts, or the sets and subsets of knowledge. But how can learners display their organization of knowledge—of cause and effect relationships, similarities and contrasts, or problems and solutions? Traditional outlines in which major topics and subtopics are grouped in a I, II, III, A, B, C order may not reveal knowledge organization. Some educators (Goetz, Alexander & Ash, 1992) believe such outlines emphasize categories of things over relationships that can impose a structure that differs from the way knowledge should actually be organized for deep understanding.

Dansereau (1988) urges teachers to model alternate strategies to help learners when they listen to presentations or read from books, which, in turn, can be used to assess the depth of understanding and organization of their knowledge base. He advocates that you assess your learners' understanding and organization of their knowledge with graphic outlines displayed as webs, much like the visual interdisciplinary thematic unit plans shown in Figure 7.3, but this time prepared by your students. Webbing is a free-form outline technique learners can use to display their level of understanding of class discussions or textbook content, as displayed in Figures 7.3A–C. Notice in each of these how the learners who drew them rose on the learning ladder from basic knowledge, requiring the memorization of facts, to simple understanding, requiring conceptualization and an understanding of relationships. The following are some rules

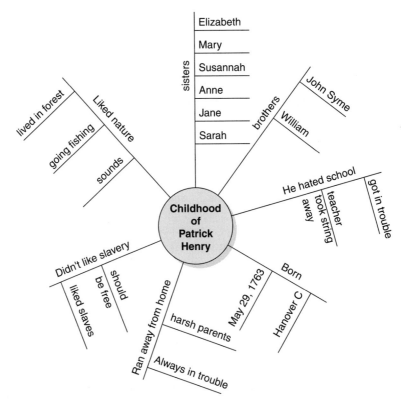

FIGURE 7.3A Example of webbing, indicating relationships.

Source: From "Cooperative Learning Strategies" by D. F. Dansereau, in Learning and Study Strategies: Issues in Assessment, Instruction and Evaluation (pp. 103–120), by C. F. Weinstein, E. T. Goetz, and P. A. Alexander (Eds.), 1988, Orlando: Academic Press. Copyright © 1988 by Academic Press. Reprinted with permission.

for communicating to your learners how to construct webs, networks, or maps for study and for assessment:

- Display only essential information or big ideas or concepts.
- Assign the central idea or concept to a central location.
- Draw arrows from the main ideas to show relationships.
- Label the arrows with key words or code letters to describe their relationship.

OPEN-BOOK QUESTIONS AND EXAMS

Having selected a topic area and identified the cognitive outcomes that you wish to assess, you have the choice to give the questions you want your learners to answer in an open-book format. Ideas for these questions can come from the text but also newspapers, news programs, technical reports and journals related to your curriculum, and your

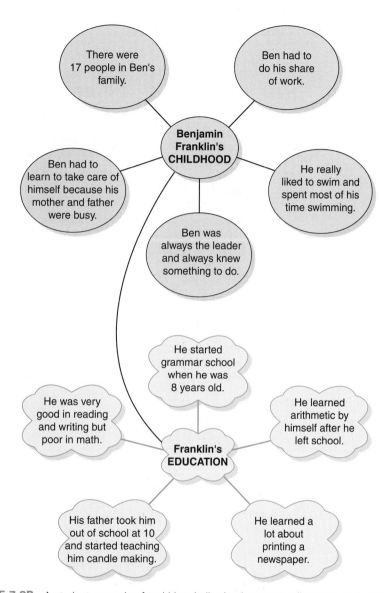

FIGURE 7.3B A student example of webbing, indicating important milestones or events.

Source: From "Cooperative Learning Strategies" by D. F. Dansereau, in Learning and Study Strategies: Issues in Assessment, Instruction and Evaluation (pp. 103–120), by C. F. Weinstein, E. T. Goetz, and P. A. Alexander (Eds.), 1988, Orlando: Academic Press. Copyright © 1988 by Academic Press. Reprinted with permission.

experiences with a variety of real-life situations in which the behaviors you want to assess are used. Your open-book questions may ask students or collaborative groups of students to prepare an outline of a presentation to a supervisory board using reference material from the text, simulate an experiment or laboratory task using data from resource tables, develop specifications for a product using a published list of industry standards, or

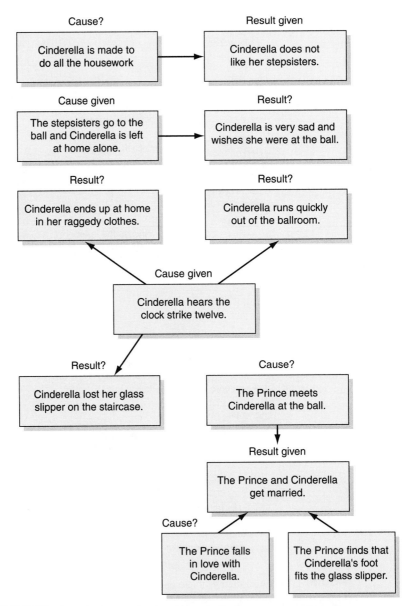

FIGURE 7.3C A student example of webbing, indicating a cause and result.

Source: From "Cooperative Learning Strategies" by D. F. Dansereau, in *Learning and Study Strategies: Issues in Assessment, Instruction and Evaluation* (pp. 103–120), by C. F. Weinstein, E. T. Goetz, and P. A. Alexander (Eds.), 1988, Orlando: Academic Press. Copyright © 1988 by Academic Press. Reprinted with permission.

develop a mass transit plan, given maps and budgetary information. You can get started on developing open-book questions by asking yourself the following questions:

What do the jobs of professionals who make their living as mathematicians, electronic technicians, journalists, food processing supervisors, etc., look and feel like?

Which of the projects and tasks of these professionals can be adapted to the knowledge and skills required by your curriculum?

Which of these skills are enhanced by being able to refer to existing data, resources, tables, charts, diagrams, etc., without having to memorize them?

Once you answer these questions a host of ideas arise. The task then becomes one of developing the open-book exam questions. The examples below illustrate different types of open-book questions.

Some Open-Book Techniques

Here is an example open-book question with explicit directions:

On pages 170–174 of your text you will find a description of a static electricity experiment. Read the description carefully. Then, using your understanding of the experiment and the principles of the electroscope in Table 5.1 in your text, answer the following questions:

(1) What would happen to the leaves of the electroscope as the charged ruler is brought closer or farther away from it? Explain why this happens.

(2) What would happen to the leaves when you touch the electroscope with the charged ruler and then touch it with your finger? Explain why this happens.

(3) What would happen when you pass the charged ruler close to the leaves but do not make contact with them? Explain why this happens.

(4) What would happen to the charged leaves when you heat the air next to them with a match? Explain why this happens.

For each question:

(a) Make a prediction about what would happen.

(b) State what you would observe.

(c) Assess whether your prediction could be supported.

Since you want the answer to show evidence of particular reasoning strategies, be sure to include explicit cues to learners to show evidence of the strategy they are using or the thinking and reasoning they went through on the way to solving the problem. Reminders like, "Show all work," "Be sure to list the steps involved," etc., will allow you better to assess both cognitive and metacognitive strategies.

Quellmalz (1991) recommends that, particularly with questions that assess analysis and comparison, you include the question, "So what?" Rather than simply list elements in an analysis or develop a laundry list of similarities and differences, learners should be asked to explain the significance of the analysis or points of comparison. Thus, questions should explicitly cue learners to explain why the various aspects of the analysis or comparison are important (e.g., "Why should the reader care about the things you analyzed?" or "Why are the similarities and differences that you discussed important for an understanding of this event?")

One very effective way of encouraging and assessing higher level thinking skills with open-book exams is through dialectical journals. The word dialectical comes from a method of argumentation originating with the ancient Greeks. This process involves the art of examining opinions or ideas logically, often by the method of question and answer so as to determine their validity. It was the practice of Socrates and his followers to conduct this process through oral discourse, but many of the same positive results can be achieved by implementing this structure into a written journal form.

In a sense, the dialectical journal is a conversation with oneself over the concepts of a given text. Here is one suggested format. Divide your examination in half vertically and title two columns as follows:

Quotation, Summary, or Paraphrase (From Text)	*Reaction, Prediction, or Analysis* (From Student)

A quotation, summary, or paraphrase from the text or related reading (e.g., relevant magazine or newspaper article) is chosen by you. A reaction, prediction or analysis to your quotation, summarization, or paraphrasing is written by the student in the column on the right. Just like the professional on the job, your students are allowed to consult the text to find material for composing their response.

This journal format should be modeled with examples and practiced with students before using it for assessment purposes. Initially students unfamiliar with this procedure may make shallow or superficial comments, often thinking that simple explication or explanation is what is wanted. Encourage students to use what is presented in the text as a starting point rather than the end point for their responses. Learning to use the text in this manner can increase the accuracy and depth of responses and encourage higher level cognition.

The dialectical procedure can be practiced in the initial stages of a new topic or unit to encourage active reading, at midpoint to see if early ideas were valid, and at the conclusion, as an open-book exam where new perspectives and deep understanding can be assessed. A good rule of thumb is to use the early dialectical journals for modeling and feedback, or to generate the exchange of ideas, and for assessment purposes at the conclusion of a topic or unit. Here are some sample dialectical entries in the form of an open-book exam.

Dialectical Open-Book Questions

Quotation, paraphrase, or summary	*Student reaction, prediction, or analysis*
"Scientists have determined that the height of a deep-water wave cannot exceed one-seventh of its wavelength if the wave's structure is to support its crest." (from a trigonometry text) Does the same principle apply to radio waves? Using examples from the text, what other factors such as wind velocity or atmospheric pressure might influence this formula?	

Quotation, paraphrase, or summary	*Student reaction, prediction, or analysis*

Quotation, paraphrase, or summary

"The reflection symmetry of living creatures like the lizard and butterfly is often called bilateral symmetry." (from an art text)

Symmetry has favorable and practical physical attributes as well as aesthetic ones. Because of this symmetry the butterfly can soar through the air and the lizard can crawl in a straight line or variations of one. From examples in the text show how we tend to lean toward symmetry in aesthetics because of its inherent usefulness.

Quotation, paraphrase, or summary

"The strength of triangular bracing is related to the SSS Postulate, which tells us that a triangle with given sides can have only one shape. A rectangle formed by four bars joined at their ends can flatten into a parallelogram, but the structural triangle cannot be deformed except by bending or stretching the bars." (from a geometry text)

From the pyramids of ancient Egypt to the Eiffel Tower in France, extending to the modest tripod of photography, or the tallest of radio towers, we see the ever-present tower. Using examples from the text, what other building or structural uses can be made of the simple triangle?

Quotation, paraphrase, or summary

"Never read feverishly, never read as though you were racing against time—unless you wish to derive neither pleasure nor profit from your reading," (from a literature text)

Could it be that pleasure and profit are connected? Do we remember things more if we take the time to enjoy them? How important are emotions to learning? According to this author, the conventional advice to read faster and more efficiently may not be so good. Can you show from any of the stories you have read that slowing down and enjoying what you are doing can increase your understanding and ability to apply what you have read?

Student reaction, prediction, or analysis

Student reaction, prediction, or analysis

Student reaction, prediction, or analysis

Since the student self-selects the material to answer the question from the text, there is already inherent interest in the content and meaning for the student.

This journal technique may be refined to meet individual instructor's needs. For example, students may be asked to choose entries which relate to a single theme or concept, such as the application of conservation practices, future uses of known scientific principles, or analysis of a historical event.

Here is another type of dialectical question. This one reverses the process by asking the student to find a quotation, paraphrase, or summary from the text that exhibits a certain principle or concept provided by you.

> *Directions:* Read the following passage from your text and choose five quotations, para-phrases, or summaries from any chapter we have studied that supports its theme.

> *Machines and tools have always been created in the image of man. The hammer grew from the balled fist, the rake from the hand with fingers, outstretched for scratching, the shovel from the hand hollowed to scoop. As machines became more than simple tools, outstripping the creators in performance, demanding and obtaining increasing amounts of power, and acquiring superhuman speed and accuracies, their outward resemblance to the natural model disappeared; only the names of the machines' parts show vestiges of the human origin. The highly complex machinery of the industrial age has arms that swing, fingers that fold, legs that support, and teeth that grind. Machines feed on material, run when things go well, and spit and cough when they don't.*

Quotation, paraphrase, or summary from text   ***Page***

1.

2.

3.

4.

5.

Now that we've studied ways of writing good essay questions in the form of extended and restricted response questions, knowledge organization, open-book exams, and dialectical journals, let's summarize with some guidelines that can help you write good essay items in all of these formats.

Guidelines for Planning Essays, Knowledge Organization, and Open-Book Questions and Exams

1. Make clear the requirements for answering your questions, but not the solution itself. While your questions should be complex, learners should not have to ques-tion whether they are finished, or whether they have provided what you want. They should, however, have to think long and hard about how to answer a question. As you refine your questions, make sure you can visualize what an acceptable answer looks like and identify the skills you can infer from it.

2. The questions should represent a valid sample from which you can make generalizations about the learner's knowledge, thinking ability, and attitudes. What essay tests lack in breadth of coverage, they make up in depth. In other words, they get your students to exhibit higher order thinking behavior in a narrow domain or skill. Thus, the type of questions you choose should be complex enough and rich enough in detail to allow you to draw conclusions about transfer and generalization to other tasks. In other words, they should be representative of other important skills that assess the essential performance outcomes you wish your learners to achieve (Shavelson & Baxter, 1992).

3. The questions should be complex enough to allow for multiple correct answers. Most assessment tends to depend on a single right answer. Essay tests, however, are designed to allow learners to demonstrate learning through a variety of paths. In science, for example, a student might choose to answer a question by emphasizing the results of an experiment from the text, showing the solution by explaining how laboratory equipment would be used to arrive at it, or by simulating data and conclusions from an experiment that would answer the question. Allowing for multiple paths to the correct answer will be more time-consuming than a multiple-choice test, but it will provide unique information about your learners' achievement untapped by other assessment methods. Shavelson and Baxter (1992) have shown that examination procedures that allow teachers to draw different conclusions about a learner's problem-solving ability lead to more analysis, interpretation, and evaluation behavior than do multiple-choice tests or restricted response essay tests.

4. The questions should yield multiple solutions where possible, each with costs and benefits. Essay questions are not a form of practice or drill. It should involve more than simple tasks for which there is one solution. Essay exams should be nonalgorithmic (the path of action is not fully specified in advance) and complex (the total solution cannot be seen from any one vantage point), and they should involve judgment and interpretation.

5. The questions should require self-regulated learning. Essay questions should require considerable mental effort and place high demands on the persistence and determination of the individual learner. The learner should be required to use cognitive strategies to arrive at a solution rather than depend on memorized content at various points in the assessment process.

6. The questions should have clear directions. Essay questions should be complex, require higher level thinking, assess multiple goals, and permit considerable latitude about how to reach these goals. Nevertheless, your questions should leave no doubt in the minds of learners about what is expected. While your students need to think long and hard about how to answer the question, they should be clear about what a good answer looks like. In other words, they should be able to explain exactly what you expect them to turn in when the exam is over.

SUMMARY

Chapter 7 introduced you to the major issues related to the construction and scoring of essay items. Its major points are as follows:

1. Essay items require that the student supply rather than select a response. The length and complexity of the response may vary, and essay items lend themselves best to the assessment of higher level cognitive skills.

2. There are two main types of essay items that are differentiated by length of response: extended response and restricted response essay items.
   a. The extended response item usually requires responses more than a page in length and may be used to assess synthesis and evaluation skills. It is usually appropriate for term papers and end-of-semester reports.
   b. The restricted response item is usually answered in a page or less. It is often used to measure comprehension, application, and analysis.

3. The type of item written is determined by the cognitive skills called for in the instructional objective.

4. Suggestions for writing essay items include the following:
   a. Identify the cognitive processes you want the student to use before you write the item.
   b. State the task clearly (i.e., focus the item), including any criteria on which the essay will be graded.
   c. Avoid beginning essay items with what, who, when, and list, unless you are measuring at the knowledge level.
   d. Ask for presentation of evidence for a controversial position, rather than asking the student simply to take a controversial position.
   e. Avoid using optional items.
   f. Establish reasonable time and/or page limits for each item.
   g. Use essays to measure learning outcomes that cannot be measured by objective items.
   h. Be sure the item matches the instructional objective.

5. Advantages of essay items over objective items include the following:
   a. Essays enable you to assess complex learning outcomes.
   b. Essays are relatively easy to construct.
   c. Essays enable you to assess communication skills.
   d. Essays eliminate student guessing.

6. Disadvantages of essay items include:
   a. Longer scoring time is needed.
   b. Scoring can be unreliable.
   c. Essays sample limited content.
   d. Answers are susceptible to bluffing.

7. Essay items should be used when:
   a. Objectives specify higher level cognitive processes and objective items are inappropriate.
   b. Few tests or items are necessary.
   c. Test security is in question.

8. Essay scoring reliability may be improved by:
   a. Writing good essay items.
   b. Using restricted range rather than extended range essays whenever appropriate.
   c. Using a predetermined scoring scheme.
   d. Implementing the scoring scheme consistently with all students.
   e. Removing or covering names on papers to avoid scoring bias.
   f. Scoring all responses to one item before scoring the next item.
   g. Keeping scores from previous items hidden when scoring subsequent items.
   h. Rescoring all papers before returning them and averaging discrepant ratings.

9. Essays may be scored according to:
   a. Simple scoring schemes that assign credit for content.
   b. Detailed scoring schemes that assign credit for content, organization, process, and any other factors that the scorer deems desirable.
   c. The rating method, in which grades are assigned on the basis of a global impression of the whole response.

10. A type of assessment for measuring the organization of knowledge in which the learner makes connections among concepts or subsets if knowledge is called webbing.

11. Open-book exams are ideal for questions that use tabular data, charts and graphs that come from the text, as well as newspapers, magazines, and reports related to your curriculum and that ask students to think about and apply information that comes from real-life situations in which the behaviors you want to assess are used.

12. One way of encouraging and assessing higher level thinking skills with an open-book exam is with dialectical journals, which involve examining the opinions or ideas of others logically, often by the method of question and answer so as to determine their validity.

FOR PRACTICE

1. Write essay test items using both an extended response format and a restricted response format. Your extended response question should be targeted to measure a synthesis or evaluation objective, while your restricted response question should be targeted to measure a comprehension, application, or analysis objective.

2. Prepare a scoring guide for your restricted response essay item using the format shown in Table 7.1.

3. Describe five scoring procedures from among those discussed in this chapter that will help ensure the reliability of scoring your essay question.

4. Give some pros and cons of the rating method, in which grades are assigned on the basis of global impressions of the whole response.

5. Prepare an open-book exam question requiring the use of specific reference material from the text (e.g., data, graphs, tables, etc.)

CHAPTER 8

PERFORMANCE-BASED ASSESSMENT

IN CHAPTER 5 (in the Writing Instructional Objectives section), you learned that there are a variety of skills that children acquire in school. Some of these require learners to acquire information by memorizing vocabulary, multiplication tables, dates of historical events, and so on. Other skills involve learning action sequences or procedures to follow when performing mathematical computations, dissecting a frog, focusing a microscope, handwriting, or typing. In addition, you learned that students must acquire concepts, rules, and generalizations that allow them to understand what they read, analyze and solve problems, carry out experiments, write poems and essays, and design projects to study historical, political, or economic problems.

Some of these skills are best assessed with paper and pencil tests. But other skills—particularly those involving independent judgment, critical thinking, and decision making—are best assessed with performance tests. Although paper and pencil tests currently represent the principal means of assessing these more complex cognitive outcomes, in this chapter we will study other ways of measuring them in more authentic contexts.

PERFORMANCE TESTS: DIRECT MEASURES OF COMPETENCE

In earlier chapters you learned that many educational tests measure learning indirectly. That is, they ask questions, the responses to which indicate that something has been learned or mastered. Performance tests, on the other hand, use direct measures of learning rather than indicators that simply suggest cognitive, affective, or psychomotor processes have taken place. In the field of athletics, diving and gymnastics are examples of performances that judges rate directly. Their scores are pooled and used to decide who, for example, earns a medal, wins first, second, third, etc., or qualifies for district or regional competition. Likewise, at band contests judges directly see and hear the competence of trombone or violin players and pool their ratings to decide who makes the state or district band and who gets the leading chairs.

Teachers can use performance tests to assess complex cognitive learning, as well as attitudes and social skills in academic areas such as science, social studies, or math. When doing so, they establish situations that allow them to observe and to rate learners directly as they analyze, problem solve, experiment, make decisions, measure, cooperate with others, present orally, or produce a product. These situations simulate real-world activities, as might be expected in a job, in the community, or in various forms of advanced training—for example, in the military, at a technical institute, during on the job training, or in college.

Performance tests also allow teachers to observe achievements, mental habits, ways of working, and behaviors of value in the real world that conventional tests may miss and in ways that an outside observer would be unaware that a "test" is going on. Performance tests can include observing and rating learners as they carry out a dialogue in a foreign language, conduct a science experiment, edit a composition, present an exhibit, work with a group of other learners in designing a student attitude survey, or use equipment. In other words, the teacher observes and evaluates student abilities to carry out complex activities that are used and valued outside the immediate confines of the classroom.

PERFORMANCE TESTS CAN ASSESS PROCESSES AND PRODUCTS

Performance tests can be assessments of processes, products, or both. For example, at the Darwin School in Winnipeg, Manitoba, teachers assess the reading process of each student by noting the percentage of words read accurately during oral reading, the number of sentences read by the learner that are meaningful within the context of the story, and the percentage of story elements that the learner can talk about in his or her own words after reading.

At the West Orient School in Gresham, Oregon, fourth-grade learners assemble a portfolio of their writing products. These portfolios include rough as well as final drafts of poetry, essays, biographies, and self-reflections. Several math teachers at Twin Peaks Middle School in Poway, California, require their students to assemble math portfolios that include the following products of their problem-solving efforts: long-term projects, daily notes, journal entries about troublesome test problems, written explanations of how they solved problems, and the problem solutions themselves.

Social studies learning processes and products are assessed in the Aurora, Colorado, Public Schools by having learners engage in a variety of projects built around the following question: "Based on your study of Colorado history, what current issues in Colorado do you believe are the most important to address, what are your ideas about the resolutions of those issues, and what contributions will you make toward the resolutions?" (Pollock, 1992). Learners answer these questions in a variety of ways involving individual and group writing assignments, oral presentations, and exhibits.

PERFORMANCE TESTS CAN BE EMBEDDED IN LESSONS

The examples of performance tests given involve performances that occurred outside the context of a lesson and which are completed at the end of a term or during an examination period. Many teachers use performance tests as part of their lessons. In fact, some proponents of performance tests hold that the ideal performance test is a good teaching activity (Shavelson & Baxter, 1992). Viewed from this perspective, a well-constructed performance test can serve as a teaching activity as well as an assessment.

For example, Figure 8.1 illustrates a performance activity and assessment that was embedded in a unit on electricity in a general science class (Shavelson & Baxter, 1992, p. 22). During the activity the teacher observes and rates the learners on the method they used to solve the problem, the care with which they measured, the manner of recording results, and the correctness of the final solution. This type of assessment provides immediate feedback on how learners are performing, reinforces hands-on teaching and learning, and underscores for learners the important link between teaching and testing. In this manner, it moves the instruction toward higher order behavior.

HANDS-ON ELECTRIC MYSTERIES INVESTIGATION

Find out what is in the six mystery boxes A, B, C, D, E, and F. They have five different things inside, shown below. Two of the boxes will have the same thing. All of the others will have something different inside.

When you find out what is in a box, fill in the spaces on the following pages.

Box A: Has _____ inside.

Draw a picture of the circuit that told you what was inside Box A.

Two batteries:

A wire:

A bulb:

How could you tell from your circuit what was inside Box A?

_____

_____

A battery and a bulb:

_____

Do the same for Boxes B, C, D, E, and F.

Nothing at all:

_____

_____

You can use your bulbs, batteries, and wires any way you like. Connect them in a circuit to help you figure what is inside.

FIGURE 8.1   An example performance activity and assessment.

Source: From Shavelson and Baxter (1992), p. 22.

Other examples of lesson-embedded performance tests might include observing and rating the following as they are actually happening: typing, preparing a microscope slide, reading out loud, programming a calculator, giving an oral presentation, determining how plants react to certain substances, designing a questionnaire or survey, solving a math problem, developing an original math problem and a solution for it, critiquing the logic of an editorial, or graphing information.

PERFORMANCE TESTS CAN ASSESS AFFECTIVE AND SOCIAL SKILLS

Teachers across the country are using performance tests not only to assess higher level cognitive skills but also noncognitive outcomes, such as self-direction, ability to work with others, and social awareness (Redding, 1992). This concern for the affective domain of learning reflects an awareness by educators that the skilled performance of complex tasks involves more than the ability to recall information, form concepts, generalize, and problem solve. It also includes the mental and behavioral habits or characteristics evident in individuals who successfully perform such complex tasks, also known as habits of mind, and interpersonal or social skills.

The Aurora Public Schools in Colorado have developed a list of learning outcomes and their indicators for learners in grades K–12. These are shown in Figure 8.2. For each of these 19 indicators a four-category rating scale has been developed to serve as a guide for teachers who are unsure of how to define "assumes responsibility" or "demonstrates consideration." While observing learners during performance tests in social studies, science, art, or economics, teachers are alert to recognize and rate those behaviors that suggest learners have acquired the outcomes.

Teachers in the Aurora Public Schools are encouraged to use this list of outcomes when planning their courses. They first ask themselves what key facts, concepts, and principles should all learners remember? In addition, they try to fuse this subject area content with the five district outcomes by designing special performance tests. For example, a third-grade language arts teacher who is planning a writing unit might choose to focus on indicators 8 and 9 to address district outcomes related to "collaborative worker," indicator 1 for the outcome of self-directed learner, and indicator 13 for the outcome "quality producer." She would then design a performance assessment that allows learners to demonstrate learning in these areas. She might select other indicators and outcomes for subsequent units and performance tests.

In summary, performance tests represent an addition to the measurement practices reviewed in previous chapters. Paper and pencil tests are the most efficient, reliable, and valid instruments available for assessing knowledge, comprehension, and some types of application. But when it comes to assessing complex thinking skills, habits of mind, and social skills, performance tests can, if properly constructed, do a better job. On the other hand, if not properly constructed, performance assessments can have some of the same problems with scoring efficiency, reliability, and validity as traditional approaches to testing. This chapter will guide you through a process that will allow you to properly construct performance tests in your classroom.

A Self-Directed Learner

1. Sets priorities and achievable goals.
2. Monitors and evaluates progress.
3. Creates options for self.
4. Assumes responsibility for actions.
5. Creates a positive vision for self and future.

A Collaborative Worker

6. Monitors own behavior as a group member.
7. Assesses and manages group functioning.
8. Demonstrates interactive communication.
9. Demonstrates consideration for individual differences.

A Complex Thinker

10. Uses a wide variety of strategies for managing complex issues.
11. Selects strategies appropriate to the resolution of complex issues and applies the strategies with accuracy and thoroughness.
12. Accesses and uses topic-relevant knowledge.

A Quality Producer

13. Creates products that achieve their purpose.
14. Creates products appropriate to the intended audience.
15. Creates products that reflect craftsmanship.
16. Uses appropriate resources/technology.

A Community Contributor

17. Demonstrates knowledge about his or her diverse communities.
18. Takes action.
19. Reflects on his or her role as a community contributor.

FIGURE 8.2 Learning outcomes of Aurora Public Schools.

DEVELOPING PERFORMANCE TESTS FOR YOUR LEARNERS

As we learned in the previous section, performance assessment has the potential to improve both instruction and learning. But as we have also learned, there are both conceptual and technical issues associated with the use of performance tests that teachers must resolve before these assessments can be effectively and efficiently used. In this chapter we will discuss some of the important considerations in planning and designing a performance test and how to score performance tests, including student portfolios. In Chapter 11 we will describe how you can include the scores from performance tests in your six-week and semester grades.

Step 1: Deciding What to Test

The first step in developing a performance test is to create a list of objectives that specifies the knowledge, skills, habits of mind, and indicators of the outcomes that will be the focus of your instruction.

There are three general questions to ask when deciding what to teach:

- What knowledge or content (i.e., facts, concepts, principles, rules) is essential for learner understanding of the subject matter?
- What intellectual skills are necessary for the learner to use this knowledge or content?
- What habits of mind are important for the learner to successfully perform with this knowledge or content?

Instructional objectives that come from answering the first question are usually measured by paper and pencil tests (discussed in Chapters 6 and 7). Objectives derived from answering questions 2 and 3, although often assessed with objective or essay-type questions, can be more appropriately assessed with performance tests. Thus your assessment plan for a unit should include both paper and pencil tests to measure mastery of content and performance tests to assess skills and habits of mind. Let's see what objectives for the latter outcomes might look like.

Performance Objectives in the Cognitive Domain   Designers of performance tests usually ask the following questions to help guide their initial selection of objectives:

- What kinds of essential tasks, achievements, or other valued competencies am I missing with paper and pencil tests?
- What accomplishments of those who practice my discipline (historians, writers, scientists, mathematicians) are valued but left unmeasured by conventional tests?

Two categories of performance skills are typically identified from such questions:

1. Skills related to acquiring information, and
2. Skills related to organizing and using information.

Figure 8.3 contains a suggested list of skills for acquiring, organizing, and using information. As you study this list, consider which skills you might use as a basis for a performance test in your area of expertise.

The following are some example objectives for performance tests from a consideration of the performance skills described in Figure 8.3.

1. Write a summary of a current controversy drawn from school life and tell how a courageous and civic-minded American you have studied might decide to act on the issue.
2. Draw a physical map of North America from memory and locate 10 cities.
3. Prepare an exhibit showing how your community responds to an important social problem of your choice.
4. Construct an electrical circuit using wires, a switch, a bulb, resistors, and a battery.
5. Describe two alternative ways to solve a mathematics word problem.
6. Identify the important variables that affected recent events in our state, and forecast how these variables will affect future events.
7. Design a freestanding structure in which the size of one leg of a triangular structure must be determined from the other two sides.

Skills in acquiring information	Skills in organizing and using information
Communicating	**Organizing**
explaining	classifying
modeling	categorizing
demonstrating	sorting
graphing	ordering
displaying	ranking
writing	arranging
advising	
programming	**Problem Solving**
proposing	stating questions
drawing	identifying problems
	developing hypotheses
Measuring	interpreting
counting	assessing risks
calibrating	monitoring
rationing	
appraising	**Decision Making**
weighing	weighing alternatives
balancing	evaluating
guessing	choosing
estimating	supporting
forecasting	electing
defending	adopting
Investigating	
gathering references	
interviewing	
using references	
experimenting	
hypothesizing	

FIGURE 8.3 Skills for acquiring, organizing, and using information.

8. Program a calculator to solve an equation with one unknown.

9. Design an exhibit showing the best ways to clean up an oil spill.

10. Prepare a visual presentation to the city council requesting increased funding to deal with a problem in our community.

Performance Objectives in the Affective and Social Domain Performance assessments not only require curriculum to teach thinking skills but also to develop positive dispositions and "habits of mind." Habits of mind include such behaviors as constructive criticism, tolerance of ambiguity, respect for reason, and appreciation for the significance of the past. Performance tests are ideal vehicles for assessing habits of mind and social skills (e.g., cooperation, sharing, and negotiation). In deciding what objectives to teach and measure with a performance test, you should give consideration to affective and social skill objectives. Following are some key questions to ask for including affective and social skills in your list of performance objectives:

- What dispositions, habits of mind, or values characterize successful individuals in the community who work in your academic discipline?

- What are some of the qualities of mind or character traits that good scientists, writers, reporters, historians, mathematicians, musicians, etc. have?
- What will I accept as evidence that my learners have or are developing these qualities?
- What social skills for getting along with others are necessary for being successful as a journalist, weather forecaster, park ranger, historian, economist, mechanic, etc.?
- What evidence will convince my learners' parents that their children are developing these skills?

Figure 8.4 displays some examples of habits of mind in checklist form that could be the focus of a performance assessment in science, social studies, and mathematics.

In Science (from Loucks-Horsley, et al., 1990. Elementary School Science for the '90's, *p. 41.)*

☐ Desiring knowledge. Viewing science as a way of knowing and understanding.

☐ Being sceptical. Recognizing the appropriate time and place to question authoritarian statements and "self-evident truths."

☐ Relying on data. Explaining natural occurrences by collecting and ordering information, testing ideas, and respecting the facts that are revealed.

☐ Accepting ambiguity. Recognizing that data are rarely clear and compelling, and appreciating the new questions and problems that arise.

☐ Willingness to modify explanations. Seeing new possibilities in the data.

☐ Cooperating in answering questions and solving problems. Working together to pool ideas, explanations, and solutions.

☐ Respecting reason. Valuing patterns of thought that lead from data to conclusions and, eventually, to the construction of theories.

☐ Being honest. Viewing information objectively, without bias.

In Social Studies (from Parker, 1990. Renewing the Social Studies Curriculum, *p. 74).*

☐ Understanding the significance of the past to their own lives, both private and public, and to their society.

☐ Distinguishing between the important and inconsequential to develop the "discriminating memory" needed for a discerning judgment in public and personal life.

☐ Preparing to live with uncertainties and exasperating, even perilous, unfinished business, realizing that not all problems have solutions.

☐ Appreciating the often tentative nature of judgments about the past, and thereby avoiding the temptation to seize upon particular "lessons" of history as cures for present ills.

In Mathematics (from Willoughby, 1990. Mathematics Education for a Changing World, *p. 14).*

☐ Appreciating that mathematics is a discipline that helps solve real-world problems.

☐ Seeing mathematics as a tool or servant rather than something mysterious or mystical to be afraid of.

☐ Recognizing that there is more than one way to solve a problem.

FIGURE 8.4 Examples of habits of mind in performance assessment.

Once you have completed Step 1, you will have identified the important knowledge, skills, and habits of mind that will be the focus of your instruction and assessment. The next step is to design the task or context in which those outcomes will be assessed.

Step 2: Designing the Assessment Context

The purpose of Step 2 is to create a task, simulation, or situation that will allow learners to demonstrate the knowledge, skills, and attitudes that they have acquired. Ideas for these tasks may come from newspapers, popular books, or interviews with professionals as reported in the media (e.g., an oil tanker runs aground and creates an environmental crisis, a drought occurs in an underdeveloped country causing famine, a technological breakthrough presents a moral dilemma). The tasks should center on issues, concepts, or problems that are important to your context area. In other words, they should be the same issues, concepts, and problems that important people who are working in the field face every day.

Here are some questions to get you started on Step 2, suggested by Wiggins (1992):

- What does the "doing of mathematics, history, science, art, writing, and so forth" look and feel like to professionals who make their living working in those fields in the real world?

- What are the projects and tasks performed by those professionals that can be adapted to school instruction?

- What are the roles—or habits of mind—that those professionals acquire that learners can re-create in the classroom?

The tasks you create may involve debates, mock trials, presentations to a city commission, re-enactments of historical events, science experiments, job responsibilities (e.g., a travel agent, weather forecaster, park ranger), etc. Regardless of the specific context, they should present the learner with a challenge.

For example, consider the following social studies performance test (adapted from Wiggins, 1992):

> *You and several travel agent colleagues have been assigned the responsibility of designing a trip to China for 12 to 14-year-olds. Prepare an extensive brochure for a month-long cultural exchange trip. Include itinerary, modes of transportation, costs, suggested budget, clothing, health considerations, areas of cultural sensitivity, language considerations, and other information necessary for a family to decide if they want their child to participate.*

Notice that this example presents learners with the following:

1. A hands-on exercise or problem to solve, which produces

2. An observable outcome or product (typed business letter, a map, graph, piece of clothing, multimedia presentation, poem, etc.), such that the teacher

3. Can observe and assess not only the product but also the process used to get there.

Designing the content for a performance test involves equal parts of inspiration and perspiration. While there is no formula or recipe to follow that guarantees a valid performance test, the following criteria can help guide you in revising and refining the task.

The Requirements for Task Mastery Should Be Clear without Revealing the Solution While your tasks should be complex, the final product should be clear. Learners should not have to question whether they are finished, or if they have provided what you want. They should, however, have to think long and hard about how to complete the task. As you refine the task, make sure you can visualize what mastery of the task looks like and identify the skills that can be inferred from it.

The Task Should Represent a Specific Activity from Which Generalizations about the Learner's Knowledge, Thinking Ability, and Habits of Mind Can Be Made What performance tests lack in breadth of coverage, they make up in depth. In other words, they allow you to observe a wide range of behavior in a narrow domain of skill. The type of tasks you choose should be complex enough and rich enough in detail to allow you to draw conclusions about transfer and generalization to other tasks. Ideally, you should be able to identify about eight to ten important performance tasks for an entire course of study (one or two a unit) that assess the essential performance outcomes you wish your learners to achieve.

The Tasks Should Be Complex Enough to Allow for Multimodal Assessment Most assessment tends to depend on the written word. Performance tests, however, are designed to allow learners to demonstrate learning through a variety of modalities. In science, for example, one could make direct observations of students while they investigate a problem using laboratory equipment, have students give oral explanations of what they did, require them to record procedures and conclusions in notebooks, prepare an exhibit of their project, and solve short-answer paper and pencil problems. This will be more time-consuming than a multiple-choice test but will provide unique information about your learners' achievement untapped by other assessment methods. Shavelson and Baxter (1992) have shown that performance tests allow teachers to draw different conclusions about a learner's problem-solving ability than do higher order multiple-choice tests or restricted response essay tests that ask learners to analyze, interpret, and evaluate information.

The Tasks Should Yield Multiple Solutions where Possible, Each with Costs and Benefits Performance testing is not a form of practice or drill. It should involve more than simple tasks for which there is one solution. Performance tests should be nonalgorithmic (the path of action is not fully specified in advance), complex (the total solution cannot be seen from any one vantage point), and involve judgment and interpretation.

The Tasks Should Require Self-Regulated Learning Performance tests should require considerable mental effort and place high demands on the persistence and determination of the individual learner. The learner should be required to use cognitive strategies to arrive at a solution rather than depend on coaching at various points in the assessment process.

Step 3: Specifying the Scoring Rubrics

One of the principal limitations of performance tests is the time required to score them. Just as these tests require time and effort on the part of the learner, they demand similar commitment from teachers when scoring them. True–false, multiple-choice, and short-answer questions are significantly easier to score than projects, portfolios, or performances. In addition, the latter accomplishments force teachers to make difficult choices over how much qualities such as effort, participation, and cooperation count in the final score.

Given the challenges confronting teachers who use performance tests, there is a temptation to limit the scoring criteria to those qualities of performance that are easiest to rate rather than the most important required for doing an effective job. Resorting to scoring what is easiest or least controversial can turn a well-thought-out and authentic performance test into an inaccurate one. Your goal when scoring performance tests is to do justice to the time spent developing them and the effort expended by students taking them. You can accomplish this by developing carefully constructed scoring systems, called rubrics.

By giving careful consideration to rubrics, you can develop a scoring system for performance tests that minimizes the arbitrariness of your judgments while holding learners to high standards of achievement. Here are some of the important considerations in developing rubrics for a performance test.

Develop Rubrics for a Variety of Accomplishments   In general, performance tests require four types of accomplishments from learners:

Products:	Poems, essays, charts, graphs, exhibits, drawings, maps, etc.
Complex cognitive processes:	Skills in acquiring, organizing, and using information (see Figure 8.3).
Observable performance:	Physical movements as in dance, gymnastics, or typing; oral presentations; use of specialized equipment as in focusing a microscope; following a set of procedures as when dissecting a frog, bisecting an angle, or following a recipe
Habits of mind and social skills:	Mental and behavioral habits, (such as persistence and cooperation) and recognition skills.

As the list suggests, the effect of your teaching may be realized in a variety of ways.

Choose a Scoring System Best Suited for the type of Accomplishment You Want to Measure   In general, there are three categories of rubrics to use when scoring performance tests: checklists, rating scales, and holistic scoring. Each has certain strengths and limitations, and each is more or less suitable for scoring products, cognitive processes, performances, and social skills.

Checklists   Checklists contain lists of behaviors, traits, or characteristics that can be scored as either present or absent. They are best suited for complex behaviors or performances that can be divided into a series of clearly defined, specific actions. Dissecting a frog, bisecting an angle, balancing a scale, making an audio tape recording, or tying a shoe are behaviors that require sequences of actions that can be clearly identified and listed on a checklist. Checklists are scored on a yes/no, present or absent, 0 or 1 point basis and should provide the opportunity for observers to indicate that they had no opportunity to observe the performance. Some checklists also include frequent mistakes that learners make when performing the task. In such cases, a score of +1 may be given for each positive behavior, −1 for each mistake, and 0 for no opportunity to observe. Figures 8.5 and 8.6 show checklists for using a microscope and a calculator.

Rating Scales   Rating scales are typically used for those aspects of a complex performance that do not lend themselves to yes/no or present/absent type judgments. The most common form of a rating scale is one that assigns numbers to categories of performance. Figure 8.7 shows a rating scale for judging elements of writing in a term paper. This scale

No opportunity to observe	Observed	
☐	☐	Wipes slide with lens paper
☐	☐	Placed drop or two of culture on slide
☐	☐	Adds a few drops of water
☐	☐	Places slide on stage
☐	☐	Turns to low power
☐	☐	Looks through eyepiece with one eye
☐	☐	Adjusts mirror
☐	☐	Turns to high power
☐	☐	Adjusts for maximum enlargement and resolution

FIGURE 8.5   Checklist for using a microscope.

No opportunity to observe	Observed	
☐	☐	Knows how to turn calculator on
☐	☐	Can "key in" ten numbers consecutively, without hitting adjacent keys
☐	☐	Can quickly add three 2-digit numbers, without error
☐	☐	Knows how to position keyboard and to rest arm and elbow for maximum comfort and accuracy
☐	☐	Knows how to reposition display screen to reduce reflection and glare, when necessary
☐	☐	Pushes keys with positive, firm motions
☐	☐	Can feel when a key touch is insufficiently firm to activate calculator

FIGURE 8.6   Checklist for using an electronic calculator.

focuses the rater's observations on certain aspects of the performance (accuracy, logic, organization, style, etc.) and assigns numbers to five degrees of performance.

Most numerical rating scales use an analytical scoring technique called primary trait scoring (Sax, 1989). This type of rating requires that the test developer first identify the most salient characteristics or primary traits of greatest importance when observing the product, process, or performance. Then, for each trait, the developer assigns numbers (usually 1–5) that represent degrees of performance.

Quality and accuracy of ideas				
1	2	3	4	5
Very limited investigation; little or no material related to the facts.		Some investigation and attention to the facts are apparent.		Extensive investigation; good detail and representation of the facts.

Logical development of ideas				
1	2	3	4	5
Very little orderly development of ideas; presentation is confusing and hard to follow.		Some logical development of ideas, but logical order needs to be improved.		Good logical development; ideas logically connected and built upon one another.

Organization of ideas				
1	2	3	4	5
No apparent organization. Lack of paragraphing and transitions.		Organization is mixed; some of the ideas not adequately separated from others with appropriate transitions.		Good organization and paragraphing; clear transitions between ideas.

Style, individuality				
1	2	3	4	5
Style bland and inconsistent, or "borrowed."		Some style and individuality beginning to show.		Good style and individuality; personality of writer shows through.

Words and phrasing				
1	2	3	4	5
Wording trite; extensive use of clichés.		Some word choices awkward.		Appropriate use of words and phrasing work to sharpen ideas.

FIGURE 8.7 Rating scale for themes and term papers that emphasizes interpretation and organization.

Figure 8.8 displays a numerical rating scale that uses primary trait scoring to rate problem solving (Szetela & Nicol, 1992). In this system, problem solving is subdivided into the primary traits of understanding the problem, solving the problem, and answering the problem. For each trait, points are assigned to certain aspects or qualities of the trait. Notice how the designer of this rating scale identified both characteristics of effective and ineffective problem solving.

Two key questions are usually addressed when designing scoring systems for rating scales using primary trait scoring:

1. What are the most important characteristics that show a high degree of the trait?

2. What are the errors most justifiable for achieving a lower score?

Answering those questions can prevent raters from assigning higher or lower scores on the basis of performance that may be trivial or unrelated to the purpose of the performance test, such as the quantity rather than quality of a performance. One of the advantages of rating scales is that they focus the scorer on specific and relevant aspects of a performance. Without the breakdown of important traits, successes, and relevant errors provided by these scales, a scorer's attention may be diverted to aspects of performance that are unrelated to the purpose of the performance test.

Holistic Scoring   Holistic scoring is used when the rater is more interested in estimating the overall quality of the performance and assigning a numerical value to that quality than assigning points for the addition or omission of a specific aspect of performance. Holistic scoring is typically used in evaluating extended essays, term papers, or some artistic performances such as dance or musical creations.

For example, a rater might decide to score an extended essay question or term paper on an A–F rating scale. In this case, it is important for the rater to have a model paper that

Understanding the problem

0 – No attempt
1 – Completely misinterprets the problem
2 – Misinterprets major part of the problem
3 – Misinterprets minor part of the problem
4 – Complete understanding of the problem

Solving the problem

0 – No attempt
1 – Total inappropriate plan
2 – Partially correct procedure but with major fault
3 – Substantially correct procedure with major omission or procedural error
4 – A plan that could lead to a correct solution with no arithmetic errors

Answering the problem

0 – No answer or wrong answer based upon an inappropriate plan
1 – Copying error, computational error, partial answer for problem with multiple answers; no answer statement; answer labeled incorrectly
2 – Correct solution

FIGURE 8.8 Analytic scale for problem solving.

exemplifies each score category. After having created or selected these models from the set to be scored, the rater again reads each paper and then assigns each to one of the categories. A model paper for each category (A–F) helps ensure that all the papers assigned to a given category are of comparable quality.

Holistic scoring systems can be more difficult to use for performances than for products. For the former, some experience in rating the performance, for example, dramatic rendition, oral interpretations, debate, etc., may be required. In these cases, audio or video tapes from past classes can be helpful as models representing different categories of performance.

Combining Scoring Systems   As suggested, good performance tests require learners to demonstrate their achievements through a variety of primary traits, for example, cooperation, research, delivery, etc. Several ratings, therefore, may need to be combined from checklists, rating scales, and holistic impressions to arrive at a total assessment. Figure 8.9 shows how scores across several traits for a current events project might be combined to provide a single performance score.

Checklist (Assign 1 or 0 points)   Total points (5)

— Interviewed four people
— Cited current references
— Typed
— No spelling errors
— Included title and summary page

Rating (Circle numbers which best represent quality of the presentation.)

Total points (9)

Persuasiveness

1	2	3
Lacks enthusiasm	Somewhat unanimated	Highly convincing

Delivery

1	2	3
Unclear, mumbled a lot	Often failed to look at audience, somewhat unclear	Clear, forceful delivery

Sensitivity to audience

1	2	3
Rarely looked at or noticed audience	Answered some questions, not always aware when audience didn't understand	Encouraged questions, stopped and clarified when saw that audience didn't understand

Holistic rating   Total points (3)

What is your overall impression of the quality of the project?

1	2	3
Below average	Average	Clearly outstanding

Total Points (17)

FIGURE 8.9   Combined scoring rubric for current events project.

Comparing the Three Scoring Systems Each of the three scoring systems has its particular strengths and weaknesses. Table 8.1 serves as a guide in choosing a particular scoring system for a given type of performance, according to the following criteria:

TABLE 8.1 The Strength of Three Performance-Based Scoring Systems According to Five Measurement Criteria

	Ease of construction	Scoring efficiency	Reliability	Defensibility	Feedback	More suitable for
Checklists	low	moderate	high	high	high	procedures
Rating scales	moderate	moderate	moderate	moderate	moderate	attitudes, products, social skills
Holistic scoring	high	high	low	low	low	products and processes

1. **Ease of construction** refers to the time involved in generating a comprehensive list of the important aspects or traits of successful and unsuccessful performance. Checklists, for example, are particularly time-consuming, while holistic scoring is not.

2. **Scoring efficiency** refers to the amount of time required to score various aspects of the performance and sum these scores into an overall score.

3. **Reliability** refers to the likelihood of two raters independently coming up with a similar score; or the likelihood of the same rater coming up with a similar score on two separate occasions.

4. **Defensibility** refers to the ease with which you can explain your score to a student or parent who challenges it.

5. **Quality of feedback** refers to the amount of information that the scoring system gives to learners or parents concerning strengths and weaknesses of their performance.

Limit the Number of Points Limit the number of points that the assessment or component of the assessment is worth to that which can be reliably discriminated. For example, 25 points assigned to a particular product or procedure assumes that the rater can discriminate 25 degrees of quality. When faced with more degrees of quality than can be detected, a typical rater may assign some points arbitrarily, reducing the reliability of the assessment.

On what basis should points be assigned to a response on a performance test? On the one hand, you want a response to be worth enough points to allow you to differentiate subtle differences in response quality. On the other hand, you want to avoid assigning too many points to a response, the complexity of which does not lend itself to complex discriminations. Assigning one or two points to a math question requiring complex problem solving would not allow you to differentiate among outstanding, above average, average, and poor responses. Yet, assigning 30 points to this same answer would seriously challenge your ability to distinguish a rating of 15 from a rating of 18. Two considerations can help in making decisions about the size and complexity of a rating scale.

The first is that a scoring model can be prepared wherein the rater specifies the exact performance—or examples of acceptable performance—that corresponds with each scale point. The ability to successfully define distinct criteria can then determine the number of scale points that are defensible. A second consideration is that, although it is customary for homework, paper and pencil tests, and report cards to use a 100 point (percent) scale, scale points derived from performance assessments do not need to add up to 100. In Chapter 11 we will indicate how to assign marks to performance tests and how to integrate them with other aspects of an overall grading system (e.g., homework, paper and pencil tests, classwork) including student portfolios.

Step 4: Specifying Testing Constraints

Should performance tests have time limits? Should learners be allowed to correct their mistakes? Can they consult references or ask for help from other learners? Were these questions asked of a multiple-choice test, most test developers would respond negatively without much hesitation. But performance tests confront the designer with the following dilemma: If performance tests are designed to confront learners with real-world challenges, why shouldn't they be allowed to tackle these challenges as real-world people do?

In the world outside of the classroom, mathematicians make mistakes and correct them, journalists write first drafts and revise them, weather forecasters make predictions and change them. These workers can consult references to help them solve problems and consult with colleagues. Why then shouldn't learners who are working on performance tests that simulate similar problems be allowed the same working (or testing) conditions? But even outside the classroom, professionals have constraints on their performance, such as deadlines, limited office space, and outmoded equipment. So how does a teacher decide which conditions to impose during a performance test? Before examining this question, let's look at some of the typical conditions imposed on learners during tests.

The following are among the most common forms of test constraints:

1. **Time.** How much time should a learner have to prepare, rethink, revise, and finish a test?
2. **Reference material.** Should learners be able to consult dictionaries, textbooks, notes, etc., as they take a test?
3. **Other people.** May learners ask for help from peers, teachers, experts, etc. as they take a test or complete a project?
4. **Equipment.** May learners use computers, calculators, etc. to help them solve problems?
5. **Prior knowledge of the task.** How much information on what they will be tested should learners receive in advance?
6. **Scoring criteria.** Should learners know the standards by which the teacher will score the assessment?

Wiggins (1992) recommends that teachers take an "Authenticity Test" to decide which of these constraints to impose on a performance assessment. His "Authenticity Test" involves answering the following questions:

1. What kinds of constraints authentically replicate the constraints and opportunities facing the performer in the real world?

2. What kinds of constraints tend to bring out the best in apprentice performers and producers?

3. What are the appropriate or authentic limits one should impose on the availability of the six resources previously listed?

Objective tests, by the nature of the questions asked, require numerous constraints during the testing conditions. Performance tests, on the other hand, are direct forms of assessment in which real-world conditions and constraints play an important role in demonstrating the competencies desired.

A FINAL WORD

Performance assessments create challenges that objective and essay tests do not. Performance grading requires greater use of judgment than do true–false or multiple-choice questions. These judgments will be more indicative of your learners' performance if (1) the performance to be judged (process and product) is clearly specified, (2) the ratings or criteria in making the judgments are determined beforehand, and (3) more than a single rater independently grades the performance and an average is taken.

Using video or audio tapes can enhance the validity of performance assessments when direct observation of performance is required. Furthermore, performance assessments need not take place at one time for the whole class. Learners can be assessed at different times, individually or in small groups. For example, learners can rotate through classroom learning centers and be assessed when the teacher feels they are acquiring mastery.

Finally, don't lose sight of the fact that performance assessments are meant to serve and enhance instruction rather than being simply an after-the-fact test given to assign a grade. When tests serve instruction, they can be given at a variety of times and in as many settings and contexts as instruction requires. Some performance assessments can sample the behavior of learners as they receive instruction or be placed within ongoing classroom activities rather than consume extra time during the day.

SUMMARY

This chapter introduced you to performance-based assessment. Its main points are as follows:

1. The four steps to constructing a performance assessment are deciding what to test, designing the assessment context, specifying the scoring rubrics, and specifying the testing constraints.

2. Some questions to ask in designing the performance assessment context are (1) what does the "doing" of math, history etc., look and feel like to professionals, (2) what projects and tasks are performed by these professionals, and (3) what roles— or habits of mind— do professionals assume?

3. A good performance assessment includes a hands-on exercise or problem, an observable outcome, and a process that can be observed.

4. A performance test can require five types of accomplishments from learners: products, complex cognitive processes, observable performance, habits of mind, and social skills. These performances can be scored with checklists, rating scales, or holistic scales.

5. Rubrics are scoring standards composed of model answers that are used to score performance tests. They are samples of acceptable responses against which the rater compares a student's performance.

6. Primary trait scoring is a type of rating that requires that the test developer first identify the most relevant characteristics or primary traits of importance.

7. Checklists contain lists of behaviors, traits, or characteristics that can be scored as either present or absent. They are best suited for complex behaviors or for performances that can be divided into a series of clearly defined, specific actions.

8. Rating scales assign numbers to categories representing different degrees of performance. They are typically used for those aspects of a complex performance, such as attitudes, products, and social skills, that do not lend themselves to yes/no or present/absent type judgments.

9. Holistic scoring estimates the overall quality of a performance by assigning a single numerical value to represent a specific category of accomplishment. They are used for measuring both products and processes.

10. Constraints that must be decided on when constructing and administering a performance test are amount of time allowed, use of reference material, help from others, use of specialized equipment, prior knowledge of the task, and scoring criteria.

FOR DISCUSSION AND PRACTICE

*1. Compare and contrast some of the reasons given to explain why we give conventional tests with those given to explain why we give performance assessments.

2. In your own words, explain how performance assessment can be a tool for instruction.

3. Using an example from your teaching area, explain the difference between a direct and an indirect measure of behavior.

4. Describe some habits of mind that might be required by professionals working in your teaching area and their importance in the workplace.

5. Describe how at least two school districts have implemented performance assessments. Indicate the behaviors they assess and by what means they are measured.

6. Would you agree or disagree with this statement: "An ideal performance test is a good teaching activity"? With a specific example in your teaching area, illustrate why you believe as you do.

7. Provide at least two learning outcomes and how you would measure them in your classroom that could indicate that a learner is (1) self-directed, (2) a collaborative worker, (3) a complex thinker, (4) a quality producer, and (5) a community contributor.

8. Describe what is meant by a "scoring rubric."

9. In your own words, how would you answer a critic of performance tests who says they do not measure generalizable thinking skills outside the classroom?

10. Identify several habits of mind and/or social skills for a unit you will be teaching that will be important to use in the real world.

11. Create a performance test of your own choosing that (1) requires a hands-on problem to solve and (2) results in an observable outcome for which (3) the process used by learners to achieve the outcome can be observed.

12. For the previous performance assessment, describe and give an example of the accomplishments—or rubrics—you would use in scoring the assessment.

13. For that same assessment, compose a checklist, rating scale, or holistic scoring method by which a learner's performance would be evaluated. Explain why you chose the scoring system you did, which may include a combination of the previously listed methods.

14. For your performance assessment, describe the constraints you would place on your learners pertaining to the time to prepare for and complete the activity; references that may be used; people who may be consulted, including other students; equipment allowed; prior knowledge about what is expected; and points or percentages you would assign to various degrees of their performance.

*Answers for Questions 1, 2, 3, 5, and 8 appear in Appendix F.

*PORTFOLIO ASSESSMENT**

AS WE SAW in the last chapter, performance assessment is a type of demonstration by which learners show their deep understanding of a particular area of learning. This demonstration is like a snapshot that captures what a learner has accomplished at a particular point in the academic year. There is another type of performance assessment that is more than a one-time picture of what a learner has accomplished. Its principal purpose is to tell a story of a learner's growth in proficiency, long-term achievement, and significant accomplishments in a given academic area. It is called portfolio assessment. The portfolio is a measure of deep understanding, like the performance demonstrations covered earlier. But, in addition, it shows growth in competence and understanding across the term or school year. Our definition of a portfolio is as follows:

> *a planned collection of learner achievement that documents what a student has accomplished and the steps taken to get there. The collection represents a collaborative effort among teacher and learner, to decide on portfolio purpose, content, and evaluation criteria.*

Portfolio assessment is based on the idea that a collection of a learner's work throughout the year is one of the best ways to show both final achievement and the effort put into getting there. You are already familiar with the idea of a portfolio. Painters, fashion designers, artisans, and writers assemble portfolios that embody their best work. Television and radio announcers compile video- and audio-taped excerpts of their best performances that are presented when interviewing for a job. A portfolio is their way of showing what they can really do.

Classroom portfolios serve a similar purpose. They show off a learner's best writing, art work, science projects, historical thinking, or mathematical achievement. They also show the steps the learner took to get there. They compile the learner's best work but they also include the works in progress: the early drafts, test runs, pilot studies, or preliminary trials. Thus they are an ideal way to assess final mastery, effort, reflection, and growth in learning that tell the learner's "story" of achievement.

The idea of classroom portfolio assessment has gained considerable support and momentum. Many school districts use portfolios and other types of exhibitions to help motivate effort and show achievement and growth in learning. While the reliability and validity of a classroom teacher's judgments are always a matter of concern, they are less

---

*This chapter was written with Martin L. Tombari. See Tombari, M. and Borich, G. (1999). Authentic assessment in the classroom: Applications and practice. Upper Saddle River, NJ: Prentice–Hall/Merrill.

so when the teacher has multiple opportunities to interact with learners and numerous occasions to observe their work and confirm judgments about their capabilities.

In this section we will first clarify what portfolio assessment is. Then, we will cover the most significant design considerations: deciding on the purpose of the portfolio; the cognitive outcomes to be assessed; who will plan it; what products to include; the criteria for assessing outcomes; the data that need to be collected to document progress, effort, and achievement; the logistics of where the products are kept; and, finally, how collaborative feedback will be given.

RATIONALE FOR THE PORTFOLIO

We believe that a portfolio's greatest potential is for showing teachers, parents, and learners a richer array of what students know and can do than paper and pencil tests and other "snapshot" assessments. If designed properly, portfolios can show a learner's ability to think and to solve problems, to use strategies and procedural-type skills, and to construct knowledge. In addition, they also tell something about a learner's persistence, effort, willingness to change, skill in monitoring their own learning, and ability to be self-reflective. One purpose for a portfolio is to give a teacher information about a learner that no other measurement tool can provide.

There are other reasons for using portfolios. Portfolios are also means to communicate to parents and other teachers the level of achievement that a learner has reached. Report card grades give us some idea of this, but portfolios supplement grades by showing parents, teachers, and learners the supporting evidence.

Portfolios are not an alternative to paper and pencil tests, essay tests, or performance tests. Each of those tools possesses validity for a purpose not served by a different tool. If you want to assess a learner's factual knowledge base (as discussed in Chapter 6), then objective-type tests are appropriate. If you are interested in a snapshot assessment of how well a learner uses a cognitive strategy, there are ways to do this that don't involve the work required for portfolio assessment. But, if you want to assess both achievement and growth in an authentic context, portfolios are a tool that you should consider.

Finally, portfolios are a way to motivate learners to higher levels of effort. They provide a seamless link between classroom teaching and assessment in a way that is consistent with modern cognitive theories of learning and instruction.

Ensuring Validity of the Portfolio

Let's say that one of the goals you have for the portfolio is to assess how well learners can communicate to a variety of audiences. However, you collect only formal samples of writing of the type you would submit to a literary journal. Or you want your math portfolio to assess growth in problem-solving ability. Yet, your evaluation criteria place too heavy an emphasis on the final solution. These are some of the pitfalls that can undermine the validity of the portfolio. In general, there are three challenges to validity that you need to address: representativeness, rubrics, and relevance.

Representativeness The best way to ensure representativeness is to be clear at the outset about the cognitive learning skills and dispositions that you want to assess and to require a variety of products that reflect these. You want the samples of writing, scientific thinking, mathematical problem solving, or woodworking to reflect the higher order thinking skills, procedural skills, or dispositions that you want the portfolio to measure.

Rubrics You have already had practice at designing rubrics in Chapter 8. The same considerations for designing clear criteria to assess complex performances or demonstrations also apply to assessing portfolios. You will want criteria for assessing both individual entries and the portfolio as a whole. You can accomplish this by developing carefully articulated scoring systems, called rubrics. By giving careful consideration to rubrics, you can develop a scoring system that minimizes the arbitrariness of your judgments while holding learners to high standards of achievement. We will look at some important considerations for developing portfolio rubrics shortly.

Relevance Assembling the portfolio shouldn't demand abilities of the learner extraneous to the ones you want to assess. A second-grade geography portfolio whose purpose is to reflect skill in map making shouldn't demand fine motor skills beyond what you would expect a 7-year-old to possess. Likewise, a junior high school science portfolio designed to reflect problem solving shouldn't require the reading of scientific journals that are beyond the ability of a ninth grader to understand. Measurement devices often fail to measure what they intend to measure (i.e. lack validity) because they require learner skills that are extraneous to those the instrument was built to measure.

DEVELOPING PORTFOLIO ASSESSMENTS

Now that you've given some consideration to validity, let's get started on building a system for portfolio assessment for your teaching area.

Step 1: Deciding on the Purposes for a Portfolio

Have your learners think about their purpose in assembling a portfolio. Having learners identify for themselves the purpose of the portfolio is one way to increase the authenticity of the task. We encourage you to use this as part of your teaching strategy. However, your learners' purposes for the portfolio (e.g., getting a job with the local news station) won't necessarily coincide with yours (e.g., evaluating your teaching). In this section we discuss how to be clear about your purposes at the outset of portfolio design.

Classroom level purposes that portfolios can achieve include the following:

- Monitoring student progress.
- Communicating what has been learned to parents.
- Passing on information to subsequent teachers.
- Evaluating how well something was taught.
- Showing off what has been accomplished.
- Assigning a course grade.

Step 2: Identifying Cognitive Skills and Dispositions

Portfolios, like performance assessments, are measures of deep understanding and genuine achievement. They can measure growth and development of competence in areas like knowledge construction (e.g. knowledge organization), cognitive strategies (analysis, interpretation, planning, organizing, revising), procedural skills (clear communication, editing, drawing, speaking, building), and metacognition (self-monitoring, self-reflection) as well as certain dispositions—or habits of mind—like flexibility, adaptability, acceptance of criticism, persistence, collaboration, and desire for mastery. Throughout this text you have had practice in specifying different types of cognitive outcomes and in planning to assess them. Apply that same practice to specifying what you want to know about your learners from their portfolios. As part of your teaching strategy, you will want to discuss these outcomes with your learners.

Step 3: Deciding Who Will Plan the Portfolio

When deciding who will plan the portfolio, consider what's involved in preparing gymnasts or skaters for a major tournament. The parent hires a coach. The coach, pupil, and parent plan together the routines, costumes, practice times, music, and so on. They are a team whose sole purpose is to produce the best performance possible. The gymnast or skater wants to be the best that he or she can be. He or she also wants to please parents and coaches and wants to meet their expectations. The atmosphere is charged with excitement, dedication, and commitment to genuine effort.

That is the atmosphere you are trying to create when using portfolios. You, the learner, and parents are a team for helping the student to improve writing, math reasoning, or scientific thinking and to assemble examples of this growing competence. Learners want to show what they can do and to verify the trust and confidence that you and their family have placed in them. The portfolio is their recital, their tournament, their competition. The principal stakeholders in the use of the portfolio are you, your learners, and their parents. Involve parents by sending home an explanation of portfolio assessment and, in addition, by asking that parents and students discuss its goals and content.

Step 4: Deciding Which Products to Put in the Portfolio and How Many Samples of Each Product

There are two key decisions to be considered: ownership and the portfolio's link with instruction. Ownership refers to your learners' perception that the portfolio contains what they want it to. You have considered this issue in Step 3. By involving learners and their parents in the planning process, you enhance their sense of ownership. You also do this by giving them a say in what goes into the portfolio. The task is to balance your desire to enhance ownership with your responsibility to see that the content of the portfolio measures the cognitive skills and dispositions that you identified in Step 3.

Both learners and their parents need to see that your class instruction focuses on teaching the skills necessary to fashion the portfolio's content. You don't want to require products in math, science, or social studies that you didn't prepare learners to create. If it's a writing portfolio, then your instructional goals must include teaching skills in writing poems, essays, editorials, or whatever your curriculum specifies. The same holds for science, math, geography, or history portfolios. In deciding what you would like to see included in your learners' portfolios, you will have to ensure that you only require products that your learners were prepared to develop.

The best way to satisfy learner needs for ownership and your needs to measure what you teach is to require certain categories of products that match your instructional purposes and cognitive outcomes, and to allow learners and parents to choose the samples within each category. For example, you may require that an eighth-grade math portfolio contain the following categories of math content (Lane, 1993):

1. "Number and operation," in which the learner demonstrates the understanding of the relative magnitude of numbers, the effects of operations on numbers, and the ability to perform those mathematical operations;

2. "Estimation," in which the learner demonstrates understanding of basic facts, place value, and operations; mental computation; tolerance of error; and flexible use of strategies; and

3. "Predictions," in which the learner demonstrates ability to make predictions based on experimental probabilities; to systematically organize and describe data; to make conjectures based on data analyses; and to construct and interpret graphs, charts, and tables.

Learners and their parents would have a choice of which assignments to include in each of the categories listed. For each sample the learner includes a brief statement about what it says about his or her development of mathematical thinking skills.

Another example could be a high school writing portfolio. The teacher requires that the following categories of writing be in the portfolio: persuasive editorial, persuasive essay, narrative story, autobiography, and dialogue. Learners choose the samples of writing in each category. For each sample they include a cover letter that explains why the sample was chosen and what it shows about the learner's development as a writer.

You will also have to decide how many samples of each content category to include in the portfolio. For example, do you require two samples of persuasive writing, one of criticism, three of dialogue, etc.? Shavelson, Gao, and Baxter (1991) suggest that at least eight products or tasks over different topic areas may be needed to obtain a reliable estimate of performance from portfolios.

Step 5: Building the Portfolio Rubrics

In Step 2 you identified the major cognitive skills and dispositions that your portfolio will measure. In Step 4 you specified the content categories that your portfolio will contain. Now you must decide what good, average, and poor performance look like for each entry in the portfolio and for the portfolio as a whole.

You already have experience with rubrics from Chapter 8. You will follow the same process here. For each cognitive learning outcome for each category of content in the portfolio, list the primary traits or characteristics that you think are important. Next, construct a rating scale that describes the range of student performance that can occur for each trait. Figures 9.1 and 9.2 show how this was done for the essay writing content area.

Essay Portfolio Rating Form.

___ First Draft
___ Second Draft
___ Final Draft

To be completed by student:

1. Date submitted: _____

2. Briefly explain what this essay says about you. _____

_____

3. What do you like best about this piece of writing? _____

_____

4. What do you want to improve on the next draft? _____

_____

5. If this is your final draft, will you include this in your portfolio and why? _____

_____

To be completed by teacher:

1. Quality of Reflection

Rating	Description
5	States very clearly what he/she likes most and least about the essay. Goes into much detail about how to improve the work.
4	States clearly what he/she likes and dislikes about the essay. Gives detail about how to improve the work.
3	States his/her likes and dislikes but could be clearer. Gives some detail about how the work will be improved.
2	Is vague about likes and dislikes. Gives few details about how essay will be improved.
1	No evidence of any reflection on the work.

2. Writing Conventions

Rating	Description
5	The use of writing conventions is very effective. No errors evident. These conventions are fluid and complex: spelling, punctuation, grammar usage, sentence structure.
4	The use of writing conventions is effective. Only minor errors evident. These conventions are nearly all effective: punctuation, grammar usage, sentence structure, spelling.
3	The use of writing conventions is somewhat effective. Errors don't interfere with meaning. These conventions are somewhat effective: punctuation, grammar usage, sentence structure, spelling.
2	Errors in the use of writing conventions interfere with meaning. These conventions are limited and uneven: punctuation, grammar usage, sentence structure, spelling.
1	Major errors in the use of writing conventions obscure meaning. Lacks understanding of punctuation, grammar usage, sentence structure, spelling.

FIGURE 9.1 Essay portfolio rating form.

3. Organization

Rating	Description
5	Clearly makes sense.
4	Makes sense.
3	Makes sense for the most part.
2	Attempted but does not make sense.
1	Does not make sense.

4. Planning (1st draft only)

Rating	Description
5	Has clear idea of audience. Goals are very clear and explicit. An overall essay plan is evident.
4	Has idea of audience. Goals are clear and explicit. Has a plan for the essay.
3	Somewhat clear about the essay's audience. Goals are stated but somewhat vague. Plan for whole essay somewhat clear.
2	Vague about who the essay is for. Goals are unclear. No clear plan evident.
1	Writing shows no evidence of planning.

5. Quality of Revision (2nd draft only)

Rating	Description
5	Follows up on all suggestions for revision. Revisions are a definite improvement.
4	Follows up on most suggestions for revision. Revisions improve on the previous draft.
3	Addresses some but not all suggested revisions. Revisions are a slight improvement over earlier draft.
2	Ignores most suggestions for revision. Revisions made do not improve the earlier draft.
1	Made only a minimal attempt to revise, if at all.

Sum of ratings _____

_____

Average of ratings: _____

_____

Comments: _____

_____

_____

_____

_____

FIGURE 9.1 *continued.*

Figures 9.3 and 9.4 show examples from a math portfolio under the content category of problem solving. The teacher wants to measure the cognitive outcomes of knowledge base, cognitive strategies, communication, and reflection.

Essay Cumulative Rating Form.

(Attach to each completed essay)

_____ Essay Sample One

_____ Essay Sample Two

Student _____

Draft 1		**Draft 2**		**Final Draft**	
Criteria	**Rating**	**Criteria**	**Rating**	**Criteria**	**Rating**
Reflection	3	Reflection	4	Reflection	3
Conventions	3	Conventions	4	Conventions	4
Organization	4	Organization	5	Organization	5
Planning	4	Planning	4	Planning	3
Average	3.5	Average	4.25	Average	3.75

Teacher: Comments on final essay development _____

_____

Student: Comments on final essay development _____

_____

Parent: Comments on final essay development _____

_____

Included in portfolio: ____ Yes

____ No

FIGURE 9.2 Essay cumulative rating form.

Once you design rubrics for each entry in the portfolio, you next design scoring criteria for the portfolio as a whole product. Some traits to consider when developing a scoring mechanism for the entire portfolio are

thoroughness

variety

growth or progress

overall quality

self-reflection

flexibility

organization

appearance

Choose among these traits or include others and build five-point rating scales for each characteristic.

The key to Step 5 is to do the following:

1. For each cognitive skill and disposition in each content area, build your scoring rubrics.

2. Put these on a form that allows you to include ratings of early drafts.

3. Prepare a rating for the portfolio as a whole.

Math Problem Solving Portfolio Rating Form.

Content Categories:

___ Problem solving   ___ Problem One

___ Numbers and operations   ___ Problem Two

___ Estimation   ___ Final Problem

___ Predictions

To be completed by student:

1. Date submitted: _____

2. What does this problem say about you as a problem solver? _____

_____

3. What do you like best about how you solved this problem? _____

_____

4. How will you improve your problem solving skill on the next problem? _____

_____

To be completed by teacher:

1. Quality of Reflection

Rating	Description
5	Has excellent insight into his/her problem-solving abilities and clear ideas of how to get better.
4	Has good insight into his/her problem-solving abilities and some ideas of how to get better.
3	Reflects somewhat on problem-solving strengths and needs. Has some idea of how to improve as a problem solver.
2	Seldom reflects on problem-solving strengths and needs. Has little idea of how to improve as a problem solver.
1	Has no concept of him- or herself as a problem solver.

2. Mathematical Knowledge

Rating	Description
5	Shows deep understanding of the problems, math concepts, and principles. Uses appropriate math terms and all calculations are correct.
4	Shows good understanding of math problems, concepts, and principles. Uses appropriate math terms most of the time. Few computational errors.
3	Shows understanding of some of the problems, math concepts, and principles. Uses some terms incorrectly. Contains some computation errors.
2	Errors in the use of many problems. Many terms used incorrectly.
1	Major errors in problems. Shows no understanding of math problems, concepts, and principles.

3. Strategic Knowledge

Rating	Description
5	Identifies all the important elements of the problem. Reflects an appropriate and systematic strategy for solving the problem; gives clear evidence of a solution process.

FIGURE 9.3   Math problem-solving portfolio rating form.

Rating	Description
4	Identifies most of the important elements of the problem. Reflects an appropriate and systematic strategy for solving the problem and gives clear evidence of a solution process most of the time.
3	Identifies some important elements of the problem. Gives some evidence of a strategy to solve the problems but process is incomplete.
2	Identifies few important elements of the problem. Gives little evidence of a strategy to solve the problems and the process is unknown.
1	Uses irrelevant outside information. Copies parts of the problem; no attempt at solution.

4. Communication

Rating	Description
5	Gives a complete response with a clear, unambiguous explanation; includes diagrams and charts when they help clarify explanation; presents strong arguments that are logically developed.
4	Gives good response with fairly clear explanation, which includes some use of diagrams and charts; presents good arguments that are mostly but not always logically developed.
3	Explanations and descriptions of problem solution are somewhat clear but incomplete; makes some use of diagrams and examples to clarify points but arguments are incomplete.
2	Explanations and descriptions of problem solution are weak; makes little, if any, use of diagrams and examples to clarify points; arguments are seriously flawed.
1	Ineffective communication; diagrams misrepresent the problem; arguments have no sound premise.

Sum of ratings: _____

Average of ratings: _____

Comments: _____

_____

_____

FIGURE 9.3 *continued.*

Step 6: Developing a Procedure to Aggregate All Portfolio Ratings

For each content category that you include in the portfolio, learners will receive a score for each draft and the final product. You will have to decide how to aggregate these scores into a final score or grade for each content area and, then, for the portfolio as a whole. Figures 9.2 and 9.4 are examples of a cumulative rating form in two content areas (essay and math) for one student. You will have one of these forms for each content area identified in Step 4. If you want a writing portfolio to include five areas of content (persuasive writing, dialogue, biography, criticism, and commentary), you will have five rating forms, each of which rates drafts and final product.

Math Problem Solving Cumulative Rating Form.

(Attach to problem-solving entries)

_____ Problem One

_____ Problem Two

_____ Final Problem

Student _____

Problem 1		Problem 2		Final Problem	
Criteria	**Rating**	**Criteria**	**Rating**	**Criteria**	**Rating**
Reflection	3	Reflection	4	Reflection	3
Knowledge	2	Knowledge	3	Knowledge	3
Strategies	2	Strategies	2	Strategies	2
Comm	2	Comm	2	Comm	2
Average	2.25	Average	2.75	Average	2.5

Teacher: Comments on problem-solving ability and improvement: _____

_____

Student: Comments on problem-solving ability and improvement: _____

_____

Parent: Comments on problem-solving ability and improvement: _____

_____

FIGURE 9.4   Math problem-solving cumulative rating form.

As you can see in Figures 9.2 and 9.4, the teacher averaged the ratings for the two preliminary drafts and the final one. The next step is to develop a rule or procedure for combining these three scores into an overall score. One procedure would be to compute a simple average of three scores. This method gives equal importance in the final score to the drafts and final product. Another procedure would be to assign greatest importance to the final product, lesser importance to the second draft, and least importance to the first draft. This is called weighting (see Chapter 11). If and how you weight scores is up to you. You might seek input from learners and parents, but there is no hard and fast rule about whether or which products in an area should be given more weight.

If you should decide to assign different importance or weight to the products in a content area, do the following:

1. Decide on the weight in terms of a percentage (e.g., first draft counts 20%, second draft counts 30%, and final draft counts 50% of final score). Make sure the percentages add up to 100%.

2. Take the average score for each product and multiply that by the weight. In our example as shown in Figure 9.2, this would involve the following calculations:

$$\text{Draft 1:} \qquad 3.50 \times 0.2 = 0.7$$
$$\text{Draft 2:} \qquad 4.25 \times 0.3 = 1.3$$
$$\text{Final:} \qquad 3.75 \times 0.5 = 1.9$$

3. Add up the products to get an overall score (e.g., 0.7 + 1.3 + 1.9 = 3.9 for the content area of essay writing). We will consider the meaning of this value shortly. (Had you not weighted, the average score would have been 3.8.)

Follow this same procedure for each content area. If you have five content areas in the portfolio, you will have five scores. Let's say that these are as follows:

Content Area	Score
Essay	3.9
Dialogue	4.0
Criticism	2.5
Biography	3.8
Commentary	2.0

The next step is to decide how to aggregate these scores. Again, you can choose to weight or not to weight. You may decide to involve learners and their parents in this decision. If you decide not to weight, the average rating for all the content areas is 3.2 (rounded to one decimal place).

Finally, assign a rating to the portfolio as a whole. Let's say that the rating came out to be a 4.5. Now you must decide how to include this rating in the overall portfolio grade. If you take an unweighted average, you assign as much importance to that one rating as you did to all the separate content ratings. That's probably not a good idea. Your average grade of 3.2 for the portfolio areas taken separately is a more reliable rating than your one rating of 4.5 for the whole portfolio. We recommend that you assign more weight to the former score than the latter—let's say 90% versus 10%:

$$3.2 \times 0.9 = 2.88$$
$$4.5 \times 0.1 = 0.45$$
$$\text{Final grade} = 2.88 + 0.45 = 3.33$$

This gives a final grade of 3.33, versus 3.85 if you had not weighted.

Now, let's consider what 3.33 (or 3.3 rounded) means in terms of the quality of the overall portfolio. In other words, how good is a 3.3 in indicating the competence of the learner? Making this decision involves evaluation.

Here is one way to assign meaning to our measurement of 3.3. Schools usually assign the following values to grades:

Grading Schemes			Meaning
90–100	A	E	Outstanding
80–89	B	S+	Above average
70–79	C	S	Average
60–69	D	S−	Below average
below 60	F	N	Failure, not at standard, etc.

When using five-point rating scales, we usually consider 3 as average, 1 as below standard, and 5 outstanding. Similarly, if you use a seven-point scale, a 3.5 would be average, ratings between 1 and 2 are below standard, and ratings between 6 and 7 are outstanding.

One way to assign value to a 3.3 would be to link the traditional grading systems and their conventional meanings to scores on the rating scale. Select a range of rating scale values that correspond to a letter or numerical grade in your school and link the two:

Average Rating	*Grade*
1.0–1.9	F, 50–59
2.0–2.5	D, 60–69
2.6–3.6	C, 70–79
3.6–4.3	B, 80–89
4.4–5.0	A, 90–100

If we use this chart, a 3.3 would represent a C grade, a numerical grade somewhere between 70 and 79, or a grade of satisfactory plus (S+). Depending on factors that we will discuss in Chapter 11, you may want to add plus and minus to your grading system. Or, decide that a C gets a grade of 75, C– gets a grade of 70, and C+ a grade of 79. Making those decisions before you begin grading the portfolios and evaluating each portfolio using the same criteria helps minimize subjectivity.

Step 7: Determining the Logistics

So far, you have accomplished these aspects of portfolio design:

1. Specified the purpose of the portfolio.
2. Identified the cognitive skills it will reflect.
3. Decided who will help plan it.
4. Decided what and how many products go in it.
5. Specified the rubrics by which to score it.
6. Developed a rating and grading scheme.

There are just a few details left.

Timelines   Your learners and their parents need to know exact dates when things are due. Point this out to your learners. This reinforces in your learners' minds the link between your teaching and what's required in the portfolio. Be prepared to revise some of your requirements. You may find that there's not enough time in the school year and not enough hours in a week for you to read all the drafts and products and get them back to your learners in a timely fashion.

How Products Are Turned in and Returned   Decide how, when, and where you want your learners to turn in their products. At the start of class? Placed in an "In" basket? Secured in a folder or binder? Returned in an "Out" basket? How will late assignments be handled? How do absent learners submit and get back assignments? Will there be penalties for late assignments?

Where Final Products Are Kept   Decide where the final products will be stored. Will it be the learner's responsibility to keep them safely at home? Or, do you want to store them so that they can be assembled easily for a final parent conference and passed on to other teachers? Remember that the products may include video or audio tapes, so a manila folder might not work. You may need boxes, filing cabinets, or closets.

Who Has Access to the Portfolio? Certainly you, learners, and parents have a right to see what's in it. But do other students, current and future teachers, or administrators? You might want learners (and their parents) to help make those decisions.

Plan a Final Conference Plan to have a final conference at the end of the year or term with individual learners and, if possible, their parents to discuss the portfolio and what it says about your learners' development and final achievement. Your learners can be responsible for conducting the conference, with a little preparation from you on how to do it. This final event can be a highly motivating force for your learners to produce an exemplary portfolio.

The following checklist will help you as you design and revise your portfolio assessment program. Consider it carefully when planning your portfolio assignment.

A Portfolio Development Checklist

1. What purpose(s) will your portfolio serve? (Check any that apply.)
   - ☐ Prepare a sample of best work for future teachers to see.
   - ☐ Communicate to parents what's been learned.
   - ☐ Evaluate my teaching.
   - ☐ Assign course grades.
   - ☐ Create collections of favorite or best work.
   - ☐ Document achievement for alternative credit.
   - ☐ Submission to a college or employer.
   - ☐ To show growth in skill and dispositions.
   - ☐ Other (specify) _____

2. What cognitive skills will be assessed by the individual entries?
   - ☐ Cognitive strategies (specify) _____
   - ☐ Deep understanding (specify) _____
   - ☐ Communication (specify) _____
   - ☐ Metacognition (specify) _____
   - ☐ Procedural skills (specify) _____
   - ☐ Knowledge construction (specify) _____
   - ☐ Other (specify) _____

3. What dispositions do you want the entries to reflect?
   - ☐ Flexibility.
   - ☐ Persistence.
   - ☐ Collaboration.
   - ☐ Acceptance of feedback.
   - ☐ Other (specify) _____

4. What criteria or rubrics will you use to judge the extent to which these skills and dispositions were achieved?

   _____

   _____

5. In rating the portfolio as a whole, what things will you look for?
   - ☐ Variety of entries.
   - ☐ Growth in reflection.
   - ☐ Growth in skill or performance.
   - ☐ Organization.
   - ☐ Presentation.

6. What kind of scale will you construct to rate the overall portfolio?

   _____

   _____

7. How will you combine all your ratings into a final grade?

   _____

   _____

8. Who will be involved in the planning process?
   - ☐ Learners.
   - ☐ Teacher.
   - ☐ Parents.

9. What content categories are included in the portfolio?

   _____

   _____

10. Will learners have a choice over content categories?
    - ☐ Yes.
    - ☐ No.

11. Who decides what samples to include in each content area?
    - ☐ Learner.
    - ☐ Teacher.
    - ☐ Parents.

12. How many samples will be included in each area?
    - ☐ One.
    - ☐ Two.
    - ☐ More than two.

13. Have you specified deadlines for the entries?
    - ☐ Yes.
    - ☐ No.

14. Have you developed forms to rate and summarize ratings for all drafts and final products?

☐ Yes (specify). _____

☐ No.

15. What are your instructions for how work gets turned in and returned?

_____

_____

16. Where will the portfolios be kept and who has access to them?

☐ Where (specify) _____

☐ When (specify) _____

17. Who will plan, conduct, and attend the final conference?

☐ Learner.

☐ Other teachers.

☐ Parents.

☐ Others (specify) _____

SUMMARY

Chapter 9 introduced you to the major issues related to the construction and scoring of portfolios. Its major points are as follows:

1. A portfolio is a planned collection of learner achievement that documents what a student has accomplished and the steps taken to get there.

2. Portfolios are a means of communicating to parents, learners, and other teachers the level of learning and performance that a learner has achieved.

3. Portfolios can measure growth and development of competence in areas such as knowledge construction (e.g., knowledge organization), cognitive strategies (analysis, interpretation, planning, organizing, revising), procedures skills (clear communication, editing, drawing, speaking), and metacognition (self-monitoring, self-reflection), as well as certain habits of mind—like flexibility, adaptability, acceptance of criticism, persistence, collaboration, and desire for mastery.

4. Portfolios are not substitutes for paper and pencil tests, essay tests, or performance tests. Each of those assessment tools possesses validity for a purpose not served by a different tool.

5. By utilizing actual tasks—projects, scripts, essays, research reports, demonstrations, models, etc.—the learner applies knowledge and understanding to exhibit the level of deep learning that has been acquired from your instruction.

6. Ownership refers to your learners' perception that the portfolio contains what they want it to. Having learners identify for themselves the purpose of the portfolio is one way to increase ownership.

7. Portfolio assessment is often the best and sometimes the only method for gauging your learners' level of deep learning. Planning and designing a portfolio assessment must be as systematic and methodical as constructing an objective test or essay exam.

8. Each cognitive skill and disposition for each portfolio content area should be identified and scoring rubrics should be developed.

9. Some traits to consider when developing a scoring mechanism for the entire portfolio are thoroughness, variety, growth or progress, overall quality, self-reflection, flexibility, organization, and appearance.

FOR PRACTICE

1. Identify three threats to the validity of a portfolio and indicate what you would do in the design of your portfolio to see that these threats are minimized.

2. Plan a real portfolio by answering each of the questions on the Portfolio Development Checklist. Check the boxes that apply and provide the necessary details, where requested.

3. Develop a portfolio rating form and cumulative rating form for the entries in your portfolio using Figures 9.1 and 9.2 as a guide. Be sure to include definitions for all the scale alternatives (e.g., 1 to 5) being rated, as illustrated in Figure 9.1.

4. Describe the procedure you will use to aggregate scores for all the portfolio ratings. By providing hypothetical ratings for the entries on your rating form, indicate, with actual numbers and averages, how you will (1) calculate weights, (2) take the average score for each entry, (3) add up all the entries to get an overall score, and (4) assign a grade symbol (e.g., A–F) to the average score.

CHAPTER 10

ADMINISTERING, ANALYZING, AND IMPROVING THE TEST OR ASSESSMENT

OVER THE LAST several chapters we have discussed various aspects of test planning and item construction. If you have written instructional objectives that include higher-level thinking, constructed a test blueprint, and written items that match your objectives, then more than likely you will have a good test or assessment. All the "raw material" will be there. However, sometimes the raw material, as good as it may be, can be rendered useless because of poorly assembled and administered paper and pencil tests. By now you know it requires a substantial amount of time to write objectives, put together a test blueprint, and write items. It is worth a little more time to properly assemble or package your test so that your efforts will not be wasted. Our goal for this chapter is to provide some suggestions to help you avoid common pitfalls in test assembly, administration, and scoring. Later in the chapter we will discuss considerations and techniques of test analysis. First, let's consider test assembly.

ASSEMBLING THE TEST

At this point let's assume you have

1. Written measurable instructional objectives;
2. Prepared a test blueprint, specifying the number of items for each content and process area; and
3. Written test items that match your instructional objectives.

Once you have completed these activities you are ready to:

1. Package the test
2. Reproduce the test

These components constitute what we are calling test assembly. Let's consider each a little more closely.

Packaging the Test

There are several packaging guidelines worth remembering, including grouping together items of similar format, arranging test items from easy to hard, properly spacing items, keeping items and options on the same page, placing illustrations near the descriptive material, checking for randomness in the answer key, deciding how students will record their answers, providing space for the test taker's name and the date, checking test directions for clarity, and proofreading the test before you reproduce and distribute it.

Group Together All Items of Similar Format   If you have all true–false items grouped together, all completion items together, and so on, the students will not have to "switch gears" to adjust to new formats. This will enable them to cover more items in a given time than if item formats were mixed throughout the test. Also, by grouping items of a given format together, only one set of directions per format section is necessary, which is another time-saver.

Arrange Test Items from Easy to Hard   Arranging test items according to level of difficulty should enable more students to answer the first few items correctly, thereby building confidence and, it is hoped, reducing test anxiety.

Space the Items for Easy Reading   If possible, try to provide enough blank space between items so that each item is distinctly separate from others. When items are crowded together, a student may inadvertently perceive a word, phrase, or line from a preceding or following item as part of the item in question. Naturally, this interferes with a student's capacity to demonstrate his or her true ability.

Keep Items and Options on the Same Page   There are few things more aggravating to a test taker than to have to turn the page to read the options for multiple-choice or matching items or to finish reading a true–false or completion item. To avoid this, do not begin an item at the bottom of the page unless you have space to complete the item. Not only will this eliminate having to carry items over to the next page, it will also minimize the likelihood that the last line or two of the item will be cut off when you reproduce the test.

Position Illustrations Near Descriptions   Place diagrams, maps, or other supporting material immediately above the item or items to which they refer. In other words, if items 9, 10, and 11 refer to a map of South America, locate the map above items 9, 10, and 11— not between 9 and 10 or between 10 and 11 and not below them. Also, if possible, keep any such stimuli and related questions on the same page to save the test taker time.

Check Your Answer Key   Be sure the correct answers follow a fairly random pattern. Avoid true–false patterns such as T F T F, etc., or T T F F, etc., and multiple-choice patterns such as D C B A D C B A, etc. At the same time, check to see that your correct answers are distributed about equally between true and false and among multiple-choice options.

Determine How Students Record Answers   Decide whether you want to have students record their answers on the test paper or on a separate answer sheet. In the lower elementary grades, it is generally a good idea to have students record answers on the test papers themselves. In the upper elementary and secondary grades, separate answer sheets can be used to facilitate scoring accuracy and to cut down on scoring time. Also, in the upper grades, learning to complete separate answer sheets will make students familiar with the process they will use when taking standardized tests.

Provide Space for Name and Date   Be sure to include a blank on your test booklet and/or answer sheet for the student's name and the date. This may seem an unnecessary suggestion, but it is not always evident to a nervous test taker that a name should be included on the test. Students are much more likely to remember to put their names on tests if space is provided.

Check Test Directions   Check your directions for each item format to be sure they are clear. Directions should specify

1. The numbers of the items to which they apply.
2. How to record answers.
3. The basis on which to select answers.
4. Criteria for scoring.

Proofread the Test   Proofread for typographical and grammatical errors before reproducing the test and make any necessary corrections. Having to announce corrections to the class just before the test or during the test will waste time and is likely to inhibit the test takers' concentration.

Before reproducing the test, it's a good idea to check off these steps. The checklist in Figure 10.1 can be used for this purpose.

Test Assembly Checklist

Put a check in the blank to the right of each statement after you've checked to see that it applies to your test.

	Yes	No
1. Are items of similar format grouped together?	___	___
2. Are items arranged from easy-to-hard levels of difficulty?	___	___
3. Are items properly spaced?	___	___
4. Are items and options on the same page?	___	___
5. Are diagrams, maps, and supporting material above designated items and on the same page with items?	___	___
6. Are answers random?	___	___
7. Have you decided whether an answer sheet will be used?	___	___
8. Are blanks for name and date included?	___	___
9. Have the directions been checked for clarity?	___	___
10. Has the test been proofread for errors?	___	___
11. Do items avoid racial and gender bias?	___	___

FIGURE 10.1   Test assembly checklist.

Reproducing the Test

Most test reproduction in the schools is done on photocopying machines. As you well know, the quality of such copies can vary tremendously. Regardless of how valid and reliable your test might be, poor copies will make it less so. Take the following practical steps to ensure that the time you spend constructing a valid and reliable test does not end in illegible copies.

Know the Photocopying Machine   Be sure you or the person you designate to do the reproduction understands how to operate the photocopying machine. There is some variation across models, and a few minutes of practice on a new machine is a worthwhile investment.

Specify Copying Instructions   If someone else will do the reproducing, be sure to specify that the copies are for an important test and not simply an enrichment exercise. Ask the clerk or aide to randomly inspect copies for legibility while running the copies and to be alert for blank or partially copied pages while collating, ordering, and stapling multipage tests.

File Original Test   Finally, retain the original or master in case you want to reuse the test or items within the test. Tell your clerk or aide to return the original to you—otherwise it may end up thrown away.

ADMINISTERING THE TEST

The test is ready. All that remains is to get the students ready and hand out the tests. Here is a series of suggestions to help your students psychologically prepare for the test:

Maintain a Positive Attitude   Try to induce a positive test-taking attitude. Of course, this consideration must be kept in mind long before the test is actually distributed. It helps to keep the main purposes of classroom testing in mind—to evaluate achievement and instructional procedures and to provide feedback to yourself and your students. Too often tests are used to punish ("Well, it's obvious the class isn't doing the readings, so we'll have a test today") or are used indiscriminately ("It's Tuesday, I guess I may as well give my class a test") or inappropriately ("I need a good evaluation from the principal; I'll give my class an easy test"). To the extent that you can avoid falling victim to such testing traps, you will be helping to induce and maintain a positive test-taking atmosphere.

Maximize Achievement Motivation   Try not to minimize the achievement aspect of the test. While you do not want to immobilize your students with fear, you do want them to try to do their best on the test. Encourage them to do so. If a student's grade will be influenced, avoid making comments such as, "We're just going to have an easy little quiz today; it's no big deal." Such an approach will probably minimize anxiety in very nervous test takers, which might improve their performance, but it may also serve to impair the test performance of students who need to take tests seriously in order to be motivated enough to do their best. In your class you will likely have both types of students. Keep your general statement about the test accurate. The test is something to be taken seriously and this should be clear to the class. Remember, you can always make reassuring or motivational comments individually to students.

Equalize Advantages   Try to equalize the advantages test-wise students have over non-test-wise students. Since you are interested in student achievement, and not how test-wise a student is (unless you are teaching a course in test-taking skills), the results will be more valid if the advantages of test-wiseness are minimized. You can do so by instructing the class when it is best to guess or not guess at an answer, and remind them about general test-taking strategies (for example: "Don't spend too much time on difficult items"; "Try all items, then return to those you are unsure of"; "Cross off options you've ruled out on matching or multiple-choice items"; "Check your answers for accuracy before turning in the test").

You may even want to take guessing into consideration when scoring the test. If time allows each student to attempt every item, a total score that is equal to the number of right answers may be perfectly adequate. In this case, students should be told to make an "educated" guess, even if they are not certain of the answer. However, the case may arise in which different students will attempt different numbers of items. This sometimes occurs when the test has a strict time limit, which may prevent some students from finishing. In this situation you may want to discourage guessing, that is, discourage the random filling out of unfinished answers seconds before the time limit is up.

A correction-for-guessing formula can be used to penalize the student for randomly answering test questions. A student's score that has been corrected for guessing will be equal to the number of questions answered incorrectly divided by the number of answer choices for an item minus 1 and, then, this amount subtracted from the total number of right answers.

$$\text{Score} = \text{Total right} - \frac{\text{Total wrong}}{\text{Number of answer choices} - 1}$$

For example, in a 50-item multiple-choice test where there are 4 possible answers and a student gets 44 answers correct, the student's score would be $44 - 6/3 = 42$. The student's score, corrected for guessing, is 42. When this formula is used, students should be encouraged to make educated guesses and to avoid randomly selecting answers.

Avoid Surprises   Be sure your students have sufficient advance notice of a test. "Pop" quizzes have little beneficial effect on overall academic achievement. They are especially problematic in junior high and high school where students have five or six different teachers. If each teacher gave pop quizzes, students would be hard pressed to be well prepared for each class each day. This is not to say that you should avoid frequent quizzes, however. When students are tested frequently, learning or study takes place at more regular intervals rather than massed or crammed the night before a test. Retention is generally better following spaced rather than massed learning.

Clarify the Rules   Inform students about time limits, restroom policy, and any special considerations about the answer sheet before you distribute the tests. Students often tune out the instructor after they receive their tests and may miss important information.

Rotate Distribution Alternate beginning test distribution at the left, right, front, and back of the class. This way, the same person will not always be the last one to receive the test.

Remind Students to Check Their Copies After handing out the tests, remind students to check page and item numbers to see that none has been omitted, and remind them to put their names on their papers.

Monitor Students Monitor students while they are completing their tests. While it would be nice to trust students not to look at one another's papers, it is not realistic. Inform students about penalties for cheating, and implement the penalties when cheating occurs. After students learn they can't get away with it, there should be little need for the penalties.

Minimize Distractions Try to keep noise and distractions to a minimum, for obvious reasons.

Give Time Warnings Give students a warning 15, 10, and 5 minutes before the time limit is up, so they are not caught by surprise at the deadline.

Collect Tests Uniformly Finally, have a uniform policy on collecting the tests. Indicate whether you want all papers or only some returned, where they are to be placed, and so forth. This not only saves time, but minimizes lost papers.

SCORING THE TEST

We discussed specific scoring recommendations for various types of objective test formats in Chapter 6 and for essay items in Chapter 7. Following are some general suggestions to save scoring time and improve scoring accuracy and consistency.

Prepare an Answer Key Prepare your answer key in advance, which will save time when you score the test and will help you identify questions that need rewording or need to be eliminated. Also, when constructing the answer key, you should get an idea of how long it will take your students to complete the test and whether this time is appropriate for the time slot you have allocated to the test.

Check the Answer Key If possible, have a colleague check your answer key to identify alternative answers or potential problems.

Score Blindly Try to score "blindly." That is, try to keep the student's name out of sight to prevent your knowledge about, or expectations of, the student from influencing the score.

Check Machine-Scored Answer Sheets If machine scoring is used, check each answer sheet for stray marks, multiple answers, or marks that may be too light to be picked up by the scoring machine.

Check Scoring   If possible, double-check your scoring. Scoring errors due to clerical error occur frequently. There is no reason to expect that you will not make such errors.

Record Scores   Before returning the scored papers to students, be sure you have recorded their scores in your record book! (Forgetting to do this has happened at least once to every teacher.)

ANALYZING THE TEST

Just as you can expect to make scoring errors, you can expect to make errors in test construction. No test you construct will be perfect—it will include inappropriate, invalid, or otherwise deficient items. In the remainder of this chapter we will introduce you to a technique called item analysis. Item analysis can be used to identify items that are deficient in some way, thus paving the way to improve or eliminate them, with the result being a better overall test. We will make a distinction between two kinds of item analysis, quantitative and qualitative. Quantitative item analysis is likely to be something new. But as you will see, qualitative item analysis is something with which you are already familiar. Finally, we will discuss how item analysis differs for norm- and criterion-referenced tests, and we provide you with several modified norm-referenced analysis methods to use with criterion-referenced tests.

Quantitative Item Analysis

As mentioned, quantitative item analysis is a technique that will enable us to assess the quality or utility of an item. It does so by identifying distractors or response options that are not doing what they are supposed to be doing. How useful is this procedure for a completion or an essay item? Frankly, it is not very useful for those types of items, but qualitative item analysis is. On the other hand, quantitative item analysis is ideally suited for examining the usefulness of multiple-choice formats. The quantitative item analysis procedures that we will describe are most appropriate for items on a norm-referenced test. As you will see, we are interested in spreading out students, or discriminating among them, with such a test. When dealing with a criterion-referenced test, qualitative and modified quantitative item analysis procedures are most appropriate.

Unfortunately, there is some terminology or jargon associated with quantitative item analysis that must be mastered. Figure 10.2 defines these terms. Study the definitions and refer to them throughout this section.

Now that you have reviewed the terms and definitions, let's see how they apply to multiple-choice items. Consider the following example. Suppose your students chose the options to a four-alternative multiple-choice item the following numbers of times: Three students chose option A; none chose B; eighteen chose the correct answer, C (marked with an asterisk); and nine chose D.

A	B	C*	D
3	0	18	9

Quantitative item analysis	A numerical method for analyzing test items employing student response alternatives or options.
Qualitative item analysis	A non-numerical method for analyzing test items not employing student responses, but considering test objectives, content validity, and technical item quality.
Key	Correct option in a multiple-choice item.
Distractor	Incorrect option in a multiple-choice item.
Difficulty index (p)	Proportion of students who answered the item correctly.
Discrimination index (D)	Measure of the extent to which a test item discriminates or differentiates between students who do well on the overall test and those who do not do well on the overall test.

There are three types of discrimination indexes:

1. *Positive discrimination index*—those who did well on the overall test chose the correct answer for a particular item more often than those who did poorly on the overall test.

2. *Negative discrimination index*—those who did poorly on the overall test chose the correct answer for a particular item more often than those who did well on the overall test.

3. *Zero discrimination index*—those who did well and those who did poorly on the overall test chose the correct answer for a particular item with equal frequency.

FIGURE 10.2 Item analysis terminology.

How does that help us? We can see immediately that B was not a very good option or distractor, because no one chose it. We can also see that more than half the class answered the item correctly. In fact, by employing the following formula, we can compute p, the item's difficulty index, which is the first step in item analysis.

$$p = \frac{\text{Number of students selecting correct answer}}{\text{Total number of students attempting the item}}$$

$$p = \frac{18}{30} = 0.60$$

From this information we learn that the item was moderately difficult (60 percent of the class got it right) and that option B ought to be modified or replaced. This is useful information, but we can learn (and need to know) more about this item. Were the students who answered it correctly those who did well on the overall test? Did the distractors fool those who did well or poorly on the test? The answers to those questions are important because they tell us whether the item discriminated between students who did well and those who did not do well on the overall test. A little confused? Let's look at it another way:

QUESTION: Why do we administer tests?

ANSWER: To find out who has mastered the material and who has not (i.e., to discriminate between the two groups).

QUESTION: Will a test discriminate between the groups better if each item on the test discriminates between those who did and did not do well on the test overall?

ANSWER: Absolutely! If more students who do well on the test overall answer an item correctly—positive discrimination index—that item helps the overall discrimination ability of the test. If this is true for all items (they are all positively discriminating), the test will do a good job of discriminating between those who know their stuff and those who don't. To the extent that students who do poorly on the overall test answer individual items correctly—negative discrimination index—the test loses its ability to discriminate.

QUESTION: How can I tell whether the key for any question is chosen more frequently by the better students (i.e., the item is positively discriminating) or the poorer students (i.e., the item is negatively discriminating)?

ANSWER: Follow the procedure described next.

Discrimination Index To determine each item's discrimination index (D), complete the following steps:

1. Arrange the papers from highest to lowest score.

2. Separate the papers into an upper group and a lower group based on total test scores. Do so by including half of your papers in each group.

3. For each item, count the number in the upper group and the number in the lower group that chose each alternative.

4. Record your information for each item in the following form (the following is data from the previous example; again the asterisk indicates the keyed option):

Example for item X (Class size = 30)

Options	A	B	C*	D
Upper	1	0	11	3
Lower	2	0	7	6

5. Compute D, the discrimination index, by plugging the appropriate numbers into the following formula:

$$D = \frac{\left(\begin{array}{c}\text{Number who got item}\\ \text{correct in upper group}\end{array}\right) - \left(\begin{array}{c}\text{Number who got item}\\ \text{correct in lower group}\end{array}\right)}{\text{Number of students in either group (if group}}$$

sizes are unequal, choose the higher number)

Plugging in our numbers we arrive at

$$D = \frac{11-7}{15} = 0.267$$

Our discrimination index (D) is 0.267, which is positive. More students who did well on the overall test answered the item correctly than students who did poorly on the overall test. Now, let's put it all together for this item.

Difficulty index (p) = 0.60

Discrimination index (D) = 0.267

An item with p = 0.60 and D = 0.267 would be considered a moderately difficult item that has positive (desirable) discrimination ability. When p levels are less than about 0.25, the item is considered relatively difficult. When p levels are above 0.75, the item is considered relatively easy. Test construction experts try to build tests that have most items between p levels of 0.20 and 0.80, with an average p level of about 0.50. All other factors being equal, the test's discrimination ability is greatest when the overall p level (difficulty) is about 0.50.

How high is a "good" discrimination index? Unfortunately, there is no single answer. Some experts insist that D should be at least 0.30, while others believe that as long as D has a positive value, the item's discrimination ability is adequate. Further complicating the issue is the fact that D is related to p. Just as a test tends to have maximum discrimination ability when p is around 0.50, so too does an individual item. It can be difficult to obtain discrimination indices above 0.30 when items are easy or difficult.

Naturally, you want your items to have as high a discrimination index as possible, but our recommendation is that you seriously consider any item with a positive D value. Based on this information, we would conclude that, in general, the item is acceptable. But we must also look at the item analysis data further to see if any distractors need to be modified or replaced.

We noted earlier that B would need to be replaced, since no one chose it. But what about A and D? Are they acceptable? The answer is yes, but can you figure out why? Because more people in the lower group chose them than did people in the upper group. This is the opposite of what we would want for the correct answer, and it makes sense. If we want more students who do well on the overall test to choose the correct answer, then we also want more students who do poorly on the overall test to choose the distractors.

Let's look at the responses for another item.

Example for item Y (Class size = 28)

Options	A*	B	C	D
Upper	4	1	5	4
Lower	1	7	3	3

The following questions will help guide us through the quantitative item analysis procedure.

1. What is the difficulty level?

$$p = \frac{\text{Number selecting correct answer}}{\text{Total number taking the test}}$$

$$p = \frac{5}{28} = 0.18$$

2. What is the discrimination index?

$$D = \frac{\text{Number correct (upper)} - \text{Number correct (lower)}}{\text{Number in either group}}$$

$$D = \frac{4-1}{14} = 0.214$$

3. Should this item be eliminated? No, since it is positively discriminating. However, it is a difficult item; only 18% of the class got it right.

4. Should any distractor be eliminated or modified? Yes; distractors C and D have attracted more students who did well on the test overall. If these distractors are modified or replaced, a good item will be made even better. Remember, in order for an item to discriminate well, more students who do well on the test should choose the correct answer than students who do poorly (the correct answer should be positively discriminating) and fewer students who do well on the test should choose each distractor than students who do poorly (the distractors should be negatively discriminating).

Example for item Z (Class Size = 30)

Options	A	B*	C	D
Upper	3	4	3	5
Lower	0	10	2	3

Again, let's ask the four basic questions to analyze item Z:

1. What is the difficulty level?

$$p = \frac{\text{Number selecting correct answer}}{\text{Total number taking the test}}$$

$$p = \frac{14}{30} = 0.467 \text{ (moderately difficult)}$$

2. What is the discrimination index?

$$D = \frac{\text{Number correct (upper)} - \text{Number correct (lower)}}{\text{Number in either group}}$$

$$D = \frac{4-10}{15} = \frac{-6}{15} = -0.40 \text{ (negatively discriminating)}$$

3. Should this item be eliminated? Yes! The item is moderately difficult (approximately 47% of the class got it right), but it discriminates negatively (D = −0.40). Remember, one of the reasons for testing is to discriminate between those students who know their stuff and those who do not. On this item more students who knew their stuff (who did well on the overall test) chose the incorrect options than the correct answer. If the test were made mostly of or entirely of items like this, the students who score high on the test, who answered the most items correctly, might be those who did not know their stuff. This is clearly what we want to avoid. An item that discriminates negatively should be eliminated.

4. Should any distractor(s) be modified or eliminated? Since we have already decided to eliminate the item, this is a moot question. However, let's look at the distractors anyway. In the case of options A, C, and D, more students who did well on the test chose each of these options than students who did poorly on the test. Each distractor discriminates positively. We want our distractors to discriminate negatively. Thus this item has nothing going for it, according to our quantitative item analysis. The correct answer, which should discriminate positively, discriminates negatively. The distractors, which should discriminate negatively, discriminate positively!

In addition to helping us decide which items to eliminate from a test before it is again administered, quantitative item analysis also enables us to make other decisions. For example, we can use quantitative item analysis to decide whether an item is miskeyed, whether responses to the item are characterized by guessing, or whether the item is ambiguous. To do so, we need only consider the responses of students in the upper half of the class. Let's see how.

Miskeying When an item is miskeyed, most students who did well on the test will likely select an option that is a distractor, rather than the option that is keyed. Consider the following miskeyed item:

> Who was the first astronaut to set foot on the moon?
> a. John Glenn
> b. Scott Carpenter
> c. Neil Armstrong
> *d. Alan Sheppard

Analyzing the responses for the *upper* half of the class, we find the following distribution:

	A	B	C	D*
Upper half	1	1	9	2

Any time most students in the *upper* half of the class fail to select the keyed option, consider whether your item is miskeyed. Remember, just as you are bound to make scoring errors, you are bound to miskey an item occasionally.

Guessing When guessing occurs, students in the *upper* half of the class respond in more or less random fashion. This is most likely to occur when the item measures content that is (1) not covered in class or the text, (2) so difficult that even the upper-half students have no idea what the correct answer is, or (3) so trivial that students are unable to choose from among the options provided. In such cases, each alternative is about equally attractive to students in the upper half, so their responses tend to be about equally distributed among the options. The following choice distribution would suggest that guessing occurred:

	A	B	C*	D
Upper half	4	3	3	3

Ambiguity   So far we have discussed using quantitative item analysis to identify miskeying and guessing. We did so by looking at response distributions for the *upper* group. With miskeying, the *upper* group chooses a distractor more frequently than the key. With guessing, each option is chosen with about equal frequency. Ambiguity is suspected when, among the *upper* group, one of the distractors is chosen with about the same frequency as the correct answer. The following distribution suggests that an item is ambiguous:

	A	**B**	**C**	**D***
Upper half	7	0	1	7

In this item, students who do well on the test but miss the item are drawn almost entirely to one of the distractors. However, quantitative analysis data can only suggest ambiguity. In the preceding item, there is no way for us to tell whether the "good" students chose distractor A because the item is deficient, or whether it was because they were distracted by an option that was plausible, but not as correct as the key.

The only way to determine whether the root of the problem is lack of mastery or a poorly written item is through qualitative item analysis, to which we turn next. Before leaving quantitative item analysis, however, a final point should be made. As you are by now aware, there can be considerable time and effort invested in quantitative item analysis by a teacher. This can be a "turnoff" to some, resulting in a teacher failing to use this very useful test analysis tool. Fortunately, with the advent of personal computers and item analysis software, the actual time spent in quantitative item analysis by the teacher may now be significantly reduced. See the sidebar (Box 10-1) to see how.

We will turn to qualitative item analysis next. However, first review what we have learned about the application of quantitative item analysis by studying Figure 10.3, the Quantitative Item Analysis Checklist.

BOX *10-1*

PCS AND TEST ASSEMBLY AND ANALYSIS

Commercial software is available that will guide the classroom teacher through the entire test construction process from writing instructional objectives, to matching items to objectives, to assembling and analyzing the test. It is this last area, test and item analysis, that the PC's power and convenience may prove most beneficial. Programs to compute item difficulty levels and discrimination indices are available, and quantitative item analyses of objective test items are now a reality for the busy classroom teacher. Programs that enable the teacher to determine the reliability of classroom tests are also available.

Statistical packages and data management programs make it possible for classroom teachers to keep accurate and comprehensive records of student performances over the course of the year, and over several years. This enables the teacher to compare classes, tests, and curricula; to identify discrepancies; and to evaluate the effects of new instructional techniques on test performance. By utilizing these PC resources the classroom teacher can objectively and scientifically analyze data from classroom tests without all the hand calculation that otherwise would be necessary. These data can enhance instruction and increase the satisfaction of pupils, parents, and administrators with the measurement process.

Quantitative Item Analysis Checklist

1. Item number   _____

2. Difficulty level: _____

$$p = \frac{\text{Number correct}}{\text{Total}} =$$

3. Discrimination index: _____

$$D = \frac{\left(\begin{array}{c}\text{Number correct} \\ \text{(upper)}\end{array}\right) - \left(\begin{array}{c}\text{Number correct} \\ \text{(lower)}\end{array}\right)}{\text{Number of students in either group}}$$

4. Eliminate or revise item? Check.
   (a) Does key discriminate positively?   _____
   (b) Do distractors discriminate negatively?   _____
   If you answer yes to both a and b, no revision may be necessary.
   If you answer no to a *or* b, revision is necessary. If you answer no to a *and* b,
       eliminate the item.

5. Check for miskeying, ambiguity, or guessing. Among the choices for the *upper group
   only*, was there evidence of:
   (a) miskeying (more chose distractor than key)?   _____
   (b) guessing (equal spread of choices across options)?   _____
   (c) ambiguity (equal number chose one distractor and the key)?   _____

FIGURE 10.3 Quantitative item analysis checklist.

Qualitative Item Analysis

As noted earlier, you already know something about qualitative item analysis. It's something you can and ought to do with items of all formats. Essentially, when we talk about qualitative item analysis, we are talking about matching items and objectives and editing poorly written items. These are activities we've discussed in Chapters 5, 6, and 7 in relation to improving the content validity of a test. We refer to them again simply because it is appropriate to edit or rewrite items and assess their content validity after a test, as well as before a test.

Let's face it. In spite of our best intentions, we end up pressed for time as the day for the test approaches. What do we do? Probably we work more quickly to assemble the test—overlooking such things as grammatical cues, specific determiners, double negatives, multiple defensible answers, and items that fail to match instructional objectives.

As a result, these faults creep into the final version of the test. It would be nice if quantitative item analysis pointed out such problems, but it does not. Quantitative item analysis is useful but limited. It points out items that have problems but doesn't tell us what the problems are. It is possible that an item that fails to measure or match an instructional objective could have an acceptable difficulty level, an answer that discriminates positively, and distractors that discriminate negatively. In short, quantitative item analysis is fallible. To do a thorough job of test analysis, one must use a combination of quantitative and qualitative item analysis, and not rely solely on one or the other. In other words, there is no substitute for carefully scrutinizing and editing items and matching test items with objectives.

Item Analysis Modifications for the Criterion-Referenced Test

The statistical test analysis method discussed earlier, called quantitative item analysis, applies most directly to the norm-referenced test. We know from Chapter 4, however, that the classroom teacher will typically use criterion-referenced tests rather than norm-referenced tests. Well, then, we can just use these same procedures for our teacher-made criterion-referenced tests. Right? Wrong!

As we will discover in later chapters, variability of scores is crucial to the appropriateness and success of norm-referenced quantitative item analysis procedures. In short, these procedures depend on the variability or spread of scores (i.e., low to high) if they are to do their jobs correctly. In a typical teacher-made criterion-referenced test, however, variability of scores would be expected to be small, assuming instruction is effective and the test and its objectives match. Thus the application of quantitative item analysis procedures to criterion-referenced measures is not appropriate, since by definition most students will answer these items correctly (i.e., there will be *minimal* variability or spread of scores). In this section we will describe several ways in which these procedures can be modified when a criterion-referenced, mastery approach to test item evaluation is employed. As you will see, these modifications are straightforward and easier to use than the quantitative procedures described earlier.

Using Pre- and Posttests as Upper and Lower Groups   The following approaches require that you administer the test as a "pretest" prior to your instruction and as a "posttest" after your instruction. Ideally, in such a situation the majority of students should answer most of your test items incorrectly on the pretest and correctly on the posttest. By studying the difference between the difficulty (p) levels for each item at the time of the pre- and posttests, we can tell if this is happening. At pretest the p level should be low (e.g., 0.30 or lower), and at posttest it should be high (e.g., 0.70 or higher). In addition, we can consider the pretest results for an item as the lower group (L) and posttest results for the item as the upper group (U), and then we can perform the quantitative item analysis procedures previously described to determine the discrimination direction for the key and for the distractors.

Example 1: *Analyze the following results.*

Numbers of students choosing option (n = 25)

Option	At pretest (Lower or L)	At posttest (Upper or U)
A	9	1
B	7	1
C	3	2
D* (key)	6	21

Step 1: Compute p levels for both tests.

	Pretest	*Posttest*
Number choosing correctly/Total number	$\dfrac{6}{25} = 0.24$	$\dfrac{21}{25} = 0.84$

This is what we would hope for in a criterion-referenced test; most students should answer the item *incorrectly* on the pretest and *correctly* on the posttest. In this case it was an improvement from 24% to 84%.

Step 2: Determine the discrimination index (D) for the key.

$$D = \frac{\text{Number correct (post)} - \text{Number correct (pre)}}{\text{Number in either group}}$$

$$D = \frac{21 - 6}{25} = \frac{15}{25} = 0.60$$

This indicates that the keyed correct option has a positive discrimination index, which is what we want.

Step 3: Determine whether each option separately discriminates *negatively*.

$$\text{Option A:} \quad D = \frac{1 - 9}{25} = \frac{-8}{25} = -0.32$$

Option A discriminates *negatively*, which is what we want; more students chose this option on the pretest (L) than the posttest (U).

$$\text{Option B:} \quad D = \frac{1 - 7}{25} = \frac{-6}{25} = -0.24$$

Option B also discriminates *negatively*.

$$\text{Option C:} \quad D = \frac{2 - 3}{25} = \frac{-1}{25} = -0.04$$

Option C also discriminates *negatively*, albeit weakly.

In summary, our modified quantitative item analysis procedures indicate the following:

1. There was a sizable increase in p value from pretest to posttest.
2. The D index for the key was positive.
3. The distractors all discriminated negatively.

If a criterion-referenced test item manifests these features, it has passed our "test" and probably is a good item with little or no need for modification. Contrast this conclusion, however, with the following item from the same test.

Example 2: *Analyze the results in the following table.*

Numbers of students choosing option (n = 25)

Option	At pretest (L)	At posttest (U)
A*	23	24
B	1	1
C	1	0
D	0	0

For this item, the pretest p level was 0.92 and the posttest level was 0.96—an increase of only 0.04, hardly an increase at all. In addition, the majority of students answered this item *correctly* on the pretest. We want *most* students to answer *incorrectly* at the pretest and correctly at the posttest!

Furthermore, the D index for the key is only 0.04:

$$D = \frac{24 - 23}{25} = \frac{1}{25} = 0.04$$

While this index is positive, and *might* be acceptable in a norm-referenced test, it is not acceptable for a criterion-referenced test.

Okay, so what D value is acceptable? Unfortunately, there is no easy answer to this question. We would suggest, however, that you look for D values of 0.40 or greater. This would mean that almost twice as many students are answering the item correctly on the posttest than on the pretest.

Finally, let's investigate our distractors. The D values for both options B and D are 0.00.

$$\text{Option B:} \quad D = \frac{1 - 1}{25} = \frac{0}{25} = 0.00$$

$$\text{Option D:} \quad D = \frac{0 - 0}{25} = \frac{0}{25} = 0.00$$

Neither of these options are useful; they both fail to differentiate between pre- and posttest. These options require modification or elimination.

Let's look at option C.

$$\text{Option C:} \quad D = \frac{0 - 1}{25} = \frac{-1}{25} = -0.04$$

This option does discriminate negatively, but weakly. Modifications to this option may increase its ability to discriminate negatively.

To evaluate this item overall, let's subject it to our three-step analysis:

1. Is there a substantial increase in p value (0.40 or more) between pre- and posttest?
   p increased from 0.92 to 0.96, hardly substantial.

2. Was D greater than 0.40 for the key?
   D was only 0.04.

3. Did all distractors discriminate negatively?
   Options B and D had zero discrimination ability; option C discriminated negatively, but only weakly.

Thus the item in Example 2 failed all the tests. Rather than modify the item, it is probably more efficient to replace it with another.

Less technical variations of modified quantitative item analysis procedures for criterion-referenced tests follow. The next two methods also have the advantage of applying to true–false, matching, and completion tests rather than to just multiple-choice tests.

Comparing the Percentage Answering Each Item Correctly on Both Pre- and Posttest If your test is sensitive to your objectives (and assuming you teach to your objectives), the majority of learners should receive a low score on the test prior to your instruction and a high score afterward. This method can be used to determine whether this is happening.

Subtract the percentage of students passing each item before your instruction from the percentage of students passing each item after your instruction. The more positive the difference, the more you know the item is tapping the content you are teaching. This method is similar to the first step as described in the preceding section.

For example, consider the following percentages for five test items:

Item	Percentage passing pretest	Percentage passing posttest	Difference
1	16	79	+63%
2	10	82	+72%
3	75	75	0%
4	27	91	+64%
5	67	53	−14%

Notice that item 3 registers no change in the percentage of students passing from before to after instruction. In fact, a high percentage of students got the item correct without any instruction! This item may be eliminated from the test, since little or no instruction pertaining to it was provided *and* most students already knew the content it represents.

Now, look at item 5. Notice the percentage is negative. That is, 14% of the class actually changed from getting the item *correct* before instruction to getting it *wrong* after. Here, either the instruction was not related to the item, or it actually confused some students who knew the correct answer beforehand. A revision of the item, the objective pertaining to this item, or the related instruction is in order.

Determining the Percentage of Items Answered in the Expected Direction for the Entire Test   Another, slightly different approach is to determine whether the entire test reflects the change from fewer to more students answering items correctly from pre- to posttest. This index uses the number of items each learner failed on the test prior to instruction but passed on the test after instruction. Here is how it is computed:

Step 1: Find the number of items each student *failed* on the pretest, *prior* to instruction, but *passed* on the posttest, *after* instruction.

Item	Bobby at pretest	Bobby at posttest
1*	Incorrect	Correct
2	Correct	Correct
3*	Incorrect	Correct
4	Correct	Incorrect
5	Incorrect	Incorrect

The asterisks indicate just the items counted in Step 1 for Bobby. This count is then repeated for each student.

Step 2: Add the counts in Step 1 for all students and divide by the number of students.

Step 3: Divide the result from Step 2 by the number of items on the test.

Step 4: Multiply the result from Step 3 by 100.

Let's see how this would work for a 25-item test given to five students before and after instruction.

Step 1: Find the number of items that students answered incorrectly prior to instruction but correctly after instruction.

Mary	18
Carlos	15
Sharon	22
Amanda	20
Charles	13

Step 2:   Add counts and divide by the number of students.

$$\frac{18 + 15 + 22 + 20 + 13}{5} = \frac{88}{5} = 17.6$$

Step 3:   Divide by number of test items. $\frac{17.6}{25} = 0.70$

Step 4:   Multiply by 100. $0.70 \times 100 = 70\%$

Seventy percent of the items on the test registered a positive change after instruction, where a positive change is defined as failing an item before instruction and passing it afterward. The greater the overall positive percentage of change, the more your test is likely to match your instruction and to be a content-valid test.

Limitations of These Modifications   One limitation of these modified quantitative item analysis procedures is that it is difficult, especially at first, to write items that virtually everyone will be successful on only after a unit of instruction. Thus you may find that in your initial efforts, 40% of your students answer an item correctly on the pretest and only 60% answer an item correctly on the posttest. This is less than optimal, but it may be a good "first try."

Another limitation is that if the unit of instruction is brief, there may be some "contamination" of the posttest by a student's recollection of responses made during the pretest. A third limitation is that we are taking a procedure that was developed for a single administration of a norm-referenced test and applying it to a criterion-referenced test administered to the same group at two different times. Finally, these modifications require two test administrations (pre and post), which will reduce the amount of time you devote to instruction.

In conclusion, it would be a mistake to uncritically apply the quantitative item analysis procedures appropriate for norm-referenced measures to criterion-referenced tests. At the same time, it would be a mistake to reject their utility. Their utility is probably strongest when tests or test items are in their early stages of use and development, and when the methods are used along with qualitative item analysis.

We have discussed quantitative and qualitative item analysis, how they apply to norm-referenced tests, and how these procedures must be modified to apply more specifically to the typical classroom test. What's left is returning the test to the students, something we like to call debriefing.

DEBRIEFING

Take a moment to think back to the times a test on which you did well was returned. Remember the happy, satisfied feeling you had? You felt good about yourself, your teacher, and the test. Of course, it was a good test because it proved that you knew your stuff. Now take a minute to think back to the times a test on which you did poorly was returned. Remember the unhappy, unsatisfied feeling you had? Were you angry or resentful? It's likely you weren't feeling very fond of yourself, your teacher, or the test—especially the test. Any time you give a test, it's likely that some students will do poorly and feel unhappy or angry as a result.

Teachers adopt their own ways of coping with complaints about a test. These range from "Your score is final, and that's it" to "I'll give everybody 10 extra points so that no one fails." We feel that neither of these positions is defensible. The first position denies or ignores reality. It is not just possible, but probable that your test has deficiencies. Refusing to examine the test with your students robs you of the opportunity to get feedback that you can use to improve or fine-tune your test before you use it again.

Furthermore, such an approach serves to antagonize and alienate students. Awarding extra credit or a make-up test may calm the angry students who did poorly but may be unfair to those who did well. As with the first approach, it robs you of the opportunity to get feedback on, and make appropriate modifications to, your test. Rather, we advocate having concern for the quality of your test and showing this concern by going over the test with your students each time you use it. Your students can actually save you time and effort by screening your test and identifying those items that are worth subjecting to the time-consuming processes of quantitative and qualitative item analysis.

If you are truly interested in improving the validity and reliability of your test, you can subject each item to both kinds of item analysis. Your reward will be a better test. Or you can find out which items your students found problematic and subject only those few items to analysis. Again, your reward will be a better test. The choice is yours, but, of course, we hope you choose to go over the test with your students later. Should you do so, consult the following suggested debriefing guidelines.

Debriefing Guidelines

Before handing back answer sheets or grades, you should do the following:

Discuss Problem Items   Discuss any items you found problematic in scoring the test. This sets the stage for rational discussion and makes for more effective consideration of the item(s) in question. Also, you are more likely to have the attention of the students than you would if they were looking over their answer sheets or thinking about the grades they received.

Listen to Student Reactions   Ask for student reactions to your comments and listen to their reactions. Again, you are setting the stage for rational discussion of the test by letting the students know you are interested in their feedback. Remember, your goal is to improve the validity and reliability of your test by improving on its weaknesses. When you or your students begin to respond emotionally, defensiveness is likely to replace listening and issues of power and control replace rational discussion. In short, improving the test may seem less important than asserting your authority. You will have plenty of opportunities to assert your authority and few opportunities to improve your test. Try to keep these issues separate, and use the few opportunities you do have for test improvement as advantageously as you can.

Avoid on-the-Spot Decisions   Tell your students that you will consider their comments, complaints, and suggestions, but you will not make any decisions about omitting items, partial credit, extra credit, and so forth until you have had time to study and think about the test data. You may want to make it clear that soliciting their comments is only for the purpose of preparing the next test, not for reconsidering grades for the present test.

Be Equitable with Changes If you decide to make changes, let your students know that any changes in scoring will apply to all students, not just those who raise objections.

After handing back answer sheets or grades, do the following:

Ask Students to Double-Check Ask students to double-check your arithmetic, and ask any who think clerical errors have been made to see you as soon as possible. Here you are presenting yourself as human by admitting that you can make errors.

Ask Students to Identify Problems If time permits, ask students to identify the items they find problematic and why they are so. Make note of the items and problems. Such items may then be discussed or worked into some new instructional objectives.

We have been suggesting that you use the time you spend returning your test as an opportunity to improve your test. To the extent that you can elicit relevant and constructive feedback from your class, you will be likely to reach this goal. In trying to remain nondefensive and emotionally detached from your test, it is useful to keep a few points in mind:

1. Your test will include at least some items that can be improved. You are human!

2. Students are criticizing your skill as a test constructor, not you as a person. Admittedly, though, frustrated students can get too personal. When this happens, try to remember what's behind it—frustration with your test.

3. The quality of an item is not necessarily related to the loudness with which complaints are made. At times, items that students loudly protest are indeed poor items. At other times, they are simply difficult or challenging items. Use quantitative item analysis to determine which is the case.

4. When it appears necessary to rescore a test or award credit, keep in mind that research has shown that rescoring tends to be highly related to the original scoring. Thus although some individual scores may change, one's rank in relation to others is not likely to change much. For all their protest, students seldom really gain much other than letting off steam.

5. Finally, keep in mind that the most important objectives for debriefing are to improve your test and to gain insight into the effectiveness and thoroughness of your instruction and to plan new objectives that can address the problems students had in learning the test content.

THE PROCESS OF EVALUATING CLASSROOM ACHIEVEMENT

Many of the various components of testing that have been presented in the last several chapters are specific and technical. You may wonder how important they are. Unfortunately, none of the major steps we have focused on can be considered optional because they are all components of a single process—the process of evaluating classroom achievement. It is important to keep this in mind since valid and reliable measurement of classroom achievement depends on each and all components. Remember, the general public is clamoring for accountability, and one of the factors for which teachers are likely to be held more and more accountable is classroom achievement. Spend the time now to master the skills involved in validly and reliably measuring classroom achievement. You will reap the benefits later. The process of measuring classroom achievement is depicted in Figure 10.4, which summarizes all of the important components of achievement testing that we have discussed thus far.

There's nothing for you to do now but go out and do it. If you've studied and worked at these chapters, you are ahead in the test construction game. What that means for you is better tests that cause fewer students and parents to complain and tests that are more valid and reliable measurements of achievement.

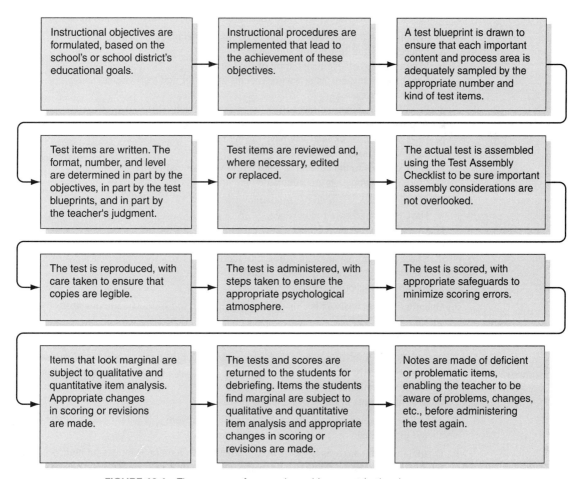

FIGURE 10.4 The process of measuring achievement in the classroom.

SUMMARY

In Chapter 10 many issues related to test assembly, administration, scoring, and analysis were covered. Major points mentioned are as follows:

1. When assembling a test:
   a. Group all items of same or similar formats together.
   b. Arrange items so that item difficulty progresses from easy to hard.
   c. Space items to eliminate overcrowding.
   d. Keep items and options on the same page.
   e. Place contextual material above the items to which they refer.
   f. Arrange answers in a random pattern.
   g. Decide how students are to record answers.
   h. Be sure to include a space for the student's name.
   i. Be sure directions are specific and accurate.
   j. Proofread your master copy before reproducing it.
   k. Check items for race or gender bias.

2. Care must be taken in reproducing the test to avoid illegible copies that would impair test validity.

3. In administering a test, make an effort to do the following:
   a. Induce a positive test-taking attitude.
   b. Maximize the achievement nature of the test.
   c. Equalize the advantages test-wise students have over non-test-wise students.
   d. Avoid surprise tests.
   e. Provide special instructions before the tests are actually distributed.
   f. Alternate your test distribution procedures.
   g. Have students check that they have the entire test.
   h. Keep distractions to a minimum.
   i. Alert students to the amount of time left toward the end of the test.
   j. Clarify test collection procedures before handing out the test.

4. In scoring the test, try to do the following:
   a. Have the key prepared in advance.
   b. Have the key checked for accuracy.
   c. Score blindly.
   d. Check for multiple answers if machine scoring is used.
   e. Double-check scores, if scored by hand.
   f. Record scores before returning the tests.

5. Quantitative item analysis is a mathematical approach to assessing an item's utility.

6. An item's difficulty level (p) is computed by dividing the number of students who answered correctly by the total number of students who attempted the item.

7. An item's discrimination index (D) is computed by subtracting the number of students who answered correctly in the low-scoring half of the class from the number of students who answered correctly in the high-scoring half of the class, and dividing the remainder by the number of students in the upper or lower group.

8. Keyed correct options should discriminate positively (positive D value), and incorrect options should discriminate negatively (negative D value).

9. Quantitative item analysis helps us decide whether to retain or eliminate an item, which distractor(s) should be modified or eliminated, whether an item is miskeyed, whether guessing occurred, and whether ambiguity is present.

10. Qualitative item analysis is a nonmathematical approach to assessing an item's utility.

11. Qualitative item analysis is performed by checking an item's content validity and inspecting it for technical faults, as outlined in Chapters 5, 6, and 7.

12. Do not apply the quantitative item analysis procedures that have been developed and proved using norm-referenced tests to criterion-referenced tests without appropriate caution and modification.

13. Several modifications of traditional norm-referenced item analysis procedures appropriate for criterion-referenced tests were discussed; they vary in their complexity.

14. These modifications to the usual quantitative item analysis procedures should be coupled with the qualitative item analysis procedures discussed in Chapters 5, 6, and 7 to properly evaluate the criterion-referenced teacher-made test.

15. After the test has been scored, but before you give students their scores:
    a. Discuss any items considered to be problematic.
    b. Listen to student concerns and try to stay unemotional.
    c. Let students know you will consider their comments but will not make any decisions affecting their scores until you have had time to reflect on their comments.
    d. Let students know that any changes made will apply equally to all students.

16. After the students are given their scores, ask them to check for clerical errors.

FOR PRACTICE

*1. Compute p, the difficulty index, for the following items. Interpret your results. (The asterisk indicates the correct option.)

a. *Options*

A	B*	C	D
10	5	8	0

b. *Options*

A	B	C*	D
4	2	16	3

*2. Compute D, the discrimination index, for the following items. Interpret your results.

(Class size = 40)

a. *Options*

	A	B	C	D*
Upper half	3	0	7	10
Lower half	5	4	9	2

(Class size = 30)

b. *Options*

	A*	B	C	D
Upper half	3	5	7	0
Lower half	8	5	1	1

*3. Identify which of the following items are likely to be miskeyed, which are likely to be susceptible to guessing, and which are probably ambiguous.

a. *Options*

	A*	B	C	D
Upper half	8	0	7	2

b. *Options*

	A	B	C*	D
Upper half	10	2	4	3

c. *Options*

	A	B*	C	D
Upper half	3	11	3	10

d. *Options*

	A*	B	C	D
Upper half	9	8	11	9

e. *Options*

	A*	B	C	D
Upper half	0	1	6	2

*4. Do a complete item analysis for the following item data. Use the Quantitative Item Analysis Checklist (Figure 10.3) as your guide, answering each of the questions indicated.

(Class size = 20)

a. *Options*

	A*	B	C	D
Upper half	3	2	3	2
Lower half	2	3	1	4

*Answers for these questions appear in Appendix F.

CHAPTER 11

MARKS AND MARKING SYSTEMS

AFTER YOU have administered your test, you score it and assign a grade to the test. This grade is not what we will be referring to in this chapter. In this chapter we will discuss several issues related to the assignment of *marks*—cumulative grades that reflect academic achievement at the end of a 6- or 9-week marking period, semester, or school year.

WHAT IS THE PURPOSE OF A MARK?

Marks are assigned to provide feedback about student *achievement*. We will reiterate this point several times in this chapter, not because it is so difficult, but because it is so often forgotten. All too often marks have been assigned as rewards and punishments. This is not what they are intended for.

Why Be Concerned about Marking?

Marks have become an accepted and expected aspect of our culture. Students come to realize very early in their educational careers that they will be graded or marked depending on their performance in school. Parents of students, having been graded themselves, realize that the marks a student receives may well affect their child's educational, occupational, and financial status by opening or closing various opportunities. Parents know that children are compared with each other through their marks. Thus marks have considerable meaning for both child and parent.

Educators also are strongly influenced by marks, often relegating pupils to faster or slower tracks, depending on their marks. Since marks carry a great deal of importance for many people, it seems sensible that care and objectivity be exercised in assigning marks. Unfortunately, this is often not the case. Rather than being assigned accurately, in hopes of presenting as valid a picture of student achievement as possible, marks are sometimes assigned in haste, or according to nebulous, undefined, and little understood "marking systems." Different marking systems have different advantages and disadvantages—some of which the average teacher often does not know. We will acquaint you with various marking systems so that you may choose the system that best fits your situation. In general, such systems compare students with other students or with established standards of knowledge, or are based on aptitude, effort, and improvement.

What Should a Mark Reflect?

What a mark should reflect depends on the subject or topic being marked. We generally talk about marks in relation to reading achievement, math achievement, and so on. However, marks are also assigned in areas like conduct, study skills, and responsibility. When marks are related to academic subjects, marks should reflect *academic achievement*, and nothing more!

Marks are assigned to provide feedback about academic achievement in order for students to be compared according to their achievement. If marks reflect only academic achievement and are assigned consistently according to a system, such marks may be compared with considerable validity (as long as the system according to which the marks are assigned is made clear). But when a single mark represents a hodgepodge of factors (e.g., achievement, attitude, attendance, punctuality, or conduct) or systems (e.g., comparisons with other students, comparisons with standards of effort, or improvement), interpretation or comparison of such marks becomes a hopeless task.

Unfortunately, the latter case characterizes some marking practices today. Different schools employ different marking systems and weigh various nonachievement factors in assigning marks, making direct and meaningful comparisons of grades from two schools difficult at best.

We are not suggesting that information about nonachievement factors, such as conduct, punctuality, and so forth, should be unreported or is unimportant. We *are* suggesting that such information should not be mixed with test scores and other indicators of academic achievement in a single grade. In other words, don't mix apples with oranges in a single mark for an academic subject. All this may seem perfectly obvious, but strange things happen when marks are assigned. It's all too tempting to use marks as vehicles to reach, or try to reach, other ends. Consider the following dialogue:

PARENT: Mr. Stokes, Jack got a D in reading this six weeks, but he's had As in reading all year. I don't understand. He seems to be reading better all the time, but I'm no teacher. What can I do to help him?

TEACHER: One thing you can do is tell him to stop looking out the window during oral reading. Some of these third graders seem to think that what is going on outside is more important than reading!

PARENT: Do you mean Jack is being disruptive in class?

TEACHER: Yes, he looks out the window, then the next thing you know another one does, then another . . .

PARENT: Have you asked him why he's doing it?

TEACHER: Of course, but it's always the same excuse—"I'm bored listening to the others read aloud what I've already read to myself."

PARENT: I see, but what about his reading ability—has it declined?

TEACHER: Oh, no! Jack's one of the top readers in the class—there's nothing he can't read.

PARENT: So he's a top reader, but he got a D in reading for not paying attention—is that it?

TEACHER: Mrs. Burns! What do you think I am? I grade on achievement—not on conduct!

PARENT: Why *did* he get the D, then? It sounds as though he was punished for not paying attention.

TEACHER: You've got it wrong. He failed to turn in two homework assignments. That's an automatic D in all my classes. Someone's got to teach these kids responsibility.

PARENT: Mr. Stokes, I know that Sarah Smith failed to turn in two homework assignments, and she got an A.

TEACHER: That's different; she pays attention during oral reading. It's obvious that she's getting more out of the class. She also tries harder, even though she's not as smart as Jack.

PARENT: Mr. Stokes, you certainly are an exceptional teacher.

TEACHER: Thank you, Mrs. Burns, but it won't work—Jack's D still stands.

Unfortunately, this type of dialogue is not uncommon. We agree with the teacher in that grades should be based on achievement, not conduct. However, it is quite clear that Jack's D is unrelated to reading achievement. By the teacher's own admission, Jack is reading well, but his classroom *behavior* is not congruent with Mr. Stokes's expectations, and he failed to turn in some homework assignments—another behavioral deficiency that Mr. Stokes equates with poor reading achievement. To what is Mr. Stokes comparing Jack's reading achievement? We can't be sure, although effort and aptitude were mentioned.

It appears that the main function of the marks in this case is punishment. Rather than providing feedback to the student about *reading* achievement, Mr. Stokes is punishing Jack for off-task behavior during class and for less than perfect compliance with his homework expectations. The major problem we see here is that the main function of grades—to provide feedback about achievement—has been lost in Mr. Stokes's zeal to change Jack's behavior. In too many cases, a single grade is used to report achievement, conduct, homework compliance, tardiness, and so on. This would be less of a problem if it were done consistently across schools. However, different schools weight each of these differently. The real point is that as long as grades continue to be based on factors other than achievement, we are robbing ourselves of the effective use of the main purpose of grading—evaluating achievement. Let's consider the different marking systems employed in schools.

MARKING SYSTEMS

Various types of marking systems have been used in the schools. They may be considered along two dimensions:

1. Type of comparison involved.
2. Type of symbol used.

Types of Comparisons

Often the type of symbol a teacher uses is determined at the school or district level—the teacher has little to say about whether an A–F; E, G, S, U; or a numerical marking system is employed. However, the classroom teacher often has more flexibility and autonomy in deciding how to assign the marks. That is, teachers often have considerable control over how they decide who gets an A or B. As mentioned earlier, marks are based on comparisons, usually from among comparisons of students with:

1. Other students.

2. Established standards.

3. Aptitude.

4. Actual versus potential effort.

5. Actual versus potential improvement.

Each of these systems has advantages and limitations. Our aim is to acquaint you with these so you may choose wisely. Whichever system you choose to employ, be sure to indicate it on the report card. Remember, the function of marking is to provide feedback on achievement. However, a grade of B based on effort versus a grade of B based on comparisons to established standards can reflect very different absolute levels of achievement. Indicating your marking system will minimize potential misinterpretations of a student's level of achievement.

Comparisons with Other Students   Certainly you have had instructors who have graded "on the curve." It almost sounds illegal, shady, or underhanded. It seems at times that this is some mysterious method by which test grades are transformed into semester marks. Basically, all that the expression "grading on the curve" means is that your grade or mark depends on how your achievement compares with the achievement of other students in your class. You may recall from Chapter 4 that such an approach is also called *norm-referenced*. Certain proportions of the class are assigned As, Bs, etc., regardless of their absolute level of performance on a test. In such a system, a student who misses 50% of the items on a test might get an A, F, or any other grade on the test depending on how his or her score of 50% compared with the scores of the other students in the class. If the score was higher than those of 95% of the students, the student would likely get an A.

Sometimes districts or schools encourage grading on the curve by specifying the percentages of students who will be assigned various grades. The following distribution is an example:

Grade	*Percentage of Students*
A	10
B	25
C	40
D	20
F	5

The main advantage of such a system is that it simplifies marking decisions. The student is either in the top 10% or he or she doesn't get an A. There is no apparent need for deliberation or agonizing over what cutoff scores should determine if students get this grade or that.

There are several disadvantages in such a system. First, this type of marking system fails to consider differences due to the overall ability level of the class. Imagine the disappointment that would result if such a system were imposed on a class of intellectually gifted students, none of whom had ever earned less than a B. Suddenly 65% would be transformed into C through F students. Regardless of achievement, in such a system some students will always get As, and some will always get Fs. Another problem involves the percentages—why not 5% As, or 15% As? The percentages are set rather arbitrarily. Furthermore, what does it mean when a student gets an A? Has the student mastered all course content? Or was the student lucky enough to be in with a class of slow learners? Such a system says nothing about absolute achievement, which makes comparisons across grades and schools difficult.

Finally, consider the teacher in such a system. No matter how well or poorly the teacher teaches, his or her students always get the same percentage of grades. There is little, if any, reward available through seeing grades on the whole improve following improved teaching. As a result, a teacher may not feel quite as motivated to improve.

Comparison with Established Standards   In a marking system using comparison with established standards, it is possible for all students to get As or Fs or any other grade in between. How much the rest of the students in the class achieve is irrelevant to a student's grade. All that is relevant is whether a student attains a defined standard of achievement or performance. We labeled this approach *criterion-referenced* in Chapter 4. In such a system, letter grades may be assigned based on the percentage of test items answered correctly, as the following distribution illustrates:

Grade	*Percentage of Items Answered Correctly*
A	85
B	75
C	65
D	55
F	Less than 55

Thus a student who answers 79% of the test items correctly earns a B, regardless of whether the rest of the class did better, worse, or about the same. Obviously, such a system requires some prior knowledge of the difficulty of the test and what level of achievement or performance is reasonable to expect.

There are several advantages to such a system. First, it is possible, in theory, for all students to obtain high grades if they put forth sufficient effort (assuming the percentage cutoffs are not unreasonably high). Second, assignment of grades is simplified. A student either has answered 75% of the items correctly or hasn't. As with comparison with other students, there is no apparent need to deliberate or agonize over assigning grades. Finally, assuming that ability levels of incoming students remain fairly constant and that tests remain comparable in validity and difficulty, teachers who work to improve teaching effectiveness should see improvement in grades with the passage of time. Presumably, this would help motivate teachers to continue working to improve their effectiveness.

As you might expect, such a system also has its drawbacks. Establishing a standard is no small task. Just what is reasonable for an A may vary from school to school and from time to time, as a result of ability levels, societal pressures, and curriculum changes. Furthermore, should the same standards be maintained for a gifted or a special education class as for an average class? Another problem is that the public and administrators often have difficulty "adjusting" to a marking system that potentially allows everyone to make an A. It is a curious fact of life that everyone presses for excellence in education, but many balk at marking systems that make attainment of excellence within everyone's reach.

Comparisons with Aptitude   Aptitude is another name for potential or ability. In aptitude-based marking systems students are compared neither to other students nor to established standards. Instead, they are compared to themselves. That is, marks are assigned depending on how closely to their potential students are achieving. Thus students with high aptitude or potential who are achieving at high levels would get high grades, since they would be achieving at their potential. Those with high aptitude and average achievement would get lower grades, since they would be achieving below their potential. But students with average aptitude and average achievement would get high grades, since they would be considered to be achieving at their potential. Such a system sounds attractive to many educators. However, serious problems exist, as Table 11.1 shows.

Table 11.1 illustrates that the concept of assigning grades based on the congruence of a student's achievement with the student's aptitude is quite sensible for high-aptitude students. Look at what happens for the low-aptitude students, however. If a student's aptitude is low enough, the student would have a hard time achieving below his or her potential. Thus the student always would be achieving at or above the expected level. Would this be fair to the moderate- and high-ability students? Perhaps more important, can you see how such a system would greatly complicate interpreting grades? For example, a C for a high-aptitude student might indicate 70% mastery, while for an average-aptitude student it might indicate 60%, and perhaps 50% mastery for the low-aptitude student. The same grade may mean very different things in terms of absolute achievement.

Other drawbacks of such a system relate to statistical considerations beyond the scope of this text that affect the reliability of such comparisons. Another is the tendency for the achievement scores of slow learners to increase and the achievement scores of fast learners to decrease when tested again. Technically this phenomenon is called the *regression toward the mean effect*—the more extreme an achievement score, the more it can be expected to "regress" or fall back toward the average or mean of all students at another testing. Finally, such a system requires more complex record keeping than the first two systems discussed. Such a system, as appealing as it is at first glance, is not practical.

TABLE 11.1 The Relationships among Aptitude, Achievement, and Marks in Marking Systems Based on Comparisons of Achievement with Aptitude

Aptitude Level	Achievement Level	Marks
High	High	High
	Average	Average
	Low	Low
Average	High	High
	Average	High
	Low	Average
Low	High	High
	Average	High
	Low	High

Comparison of Achievement with Effort   Systems that compare achievement with effort are similar to those that compare achievement with aptitude. Students who get average test scores but have to work hard to get them are given high marks. Students who get average scores but do not have to work hard to get them are given lower grades.

Several problems plague marking systems that are based on effort. First, we have no known measure of effort. Unlike aptitude, for which reliable and valid measures exist, effort is at best estimated by informal procedures. Second, within such a system children are punished for being bright and catching on quickly, while other children are rewarded for taking a long time to master concepts. Third, there is the old problem of the marks not representing academic achievement. Effort may cover up academic attainment, making marks all the more difficult to interpret. Finally, record keeping is once again complex.

The advantage cited for grading based on effort is that it serves to motivate the slower or turned off students, but it may also serve to turn off the brighter students who would quickly see such a system as unfair. Whatever the case, the primary function of marking—to provide feedback about academic achievement—is not well served by such a system.

Comparison of Achievement with Improvement   Marking systems may compare the amount of improvement between the beginning (pretest) and end (posttest) of instruction. Students who show the most progress get the highest grades. An obvious problem occurs for the student who does well on the pretest. Improvement for such a student is likely to be less overall than for a student who does poorly on the pretest. In fact, some bright students have been known to "play dumb" on pretests when such systems are in force. Other shortcomings of these systems include the statistical problems we mentioned before in regard to comparisons with aptitude (i.e., unreliability of such comparisons and regression toward the mean) and unwieldy record keeping.

Which System Should You Choose?

We have seen that each system has significant drawbacks as well as advantages. Which should you choose? In our opinion, comparisons with established standards would best suit the primary function of marking—to provide feedback about academic achievement. Once standards are established, comparisons among schools and students may be more easily made. It seems to us that such a system has the best chance of reducing misinterpretation of marks.

In reality, many schools and districts have adopted multiple marking systems, such as assigning separate grades for achievement and effort or for achievement, effort, and improvement. Others are now considering separate grades for paper and pencil tasks and performance and portfolio assessments, such as those we have considered in Chapters 8 and 9. As long as the achievement portion of the grade reflects only achievement, such systems seem to be reasonable. Two disadvantages of such systems are worth noting, however. First, they double or triple the number of grades to be assigned and interpreted, leading to an increase in record keeping and interpretation time. Second, unless the purpose of each grade is explained very clearly on the report card, marking systems are often difficult for parents to decipher.

Types of Symbols

Within marking systems, a variety of symbols have been used. Some of the more common types are discussed in this section.

Letter Grades   Letter grades are the most common symbol system. Many American schools use the letters A–F to report marks. Often, plus and minus symbols are used to indicate finer distinctions between the letter grades. This system, along with its variations (E, G, S, U for excellent, good, satisfactory, or unsatisfactory), has several advantages that have led to its widespread adoption and continuing popularity.

First, the letter system is widely understood. Students, teachers, parents, administrators, and employers understand, at least in a general sense, that grades of A represent excellent or exceptional performance and grades of D or F represent marginal or poor performance. Second, such a system is compact, requiring only one or two spaces to report a summary mark of an entire semester's work. Third, such a system has just about the optimal number of levels of judgment humans can effectively exercise (Miller, 1956). It can have as few as 5 or as many as 15 if plus and minus signs are used.

Limitations of the system are worth considering. First, the specific meaning of letter grades varies from class to class and from school to school. Different schools and districts tend to use different marking systems and, as will be discussed later in this chapter, also tend to combine and weight the components of a mark differently. Consequently, a grade of A in one school or district may represent performance similar to a grade of B or even C in another.

Second, letter grades fail to clearly indicate the student's actual level of mastery. There is often a considerable difference between the achievement of a "low-B" student and that of a "high-B" student. Finally, because of this, averaging of letter grades often results in a loss of information or misinterpretation of the student's actual achievement. When averaging letter grades, it is necessary to go back to the actual numerical grades to obtain the correct average.

Numerical Grades   The numerical symbol system is another type of mark commonly used in the schools. Such systems usually employ 100 as the highest mark, and report cards often carry letter grade equivalents for the range of numerical grades. For example,

Numerical Grade	Letter Grade
90–100	A
80–89	B
70–79	C
60–69	D
Below 60	F

Numerical grades have three main advantages. First, like letter grades, they provide a convenient summary mark for a semester's or year's work. Second, unlike letter grades, numerical grades are easily averaged to obtain the "correct" final marks. Third, they are widely understood—most pupils and parents realize there are substantial differences between a mark of 95 and one of 75.

There are also disadvantages to such a system. First, the discriminations are finer than humans can really make (Miller, 1956). No one can make 40 reliable distinctions between grades from 61 to 100. Another way of saying this is that it is not possible to determine the real difference between a grade of 67 and a grade of 68 or between a grade of 95 and a grade of 96. Second, as with letter grades, we are never sure just what a grade means, since standards may vary considerably from school to school.

Other Symbols   Pass–fail (P–F) grading reached its popularity peak in the 1970s. Fewer schools exclusively employ this approach today because of its shortcomings. One shortcoming is that such symbols do not provide enough information: P could mean the student exhibited anywhere from exceptional to marginal performance in the class. This makes it difficult for employers and admissions officers to evaluate applicants. Students themselves have complained about the same lack of information—they really do not know how well they did. Finally, students tend to do the minimum necessary to earn a P under such systems. When used, pass–fail approaches should at least elaborate the strengths and weaknesses on which the mark was based.

Checklists   A common adjunct to a letter, numerical, or pass–fail symbol system is a checklist. Since those symbol systems may fail to define just what a student can or cannot do, many report cards now include skill checklists to go along with their grade symbols for each subject. Checklists are also used to provide information about nonacademic aspects of the child. For example, checklists often are provided to identify problems in the areas of conduct, social skills, responsibility, and organization. Properly utilized checklists represent useful supplements to letter or numerical grades and can convey much more detailed information about the student without contaminating or confusing the interpretation of a student's overall achievement level.

As mentioned at the beginning of this chapter, districts and schools usually decide which symbol system teachers must use. In such situations you have little choice but to employ the required system. It is more likely, though, that you will have some say about how the marks are actually assigned (i.e., what you will compare student achievement with). Now that you have been exposed to the pros and cons of various systems, you should be able to make better use of any marking or symbol system you are required—or choose—to use. However, there are a number of technical considerations regarding the combining and weighting of the components of a mark that must be considered before we leave this topic. The following discussion covers points that, unfortunately, most classroom teachers are unaware of regarding marks. Master the points and procedures covered, and you will have yet another important tool to add to your growing expertise in classroom measurement and evaluation.

COMBINING AND WEIGHTING THE COMPONENTS OF A MARK

As we mentioned, the classroom teacher seldom has control over the symbol system employed but may have latitude insofar as deciding on the type of comparison used to assign marks at the end of a marking period. But how does a teacher go about combining the grades from two quizzes, one major test, a performance assessment, several home-work assignments, and a term paper into a mark without allowing one or more of these factors to influence the final mark too heavily or lightly? Recall the example at the begin-ning of this chapter. Mr. Stokes said that Jack's failure to turn in two homework assignments earned him "an automatic D," regardless of Jack's achievement on tests, oral reading, papers, etc. While Mr. Stokes later contradicted himself on this point, there are some teachers who do adhere to such or similar practices. This is an example of allowing a component of a mark to influence that mark too heavily. Remember that the main purpose of marks is to provide feedback about student achievement.

It goes without saying that such feedback is beneficial only if it is accurate. To attain this goal, each component of a final mark (tests, quizzes, homework assignments, papers, etc.) should affect the final mark *only to the appropriate extent*. At first glance it might seem simple enough to do this by weighting components considered more impor-tant (e.g., a final test grade) more heavily than components considered less important (e.g., homework grades) in computing the final mark. While differential weighting of components is an important step in arriving at an accurate, fair, and just final mark, it is only one step of several that must be taken, and taken carefully, to prevent a final mark from misrepresenting student achievement. Unfortunately, failure to recognize this fact is widespread in classrooms today. As a result, feedback provided about student achieve-ment through final marks is often distorted. It may be argued that distorted feedback is more troublesome than no feedback at all. To sensitize you to the complexity of what appears to be a simple issue, consider the following scenario.

Who Is the Better Teacher?

Mr. Nickels and Ms. Dimes, history teachers at different high schools in the same district, decided prior to the school year to collaborate in developing their instructional objectives, methods, tests, quizzes, and assignments for the upcoming school year. Since they always had similar students in the past, in terms of background and aptitude, they saw no problem in reducing their workload by using the same objectives, methods, and measure-ment instruments for both of their classes. They did have some concerns about students from the different schools "finding out" that they were using the same materials and sharing them, but they decided that this potential problem could be avoided by adminis-tering the quizzes and tests at the same time and by giving out assignments on the same day. Pleased that they had ironed out all the wrinkles, they agreed to meet at the end of the semester to compare marks. They expected that the marks would be about the same, on average, for both classes, since the marking symbols and the marking system they were required to use by the district were the same in both of their schools, and they both considered quizzes and test grades to be more important than homework or term paper grades. They agreed to weight their students' quiz and test grades twice as heavily in computing their final marks.

Mr. Nickels and Ms. Dimes both prided themselves on their ability and dedication as teachers. They decided that this would be a good opportunity to determine who was the "better" teacher. Since their classes would be similar, and since they would both be using the same objectives, methods, measurement instruments, and weights for the various components that would go into their students' marks, they agreed that any significant difference in the marks earned by their classes must reflect differences in teaching ability and/or effectiveness. To spice things up a bit, they agreed to wager a cheeseburger on the outcome. The competition was on, and both Mr. Nickels and Ms. Dimes anticipated their own students earning the higher marks. Each teacher expected to earn a cheeseburger at the end of the semester.

At their end-of-semester meeting, however, Mr. Nickels was shocked to find that on the average Ms. Dimes's students earned marks that were one-half to a full letter grade higher than those earned by his students. Not panicking, he applied what he had learned in his college tests and measurements class. Mr. Nickels compared aptitude test scores for the two classes, hoping that by chance there would be some difference in aptitude between these two classes and their previous classes. He expected he would find significantly higher aptitude scores for Ms. Dimes's class, which would explain why their semester marks were higher than those of his class. After comparing aptitude scores for the two classes, however, Mr. Nickels found them to be quite comparable. "I could have told you that," responded Ms. Dimes somewhat haughtily.

Unwilling to concede and suspicious by nature, Mr. Nickels next suggested that Ms. Dimes must have "fixed" things by changing the curriculum—perhaps only covering two-thirds of the material he covered. This would have enabled her students to have more time to master the material and thereby earn higher grades. Offended by this challenge to her integrity, Ms. Dimes tossed her objectives, curriculum guide, and all the semester's assignments, quizzes, and tests to Mr. Nickels. "Read 'em and weep!" she exclaimed. And Mr. Nickels did ... at first. After comparing the materials piece by piece with his own, he found them to be identical. Next, however, he laboriously compared the test and quiz grades for both classes, since this is what both he and Ms. Dimes agreed would be the major basis for the marks of their students. To his relief he discovered that the scores from both classes on the tests and quizzes *were about the same.*

"Look here, Ms. Dimes! The test and quiz grades for both classes are the same— you must have made a mistake in computing your marks," said Mr. Nickels. "Impossible, I triple-checked all my computations," stated Ms. Dimes firmly. However, when she compared the grades herself she agreed that Mr. Nickels was correct. The test and quiz grades were similar, yet she had assigned marks that on the average were one-half to a full letter grade higher than those assigned by Mr. Nickels.

Both teachers were confused. Not only were they unable to settle their bet, they were puzzled as to how such a situation could occur. They decided to review the procedures they used to combine and weight the marks their pupils had obtained. What they learned from this review is described in the next section.

Combining Grades from Quizzes, Tests, Papers, Homework, Etc., into a Single Mark

Let's consider a set of grades earned by a typical student in Mr. Nickels's class, who earned a mark of B, and a set of grades of a typical student in Ms. Dimes's class, who also earned a B (see Table 11.2). Remember, both teachers used the same measurement instruments and applied the same scoring schemes to those instruments. Also, consistent with good measurement practice, they included only *achievement* factors in assigning their marks, not *nonachievement* factors such as attendance, conduct, appearance, effort, etc.

TABLE 11.2 Grades of Nickels's and Dimes's Students

	Student (Nickels's)	Student (Dimes's)
Semester test (75-100)	86	76
Quiz no. 1 (5–10)	9	5
Quiz no. 2 (5–10)	9	7
Homework (15–25)	18	25
Paper (15–25)	18	25
Total points earned	**140**	**138**

Note: The lowest and highest scores for each component are in parentheses.

Simply looking at the data in Table 11.2 indicates that student performance was different in an important way. Ms. Dimes's student obtained very low test and quiz grades but had very high homework and term paper grades, while Mr. Nickels's student displayed an opposite tendency. Yet both earned about the same number of overall points out of a possible 170, and both received Bs. Since both teachers emphasize test and quiz grades over homework and term paper grades, this doesn't make sense, especially when one considers that Ms. Dimes's student had the lowest grade on one quiz and the second lowest grade on the final test—yet still earned a mark of B! To understand how this happened we must consider how the obtained component scores were combined and weighted by the teachers.

Ms. Dimes, doing what most teachers commonly do in such situations, simply assigned double weight to the quiz and test scores and then added the scores:

$$(76 \times 2) + (5 \times 2) + (7 \times 2) + 25 + 25 = 226$$

Next she divided this number by the total number of points possible, $(100 \times 2) + (10 \times 2) + (10 \times 2) + 25 + 25 = 290$, to arrive at the percentage of points earned by the student:

$$(226/290) \times 100 = 78\%.$$

Since the district mandated that students who earn 78–88.99% of possible points be assigned a B, she assigned a mark of B to this student and followed the same procedure for all her students. Thus even though Ms. Dimes herself believes that test and quiz performance is most important, and "weighted" those scores to reflect her belief, this student ended up with a grade of B in spite of having the lowest grade on one of the quizzes and close to the lowest grade on the final test! Unknowingly and unintentionally, Ms. Dimes is employing a combining and weighting procedure that contradicts her beliefs and her intent.

Mr. Nickels assigned the *same weight* to the various components as did Ms. Dimes. However, he recalled that in his tests and measurements class his instructor emphasized the importance of considering the *variation*, or *range*, of the scores, not just the scores themselves, in combining component scores into a *composite score*. Mr. Nickels also recalled that the reason for this is that *it is the extent of the variability of the scores of each component that largely determines the extent of the component's contribution to the composite score, NOT simply the weight attached to the component.*

Notice that each of the grade components was scored using scales of different ranges. The range is obtained by subtracting the lowest score from the highest score. A more accurate estimate of variation, called the *standard deviation* (covered in Chapter 13), is actually preferable to the range when combining component scores into a composite score. However, the range is an adequate estimate for most classroom purposes and is less time-consuming and easier to compute than the standard deviation. Here are the ranges for the five score components:

Component	Range
Semester test	$100 - 75 = 25$
Quiz no. 1	$10 - 5 = 5$
Quiz no. 2	$10 - 5 = 5$
Homework	$25 - 15 = 10$
Paper	$25 - 15 = 10$

After determining the range for each of the components, Mr. Nickels decided to *equate the variability of each component before he could double the weights of the quizzes and the tests.* Since the semester test had the greatest range, 25 points, he did so by multiplying the quizzes by 5, the homework grade by 2.5, and the paper grade by 2.5. This procedure *equated* the variability of the scores (i.e., all components then had a range of 25 points). Only then did he *weight* the scores by multiplying the quiz and test scores by 2. Table 11.3 illustrates the procedure followed by Mr. Nickels. The maximum number of points possible, after equating and weighting, is 525 (200 + 100 + 100 + 62.5 + 62.5 = 525). Dividing the points earned by the points possible gives us the student's percentage:

$$(442/525) \times 100 = 84.19\%$$

Recalling that the district's policy is to assign a B to all students who earn between 78% and 88.99% of possible points, Mr. Nickels assigned a mark of B to this student—

TABLE 11.3 Weighting Procedure Followed by Mr. Nickels

	Score	×	Equating factor	=	Equated score	×	Weight	=	Weighted score
Semester test	86	×	1		86	×	2		172
Quiz no. 1	9	×	5		45	×	2		90
Quiz no. 2	9	×	5		45	×	2		90
Homework	18	×	2.5		45	×	1		45
Paper	18	×	2.5		45	×	1		45
Total									**442**

the same mark assigned by Ms. Dimes to her student, in spite of this student's significantly better test and quiz performance.

Which procedure best achieved the goals of the teacher, that is, to weight test and quiz performance *twice* as heavily as homework and term paper performance? Which procedure do you think is more fair? Which procedure is less likely to result in a storm of protest from the students, who will invariably compare their scores and marks?

Let's consider one more example. This time let's compare the effects of Mr. Nickels's correct procedure on the mark earned by Ms. Dimes's student, as shown in Table 11.4.

TABLE 11.4 Effect of Mr. Nickels's Correct Procedure on Ms. Dimes's Student's Mark

	Score	×	Equating factor	=	Equated score	×	Weight	=	Weighted score
Semester test	76	×	1		76	×	2		152
Quiz no. 1	5	×	5		25	×	2		50
Quiz no. 2	7	×	5		35	×	2		70
Homework	25	×	2.5		62.5	×	1		62.5
Paper	25	×	2.5		62.5	×	1		62.5
Total									**397.0**

Dividing the total points earned after equating and weighting (397) by the total points possible (525) gives us the percentage of points earned:

$$(397/525) \times 100 = 75.6\%$$

According to the district's policy, this student mark would be a C. Clearly, it is more fair that this student, who has such low test and quiz grades, be assigned a lower semester mark than a student whose test and quiz grades are significantly higher.

We hope that this example has sensitized you to a potential problem in assigning semester or grading period marks. When developing a composite mark from scores with different ranges or variation, remember to *equate before you weight* to avoid the problem encountered by Ms. Dimes.

However, in the face of the increasing demands placed on today's classroom teacher, finding the time to go through the outlined procedures may prove to be frustrating. Furthermore, in these examples we have only considered a limited sample of mark components: test, quiz, homework, and paper. Today, most teachers also have to include marks for performance assessments, portfolios, and notebooks in their composite semester or other marking period summary marks. As important as it may be to accurate measurement, remembering to equate all these components before you weight may be lost in the face of the other important instructional, administrative, and legal considerations (see Chapter 1) that today's classroom teacher is faced with. To guard against such an oversight we will next present equating procedures that are less computationally complex, less time-consuming, and, we believe, more congruent with the typical teacher's intuitive marking practices.

PRACTICAL APPROACHES TO EQUATING BEFORE WEIGHTING IN THE BUSY CLASSROOM

The approaches we present in this section represent compromises between the equating approach taken by Mr. Nickels and the nonequating approach taken by Ms. Dimes. Technically, even Mr. Nickels's approach is a compromise since, from a statistical perspective, the standard deviation rather than the range is the preferred variability measure to be used in developing a composite score or mark. We believe that the following methods represent an efficient way for busy teachers to incorporate equating considerations (although they are approximations) into their marking procedures. By presenting these methods we hope to minimize the likelihood that equating will be overlooked completely.

Performance and portfolio assessments require a substantial commitment of teacher time and learner-engaged time. Consequently, a teacher who decides to use them should ensure that the performance assessment has substantial weight in the 6-week or final report card grade. The following equating methods lend themselves well to the relatively straightforward inclusion of these important additional measures to the traditional test, quiz, homework, and paper components of a mark.

Front-End Equating

The front-end equating approach requires that you immediately convert all grades assigned to a 100-point scale (i.e., a percentage) by dividing the number of points obtained on every component by the total number of points possible and multiplying by 100. For example, a student who obtains 37 of 50 possible points on a performance assessment would be assigned a grade of 74:

$$(37/50) \times 100 = 74\%$$

This is a very common practice followed by many teachers. If all components (e.g., tests, quizzes, etc.) are similarly converted then all grades will be on the same 100-point scale. Each component will then have the same potential range of 100 points; you have thereby equated the scores without having to go through Mr. Nickels's more time-consuming (but more technically correct) procedure.[1] Computing the composite mark, then, simply involves averaging the grades for each component, multiplying these averages by the weight assigned to the component, and adding the products to determine the final grade. Figure 11.1 provides examples of three formulas to accomplish this.

---

[1] This approach and the following approach are intended to promote comparable variation in scale scores across components that will be combined into a final mark. They assume that the variation of actual scale scores for each component will be approximately the same, that is, that you use the full or comparable portions of the scale across components.

Marking Formula Example #1:

This formula is known as the "One, Two, Three Times Plan."

Homework and classwork:

All grades recorded for homework and claswork will be totaled and averaged. The average grade will count once (one-sixth of the six-week mark).

Example homework and classwork grades:

84, 81 88, 92, 96, 85, 78, 83, 91, 79, 89, 94 = 1040/12 = 86.7 = 87 average

Quizzes:

All of the quizzes are totaled and averaged. This average grade will count two times (one-third of the six-week mark).

Example quiz grades:

82, 88, 80, 91, 78, 86 = 505/6 = 84.2 = 84 average

Performance assessments:

All of the performance assessment grades will be totaled and averaged. This average grade will count three times (one-half of the six-week mark).

Example performance assessment grades:

81, 91, 86 = 258/3 = 86 average

Then, the six-week mark would be computed as follows:

87 (one time) + 84 + 84 (two times) + 86 + 86 + 86 (three times) = 513/6 = 85.5 = 86 as the six-week mark.

Marking Formula Example #2:

This formula is known as the "Percentages Plan."

A teacher determines a percentage for each component. For example, homework and classwork will count for 20 percent of the grade: quizzes will count for 40 percent of the grade; and performance assessments will count for 40 percent of the grade.

Using the same scores as previously listed, a student's mark would be computed as follows:

20% of the 86.7 for homework and classwork is 17.3,

40% of the 84.2 for quizzes is 33.7, and

40% of he 86 for performance assessments is 34.4

17.3 + 33.7 + 34.4 = 85.4 as the six-week mark.

(This mark differs from the mark obtained from Example #1 because the weight put on each component differs in the two examples.)

Marking Formula Example #3:

This formula is known as the "Language Arts Plan."

A language arts teacher determines that the publishing, goal meeting, journal, and daily process grades each count one-fourth (25 percent) of the six-week mark.

A language arts mark will be computed as follows:

The publishing grade, issued at the end of the six-week period, is 88.

The goal meeting grade, issued at the end of the six-week period, is 86.

The journal grades are: 82 + 92 + 94 + 90 + 88 + 86 = 532/6 = 88.7 = 89.

The daily process grades are: 78 + 82 + 94 + 94 + 91 + 86 = 525/6 = 87.5 = 88.

The six-week mark would be: 88 + 86 + 89 + 88 = 351/4 = 87.75 = 88.

FIGURE 11.1 Three examples of different front-end ways to equate and weight a six-week mark based on grades from a 100-point scale.

Back-End Equating

With the "back-end" approach you decide how many points each component of your marking system is worth on a case-by-case basis. You may want some tests to be worth 40 points, some 75, some 14, and so on, since the total point value should depend on the complexity of the items and the number of discriminations you can reliably make, rather than a multiple of 5 or 10, as is common practice. Similarly, some homework assignments may be worth 10 points, or 7 points; portfolios may be worth 23 points, or 64 points, and so on. The front-end approach requires you to convert the scores to percentages before combining them. As we shall see, this approach addresses this consideration at the back end rather than the beginning of the process. Both approaches will lead to the same outcome, so experiment with both until you find one that best fits your style. Here are the procedures involved in setting up a "back-end" marking scheme for a 6-week marking period.

Step 1: Identify the components of your marking system and assign each component a weight. Recall that a weight is the percentage of total points a particular component carries. For example,

Component	Weight
Homework	15%
Objective tests	20%
Performance tests	20%
Portfolio	20%
Classroom work	15%
Notebook	10%
	100%

Step 2: Record the actual points earned out of the total possible in the grade book. Leave a column for totals. These scores are illustrated in Fig. 11.2. As you can see, each component and each separate assignment have varying numbers of points possible to be earned. Assign possible points for each component based on the length of the assignment, your ability to make reliable distinctions, etc.

Step 3: Total the actual points earned for each component and divide this by the possible points and multiply by 100. The results represent the percentage of points earned for each particular component. In our example from Fig. 11.2, Cornell and Rosie earned the following total points:

	Cornell	Rosie
Homework	50/70 = 71	55/70 = 79
Objective tests	45/60 = 75	35/60 = 58
Performance tests	33/40 = 83	39/40 = 98
Portfolio	18/20 = 90	15/20 = 75
Classroom work	39/50 = 78	37/50 = 74
Notebook	5/10 = 50	8/10 = 80

Component	Dates	Cornell	Rosie
Homework	8/20	10/10	10/10
	9/7	8/10	5/10
	9/14	14/15	12/15
	9/20	10/10	8/10
	9/28	8/15	12/15
	10/6	0/10	8/10
	Total	**50/70**	**55/70**
Objective tests	9/17	20/30	15/30
	10/7	25/30	20/30
	Total	**45/60**	**35/60**
Performance tests	9/23	15/20	20/20
	10/8	18/20	19/20
	Total	**33/40**	**39/40**
Portfolio	**10/7**	**18/20**	**15/20**
Classwork	9/2	9/10	8/10
	9/6	7/15	14/15
	9/14	10/10	0/10
	9/23	9/10	10/10
	10/5	4/5	5/5
	Total	**39/50**	**37/50**
Notebook	**10/8**	**5/10**	**8/10**

FIGURE 11.2 Sample grade recording sheet, first six weeks.

Step 4: Multiply each of these percentages by the weights assigned, as shown here, and then sum the products.

	Cornell	*Rosie*
Homework	$71 \times 0.15 = 10.6$	$79 \times 0.15 = 11.8$
Objective tests	$75 \times 0.20 = 15.0$	$58 \times 0.20 = 11.6$
Performance tests	$83 \times 0.20 = 16.6$	$98 \times 0.20 = 19.6$
Portfolio	$90 \times 0.20 = 18.0$	$75 \times 0.20 = 15.0$
Classroom work	$78 \times 0.15 = 11.7$	$74 \times 0.15 = 11.1$
Notebook	$50 \times 0.10 =\ 5.0$	$80 \times 0.10 =\ 8.0$
Totals	**76.9**	**77.1**

Step 5: Record the 6-week mark either as a letter grade (e.g., A = 90 − 100, B = 80 − 89.99, etc.) or as the total (i.e., percentage) for each student, depending on your district's policy.

SUMMARY

This chapter introduced you to various issues related to marks and marking systems. Its major points are as follows:

1. Marks are used to provide information about student achievement.

2. Marks should reflect academic achievement and nothing more. Grades for attitude, effort, improvement, conduct, and so on should be recorded separately from marks.

3. Marks often reflect factors other than achievement and are often assigned according to a variety of marking systems. This makes valid comparisons of marks across schools, and even across teachers, difficult at best.

4. Several types of marking systems are employed in the schools today. These involve comparison of a student with:

   a. Other students (grades depend on how well the student did compared with other students).
   b. Established standards (grades depend on how well a student's performance compares with pre-established standards).
   c. Aptitude (grades depend on how consistent a student's actual achievement is with his or her achievement potential).
   d. Effort (grades depend on how hard the student works).
   e. Improvement (grades depend on how much progress a student makes over the course of instruction).

5. Each system has its advantages and disadvantages, but marking based on comparisons with established standards seems to best fit the main function of marks—to provide feedback about academic achievement.

6. The symbols most commonly used in marking systems are letter grades (A–F, E–U) and numerical grades (0–100). Such symbol systems are often combined with checklists to provide specific information about such factors as skill level, conduct, and attitude.

7. When combining grades from quizzes, tests, papers, homework, etc., that have different ranges or variation, and which are not on 100-point scales, equate the variability of each component before weighting and computing the final mark.

8. A practical alternative to this technique is to use the front-end or back-end equating approaches. These approaches yield approximate but similar outcomes, and they are less time-consuming ways to equate scores from quizzes, tests, homework, performance assessments, portfolios, and notebooks.

FOR PRACTICE

1. List the pros and cons of each of the following types of marking systems:

a. Comparison with other students.

b. Comparison with established standards.

c. Comparison of achievement with one's own aptitude.

d. Basing grades on effort.

e. Basing grades on improvement.

2. Create a numerical scale for measuring effort and another for measuring improvement. For each level of the scale, indicate the type of behavior(s) you are looking for. What might be another way of measuring those two qualities?

3. Choose the most appropriate marking system from among the following pairs of symbol systems and give reasons for your choices.

a. A–F and 0–100

b. 0–100 and P–F

c. E–U and P–F

4. The school in which you will teach will probably have an established marking system to report subject matter grades. With what behaviors might you augment this marking system to report to students and parents additional information you think is important? How would you measure these additional behaviors?

*****5.** Using the following scores obtained from a single student, use both the front-end and back-end methods to determine an overall mark: Quiz, 10 out of 15; test, 32 out of 50; paper, 8 out of 10; homework, 80 out of 100; portfolio, 9 out of 10. You decided that the quiz, test, paper, homework, and portfolio would be weighted 15, 30, 30, 10, and 15% of the final mark, respectively. What is the final numerical mark? What letter grade would be assigned if A = 90–100, B = 80–89.99, C = 70–79.99, D = 65–69.99, and F = 64.99 and below? Why does the same numerical mark result from both the front-end and back-end approaches?

* Answer for question 5 appears in Appendix F.

CHAPTER 12

SUMMARIZING DATA AND MEASURES OF CENTRAL TENDENCY

FOR MANY, the term statistics forebodes evil. It is probably one of the most misunderstood terms in education. A statistician, or statistical expert, is stereotypically seen as a social isolate who lacks a sense of humor, speaks in strange tongues, and knows how to make numbers say whatever he or she desires them to say. Indeed, in some doctoral programs, courses in statistics are acceptable as substitutes for foreign languages! Having taught statistics courses, both authors are keenly aware of the anxiety and/or resentment many students feel when they are required or encouraged to take their first statistics course. As we mentioned in Chapter 1, however, fewer than 1% of the students we have taught fail courses in tests and measurement because of statistics. Then why are students so anxious about statistics?

The answer, we believe, lies in the misconceptions students have about statistics and statisticians. Let's clarify some things. We do not intend that you become full-fledged statisticians after completing this section of the text. In fact, a complete program of graduate study is usually necessary before one can call oneself a statistician. Perhaps you know students who suffered through an introductory statistics course. Will you have to undergo the trauma they may have undergone? Again, the answer is no. Even courses in introductory statistics treat this topic in much greater depth than is necessary for a course in tests and measurement. If you did well on the self-test and review in Appendix A, you have little to fear. If you failed to do well, brush up on the fundamentals presented in Appendix A until you do perform well. After you completed the review it should have been apparent that the four basic functions—addition, subtraction, multiplication, and division—will suffice for the statistics we will deal with. Master these operations, and with a little work (and an open mind), mastery of statistics at the tests and measurement level will soon follow.

WHAT ARE STATISTICS?

Thus far we have been talking about statistics in general. In reality, there are two types of statistics: descriptive and inferential. For our purposes we will deal entirely with the "easy" side of statistics, descriptive statistics. Inferential statistics are more complicated and are best taught in more advanced courses.

Descriptive statistics are simply numbers, for example, percentages, numerals, fractions, and decimals. These numbers are used to describe or summarize a larger body of numbers. For example, if you wanted to give someone an indication of how your grades have been in college, you could list all your courses and the grade you received in each course, or you could simply report your grade point average (GPA). Both approaches have advantages and disadvantages, of course, but we think you will agree that reporting your GPA would normally be the most useful approach. In this example, the GPA is a descriptive or summary statistic, since it describes or summarizes extensive data.

In the classroom the typical teacher has from 25 to 30 pupils. When a test is administered to the class, 25 to 30 test scores result. If a teacher gives 10 tests over the year, 250 to 300 test scores result. Naturally, these scores would be recorded in the teacher's grade book, but when it comes time to report grades to parents at the end of the year, are they all reported? Obviously not. Instead, teachers report descriptive or summary statistics—that is, grades—probably without realizing they are reporting statistics!

Any time you deal with averages (GPAs, batting averages), rates (death rates, birth rates), or other numbers used to describe or summarize a larger body of numbers, you are dealing with descriptive or summary statistics. All of us deal with statistics daily. One of our goals for this chapter is to make you better users and consumers of such information. We hope to do this by going a little beyond common sense statistics and looking at statistics and their uses more systematically.

WHY USE STATISTICS?

As we said, the term statistics is frequently misunderstood. Although some people want nothing to do with statistics, statistics are important and appear to be an increasingly important aspect of our personal as well as professional lives. Any time you read, hear, or see "a 70% chance of rain" or "82% of doctors surveyed recommend" or "an EPA average of 32 miles per gallon," you are being exposed to statistics. Exposure to statistics will not go away. The ability to understand and profit from everyday statistics is well within your reach. You will become a better interpreter of educational data (and thus a better teacher) by mastering the statistical concepts presented in this section of the text.

You will also become a better consumer of everyday data presented in advertising, public relations, opinion polls, and so forth. Much of what you learn in teacher training may seem to have little application outside the classroom. This is not the case for statistics. Master the concepts in this chapter and they will serve you throughout your personal and professional life.

With increasing calls for accountability, it will become all the more important that classroom teachers understand the statistics reported to them and the statistics they report to others. Needless to say, the teacher who understands the uses and limitations of various kinds of statistical data will have a decided advantage over the teacher who lacks such understanding. While your professional survival and development may not depend entirely on a working knowledge of statistics, they may certainly be enhanced by it.

TABULATING FREQUENCY DATA

The classroom teacher normally deals with a large amount of data, usually in the form of test scores. As more and more scores accumulate, it gets more and more difficult to make sense of the data. It becomes more and more difficult to answer questions such as the following:

How many people are above average?

How many scored above the cutoff passing score?

Did most of the class do well on the test?

What is the highest or lowest score?

Keeping these questions in mind, consider the following set of scores obtained by 25 sixth-grade children on a math test:

36	63	51	43	93
54	48	84	36	45
57	45	48	96	66
54	72	81	30	27
45	51	47	63	88

Without doing anything to these test scores, are you able to answer the questions? You cannot answer the first two questions until you compute the average score and establish the cutoff or passing score. But what about the last two questions?

You can eventually answer these questions, but it takes a lot of time to do so. In arriving at answers to the last two questions, you probably resorted to some sort of strategy to organize the data so they make sense. For example, to determine whether "most of the class did well" you may have crossed off and counted the number of scores in the 80s and 90s.

Whatever the strategy you used, you used it because the 25 scores, as they stood, were difficult to make sense of or to interpret. Next we will consider several systematic ways to make sense of an unwieldy group of numbers. We will be organizing or introducing some sort of order to unorganized, unordered test scores. The first method is to simply list the scores in ascending or descending numerical order.

The List

Let's list our set of 25 scores in descending order:

96	72	54	48	43
93	66	54	47	36
88	63	51	45	36
84	63	51	45	30
81	57	48	45	27

Introducing some order or "sense" into this group of scores makes trends, patterns, and individual scores easier to find and to interpret. At a glance we can now determine the highest score, lowest score, and even the middle score. We can easily see that only five students scored above 80 on the test. Listing has helped us organize this set of scores. But what if we had 50 scores, or 100 scores, or 1000 scores?

As the number of scores increases, the advantage of simply listing scores decreases. Many scores will repeat themselves several times. It becomes more and more difficult to make sense of data when the number of scores would require a lot of paper. Also, when you list data there are usually many missing scores (e.g., 95, 94, 92, 91, 90, 89, 87, and so on, in the previous example). Failure to consider these missing scores can sometimes result in a misrepresentation of the data.

To sum up, a simple list summarizes data conveniently if N, the number of scores, is small. If N is large, however, lists become difficult to interpret. Trends are not always very clear, numbers tend to repeat themselves, and there are usually a lot of missing scores. Next we will consider a *simple frequency distribution*. This approach to tabulating data considers all scores, including those that are missing.

The Simple Frequency Distribution

Inspecting the simple frequency distribution in Table 12.1 may cause as much or more confusion as the original group of 25 unorganized scores. Usually, for classroom purposes, a simple frequency distribution is too unwieldy. Unless your tests yield a narrow spread of scores, simple frequency distributions tend to be so lengthy that it is difficult to make sense of the data, which is what we are trying to do. Seldom will a simple frequency distribution prove useful in the average classroom.

In summary, a simple frequency distribution will summarize data effectively *only* if the spread of scores is small. If there is a large amount of variation in test scores, a simple frequency distribution usually results in a table similar to Table 12.1, full of zeros in the frequency column and with so many categories that it becomes difficult to interpret the data. Fortunately, a variation of the simple frequency distribution, called the *grouped frequency distribution*, eliminates these shortcomings and can be quite useful in the classroom. Let's consider this variation.

The Grouped Frequency Distribution

The grouped frequency distribution method of tabulating data is very similar to the simple frequency distribution, except that ranges or intervals of scores are used for categories rather than considering each possible score as a category. The following is a grouped frequency distribution for the 25 scores we've been talking about:

Interval	f
91–97	2
84–90	2
77–83	1
70–76	1
63–69	3
56–62	1
49–55	4
42–48	7
35–41	2
28–34	1
21–27	1

TABLE 12.1 Simple Frequency Distribution

X (Score)	f (Frequency)	X (Score)	f (Frequency)
96	1	61	0
95	0	60	0
94	0	59	0
93	1	58	0
92	0	57	1
91	0	56	0
90	0	55	0
89	0	54	2
88	1	53	0
87	0	52	0
86	0	51	2
85	0	50	0
84	1	49	0
83	0	48	2
82	0	47	1
81	1	46	0
80	0	45	3
79	0	44	0
78	0	43	1
77	0	42	0
76	0	41	0
75	0	40	0
74	0	39	0
73	0	38	0
72	1	37	0
71	0	36	2
70	0	36	0
69	0	34	0
68	0	33	0
67	0	32	0
66	1	31	0
65	0	30	1
64	0	29	0
63	2	28	0
62	0	27	1

Contrast this grouped frequency distribution with the simple frequency distribution and with the listing of scores. The grouped frequency distribution has two major advantages over the listing and the simple frequency distribution. It compresses the size of the table and makes the data much more interpretable. At a glance it becomes apparent that most of the class (as indicated by the numbers in the frequency column) obtained scores of 55 or below. If we add the numbers in the f column, we can see specifically that 15 (4 + 7 + 2 + 1 + 1 = 15) of the 25 students in the class scored 55 or below. That is, four students scored between 49 and 55, seven scored between 42 and 48, two scored between 35 and 41, one scored between 28 and 34, and one scored between 21 and 27.

Since most of the class scored 55 or lower, one interpretation the grouped frequency distribution helps us make is that the test may have been too difficult. However, at least three other possible interpretations are suggested: Perhaps the students simply failed to prepare for the test; perhaps the students need more instruction in this area because they are slower than the teacher expected them to be; perhaps the instruction was ineffective or inappropriate.

Whichever of these interpretations is correct is irrelevant to us at the moment. What is important is that once we construct a grouped frequency distribution, it quickly becomes apparent that the class did not do well on the test. We may have arrived at the same conclusion after looking at the listing of scores or at the simple frequency distribution, but it certainly would take longer. Thus a grouped frequency distribution does help us make sense of a set of scores. But there are also disadvantages to using a grouped frequency distribution.

The main disadvantage of a grouped frequency distribution is that information about individual scores is lost. As a result, the information we deal with becomes less accurate. Consider the interval of scores 49–55 in the previous grouped frequency distribution. We see that four scores fell in this interval. However, exactly what were these scores? Were they 49, 51, 53, and 55? Or were they 49, 50, 51, and 54? Or were all four scores 49? Or were two scores 52 and two scores 53? Or 51? The four scores could be any conceivable combination of scores. Without referring to the original list of scores, we cannot tell.

While a grouped frequency distribution compresses table size and makes data easier to interpret, it does so at the expense of accuracy and information about individual scores. Usually the advantages of constructing grouped frequency distributions are great enough to offset the disadvantages. Next we will consider the steps involved in actually constructing a grouped frequency distribution.

Steps in Constructing a Grouped Frequency Distribution

Step 1: Determine the range of scores (symbolized by R). The range (or spread) of scores is determined by subtracting the lowest score (L) from the highest score (H).

Formula	*Application*
R = H − L	R = 96 − 27 = 69

The range of scores for the 25 sixth graders is 69.

Step 2: Determine the appropriate number of intervals. The number of intervals or categories used in a grouped frequency distribution is somewhat flexible or arbitrary. Different authorities will suggest that you select from among 5, 10, or 15 intervals, or 8, 10, 12, or 15 intervals, and so on. In our example we used 11 intervals. Well, then, what is "correct"?

As we said, this decision is somewhat arbitrary. In making such decisions, though, be sure to use as many categories or intervals as are necessary to demonstrate variations in the frequencies of scores. In other words, if you decide to use five intervals and find that for an N of 25 scores there are frequencies of five in each interval, the number of intervals is too small. Increasing the number of intervals to 10 in this case should result in different frequencies for each interval. Selecting too many intervals is also a possibility.

Generally, if you find more than one interval with zero in the frequency column, you have decided on too many intervals. If this all sounds confusing, that's because in some ways it is. The bottom line is that sometimes it is necessary to experiment a little. You may have to vary the number of intervals until you find the number you feel best represents your data. It is generally best to begin with 8 or 10 intervals when constructing a grouped frequency distribution for a group of 25 to 30 scores, the typical number of scores resulting from a classroom test. Increase the number of intervals for larger score sets.

Step 3: Divide the range by the number of intervals you decide to use and round to the nearest odd number. This will give you i, the interval width:

Formula	*Application*
$i = \dfrac{R}{\text{number of intervals}}$	$i = \dfrac{69}{10}$
	$= 6.9$ (rounded to nearest odd number $= 7$)

The width of the interval is 7. If we decided to use 8 for our number of intervals we would arrive at a wider interval width.

Formula	*Application*
$i = \dfrac{R}{\text{number of intervals}}$	$i = \dfrac{69}{8}$
	$= 8.6$ (rounded to nearest odd number $= 9$)

If we decide to use 15 intervals, we would arrive at a narrower interval width than we would with 10 or 8 intervals.

Formula	*Application*
$i = \dfrac{R}{\text{number of intervals}}$	$i = \dfrac{69}{15}$
	$= 4.6$ (rounded to nearest odd number $= 5$)

You can see there is an inverse relationship between the number of intervals and the width of each interval. That is, as fewer intervals are used, the width of each interval increases; as more intervals are used, the interval width decreases. Also, keep in mind that as i, the interval width, increases, we lose more and more information about individual scores.

Step 4: Construct the interval column making sure that the lowest score in each interval, called the lower limit (LL), is a multiple of the interval width (i). The upper limit of each interval (UL) is one point less than the lower limit of the next interval. All this means is that the lowest score of each interval should be a value that is equal to the interval width times 1, 2, 3, etc. With an interval width of 7, the LL of each interval could be 7, 14, 21, etc. (7×1, 7×2, 7×3, etc.). However, we eliminate those intervals below and above the intervals that include or "capture" the lowest and highest scores. Consider the following sets of intervals for which the highest score was 96 and the lowest score was 27:

Lower Limit	*Upper Limit*	
112	118	
105	111	
98	104	
91	97	← Highest score captured;
84	90	eliminate all intervals above.
77	83	
70	76	
63	69	
56	62	
49	55	
42	48	
35	41	
28	34	
21	27	← Lowest score captured;
14	20	eliminate all intervals below.
7	13	

We retain only the intervals 21–27 through 91–97. Thus, the interval column of our grouped frequency distribution should look like this:

Intervals
91–97
84–90
77–83
70–76
63–69
56–62
49–55
42–48
35–41
28–34
21–27

Step 5: Construct the f, or frequency, column by tallying the number of scores that are captured by each interval.

Intervals	Tally	f
91–97	||	2
84–90	||	2
77–83			1
70–76			1
63–69	|||	3
56–62			1
49–55	|||	4
42–48	|||| ||	7
35–41	||	2
28–34			1
21–27			1

Next, simply eliminate the tally column and you have a grouped frequency distribution.

However, didn't we decide we wanted 10 intervals? How is it we ended up with 11? The answer to the first question is yes, but it is not unusual to end up with one more or one less interval than you intended. This happens because of what we often end up doing at Step 3.

Step 3. We round to the nearest odd number. The inaccuracy we introduce by rounding to the nearest odd number is multiplied by the number of intervals (since in effect we do this for each interval). The result is that the range from the upper limit of the highest interval to the lower limit of the lowest interval is greater than the range from the highest score to the lowest score. In our example:

$$
\begin{array}{lr}
\text{Upper limit of highest interval} & 97 \\
\text{Lower limit of lowest interval} & \underline{-21} \\
& 76 \\
\\
\text{High score} & 96 \\
\text{Low score} & \underline{-27} \\
& 69
\end{array}
$$

Notice the difference between 76 and 69. The extra interval is needed to include the extra values. Fortunately, ending up with one more or one less interval than we intended is not a serious problem. We need only be aware of it, not unduly concerned with it.

Before we leave grouped frequency distributions, let's clarify one more point. In Step 3 we said "round to the nearest odd number." There is no sound mathematical reason for this recommendation. Rather, it serves to simplify determining the midpoint of the interval. While the midpoint is of little importance for grouped frequency distributions, it is important in the construction of a *frequency polygon*, a graphical representation of a grouped frequency distribution, which we will consider next.

GRAPHING DATA

"A picture is worth a thousand words" is a well-worn expression, but it is especially applicable to statistics. Some of you may have the ability to extract meaning from groups of numbers, but others, the authors included, need to see graphical representations before such data can be meaningful. In any case, a graph will almost always clarify or simplify the information presented in a grouped frequency distribution. There are three types of graphs we will consider: the *bar graph*, or *histogram*; the *frequency polygon*; and the *smooth curve*.

The Bar Graph, or Histogram

The bar graph, or histogram, is the type of graph used most frequently to convey statistical data. The histogram in Fig. 12.1 is based on the grouped frequency distribution used earlier to represent the scores of 25 sixth graders.

In constructing a histogram, or bar graph, several guidelines, which are listed in Fig. 12.2, should be followed. The interpretation of bar graphs is straightforward. The higher the column, the greater the number of scores falling in that interval. The lower the column, the fewer the number of scores falling in that interval.

The Frequency Polygon

Technically, a frequency polygon is best used for graphically representing what are called continuous data, such as test scores. Continuous data usually represent entities that can be expressed as fractions or parts of whole numbers, for example, achievement test scores and grade point averages. Histograms are best used for graphically representing discrete or noncontinuous data. Discrete or noncontinuous data represent entities that usually cannot be expressed as fractioned parts of anything and, hence, signify different dimensions, for example, Catholics, Protestants, and Jews. However, we need not be overly concerned with discriminating between continuous and discrete data because much overlap exists in the actual ways these two types of graphs are used.

For our purposes, what is the critical difference between a histogram and a frequency polygon? The answer is that a frequency polygon is an alternative way of

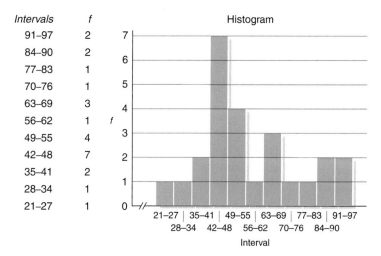

FIGURE 12.1 Histogram based on a grouped frequency distribution.

1. The vertical axis should be three-fourths as long as the horizontal axis to help prevent misrepresenting the data.

2. Scores are listed along the horizontal axis and increase from left to right. Frequencies are listed along the vertical axis and increase from bottom to top.

3. Double slash marks (//) are used to indicate breaks in the sequence of numbers (horizontal axis) or in the sequence of frequencies (vertical axis).

4. Points in the scales along the axes are expanded or compressed so that the range of scores and frequencies fit within the "three-fourths" guideline given above.

5. If an interval or intervals with frequencies of zero occur, these *must not* be omitted from the horizontal axis. To do so misrepresents the data. The following example illustrates this point.

FIGURE 12.2   Guidelines for constructing a histogram.

representing a grouped frequency distribution. It uses straight lines to connect the midpoint (MP) of each interval rather than bars or columns to show the frequency with which scores occur. The grouped frequency distribution with midpoints and the frequency polygon shown in   Fig. 12.3 represent the same group of scores we have been considering.

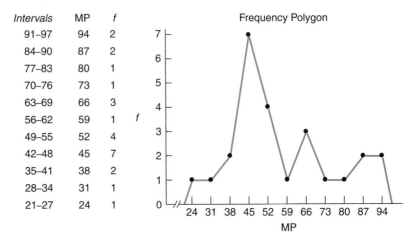

FIGURE 12.3   A grouped frequency distribution and frequency polygon.

Interpretation of the frequency polygon is similar to that of the histogram. The higher or lower the dots, the greater or lesser the number of scores in the interval.

Comparing the frequency polygon with the histogram demonstrates the same pattern of scores (see Figs. 12.1 and 12.3). This is a perfectly logical finding, since they were both constructed from the same grouped frequency distribution, except that we add a midpoint column to construct a frequency polygon.

Determining the MP is straightforward and results in a whole number if the interval width is an odd number. Its determination results in a fractional number if the interval width is an even number. In either case, the midpoint is simply the middle score in each interval. If you mistrust your ability to determine the middle score in an interval, you can check yourself mathematically. Simply add the lower limit (lowest score in the interval) to the upper limit (highest score in the interval) and divide the sum of these two scores by 2.

Formula	*Application*

$$MP = \frac{LL + UL}{2}$$

Top interval:

$$MP = \frac{91 + 97}{2} = \frac{188}{2} = 94$$

Second from top:

$$MP = \frac{84 + 90}{2} = \frac{174}{2} = 87$$

Guidelines for constructing a frequency polygon appear in Fig. 12.4. Notice that they are similar to those for histograms.

The Smooth Curve

Thus far we have discussed two graphical ways of depicting data represented by a grouped frequency distribution: the histogram and the frequency polygon. Our topic for this section, the *smooth* or *smoothed* curve, is not really an appropriate way to represent data from grouped frequency distributions, since an accurate smooth curve requires that advanced mathematical calculations be computed. Nevertheless, we will make great use of a smooth curve as a general representation of groups of scores. An example of a smooth curve is provided in the following graph:

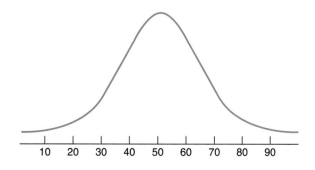

1. Construct the vertical axis three-fourths as long as the horizontal axis.

2. List scores along the horizontal axis and increasing from left to right, and list frequencies along the vertical axis, increasing from bottom to top.

3. Double slash marks (//) are used to indicate breaks in the sequence of numbers between scores and/or frequencies and zero points.

4. Points in the scales along the axes are expanded or compressed to fit the "three-fourths" guideline.

5. When intervals of zero frequency occur, the midpoints *must not* be omitted from the horizontal axis and the lines connecting the dots must be brought down to the baseline to represent zero frequencies.

6. The lines should also be brought down to the baseline halfway into the intervals above and below the highest and lowest intervals, as noted in the diagram below:

This guideline represents more of an aesthetic than a statistical consideration. A frequency polygon "tied" to the baseline has a better or more complete appearance, as shown below.

FIGURE 12.4 Guidelines for constructing a frequency polygon.

The curve represents a set of data. Note that it closely resembles a frequency polygon except that the *f*, or frequency, axis is omitted, and curved rather than straight lines are used. Although the *f* column is omitted, we can still make decisions about the frequency of occurrence of certain scores on the basis of the height of the curve. That is, scores in the 40–60 range were obtained by large numbers of students, while very few students obtained scores below 20 or above 80. With a histogram or frequency polygon we could determine *exactly* how many students scored between 40 and 60 or above 80 or below 20 by referring to the *f* axis. However, we are willing to sacrifice this accuracy when dealing with smooth curves because we use these curves to depict the *shape* of a distribution rather than to accurately represent the data.

Smooth curves can easily be developed from existing histograms or frequency polygons by connecting the high points of the bars or midpoints of the intervals, as shown in Fig. 12.5. Follow these two guidelines in constructing smooth curves:

1. Be sure your score axis increases from left to right.

2. Be sure the "tails" or ends of the curves come close to, but do not touch, the baseline.

Remember, although we use smooth curves to give us an idea of the shape of a distribution, they also enable us to make general statements about the frequency of scores.

FIGURE 12.5   Smooth curves.

The higher the curve, the more frequently the same scores occur. The lower the curve, the less frequently the same scores occur. Next, let's consider two major characteristics of distributions: symmetry and skewness.

Symmetrical and Asymmetrical Distributions   There are two major types of distributions: symmetrical and asymmetrical. In a symmetrical distribution each half or side of the distribution is a mirror image of the other side. An asymmetrical distribution, on the other hand, has nonmatching sides or halves. Both types of distributions are illustrated in the following graphs:

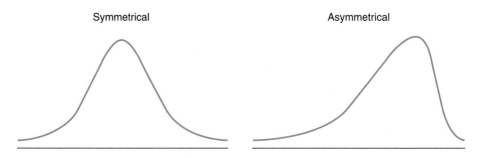

Symmetrical distributions can come in a variety of configurations. As illustrated, they may appear peaked, flattened, or somewhere in between:

All three of these are symmetrical distributions. The distribution on the right, however, has special significance. It is a special kind of symmetrical distribution called a normal distribution. It has some unique characteristics that make it among the most important distributions in statistics. Practice drawing this distribution. You will be called on to draw it many times before leaving this section of the book. Technically, the normal distribution follows very precise mathematical rules, but as long as you can approximate the illustration you need not worry about its precise mathematical properties. We will have more to say about the normal curve later.

Positively and Negatively Skewed Distributions   There are also two types of skewness: positive skewness and negative skewness. A positively skewed distribution results from an asymmetrical distribution of scores. In this case, the majority of scores fall below the middle of the score distribution. There are many low scores, but few high scores. A positively skewed distribution is illustrated as follows:

low   high

Scores

In a classroom testing situation a positively skewed distribution indicates the class did poorly on the test (a majority of low scores and few high scores). The reasons for such poor performance could include these: the test was too difficult, teaching was ineffective, the students didn't study, or not enough time was allowed. A positively skewed distribution does not tell you why the class did poorly; it only informs you of the fact that they did.

A negatively skewed distribution also results from an asymmetrical score distribution. In this type of distribution the majority of scores fall above the middle of the score distribution. There are many high scores, but few low scores. A negatively skewed distribution is illustrated as follows:

low   high

Scores

One interpretation attached to a negatively skewed distribution is that the class did well on the test (a majority had high scores and few had low scores). Again, there could be many reasons for this. The test may have been too easy, too much time may have been allowed, the class may be exceptionally bright, and so forth. Distributional shapes only describe data. They do not explain why the data take their shape.

We have discussed the what and why of statistics and have described methods for tabulating and depicting data. Next we will discuss what are probably the most widely used (and frequently misunderstood) summary statistics, *measures of central tendency*.

MEASURES OF CENTRAL TENDENCY

There are three measures of central tendency: the mean, the median, and the mode. We will define each in turn, give an example or examples of its computation, and discuss its characteristics. The main point to remember about these measures is that they represent our best bet when we must rely on a single score to represent an entire distribution. Since we have three measures of central tendency, it may occur to you that each is more or less applicable in different situations. But before we go any further, test yourself to see if you are on top of the statistical jargon we have already presented. If you can define the terms listed in Fig. 12.6, the jargon checklist, you are in good shape. If not, review these terms and commit them to memory to build your vocabulary and to prepare yourself to learn more terms later.

The Mean

Have you ever computed your grade average in elementary school, your GPA in college, your field goal average in basketball, or any other average? The mean is nothing more than the average of a group of scores:

Average = mean

The symbol we will use for the mean is M, the symbol that has been adopted in the American Psychological Association's style manual (APA, 2004) to represent the mean. In previous editions of this text we have used $\overline{X}$ (pronounced "X bar") to represent the mean. Some texts continue to $\overline{X}$ rather than M to symbolize the average or mean score, but most now use M, and so will we. Just in case you have forgotten how, we will compute a mean (our sneaky way of introducing a formula with a couple of other unfamiliar symbols). The formula and its plain English interpretation appear here:

Formula	*Plain English Version*
$M = \dfrac{\Sigma X}{N}$	$Average = \dfrac{\text{sum of all the scores}}{\text{total number of scores}}$

The formula looks impressive. But as you can see, it (like all mathematical formulas) is only a shorthand way of describing the process you go through to compute an average. Let's have a closer look at the terms in the formula:

- M   Symbol for the mean or arithmetic average
- Σ Sigma symbol used in mathematics that tells you to sum up whatever follows it

Statistics	Frequency (*f*)
List	Midpoint (MP)
Simple frequency distribution	Histogram
Grouped frequency distribution	Frequency polygon
N	Smooth curve
Range (R)	Symmetrical distribution
Interval (*i*)	Normal distribution
Lower limit (LL)	Positively skewed distribution
Upper limit (UL)	Negatively skewed distribution

FIGURE 12.6   Jargon checklist.

X   Symbol we will use from now on to represent a test score

N   Total number of scores in a distribution

Thus Σ tells you to sum up the test scores, and $\Sigma X/N$ tells you to sum up the test scores and divide this value by the total number of scores in the distribution. Let's work an example for the following set of scores: 90, 105, 95, 100, and 110.

Example	*Application*
$$M = \frac{\Sigma X}{N}$$	$$M = \frac{\Sigma X}{N}$$
	$$M = \frac{90 + 105 + 95 + 100 + 110}{5}$$
	$$M = \frac{500}{5}$$
	$$M = 100$$

The mean has several characteristics that make it the measure of central tendency most frequently used. One of these characteristics is stability. Since each score in the distribution enters into the computation of the mean, it is more stable over time than other measures of central tendency, which consider only one or two scores.

Another characteristic is that the sum of each score's distance from the mean is equal to zero. Presently, this is probably quite meaningless to you. However, it is a key concept in more advanced statistical operations. We will discuss this characteristic and its importance shortly.

A third characteristic of the mean is that it is affected by extreme scores. This means that a few very high scores in a distribution composed primarily of low scores (a positively skewed distribution) or a few very low scores in a distribution composed primarily of high scores (a negatively skewed distribution) will "pull" the value of the mean down or up toward the extreme score or scores. Table 12.2 illustrates this point. Since the mean is affected by extreme scores, it is usually not the measure of choice when dealing with skewed distributions. In such cases a measure that is more resistant to extreme scores is required. Our next topic for discussion, the median, represents such a measure.

The Median

The median is the second most frequently encountered measure of central tendency. The median is the score that splits a distribution in half: 50% of the scores lie above the median, and 50% of the scores lie below the median. Thus the median (abbreviated MDN) is also known as the 50th percentile. You may also think of the median as the middle score, since it is the score, or value, that falls in the middle of the distribution of scores.

For most classroom purposes simple methods may be used to determine the median. When the score distribution contains an odd number of scores, the median is the score that has equal numbers of scores above and below it. The following example describes the steps involved in determining the median when N, the total number of scores in the distribution, is odd.

TABLE 12.2 The Effect of Extreme Scores on the Mean

Original set of scores	Add an extremely low score	Add an extremely high score
90	90	90
105	105	105
95	95	95
100	100	100
$\underline{+110}$	110	110
$\Sigma X = 500$	$\underline{+20}$	$\underline{+200}$
	$\Sigma X = 520$	$\Sigma X = 700$
$M = \dfrac{\Sigma X}{N}$	$M = \dfrac{\Sigma X}{N}$	$M = \dfrac{\Sigma X}{N}$
$M = \dfrac{500}{5}$	$M = \dfrac{520}{6}$	$M = \dfrac{700}{6}$
$= 100$	$= 86.67$	$= 116.67$

Example: *Determine the median for the following set of scores: 90, 105, 95, 100, and 110.*

Steps

1. Arrange the scores in ascending or descending numerical order (don't just take the middle score from the original distribution).

2. Circle the score that has equal numbers of scores above and below it; this score is the median.

Application

   110

   105

   (100) $= MDN$

   95

   90

      When N is even, the procedure is a bit more complicated. In this case, select the *two* scores in the middle that have equal numbers of scores above and below them. Taking the average of these two scores will give you the median. These steps are illustrated in the following example.

Example: *Determine the median for the following set of scores: 90, 105, 95, 100, 110, and 95.*

Steps

1. Arrange the scores in numerical order.

2. Circle the *two* middle scores that have equal numbers of scores above and below them.

3. Compute the average of those two scores to determine the median.

Application

110

105

100
95 } Two middle scores: $\frac{95 + 100}{2} = \frac{195}{2} = 97.5 = MDN$

95

90

In this example the two middle scores are different scores, and the median is actually a decimal rather than a whole number (integer). This can be confusing unless you remember that the median is a value, but not necessarily a score. In the classroom, test scores are almost always integers. So it is possible, in a situation like this, for the value of the median to be neither a score actually obtained by a student in the class nor a whole number!

Sometimes, when the number of scores is even, more than two students who are in the middle of a distribution obtain the same score. Which scores do you use? In such cases keep in mind that it is only the values of the two middle scores that are important to determining the median, not who they were obtained by. For example, if Julio, Janelle, Joe, Jill, and Juanita all score in the middle of the classroom test distribution it does not matter whether you use Julio and Janelle's scores, or Jill and Juanita's, etc. to determine the median, because it is the score value that is relevant, not the student who obtained it. For example;

Students	*Scores*	
Julio	100	Median = (100 + 100)/2 = 200/2 = 100,
Janelle	100	if Julio's and Janelle's scores are used
Joe	100	
Jill	100	Median = (100 + 100)/2 = 200/2 = 100,
Juanita	100	if Jill's and Juanita's scores are used

Next, let's put all five of these scores into a distribution and compute the MDN when N is even.

Example: *Determine the median for the following set of scores: 100, 90, 100, 105, 100, 95, 100, 110, 95, and 100.*

Steps

1. Arrange the scores in numerical order.
2. Circle the two middle scores that have equal numbers of scores above and below them.
3. Compute the average of those two scores to determine the median.

Application

Students	Scores
Bo	110
Deanna	105
Julio	100
Janelle	100
Joe	100
Jill	100
Juanita	100
Thomas	95
Dara	95
Richard	90

Two middle scores: $\dfrac{100 + 100}{2} = \dfrac{200}{2} = 100 = \text{MDN}$

In this case the median is a whole number and has the same value as the five middle, or tied, scores. Tied scores are a common occurrence and when they are in the middle of a distribution the median will always be a whole number. When the middle scores are not tied, the median will be a decimal.

The median determination methods we have provided are useful for classroom purposes, although other computational methods also exist. For technical reasons that we do not need to be unduly concerned about, the method we just described to determine the median when we have an even number of scores may, at times, overestimate or underestimate by a fraction the actual value of the median. This can occur only when more than two scores around the center of the distribution are the same. An example of this more complex, but sometimes more accurate, approach to determining the median when there are multiple tied scores in the middle of the distribution can be found in Appendix C, if you are interested.

The main characteristic of the median is that it is not affected by extreme scores. This is because only the middle or two middle scores are considered in determining the median. Let's consider the following examples:

Original Set of scores	*Substitute an Extremely High Score*	*Substitute an Extremely Low Score*
110	**600**	110
105	105	105
100	100	100
100	100	100
95	95	90
90	90	**5**

$$\text{MDN} = \frac{100 + 100}{2} = 100 \qquad \text{MDN} = \frac{100 + 100}{2} = 100 \qquad \text{MDN} = \frac{100 + 100}{2} = 100$$

Since the median is not affected by extreme scores, it represents central tendency better than the mean when distributions are skewed. In skewed distributions the mean is pulled toward the extremes, so that in some cases it may give a falsely high or falsely low estimate of central tendency. Since the median, on the other hand, is the score above and below which half the scores lie, it always indicates the center of the distribution, as illustrated by the following diagrams:

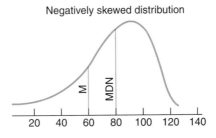

In the positively skewed distribution the few scores of 100 or above pull M toward them. The mean presents the impression that the typical student scored about 80 and passed the test. However, the MDN shows that 50% of the students scored 60 or below. In other words, not only did the typical students fail the test (if we consider the middle student typical), but the majority of students failed the test (assuming a score of 60 is failing, of course).

In the negatively skewed distribution the few scores of 40 or below pull the mean down toward them. Thus the mean score gives the impression that the typical student scored about 60 and failed the test. Again, the median contradicts this interpretation. It shows that 50% of the students scored 80 or above on the test and that actually the majority of students passed the test.

As you can see, it is important that the median be considered when skewed distributions are involved. Too often, however, only the average or mean is reported when statistics are presented, without regard for the shape of the distribution.

Percentiles   Now that we have introduced the idea of the median as the 50th percentile, it is only a small step to finding out how to determine the score that represents any desired percentile in a frequency distribution. Although a percentile is not considered a measure of central tendency unless it is the 50th percentile, the calculation of other percentiles is very similar to that of the median. A percentile is a score below which a certain percentage of the scores lie. In the case of the median, we saw that 50% of the total number of cases were lower (and higher) than the median. Percentiles divide a frequency distribution into 100 equal parts. Percentiles are symbolized $P_1, P_2, \ldots P_{99}$. P_1 represents that score in a frequency distribution below which 1% of the scores lie. P_2 represents that score in a frequency distribution below which 2% of the scores lie. P_{99} represents that score in a frequency distribution below which 99% of the scores lie.

A score can be calculated for each percentile from P_1 to P_{99} in a manner similar to the way the median—or 50th percentile (or P_{50})—was calculated for a distribution with an even number of scores. That is;

1. Arrange the scores in numerical order.

2. Counting up from the bottom, find the point below which the desired percentage of scores falls.

3. Circle the two scores that surround this point.

4. The average of this pair of scores will be the percentile of interest.

For example, for the following data, P_{75} and P_{25} would be determined in the following manner:

115

110

110
110      $P_{75} = (110 + 110)/2 = 220/2 = 110$

105

100

100

95

95
90      $P_{25} = \dfrac{95 + 90}{2} = 92.5$

90

85

As you can see from these examples, when the two scores used to determine a percentile are tied values, the percentile will be an integer, but if the two values are not tied, the percentile will be a decimal. If this is confusing, please review the procedures for determining the median when the middle values are tied and untied for clarification. As we mentioned with regard to the methods we used to determine the median, more complex, specific procedures exist to compute percentiles, but for classroom purposes this approach should be sufficient.

Finally, we will consider the last measure of central tendency—the mode.

The Mode

The *mode* is the least reported measure of central tendency. The mode, or modal score, in a distribution is the score that occurs most frequently. However, a distribution may have one score that occurs most frequently (unimodal), two scores that occur with equal frequency and more frequently than any other scores (bimodal), or three or more scores that occur with equal frequency and more frequently than any other scores (multimodal). If *each* score in a distribution occurs with equal frequency, the distribution is called a rectangular distribution, and it has *no mode*.

The mode is determined by tallying up the number of times each score occurs in a distribution and selecting the score that occurs most frequently. The following examples are illustrative:

Example: *What is the mode of this score distribution: 90, 105, 95, 100, and 100?*

X	Tally	
105	I	
100	II	Mode = 100
95	I	This is a unimodal distribution.
90	I	

Example: *What is the mode for this set of scores: 90, 110, 95, 100, 110, 90, 105, 100, 110, and 95?*

X	Tally	
110	III	
105	I	
100	II	Mode = 100
95	II	This is a unimodal distribution.
90	II	

Example: *What is the mode for this set of scores: 6, 9, 1, 3, 4, 6, and 9?*

X	Tally	
9	II	
6	II	
4	I	Mode = 6 and 9
3	I	This is a bimodal distribution.
1	I	

The mode has the advantage of being easy to determine. If you know how to count you can determine a mode! However, it is the least used of the measures of central tendency because of a serious shortcoming. The mode is the least stable measure of central tendency. A few scores can influence the mode considerably. Consider the following:

Original Set of Scores			*Add a Few Scores* *(e.g., 90, 70, 70, 70, and 90)*	
X	Tally		X	Tally
105	I		105	I
100	II		100	II
95	I		95	I
95	I		90	III
			70	III
Mode = 100			Mode = 70 and 90	

Because of this unfortunate characteristic, the mode usually is not used as the only measure of central tendency. An exceptional case, however, is the normal distribution because in a normal distribution all three measures of central tendency have the same value.

The Measures of Central Tendency in Various Distributions

As was mentioned, the mean, median, and mode all have the same value in a normal distribution, which is illustrated here:

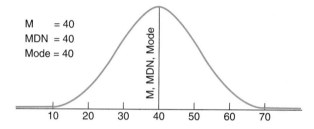

In a positively skewed distribution, the mean usually has the highest value of all the measures of central tendency, the mode the lowest, and the median the middle or intermediate value:

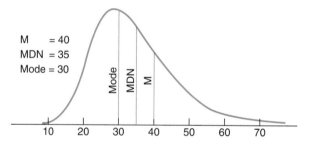

Just the opposite occurs in a negatively skewed distribution. In a negatively skewed distribution, the mean usually has the lowest value, the mode the highest, and the median the middle or intermediate value:

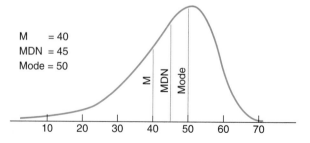

Knowing the relationships of the measures of central tendency to these distributions enables you to place these measures in their appropriate position when a distribution's shape is known. The opposite is also true. Knowing the values of the measures of central tendency enables you to determine the shape of the distribution. For example, if the mean = 47, median = 54, and mode = 59, what is the shape of the distribution? You know it is not normal (since the values are different). But, before you guess at whether it's positively or negatively skewed, take the uncertainty or guesswork out of the question. How? The answer to this and many other questions concerning statistical principles is to draw a picture.

Example: *What is the shape of a distribution with a mean of 47, median of 54, and mode of 59?*

Steps
1. Examine the relationship among the three measures of central tendency.
2. Draw a picture (baseline first); then mark the measures of central tendency in the appropriate spaces. Draw in the curve. Remember the high point of the curve is the mode.
3. Evaluate the curve to arrive at the answer, in this case, negatively skewed.

Application

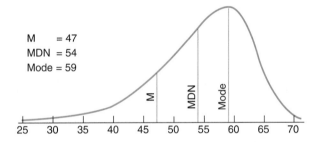

M   = 47
MDN = 54
Mode = 59

We've been discussing estimates of one important aspect of a distribution. Estimates of central tendency represent good bets about the single value that best describes a distribution. But some good bets are better than others. In the next chapter we will consider statistics that indicate how adequate our good bets really are. These are estimates of variability.

SUMMARY

This chapter introduced you to various methods of tabulating and graphing data and to the measures of central tendency. Its major points are as follows:

1. Descriptive statistics are numbers used to describe or summarize a larger body of numbers.

2. Data are tabulated to introduce some order to the data and make them more interpretable. Three methods of tabulating data are listing, simple frequency distributions, and grouped frequency distributions.

3. While each method has its advantages and disadvantages, the grouped frequency distribution is usually most appropriate for classroom use.

4. The following steps are followed in constructing a grouped frequency distribution:
   a. Determine the range.
   b. Determine the number of intervals.
   c. Divide the range by the number of intervals and round to the nearest odd number to get the interval width (i).

    d. Develop the interval column, being sure the lower limit of each interval is a multiple of i.

    e. Tally the scores in each interval to get f, the frequency column.

5. Data from grouped frequency distributions may be graphically represented by histograms or frequency polygons.

6. Histograms, or bar graphs, use columns of varying height to represent the frequencies in each interval.

7. Frequency polygons use straight lines to connect the midpoints of each interval, which vary in height depending on the frequency of scores in the interval.

8. The following general guidelines apply to the construction of both histograms and frequency polygons:

    a. Make sure the vertical axis is two-thirds to three-quarters as long as the horizontal axis.

    b. List scores along the horizontal axis, frequencies along the vertical axis, and label the axes clearly.

    c. Use double slash marks (//) to indicate breaks in any number sequences.

    d. Do not omit intervals with frequencies of zero.

9. A smooth curve is usually drawn to represent a distribution's shape, although decisions about frequency of occurrence of scores or scores in intervals can be made by looking at the height of the curve. The f axis is omitted in a smooth curve.

10. In a symmetrical distribution, each half or side of the distribution is a mirror image of the other, unlike in an asymmetrical distribution.

11. A normal distribution is a special type of symmetrical distribution.

12. An asymmetrical distribution in which most scores are low is called a positively skewed distribution. The tail in such a distribution is toward the high scores.

13. An asymmetrical distribution in which most scores are high is called a negatively skewed distribution. The tail in such a distribution is toward the low scores.

14. One of the measures of central tendency (mean, median, and mode) is used to represent a distribution when a single value must be used. Such a measure is our "best bet" about the overall distribution.

15. The mean, or the arithmetic average, of a set of scores is determined by summing all the scores and dividing by the number of scores.

16. The mean has several important characteristics. Of the measures of central tendency it is the most stable, the sum of the deviations of each score from the mean always equals zero, and it is affected by extreme scores.

17. Since the mean is affected by extreme scores, it is not the measure of central tendency of choice for skewed distributions.

18. The median is the score that splits a distribution in half. It is also known as the middle score, or the 50th percentile.

19. The median is determined by finding the score or value that has equal numbers of scores above or below it. In certain cases when there are multiple tied scores in the middle of the distribution the most accurate way of determining the median is through interpolation (see Appendix C).

20. The most important characteristic of the median is that it is not affected by extreme scores. Thus it is the measure of central tendency of choice in a skewed distribution.

21. The mode is the score in a distribution that occurs most frequently.

22. The mode is determined by counting the number of times scores occur and selecting the score(s) that occurs most frequently. A distribution may have more than one mode.

23. The major characteristic of the mode is its instability. Seldom is the mode, by itself, acceptable as a measure of central tendency.

24. In a normal distribution, the mean, median, and mode have the same value.

25. In a positively skewed distribution, the mean has the highest and the mode the lowest value of the measures of central tendency. The median has an intermediate value.

26. In a negatively skewed distribution, the mean has the lowest value and the mode the highest value of the measures of central tendency. Again, the median has an intermediate value.

FOR PRACTICE

*1. An achievement test designed to measure the level of arithmetic achievement among students in the middle of the third grade is administered to three classes of equal size: one first-grade class, one third-grade class, and one fifth-grade class. The test is administered in the middle of the school year. Other things being equal, what sort of distribution would you predict for each of the three classes? Sketch a distribution of the shape you would expect for each grade. On each of your three sketches, indicate the probable location of the three measures of central tendency.

*2. Mr. Martin's best reading group obtained the following scores on an achievement test:

85, 90, 90, 92, 94, 94, 96, 97, 97, 98

Mr. Scott's best reading group obtained the following scores on the same achievement test:

61, 85, 90, 90, 92, 93, 94, 97, 97, 97

For each group, determine the following:
a. N
b. R
c. M
d. MDN
e. Mode
f. Why is there so much difference in means?
g. Which measure of central tendency should be used to compare these distributions?

*3. For the following group of 30 scores, construct three grouped frequency distributions with different numbers of intervals. Graph your data, using both a histogram and a frequency polygon. Decide which frequency distribution best represents the data.

60, 60, 63, 68, 70, 72, 75, 75, 75, 76, 76, 77, 78, 80, 83, 83, 84, 88, 93, 93, 93, 94, 94, 94, 94, 95, 97, 98, 100, 100

*4. Match the terms in Column B with the characteristics listed in Column A. The options from Column B may be used more than once.

Column A	Column B
1. Least stable measure of central tendency	**a.** Mean
	b. Median
2. More than one possible in same distribution	**c.** Mode
3. Most influenced by extreme scores	
4. Also known as the 50th percentile	
5. Measure of choice in skewed distributions	

*5. Find P_{25} and P_{50} in the following distribution of scores:

115, 112, 110, 108, 106, 104, 100, 100, 98, 96, 96, 94, 93, 91, 90, 88

*6. Indicate the type of distribution to which each of these sets of data refer:

a. M = 78.37, MDN = 78.37, mode = 78.37

b. M = 374.3, MDN = 379.7, mode = 391.3

c. M = 109.5, MDN = 107.4, mode = 107.4

*7. For the following sets of data, which method of tabulating data would be most appropriate? Why?

a. 70, 70, 70, 71, 72, 72, 73, 73, 73, 73, 74

b. 39, 47, 67, 51, 92, 60, 75

c. 35, 88, 85, 45, 49, 52, 69, 71, 49, 50, 90, 72, 79, 36, 43, 52, 92, 81, 80, 47, 55, 60, 72, 94, 91, 53, 48, 72

*Answers for these questions appear in Appendix F.

CHAPTER 13

VARIABILITY, THE NORMAL DISTRIBUTION, AND CONVERTED SCORES

IN CHAPTER 12 we learned that measures of central tendency can be used to describe a distribution. However, an estimate of the variability, or spread, of scores is needed before we can compare scores within and between distributions. For example, suppose we have the following data: M = 160, MDN = 170, and mode = 180. After drawing a curve, we know that the distribution is negatively skewed. What we don't know is how spread out, dispersed, or variable the scores are. For this we would at least need to know the range of obtained scores. Were all the scores between 100 and 200? 50 and 250? 150 and 190? Without an estimate of variability, we don't know which of the following three negatively skewed distributions best fits the data:

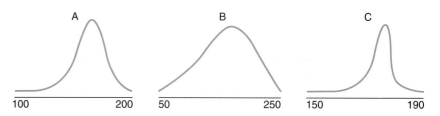

In A, the scores vary between about 100 and 200; in B, between 50 and 250; and in C between 150 and 190. In other words, it's possible for two or more distributions to have the same values for the mean, median, and mode but be different in the way their scores are spread out around these measures. This is why we must have an estimate of variability. This estimate helps us determine how compressed or expanded the distributions are.

THE RANGE

The easiest estimate of variability to compute is one we've already been exposed to: the range (R). The range is determined by subtracting the lowest score from the highest score.[1]

[1] Sometimes the range is defined as the lowest score subtracted from the highest score plus 1. This is called the inclusive range. It is the statistic most often referred to in introductory statistics texts and is based on mathematical concepts that need not concern us here.

This is what you did as the first step in constructing a grouped frequency distribution. Ease of computation does not offset the major drawbacks of the range as an estimate of variability, however. Since the range is dependent only on the low and high scores, it is often unstable and is useful only for gross ballpark estimates of variability. If an extreme score is present, R can be very misleading. Consider the following example.

Example: *Compute the range for the following set of data: 11, 11, 11, 11, 12, 12, 13, 14, 14, 14, 15, 15, 15, 15, 16, 17, 18, 18, 18.*

$R = H - L$
$R = 18 - 11 = 7$

Now substitute one extreme score, 96, for one of the scores of 18 and compute the range: 11, 11, 11, 11, 12, 12, 13, 14, 14, 14, 15, 15, 15, 15, 16, 17, 18, 18, 96.

$R = H - L$
$R = 96 - 11 = 85$

This single extreme score increased R by 78 points and gives the impression that there is a large spread of scores when, with the exception of the single extreme score, there is actually very little.

THE SEMI-INTERQUARTILE RANGE (SIQR)

The semi-interquartile range (SIQR) compensates for the sensitivity of the range to extreme scores by preventing extreme scores from influencing its computation. The SIQR computation is determined by the middle 50% of the scores in a distribution. The lower 25% and upper 25% do not enter into its final computation. The formula for the SIQR is presented here:

$$\text{SIQR} = \frac{Q_3 - Q_1}{2}$$

In this formula Q_3 stands for the third quartile and Q_1 stands for the first. Quartiles, like the median, are points in a distribution below which a certain percentage of scores lie. In fact the median, or 50th percentile, is the same as Q_2 or the second quartile.

Q_1 is the point below which 25% of the scores lie, and Q_3 is the point below which 75% of the scores lie. The same process we used in Chapter 12 to determine a percentile is used to determine Q_1 and Q_3 (since Q_1 is the same as P_{25} and Q_3 is the same P_{75}), as illustrated by the following example.

Example: *Determine the semi-interquartile range for the following set of scores: 85, 115, 90, 90, 105, 100, 110, 110, 95, 110, 95, 100.*

Process

1. Determine Q_1 and Q_3 by employing the steps used to determine the median (Q_2) for a distribution with an even number of scores.

a. Arrange scores in numerical order.
b. Counting up from the bottom, find the points below which 25% of the score values and 75% of the score values fall (theoretically, that is, since we are talking about values rather than the actual scores).
c. Circle the two scores that surround these points.
d. The averages of each of these two pairs of scores are Q_1 and Q_3.

$$115$$
$$110$$
$$Q_1 \cdots \left. \begin{array}{c} \boxed{110} \\ \boxed{110} \end{array} \right\} \quad Q_3 = \frac{110 + 110}{2} = 110$$
$$105$$
$$100$$
$$100$$
$$95$$
$$Q_1 \cdots \left. \begin{array}{c} \boxed{95} \\ \boxed{90} \end{array} \right\} \quad Q_1 = \frac{95 + 90}{2} = 92.5$$
$$90$$
$$85$$

2. Plug Q_1 and Q_3 into the formula and determine the SIQR.

Formula	*Application*
$\text{SIQR} = \dfrac{Q_3 - Q_1}{2}$	$\text{SIQR} = \dfrac{110 - 92.5}{2}$
	$= \dfrac{17.5}{2}$
	$= 8.75$

Although the SIQR has the advantage of not being influenced by extreme scores, it has the disadvantage of being determined ultimately by only *half* the scores in a distribution. Any time all scores in a distribution do not enter the computation of a statistic, an element of error is introduced. Although the SIQR is a better estimate of variability than the range, it is not as good or as stable as the estimate of variability known as the standard deviation. The standard deviation, like the mean, considers all scores in its computation. As a result, it is the most commonly used estimate of variability. When the SIQR is reported it usually accompanies the median, which is not surprising since they share part of the same computational process. Next we will consider the standard deviation, which we will symbolize as SD.

THE STANDARD DEVIATION

As mentioned, the *standard deviation* (SD) includes all scores in a distribution in its computation. The SD is normally reported as the estimate of variability that accompanies the mean in describing a distribution.

Remember, we said an estimate of variability tells us how poor our best bet is as a single value with which to describe a distribution. Consider the following three distributions:

A	B	C
38	20	25
34	20	24
26	20	23
24	20	22
20	20	21
20	20	19
16	20	18
14	20	17
6	20	16
2	20	15
$\Sigma X = \overline{200}$	$\Sigma X = \overline{200}$	$\Sigma X = \overline{200}$

$$M_A = \frac{\Sigma X}{N} \qquad M_A = \frac{\Sigma X}{N} \qquad M_A = \frac{\Sigma X}{N}$$

$$= \frac{200}{10} \qquad\qquad = \frac{200}{10} \qquad\qquad = \frac{200}{10}$$

$$= 20 \qquad\qquad = 20 \qquad\qquad = 20$$

Although the distributions are composed of many different scores, they all have the same mean value. In distribution B, this best bet is right on the mark. Our mean value of 20 perfectly represents each and every score in the distribution, simply because each score in the distribution is 20. What about our best bets in A and C? How good or poor are they?

From these cases we can easily see that the mean is a better estimate of the scores in distribution C than in distribution A. We know this because none of the scores in C is more than five points away from the mean. In distribution A, on the other hand, 6 of the 10 scores are six or more points away from the mean. Using this information, we can conclude that there is less variability, spread, or dispersion of scores in C. But just how much less variable is C than A? And what if there were less of a discrepancy in scores between A and C? How could we determine which was more or less variable?

With only this information, it would be difficult if not impossible to answer these questions. We need a reliable index of variability that considers all scores. Let's develop one by putting down on paper what we did when we compared A and C.

First, we looked at each distribution to see how far away each score was from the mean. We can do this more formally by subtracting the mean from each score $(X - M)$. We'll call this distance the score's *deviation* from the mean and use the symbol x (lower-case) to represent such deviation scores. Thus $X - M = x$, which is illustrated here:

A		C	
X – M =	x	X – M =	x
38 – 20 =	18	25 – 20 =	5
34 – 20 =	14	24 – 20 =	4
26 – 20 =	6	23 – 20 =	3
24 – 20 =	4	22 – 20 =	2
20 – 20 =	0	21 – 20 =	1
20 – 20 =	0	19 – 20 =	–1
16 – 20 =	–4	18 – 20 =	–2
14 – 20 =	–6	17 – 20 =	–3
6 – 20 =	–14	16 – 20 =	–4
2 – 20 =	–18	15 – 20 =	–5

This is just what we did before, except it was done in our heads. Since we want a single number or index to represent the deviations, why don't we just sum the x column, being careful to note the sign of the number, and then average the result? Let's do this:

A	C
x	x
18	5
14	4
6	3
4	2
0	1
0	–1
–4	–2
–6	–3
–14	–4
–18	–5
$\dfrac{\Sigma x}{N} = 0$	$\dfrac{\Sigma x}{N} = 0$

Because the positive and negative numbers cancel one another out, the sum of both x columns is zero. Remember the characteristics of the mean? One of them is that the sum of the deviations from the mean always equals zero. Now you can see what is meant by this characteristic. This characteristic holds true for all shapes and sizes of distributions without exception. We cannot use Σx or even the average deviation, $\Sigma x/N$, as our index of variability, as promising as these two indices might appear at first glance.

Fortunately mathematics provides us with a way out of this dilemma. An index of variability based on deviation scores that we can use is computed in much the same fashion. There are two differences, however. First, let's square all the individual deviation scores and then sum them, as illustrated here:

	A				*C*		
X − M =	*x*	x^2		X − M =	*x*	x^2	
38 − 20 =	18	324		25 − 20 =	5	25	
34 − 20 =	14	196		24 − 20 =	4	16	
26 − 20 =	6	36		23 − 20 =	3	9	
24 − 20 =	4	16		22 − 20 =	2	4	
20 − 20 =	0	0		21 − 20 =	1	1	
20 − 20 =	0	0		19 − 20 =	−1	1	
16 − 20 =	−4	16		18 − 20 =	−2	4	
14 − 20 =	−6	36		17 − 20 =	−3	9	
6 − 20 =	−14	196		16 − 20 =	−4	16	
2 − 20 =	−18	324		15 − 20 =	−5	25	
		$1144 = \Sigma x^2$				$110 = \Sigma x^2$	

The next step is to find the average of the sum of the squared deviation scores:

A	*C*
$\dfrac{1144}{10} = 114.4$	$\dfrac{110}{10} = 11.0$

These estimates of variability are useful in more advanced statistical computations and have a special name. The average of the sum of the squared deviation scores is called the *variance*. By themselves these estimates are not very useful because they represent squared units, not the units we started with. To return the values to units representative of our original data we must extract their square roots:

A	*C*
$\sqrt{114.4} = 10.7$	$\sqrt{11.0} = 3.32$

These values—10.7 for distribution A and 3.32 for distribution C—are the indices we've been looking for. They are based on all the scores in a distribution and are on the *same scale* of units as our original set of data. These values are the standard deviations for distributions A and C.

The following formula is simply a shorthand mathematical way of representing what we have just done for distributions A and C:

$$SD = \sqrt{\frac{\Sigma(X - M)^2}{N}}$$

or, since X − M = *x*,

$$SD = \sqrt{\frac{\Sigma x^2}{N}}$$

These formulas are equivalent. In other words, they tell you that to find the standard deviation you must square each deviation score, sum the squares of the deviation scores, divide this value by the number of scores in the distribution, and find the square root of that final value. Just to be sure you understand the process, we will work one more example and follow each of the steps.

The Deviation Score Method for Computing the Standard Deviation

Example: *Determine the standard deviation for the following set of scores: 92, 100, 90, 80, 94, 96.*

Process

1. Determine the mean.

100
96
94

$$M = \frac{\Sigma X}{N}$$

92

$$M = \frac{552}{6}$$

90

$\underline{80}$

$\Sigma X = 552$ $M = 92$

2. Subtract the mean from each raw score to arrive at the deviation scores. (As a check on your computations, sum the x column to see if it equals zero.)

$X - M =$	x
$100 - 92 =$	8
$96 - 92 =$	4
$94 - 92 =$	2
$92 - 92 =$	0
$90 - 92 =$	-2
$80 - 92 =$	$\underline{-12}$
$\Sigma x =$	0

3. Square each deviation score and sum the squared deviation scores.

$X - M =$	x	x^2
$100 - 92 =$	8	64
$96 - 92 =$	4	16
$94 - 92 =$	2	4
$92 - 92 =$	0	0
$90 - 92 =$	-2	4
$80 - 92 =$	$\underline{-12}$	$\underline{144}$
		$\Sigma x = 232$

4. Plug the Σx^2 into the formula and solve for the SD.

$$SD = \sqrt{\frac{\Sigma x^2}{N}} = \sqrt{\frac{232}{6}} = \sqrt{38.67} = 6.22$$

The Raw Score Method for Computing the Standard Deviation

The following formula is another, quicker way of representing what we have just done for distributions A and C. It is called the raw score formula for the standard deviation, since it uses only the raw scores and does not require the more laborious process of finding deviations from the mean. Here is the raw score formula for calculating SD:

$$SD = \sqrt{\frac{\Sigma X^2 - (\Sigma X)^2/N}{N}}$$

where

ΣX^2 = each raw score squared and then summed

(ΣX^2) = the square of the sum of the raw scores (i.e., add the scores, then square the total)

N = the number of pupils

Both the more cumbersome deviation method and the shorter raw score method of computing the standard deviation will give you the same result; keep in mind that the raw score formula will be easier to use. Just to be sure you understand the process of obtaining a standard deviation. We will use the raw score formula to work one more example.

Example: *Determine the standard deviation for the following set of scores: 10, 12, 15, 13, 20, 14, 15, 14, 18, 13.*

Process

1. Determine the square of each raw score.

X	X^2
10	100
12	144
15	225
13	169
20	400
14	196
15	225
14	196
18	324
13	169

2. Sum both the raw scores (X) and the squared scores (X^2)

X	X^2
10	100
12	144
15	225
13	169

20	400
14	196
15	225
14	196
18	324
13	169
$\Sigma X = 144$	$\Sigma X^2 = 2{,}148$

3. Square the sum of the raw scores.

$$(\Sigma X)^2 = 144^2 = 20{,}736$$

4. Find N, the number of scores.

$$N = 10$$

5. Plug ΣX^2, $(\Sigma X)^2$, and N into the formula and solve for the SD.

$$SD = \sqrt{\frac{\Sigma X^2 - (\Sigma X)^2/N}{N}}$$

$$= \sqrt{\frac{2148 - (20{,}736)/10}{10}}$$

$$= \sqrt{\frac{2148 - 2074}{10}}$$

$$= \sqrt{\frac{74}{10}}$$

$$= \sqrt{7.4}$$

$$= 2.72$$

Since the SD is an estimate of score variability or spread, it stands to reason that large SD values indicate greater score variability than do small SD values. In other words, when the SD is small, scores tend to cluster closely around the mean. Such a distribution is said to be homogeneous and tends to have a compressed shape, whether it is symmetrical or skewed. Three examples of homogeneous distributions with compressed shapes are pictured here:

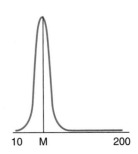

In those examples the mean is a very good bet as the single value that best represents all the scores in each distribution. Our best bet is much poorer when distributions have large standard deviations. Such distributions have a lot of variability or spread of scores and all have an expanded appearance. These are called heterogeneous distributions. Three examples follow:

To sum up, measures of central tendency help us determine whether a distribution is symmetrical or skewed. Measures of variability help us determine more precisely whether these distributions appear compressed (small SD) or expanded (large SD). The SD also has a very important role in a special kind of symmetrical distribution. This is called the *normal distribution*, and it is to this topic that we now turn.

THE NORMAL DISTRIBUTION

The normal distribution is a special kind of symmetrical distribution that represents specific mathematical properties. This distribution has special importance for us because it is the model we most frequently use to make comparisons among scores or to make other kinds of statistical decisions. It is important, however, to note that the normal distribution is hypothetical. No distribution of scores matches the normal distribution perfectly. However, many distributions or scores in education come close to the normal distribution, and herein lies its value. The following example shows a distribution of Stanford–Binet IQ scores for a large number of students:

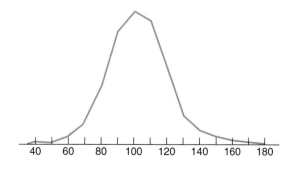

Looking at the figure you can see that although the IQ distribution differs somewhat from the symmetrical, normal distribution, it is close enough that we do not lose too much accuracy by using the normal distribution as a model for the actual distribution. Many other characteristics of individuals also come close enough to the normal distribution for it to be used as a model for these distributions. Besides IQ, examples of these include most kinds of achievement and physical characteristics (e.g., height and weight). The accuracy we sacrifice by employing a slightly inaccurate model is offset by the advantages of being able to make statistical and measurement decisions based on a *single* standard for comparison, the normal distribution. Before we can make such decisions, though, we must become familiar with the fixed properties of the normal distribution.

Properties of the Normal Distribution

The curve drawn here represents the normal distribution.

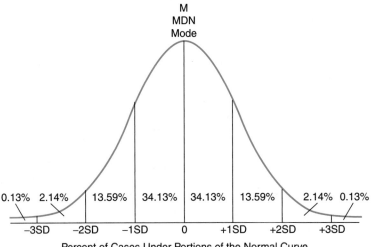

Percent of Cases Under Portions of the Normal Curve

Notice in the curve that the mean, median, and mode all coincide. This, of course, will occur whenever a distribution is normal. The percentages show how many cases fall under portions of the curve.

Now add up the percentages you see above the baseline between three SD units below and three SD units above the mean. Notice that more than 99.7%, or almost all scores in the normal distribution, fall between three standard deviation units below the mean and three standard deviation units above the mean. Now look at the area of the curve between the mean and one SD above the mean. The 34.13% you see in this area indicates the percentage of cases that fall between the mean value and the value of the mean *plus* the value of one standard deviation unit in a normal distribution of scores. For example, if we were using the normal curve as a model for a distribution with a mean of

61 and a standard deviation of 7, we would expect 34.13% (about 34% or one-third) of the scores in this distribution to fall between 61 and 68, as the following illustration shows:

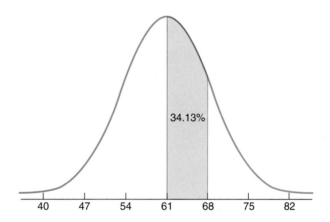

Notice also that for a distribution with a mean equal to 61 and a standard deviation equal to 7, seven points are added for each standard deviation unit above the mean (68, 75, 82), and seven points are subtracted from the mean for each standard deviation unit below the mean (54, 47, 40). Thus we can see that *about* 68% or *about* two-thirds of the scores in this distribution fall between 54 and 68, as shown here:

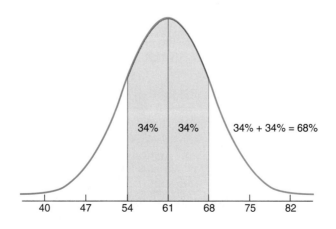

The interval between the mean and 75 represents what percentage of scores? We know what percentage of cases fall in each interval of the normal curve, so we can easily find the answer. The answer is about 48%, as shown in the following illustration:

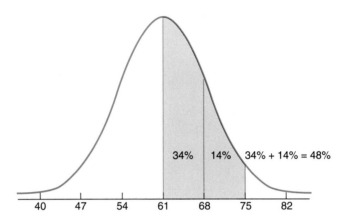

We can also use the normal curve to determine the percentage of scores above or below a certain score. The interval above 47 represents what percentage of scores? The answer, about 98%, is illustrated next:

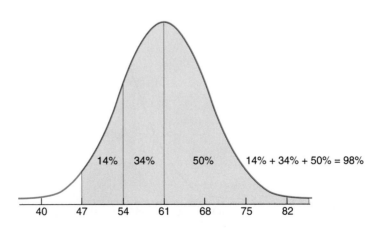

The interval below 68 represents what percentage of scores? The answer is about 84%, as shown in the following illustration:

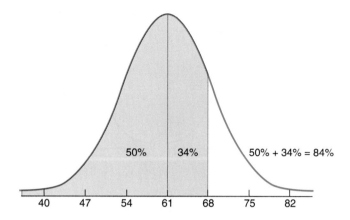

In other words, in a distribution with a mean of 61 and a standard deviation of 7, a score of 68 is at the 84th percentile. Recall that a percentile, like a quartile, is the point below which a given percentage of scores lie. If you wanted to determine the score at the 16th percentile, you would find that score below which there is 16% of the area under the normal curve, as illustrated here:

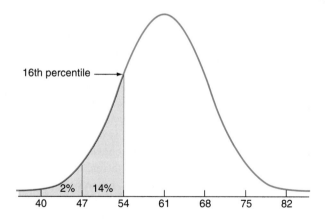

Assuming that test scores for a group of students were normally distributed—that is, if they conformed to a normal curve or close approximation of it—the standard deviation of that group could be converted to numbers and percentages of students scoring above or below certain score points. Before illustrating this concept, however, we must know how to accomplish this conversion.

CONVERTED SCORES

Thus far, we have talked about scores that come directly from tests. These actual or obtained scores are called *raw* scores. Consider the following:

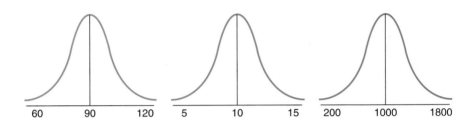

In these illustrations all three distributions have the same shape, but their means and standard deviations are different, which is often what happens because tests have different ranges of scores. The example illustrates what we are up against when we try to compare scores from different tests.

The following example shows the process necessary to compare scores from distributions with different means and standard deviations.

> *John obtained a score of 85 on his psychology midterm and 90 on his history midterm.*
> *On which test did he do better compared to the rest of the class?*

At first glance you might say he did better in history. Well, this may be true, but how do you know? If you did say history, chances are you're treating the raw scores as percentages. Most of us are accustomed to test scores being converted to percentages before they are reported to us, but this is not always the case. John's score of 85 *may* mean he answered 85 out of 100 correctly, or it *may* mean he answered 85 out of 85 correctly, or 85 out of 217! Similarly, his history score may indicate he answered 90 out of 100, 90 out of 90, or 90 out of 329 items correctly. The point is that without additional information, we can't say which of these scores is higher or lower. With only raw scores reported, we *cannot* determine whether these scores are low, high, or intermediate. We need more information. Raw scores, by themselves, are *not* interpretable. This is an important but often overlooked point. Let's add some information.

The information we have—the raw scores—exists as part of two distributions: one for psychology and one for history. The distributions consist of the raw scores obtained by *all* the students who took these tests. If we can determine where John's scores fall in these distributions, we should be able to answer our question. First we need information that describes each distribution. As we now know, the mean and standard deviation are necessary to describe a distribution. If we have the mean and the standard deviation for each distribution, we should be able to answer our question. Let's add the information we need, but one piece at a time. First we will add the means. The mean in psychology was

75, and the mean in history was 140. Before we go any further, let's organize our data and examine them carefully.

Psychology	*History*
X = 85	X = 90
M = 75	M = 140

We see that John's score was 10 points above the class mean in psychology and 50 points below the class mean in history. Clearly, compared with the rest of the class, he performed better in psychology than in history. We have answered our question without even using the standard deviation of these distributions. Well, then, of what value is the standard deviation? As we will soon see, the standard deviation will enable us to pinpoint the percentage of scores above or below each of these scores. At first glance it may appear that John's history score is far below average, maybe even the lowest in the class. However, we don't know for sure because we have no idea how spread out or variable the history scores were.

Consider the following illustrations:

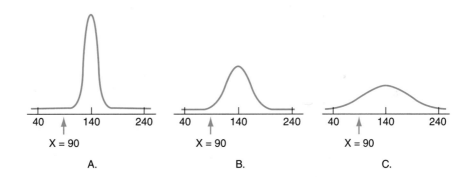

If the history scores are distributed as they are in the left-hand graph, then a score of 90 may indeed be among the lowest in the class. If the distribution looks like the middle graph, 90 will not be the lowest score. In the distribution in the right-hand graph, we can expect a fair percentage of scores to be lower than 90. Similarly, we don't know if John's psychology score of 85 is far above average or only a little above average, simply because we don't know how spread out the distribution is. We will now add the standard deviations and pinpoint the locations of John's scores in their respective distributions.

The standard deviation in psychology was 10, and the standard deviation in history was 25. Again, let's organize our data before we do anything else.

Psychology	*History*
X = 85	X = 90
M = 75	M = 140
SD = 10	SD = 25

Next, let's construct curves to represent these data, assuming the scores are normally distributed.

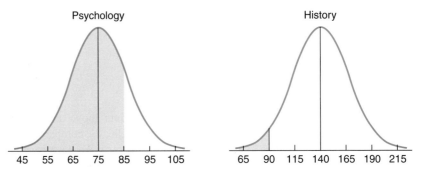

The shaded area in each distribution represents the proportion of scores below John's score. We can see that his psychology score is one standard deviation above the mean, and his history score is two standard deviations below the mean. To determine exactly what percentage of scores is lower than John's scores, all we need to do is consult the normal curve diagram to determine the percentage of cases lower than one standard deviation unit above the mean (for psychology) and lower than two standard deviation units below the mean (for history).

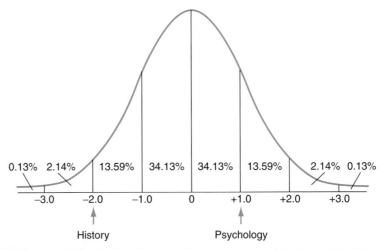

This diagram is identical to the normal curve presented in the section "Properties of the Normal Distribution." The normal curve is used when we need a common basis on which to compare scores from distributions with different means and standard deviations. Examining this distribution we can see that about 84% of the class scored lower than John in psychology, while only about 2% scored lower in history. As compared with the rest of the class, his performance in psychology was far better than his performance in history. In psychology he scored at the 84th percentile, and in history he scored at the 2nd.

z-Scores

Now we have very specific information about John's performance. We had to collect the proper data (means and standard deviations for each distribution) and determine how far above or below the mean in standard deviation units each score was in order to determine the percentage of scores below (or above) the obtained raw scores. It took a while, but we got there! Fortunately there is a mathematical shortcut. A relatively simple formula enables us to determine a score's exact position in the normal distribution quickly. The formula is called the z-score formula, and it converts raw scores into what are called z-scores. These are scores that tell us how far above or below the mean in standard deviation units raw scores lie:

$$z = \frac{X - M}{SD}$$

where:

z = z-score

X = obtained raw score

M = mean score

SD = standard deviation

This formula enables us to convert raw scores from any distribution to a common scale, regardless of its mean or standard deviation, so that we can easily compare such scores. This eliminates the confusion that would ordinarily result from such comparisons. As we mentioned, this formula is a shortcut method of doing what we just did in step-by-step fashion.

In case you don't believe us, let's work through the same example, this time using the z-score formula.

John obtained a score of 85 on his psychology midterm and 90 on his history midterm. On which test did he do better compared to the rest of the class?

The first thing we should do is to organize the relevant information. We already have the raw scores, the mean, and the standard deviation.

Psychology	*History*
X = 85	X = 90
M = 75	M = 140
SD = 10	SD = 25

Once we have all the necessary data—the obtained score, mean, and standard deviation for each distribution—we are ready to plug the data into the z-score formula, obtain z-scores for each raw score, and compare these using the z-score distribution:

Psychology	*History*
$z = \dfrac{X - M}{SD}$	$z = \dfrac{X - M}{SD}$
$= \dfrac{85 - 75}{10}$	$= \dfrac{90 - 140}{25}$
$= \dfrac{10}{10}$	$= \dfrac{-50}{25}$
$= +1.0$	$= -2.0$

As you can see, we were quickly able to get the same results as before by using the mathematical formula (i.e., John's scores in psychology and history are +1 and −2 SDs from the mean, respectively). We can now use the properties of the normal curve to answer a variety of questions about these scores. For example,

What percentage of scores fall higher? Lower?

At what percentile do the scores lie?

How much better than average were the scores? How much poorer?

Just to make sure you understand the *z*-score concept, let's work through two examples.

Example: *On a 70-item test Mary obtained a score of 49. The test had a mean of 40 and a standard deviation of 3. What percentage of the class scored higher than Mary?*

Process

1. Organize the relevant information.

$$X = 49$$
$$M = 40$$
$$SD = \ 3$$

2. Convert to *z*-scores.

$$z = \frac{X - M}{SD}$$

$$= \frac{49 - 40}{3} = \frac{9}{3} = +3.0$$

3. Use the normal curve to answer questions about comparisons, percentages, or percentiles.

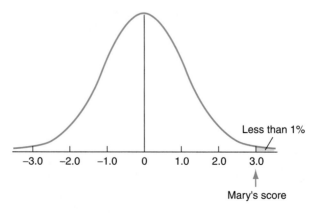

Less than 1%

−3.0   −2.0   −1.0   0   1.0   2.0   3.0

Mary's score

The shaded area in the z-score distribution indicates the percentage of obtained scores that were higher than Mary's. In other words, less than 1% (or, more accurately, 0.13% or less) of the individuals who took the test scored higher than Mary.

Example: *On the verbal portion of the Scholastic Assessment Test (SAT) Pete obtained a score of 350. The mean of the SAT-V is 500, and its standard deviation is 100. The college Pete wants to go to will not accept applicants who score below the eighth percentile on the SAT-V. Will Pete be accepted by this college?*

Process

1. Organize data.

$$X = 350$$
$$M = 500$$
$$SD = 100$$

2. Complete the z-score.

$$z = \frac{X - M}{SD}$$

$$= \frac{350 - 500}{100} = \frac{-150}{100} = -1.5$$

3. Use the normal curve properties to draw conclusions.

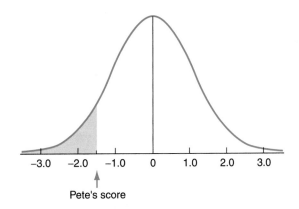

Pete's score

So far we have not had to deal with z-scores containing decimals. We can see that the shaded area in the curve represents the percentage of scores below Pete's score. The question is, does this shaded area represent at least 8% of the scores obtained by others? If it does, Pete's score is at or above the eighth percentile, and he will be accepted. If it represents less than 8%, Pete's score is below the eighth percentile, and he will not be accepted.

In an introductory statistics course you would learn to determine exactly what percentage of the z-score distribution falls below a z-score of 1.5, but we will settle for an estimate. Let's go ahead and estimate, considering the following illustration:

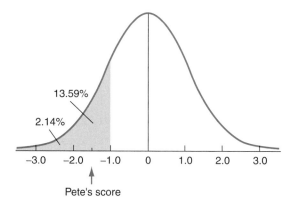

13.59%

2.14%

−3.0   −2.0   −1.0   0   1.0   2.0   3.0

Pete's score

We know that about 2% of the scores fall below two z-score units below the mean and that about 14% fall between one and two z-score units below the mean. A common mistake is to erroneously assume that since −1.5 is halfway between −1.0 and −2.0, about 7% of the scores fall between −1.0 and −1.5 and another 7% fall between −1.5 and −2.0. This reasoning would be correct if the proportions of the curve between −1.0 and −1.5 and between −1.5 and −2.0 were the same. The following illustration shows, however, that a greater proportion of scores falls between −1.0 and −1.5 than falls between −1.5 and −2.0.

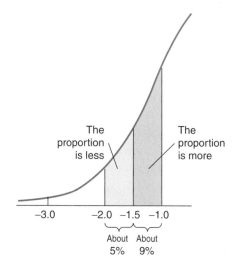

The proportion is less

The proportion is more

−3.0   −2.0 −1.5 −1.0

About   About
5%   9%

Remember, we are dealing with a curve, not with a histogram! If we were dealing with a histogram, splitting the percentage in half would be correct. Since we are not dealing with a histogram, we must estimate the proportions any time we have a z-score that results in a decimal number.

Now, returning to our example, we see that about 7% (2% below $z = -2\%$ and 5% between $z = -1.5$ and $z = -2.0$) of SAT-V scores fall below 350. Pete's score is below the eighth percentile. He will not be accepted by the college.

T-Scores

In working through this last example, at times you may have been confused about the negative numbers or may have forgotten that you were dealing with negative numbers. To avoid this difficulty, statisticians often convert z-scores to T-scores. T-scores are identical to z-scores, except that the T-score distribution has a mean of 50 and a standard deviation of 10. Our z, or normal curve distribution, had a mean of 0 and a standard deviation of 1.0. In the T-score distribution, negative numbers are eliminated except in those extremely rare cases where raw scores more than five standard deviations below the mean are obtained. To convert a raw score to a T-score you must first convert to a z-score. The formula for a T-score is

$$T = 10z + 50$$

This formula says multiply the z-score by 10 and add 50 to this value to obtain the equivalent T-score. Let's convert John's psychology z-score of +1.0 and history score of −2.0 to T-scores.

Psychology	*History*
$T = 10z + 50$	$T = 10z + 50$
$= 10(1.0) + 50$	$= 10(-2.0) + 50$
$= 10 + 50$	$= (-20) + 50$
$= 60$	$= 30$

Thus a z-score of 1.0 is equivalent to a T-score of 60, and a z-score of −2.0 is equivalent to a T-score of 30. Notice that the negative number has been eliminated. The following illustration shows the relationship between z-scores and T-scores:

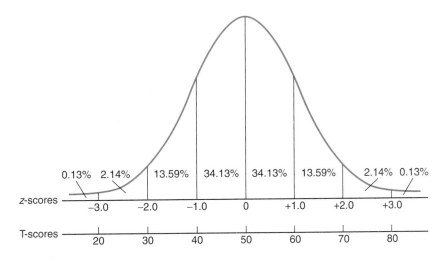

Thus far we have considered statistical methods of tabulating and graphing data, the measures of central tendency and variability, the normal distribution, and converted scores. In the next chapter we will consider another statistic, one that enables us to indicate how closely related or associated different sets of scores are.

SUMMARY

This chapter introduced you to the concept of score variability, methods to compute estimates of variability, the normal distribution, and converted scores. Its major points are as follows:

1. Variability is the term we use to describe how spread out or dispersed scores are within a distribution.

2. The range, a gross estimate of variability, is determined by subtracting the lowest score from the highest score in the distribution.

3. The semi-interquartile range (SIQR), which is usually reported along with the median, is determined by subtracting the value for the first quartile from the value for the third quartile and dividing the remainder by two.

4. The standard deviation (SD) is usually reported along with the mean and is our best estimate of variability. It is determined by subtracting the mean from each raw score to obtain a deviation score (x), squaring each deviation score, summing the squared deviation scores, dividing the total by the number of scores, and then determining the square root of this value.

5. Distributions with small standard deviations have a compressed appearance and are called homogeneous distributions.

6. Distributions with large standard deviations have a more expanded appearance and are called heterogeneous distributions.

7. The normal distribution is a specific type of symmetrical distribution that is mathematically determined and has fixed properties.

8. Although the normal distribution is hypothetical, it approximates the distribution of many test scores, enabling us to use it as a model on which to base statistical decisions.

9. We use the normal distribution as our basis for comparing scores from distributions with different means and standard deviations.

10. We do so by converting raw scores from different distributions to either z-scores or T-scores and using these converted scores as the baseline for the normal distribution. This enables us to compare scores from different distributions on a single distribution with a single mean and standard deviation.

11. Determine z-scores by subtracting the mean for the distribution from the raw score and dividing by the standard deviation of the distribution.

12. Determine T-scores by first computing the corresponding z-score for a raw score and then multiply the z-score by 10 and add 50 to the product.

13. The main advantage of the T-score over the z-score is the elimination of negative numbers.

FOR PRACTICE

*1. For this set of scores (5, 6, 6, 4, 5, 1, 2, 3, 5, 3), compute the following:

a. N

b. Mode

c. Median

d. Mean

e. Standard deviation

f. Variance

g. Range

*2. Given M = 100 and SD = 10,

a. Convert these raw scores into z-scores: 120, 132, 140, and 145.

b. Convert these z-scores into raw scores: −2.5, 0.6, 1.25, and 2.15.

c. Convert these T-scores into raw scores: 75, 38, 35, and 28.

d. What percentages of scores lie between the following scores?

  75– 90

  90–120

  100–110

  112–125

*3. A normal score distribution has a mean of 100 and a standard deviation of 15.

a. What z-score is the equivalent of a raw score of 120?

b. What raw score is most equivalent to a T-score of 33?

c. Approximately what percentage of scores lie below a score of 85?

*4. A pupil obtains a raw score of 82 on a test with a mean of 100 and a standard deviation of 12. His score corresponds to what T-score?

*Answers for these questions appear in Appendix F.

*5. The mean for the following distribution is 80 and the standard deviation is 12. Assuming a normal distribution, compute or determine the z-scores and T-scores for the following students:

Student	Score
John	68
Mary	104
Jim	86
Claire	62

*6. The following are the means and standard deviations of some well-known standardized tests, referred to as Test A, Test B, and Test C. All three yield normal distributions.

Test	Mean	Standard Deviation
Test A	500	100
Test B	100	15
Test C	60	10

a. A score of 325 on Test A corresponds to what score on Test C? A score of 640 on Test A corresponds to what score on Test B?

b. The counselor told Sally that she had scored so high on Test A that only 2 people out of 100 would score higher. What was Sally's score on Test A?

CHAPTER *14*

CORRELATION

OUR LAST statistical topic is correlation. Thus far we have discussed statistics that are used to describe distributions and the position of individual scores within a distribution. There are times, though, when we are interested in the extent to which an individual's position or rank in one distribution is similar or dissimilar to his or her position or rank in a different distribution. That is, at times we want to determine how closely scores in *different* distributions are related to one another. Or, simply, we wish to know if individuals with high scores in distribution A tend also to obtain high scores in distribution B.

These and similar issues are concerned with the extent to which two different distributions of scores correlate. A statistic called a *correlation coefficient* (symbolized by r) helps us address general issues like those just mentioned or answer specific questions like those that follow:

> Are athletes really poor scholars?
>
> If you do poorly on the verbal portion of the SAT, are you likely to do poorly on the quantitative portion?
>
> Do students with high grades in high school really tend to get high grades in college?

In this first question what is being asked is whether individuals who score high in a distribution of ratings pertaining to physical ability tend to score low in a distribution of ratings pertaining to intellectual ability. Using information gained from the previous chapter we can illustrate this as follows:

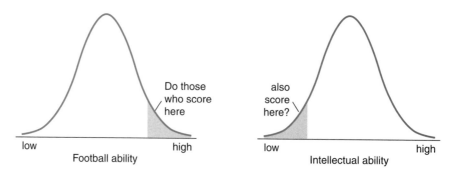

This question asks whether there is a *negative* correlation between the two. Are high scores in one distribution associated with low scores in the other?

The next question asks whether those who score low in the SAT-V distribution also score low in the SAT-Q distribution. Here, too, we can illustrate the question being asked, but note the difference from our previous illustration:

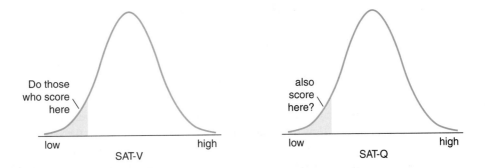

This question asks whether there is a *positive* correlation between the two distributions of scores.

Our last question asks whether students with high grades in high school also tend to receive high grades in college. This issue could be illustrated in the same manner as before:

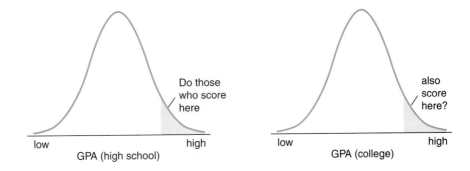

It asks whether there is a *positive* correlation between the two distributions. In other words, are high scores in one distribution associated with high scores in the other distribution?

THE CORRELATION COEFFICIENT

As we have seen, distributions can correlate positively or negatively. They may also not correlate at all! The correlation coefficient (r) tells us at a glance the strength and direction (positive or negative) of the relationship between distributions. Correlation coefficients range from −1.0 to +1.0. The closer a coefficient gets to −1.0 or to +1.0, the stronger the relationship. The sign of the coefficient tells us whether the relationship is positive or negative. The following examples are illustrative of correlation coefficients:

Coefficient	Strength	Direction
$r = -.85$	Strong	Negative
$r = +.82$	Strong	Positive
$r = +.22$	Weak	Positive
$r = +.03$	Very weak	Positive
$r = -.42$	Moderate	Negative

Strength of a Correlation

The previous coefficients are described as ranging from very weak to strong. You may ask yourself, "How high must r be for it to be strong?" Well, there is no cut and dried answer to this question because an $r = .40$ may be considered strong for one set of data (e.g., correlation of IQ scores and "happiness") and very weak for another (e.g. , correlation of scores from two standardized achievement tests). In other words, we must always consider the distributions with which we are dealing before deciding whether an r is weak, moderate, or strong. If our distributions are composed of scores arrived at by fairly objective means, such as standardized achievement tests, we require r values to be fairly high (e.g., .80 or more) before we call them strong. When distributions are composed of scores arrived at by subjective means, such as ratings of happiness, job success, or maturity, we usually consider much lower r values (e.g., .50 to .60) as indicative of the presence of a strong relationship between the distributions in question.

Direction of a Correlation

The following illustrates the possible relationships between distributions that will result in positive or negative correlation coefficients. A positive correlation exists when:

1. High scores in distribution A are associated with high scores in distribution B.

2. Low scores in distribution A are associated with low scores in distribution B.

A negative correlation exists when:

1. High scores in distribution A are associated with low scores in distribution B.

2. Low scores in distribution A are associated with high scores in distribution B.

A common example of a positive correlation is the relationship between height and weight. As people *increase* in height, they tend to *increase* in weight, and vice versa. A real-life example of negative correlation is the relationship between the number of cigarettes smoked per day and life expectancy. As the number of cigarettes smoked per day *increases*, life expectancy *decreases*, and vice versa. Fortunately, for those who are smokers, the correlation is not very strong.

When there is no systematic relationship between two distributions, correlation coefficients around .00 are found. These indicate that high scores in distribution A are likely to be associated with *both* high and low scores in distribution B, and vice versa. In other words, there is no consistent pattern.

Scatterplots

As we have noted, the strength and direction of a relationship between two distributions can be determined by a correlation coefficient. Scatterplots also enable us to determine the strength and direction of a correlation, but in a less formal manner. A scatterplot is nothing more than a graphical representation of the relationship between two variables representing the scores in two distributions.

Suppose we are interested in determining whether there is a relationship between number of touchdowns scored and academic achievement. To do so, we randomly select five running backs from past football teams, count up the number of touchdowns they scored, and obtain copies of their transcripts. Although it is not necessary to do so, for illustrative purposes we will then rank each player on the two variables in question: touchdowns scored and GPA.[1] The results might look something like those in Fig. 14.1; which is a scatterplot of the data for each individual player. This graph indicates there is a *perfect negative* correlation ($r = -1.0$) between rank in touchdowns and rank in GPA. The player ranked highest in touchdowns is ranked lowest in GPA, and vice versa. There is a *perfect* correlation because all the plotted points can be connected by a straight line. We can tell it is a *negative* correlation because the slope of the scatterplot descends from left to right.

Let's collect the same data from another school, one that emphasizes academics and not football. These data are represented in Fig. 14.2. The scatterplot in Fig. 14.2 indicates a *perfect positive* correlation ($r = 1.0$) between these variables. The player ranked lowest in touchdowns was also ranked lowest in GPA. The player ranked highest in touchdowns was also ranked highest in GPA. This is a *perfect* correlation because, again, the points are connected by a straight line. However, this time we can see the correlation is *positive* because the slope of the scatterplot ascends from left to right.

As you might have suspected, both of these examples are unrealistic. Perfect correlations, whether positive or negative, seldom occur. Normally one ends up with r values

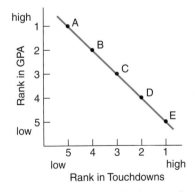

Player	Rank in Touchdowns	Rank in GPA
A	5 (lowest)	1 (highest)
B	4	2
C	3	3
D	2	4
E	1 (highest)	5 (lowest)

FIGURE 14.1 A scatterplot indicating a perfect negative correlation.

[1] We could also have used the unranked, or raw score, data. Our choice of data will determine the type of correlation coefficient that we compute and the symbol used to denote it, as we explain later.

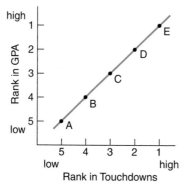

Player	Rank in Touchdowns	Rank in GPA
A	5 (low)	5 (low)
B	4	4
C	3	3
D	2	2
E	1 (high)	1 (high)

FIGURE 14.2 A scatterplot indicating a perfect positive correlation.

somewhere between −1.0 and +10. Consider in Fig. 14.3 data collected from a third school. The scatterplot in this figure represents a *positive* correlation. However, it is not a perfect correlation because the points are "scattered" around the line rather than falling on the line. The line drawn through the points, called the regression line, is mathematically determined and is included here only to highlight the degree to which the data points slope upward or downward.

These data yield an *r* of .42. You can estimate the position of a regression line by drawing a straight line through the scattered points that best fits the movement of data upward (positive correlation) or downward (negative correlation). This movement is actually the rate at which rank in touchdowns changes relative to rank in GPA as we move from one individual to another. You may also enclose scattered data points with an ellipse, as we have done, to highlight the *strength* of the relationship. As the data points form a tighter and tighter ellipse, the correlation gets stronger. This is illustrated by the scatterplots in Fig. 14.4. Notice that when *r* approaches zero, a circle rather than an ellipse may better capture all the data points. As these examples illustrate, we often deal with correlations less than +1.0 or −1.0 because people do not

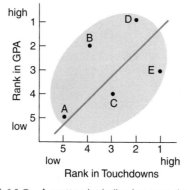

Player	Rank in Touchdowns	Rank in GPA
A	5 (low)	5
B	4	2
C	3	4
D	2	1
E	1 (high)	3

FIGURE 14.3 A scatterplot indicating a weaker positive correlation.

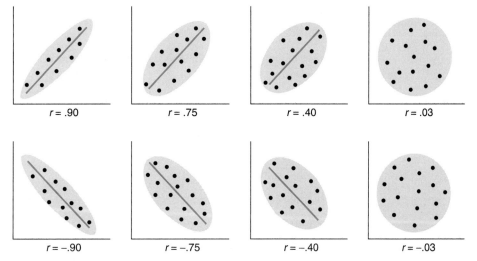

FIGURE 14.4 Scatterplots for a variety of correlations.

conform to strict rules governing relationships among their abilities and other characteristics. Instead, relationships occur according to general trends with lots of
exceptions. For example, there is a positive relationship between height and weight.
Tall people tend to weigh more than short people. However, there are reversals to this
trend (or exceptions to the rule): tall, skinny folks and short, stout folks. The more
reversals or exceptions present in relationships, the weaker the correlation between the
variables.

Where Does *r* Come From?

The correlation is determined through any one of a variety of mathematical formulas. One
of these uses data that have been ranked, rather than raw scores—data like those
presented in Fig. 14.1. This type of correlation coefficient is called a rank difference
correlation[2], which has the following formula:

$$r_\rho = 1 - \frac{6\Sigma D^2}{N(N^2 - 1)}$$

where

r_ρ = rank difference coefficient of correlation
Σ = sum of
D = difference between a pair of ranks
N = number of pupils

---

[2] The rank difference correlation is one of several different types of correlations. The Greek letter rho (ρ) is
used to identify a rank difference correlation.

The results of this formula for the rank difference coefficient when applied to the data presented in Fig. 14.1 are as follows:

Rank in Touchdowns	Rank in GPA	Difference between Ranks	D^2
5	1	4	16
4	2	2	4
3	3	0	0
2	4	2	4
1	5	4	16
			$\Sigma D^2 = 40$

$$r_\rho = 1 - \frac{6(40)}{5(25 - 1)}$$

$$= 1 - \frac{240}{120} = 1 - 2 = -1.0$$

The calculation of another type of correlation coefficient, called the Pearson product–moment correlation coefficient, is illustrated with an example in Appendix D. The advantage of the rank difference correlation is that it can be used with small numbers of subjects, whereas the Pearson product–moment correlation must be used with larger numbers of scores, usually 30 or more pairs of scores. Generally, when this number of scores is obtained, the Pearson product–moment correlation (symbolized simply as r) is easier to use and more accurate. However, since few teachers are ever called on to actually compute a correlation coefficient, especially on large numbers of students, we will not concern ourselves with computations for the Pearson product–moment correlation in this chapter. More important is your ability to understand and interpret correlation coefficients. Thus far we have described what a correlation is and we have considered the numerical and graphical representations of correlations. Next, let's consider a frequently misunderstood aspect of correlation.

Causality

Correlation does not imply causality. That is, a correlation only indicates that some sort of relationship or association exists between two distributions. It does not mean that one distribution of scores *causes* the other distribution of scores. This may seem perfectly logical and sensible to you. Yet, one of the most frequent misinterpretations in statistics (and in education) is to infer that because two variables are correlated with one another, one variable causes the other. It is possible that one variable may cause another, and thus account for the relationship between the two. However, it is just as possible, and usually more likely, that the two variables are correlated with each other because of the effects of some third unidentified variable. That is, a third variable is actually causing one or both conditions, thus making it appear as though the first variable is causing the second.

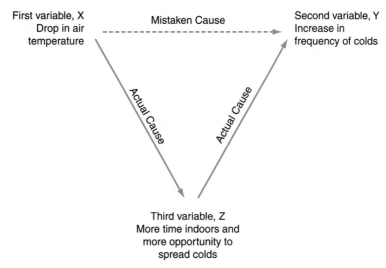

FIGURE 14.5 One way a third variable may affect conclusions about causality.

For example, there is a negative correlation between air temperature and frequency of colds. As air temperature decreases, the number of people who catch colds increases. Thus one might infer, incorrectly, that a drop in air temperature will cause colds. While this is a possibility, it is much more likely that the effect is the result of the effects of a third variable. That is, rather than a drop in air temperature causing an increase in colds, it may be that a drop in air temperature causes people to stay indoors and come in contact with each other more frequently, which causes an increase in colds. Figure 14.5 illustrates the probable sequence of events.

Two variables may also correlate with one another because a third variable affects them both. For example, head size correlates with mental age. However, this does not mean that increases in head size cause increases in mental age. Both of these are affected by a third variable, chronological age, shown in Fig. 14.6.

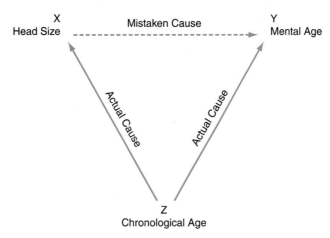

FIGURE 14.6 Another way a third variable may affect conclusions about causality.

To sum up, in and of themselves, correlation coefficients alone can never be used to prove causality. Now that we are aware of this common misinterpretation, let's consider some other cautions.

Other Interpretive Cautions

Coefficient of Determination   A correlation coefficient of .83 is referred to as "point eight three," *not* as 83%. Furthermore, to make comparative decisions about the relative strength of correlation coefficients, it is insufficient to simply compare the coefficients themselves. Instead, it is necessary to square the coefficient and multiply the result times 100. The result of this operation is called the *coefficient of determination*. The coefficient of determination is the percentage of variability (see Chapter 13) in one variable that is associated with or determined by the other variable. The following computations of the coefficient of determination demonstrate that a correlation coefficient of .80 is *four* times as strong as a coefficient of .40 and *sixteen* times as strong as a coefficient of .20.

Correlation Coefficient (r)	r^2	$r^2 \times 100$	*Coefficient of Determination*
.80	.64	64	64%
.40	.16	16	16%
.20	.04	4	4%

The coefficient of determination is an important concept in more advanced statistical operations. For our purposes we need to keep in mind only that correlation coefficients are not percentages and that we must convert correlation coefficients to the coefficient of determination *before* we can make decisions about their relative strength.

Curvilinearity   All the scatterplots we have discussed thus far are plots of variables that have *linear* relationships with each other. In a linear relationship, scores on variables A and B either increase or decrease at approximately the same rate throughout the entire range of scores. That is, they progressively move up or down together in the same way regardless of whether they are at the low, middle, or high end of the score continuum. In a *curvilinear* relationship, scores on variables A and B may increase together at first and then decrease, or they may decrease at first and then increase, depending on whether the scores are at the low, middle, or high end of the score distribution. The curvilinear relationship between anxiety and test performance (Duffy, 1972) is depicted in the scatterplot here:

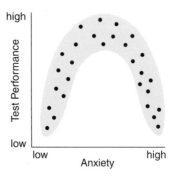

When data are related to each other in curvilinear fashion, a curved regression line fits the data better than a straight regression line. This curvilinear relationship between anxiety and test performance indicates that increases in anxiety are positively associated with test performance up to a point, after which the association between anxiety and test performance is negative. When plotted, such data take on a boomerang shape. While it is possible to compute a correlation coefficient for such data, the coefficient is of a special type. For curvilinear data, computing a rank-difference or Pearson coefficient like we would for linear data will yield an artificially low r. Thus it is always a good idea to plot and inspect data before deciding on the type of correlation coefficient to compute or use.

Truncated Range   Normally we compute correlation coefficients across the range of all possible values for variables A and B. At times, though, we may desire or be forced to consider only a part of all the possible values (e.g., just low-ranked or high-ranked individuals). Here we are dealing with a truncated or restricted range of scores. When only a portion of the entire range of scores is considered, the strength of the correlation coefficient goes down. The following scatterplots illustrate this phenomenon. The first scatterplot illustrates the relationship between IQ scores and standardized test scores.

However, let's say that we are concerned only with the relationship between high scores on both tests (indicated by the broken lines demarcating the upper right-hand section of the scatterplot). The correlation between only the high scores is much weaker than the correlation between scores across the entire range. This is illustrated in the next scatterplot, which is an enlargement of the upper right-hand section of the previous scatterplot.

This completes our chapters on statistics. We trust you now have a good working knowledge of the concepts and methods presented. If so, you are ready to apply some of these concepts and methods in the following chapters. If not, now is the time to review. The remainder of the text will be a lot easier to understand if you take the extra time to master these concepts.

SUMMARY

In this chapter you were introduced to a number of considerations related to the topic of correlation. The major points are as follows:

1. Correlation refers to the extent to which two distributions are related or associated. That is, it refers to the extent to which scores in one distribution vary depending on the variation of scores in the other distribution.

2. The extent of correlation is indicated numerically by a correlation coefficient (r) and graphically by a scatterplot.

3. When high scores in one distribution tend to be associated with low scores in another distribution, and vice versa, the correlation is negative.

4. When high scores in one distribution tend to be associated with high scores in another distribution (with the same being true for low and moderate scores), the correlation is positive.

5. Correlation coefficients may range from −1.0 (perfect negative correlation) to +1.0 (perfect positive correlation). A correlation of .00 indicates a complete absence of relationship or association.

6. The size of the number of the correlation coefficient indicates the strength of the correlation (higher numbers indicate stronger correlation), and the sign indicates the direction (positive or negative).

7. Scatterplots range from straight lines indicative of a perfect correlation to ellipses that approach circles. The tighter the ellipse, the stronger the correlation; the more circular the ellipse, the weaker the correlation.

8. The fact that two variables are correlated with one another does not necessarily mean that one variable causes the other. Often the correlation is the result of the effects of a third variable.

9. To compare the relative strength of correlation coefficients it is necessary to square the coefficients, resulting in coefficients of determination. Correlation coefficients are not percentages; coefficients of determination are.

10. When two distributions are linearly related, scores increase or decrease across the range of scores.

11. When two distributions have a curvilinear relationship, scores in one distribution may increase and then decrease, or vice versa, while scores in the other distribution consistently increase or decrease.

12. Since a linear correlation coefficient will underestimate the strength of a curvilinear relationship, it is wise to construct a scatterplot before computing a correlation coefficient to determine whether a linear correlation coefficient is appropriate.

13. When only a portion of the entire range of scores for a distribution is considered (e.g., only high or low scores) in computing a correlation coefficient, the strength of the correlation coefficient decreases. This effect is due to use of a truncated range of scores rather than the entire range of scores.

FOR PRACTICE

1. After pairing each X score with each Y score in the order given, construct a scatterplot of the data.

X: 15, 15, 15, 15, 30, 30, 30, 30, 45, 45, 45, 45, 60, 60, 60, 60, 75, 75, 75, 75

Y: 1, 2, 1, 3, 12, 10, 13, 15, 19, 18, 20, 21, 15, 11, 12, 12, 2, 3, 1, 2

*2. Does the scatterplot in Question 1 indicate that the data are linear or curvilinear? If X represents age and Y represents average annual income in thousands of dollars, describe this relationship in words.

*3. Using the formula given in Appendix D, compute a Pearson product–moment correlation coefficient for the following data.

X: 10, 8, 14, 6, 4, 8, 7, 3, 7, 10

Y: 12, 7, 13, 8, 7, 6, 6, 4, 9, 11

How would you describe the direction and size of this relationship?

*4. Compute the coefficient of determination for the data in Question 3.

*5. In the following matching exercise, Column A contains scatterplots and Column B contains correlation coefficients. Indicate which of the correlation coefficients in Column B most closely approximates the scatterplots in Column A by putting its number in the space to the left of the scatterplot. Each of the options may be used only once or not at all.

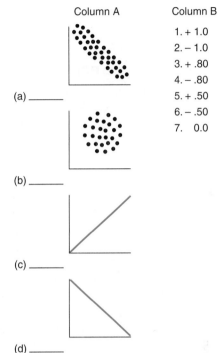

Column A   Column B

(a) _____   1. + 1.0
                   2. – 1.0
                   3. + .80
                   4. – .80
(b) _____   5. + .50
                   6. – .50
                   7.   0.0

(c) _____

(d) _____

*6. A researcher finds a high positive correlation between shoe size and vocabulary size in elementary school pupils. The researcher concludes that big feet cause big vocabularies. Do you agree or disagree? If so, why? If not, why not?

*7. Explain why the use of a truncated range of scores will result in a lower correlation between the variables in question than if the distribution were not truncated.

*Answers for questions 2 through 7 appear in Appendix F.

CHAPTER 15

VALIDITY EVIDENCE

IN THE PREVIOUS three chapters we introduced you to the field of statistics. In this and subsequent chapters we will show you how to use some of this newly acquired knowledge to evaluate tests. In short, we will show you how statistical tools are applied to test results to determine the degree of confidence we can place in the results.

WHY EVALUATE TESTS?

If a test shows that 60% of the students in our third-grade class are reading below grade level, should we be seriously concerned? Your initial response might be an unqualified yes, but we would say not necessarily. We would be worried only if we had confidence in the results of our test. We have such confidence only when we are reasonably sure a test measures the skill, trait, or attribute it is supposed to measure; when it yields reasonably consistent results for the same individual; and when it measures with a reasonable degree of accuracy. That is, we should seriously consider using test results only from tests that yield sufficient evidence that they are valid, reliable, and accurate for the purposes they are used for, and for the persons they are used with. As we discussed at some length in Chapter 1, a test may be used for more than one purpose and with people who have different characteristics, and the test may be more or less valid, reliable or accurate when used for different purposes and with different persons. In general, we can define validity, reliability, and accuracy as follows:

1. *Validity:* Does the test measure what it is supposed to measure?
2. *Reliability:* Does the test yield the same or similar score rankings (all other factors being equal) consistently?
3. *Accuracy:* Does the test score fairly closely approximate an individual's true level of ability, skill, or aptitude?

To be a "good" test, a test ought to have adequate evidence for its validity, reliability, and accuracy for the purpose it is being used for, and for the persons it is being used with. In this chapter we will see how statistics help us determine the extent to which tests possess validity evidence.

TYPES OF VALIDITY EVIDENCE

A test has validity evidence if we can demonstrate that it measures what it says it measures. For instance, if it is supposed to be a test of third-grade arithmetic ability, it should measure third-grade arithmetic skills, not fifth-grade arithmetic skills and not reading ability. If it is supposed to be a measure of ability to write behavioral objectives, it should measure that ability, not the ability to recognize bad objectives. Clearly, if a test is to be used in any kind of decision making, or indeed if the test information is to have any use at all, we should be able to identify the types of evidence that indicate the test's validity for the purpose it is being used for.

Content Validity Evidence

There are several ways of deciding whether a test has sufficient validity evidence. The simplest is content validity evidence. The content validity evidence for a test is established by inspecting test questions to see whether they correspond to what the user decides should be covered by the test. This is easiest to see when the test is in an area such as achievement, where it is fairly easy to specify what should be included in the content of a test. It is more difficult if the concept being tested is a personality or aptitude trait, as it is sometimes difficult to specify beforehand what a relevant question should look like. Another problem with content validity evidence is that it gives information about whether the test *looks* valid, but not whether the reading level of the test is too high or if the items are poorly constructed. A test can sometimes look valid but measure something entirely different than what is intended, such as guessing ability, reading level, or skills that may have been acquired before instruction. Content validity evidence is, therefore, more a minimum requirement for a useful test than it is a guarantee of a good test.

In the context of classroom testing, content validity evidence answers the question "Does the test measure the instructional objectives?" In other words, a test with good content validity evidence matches or fits the instructional objectives. In a high-stakes testing context, content validity evidence answers the question "Does the test align with state academic standards?"

Criterion-Related Validity Evidence

A second form of validity evidence is criterion-related evidence. In establishing criterion-related validity evidence, scores from a test are correlated with an external criterion. There are two types of criterion-related validity evidence: concurrent and predictive.

Concurrent Criterion-Related Validity Evidence Concurrent criterion-related validity evidence deals with measures that can be administered at the same time as the measure to be validated. For instance, the Stanford–Binet V and the Wechsler Intelligence Scale for Children–IV (WISC–IV) are well-known, widely accepted IQ tests. Therefore, a test publisher designing a short screening test that measures IQ might show that the test is highly correlated with the WISC–IV or the Binet V, and thus establish concurrent criterion-related validity evidence for the test. Unlike content validity evidence, criterion-related validity evidence yields a numeric value, which is simply a correlation coefficient. When used to illustrate validity evidence the correlation coefficient is called a *validity coefficient.*

The concurrent validity evidence for a test is determined by administering both the new test and the established test to a group of respondents, then finding the correlation between the two sets of test scores. If there exists an established test (criterion) in which most people have confidence, criterion-related validity evidence provides a good method of estimating the validity of a new test for this use. Of course, usually there is some practical advantage of having a new test—it is less expensive to give, or shorter, or can be administered to groups. Otherwise, it would be easier simply to use the established test. The following example illustrates how concurrent validity evidence might be established for a new third-grade math test.

> *The Goodly Test of Basic Third-Grade Math has been around a long time, but it takes 60 minutes to administer. Being pressed for teaching time, you develop another test that takes only 20 minutes to administer and call it the Shorter and Better Test of Basic Third-Grade Math. With visions of fame and wealth you send it off to a test publisher.*
>
> *The publisher writes back to ask whether the test is as good as the Goodly Test: "No point marketing a test that isn't at least as good as the Goodly."*

To address this challenge, you would determine the test's concurrent validity evidence by giving both the Goodly and the Shorter and Better to the same group of students and calculating a correlation coefficient between scores on the two tests. If the same students rank similarly on both tests, indicated by a high correlation, the new test could be said to have concurrent validity evidence for this use. Consider the following hypothetical data:

Student	*Score on Goodly*	*Score on Shorter and Better*
Jim	88	37
Joan	86	34
Don	77	32
Margaret	72	26
Teresa	65	22
Victor	62	21
Veronica	59	19
Wilson	58	16

Since the correlation in this instance is likely to be very high (notice that, for the data shown, everyone maintains the same rank across tests), the concurrent validity evidence for the Shorter and Better Test has been established. The publisher will be impressed and you will soon be famous.

Predictive Validity Evidence   Predictive validity evidence refers to how well the test predicts some future behavior of the examinees. This form of validity evidence is particularly useful and important for aptitude tests, which attempt to predict how well test takers will do in some future setting. The SAT-II, for instance, is frequently used to help decide who should be admitted to college. It would be desirable, therefore, for it to do a good job of predicting success in college. If a personality test is used to choose among various types of therapy for mental patients, it is desirable that it have good predictive validity evidence for that purpose. That is, it should predict who will do well with what kind of therapy. The predictive validity evidence of a test is determined by administering the test to a group of subjects, then measuring the subjects on whatever the test is supposed to predict after a period of time has elapsed. The two sets of scores are then correlated, and the coefficient that results is called a *predictive validity coefficient*.

If a test is being used to make predictions, an effort should be made to find its predictive validity evidence for the setting in which it will be used. High predictive validity evidence provides a strong argument for the worth of a test, even if it seems questionable on other grounds. In such a situation you might argue about whether it is being used to predict something worthwhile, but you can't argue about whether the test does a good job of predicting. The following example illustrates the concept of predictive validity evidence:

"Psychics predict blizzard for Houston on July 4th!" You have likely seen similar predictions in various tabloids while waiting in checkout lines at supermarkets. Are they valid? Initially you'd probably say no, but how can you be sure? The only answer is to wait and see if the predictions come true. With a test, similar reasoning applies. Just because a test is named the Test to Predict Happiness in Life doesn't mean it can (or cannot). More likely than not, we would be inclined to say it can't. But again, the only way to be sure is to wait for a period of time and see if the individuals for whom the test predicts happiness are actually happy.

Both predictive and concurrent criterion-related validity evidence yield numerical indices of validity. Content validity evidence does not yield a numerical index, but instead yields a logical judgment as to whether the test measures what it is supposed to measure, based on a systematic comparison of the test to the domain it is intended to measure. However, all three of these indices—content, concurrent, and predictive—assume that some criterion exists external to the test that can be used to anchor or validate the test. In the case of content validity evidence for a classroom achievement test, it was the instructional objectives (or state academic standards) that provided the anchor or point of reference; in the case of concurrent validity evidence, it was another well-accepted test measuring the same thing; and in the case of predictive validity evidence, it was some future behavior or condition we were attempting to predict. However, if a test is being developed to measure something not previously measured, or not measured well, and no criterion exists for anchoring the test, another kind of validity evidence must be obtained. This type of validity evidence is called *construct validity evidence*.

Construct Validity Evidence

A test has construct validity evidence if its relationship to other information corresponds well with some theory. A theory is simply a logical explanation or rationale that can account for the interrelationships among a set of variables. Many different kinds of theories can be used to help determine the construct validity evidence of a test. For instance, if a test is supposed to be a test of arithmetic computation skills, you would expect scores on it to improve after intensive coaching in arithmetic, but not after intensive coaching in a foreign language. If it is a test of mechanical aptitude, you might expect that mechanics would, on the average, do better on it than poets. You might also expect that it would have a *low* correlation with scores on a reading test, since it seems reasonable to assume that reading ability and mechanical ability are not highly related.

In general, any information that lets you know whether results from the test correspond to what you would expect (based on your own knowledge about what is being measured) tells you something about the construct validity evidence for a test. It differs from concurrent validity evidence, in that there is no accepted second measure available of what you're trying to measure, and from predictive validity evidence, in that there is no measure of future behavior available.

Already in this chapter we have had to introduce some new terms and concepts. Before proceeding, be familiar with them, and if necessary, reread our presentation on validity evidence. Before you do, let's try to understand at a commonsense level what we've been saying.

WHAT HAVE WE BEEN SAYING? A REVIEW

A test should ideally do the job it's intended to do. It should measure what it's supposed to measure. In other words, we should be able to collect evidence of its validity for a particular use. The following three questions are equivalent:

1. Is the test valid for the intended purpose?
2. Does the test measure what it is supposed to measure?
3. Does the test do the job it was designed to do?

It makes no sense to prepare or select for the classroom a test designed to measure something other than what has been taught. If we want to measure someone's height, does it make sense to use a scale? A ruler, yardstick, or a tape measure would certainly be more appropriate. Similarly, if we are interested in knowing whether our students can multiply two-digit numbers, would it make sense to administer a test that focuses on addition of two-digit numbers? The appropriate measure would be a test that includes items on two-digit multiplication. Such a test would *do the job it's supposed to do*. It would have content validity evidence.

For achievement tests, content validity evidence is most important because the "job" of an achievement test is to measure how well the content taught has been mastered. The best way to ensure that a test has content validity evidence is to be sure its items match or measure the instructional objectives. Recall that in Chapter 5 we discussed ways to check whether items match objectives. Now, let's review predictive validity evidence.

Consider a situation in which the purpose of a test is to identify those individuals who are likely to stay with a company for at least three years. A valid test in this case would accomplish this purpose. But just what is the purpose? Is it to measure how well certain concepts have been mastered? No, the purpose is to predict who will last three years and who won't. A different kind of validity evidence is necessary—predictive validity evidence.

In this situation we are interested only in finding a measuring instrument that correlates well with length of time on the job. We don't care whether it is an IQ test, math test, reading test, vocational test, visual–motor integration test, or whatever. The purpose is to predict who will last three years. If the math test correlates .75 with length of time on the job and the vocational test correlates .40 with length of time on the job, which test has the better predictive validity evidence? The math test, of course, because it would provide us with the most accurate prediction of future behavior.

In the case of concurrent validity evidence, the purpose of a test is to approximate the results that would have been obtained had a well-established test been used. In other words, if the ranking of students with the new or shorter test *concurs* with the rankings of students on the older, standard test, then the new or shorter test has concurrent validity evidence. Remember, unless a new test does something more easily or better than an established measure, there is no point in constructing a new test!

Finally, let's think about construct validity evidence. Construct validity evidence is important in establishing the validity of a test when we cannot anchor our test either to a well-established test measuring the same behavior or to any measurable future behavior. Since we do not have these anchoring devices to rely on, we can only create verbal and mathematical descriptions or theories of how our test behavior (called a construct) is either likely to change following or during certain situations or likely to be related to other constructs. If a test of our theory reflects or demonstrates the relationships specified, the new measure has construct validity evidence. Unlike predictive and concurrent validity evidence, not one but many correlation coefficients emerge from a construct validation study. The actual process used to assess construct validity evidence can be lengthy and complex and need not concern us here. Figure 15.1 summarizes our discussion of the types of validity evidence most relevant in the classroom. Believe it or not, our presentation of test validity has been quite superficial as far as measurement theory goes. If you are interested in a more intensive discussion of any of these topics you can consult one or more of the measurement texts listed in Appendix E. Next we will discuss the role of validity coefficients in evaluating tests.

INTERPRETING VALIDITY COEFFICIENTS

Now that we have discussed and reviewed the concepts of content, concurrent, and predictive validity evidence, we can begin to put these concepts to use in evaluating educational tests. Remember, validity coefficients enable us to estimate the extent to which a test measures what it is supposed to measure. Let's consider the role of validity coefficients in making decisions about tests.

Content Validity Evidence

If you are wondering why content validity evidence is included in this section, you are probably grasping more of what has been presented than you may realize. Procedures to determine a test's content validity evidence do *not* yield validity coefficients. Content validity evidence is established by comparing test items with instructional objectives (e.g., with the aid of a test blueprint) to determine whether the items match or measure the objectives. After such an examination takes place, a test is judged either to have or not to have content validity evidence for a particular use. No correlation coefficient is computed. Instead, human judgment is relied upon.

	Ask the question:	*To answer the question:*
• Content Validity Evidence	Do test items match and measure objectives?	Match the items with objectives.
• Concurrent Criterion-Related Validity Evidence	How well does performance on the new test match performance on an established test?	Correlate new test with an accepted criterion, for example, a well-established test measuring the same behavior.
• Predictive Criterion-Related Validity Evidence	Can the test predict subsequent performance, for example, success or failure in the next grade?	Correlate scores from the new test with a measure of some future performance.

Remember. Predictive validity evidence involves a time interval. A test is administered and, after a period of time, a behavior is measured which the test is intended to predict. For example:

Remember. Concurrent validity evidence does not involve a time interval. A test is administered, and its relationship to a well-established test measuring the same behavior is determined. For example:

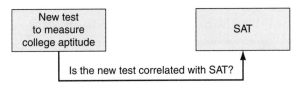

FIGURE 15.1   Review of validity evidence.

Concurrent and Predictive Validity Evidence

Concurrent and predictive validity evidence require the correlation of a predictor or concurrent measure with a criterion measure. These types of validity evidence do yield numerical coefficients. Using our interpretation of these coefficients, we can determine whether a test is useful to us as a predictor or as a substitute (concurrent) measure. In general, the higher the validity coefficient, the better the validity evidence for the test is. However, several principles must be considered in evaluating validity coefficients.

PRINCIPLE 1: Concurrent validity coefficients are generally higher than predictive validity coefficients. This does *not* mean, however, that the test with the higher validity coefficient is more suitable for a given purpose.

The rationale for this principle is that in establishing concurrent validity evidence, no time interval (or a very small time interval) is involved between administration of the new test and the criterion or established test. Thus the chances that the behavior of individuals measured on both the new test and the criterion test has changed between testings is negligible. On the contrary, predictive validity evidence coefficients are by definition susceptible to such changes. Lifestyle, personality, and attitudinal or experiential changes may alter an individual's rank on a criterion measure two years from now from what it was at the initial testing. Thus a *decline* in the size of the correlation between the test and a measure of future performance would be expected as the time interval between the two measurements increases.

Generally, concurrent validity coefficients in the .80 and higher range and predictive validity coefficients in the .60 and higher range are considered encouraging. However, judgments about the strength of a validity coefficient must consider the attributes being measured. If a new achievement test reports a concurrent validity coefficient of .60 with an established achievement test, we probably would not consider using the new achievement test; we would look for higher correlations because correlations between achievement tests are generally higher. On the other hand, if a new college selection test correlated .60 with college GPA, the new test might be considered suitable for use as a college selection test, because correlations between such tests and GPA are generally much lower. In other words, the *purpose* of the test as well as the size of the validity coefficient must be considered in evaluating the test's validity evidence.

> PRINCIPLE 2: Group variability affects the size of the validity coefficient. Higher validity coefficients are derived from heterogeneous groups than from homogeneous groups.

If the college selection test mentioned before was administered to *all* high school seniors in a district (a heterogeneous group) and if all these students went to the same four-year college, the obtained validity coefficient would be higher for this group than if the test were administered only to high school seniors in the top 10% of their class (a homogeneous group). At first glance this may not seem to make sense. The picture becomes clear, however, if we think about how changes in the rankings of individuals on the two measures are affected by the variability of these distributions. In the heterogeneous group, students who are at the top of their high school class are likely to score high on the test and have high college GPAs. Students at the bottom of the class are likely to score low and have low college GPAs. That is, the likelihood of major shifting in ranks occurring is small. It's not likely that students who score low on the test will have high GPAs and vice versa, as is illustrated in Fig. 15.2. Although some shifting in ranks or position might be expected, as indicated by the arrows in Fig. 15.2, dramatic shifts would be unlikely. While it might be possible for our lowest scoring student on the selection test (Student A) to obtain a 3.5 GPA, it would be unlikely.

But what happens when the variability of the group is greatly reduced, creating a homogeneous group composed only of the top 10% of the high school seniors? Now we would expect a pronounced shifting of ranks or positions to take place. This is likely to occur because the students are all ranked so closely together on the selection test that even small differences between their ranks on GPA will lower the size of the validity coefficient. This is illustrated in Fig. 15.3.

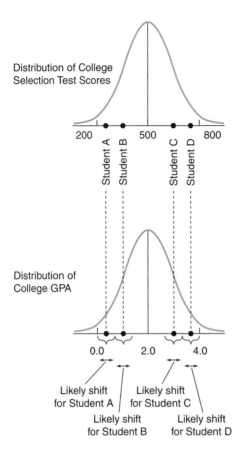

FIGURE 15.2 Comparison of probable rankings between college selection test scores and college GPA for four students from a heterogeneous group.

Compare the overlap, or possible shifting in ranks, for this group to the possible shifting in ranks for the heterogeneous group. The width of the arrows has not changed, but their significance has. There is much more likelihood of dramatic shifts occurring among the students in this homogeneous group. They are so much alike in ability that the test is unable to discriminate among those individuals in the high-ability group who will rank low, middle, or high in their GPAs, since the range of GPAs for this group is only about 3.5 to 4.0. When test scores or criterion measures are more heterogeneous, however, the test is able to discriminate among those who will rank low, moderate, or high in GPAs. In such a case, GPAs might range from 0.0 to 4.0.

In evaluating the adequacy of a test's validity coefficient, it is necessary to consider the variability of the group from which the coefficient was derived. For example, critics who discourage using the SAT-II as a criterion for college admission often point out that its predictive validity evidence coefficient is only about .40. What they may fail to consider, however, is that the coefficient is not based on all high school students, but only on those who took the test and actually went to college. This is a far more homogeneous group than the entire body of high school students. Thus its predictive validity evidence coefficient is smaller than would be expected if it were based on *all* high school students.

FIGURE 15.3 Comparison of probable rankings between college selection test scores and college GPA for four students from a homogeneous group (upper 10% of senior class).

> PRINCIPLE 3: The relevance and reliability of the criterion should be considered in the interpretation of validity coefficients.

Wherever predictive validity evidence is being considered, it is necessary to be aware that the size of the resulting coefficient is dependent on both the reliability of the predictor *and* the criterion measure. If you are using a test to predict whether someone will last for three years on a job, your criterion is easy to measure, and your criterion measure would be dependable. For this measure you need simply to determine whether someone is employed after three years. Unfortunately, in many cases criterion measures are not so simple. For example, let's say you want to establish the predictive validity evidence of a test to predict job success, rather than simply whether or not someone is employed after three years. What does job success mean? Herein lies the problem of selecting a criterion measure. Is it best measured by salary scale? Number of promotions? Amount of sales? Merchandise produced? Supervisor ratings? Peer ratings? All of these? We could probably go on and on, but the point is that criterion measures that are meaningful are often difficult to identify and agree upon. Each of the criterion measures mentioned may be an important *aspect* of job success, but none is *equivalent* to job success. Ideally you would want to collect many measures of job success and determine their relationship to the test. In reality, however, such a thorough approach might be impossible due to financial or time constraints. What typically happens in a predictive validity investigation is that one or two of what are considered to be relevant criterion measures are selected and correlated with the predictor. Naturally, such a compromise limits somewhat the weight that one might attach to predictive validity coefficients, since not all relevant aspects of the criterion are considered.

If a test has a predictive validity coefficient of .60 with salary after three years, but coefficients of .20 with supervisor ratings and .16 with peer ratings, we would question the test's validity evidence. Since salary typically increases from year to year, often independent of success on the job, the correlation with salary might not be very meaningful, since salary may not be all that *relevant*. On the other hand, supervisor and peer ratings may be more relevant measures. However, our test's correlation with those measures is little more than what might occur by chance. Since the test does not correlate highly with more relevant criteria, we might question its predictive validity evidence. However, to do so without considering the dependability of the criterion measure we have chosen would be a mistake.

To correlate highly or even moderately with each other, measures must be dependable or fairly stable (i.e., *reliable*). If ratings by supervisors or peers vary greatly from rating period to rating period, then any attempt to correlate such ratings with a predictor will yield low correlation coefficients—even if the predictor is highly reliable. If an employee gets a high rating from one peer or supervisor and a low rating from another, how can the predictor possibly predict a rating? The answer is that it can't. Some evidence of stability or reliability in a criterion measure is necessary before we can conclude that a predictor which correlates poorly with a criterion measure is actually a poor predictor and not a reflection of an unreliable criterion measure.

We have intended this discussion to alert you to the importance of studying carefully any and all statistical data presented in test manuals. Where predictive validity coefficients are reported, check the adequacy (the relevance) of the criterion measure and its dependability (the reliability) before drawing any conclusions about the validity evidence for the predictor.

SUMMARY

This chapter introduced you to the major types of validity evidence and some principles to be considered in interpreting validity coefficients. The major points are as follows:

1. To be considered seriously, test results should have adequate validity evidence and be reliable.

2. A valid test measures what it is supposed to measure.

3. Content validity evidence is assessed by systematically comparing a test item with instructional objectives to see if they match. Content validity evidence does not yield a numerical estimate of validity.

4. Criterion-related validity evidence is established by correlating test scores with an external standard or criterion to obtain a numerical estimate of validity evidence.

5. There are two types of criterion-related validity evidence: concurrent and predictive.
    a. Concurrent validity evidence is determined by correlating test scores with a criterion measure collected at the same time.
    b. redictive validity evidence is determined by correlating test scores with a criterion measure collected after a period of time has passed.

6. Construct validity evidence is determined by finding whether test results correspond with scores on other variables as predicted by some rationale or theory.

7. In interpreting validity evidence, the following principles should be kept in mind:
   a. The adequacy of validity evidence depends on both the strength of the validity coefficient and the purpose the test is being used for.
   b. Group variability affects the strength of the validity coefficient.
   c. Validity coefficients should be considered in terms of the relevance and reliability of the criterion or standard.

FOR PRACTICE

*1. A teacher who is a friend of yours has just developed a test to measure the content in a social studies unit you both teach. His test takes 30 minutes less time to complete than the test you have used in the past, and this is a major advantage. You decide to evaluate the new test by giving it and the old test to the same class of students. Using the following data, determine if the new test has concurrent validity evidence.

a. Scores on the new test: 25, 22, 18, 18, 16, 14, 12, 8, 6, 6

b. Scores for the same students on the old test: 22, 23, 25, 28, 31, 32, 34, 42, 44, 48

*2. Indicate how and with what types of tests you would evaluate the predictive and construct validity evidence of the new social studies test in Question 1.

*3. Examine the validity coefficients of the following tests and, assuming they have content validity evidence, determine which are suitable for use. State your reasons. What is unusual about Test C?

	Test A	Test B	Test C
Concurrent validity coefficient	.90	.50	.75
Predictive validity coefficient	.72	.32	.88

*4. Assuming the following tests measure the same content and assuming all other things are equal, rank them in terms of their overall acceptability for predicting behavior in upcoming years.

*Answers for these questions appear in Appendix F.

	Test A	Test B	Test C
Concurrent validity coefficient	.90	.80	.85
Predictive validity coefficient (one-month interval)	.50	.65	.60
Predictive validity coefficient (six-month interval)	.40	.10	.55

*5. What types of validity evidence go with the following procedures?

a. Matching test items with objectives.

b. Correlating a test of mechanical skills after training with on-the-job performance ratings.

c. Correlating the short form of an IQ test with the long form.

d. Correlating a paper and pencil test of musical talent with ratings from a live audition completed after the test.

e. Correlating a test of reading ability with a test of mathematical ability.

f. Comparing lesson plans with a test publisher's test blueprint.

*6. The principal is upset. The results of the four-year follow-up study are in. The correlation between the grades assigned by you to your gifted students and their college GPA is lower than the correlation between grades and college GPA for nongifted students. The principal wants to abandon the gifted program. How would you defend yourself and your program?

CHAPTER 16

RELIABILITY

THE **RELIABILITY** of a test refers to the consistency with which it yields the same rank for individuals who take the test more than once. In other words, a test (or any measuring instrument) is reliable if it consistently yields the same, or nearly the same, ranks over repeated administrations during which we would not expect the trait being measured to have changed. For instance, a bathroom scale is reliable if it gives you the same weight after five weighings in a single morning. If the five weights differ by several pounds, the scale is not especially reliable. If the five weights differ by 25 pounds, it is extremely unreliable. In the same manner, scores from educational tests may be very reliable, fairly reliable, or totally unreliable. For instance, if a multiple-choice test given to a class were so difficult that everyone guessed at the answers, then a student's rank would probably vary quite a bit from one administration to another and the test would be unreliable.

If any use is to be made of the information from a test, it is desirable that the test results be reliable. If the test is going to be used to make placement decisions about individual students, you wouldn't want it to provide different rankings of students if it were given again the next day. If a test is going to be used to make decisions about the difficulty level of your instructional materials, you wouldn't want scores from the test to indicate that the same materials are too difficult one day and too easy the next. In testing, as in our everyday lives, if we have use for some piece of information, we would like that information to be stable, consistent, and dependable.

METHODS OF ESTIMATING RELIABILITY

There are several ways to estimate the reliability of scores from a test. The three basic methods most often used are called *test–retest*, *alternative form*, and *internal consistency*.

Test–Retest or Stability

Test–retest is a method of estimating reliability that is exactly what its name implies. The test is given twice and the correlation between the first set of scores and the second set of scores is determined. For example, suppose a math test given to six students on Monday is given again on the following Monday without any math having been taught in between these times. The six students make the following scores on the test:

Student	First Administration Score	Second Administration Score
1	75	78
2	50	62
3	93	91
4	80	77
5	67	66
6	88	88

The correlation between these two sets of scores is .96. It could be concluded that scores from this test are quite reliable.

The main problem with test–retest reliability data is that there is usually some memory or experience involved the second time the test is taken. That means that the scores may differ not only because of the unreliability of the test, but also because the students themselves may have changed in some way. For example, they may have gotten some answers correct on the retest by remembering or finding answers to some of the questions on the initial test. To some extent this problem can be overcome by using a longer interval between test administrations, to give memory a chance to fade. However, if the interval is too long, the students may have changed on the trait being measured because of other factors, for example, reading in the library, instruction in other courses, seeing a film, and so on. So, in considering test–retest reliability coefficients, the interval between testings must also be considered. In general, the longer the interval between test and retest, the lower the reliability coefficient will be. Test–retest reliability is illustrated in Fig. 16.1.

To determine test–retest reliability, the same test is administered twice to the same group of students, and their scores are correlated. Generally, the longer the interval between test administrations, the lower the correlation. Since students can be expected to change with the passage of time, an especially long interval between testings will produce a "reliability" coefficient that is more a reflection of student changes on the attribute being measured than a reflection of the reliability of the test.

This time interval reflects the reliability of the test.	January 1 Test A	February 1 Test A
	Correlation, $r = .90$	
This time interval reflects the reliability of the test plus unknown changes in the students on the attribute being measured.	January 1 Test A	June 1 Test A
	Correlation, $r = .50$	

FIGURE 16.1   Test–retest reliability.

Alternate Forms or Equivalence

If there are two equivalent forms of a test, these forms can be used to obtain an estimate of the reliability of the scores from the test. Both forms are administered to a group of students, and the correlation between the two sets of scores is determined. This estimate eliminates the problems of memory and practice involved in test–retest estimates. Large differences in a student's score on two forms of a test that supposedly measures the same behavior would indicate an unreliable test. To use this method of estimating reliability, two equivalent forms of the test must be available, and they must be administered under conditions as nearly equivalent as possible. The most critical problem with this method of estimating reliability is that it takes a great deal of effort to develop *one* good test, let alone two. Hence, this method is most often used by test publishers who are creating two forms of their test for other reasons (e.g., to maintain test security). Figure 16.2 illustrates alternate-forms reliability.

Internal Consistency

If the test in question is designed to measure a single basic concept, it is reasonable to assume that people who get one item right will be more likely to get other, similar items right. In other words, items ought to be correlated with each other, and the test ought to be internally consistent. If this is the case, the reliability of the scores for the test can be estimated by the internal consistency method. One approach to determining a test's internal consistency, called *split halves*, involves splitting the test into two equivalent halves and determining the correlation between them. This can be done by assigning all items in the first half of the test to one form and all items in the second half of the test to the other form. However, this approach is only appropriate when items of varying difficulty are randomly spread across the test. Frequently they are not; easier items are often found at the beginning of the test and difficult items at the end. In these cases the best approach would be to divide test items by placing all odd-numbered items into one half and all even-numbered items into the other half. When this latter approach is used, the reliability data are called *odd–even reliability*.

Split-Half Methods   To find the split-half (or odd–even) reliability, each item is assigned to one half or the other. Then, the total score for each student on each half is

To determine alternate-forms reliability of a test, two different versions of the same test are administered to the same group of students in as short a time period as possible, and their scores are correlated. Efforts are made to have the students complete one form of the test in the morning and another, equivalent form of the test in the afternoon or the following day.

June 1, morning   June 1, afternoon
Test A (Form X)   Test A (Form Y)

Correlation, $r = .80$

FIGURE 16.2   Alternate-forms reliability.

determined and the correlation between the two total scores for both halves is computed. Essentially, a single test is used to make two shorter alternative forms. This method has the advantage that only one test administration is required and, therefore, memory or practice effects are not involved. Again, it does not require two tests. Thus it has several advantages over test–retest and alternate-form estimates of reliability. Because of these advantages, it is the most frequently used method of estimating the reliability of classroom tests. This method is illustrated in Fig. 16.3.

Internal consistency calculated by this method is actually a way of finding alternate-form reliability for a test half as long as the original test. However, since a test is usually more reliable if it is longer, the internal consistency method *underestimates* what the actual reliability of the full test would be. The split-half (or odd–even) reliability coefficient should be corrected or adjusted upward to reflect the reliability that the test would have if it were twice as long. The formula used for this correction is called the Spearman–Brown prophecy formula. It is

$$r_w = \frac{2r_h}{1 + r_h}$$

where r_w is the correlation for the *whole* test and r_h is the correlation between the two *halves* of the test. The result of applying this formula gives the predicted split-half (or odd–even) reliability coefficient for a test twice as long as either of its halves. In almost all cases, it will increase the size of the reliability coefficient from that computed for the two half tests.

Kuder–Richardson Methods   Another way of estimating the internal consistency of a test is through one of the Kuder–Richardson methods. These methods measure the extent to which items within one form of the test have as much in common with one another as do the items in that one form with corresponding items in an equivalent form. The strength of this estimate of reliability depends on the extent to which the entire test represents a *single*, fairly consistent measure of a concept. Normally Kuder–Richardson techniques will yield estimates of reliability somewhat lower than those of split halves, but higher than test–retest or alternate-form estimates. These procedures are sometimes called item–total correlations.

The internal consistency of a test is determined from a *single* test administration. Hence, it does not involve a time interval as do the test–retest and alternate-form methods. The test is split into two equal parts and the total scores for each student on each half of the test are correlated. The internal consistency method of determining reliability is appropriate only when the test measures a unitary, homogeneous concept (e.g., addition or finding the least common denominator) and not a variety of concepts.

Half of Test A	Half of Test A
(e.g., even-numbered items)	(e.g., odd-numbered items)

Correlation, $r = .75$

FIGURE 16.3   Internal consistency reliability (odd–even method).

There are several ways to determine the internal consistency of a test using Kuder–Richardson procedures. Of these, two are frequently seen in test manuals. The first is more difficult to calculate since it requires the percentage of students passing each item on the test. It is, however, the most accurate and has the name KR20 (Kuder–Richardson formula 20). The resulting coefficient is equal to the average of all possible split-half coefficients for the group tested. The second formula, which is easier to calculate but slightly less accurate, has the name KR21. It is the least cumbersome of the KR formulas and requires a knowledge only of the number of test items (n), the mean of the test (M), and its standard deviation (s). The formula for KR21 is

$$KR_{21} = \frac{n}{n-1}\left(\frac{1 - M(n-M)}{ns^2}\right)$$

KR21 tends to produce a smaller (less accurate) coefficient than KR20 but has the advantage of being easier to calculate. Test publishers often report a Kuder–Richardson coefficient, so it is important that you recognize it and know something about it.

Before leaving the topic of internal consistency we need to mention one other coefficient because of its frequent use. This coefficient, called coefficient Alpha, is closely related to Kuder–Richardson procedures but has the advantage of being applicable to tests that are multiple scored, that is, that are not scored right or wrong or according to some other all-or-none system. For example, on attitude or personality surveys the respondent may receive a different numerical score on an item depending on whether the response "all," "some," "a little," or "none" is checked. In such cases our previous methods of determining internal consistency would not be applicable and the coefficient Alpha should be used. Coefficient Alpha is laborious to compute, so its computation is best left to a computer program or the test publisher. Its interpretation is not difficult, however, because it is interpreted the same way as the Kuder–Richardson methods and therefore may be taken as an index of the extent to which the instrument measures a single, unified concept.

Problems with Internal Consistency Estimates

Internal consistency techniques are useful and popular measures of reliability because they involve only one test administration and are free from memory and practice effects. However, there are some problems with these methods. First, they should only be used if the entire test consists of similar items measuring a single concept. Thus they *would* be appropriate for use on a spelling test, but *not* for a language test involving a spelling section, a reading comprehension section, and a composition section.

A second problem is that measures of internal consistency yield inflated estimates of reliability when used with *speeded* tests. A speeded test consists entirely of easy or relatively easy item tasks with a strict time limit. On such a test, test takers are expected to correctly answer most items attempted. Ranks or grades are usually assigned mostly on the basis of the number of items attempted (since the items are easy, most attempts are successful), rather than on mastery of the subject areas, written expression, and so forth. Examples of speeded tests are typing tests or such manual dexterity tests as screwing nuts on bolts or putting square pegs in square holes.

Speeded tests may be thought of in contrast to *power tests*. Power tests have difficult items, or items varying in difficulty, but have such generous time limits that most students have an opportunity to attempt most or all of the items. With a power test, ranks or grades are assigned based mostly on the quality or "correctness" of answers, rather than on the number of items attempted. Examples of power tests are essay tests, word problems, and reasoning tasks. In reality, most tests are a combination of power *and* speed tests. The typical classroom or standardized achievement test is partially a speeded test (e.g., some easy items, fairly strict time limits) and partially a power test (e.g., items range in difficulty and most students are expected to attempt most items in the allotted time).

Why is this important? Recall that we said that measures of internal consistency yield inflated estimates of reliability when used with speeded tests. Since most achievement tests are partially speeded, estimates of internal consistency reliability that are computed for such tests will also be somewhat inflated. Naturally, they will not be as falsely high as they would be for a *pure* speeded test, but they will be high enough to suggest that the test scores are more reliable than they actually are. For this reason, it is always preferable to look for a second estimate of reliability (e.g., test–retest or alternate form) rather than relying on the internal consistency method to evaluate the reliability of a test's scores. In Chapter 17 we will also see that internal consistency measures are not as sensitive to errors in test construction, administration, and scoring as are other types of reliability data.

INTERPRETING RELIABILITY COEFFICIENTS

In Chapter 15 we discussed several principles relevant to the interpretation of validity coefficients. These were provided to give you some guidelines with which to consider the validity evidence of a test. In this chapter we will discuss several principles related to the interpretation of reliability coefficients, which should prove useful as guidelines in evaluating the reliability of scores from a test.

Our first principle relates to the effect of group variability on the size of the reliability coefficient. It should sound familiar, since we considered this concept in discussing the interpretation of validity coefficients.

> PRINCIPLE 1: Group variability affects the size of the reliability coefficient. Higher coefficients result from heterogeneous groups than from homogeneous groups.

Rather than present our rationale for this principle, we suggest that you might want to refresh your memory by reviewing Principle 2 from the previous chapter. The concept applied here is exactly the same, except that it refers to repeated administrations of the same test, or to alternate forms of the same test, rather than predictor and criterion measures. Figures 16.4 and 16.5 illustrate Principle 1 applied to test–retest reliability.

> PRINCIPLE 2: Scoring reliability limits test score reliability. If tests are scored unreliably, error is introduced that will limit the reliability of the test scores.

Recall that in Chapters 7, 8, and 9 we emphasized how important it is to make essay, performance, and portfolio scoring as reliable as possible. If there is little agreement among scorers about the "correctness" of an answer, scores for an otherwise good test or assessment may not have sufficient reliability. Stated another way, if scoring reliability is .70, then .70 becomes the *maximum* possible reliability of the test scores. In

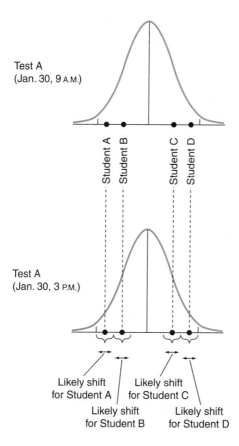

Test A
(Jan. 30, 9 A.M.)

Student A
Student B
Student C
Student D

Test A
(Jan. 30, 3 P.M.)

Likely shift
for Student A

Likely shift
for Student C

Likely shift
for Student B

Likely shift
for Student D

FIGURE 16.4 Comparison of probable rankings for repeated administrations of the same test (or alternate forms of the same test) for four students from a heterogeneous sample.

reality, it would be even lower since other sources of error would add to the unreliability of the test scores. This is why objectivity in scoring and clerical checks are important. Before dismissing a test as yielding scores that are too unreliable for your purposes, check its scoring reliability. It may be that improvements in scoring procedures will result in a reliability increment large enough to make the test usable.

> PRINCIPLE 3: All other factors being equal, the more items included in a test, the higher the reliability of the scores.

There are several reasons for this principle. First, the number of items increases the potential variability of the scores (i.e., group variability will increase). According to Principle 1, this will lead to an increase in the stability of ranks across administrations and increased reliability. Second, when more items are added to a test, the test is better able to sample the student's knowledge of the attribute being measured. For example, a 10-item test about the presidents of the United States will provide a more reliable and representative sample of student knowledge of U.S. presidents than a 2-item test. With a 2-item test, a student might get lucky and guess correctly twice, earning a perfect score. Furthermore, such a limited sample may penalize better prepared students since its narrow focus may miss much of what they have mastered. It should be noted that Principle 3 is the basis of the Spearman–Brown prophecy formula we introduced earlier.

FIGURE 16.5 *Comparison of probable rankings for repeated administrations of the same test (or alternate forms of the same test) for four students from a homogeneous sample.*

A caution is in order, however. Simply increasing the number of items on a test will not *necessarily* increase reliability of the test's scores. For example, if the extra items are ambiguous or otherwise poorly written items, then score reliability would likely *decrease*. Only if the added items are at least the equivalent of those in the original test will score reliability increase.

In interpreting the reliability of a test's scores, always consider its length. A very short test with a score reliability of .80 may, with only a few more items added, turn out to measure some trait just as well as or better than a longer test with a score reliability of .90.

PRINCIPLE 4: Reliability of test scores tends to decrease as tests become too easy or too difficult.

As tests become very easy (nearly everyone answers all of the items correctly) or very difficult (nearly everyone answers all of the items incorrectly), score distributions become homogeneous, which is illustrated by Fig. 16.6. By referring to Principle 1, we can conclude that when distributions are homogeneous, significant shifting of ranks and a lowering of the correlation coefficient will occur. Another factor worth considering is that when tests are made very difficult, guessing is encouraged. This is another source of error that serves to lower test score reliability even further. Hence, both very easy and very difficult tests will have low score reliabilities. Because of error due to guessing, score reliability for very difficult tests will be even less than for very easy tests.

FIGURE 16.6 Score distributions for very easy and very difficult tests.

SUMMARY

This chapter introduced you to the concept of reliability, various methods of estimating reliability, and several principles to be considered in interpreting reliability coefficients. Its major points are as follows:

1. Reliability refers to the stability of a test score over repeated administrations. A reliable test will yield stable scores over repeated administrations, assuming the trait being measured has not changed.

2. Test–retest estimates of reliability are obtained by administering the same test twice to the same group of individuals, with a small time interval between testing, and correlating the scores. The longer the time interval, the lower test–retest estimates will be.

3. Alternate-form estimates of reliability are obtained by administering two alternate or equivalent forms of a test to the same group and correlating their scores. The time interval between testings is as short as possible.

4. Internal consistency estimates of reliability fall into two general categories: split-half or odd–even estimates and item–total correlations, such as the Kuder–Richardson procedure. These estimates should be used only when the test measures a single or unitary trait.

5. Split-half and odd–even estimates divide a test into halves and correlate the halves with one another. Because these correlations are based on half tests, the obtained correlations underestimate the reliability of the whole test. The Spearman–Brown prophecy formula is used to correct these estimates to what they would be if they were based on the whole test.

6. Kuder–Richardson methods determine the extent to which the entire test represents a single, fairly consistent measure of a concept.

7. Internal consistency estimates tend to yield inflated reliability estimates for speeded tests.

8. Since most achievement tests are at least partially speeded, internal consistency estimates for such tests will be somewhat inflated.

9. In interpreting reliability coefficients the following principles should be considered:

    a. Group variability affects test score reliability. As group variability increases, reliability goes up.

    b. Scoring reliability limits test score reliability. As scoring reliability goes down, so does the test's reliability.

    c. Test length affects test score reliability. As test length increases, the test's reliability tends to go up.

    d. Item difficulty affects test score reliability. As items become very easy or very hard, the test's reliability goes down.

FOR PRACTICE

*1. All other things being equal, which test—A, B, or C—would you use?

Type of Reliability	Test A	Test B	Test C
Split-half reliability coefficient	.80	.90	.85
Test–retest reliability coefficient	.60	.60	.75
Alternate-forms reliability	.30	.60	.60

*2. If the unadjusted odd–even reliability for a test's scores is .60, what is its true reliability?

*3. What reliability coefficient would be least appropriate in each of the following situations?

a. The test is speeded.

b. The test measures heterogeneous topics.

c. Students can easily learn the answers from taking the test.

*4. Assuming that the scores for the following tests all had exactly the same internal consistency reliability coefficient of .75, and assuming all other things are equal, which test—A, B, or C—would you use?

Aspect of Test	Test A	Test B	Test C
Content	Homogeneous	Heterogeneous	Homogeneous
Test length	50 items	25 items	100 items
Difficulty	Average	Difficult	Average
Speed/power	Speeded	Speed and power	Power

*5. For each of the following statements indicate which type of reliability is being referred to from among the four alternatives that follow:

> Test–retest   Alternate-forms (long interval)
>
> Alternate forms   Split-half

a. "Practice effects" could most seriously affect this type of reliability. _____

b. This procedure would yield the lowest reliability coefficient. _____

c. Requires the use of a formula to adjust the estimate of the reliability to that for a total test. _____

d. Should be used by teachers who want to give comparable (but different) tests to students. _____

e. Changes due to item sampling will not be reflected. _____

*6. Test A and Test B both claim to be reading achievement tests. The technical manual for Test A reports a test–retest reliability of .88, and the technical manual for Test B reports split-half reliability of .91. Test B has good content validity evidence with Mr. Burns's classroom objectives. Test A has good concurrent validity evidence with a recognized reading test, but measures several skills not taught by Mr. Burns. If Mr. Burns wishes to evaluate progress over his course of instruction, which test should be used for both his pretest and posttest?

*7. Test A and Test B both claim to be reading readiness tests for use in placing children in first-grade reading groups. Neither test reports validity data. The technical manual for Test A reports an internal consistency reliability of .86, and the technical manual for Test B reports a test–retest reliability of .70. If a first-grade teacher came to you for advice on test selection, what would be your recommendation?

*Answers for these questions appear in Appendix F.

ACCURACY AND ERROR

WHEN IS A test score inaccurate? Almost always. Surprised? If you are, you have reason to be. We have learned (or have been programmed) to put a great deal of faith in test scores. In fact, to some individuals test results represent the ultimate truth. Our position is that tests and the scores they yield are fallible. They come with varying degrees of "goodness," but no test or score is completely valid or reliable. In other words, all tests and scores are imperfect and are subject to error.

If most or all test scores were perfectly reliable, we could put a great deal of confidence in a person's score from a single test. If Student A scores 75 on a test with perfectly reliable scores, then 75 is his or her "true" score. However, most test scores are not perfectly reliable—in fact, most test scores are a long way from being perfectly reliable. Therefore when Student A scores 75 on a test, we only hope that his or her true score—his or her actual level of ability—is somewhere around 75. The closer the score reliability of a test is to perfect, the more likely it is that the true score is very close to 75.

Later in this chapter we will introduce a special statistic that will enable you to estimate the *range* of scores within which lies an individual's true score or true level of ability. This is the extent of the precision we can realistically arrive at in interpreting test scores. In other words, a score from any test is our best guess about an individual's true level of knowledge, ability, achievement, and so forth and, like all guesses, the guesses we make can be wrong.

All tests are subject to various sources of error that impair the reliability of their scores and, consequently, their accuracy. Logically, if we understand these sources of error in test scores, we should be able to minimize them in constructing tests and thereby improve test score reliability. But just what is "error" in testing?

ERROR—WHAT IS IT?

"I've made a mistake." We have all said this aloud or to ourselves at one time or another. In other words, we've made an error—we have failed to do something perfectly, or as well as we would like to have done it. The notion of error in testing is very similar. No test measures perfectly, and many tests fail to measure as well as we would like them to. That is, tests make "mistakes." They are always associated with some degree of error. Let's look at a test score more closely.

Think about the last test you took. Did you obtain exactly the score you thought or knew you deserved? Was your score higher than you expected? Was it lower than you expected? What about your *obtained* scores on all the other tests you have taken? Did they *truly* reflect your skill, knowledge, or ability, or did they sometimes underestimate your knowledge, ability, or skill? Or did they overestimate? If your obtained test scores did not always reflect your true ability, they were associated with some error. Your obtained scores may have been lower or higher than they should have been. In short, an *obtained score* has a *true* score component (actual level of ability, skill, knowledge) and an *error* component (which may act to lower or raise the obtained score).

Can you think of some concrete examples of a type of error that lowered your obtained score? Remember when you couldn't sleep the night before the test, when you were sick but took the test anyway, when the essay test you were taking was so poorly constructed it was hard to tell what was being tested, when the test had a 45-minute time limit but you were allowed only 38 minutes, or when you took a test that had multiple defensible answers? Each of these examples illustrates various types of error. These and perhaps other sources of error prevented your "true" score from equaling your obtained score. Another way of saying this is simply that your obtained score equaled your true score *minus* any error.

Now, what about some examples of situations in which error operated to *raise* your obtained score above your actual or "true" level of knowledge, skill, or ability? In short, what about the times you obtained a higher score than you deserved? Never happened, you say! Well, what about the time you just happened to see the answers on your neighbor's paper, the time you got lucky guessing, the time you had 52 minutes for a 45-minute test, or the time the test was so full of unintentional clues that you were able to answer several questions based on the information given in other questions? Remember the principal we described in Chapter 2 who "helped" students taking high-stakes tests? Each of these examples illustrates error. Again, because of this error your true score was not reflected in your obtained score. You received a higher score than you deserved! In these cases your obtained score equaled your true score *plus* any error.

Then how does one go about discovering one's true score? Unfortunately, we do not have an answer. The true score and the error score are both theoretical or hypothetical values. We never actually know an individual's true score or error score. Why bother with them then? They are important concepts because they allow us to illustrate some important points about test score reliability and test score accuracy. For now, simply keep in mind the following:

$$\text{Obtained score} = \text{true score} \pm \text{error score}$$

Table 17.1 illustrates the relationship among obtained scores, true scores, and error. In considering the table, remember that the *only* value in the table we are sure about is the obtained score value. We *never* know what the exact true scores are or what the exact error scores are. This is probably one of the most difficult concepts you have to master.

According to Table 17.1, Donna, Gary, and Marsha each obtained higher scores than they should have. These students had error work to their advantage in that their obtained scores were higher than their true scores.

On the other hand, Jack, Phyllis, and Milton each obtained lower scores than they should have. These students had error work to their disadvantage in that their obtained scores were *lower* than their true scores. Unfortunately, as noted earlier, we never actually know what an individual's true and error scores are. The values shown in our table are hypothetical values used to impress on you the fact that *all* test scores contain error. If you understand the notion of test error, you already have an intuitive understanding of our next topic, the standard error of measurement.

TABLE 17.1 **The Relationship among Obtained Scores, Hypothetical True Scores, and Hypothetical Error Scores for a Ninth-Grade Math Test**

Student	Obtained Score	True Score[a]	Error Score[a]
Donna	91	88	+3
Jack	72	79	−7
Phyllis	68	70	−2
Gary	85	80	+5
Marsha	90	86	+4
Milton	75	78	−3

[a] Hypothetical values.

THE STANDARD ERROR OF MEASUREMENT

The standard error of measurement of a test (abbreviated S_m) is the standard deviation of the *error scores* of a test. In the following calculations, S_m is the standard deviation of the error score column. It is determined in the same manner you would determine a standard deviation of any score distribution. Review the following calculations to confirm this. We will use error scores from Table 17.1: 3, −7, −2, 5, 4, −3.

Step 1: Determine the mean.

$$M = \frac{\Sigma X}{N} = \frac{0}{6} = 0$$

Step 2: Subtract the mean from each error score to arrive at the deviation scores. Square each deviation score and sum the squared deviations.

$X - M =$	x	x^2
$+3 - 0 =$	3	9
$-7 - 0 =$	−7	49
$-2 - 0 =$	−2	4
$+5 - 0 =$	5	25
$+4 - 0 =$	4	16
$-3 - 0 =$	−3	9
	$\Sigma x^2 =$	112

Step 3: Plug the x^2 sum into the formula and solve for the standard deviation.

$$\text{Error score SD} = \sqrt{\frac{\Sigma x^2}{N}} = \sqrt{\frac{112}{6}} = \sqrt{18.67} = 4.32 = S_m$$

The standard deviation of the error score distribution, also known as the standard error of measurement, is 4.32. If we could know what the error scores are for each test we administer, we could compute S_m in this manner. But, of course, we never know these error scores. If you are following so far, your next question should be, "But how in the world do you determine the standard deviation of the error scores if you never know the error scores?"

Fortunately, a rather simple statistical formula can be used to estimate this standard deviation (S_m) without actually knowing the error scores:

$$S_m = SD\sqrt{1 - r}$$

where r is the reliability of the test and SD is the test's standard deviation.

Using the Standard Error of Measurement

Error scores are assumed to be random. As such, they cancel each other out. That is, obtained scores are inflated by random error to the same extent as they are deflated by error. Another way of saying this is that the mean of the error scores for a test is zero. The distribution of the error scores is also important, since it approximates a normal distribution closely enough for us to use the normal distribution to represent it. In summary, then, we know that error scores (1) are normally distributed, (2) have a mean of zero, and (3) have a standard deviation called the standard error of measurement (S_m). These characteristics are illustrated in Fig. 17.1.

Returning to our example from the ninth-grade math test depicted in Table 17.1, we recall that we obtained an S_m of 4.32 for the data provided. Figure 17.2 illustrates the distribution of error scores for these data. What does the distribution in Fig. 17.2 tell us? Before you answer, consider this: The distribution of error scores is a normal distribution. This is important since, as you learned in Chapter 13, the normal distribution has characteristics that enable us to make decisions about scores that fall between, above, or below different points in the distribution. We are able to do so because fixed percentages of scores fall between various score values in a normal distribution. Figure 17.3 should refresh your memory.

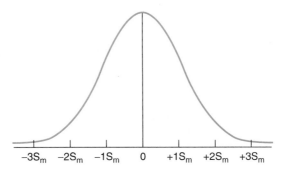

-3S_m   -2S_m   -1S_m   0   +1S_m   +2S_m   +3S_m

FIGURE 17.1   The error score distribution.

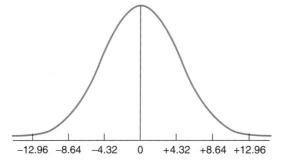

FIGURE 17.2 The error score distribution for the test depicted in Table 17.1.

−12.96 −8.64 −4.32 0 +4.32 +8.64 +12.96

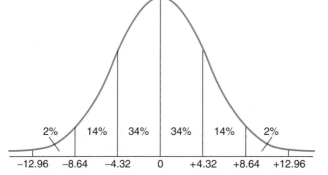

FIGURE 17.3 The error score distribution for the test depicted in Table 17.1 with approximate normal curve percentages.

2% 14% 34% 34% 14% 2%

−12.96 −8.64 −4.32 0 +4.32 +8.64 +12.96

In Fig. 17.3 we listed along the baseline the standard deviation of the error score distribution. This is more commonly called the *standard error of measurement* (S_m) of the test. Thus we can see that 68% of the error scores for the test will be no more than 4.32 points higher or 4.32 points lower than the true scores. That is, if there were 100 obtained scores on this test, 68 of these scores would *not* be "off" their true scores by more than 4.32 points. The S_m then, tells us about the distribution of obtained scores around true scores. By knowing an individual's true score we can predict what his or her obtained score is likely to be.

The careful reader may be thinking, "That's not very useful information. We can never know what a person's true score is, only their obtained score." This is correct. As test users, we work only with obtained scores. However, we can follow our logic in reverse. If 68% of obtained scores fall within $1S_m$ of their true scores, then 68% of true scores must fall within $1S_m$ of their obtained scores. Strictly speaking, this reverse logic is somewhat inaccurate when we consider individual test scores. However, across all test scores, it would be true 99% of the time (Gullikson, 1987). Therefore the S_m is often used to determine how test error is likely to have affected individual obtained scores.

Let's use the following number line to represent an individual's obtained score, which we will simply call X:

−5 −4 −3 −2 −1 X 1 2 3 4 5

That is, X plus or minus 4.32 (±4.32) defines the range or band, which we are about 68% sure contains this individual's true score. Extending this reasoning, we can construct a similar band around *any* obtained score to identify the range of scores that, at a certain level of confidence, will capture or span an individual's true score. Stated another way, if a student obtains a score of X on a test, the student's true score on the test will be within $\pm 1S_m$ of X about 68% of the time. We know this to be the case since error (the difference between obtained and true scores) is normally distributed. We can conceptualize what we have been describing by considering error to be normally distributed around any obtained score. Returning once again to our ninth-grade math test (Table 17.1), we see that Marsha had an obtained score of 90. We also know that the S_m for the test was 4.32. Knowing the data, and that error is normally distributed, we can graphically depict the distribution of error around Marsha's obtained score of 90 as shown in Fig. 17.4. Figure 17.5 illustrates the distribution of error around an obtained score of 75 for the same test.

77.04   81.36   85.68   90   94.32   98.64   102.96

We are about 68% sure that Marsha's true score lies between 85.68 and 94.32.

FIGURE 17.4 The error distribution around an obtained score of 90 for a test with $S_m = 4.32$.

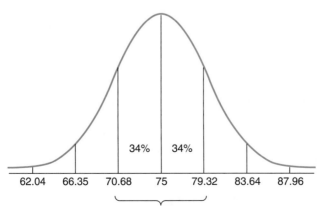

62.04   66.35   70.68   75   79.32   83.64   87.96

We are about 68% sure that someone with an obtained score of 75 has a true score between 70.68 and 79.32

FIGURE 17.5 The error distribution around an obtained score of 75 for a test with $S_m = 4.32$.

Why all the fuss? Remember our original point. All test scores are fallible; they contain a margin of error. The S_m is a statistic that estimates this margin for us. We are accustomed to reporting a single test score. Considering the S_m, that is, reporting a range of scores that spans or captures an individual's true score, helps us present a more realistic picture of someone's obtained scores. From our last two examples we could conclude with 68% certainty that for a distribution with a standard error of measurement of 4.32, each student's true score would be captured by a range of scores 4.32 from his or her obtained score. Left unsaid was the fact that we would probably be wrong in drawing such a conclusion 32% of the time! Even though we report a band of scores 8.64 points wide around a single score, we will still draw an incorrect conclusion 32% of the time.

This is *not* an exceptional case. Even the *best* tests often have S_m of from three to five points (more or less, depending on the scale). In education we have long had a tendency to *overinterpret* small differences in test scores since we too often consider obtained scores to be completely accurate. Incorporating the S_m in reporting test scores greatly minimizes the likelihood of overinterpretation and forces us to consider how fallible our test scores are. After considering the S_m from a slightly different angle, we will show how to incorporate it to make comparisons among test scores. This procedure is called *band interpretation*. First, however, let's sew up a few loose ends about S_m.

More Applications

Let's look again at the formula for the standard error of measurement:

$$S_m = SD\sqrt{1-r}$$

We know that an obtained score, X, $\pm 1S_m$ will span or capture the true score 68% of the time. Extending this thinking further, we know that the range of scores covered by $X \pm 2S_m$ will capture the true score 95% of the time. Finally, we know that the range of scores covered by $X \pm 3S_m$ will capture the true score more than 99% of the time. Figure 17.6 illustrates these relationships.

Let's work an example. Scores for a test have a standard deviation of 5 points and a reliability of .75. The standard error of measurement of the test is

$$S_m = 5\sqrt{1-.75} = 5\sqrt{.25} = 2.5$$

If a student obtains a score of 80 on the test, you know that his or her true score lies between

77.5 and 82.5 ($X \pm 1S_m$) 68% of the time

75 and 85 ($X \pm 2S_m$) 95% of the time

72.5 and 87.5 ($X \pm 3S_m$) 99% of the time

The expressions "68% of the time," "95% of the time," and so on refer to the hypothetical situation in which the student is given the test many times. In this case, the student could

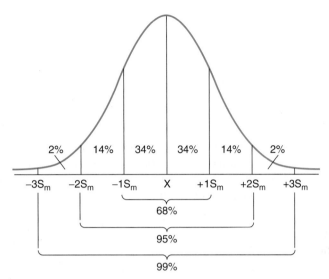

FIGURE 17.6 The area or bands for a given obtained score that are 68%, 95%, and 99% sure to span the true score.

expect that his or her true score would be within the interval a certain percentage of the total number of times the test was taken.

Here's another example. A teacher gets back the results of class IQ tests. The IQ test given to the students has a standard deviation of 15 and the scores have a test–retest reliability of .84. Therefore the test has a standard error of measurement of 6. The teacher then knows that of the children who made an IQ score of 100, about 68% have a true score between 94 and 106; 95% have a true IQ score between 88 and 112; and 99% have a true IQ score between 82 and 118. For one particular child with an IQ of 100, the teacher knows that probably the true IQ is between 94 and 106, but 32% of the time $(100 - 68 = 32)$ it will be even further than that from 100. Thus the teacher has some idea of just how much confidence to place in the score. That is, the teacher has an idea about the accuracy of the score.

If test scores are perfectly reliable $(r = 1.0)$, a student will always get exactly the same score. In this case the S_m is zero, as can be seen by substituting a coefficient of 1.0 in the formula for S_m. If test scores are very close to perfectly reliable, the S_m will be very small, and we can assume the student's obtained score is very close to his or her true score. If test scores are not reliable, the S_m will be nearly as big as the standard deviation, and we can assume the student's obtained score is not a good approximation of his or her true score. The relationships among true scores, error scores, obtained scores, and score reliability are illustrated next.

Scores From Test K are Perfectly Reliable (r = 1.00) In other words, a student's ranking on repeated administrations of Test K *never changes*. There is no error, and as a result the student's true score equals the obtained score *and* there is *no* error score distribution. Thus S_m is zero.

Proof

$$Sm = SD\sqrt{1 - r}$$

$$= SD\sqrt{1 - 1.0}$$

$$= SD\sqrt{0}$$

$$= 0$$

Scores From Test L are Totally Unreliable (r = .00)   In other words, a student's ranking on repeated administrations of Test L is *likely to vary across the range of possible rankings*. If the student is ranked first on one administration, he or she could easily be ranked last on the next administration. Because there is *so much error* present, the S_m will be the same as the SD of the test.

Proof

$$Sm = SD\sqrt{1 - r}$$

$$= SD\sqrt{1 - .00}$$

$$= SD\sqrt{1}$$

$$= SD(1)$$

$$= SD$$

In reality, neither of the examples presented here actually occur. So, the S_m typically takes on a value greater than zero and smaller than the test's standard deviation. As score reliability increases, S_m decreases, and as score reliability decreases, the S_m increases. In summary, the S_m can be thought of as a measure of the accuracy of a test score. The larger the S_m the less accurate the score. The smaller the S_m the more accurate the score.

Standard Deviation or Standard Error of Measurement?

Until you have a working familiarity with these concepts, you can expect to confuse the standard deviation (SD) with the standard error of measurement (S_m). Don't despair! The two have some similarities, but they are very different. Both are measures of score variability, but of different kinds of scores. The standard deviation is a measure of variability of raw scores for a *group* of test takers. It tells you how spread out the scores are in a distribution of raw scores. You learned to compute and interpret standard deviations in Chapter 13. The standard error of measurement, however, is the standard deviation of the hypothetical *error* scores of a distribution. This is what you learned to compute and interpret in *this* chapter. Think about what you have just read:

Standard deviation (SD) is the variability of *raw* scores.

Standard error of measurement (S_m) is the variability of *error* scores.

The standard deviation is based on a group of scores that *actually exist*. The standard error of measurement is based on a group of scores that is *hypothetical*.

WHY ALL THE FUSS ABOUT ERROR?

In reality, an individual's obtained score is the best estimate of an individual's true score. That is, in spite of the foregoing discussion, we usually use the obtained score as our best guess of a student's true level of ability. Well, why all the fuss about error then? For two reasons: First, we want to make you aware of the fallibility of test scores, and, second, we want to sensitize you to the factors that can affect scores. Why? So they can be better controlled. Now you know how to determine how wide a range of scores around an obtained score must be to be 68% sure that it captures the true score. Controlling error can help narrow this range, thereby increasing the utility of test results. Let's consider error more closely.

The sources of error can be classified into the following categories:

1. Test takers.
2. The test itself.
3. Test administration.
4. Test scoring.

Error within Test Takers

The source of error within test takers could be called intra-individual error. Earlier, we talked about several within-student factors that would likely result in an obtained score lower than a student's true score. The examples we used were fatigue and illness. We also noted that accidentally seeing another student's answer could be a factor that might result in an individual's obtained score being higher than his or her true score. Situations such as these are undesirable since they have unpredictable effects on test performance, and as a result the reliability and accuracy of the scores yielded by the test suffer. They are usually temporary situations, affecting a student on one day but not on another. Any temporary and unpredictable change in a student can be considered intra-individual error or error within test takers. Remember, we are *not* saying anything about actual errors or mistakes test takers make in responding to test items. Rather, we are talking about factors that change unpredictably over time and, as a result, impair consistency and accuracy in measurement.

Error within the Test

We may refer to error within the test as an intratest or within-test error. The poorly designed essay test that results in an obtained score lower than a true score and the poorly written test replete with clues that results in an obtained score higher than a true score are both examples of this source of error.

There are many, many ways to *increase* error within the test. The following is only a partial list:

Trick questions.

Reading level that is too high.

Ambiguous questions.

Items that are too difficult.

Poorly written items.

To the extent that test items and tests are poorly constructed, test score reliability and accuracy will be impaired.

Error in Test Administration

Misreading the amount of time to be allotted for testing is an example of error in test administration that could raise or lower obtained scores in relation to true scores. There are, however, a variety of other direct and indirect test administration factors to be considered, including physical comfort, instructions and explanations, and test administration attitudes.

Physical Comfort   Room temperature, humidity, lighting, noise, and seating arrangement are all potential sources of error for the test taker.

Instructions and Explanations   Different test administrators provide differing amounts of information to test takers. Some spell words, provide hints, or tell whether it's better to guess or leave blanks, while others remain fairly distant. Naturally, your score may vary depending on the amount of information you are provided.

Test Administrator Attitudes   Administrators will differ in the notions they convey about the importance of the test, the extent to which they are emotionally supportive of students, and the way in which they monitor the test. To the extent that these variables affect students differently, test score reliability and accuracy will be impaired.

Error in Scoring

With the advent of computerized test scoring, error in scoring has decreased significantly. However, even when computer scoring is used, error can occur. The computer, a highly reliable machine, is seldom the cause of such errors. But teachers and other test administrators prepare the scoring keys, introducing possibilities for error. And students sometimes fail to use No. 2 pencils or make extraneous marks on answer sheets, introducing another potential source of scoring error. Needless to say, when tests are hand scored, as most classroom tests are, the likelihood of error increases greatly. In fact, because you are human, you can be sure that you will make some scoring errors in grading the tests you give.

These four sources of error—the test takers, the test, the test administration, and the scoring—are factors that can increase the discrepancy between an individual's obtained score and his or her true score. To the extent that these sources of error are present, individual and group scores will be prone to error, and therefore less accurate. We can take measures to minimize error within the test, the test administration, and the scoring, but we can never eliminate such error completely. Generally, error due to within-student factors is beyond our control.

These sources of error also affect the different types of reliability coefficients we have discussed. Next we consider the extent to which our four sources of error influence the test–retest, alternate-forms, and internal consistency methods of estimating reliability.

SOURCES OF ERROR INFLUENCING VARIOUS RELIABILITY COEFFICIENTS

Test–Retest

If test–retest reliability coefficients are determined over a short time, few changes are likely to take place *within students* to alter their test scores. Thus short-interval test–retest coefficients are not likely to be affected greatly by within-student error. However, as the time interval involved increases, it becomes more and more likely that significant changes will occur in the test takers. Correspondingly, test scores will be increasingly affected by those changes and the test–retest reliability coefficient will be lowered. This lowered score reliability may be more a result of new learning on the part of the students than it is an indication of the unreliability of the test items.

Since the *same* test is administered twice in determining test–retest reliability, error within the test itself (e.g., from poorly worded or ambiguous items) does not affect the strength of the reliability coefficient. Any problems that do exist in the test are present in both the first and second administrations, affecting scores the same way each time the test is administered. As long as similar administration and scoring procedures are followed, administration and scoring errors are likely to contribute only minimally to error. However, if there are significant changes in either or both, these can contribute significantly to error, resulting in a lower estimate of test–retest score reliability.

Alternate Forms

Since alternate-forms reliability is determined by administering two different forms or versions of the same test to the same group close together in time, the effects of within-student error are negligible. Students usually do not change significantly between morning and afternoon or from one day to the following day. Granted, students may be more fatigued when taking Form B of a test immediately after taking Form A. However, those factors can be controlled by splitting the test administration across groups of students, as suggested in Table 17.2.

TABLE 17.2 Splitting Same-Day Alternate-Form Administrations across Groups

A.M. **Group**	P.M. **Group**
Students whose last names begin with A–K get Form A.	Students whose last names begin with A–K get Form B.
Students whose last names begin with L–Z get Form B.	Students whose last names begin with L–Z get Form A.

Error within the test, however, has a significant effect on alternate-forms reliability. Unlike test–retest reliability, error within the test is *not* the same between test administrations. Error within Form A combines with error within Form B to have an effect on alternate-forms reliability. By now you are aware of how difficult it is to construct one good test, much less two! Yet, this is just what is necessary for acceptable alternate-forms score reliability.

As with test–retest methods, alternate-forms score reliability is not greatly affected by error in administering or scoring the test, as long as similar procedures are followed. Since within-test error is considered by alternate-forms estimates, these estimates normally have the lowest numerical index of score reliability.

Internal Consistency

With test–retest and alternate-forms reliability, within-student factors affect the method of estimating score reliability, since changes in test performance due to such problems as fatigue, momentary anxiety, illness, or just having an "off day" can be doubled because there are two separate administrations of the test. If the test is sensitive to those problems, it will record different scores from one test administration to another, lowering the reliability (or correlation coefficient) between them. Obviously, we would prefer that the test not be affected by those problems. But if it is, we would like to know about it.

With internal consistency reliability, neither within-student nor within-test factors are affected by the method of estimation. Since there is a single test administered, no changes in students should occur, and any errors within the test will occur only once. Similarly, since there is but a single administration and scoring procedure, administration and scoring errors are held to a minimum.

Measures of internal consistency, then, are influenced by the *fewest* of the four sources of error affecting test score reliability. Thus we would expect such measures to yield *higher* reliability coefficients than test–retest or alternate-forms estimates. This is important in evaluating test data presented in standardized test manuals. If a test publisher presents only internal consistency estimates of score reliability, the publisher has failed to indicate how consistent the obtained scores from the test are likely to be over time. Also unknown is whether any parallel or alternative forms being offered are equivalent to one another. Simply saying there are two alternate, equivalent, or parallel forms is not sufficient. To evaluate their equivalence there must be an estimate of alternate-forms reliability.

By itself, then, an internal consistency reliability coefficient—high though it may be—does not provide sufficient evidence of a test's score reliability. When you must have an estimate of a test's score reliability and can give only a single administration (such as with a typical teacher-made test), measures of internal consistency can be useful. However, any well-constructed standardized test must provide more than just information on the test's internal consistency. A measure of the test's score reliability over time (i.e., test–retest reliability) and, if the test advertises alternate forms, an estimate of the equivalence of the forms being offered (i.e., alternate-forms reliability) must be provided.

The influence of the four sources of error on the test–retest, alternate-forms, and internal consistency methods of estimating test score reliability are summarized in Table 17.3.

TABLE 17.3 Extent of Error Influencing Test–Retest, Alternate-Forms, and Internal Consistency Methods of Score Reliability

Reliability measure	Type of Error			
	Within Student	Within Test[a]	Administration	Scoring
Test–retest, short interval	Minimal	Minimal	Minimal[b] or moderate[c]	Minimal[d] or moderate[e]
Test–retest, long interval	Extensive	Minimal	Minimal[b] or moderate[c]	Minimal[d] or moderate[e]
Alternate forms, short interval	Minimal	Moderate[b] or extensive[c]	Minimal[b] or moderate[c]	Minimal[d] or moderate[e]
Alternate forms, long interval	Extensive	Moderate[b] or extensive[c]	Minimal[b] or moderate[c]	Minimal[d] or moderate[e]
Internal consistency	Minimal	Minimal	Minimal	Minimal

[a] Assuming test is well constructed.
[b] If test is standardized.
[c] If test is teacher-made.
[d] If test is objective.
[e] If test is subjective.

BAND INTERPRETATION

We have learned how to use the standard error of measurement, S_m, to more realistically interpret and report single test scores. In this section we will show you how to use the standard error of measurement to more realistically interpret and report groups of test scores.

Let's consider the following example: John obtained the following scores on an end-of-year achievement test:

Subtest	Score
Reading	103
Listening	104
Writing	105
Social Studies	98
Science	100
Math	91

Note: M = 100 and SD = 10 for all subtests.

Suppose you have a parent conference coming up, and John's parents want you to interpret his scores to them. What would you say? Would you say that he did best in Writing and poorest in Math? Would you say that the differences among the scores are likely due to measurement error, or do they represent actual differences in achievement?

It seems likely that John's parents would know from looking at the scores what John did best in and what he did poorest in. If they had some statistical sophistication, as you now have, they might even be able to conclude that his Math score is at about the 19th percentile and that his Reading score is at about the 69th percentile—a difference between the two tests of 50 percentile points. This appears to be a rather dramatic difference indicating a real difference in achievement. But how can we be sure the difference is not due to error? Granted it seems to be so large a difference that it probably is a "real" difference rather than a "chance" (i.e., due to error) difference. But what about the difference between Writing (69th percentile) and Science (50th percentile)? Is this difference a "real" or a "chance" one? In short, how large a difference do we need between test scores to conclude that the differences represent real and not chance differences? As you might have guessed, we can employ the standard error of measurement to help us answer these questions. The specific technique we will be discussing is called *band interpretation*. This technique lends itself quite well to the interpretation of scores from test batteries. Here is a step-by-step approach to band interpretation.

Technically, the approach we will be describing fails to consider the problem of the *reliability of the difference scores*. That advanced statistical concept basically states that in comparing scores from two tests (or subtests), the reliability of the difference between the two scores will be less than the reliability of each of the two scores. Thus less confidence should be placed in the difference score than in either of the individual scores. For those who may be interested, the formula to compute the reliability of the difference score is as follows:

$$r_{Diff} = \frac{(r_{11} + r_{22})/2 - r_{12}}{1 - r_{12}}$$

where r_{11} is the reliability of one measure, r_{22} is the reliability of the other measure, and r_{12} is the correlation between the two measures.

Our approach, band interpretation, represents a practical compromise between that statistically correct approach and the all-too-common acceptance of difference scores as being reliable.

Steps: Band Interpretation

List Data   List subtests and scores and the M, SD, and reliability (*r*) for each subtest. For purposes of illustration, let's assume that the mean is 100, the standard deviation is 10, and the score reliability is .91 for all the subtests. Here are the subtest scores for John:

Subtest	Score
Reading	103
Listening	104
Writing	105
Social Studies	98
Science	100
Math	91

Determine S_m   Since SD and *r* are the same for each subtest in this example, the standard error of measurement will be the same for each subtest.

$$Sm = SD\sqrt{1 - r}$$

$$= 10\sqrt{1 - .91} = 10\sqrt{.09} = 3$$

Add and Subtract S_m   To identify the band or interval of scores that has a 68% chance of capturing John's true score, add and subtract Sm to each subtest score. If the test could be given to John 100 times (without John learning from taking the test), 68 out of 100 times John's true score would be within the following bands:

Subtest	Score	68% Band
Reading	103	100–106
Listening	104	101–107
Writing	105	102–108
Social Studies	98	95–101
Science	100	97–103
Math	91	88–94

Graph the Results   On each scale, shade in the bands to represent the range of scores that has a 68% chance of capturing John's true score (see example above).

Interpret the Bands   Interpret the profile of bands by visually inspecting the bars to see which bands overlap and which do not. Those that *overlap* probably represent differences that likely occurred by *chance*. For example, scores in Reading, Listening, Writing, and Science may differ from one another only by chance, in spite of the fact that John's Science score of 100 was five points lower than his Writing score of 105, a difference of half a standard deviation. We arrive at this conclusion because there is at least some overlap among the bands for each of these subtest scores. Thus we could say John's level of achievement is similar in each of these subjects.

However, we can see a large difference in John's Math achievement compared to these same four subtests. Since there is no overlap, we will consider this difference a *real*, not a chance, difference. Social Studies shows a *real* difference compared to Writing (again, no overlap), but only a *chance* difference compared to Reading, Listening, and Science (again, because there is overlap).

Getting the hang of it? Band interpretation is one of the most realistic and appropriate ways to interpret scores from test batteries, since it considers the error that is always present in testing. Work with it and you will reduce the natural tendency to put too much weight on small or chance differences among scores.

So far we have used the subtest score plus and minus the standard error of measurement to identify whether a real difference exists among subtest scores. We have constructed ranges of scores around each obtained score in which we are 68% sure the individual's true score lies. Recall from our earlier discussion of S_m, though, that by adding and subtracting twice the value of S_m to the obtained subtest score, we can construct an interval or range of scores within which we are 95% sure the individual's true score lies. Naturally, this would create a much wider band for each obtained score, which has the effect of making overlap much *more* likely. This means "real" differences would be less likely to appear. That is, if we use the 95% rule by adding $2S_m$ to and subtracting $2S_m$ from each score instead of adding and subtracting only one standard error of measurement, we may have very different interpretations of the same test scores. Let's see what kind of difference this makes. Figure 17.7 compares and contrasts the 68% and 95% approaches.

Now let's compare conclusions. At the 68% level, we concluded that there was a significant discrepancy between John's Math achievement and all his other subjects (there is no overlap between his Math score interval and any other subtest score interval). We also concluded that there was a real difference (i.e., no overlap) between John's Social Studies achievement and his Writing achievement. All other differences were attributed to chance (i.e., there was overlap).

Now look at the 95% profile in Fig. 17.7. In essence we have doubled the width of each band in order to become more confident that we have really captured John's true score within each subtest interval. With this more conservative approach to test interpretation, the real differences decline sharply. We use the word conservative with the 95% approach since the odds of John's true score falling outside the band are only 1 in 20 or a probability of .05 with the 95% approach, but 1 in 3 or a probability of about .32 with the 68% approach. We are, therefore, *more confident* that John's true score is within the band with the 95% approach. Since the bands will be larger, the only real differences we find at the 95% level are between John's Math achievement and his achievement in Listening and in Writing. All the other bands overlap, suggesting that at the 95% level the differences in obtained scores are due to chance. If we employ the more conservative 95% approach, we would conclude that even though the difference between John's obtained Reading and Math scores is 12 points ($103 - 91 = 12$, a difference of 1.2 standard deviations), the difference is due to chance, not to a real difference in achievement.

Why bother with the 95% level, then? Well, if you are going to make important decisions about a student, a conservative approach appears warranted. In short, if you are concerned about the effects of a "wrong" decision (i.e., saying a real difference in achievement exists when it is really due to chance), take the conservative approach. On the other hand, if little is at risk for the student (or yourself), then the less conservative 68% approach is probably warranted. To make it simpler yet, let differences at the 68% level be a signal to you; let differences at the 95% level be a signal to the school and to the parents.

In the next chapter we will describe an application of band interpretation in which we believe the more conservative 95% approach should typically be employed. This will be in relation to determining real differences between a student's potential for achievement, called *aptitude*, and actual achievement. This approach, known as the severe discrepancy model, has been the basis for determining whether students are eligible for special education under the Specific Learning Disability (SLD) category (see Chapter 20) since the mid-1970s.

Subtest	Score*	68% range $(X \pm 1S_m)$	95% range $(X \pm 2S_m)$
Reading	103	100–106	97–109
Listening	104	101–107	98–110
Writing	105	102–108	99–111
Social Studies	98	95–101	92–104
Science	100	97–103	94–106
Math	91	88–94	85–97

*M = 100,   SD = 10

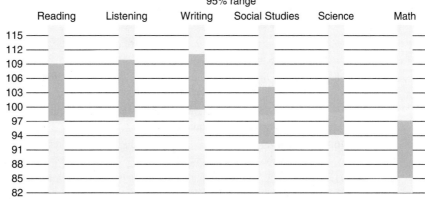

FIGURE 17.7   Comparison of the 68% and 95% methods of band interpretation.

A FINAL WORD

Technically, there are more accurate statistical procedures for determining real differences between an individual's test scores than the ones we have been able to present here. These procedures, however, are time-consuming, complex, and overly specific for the typical teacher. Within the classroom, band interpretation, properly used, makes for a practical alternative to those more advanced methods and is superior to simply comparing individual scores.

Before we complete this chapter, answer the questions—using the 95% approach—that we raised at the beginning of the last section. To refresh your memory, here they are:

Is there a real difference between John's Reading score and his Math score?

Is there a real difference between John's Writing score and his Science score?

SUMMARY

Chapter 17 presented the concepts of accuracy and error, the statistic used to represent error (the standard error of measurement), and the four sources of error in measurement. Its major points are as follows:

1. No test is perfectly reliable, and therefore no test is perfectly accurate. All tests are subject to error.

2. Error is any factor that leads an individual to perform better or worse on a test than the individual's true level of performance.

3. An obtained score for a test contains two components: one reflects the individual's true level of performance, and the other reflects the error associated with the test that prevents the individual from performing at exactly his or her true level of ability.

4. An individual's true score and error score are hypothetical. We can never be sure exactly what they are.

5. The standard error of measurement (S_m) is the standard deviation of the error score distribution of a test.

6. The standard error of measurement for a test can be determined mathematically if we know the test's standard deviation and reliability.

7. The error distribution is normally distributed and has a mean of zero, and its standard deviation is the standard error of measurement.

8. We can be 68% sure an individual's true score lies in the range between one S_m above and one S_m below that individual's obtained score.

9. We can be 95% sure a true score lies in the range of scores between two S_m above and two S_m below the obtained score.

10. We can be 99% sure a true score lies in the range of scores between three S_m above and three S_m below the obtained score.

11. Using the S_m in interpreting scores helps us avoid overinterpreting small differences among test scores.

12. Accuracy increases and the S_m decreases as reliability increases.

13. The S_m refers to the variability of error scores; the SD refers to the variability of raw scores.

14. We can improve test accuracy by controlling the sources of error in testing.

15. Error is classified into four categories:
    a. Error within test takers.
    b. Error within the test.
    c. Error within the test administration.
    d. Error within scoring.

16. Error within the test takers refers to changes in the student over which the test administrator has no control.

17. Error within the test refers to technical problems in the test. The test developer has considerable control over this source of error.

18. Error within the test administration refers to physical, verbal, and attitudinal variables that vary from administration to administration and affect test scores. The administrator can minimize this source of error by standardizing administration procedures.

19. Error in scoring typically refers to clerical errors that influence test scores. The test administrator can control this source of error by using objective items and clerical checks or by using computer scoring.

20. Different estimates of score reliability are differentially affected by the various sources of error.

21. Test–retest score reliability is most susceptible to error within test takers.

22. Alternate-forms score reliability is most affected by error within the two forms of the test. As a result, it usually yields lower score reliability estimates than test–retest or internal consistency estimates.

23. Since only one administration and one test are necessary for internal consistency estimates, this approach is least affected by error. As a result, internal consistency estimates of score reliability typically will be higher for the same test than for test–retest or alternate-forms score reliability estimates.

24. Band interpretation is a technique that the teacher can use to help separate real differences in student achievement from differences due to chance. This approach helps prevent over-interpretation of small differences among subtests in achievement test batteries.

FOR PRACTICE

*1. Calculate the standard error of measurement for a test with a standard deviation of 10 and a score reliability of .84. Draw a normal curve picturing the error score distribution in units of the standard error of measurement.

*2. Suppose an individual received a score of 16 on the test in Question 1. Calculate the range or band within which we could be 95% sure that this individual's true score is contained. What would this range or band be if we wanted to be 99% sure this individual's true score is contained within it? To be 68% sure?

*3. What are the four sources of error that increase the discrepancy between an individual's obtained score and his or her true score? Give a specific example of each.

*4. Indicate the extent to which (a) within-student, (b) within-test, (c) administration, and (d) scoring error affects each of the following methods of determining reliability:
a. Test–retest, short interval
b. Test–retest, long interval
c. Alternate forms, short interval
d. Alternate forms, long interval
e. Internal consistency

*5. Construct a subtest profile with bands for each of the following subtests taken by a particular student. Assume the mean is 50, the standard deviation is 8, and the reliability is .91 for all the tests. Construct your bands so that they have a 68% chance of capturing this individual's true scores. How would you interpret the differences between subtests to this student's parents?

Subtest	Score
Reading	56
Listening	50
Writing	61
Social Studies	35
Science	60
Math	56

*6. The following table lists the scores obtained by Tom and Mary on five different tests. At the 99% level, indicate which tests showed real differences in performance between Tom and Mary.

Test	S_m	Tom	Mary
A	5.5	80	60
B	16.0	150	165
C	3.4	32	35
D	30.0	620	679
E	8.0	89	103

*7. The following score reliability coefficients were reported for a test administered to a single class. How do you account for the differences?

Test–retest (30 days)	$r = .90$
Alternate forms	$r = .84$
Split-half (corrected using the Spearman–Brown formula)	$r = .93$

*8. Consider the following information from two tests:

Test	Mean	Reliability	SD
A	100	.91	20
B	100	.75	10

On which test would an individual's score fluctuate the most on repeated test administrations? Explain why.

* Answers for these questions appear in Appendix F.

CHAPTER 18

STANDARDIZED TESTS

WITH THE EXCEPTION of our review of high-stakes testing, we have limited our discussion of testing and measurement to teacher-constructed tests thus far—and with good reason. The average teacher uses teacher-made tests for most classroom testing and decision making. However, teachers are also required at least once a year to administer *standardized* tests, evaluate the results of such tests, and interpret the results to interested and sometimes concerned parents. Table 18.1 compares standardized achievement tests with teacher-made achievement tests.

Today, standardized tests are also at the heart of the high-stakes testing (HST) movement and the accountability requirements of the No Child Left Behind Act (NCLB). HST, described in detail in Chapter 2, can affect student promotion and graduation; teacher and principal evaluation, contract extensions, and cash incentives; and public recognition or humiliation for schools and districts. But using HST for such important purposes may not always be appropriate (see Chapter 1 sidebar, Box 1-1). With so much riding on standardized test results today, it is increasingly important for you to know the advantages, limitations, and uses of standardized tests and to learn how to interpret their results appropriately. Before we consider these issues, however, let's find out what a standardized test is.

WHAT IS A STANDARDIZED TEST?

Standardized achievement tests often take years to construct as opposed to a few days for a teacher-made test. They are called *standardized* because they are administered and scored according to *specific* and *uniform* (i.e., standard) procedures. In other words, a standardized achievement test administered and scored in Buffalo, New York, would be administered and scored in exactly the same manner in New York City, Chicago, Los Angeles, or anywhere else in the United States. Because of these standardization procedures, measurement error due to administration and scoring is reduced, which increases score reliability.

Standardized tests are constructed by test construction specialists, usually with the assistance of curriculum experts, teachers, and school administrators. They may be used to determine a student's level of performance relative to (a) the performance of other students of similar age and grade or (b) a criterion, such as state academic standards (see Chapter 2). When standardized tests are used to compare performance to students across the country they are called standardized norm-referenced tests, and when they are used to determine whether performance meets or exceeds criteria like state standards they are called standardized criterion-referenced tests.

TABLE 18.1 **A Comparison of Standardized and Teacher-Made Achievement Tests**

	Standardized Achievement Tests	Teacher-Made Achievement Tests
Learning outcomes and content measured	Measure general outcomes and content appropriate to the majority of schools in the United States. They are tests of general skills and understanding that tend not to reflect specific or unique emphases of local curricula.	Well adapted to the specific and unique outcomes and content of a local curriculum. They are adaptable to various sizes of work units, but tend to neglect complex learning outcomes.
Quality of test items	Quality of items generally is high. Items are written by specialists, pretested, and selected on the basis of the results of a quantitative item analysis.	Quality of items is often unknown. Quality is typically lower than that of standardized tests due to the limited time of the teacher.
Reliability	Reliability is high, commonly between .80 and .95, and frequently above .90.	Reliability is usually unknown, but can be high if items are carefully constructed.
Administration and scoring	Procedures are standardized; specific instructions are provided.	Uniform procedures are possible, but usually are flexible and unwritten.
Interpretation of scores	Scores can be compared to norm groups. Test manual and other guides aid interpretation and use.	Score comparisons and interpretations are limited to local class or school situation. Few, if any, guidelines are available for interpretation and use.

Source: Adapted with permission of Prentice-Hall, Inc., from *Measurement and Assessment in Teaching*, 8th ed., by Robert L. Linn and Norman E. Gronlund.

In Chapter 2 we mentioned that all 50 states and the District of Columbia now employ some form of high-stakes test. All these tests are standardized in terms of their administration and scoring, and they are carefully constructed. However, some high-stakes tests are norm-referenced (e.g., the Terra-Nova, Second Edition; the Stanford Achievement Test, Ninth Edition) while others are criterion-referenced (e.g., the Texas Assessment of Knowledge and Skills, or TAKS; the Massachusetts Comprehensive Assessment System of Skills, or MCAS). While much of what we discuss in this chapter applies to both norm- and criterion-referenced standardized tests, our primary focus will be on norm-referenced standardized tests.

Scores for students taking a norm-referenced standardized test are determined by comparing their obtained scores to a nationally representative sample, or norm group, that also took the test under standardized conditions. Thus scores for standardized, norm-referenced test takers are determined by comparing their scores to a norms table based on the performance of the norm group, or normative sample. Standardized testing is not limited to achievement measurement. Other standardized tests include tests of academic and general aptitude, personality, interest, and other characteristics. We will review each category and examples of each type of test in Chapter 19.

Do Test Stimuli, Administration, and Scoring Have to Be Standardized?

When the principal we described in Chapter 2 decided to "help" some students taking a standardized achievement test by telling them to change their answers, she seriously compromised the utility of the test results for the students. Since the conditions under which the students took the test varied from the conditions under which other students took the test, we cannot validly compare performances. Did the actions of the principal really "help" these students by invalidating their test results?

When standardized achievement tests are appropriately employed, test results from different students, classes, schools, and districts can be more easily and confidently compared to one another, or to state standards, than would be the case with different teacher-made tests. Imagine the difficulty in comparing teacher-made test results from Mrs. Smith's fifth-grade class in Orlando with results from Mrs. Wilson's fifth-grade class in Seattle. Not only would the test items be different, but the length of the test, the amount of time allowed, the instructions given by the teacher, and the scoring criteria would also be different. In short, there would be little or no basis for comparison. Standardization of achievement test stimuli and administration and scoring procedures reduces measurement error (see Chapter 17) and enables students evaluated with the same test under the standardized conditions to be compared with one another, or state standards, over time and across classes, schools, districts, and states.

Standardized Testing: Effects of Accommodations and Alternate Assessments

Under the 2004 reauthorization of the Individuals with Disabilities Education Act (IDEA–04) and the No Child Left Behind Act (NCLB), students with disabilities must now participate in annual state and district-wide achievement assessments. Prior to the passage of the previous version of IDEA in 1997, students with disabilities often were excluded from annual achievement assessments. Congress was concerned that the exclusion of children with disabilities from annual achievement assessments impeded assessment of the educational progress of children with disabilities and the development of an accountability system to ensure their achievement. Congress's intent in requiring that children with disabilities participate in these annual assessments was to increase accountability by enabling comparisons to be made for individual students to state standards over time and across students, schools, and districts. By enabling such comparisons, Congress also intended to enhance educational outcomes for children with disabilities.

Congress recognized that the very disabilities that qualify students for special education services may interfere with standardized achievement test performance (e.g., visual or hearing impairments, learning disabilities, health or emotional conditions). Thus IDEA–04 allows students with disabilities to (a) take the same annual state tests that regular education students take, (b) take the tests with alterations to the test stimuli and administration procedures (i.e., accommodations), or (c) take an alternate assessment approved by the state.

The requirement for accommodations and alternative assessments was well intended and seemingly appropriate. Requiring a visually impaired special learner to take the test under the same conditions as a non-visually impaired student likely would limit the performance of the visually impaired student by comparison. The allowance for accommodations and alternate assessments was included in IDEA to "level the playing field" for children with disabilities during annual assessments.

Although Congress was well intended in encouraging accommodations and alternate assessments, such alterations preclude the very comparisons Congress intended to enable! Without ongoing, systematic evaluation, no one can be certain how alteration of test stimuli, changes in administration procedures, or alternate assessments may affect test performance. Thus the performance of children with disabilities evaluated under nonstandardized conditions may not be directly comparable with (a) their own past or future performance, (b) the performance of other students with disabilities, or (c) students evaluated under standardized conditions.

We will discuss IDEA–04 and its broad implications for general education teachers, testing, and assessment more fully in Chapters 20 and 21. The point is that even when decision makers have good intentions, the purposes and procedures related to standardized testing continue to be misunderstood and misapplied at local, state, and national levels. When this happens the potential for misuse and abuse of the potentially useful tool called a standardized test increases, and often it is the test that ends up being blamed for any confusion or controversy which results.

Fortunately, learning to use standardized test results appropriately is not an overwhelming task. In this chapter we will present the principles that comprise good practice with standardized tests. Learn them and follow them (even if others do not!) and you will find that appropriately used standardized tests can be valuable measurement tools. Again, although our primary focus is on the interpretation of standardized norm-referenced test scores, much of what we discuss also applies to standardized criterion-referenced tests.

USES OF STANDARDIZED ACHIEVEMENT TESTS

In Chapter 3 we discussed educational decision making. We concluded that teacher-made measurement instruments are useful for most educational decisions. Historically, standardized tests were used to compare test scores over time or across students, classes, schools, or districts. Today, standardized tests also are used to make "high-stakes" decisions (e.g., promotion, graduation, teacher and principal ratings and incentives, and school and district evaluations). In some cases standardized achievement tests also are used diagnostically, to help educators identify student strengths and weaknesses or to evaluate specific programs and curricula. Group administered standardized achievement tests are most useful for comparative purposes. This is quite different from the main uses of teacher-made tests, which are to determine pupil mastery or skill levels, to assign grades, and to provide students and parents with feedback. Why, then, would the classroom teacher administer a standardized test? To compare this year's students with last year's? To compare class A with class B? Yes, but the most accurate answer is more likely that the classroom teacher administers standardized achievement tests because he or she is required to do so because it is required under NCLB and by state laws. This is the case in all school districts in the country today. However, the trend toward increased standardized testing predates NCLB. Morrison (1992) reviewed statistics published by the U.S. Department of Education and found that revenue from standardized test sales increased by 150% between 1960 and 1989, while student enrollment only grew by 15%. With the recent surge in high-stakes testing we believe the amount of testing taking place in the schools is now even higher than in 1989. Cizek (1998) estimated that standardized tests were administered to 140 million to 400 million students worldwide.

Part of the reason for the increase in standardized testing is the current trend toward increasing accountability and high-stakes testing. As teacher salaries and school taxes increase, taxpayers demand more justification for how their tax dollar is spent. By and large, taxpayers will support higher teacher salaries if teacher effectiveness increases, or at least remains constant. One indicator of teaching effectiveness, limited though it is, is standardized achievement test scores. As long as the public wants standardized achievement tests administered in the schools, the public will elect school board members who feel similarly, who will in turn choose school administrators who feel similarly, and those administrators will, in turn, require teachers to administer standardized achievement tests in their classrooms.

Accountability also includes evaluation of various federal and state programs. Most, if not all, such programs require that standardized achievement tests be administered as part of the program's evaluation. Further funding may depend on the results of these tests.

What this boils down to is that citizens, school administrators, special project personnel, and administrators of federal programs want to be able to compare students, schools, and districts with one another in order to make judgments concerning the effectiveness of school-wide or district-wide programs and practices. Standardized achievement tests enable them to do so. As long as this objective remains, standardized test administration and interpretation will be a necessary part of teaching. Hence, the classroom teacher must learn to administer and interpret these tests.

WILL PERFORMANCE AND PORTFOLIO ASSESSMENT MAKE STANDARDIZED TESTS OBSOLETE?

The status quo regarding the nationwide reliance on standardized multiple-choice and similar format tests to evaluate American education is changing. As we noted in Chapters 1, 8 and 9, pressure is mounting to use performance and portfolio assessments (i.e., authentic assessments) to supplement traditional tests, both standardized and teacher-made. And pressure to increasingly use performance and portfolio assessments to evaluate students and programs is being felt at all levels—local, state, and national. Does this mean that the utility and employment of standardized tests will decrease? While some would say yes, we do not think so.

First, administering standardized performance and portfolio assessments for all pupils would be extremely time-consuming and demanding on teachers, and far more expensive than traditional standardized testing. Second, for performance and portfolio assessment to be useful in comparing schools or districts on a state or national level, procedures will need to be developed that meet appropriate psychometric standards. Since standards for performance and portfolio assessments are not yet universally accepted, it is likely to be some time until procedures can be established that adhere to them. And third, when performance and portfolio procedures that meet appropriate standards are developed, they will provide a different kind of information than that provided by traditional standardized tests, rather than replace the information provided by standardized tests.

Thus there will almost certainly be the room and the need for both assessment approaches—traditional standardized and performance- and portfolio-based—in the schools of the future. In the meantime, a primary need facing the new teacher will be to learn how to use and interpret traditional standardized tests. As will be discussed later in this chapter, this will also put you a step ahead when adequate standardized performance and portfolio assessment systems become a reality.

ADMINISTERING STANDARDIZED TESTS

Recall our discussion of reliability and error in Chapters 16 and 17. We identified four major sources of error associated with measurement:

1. Errors within the student (illness, fatigue).
2. Errors within the test (poor items).
3. Errors in administration (too little time, too many hints).
4. Errors in scoring (clerical errors).

A standardized test, because it has been carefully prepared over several years, generally will have carefully constructed items, thereby minimizing error within the test. This is certainly the case for standardized norm-referenced tets, although some state standardized criterion-referenced tests may not be as carefully constructed. Since such tests usually are machine scored, clerical errors in scoring are minimized. Little can be done in standardized test situations to minimize within-student error, but standardized tests do minimize error in test administration. Figure 18.1 provides an example of how a standardized test minimizes error in test administration. Notice the specific directions that are given the test administrator as to what to say and what to do during the test. The best way to guard against error in test administration is to instruct *everyone* to administer the test in exactly the same way. Instructions such as these attempt to promote uniformity in how the test is administered across teachers, schools, and districts. If performance and portfolio assessment comes to be used for comparisons between students in different localities, similar standardized instructions and conditions under which performances and portfolios must be demonstrated will be necessary. Figure 18.2 also provides some helpful hints to keep in mind when administering standardized tests.

The last point in Fig. 18.2 bears further emphasis. It is not uncommon for well-intended classroom teachers to "individualize" the test administration by helping slower students or by pushing faster students. This is a violation of standardized testing procedure. The test and its administration and scoring are called *standardized* because everyone gets the same treatment. This sameness is what allows reliable comparisons to be made.

READING/LANGUAGE ARTS

Check to see that each student has his or her own test book. Students should have filled in the student-identifying information on the inside front cover of their test books.

SAY Open your test book to Page 1 in the Reading/ Languages Arts test. Be sure to stay on the pages that say "Reading/Language Arts" at the bottom of the page.

Check to see that all students are in the right place in their test book.

It is helpful to hold up a folded test book as you read the test directions. That way students will be able to check to be sure they are on the correct page.

SAY In this test, you will mark your answer in the test book. Some of the sections in the Reading/ Language Arts test have letters inside ovals to indicate the answer choices. You will need to choose one answer for each question.

To mark an answer, fill in the oval for the answer you choose. Make your mark heavy and dark, and do not make any other marks on the page. If you want to change an answer, completely erase the mark you made before making a new mark.

Are there any questions?

Following the instructions exactly ensures similar testing conditions in all classrooms. Test directions should be read as written.

FIGURE 18.1 Directions read aloud to students taking the Comprehensive Tests of Basic Skills (CTBS).

Source: From *Comprehensive Tests of Basic Skills, Examiners' Manual, Form S, Level B.* Reproduced with permission of McGraw-Hill School Publishing Company.

Do

- Read the manual *before* test administration day.
- Be sure you have been given the correct form for your grade level.
- Adhere strictly to the administration instructions.

Don't

- Try to minimize the achievement nature of the test.
- Deviate from the standardized administration instructions (i.e., do *not* allow more time, give hints, spell words, define words, etc.)

FIGURE 18.2 Dos and Don'ts in administering standardized tests.

Unfortunately, as the use of standardized testing has grown because of HST and NCLB requirements, there has been a corresponding increase in violations of standardized test administration procedures intended to increase scores. A number of examples of these practices were reviewed in Chapter 2. Even more troubling, these violations may be subtly or openly supported and encouraged by school and district administrators.

Regardless of whether the teacher or administrator is naive or well intended, such violations compromise the very reason the tests are administered, which is to allow reliable and valid comparisons of pupil achievement to be made.

TYPES OF SCORES OFFERED FOR STANDARDIZED ACHIEVEMENT TESTS

In this section we will consider the types of scores offered for standardized norm-referenced tests: grade equivalents, age equivalents, percentiles, and standard scores.

Grade Equivalents

Grade-equivalent scores are among the most widely used vehicle to report test results. They are also likely to be those most often misinterpreted. Grade equivalents are deceptively simple to interpret, on the surface. Consider the following statement:

> *Danielle obtained a Math Computation grade-equivalent score of 7.6 (seventh grade, sixth month) on the California Achievement Test (CAT). That means that even though she's only in fourth grade, she can do math at the seventh-grade level.*

Do you agree with this statement? If you do, you have fallen victim to the most common kind of misinterpretation regarding grade-equivalent scores. Danielle's obtained score is the score that the publisher *estimates* would be obtained by the average seventh grader during the sixth month of school. It does not necessarily mean that Danielle is ready for seventh-grade math! She may not necessarily have mastered the prerequisites for success in seventh grade or even sixth grade! All we know for sure is that a fourth grader who obtains a math grade equivalent of 7.6 is *well above average* in math. This is not the same as saying the student is ready for seventh-grade math work. In fact, we don't even know how seventh graders would do on this test since it is unlikely that any seventh grader took the test! To understand the statement, we must consider the way in which grade-equivalent scores are determined.

Usually a test is administered to the targeted grade (e.g., fourth grade) plus the grades immediately below and above the targeted grade (e.g., third and fifth grades). Thus grade equivalents are based on actually obtained scores only for students one grade level below to one grade level above the grade being tested. Scores appearing in grade-equivalent norms tables that are more than one grade level below or above the grade being tested are *estimated*—they are extrapolated from the obtained scores. This is where the problem lies. Much higher or lower grade equivalents than average represent only relative degrees of performance. They say nothing about specific skills mastered or about deficiencies.

Unfortunately, the problems related to grade equivalents do not end there. Others are listed here:

1. Apparently equal differences in scores do not necessarily reflect equal differences in achievement. For example, growth in reading comprehension from 2.6 to 3.6 will likely not mean the same degree or amount of growth as growth in reading comprehension from 7.6 to 8.6. It is likely that the one year's improvement is attributable to different factors in each case.

2. Grade equivalents are meaningless unless a subject is taught across all grades. Why report a physics grade equivalent of 6.2 when physics is taught only during the 12th grade? What does it mean to say your performance in physics is equivalent to that of a beginning sixth grader?

3. Grade equivalents are often misinterpreted as *standards* rather than norms. That is, teachers often forget that grade equivalents are averages—about half the students will score above and half below grade placement (depending on aptitude, of course!).

4. Grade equivalents may not be directly comparable across school subjects. That is, a fifth grader who is one year behind grade placement in reading is not necessarily as far behind in reading as he or she may be in math, even though he or she is one year behind in math, too. This is because growth in different subjects occurs at different rates. Equal levels of growth or deficiency, as indicated by grade-equivalent scores, may mean quite different things.

In spite of these shortcomings, grade equivalents continue to be popular. Our recommendation is that if you use them, you should carefully consider the cautions we have outlined. In general, they are more useful for the elementary grades, where they can be used to compare growth across a common core of subjects. In spite of this, remember that we cannot be very confident in the equality of the units, their equivalence across subjects, or their meaningfulness when grade equivalents far above or below grade placement are obtained.

Age Equivalents

Age-equivalent scores are very similar to the grade-equivalent scores just discussed. Age-equivalent scores are determined in a fashion similar to that described for grade equivalents. That is, samples of 7-, 8-, and 9-year-olds might be tested and average scores for each age determined. Scores for younger or older students would then be estimated or extrapolated from those scores. Problems similar to those affecting grade equivalents affect age equivalents, as outlined here:

1. Equal differences in scores may not reflect equal differences in achievement. In other words, does growth from age 6 to age 7 represent the same amount of growth as from age 10 to 11? It may or may not, depending on the trait being measured. Furthermore, growth in most traits slows down or stops during the teens or early 20s. In other words, a year's growth in reading after age 17 is likely to be very different from a year's growth in reading at age 7.

2. Age equivalents are only meaningful if subjects are taught across all grades. It makes little sense to say someone has an age equivalent of 16.9 in subtraction.

3. Age equivalents may be misinterpreted as standards, rather than as averages or norms.

4. Growth across subjects may vary greatly, even if age equivalents show equal growth. A year's increase in language age equivalent does not necessarily mean the same thing as a year's increase in science age equivalent.

Unlike grade equivalents, age equivalents have *not* attracted widespread acceptance in the schools. Like grade equivalents, they are most useful in the elementary grades to compare growth across a common core of subjects. These shortcomings should always be considered in interpreting age equivalents.

Percentile Ranks

With grade- and age-equivalent scores we indicate the grade or age group in which a student's test performance would be considered average. That is, if a student obtains a grade-equivalent score of 4.5, we can say the student did as well on the test as an average fourth grader during the fifth month of school. At times, however, we are not interested in making such comparisons. In fact, we would go so far as to say that in most cases we are more interested in determining how a student's performance compares with that of students in his or her own grade or of the same age. Percentile ranks enable us to make such comparisons.[1]

Percentile ranks are a substantial improvement over grade and age equivalent scores in that they do not suffer from the many limitations of grade and age equivalents. Since comparisons are within grade, it does not matter whether subjects are taught across grades, and since growth is only relative to others in the grade, the problem of growth being unequal at different grade levels is avoided. In addition, percentile ranks are less likely to be considered as standards for performance. However, percentile ranks do have two major shortcomings:

1. Percentile ranks are often confused with *percentage correct*. In using percentile ranks, be sure you are communicating that a percentile rank of 62, for example, is understood to mean that the individual's score was higher than 62% of the people who took the test or, conversely, that 62% of those taking the test received scores lower than this individual. Commonly, a score at the 62nd percentile is misinterpreted to mean the student answered only 62% of the items correct. A score at the 62nd percentile might be equivalent to a B or a C, whereas a score of 62% would likely be an F.

2. Equal differences between percentile ranks do *not* necessarily indicate equal differences in achievement. To refresh your memory, review the section on percentiles in Chapter 12. Briefly, in a class of 100 pupils, the difference in achievement between the 2nd percentile and 5th percentile is substantial, whereas the difference between the 47th and 50th is negligible, assuming a normal distribution. Interpretation of percentile ranks has to consider that units toward the tails of the distribution tend to be spread out, while units toward the center tend to be compressed, as illustrated in Fig. 18.3. As long as these limitations are considered, percentiles represent a useful type of score to employ in interpreting standardized test results.

[1] You may be wondering what the difference is between percentiles and percentile ranks. Percentiles and percentile ranks have slightly different meanings. In finding *percentiles*, one starts with the percentile desired (e.g., P_{25}, P_{50}, P_{75}, etc.) and then finds the score value below which there is that percentage of cases (e.g., 25% of the class scored below a score of 70). In finding *percentile ranks*, the reverse direction is taken: One starts with all the score values and then finds the percentage of cases falling below each value. Percentile ranks are generally determined by all the scores in a distribution at the same time.

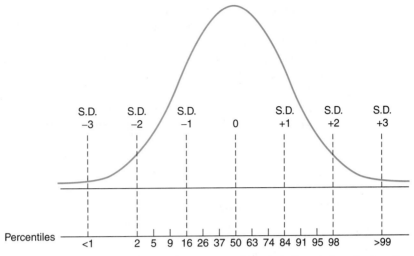

FIGURE 18.3   Normal curve with approximate percentile ranks indicated along the baseline.

Standard Scores

Like percentile ranks, standard scores compare a student's performance to that of other students at the same grade level. The problem of equal differences between units not representing equal differences in achievement is overcome through the use of standard scores. Computation of such converted scores was discussed in Chapter 13, and you might want to review the relevant sections of that chapter. Recall that the z-score is the basic type of standard score, and all other standard scores are derived from it. This is an important consideration to keep in mind since many test publishers "create" new types of standard scores with various means and standard deviations when they publish new tests (e.g., *Developmental Standard Scores* on the Iowa Tests of Basic Skills, or *Expanded Standard Scores* on the Comprehensive Tests of Basic Skills). You need not be overwhelmed by such scores since conceptually they are identical to z-scores.

Similar to, but different from, z-scores is a special type of standard score called *stanines*. Stanines are ranges or bands within which fixed percentages of scores fall. They are determined by dividing the normal curve into nine portions, each being one-half standard deviation wide. Stanines and the percentage of cases within each stanine are indicated here:

Stanine	Percentage of Cases
1	4 (lowest)
2	7
3	12
4	17
5	20
6	17
7	12
8	7
9	4 (highest)

Stanines have a mean equal to 5 and a standard deviation equal to 2. Each stanine is one-half standard deviation wide. Interpreting stanines is straightforward in that a student is simply described as being "in" the second stanine, ninth stanine, etc. A major advantage of stanines is that, since they are intervals or bands, they tend to minimize overinterpretation of data. Also, since they only require single-digit numbers, they are useful for situations where recording space is limited.

Standard scores represent the ultimate in standardized test score interpretation. However, there is one factor that limits their widespread adoption: Most educators, parents, and students do not understand how to use standard scores. As a result, few schools or districts request standard scores from test publishers. As we will demonstrate, however, standard scores can save time and effort in determining aptitude–achievement discrepancies. They also allow for easy comparison of scores both within and across pupils, either over time or across subjects.

Having had a course in tests and measurements, you are now able to make use of standard scores to make sense out of standardized test scores. Keep in mind that such scores are not understood by most parents and students and as a result are not a good medium to use in reporting standardized test results. What should you use, then? In our opinion, grade and age equivalents lend themselves too easily to misinterpretation and have too many limitations. As we mentioned, standard scores would be our choice but may be too complicated for use by the general public. We recommend, therefore, that you use percentile ranks when reporting and interpreting standardized test results to parents. Be sure, however, to consider the limitations we mentioned regarding percentile ranks in making such interpretations. Next, we will turn to the important topic of test interpretation and provide examples of standardized test score reports from publishers to familiarize you with the variety of reports available.

INTERPRETING STANDARDIZED TESTS: TEST AND STUDENT FACTORS

Standardized tests, although less useful for day-to-day instructional decision making than teacher-made tests, can be very useful for selection, placement, and diagnostic decisions and for providing feedback to parents and students. As we know, standardized tests are now also widely used for accountability purposes. Unfortunately, standardized test interpretation is by no means a straightforward task. Standardized or not, tests are fallible and require thoughtful and considerate use. To acquire the skill of properly using standardized tests, you must consider certain factors. These factors can be classified into two categories: test-related and student-related.

Test-Related Factors

Test-related factors can limit the interpretability of the test's results due to problems inherent in the test itself, its use, or its administration or scoring. They can be addressed by asking the following questions: Does the test have acceptable score reliability and criterion-related validity evidence? Does the test have content validity evidence for my instructional objectives, or for state academic standards? Was the test's norm group composed of students similar to my class (for standardized norm-referenced tests)? Were the standardized administration procedures followed? Let's consider each of these questions.

Does the test have acceptable score reliability and criterion-related validity evidence?

This question highlights the need to know how valid, reliable, and accurate a test is. In Chapters 15, 16, and 17 we discussed validity evidence, reliability, and accuracy. We can review the evidence for a test's reliability, accuracy, and validity from information contained in the administrator's manual or the technical manual accompanying the standardized test. Let's consider this information.

Reliability   An acceptable standardized test should have the following score reliability coefficients:

.95 for internal consistency,

.90 for test–retest, and

.85 for alternate forms.

If your test has coefficients this high, you can feel confident that scores from the test are reliable. Of course, there is nothing sacred about these particular coefficients. If your test scores have coefficients of .92 for test–retest reliability, .93 for internal consistency, and .82 for alternate forms, it will still have good score reliability.

Accuracy   If test scores are reliable, they are also accurate. That is, obtained results close to an individual's true level of achievement are likely. Under the section "Standard Error of Measurement" in the administrator's or technical manual you will find a numerical value that will enable you to determine the range of scores within which an individual's true score is likely to lie. Recall from Chapter 17 that this range of scores can be determined at the 68%, 95%, and 99% levels of confidence.

Criterion-Related Validity Evidence   Recall that criterion-related validity evidence may be of two types: predictive and concurrent. Since standardized achievement tests are used to assess past learning, it makes little sense to report predictive validity coefficients for them. However, concurrent validity coefficients are often reported. These are numerical estimates of the extent to which a test correlates with another established test or tests. However, using such coefficients to determine an achievement test's validity is difficult. Since the content and specificity of the different tests will vary, a valid achievement test may yield concurrent validity coefficients of .60 with Test X and .90 with Test Y, and still be a good achievement test. The reason for the discrepancy may reflect a closer match in content and specificity between your test and Test Y, and less of a match with Test X. For this reason, it is *most* important to evaluate the content validity evidence of standardized achievement tests. This is the same as the concept of a high-stakes test's alignment with state standards, as was discussed in Chapter 2. Concurrent validity evidence is of secondary importance. Of course, one would be very suspicious of an achievement test that yielded a concurrent validity coefficient of less than .50 with an established standardized achievement test that measures the same objectives or state standards.

Does the test have content validity evidence for my instructional objectives, or for state academic standards?

A numerical estimate of validity showing that Test A correlates highly with Test B is not evidence that either test has content validity for your instructional objectives. Only by matching items with your objectives, or with state standards, can you determine whether a standardized achievement test has content validity evidence. Furthermore, remember that a test score reliability does not ensure the test is valid. If the test has several items covering dictionary skills and you have not taught such skills, the case for content validity evidence of the test for your class has been weakened. That is, if the test does not measure or match your objectives and your instruction, the test's results will be ambiguous, regardless of score reliability or accuracy.

Was the test's norm group composed of students similar to my class (for standardized norm-referenced tests)?

When the pilot or preliminary version of a standardized test is constructed, it is often administered to a test or pilot group of students. Revisions are made as indicated, and then it is administered to a *norming group* or *normative sample*. A norms table (essentially a frequency distribution; see Chapter 12) for the test is then compiled, based on the performance of this sample of the test.

A norms table provides you with a variety of kinds of information. Some norms tables enable you to determine the proportion of test takers who scored above, at, or below the various scores possible on the test. In addition, norms tables usually enable you to convert raw scores to percentiles and a variety of standard scores. Table 18.2 is a norms table that enables conversion from raw scores on various subtests to what are called "scale scores," and also includes two types of estimates of the standard error of measurement for each scale score. For standardized norm-referenced tests, scale scores, like any of a number of other standard scores developed by test publishers (e.g., GRE scores, SAT scores, Expanded Standard scores) are all variations of the z-scores discussed earlier. Most publishers of standardized norm-referenced tests develop their own versions of standard scores. However, all of these scores conform to the z-score interpretations presented earlier, albeit with different means and standard deviations.

Knowing what kind of students made up the norm group of a standardized norm-referenced test is important. This is the group with which you will be comparing your students in interpreting their scores. If the test you administer to your upper-income class was normed on a sample of low-income children from impoverished backgrounds, and your class scored somewhat higher than 50% of the norm group, would you interpret the findings to mean exceptional performance? Hopefully not. Since children who were raised in impoverished, low-income families tend to score low on standardized tests, we would expect children from upper-income families to score considerably higher regardless of instructional method or the academic potential of the children involved. Such a comparison would be inappropriate. Similarly, it would be inappropriate to compare the performance of low-income children to a norm group composed entirely of upper-income children. The low-income group would be expected to fare poorly in comparison, again, regardless of instructional methods or academic potential.

TABLE 18.2 Raw Score to Scale Score with SEM for Raw Score and Pattern (IRT) Scoring Methods: Complete Battery, Form A, Level 12

Raw Score	Reading SS	Reading RS SEM	Reading IRT SEM	Vocabulary SS	Vocab RS SEM	Vocab IRT SEM	Language SS	Lang RS SEM	Lang IRT SEM	Lang Mech SS	LM RS SEM	LM IRT SEM	Math SS	Math RS SEM	Math IRT SEM	Math Comp SS	MC RS SEM	MC IRT SEM	Science SS	Sci RS SEM	Sci IRT SEM	Social Studies SS	Soc RS SEM	Soc IRT SEM	Spelling SS	Sp RS SEM	Sp IRT SEM	Word Analysis SS	WA RS SEM	WA IRT SEM	Raw Score
0	423	135	128	434	100	82	424	126	113	445	117	105	347	125	105	360	119	103	361	132	119	395	132	120	405	124	96	462	96	67	0
1	423	135	128	434	100	82	424	126	113	445	117	105	347	125	105	360	119	103	361	132	119	395	132	120	405	124	96	462	96	67	1
2	423	135	128	434	100	82	424	126	113	445	117	105	347	125	105	360	119	103	361	132	119	395	132	120	405	124	96	462	96	67	2
3	423	135	128	434	100	82	424	126	113	445	117	105	347	125	105	360	119	103	372	120	108	395	132	120	405	124	96	462	96	67	3
4	423	135	128	475	59	41	424	126	113	466	96	84	347	125	105	419	60	44	434	58	47	395	132	120	455	74	49	462	96	67	4
5	423	135	128	500	34	24	424	126	113	521	41	29	347	125	105	444	35	26	457	35	30	466	62	49	484	45	34	507	51	30	5
6	423	135	128	515	27	20	424	126	113	537	25	20	347	125	105	460	28	22	472	26	23	491	36	29	503	33	27	528	35	23	6
7	469	88	82	528	24	19	458	92	79	548	20	16	347	125	105	473	24	20	483	22	19	505	25	21	517	28	24	544	29	22	7
8	516	42	35	540	23	19	499	52	38	557	17	14	347	125	105	485	22	18	492	19	17	515	20	18	529	24	22	557	25	21	8
9	539	27	22	551	20	18	517	34	26	564	16	14	368	104	84	495	20	17	500	18	16	523	17	15	541	22	19	569	22	19	9
10	540	20	16	562	20	18	528	25	21	571	16	13	408	65	45	505	18	17	508	17	16	530	16	14	551	21	19	578	19	18	10
11	547	16	14	573	19	17	538	21	17	578	15	13	428	45	31	514	17	16	516	17	15	536	14	13	561	20	19	587	17	16	11
12	552	14	12	583	19	17	545	18	16	586	15	13	441	34	25	523	16	14	523	17	15	542	14	13	571	20	18	595	16	15	12
13	557	13	11	583	19	17	545	18	16	586	15	13	452	28	22	531	15	13	530	17	15	548	13	12	581	19	18	603	15	14	13
14	562	12	10	604	19	18	558	15	13	602	16	15	461	25	19	539	14	13	538	17	16	553	13	12	591	19	18	611	15	14	14
15	566	11	10	615	19	18	564	14	13	611	17	16	469	22	18	548	14	14	546	17	16	559	13	12	603	20	19	618	15	14	15
16	570	11	9	627	19	18	570	14	12	623	19	17	476	20	17	557	15	14	554	18	17	564	13	13	616	22	21	627	15	15	16
17	574	10	9	641	20	19	575	14	12	636	20	18	482	19	16	567	16	14	563	19	17	571	15	13	633	27	25	637	17	16	17
18	578	10	9	657	24	22	581	14	12	652	22	20	488	18	15	579	16	15	573	20	19	577	15	14	664	43	39	650	20	19	18
19	582	10	9	685	39	35	587	14	12	676	31	28	494	17	15	595	21	19	585	22	21	585	16	15	700	71	66	671	28	27	19
20	585	10	9	705	54	49	593	14	13	695	42	38	499	16	14	630	56	48	600	26	24	594	18	16				699	47	45	20
21	590	10	9				599	15	13				504	15	14				619	31	29	606	21	19							21
22	594	11	10				607	16	14				509	15	14				648	42	39	621	24	23							22
23	599	11	10				615	18	16				513	14	13				703	69	65	641	30	28							23
24	604	12	11				626	20	18				518	14	13				743	92	88	675	43	40							24
25	609	12	11				639	24	22				522	13	12							720	81	72							25
26	616	13	13				658	29	27				527	13	12																26
27	623	14	13				688	38	37				531	13	12																27
28	632	15	14				706	47	45				535	12	12																28
29	642	17	16										539	12	11																29
30	655	20	19										543	12	11																30
31	676	27	26										548	12	11																31
32	722	59	58										552	12	11																32
33													556	12	11																33
34													561	12	11																34
35													565	12	12																35
36													570	12	12																36
37													575	13	12																37
38													581	13	13																38
39													587	14	13																39
40													593	15	14																40
41													601	16	15																41
42													609	17	16																42
43													619	19	18																43
44													631	21	20																44
45													647	25	24																45
46													674	35	34																46
47													720	69	67																47

Source: Adapted from *Comprehensive Tests of Basic Skills, Examiners' Manual, Form A, Level 12.* Reproduced with permission of McGraw–Hill School Publishing Company.

Fortunately, most norm groups are not composed of such homogeneous groups of students. Most standardized test publishers are careful to select norm groups that are representative of the general U.S. population. This means the sample is scientifically chosen to be as similar to the general U.S. population as possible in terms of sex, ethnicity, region, income, etc. A nationally representative sample increases the usefulness of the test for making comparisons with your class. Often a compromise must be reached in creating a norms table. In trying to closely represent the U.S. norm, we create a norms table that may not represent the unique characteristics of any individual classroom. To the extent your class fails to approximate the U.S. population in general, the comparisons you make to a nationally representative norm will be less valid.

Trying to assess progress in a class for the intellectually gifted by comparing test scores to a national norm, therefore, would not be appropriate. All or most students would score high in comparison. This is *not necessarily* because the students are working hard, or because their teachers are effective. It may simply be the result of choosing an inappropriate standard for comparison, in this case a norm group composed of the general population of students, not gifted students. Although the gifted students may seem to be doing very well by comparison, it would be difficult to discriminate among them, since all or most would score at or near the ceiling for the test.

A similar case could be made for the inappropriateness of comparing a class composed entirely, or mainly, of low-income, low-achieving students to a norm group representative of the national population. Such a class would score very low by comparison—probably so low as to make discrimination among students in the class difficult.

Most teachers, however, do not have uniformly high- or low-achieving students in their classes. How, then, can teachers in such classes tell how appropriate the comparisons they make are? Fortunately, there is an answer.

The teacher knows approximately what his or her class composition is with respect to income and ethnicity. The teacher can then find the composition of the norm group by reading the "Norm Group" description section in the appropriate manual accompanying the standardized test. An example of such a description is presented in Fig. 18.4. After studying the description, you can compare your class to the norm group. The closer the correspondence between the class and the norm group, the more confidence you can place in interpreting results using the norms table. The more the discrepancy between the table and the norm group, the less confidence you can place in interpretations based on the norms table. This is a judgment that one gets better at with time and practice.

But what if you decide there is a large discrepancy between the norm group and your class? Is there any way to better interpret the standardized test results? There are other options. Test publishers are now beginning to publish specialized norms tables, and one can always consider the option of establishing local norms.

Specialized Norms Tables   In recognition of our nation's increasing language and sociocultural diversity, standardized test publishers are now beginning to offer specialized norms tables to supplement the nationally representative norms tables they have always offered. Specialized norms may be found in some standardized test manuals or may be available on request from the test publisher. Specialized norms tables for students for whom English is a second language, for students in low-achieving schools, for students from low socioeconomic backgrounds, and for others may be available, depending on the

The norms for this test are derived from a sample of 13,000 students in grades K–12. Approximately 1,000 students were included for each grade level (K–12). Only students who never repeated or skipped a grade were included. Their ages ranged from 5–19. The test was administered to the sample in spring 2000. The sample was stratified to be representative of the U.S. population according to gender, parental income, parental education, ethnicity, and geographic region. The actual composition of the standardization sample is described next.

Gender: Approximately equal numbers of males and females were included (6,432 boys and 6,568 girls) in the overall sample. At each grade level the number of males and females in the grade samples did not differ by more than 50.

Parental Income: Approximately 10% of the sample had parental income of $80,000 or more, 60% had incomes ranging from $30,000 to $79,999, and 30% had incomes under $30,000. These proportions (plus or minus 1.5%) were maintained at each grade level.

Parental Education: 28% of the parents whose children were included in the sample completed four or more years of college, 16% had some college, 32% completed high school or had a high school equivalency diploma, and 24% did not complete high school.

Ethnicity: 66% of the sample was Caucasian, 15% African-American, 13% Hispanic-American, and 4% Asian-American, with other ethnic groups comprising the remaining 2%.

Region: 26.5 of the sample came from the northeast, 23% from the southeast, 24.5% from the northwest, and 26% from the southwest regions of the United States.

FIGURE 18.4 An example of a norm group description that would be found in a standardized test manual.

publisher. It is important to note, however, that the sizes of the samples for these specialized norms tables will be smaller than the size of the nationally representative sample, and may be substantially smaller. Therefore we must not be overconfident about the accuracy of scores obtained from such specialized norm groups, or any comparisons or decisions we make that are based on specialized norms tables.

Local Norms When a class, school, or district is substantially different from the normative sample, local norms may enable better use of test results. It should be noted, however, that we are not suggesting that local norms should be substituted for national norms. We are suggesting that local norms are useful tools that can, in some situations, increase the interpretability of test scores. They do so by enabling more meaningful comparisons to be made among and within unique students, classes, and schools. Since such norms are established on relatively homogeneous groups, they enable better comparisons within such groups, but they do not allow broader or national comparisons to be made. Table 18.3 compares and contrasts national and local norms.

Establishing Local Norms Although establishing norms generally will be the responsibility of the school district's support staff, they are fairly easy to develop. To construct a local norms table, use the following procedures:

1. Collect scores for all individuals in the local group.

TABLE 18.3   **A Comparison and Contrast of National and Local Norms**

	National Norms	Local Norms
Composition	Large numbers of students of various ethnicity and income selected to represent U.S. population.	All students in a specific school or district.
Use	Compare local performance to a national norm.	Compare local performance to a local norm.
Advantage	Allows broad, general comparisons in areas of broad concern (e.g., college entrance, scholarships).	Allows comparisons in areas of local or immediate concern (e.g., academic gain within homogeneous groups, placement in local classes).
Disadvantage	Not useful in comparisons when relatively homogeneous groups are involved.	Not useful for making broad comparisons at a national level.

2. Tally all the obtained scores.

3. Construct a simple frequency distribution (refresh your memory by rereading this procedure in Chapter 12).

4. Compute percentile ranks for each score in the table (see Chapter 12).

5. Refer to the table as you would a national norms table.

Interpreting a Norms Table   A national norms table like the one shown in Table 18.2 can be confusing and intimidating at first glance. The key to successfully maneuvering through a norms table to convert raw scores to standard scores or other converted scores is to first understand how the table is organized. Table 18.2 lists the CTBS skill areas across the top row. These include Reading, Vocabulary, Language, Language Mechanics, Mathematics, and several other skill areas.

To convert a raw score to a scaled score (SS), find the student's subtest raw score in either the left or right columns, whichever is closest to the column for the subtest you are interested in, and look along a straightedge (e.g., a ruler) to find the scaled score that corresponds to the raw score in question. For example, a student with a raw score of 25 in Reading would have a scaled score of 609, a student with a raw score of 15 in Spelling would have a scaled score of 591, and a student with a raw score of 11 in Mathematics Computation would have a scaled score of 514.

Let's turn to the final question addressing test-related factors that influence standardized test interpretation:

Were standardized administration procedures followed?

Here, the teacher needs to think back to the day the test was administered. Were any required procedures or wording altered or omitted? Was extra time or too little time afforded? Was help made available above and beyond what was permissible according to the test manual? If no such violations occurred, no more need be done about this consideration. If one or more violations did occur, the teacher must realize that reliability and validity have been affected to some unknown extent. Obviously, this reduces the confidence you can place in the test results. Since you will never be sure how reliability and validity has been affected by such violations, or be certain the violations resulted in increased or decreased scores, there is little you can do to correct for such errors—except, of course, to prevent them.

This completes our discussion of test-related factors to be considered in interpreting standardized tests. Now let's consider several equally important student-related factors.

Student-Related Factors

The variety of student-related factors that can affect test score interpretation can be divided into several categories: language and sociocultural; age, gender, and development; motivation; emotional state on the test day; disabilities; and aptitude.

Language and Sociocultural   For decades there has been a steady flow of immigrants from non–English-speaking countries into the United States. Most would agree that there are legal, moral, and practical reasons why non–English-speaking children of these immigrants should be educated in our schools. Thus we have seen considerable growth in the language and cultural diversity of our classrooms over the last couple of decades. There are no signs of abatement in immigration trends.

In Chapters 1 and 4 we discussed the importance of considering a student's language proficiency and sociocultural context in relation to norm- and criterion-referenced test selection and the interpretation and assessment process. We asked whether Svetlana, a recent Russian immigrant with limited English proficiency, or Diana, a recent immigrant from England with excellent proficiency in English, would be expected, all other factors being equal, to score higher on a standardized test in English. Our obvious conclusion was that Diana would score higher simply because she could read and comprehend the test questions far more easily, accurately, and quickly than Svetlana.

Yet, there have been many instances where well-intentioned but unthinking or naive individuals have administered standardized and teacher-made tests in English to students with limited English proficiencies. Worse, when students with limited English proficiency obtain scores on tests in English that are below national norms, or fail to meet proficiency criteria, they have at times been labeled as slow learners, learning disabled, or mentally retarded.

Sociocultural factors beyond language factors also can negatively affect a child's performance on a standardized test. In our culture, competitiveness, assertiveness, frequent testing, and the use of tests to determine entry into schools, trades, and professions have been accepted and are valued. As a result, parents and students raised in our culture have learned to recognize the "demands" of the typical testing situation. Another way of saying this is that they have become "acculturated" into our competitive, test-oriented culture.

Immigrants may lack this acculturation if their native culture places less emphasis and importance on competitiveness and testing. For example, parents and students from our majority culture realize that students must prepare for a test, concentrate and work quickly and accurately during the test, and insist on equitable treatment from the test administrator. Children from other cultures may not even be aware of these expectations, much less agree with or be prepared to accomplish them. Thus their behavior during important testing situations may be discrepant with expectations based on children who have been acculturated to testing, and may be interpreted negatively by educators. Other factors also may affect test behavior and performance among students who are not from the majority culture. Some examples include hunger and poor nutrition, poverty, the importance placed on achievement in the family, and a variety of other behavioral differences across cultures (e.g., assertiveness, competitiveness, and compliance with authority figures).

In summary, language proficiency and a variety of sociocultural factors can negatively affect test behavior and standardized test performance. Language proficiency and sociocultural differences from the majority culture should always be considered in planning for, selecting, administering, and interpreting standardized test results.

Age, Gender, and Development An awareness of individual differences has influenced educational practice for many years. We read and hear about students being visual or auditory learners, high or low IQ, advanced or delayed, and so forth. Yet we sometimes fail to consider three of the most obvious of the individual differences among children—age, gender, and stage of development.

Typically, norms tables are broken into three or four sections to correspond to various times of the year. Students are expected to know more, and therefore answer more items correctly, in May than in October, due to the effects of schooling. This makes sense, of course, but what about the case of a first grader who turns six the day before school starts, compared to the first grader who turns seven the day after school starts? Should both students, all other factors except age being equal, be expected to improve their test scores equally? If you are familiar with younger elementary-age children, your answer would likely be a firm no. Five-, six-, and seven-year-olds show very different rates of development in different areas. Furthermore, there are differences that correlate with gender. Girls tend to master verbal skills and reading earlier than boys. Norms tables for achievement tests may not take such factors into account. The reasons for academic performance are complex and, of course, involve more than just age, gender, and stage of development. Do not treat them as though they alone determine test performance, but do not neglect those factors in interpreting standardized test scores.

Motivation Ever find it hard to be "up" for a test? If you are like most of us, it happens from time to time. At those times your performance is less likely to reflect your actual level of achievement than if you were up for the test. Most pupils have little trouble getting ready for a teacher-made achievement test—they know that their grades depend on it. With standardized tests, however, motivation can be a problem.

Both pupils and their parents have made more sophisticated use of standardized tests over the last few years. Many parents realize that such tests do not affect a child's grades in school, but at the same time they may not realize that such results may be used for instructional grouping and high-stakes decisions that will affect their child later. Believing standardized tests are not important often leads pupils to take a "who cares?" attitude toward standardized tests. Such an attitude is sometimes unintentionally transmitted by teachers in an effort to minimize the anxiety some pupils experience over tests. The result can be a decline in motivation and a consequent decline in performance.

Emotional State on the Test Day　Just as teachers get emotionally upset from time to time, so do their students. This does not simply refer to students who are nervous about the test, but to students who may be undergoing severe stress for personal reasons, such as an argument before the test, a dispute at home, or some destabilizing event within the family. One cannot function at one's best when depressed, angry, or very nervous. When you find these characteristics exhibited by a student before or during the test, make a note of it and consider it when you interpret the student's test performance at a later date.

Disabilities　There is a sizable percentage of students in the public schools who suffer from physical and/or emotional problems that hinder academic achievement. In the past, children with disabilities were often excluded from annual state- and district-wide standardized assessments. As we mentioned at the beginning of this chapter, beginning with the passage of the 1997 Amendments to the Individuals with Disabilities Education Act (IDEA–97), and reinforced by NCLB in 2002, and IDEA–04 students with disabilities must now participate in annual academic assessments, albeit with accommodations or through alternate assessments. This well-intended participatory requirement attempted to minimize disability-related impediments to performance on annual assessments by encouraging accommodations and alternative assessments to standardized tests. However, such accommodations and alternative assessments will limit comparability of scores for children with disabilities with one another, with themselves over time, and across classes, schools, districts, and states. This issue was mentioned at the beginning of this chapter and will be discussed again in Chapter 21.

Aptitude　*Aptitude* and *potential* can be considered synonymous for our purposes. They refer to the maximum we can expect from a student, as indicated by a student's score on a test of academic aptitude or potential. Such tests are often referred to as IQ tests, intelligence tests, or cognitive tests. IQ tests will be discussed in more depth in Chapter 19. The academic aptitude, or IQ, test provides us with an estimated ceiling for a student's academic performance. The achievement test, on the other hand, measures actual academic performance.

Traditionally, students have been labeled overachievers or underachievers when achievement scores are discrepant with academic aptitude scores. Figure 18.5 illustrates an underachiever, an overachiever, and a student achieving at expectancy. Student A in Fig. 18.5 is a student with considerable potential who is not achieving his or her potential. Student B is a student with moderate potential who is achieving above his or her potential. More accurately, this "overachiever" is a student whose obtained aptitude score (not necessarily true score) is lower than his or her obtained achievement score. Student C represents a student achieving at the level we would expect, given his or her aptitude score. The obtained aptitude score is equivalent to the obtained achievement score.

Obviously, it is necessary to have an aptitude score to enable you to determine whether a student is achieving at *expectancy* (the level you would expect, given the student's aptitude) or whether a *discrepancy* exists between aptitude and achievement. However, school district policies vary in requiring the administration of aptitude tests. Depending on your district, you may have aptitude tests administered to students every few years, or only in the fourth and ninth grades, or not at all. If you find aptitude test scores in your students' folders, you can use them to enhance your achievement test interpretation. However, be careful not to simply label your students underachievers or overachievers.

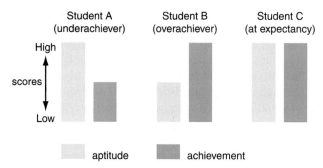

FIGURE 18.5 Relative levels of aptitude and achievement for an underachiever, an overachiever, and a student achieving at expectancy.

Most aptitude tests yield more than one overall IQ score. Many yield a *verbal* and a *nonverbal* score, or a *language* and a *nonlanguage* score, or a *verbal* and a *quantitative* score. Quantitative scores represent general math or number ability. When the aptitude or IQ test yields a verbal score and a nonverbal score or a quantitative score, more relevant comparisons are possible than when only one overall score is reported. Consider the following example.

> *Donna, a new fifth grader, obtained the following scores on the Cognitive Abilities Test (an aptitude test) at the beginning of fourth grade (note: M = 100, SD = 15).*
>
> *Verbal = 100*
>
> *Quantitative = 130*
>
> *Donna's scores on the California Achievement Test (CAT) given at the end of fourth grade are as follows:*

	Percentile Rank
Reading Vocabulary	*66*
Reading Comprehension	*60*
Reading Total	*63*
Math Concepts	*99*
Math Computation	*99*
Math Total	*99*

> *Donna's parents have requested a conference with you. They want you to push her harder in reading until her reading scores match her math scores, which have been superior.*

What would you do? How would you interpret Donna's scores? Would you push her in reading? Before you answer those questions, let's make Donna's data interpretable. We can do so by using bar graph comparisons to illustrate the concepts of underachievement and overachievement.

We know that an obtained IQ score of 100 is at the 50th percentile on an IQ test with a mean of 100 and a standard deviation of 15. We also know that on the same test an IQ score of 130 is at the 98th percentile, two standard deviations above the mean. In the graphs in Fig. 18.6 our percentile scales do not correspond directly to each other, but that

FIGURE 18.6 A comparison of Donna's aptitude and achievement scores.

is of little consequence since we are not interested in comparing reading with math. Rather, we are interested in comparing verbal aptitude with reading total, both of which are on the same scale, and quantitative aptitude with math total, which are also on a common scale.

From the graphs, we would conclude that Donna's obtained math achievement score actually *exceeds* the obtained math aptitude score. According to our popular but somewhat misleading terminology, she is "overachieving" in math. Unless she is paying a high price socially or emotionally for working so hard at math, we see no problem here. Hence, the qualifier "over" in the word *overachiever* should not imply a negative valuation of what has been accomplished by this student. But Donna's parents are not concerned with her math achievement; they are concerned with her reading achievement. They want her pushed, which suggests they feel she can do better than she has in the past. That is, Donna's parents feel she is underachieving in reading. Is she?

On the basis of a comparison of her obtained verbal aptitude score and her obtained reading achievement score, our conclusion would have to be no. In fact, Donna is "overachieving" in reading, too. That is, her obtained reading achievement score exceeds her obtained verbal aptitude score; she is actually performing above expectancy. Would you agree that she needs to be pushed? By now, we should hope not. In fact, you might suggest to Donna's parents that they ease up, using your skills in the interpretation of standardized test results to substantiate your suggestion.

Aptitude–Achievement Discrepancies[2]

What we have been doing is making a general or global decision about whether Donna is achieving at her expected level, as indicated by her aptitude score. In other words, are there any differences between her aptitude and her achievement? When these differences are large enough to indicate substantial variation in the traits being measured, we call them *aptitude–achievement discrepancies*.

[2] The following discussion assumes high difference score reliability. Unfortunately, difference scores often are less reliable than the reliability of the aptitude or achievement tests that are used to determine them. The formula for determining reliability of difference scores is presented in the section on band interpretation of scores in Chapter 17. The procedures described in the section are intended to provide the regular classroom teacher with an easy-to-use standard for identifying students who may be in need of further testing or diagnosis. They are not intended to classify a student on the basis of aptitude-achievement discrepancy.

But when is a difference a discrepancy? How large must the gap be before we call a difference a discrepancy? Does this begin to sound familiar? We hope so, but if it does not, this next question should help: How large a difference do we need between an aptitude score and an achievement score before we can conclude that the difference is due to a "real" discrepancy rather than a "chance" difference? In Chapter 17 we learned how to use the standard error of measurement (S_m) and band interpretation to discriminate real from chance differences among subtests in an achievement test battery. This same principle can be applied to discriminate real discrepancies from chance differences when dealing with aptitude and achievement test scores.

We will consider an example in a moment, but first let's review one aspect of band interpretation. Recall that we can use the 68% (score $\pm$ 1S_m) or 95% (score $\pm$ 2S_m) methods, depending on how conservative we want to be regarding the educational decisions to be made. If such findings are kept within the classroom and little of consequence is to follow from a band interpretation, or if comparisons are limited to those among subtests on an achievement battery, the 68% approach may be appropriate.

Beyond the confines of your own classroom, however, important educational decisions or conclusions may be based on comparisons between achievement and aptitude. Indeed, for individual students, demonstration of a *severe* aptitude–achievement discrepancy has been required by federal law since 1977 to qualify a student to receive special educational services as child with a Specific Learning Disability (SLD). With the passage of IDEA–04, however, the discrepancy approach to SLD eligibility decision-making was made optional. Instead, states now have three options for SLD determination: continuing to use the discrepancy approach, employing a response to instruction/intervention (RTI) approach, or using a combination of both approaches (see Chapter 20 for more detail). Regardless, of the SLD determination method used in your state or district, the special education referral process often begins with a teacher suspecting that a student is not achieving at an average rate, or up to his or her potential. Thus we would strongly encourage you to use the more conservative 95% approach any time you consider making a special education referral based on aptitude–achievement discrepancies you have observed.

Let's turn to an example that illustrates how aptitude–achievement discrepancies are determined. Table 18.4 lists scores obtained by three students on the California Achievement Test and an aptitude test, the Cognitive Abilities Test. Inspect the table. Are there any aptitude–achievement discrepancies? Are you having trouble answering?

Before going any further, let's try to make some sense out of the table. Provided are three types of scores for the California Achievement Test: grade equivalents, percentile ranks, and standard scores. It is more often the case than not that several scores are reported for each student. However, aptitude scores, like those in our table from the Cognitive Abilities Test, are typically reported in standard scores only. The first step in determining aptitude–achievement discrepancies is to be sure both sets of scores are on the same scale. If for some reason standard scores are not included on your score report, request a copy of the test manual and convert the scores you do have (e.g., either grade or age equivalents, or percentiles) to standard scores. Such conversions normally require using only the appropriate table or tables in the manual. Instructions on how to perform the necessary operations will be provided in the manual, and they likely will differ somewhat from test to test.

TABLE 18.4 Scores for Max, Betty, and Robert Reported in Standard Scores (SS), Percentile Ranks (%), and Grade Equivalents (GE)

	California Achievement Test																		Cognitive Abilities Test	
	Reading Recognition			Reading Comprehension			Reading Total			Math Concepts			Math Computation			Math Total				
Name	GE	%	SS*	GE	%	SS*	GE	%	SS*	GE	%	SS*	GE	%	SS*	GE	%	SS*	Verbal*	Quanti-tative*
Max	2.2	13	82	2.3	15	83	2.2	14	82	1.9	9	79	2.5	17	85	2.2	13	85	81	89
Betty	2.9	25	89	3.3	34	94	3.1	30	92	3.2	32	93	3.6	42	97	3.4	37	95	112	120
Robert	5.4	84	116	5.8	89	121	5.6	87	118	4.6	68	107	4.8	73	109	4.7	70	108	114	118
	$S_m = 3.5$			$S_m = 3.0$			$S_m = 3.3$			$S_m = 3.5$			$S_m = 2.5$			$S_m = 3.0$			$S_m = 3.5$	$S_m = 3.5$

*M = 100, SD = 15.

Note: S_m is in standard score units. The values provided are illustrative estimates only. Actual values will differ somewhat.

After you have converted all scores to standard scores, the remaining steps are very similar to those we followed in the section on band interpretation in Chapter 17. Once our scores are all on the same scale, determine the S_m for each subtest. This is important because each subtest will have a somewhat different S_m. Do not use the S_m for the whole test, as this would give an inaccurate or misleading interpretation in many cases. In Table 18.4 the S_m is listed under each subtest. While the S_m is usually not included in score reports, you can find the S_m for each subtest in the test manual. You could also compute the S_m for each subtest, using the formula from Chapter 17: $S_m = SD\sqrt{1-r}$. To do so, you would need to look up the reliability of each subtest in the manual.

After determining the S_m for each subtest, add and subtract $2S_m$ to each obtained score. This gives us the range of scores for each subtest within which we are 95% sure the student's true score lies. Remember, we are advising use of the more conservative 95% approach in determining aptitude–achievement discrepancies. Using Table 18.4, here are the data for Betty's reading and verbal IQ scores:

Name	Subtest	Obtained Score	S_m	95% Range
Betty	Verbal IQ	112	3.5	105–119
	Reading Recognition	89	3.5	82–96
	Reading Comprehension	94	3.0	88–100
	Reading Total	92	3.3	85.4–98.6

Now we are ready to complete our band interpretation and identify any aptitude–achievement discrepancies. Transfer your data to a table like the one used in Chapter 17, as shown in Table 18.5. Inspection of the bands in Table 18.5 reveals there are real differences between Betty's verbal aptitude or IQ and her reading achievement. Even though we have used the conservative 95% approach, there is no overlap between her verbal

TABLE 18.5   **Band Interpretation of Betty's Verbal IQ and Reading Scores (95% Level)**

	Subtests		
Verbal IQ	Reading Recognition	Reading Comprehension	Reading Total

aptitude and her reading achievement. We could state with considerable confidence that a difference this large indicates a real discrepancy.

Keep in mind, however, that when an aptitude–achievement discrepancy is found, the teacher's task is only beginning. Why the discrepancy exists must be determined, and then appropriate steps taken to remediate it.

This concludes our discussion of aptitude–achievement discrepancies. Recall why we began this discussion: to consider comparing actual student achievement to individual potentials, not just to one another or to a local or national norm. Students have differing levels of potential, and searching for aptitude–achievement discrepancies helps sensitize you to these differences. Instructional planning and standardized score interpretation are facilitated and aided when student achievement is considered in relation to potential, not simply in relation to norms. The beneficiaries of such an approach to standardized test interpretation are likely to be both you and your students.

Do I really have to consider test- and student-related factors in standardized test interpretation?

Yes! We have discussed several test-related and student-related factors in this chapter that can affect the usefulness of standardized tests (i.e., their validity, reliability, and accuracy). And, because the consideration of these factors may be omitted when highly visible high-stakes testing results are released, you may believe they are not important or not applicable to high-stakes tests! This is simply not true. All tests provide only estimates of performance, and all are affected by the test and by student-related factors like those we have covered in this chapter.

It may seem as though these factors are too many and too complex to deal with every time you have to interpret standardized test scores. However, with time and practice they become second nature—if you make yourself consider them in your initial attempts at standardized test interpretation. We will present dialogues in the next section that illustrate this point. They will provide examples of how these factors can be vital to sound educational decision making in what sometimes can become emotion-laden parent conferences, and they demonstrate how these factors can be integrated with marks or grades from teacher-made tests, performance-based assessments and background information to clarify your students' performance to parents. We consider this to be best practice, and an illustration of the assessment process that we described in Chapter 1, rather than just testing or just assessment.

INTERPRETING STANDARDIZED TESTS: PARENT–TEACHER CONFERENCES AND EDUCATIONAL DECISION MAKING

We have defined what standardized tests are; described their various uses; and discussed important considerations in administering standardized tests, the types of scores reported for standardized tests, and various test-related and student-related factors that can affect the reliability and accuracy of standardized tests. If it seems as though we have covered a lot of territory in this chapter, your perceptions are correct. In this section we will integrate and apply this information to actual, real-world situations. As with our previous examples, these will not be exaggerated or hypothetical situations. They have occurred with one or both authors, and at some point you may be confronted by similar situations. Our intent in including these examples is to provide you with information necessary to use test data effectively, and not to misuse it. Keep in mind our main point. Tests are tools that may be used correctly or incorrectly. The following examples show how they can work to your advantage as well as your disadvantage.

An Example: Pressure to Change an Educational Placement

(Miss Garza, the seventh-grade math teacher, is grading papers in her office when Jackie, one of the students in her Introductory Algebra class, walks in. Looking sad and forlorn, Jackie asks Miss Garza if she can speak with her.)

JACKIE: Miss Garza, can I transfer out of Introductory Algebra and get into Fundamentals of Math? *(Introductory Algebra is the standard-level mathematics class for seventh grade; Fundamentals of Math is a remedial math class designed for students with limited mathematical aptitude and achievement.)*

MISS GARZA: You want to switch out of Algebra and into Fundamentals! Why, Jackie?

JACKIE: Well, you know that I barely passed Algebra for the first six weeks, and I'm failing it for the second six weeks. I just don't get it. It's too hard for me. I'm not good in math.

MISS GARZA: Well, Jackie, why is that? You have always done well in math in the past, as your record indicates, and that's on both standardized achievement tests and your grades in math up to this point. Are you studying? It sure doesn't look it from your test performance, and as you know, you failed to turn in most of the assignments.

JACKIE: The reason I don't turn in the assignments is because they are too hard. That's my whole point. I just can't understand algebra. It's too hard for me. It's really making me depressed. If I can't get out of algebra I'm going to fail it. That means I'll not only be ineligible to play volleyball for the school, but I'll also be grounded until I bring my grades back up.

MISS GARZA: Jackie, how do you think transferring into Fundamentals is going to help you?

JACKIE: Well, I'll be able to play volleyball, I won't be grounded, and then I won't feel depressed.

MISS GARZA: Well, Jackie, this is an important decision, and I think your parents should be involved. This decision has a big potential impact on your future, not just in terms of sports and whether you're grounded but on whether you take the right courses needed in high school and to get into college. So I'm going to give your parents a call and set up a conference to review this with them.

JACKIE: Why do you have to do that?

MISS GARZA: This decision is one that you and I should not make until we consult with your parents and review your entire record.

JACKIE: Well, I thought teachers were supposed to be here to help students. If you get my parents involved in this, it's not going to help at all. They're probably going to say they want me to stay in Algebra because they don't care whether I pass or fail anyway. They just want something to complain about.

MISS GARZA: Well, that may or may not be the case, but the bottom line is that we're not making any decisions about transferring you out of Algebra until all the information is reviewed with your parents.

(Jackie grabs her books quickly and storms out of Miss Garza's room without saying goodbye. Miss Garza then contacts Mrs. Williams, Jackie's mother, and lets her know that she would like to get up a conference as soon as possible to review Jackie's math performance. A parent conference is arranged, and the next dialogue describes the interchange between Miss Garza and Mr. and Mrs. Williams.)

(After exchanging pleasantries, Miss Garza informs the parents about Jackie's request to switch from Algebra to Fundamentals.)

MR. WILLIAMS: Oh, why does she want to do that?

MRS. WILLIAMS: She's failing, isn't she?

MISS GARZA: Well, I'm afraid so. For the first six weeks she barely passed, and this six weeks her grades are well below passing. Unless she really gets to work, gets her homework completed, and prepares properly for the tests, she's not likely to pass for this six weeks.

MR. WILLIAMS: Well, let's go ahead and transfer her into Fundamentals, then. As you know, with the present school policy, if she fails she'll be ineligible to play volleyball.

MISS GARZA: I realize that, Mr. Williams. However, I'm concerned that if we take this step, we may send her the wrong message for the future.

MRS. WILLIAMS: What do you mean? You want her to fail? She just loves to play sports, and it would kill her to have to sit out because of ineligibility.

MISS GARZA: Well, Mr. and Mrs. Williams, you're Jackie's parents, and I think you should have the final say on this matter. My concern is that Jackie has worked herself into a corner and is trying to take the easy way out, rather than putting together an effective plan to solve the problem herself. If this is the way she solves her problem now, I'm concerned she'll continue to do the same in the future.

MR. WILLIAMS: Maybe you just don't like Jackie. Is that it?

MISS GARZA: Mr. Williams, if I didn't like Jackie and if I wasn't concerned for her future, I wouldn't have called you, I wouldn't have set up this conference, and I wouldn't have collected all the information I've gotten for us to review. My hope is that we can review her records, including her report cards and standardized test results, and make an informed decision that is most likely to benefit Jackie in the long run, rather than a hasty and impulsive one based on emotion rather than reason.

MRS. WILLIAMS: Are you saying Jackie has emotional problems?

MISS GARZA: No, Mrs. Williams. I'm not qualified to make a diagnosis or decision about emotional problems. However, I have taught middle school for a number of years, and situations like this come up frequently. Adolescence is a difficult time, for both students and their parents, and the patterns that we put in place early in adolescence tend to repeat themselves later on. My concern is that Jackie has more than ample ability to handle Introductory Algebra, but she currently is unwilling to put in the time and effort required. If she lacked the mathematical or intellectual aptitude, or if it were evident that other factors might be contributing to her academic difficulties, I would not have suggested a conference.

MR. WILLIAMS: Okay, let's see what information you have. I know what her report card says, but I don't know anything about the standardized test scores she brought home.

(Miss Garza then describes how standardized tests are constructed and what their scores are designed to represent. Subsequently, she reviews scores from the group IQ test that Jackie took in fifth grade, as well as the year-end standardized test scores from first through sixth grade. Miss Garza then indicates these scores on a piece of paper, as illustrated in Fig. 18.7).

		Percentile Scores		
Grade	Test	Math Computation	Concepts	Math Total
1	ITBS	91	81	86
2	ITBS	94	90	93
3	ITBS	85	83	84
4	ITBS	32	14	24
5	CogAT	—	—	88
5	ITBS	90	85	87
6	ITBS	88	82	85

FIGURE 18.7   Jackie Williams: test scores from first through sixth grades.

(After reviewing the data, Miss Garza points out that almost all the scores are at or above the 80th percentile. This, she says, indicates that Jackie's mathematical aptitude and achievement are well above average. Thus there is no evidence that suggests that she should be unable to handle the Introductory Algebra course because of a lack of aptitude or ability.)

MR. WILLIAMS: Wait a minute! What about her scores in fourth grade? They're not at the 80th percentile; they're way down at the 24th percentile. How do you explain that? If she has such great aptitude and achievement, how could she do so badly on that test?

MISS GARZA: I really don't know, Mr. Williams. However, there are any number of reasons why a student may do poorly on a standardized test administration. *(She then shares with the Williamses a copy of Fig. 18.8.)*

MISS GARZA: As you can see, interpreting standardized tests is not as simple as it might first appear. The reliability and validity of any score or group of scores depends on a number of factors related to the test and a variety of factors related to the student. Since the test was the fourth-grade version of the Iowa Test of Basic Skills, the same test that she took before and after fourth grade, we can pretty well rule out test-related factors as being contributory to her poor performance. If, on the other hand, for some reason the district had administered a completely different test, which may have had less direct applicability to the district's instructional objectives, that factor might explain the decline. I would conclude that some factor other than her ability was probably the cause.

MRS. WILLIAMS: Aren't these the tests that are administered over a three-day period in April?

MISS GARZA: Yes, that's right.

MR. WILLIAMS: *(Looking empathically at his wife)* Wasn't it in April of Jackie's fourth-grade year that your mother died?

MRS. WILLIAMS: Yes, it was. And you know how devastated Jackie was when her grandmother died. *(Looking at Miss Garza)* They were very close.

Test-related factors

1. Does the test have acceptable reliability and criterion-related validity evidence?
2. Does the test have content validity evidence for my instructional objectives?
3. Was the test's norm group composed of students similar to my class?
4. Were standardized procedures followed?

Student-related factors

1. Language and sociocultural
2. Age, sex, and development
3. Motivation
4. Emotional state on the test date
5. Disabilities
6. Aptitude

FIGURE 18.8 Factors to consider in interpreting standardized test scores.

MR. WILLIAMS: Miss Garza, do you think that could explain why she did so poorly that year?

MISS GARZA: Well, I can't be sure, but it sounds reasonable.

MRS. WILLIAMS: Yes, it does. What other information do you have?

(Miss Garza then reviews with the parents Jackie's grades in math from her previous report cards. These range from straight A's from first through fourth grade, through A's and B's in fifth and sixth grade. Jackie's first D in math was in her first six weeks of seventh-grade Algebra. Miss Garza points out that, with the exception of the D, these grades are completely consistent with what would be expected from an individual with standardized test scores at the 80th percentile.)

MISS GARZA: So, from all the evidence we have available, we have a consistent pattern except for the fourth-grade standardized test. So you see why I'm concerned that we may be allowing Jackie to avoid responsibility and take the easy way out by transferring into Fundamentals. More important, this will put her behind her peers and make it difficult for her to have the same advantages they have in high school and college.

MR. WILLIAMS: What! How can that be? How can what you take in seventh grade affect you in college?

MISS GARZA: Well, if Jackie goes into Fundamentals now, that means she'll take Introductory Algebra or Consumer Math next year. As a result, during her first year in high school she will be enrolled in one of the lower or remedial math classes, such as Beginning Algebra or Math in Life, rather than Algebra 1.

MRS. WILLIAMS: This is confusing. Are you telling me that ninth-grade Beginning Algebra is a remedial class rather than the beginning or entry level algebra class?

MISS GARZA: That's right, Mrs. Williams. Students who pass Introduction to Algebra in seventh grade will go on to Geometry in eighth grade, Algebra I in ninth grade, Geometry in tenth grade, Algebra II in eleventh grade, and either Trigonometry, Calculus, or one of the other options during twelfth grade.

MR. WILLIAMS: So if she gets off this track, she would end up basically being a year behind in math when she graduates.

MISS GARZA: That's right, Mr. Williams.

MR. AND MRS. WILLIAMS: *(Together)* We'll talk to her!

The situation described is not designed to provide a complete and detailed diagnosis or intervention plan for Jackie. Rather, it is to illustrate what has been presented in this and other chapters. Without examining the cumulative record of test scores, report cards, and the factors identified in Fig. 18.8, neither Miss Garza, the parents, nor Jackie would be likely to make an informed decision. An individual grade, such as Jackie's grade in Algebra, or a standardized test score, such as her test score in fourth grade, should not be the basis on which important educational decisions are made. Instead, defensible educational decisions require that all sources of data be considered, including standardized test scores, report cards, classroom grades, and relevant background information. This is your best safeguard to ensure an informed parent–teacher conference.

Obviously, Jackie will not be happy with the decision. However, Jackie is also a seventh grader who is unaware of the long-term ramifications of transferring into the remedial class at this point. In her mind the transfer would clearly be the best option, since it would lead to resolution of all her problems and would require very little in the way of commitment on her part. All too often, educators find themselves in the position of making decisions in order to please parents or students, without considering the appropriateness of all the data on which the decisions are based as well as the short- and long-term consequences of those decisions. In a case such as this, it is likely that if Jackie's parents sit down with her and discuss the short- and long-term consequences of their decision and provide the proper support, the outcome will be a positive one.

A Second Example: Pressure from the Opposite Direction

Mr. Buckley is your school's teacher for talented and gifted (TAG) students. Each year, it is his job to review the parent and teacher nominations of students for this program, which is designed for students who have significantly above average aptitude or achievement in language arts, math, or science. One of the main reasons Mr. Buckley was given this job was that he made a favorable impression on the principal and school board when they were interviewing for the position. He explained that his approach to making selections would be "data based." That is, he planned to review each child's cumulative folder and would be looking for not just an isolated test score, grade, or assignment that was well above average but a consistent pattern across standardized tests, grades, and work samples that indicated high aptitude and/or achievement. District administrators and the school board, well aware of the district's high socioeconomic status, felt quite comfortable with his approach, since it would give them something to fall back on when parents complained that their child was not selected for the TAG program. The dialogue that follows took place between Mr. Buckley and Mr. and Mrs. Miller after the Millers found out that their son, Bart, was not selected for the TAG program.

MR. MILLER: Well, Mr. Buckley, since we called this meeting, I may as well lay out our agenda. We were very, very disappointed that Bart was excluded from the TAG program. We are his parents, and we know quite well Bart's exceptional capacity, not just in math, but in language and science as well. He was a straight A student last year, you know! If that's not indicative of his appropriateness for your program, then I don't know what is. We were surprised when we heard he was excluded, and, quite frankly, we would like for you to show us exactly why he was excluded.

MRS. MILLER: By the way, Mr. Buckley, we may be new to this district, but we know how things like this are handled. We've heard from a lot of different people that in this district it's not what you know but who you know that counts. I want you to know in advance that we have already consulted with our attorney, who will be interested in what you have to say this afternoon. By the way, both my husband and I have a professional interest in what you have to tell us as well. I have a master's degree in education and my husband teaches at the university.

MR. BUCKLEY: I didn't know that, but it should facilitate our ability to communicate. I'm glad to have individuals like you to talk with, since usually I have to spend a great deal of time explaining things and providing background information. In fact, let me just give you a copy of the criteria I use in selecting students for the TAG program. (*Mr. Buckley then gives Mr. Miller a checklist that illustrates the many objective criteria that students must meet to qualify for TAG.*)

MR. MILLER: (*With a wide-eyed look of surprise on his face*) Um, uh ... um ... um ... Well, okay, let's get on with it.

MR. BUCKLEY: As you know, the TAG program is designed to provide an accelerated curriculum to students who have documented aptitude and/or achievement above the 95th percentile. For a measure of aptitude, we use the IQ or academic aptitude test scores that are in the student's file. For a measure of achievement, we use the standardized, norm-referenced tests that are administered every April, the state high-stakes tests that are used to meet No Child Left Behind accountability requirements, and, for a measure of day-to-day performance, we use grades and work samples from the classroom. Once nominations are received from teachers and parents, the process, although time-consuming, is straightforward. The student's file is reviewed, and if the student demonstrates consistent aptitude and achievement above the 95th percentile, with commensurate classroom grades and work performance, the student is selected for the TAG program. Since there is a lot of information in Bart's file, I have taken the liberty of summarizing his aptitude and achievement score performance and his grades in the various subjects. Here's what it looks like. (*Mr. Buckley then provides Mr. and Mrs. Miller with a copy of the summary sheet in Fig. 18.9.*)

MR. BUCKLEY: As you can see, Mr. and Mrs. Miller, except for the straight A's he received for the last two grading periods last year, Bart's achievement has been in the average to slightly above average range. Consequently, it would be inappropriate

			Percentiles		
Grade Level	Test	Math	Language	Science
1	SRA	60	52	49
2	SRA	68	46	53
3	SRA	58	59	63

	Grade Level	1st Six Weeks	2nd Six Weeks	3rd Six Weeks	4th Six Weeks	5th Six Weeks	6th Six Weeks
Math	1	B	C	B	B–	C	B
	2	A	B	B–	C	C	C
	3	C	C	B–	C	A	A
Language	1	A	B	B	B+	B	B–
	2	B	B+	A–	B	B–	C
	3	B	B-	C+	C	A	A
Science	1	A	B	C	D	D	C
	2	C	C	B–	C	C	C
	3	B–	B–	B	C	A	A

FIGURE 18.9   Bart Miller: test scores and six-week marks from first through third grades.

and maybe even damaging to Bart to enroll him in the TAG program, since essentially he would be competing with students who are more advanced in achievement and aptitude. While we can't be sure, this likely would affect his self-confidence, self-esteem, social life, and a variety of other factors in a way that could actually slow his academic progress.

(Mr. and Mrs. Miller look at each other, with pained expressions on their faces.)

MRS. MILLER: *(clearing her throat)* Well, I ... I see what you're saying, Mr. Buckley. But he got straight A's during those last two grading periods last year. I always thought that straight A's meant exceptional performance, and exceptional performance is what the TAG program is all about, isn't it?

MR. BUCKLEY: Yes, it is about exceptional performance, but it's also about exceptional demands being placed on students. That is, students in the TAG program are expected to do more work, complete it more quickly, and meet a higher level of expectations than students in the regular program. If there were any data that supported Bart's ability to profit from such a placement, I would have gone along with your recommendation.

MR. MILLER: Wait a minute—it wasn't just our recommendation. Miss Peterson, his teacher last year, recommended him, too!

MR. BUCKLEY: Yes, I realize that. I have the recommendation here. I also have 14 other recommendations from Miss Peterson for the TAG program. In addition, I've reviewed the grades given by Miss Peterson to all 25 students in her class during those two six-week periods last semester.

MR. MILLER: And . . . .

MR. BUCKLEY: Nearly every student in the class received straight A's during those last two six-week grading periods. These data make it difficult to know how Bart would perform under different circumstances such as the TAG program.

MRS. MILLER: I was hoping that starting to get A's like that meant Bart was a late bloomer.

MR. BUCKLEY: I understand. But, as you can see from the data, with the exception of these two grading periods, Bart's performance is in the average to only slightly above average range. Rather than subjecting him to an accelerated program at this time, I believe keeping him in the regular class might be more beneficial.

MR. MILLER: Thanks very much for your time and the reasonable approach you've taken. I guess I should have looked at the whole picture instead of just a part of it before getting angry.

How do you think these conferences would have ended if Miss Garza or Mr. Buckley had failed to consider all the data pertaining to aptitude, achievement, and classroom performance? Would Jackie have dropped out of Algebra? Would Bart have been placed in the TAG program? How would the parents, teachers, and students have felt about the decisions? How would each child's educational, psychological, and/or social development have been affected by these decisions?

Of course, there may be many and varied responses to these questions. We are not implying that the proper use of test data will *ensure* a child's success or ensure errorless decision making. But we are saying that the proper use of tests will increase the likelihood of a child's success. At some point you may be in situations similar to the ones in which Miss Garza and Mr. Buckley found themselves. If you collect and organize *all* your data, and consider the relevant test- and student-related factors that may affect them, you are more likely to help parents and students make decisions that are to their benefit in the long run rather than only in the short run.

Next we will study a few of the many types of individual student score reports that are available from publishers of standardized tests. Each type of report provides different information and will be better suited for some decisions than for others. Knowing what each type of report provides and how the data may be used will enable you to fine-tune your feedback to parents at conferences, since, as you will see, certain reports can provide a wealth of information about a student's achievement.

INTERPRETING STANDARDIZED TESTS: SCORE REPORTS FROM PUBLISHERS

Test publishers offer a variety of reports for test users, ranging from the small press-on labels illustrated in Fig. 18.10 containing only identification information and a single type of test score to comprehensive reports such as those illustrated in Figs. 18.11 and 18.12. The press-on labels are designed to be affixed to report cards or cumulative folders to provide a concise norm-referenced record of past or current achievement. Comprehensive individual score reports are designed to provide more specific, criterion-referenced information to help teachers diagnose a student's specific strengths and weaknesses. With proper interpretation they can also help students and parents understand how uniformly a child is achieving in the many subskill areas that are part of the child's curriculum.

Although individual score reports differ from publisher to publisher, they commonly report the following:

> Identification information (pupil's name, birth date, teacher's name, school, grade, test date).

NAME JACKSON, THOMAS		**Tests of Achievement and Proficiency**						Grade 09	Test Date 05/92
Scores Reported	Reading	Written Expression	Math	Core Total	Social Studies	Science	Info Process -ing	Com- posite	
NPR	53	59	70	61	53	25	50	56	

FIGURE 18.10 A press-on label for the Tests of Achievement and Proficiency (TAP).

Requested scores (raw scores, grade equivalents, percentile ranks, standard scores, and scores developed by the publisher are common for standardized norm-referenced tests; for high-stakes tests mastery information is usually provided).

The Riverside Publishing Company
a Houghton Mifflin company

Actual size 8.5" x 11"

The Student Criterion-Referenced Skills Analysis Report is available for *ITBS, TAP, ITED* and the achievement portion of combined achievement/ability testing.

This is an excellent report for individual student evaluation because it permits criterion-referenced interpretation of student performance.

A Plan 2 provides 2 copies of this report for each student. Scores reported are main score (GE or SS), NPR, and NS. Stanines can be suppressed.

B With custom reporting, up to any of four scores can be reported for each test, total, and composite, and as many additional copies as desired can be ordered by indicating your preferences on the OSS. This report may be obtained for any group of students by subpopulating.

C The number of students in the class who took each test is provided.

D For each test and skill category, the number of items, the number attempted, the number correct and percent correct for the student, the class and the nation are provided.

E Skill categories on which an individual student's performance is considerably above or below the student's overall score are flagged with a plus (+) or minus (–). These indicators of strengths or weaknesses can be suppressed by checking the appropriate box on the OSS.

F Performance on items measuring Thinking Skills is reported.

FIGURE 18.11 A criterion-referenced skill analysis for a fourth-grader for the Iowa Tests of Basic Skills (ITBS).

Source: Adapted from *Riverside 95* Catalog. Copyright © 1995. Reprinted with the permission of the publisher, The Riverside Publishing Company, 425 Spring Lake Drive, Itasca, IL 60143. All rights reserved.

A breakdown of the student's performance by subskill areas (see Fig. 18.11) or a bar or line graph profile to enable quick visual comparisons of performance across the many skill areas assessed (see Fig. 18.12).

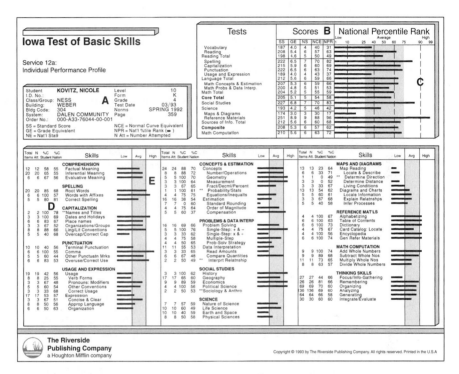

The Individual Performance Profile (Service 12a) and Group Performance Profile (Service 12b) are available for *ITBS, TAP, ITED* and the achievement portion of combined achievement/ability testing.

Teacher and parents are the primary users of the 12a Individual Profile. The 12b Group Profile is most often used by administrators and curriculum specialists. Both are useful to analyze relative strengths and weaknesses, and to develop strategies for groups or individuals.

A Two copies of the 12a are provided for each student and two copies of the 12b are provided for each class, building, and system with Plans 4 and 5. On the 12b Group Profile, a summary profile by class, by building, and by system is provided.

B Reports main score (GE or SS as selected in step 4 on the OSS, NPR, and NS (unless NS is suppressed in step 4) for both services. With custom reporting, up to any four scores can be selected for each test, total and composite, and as many additional copies as desired can be ordered by indicating your preference on the OSS.

C Local or national PRs and predicted achievements may be graphed on Service 12a using a bar graph. A 50% confidence interval band may be selected if NPRs are reported. Choose by checking the appropriate box on the OSS.

D For 12a, the number of items, number attempted, and the percent correct for the student and the nation for each skill category are reported. The 12b Group Profile reports average class, building, or system percent correct for each skill category in place of the student data.

E On 12a, a graph highlights the student's strengths and weaknesses by comparing the student to the national percent correct for each skill category. On the 12b Group Profile, the percentage of local students scoring Low, Average, and High for each skills calculated and reported. The local percentages can be compared with the national norm group percentage.

FIGURE 18.12 An individual performance profile for a fourth-grader for the Iowa Tests of Basic Skills (ITBS).

Source: Adapted from *Riverside 95* Catalog. Copyright © 1995. Reprinted with the permission of the publisher, The Riverside Publishing Company, 425 Spring Lake Drive, Itasca, IL 60143. All rights reserved.

As mentioned, these standardized test reports can help you understand a pupil's strengths and weaknesses, especially when coupled with teacher-made tests. In addition to having diagnostic utility, such reports also provide helpful comparative, placement, and even mastery information. After analyzing the kind of data press-on labels provide, we will study the data provided in two examples of these detailed reports.

The Press-On Label

Figure 18.10 illustrates the simplest type of publisher score report, the press-on label. Typically these labels are ordered by a district for each pupil and are attached to report cards and cumulative school folders. The label in Fig. 18.10 includes Thomas's national percentile rank, compared to the norm group of ninth graders, across the various subtests of the Tests of Achievement and Proficiency (TAP).

Any questions that Thomas or his parents have about his performance in the various subject areas compared to national standards should be fairly easy to answer based on this information. However, just to be sure, let's consider a couple of possible situations. Try responding to the following interpretive exercise before looking at the authors' responses. After you have responded, compare your reactions with the authors' responses. If you have difficulty determining why the authors respond the way they do, review the relevant sections of this text before proceeding further.

Interpretive Exercise

1. Parent: "Except for two of the subtests, this looks just like Thomas's score reports from previous years. Thomas has always done better in reading than writing until this test. We'd better get him a tutor in reading because this shows he's falling behind."

2. Thomas: "I was sick when I took the TAP, so the low score on Science must be because of that. I know all about science stuff and don't need to worry about it."

Authors' Responses

1. Although Thomas's percentile rank in Reading (53) is lower than his percentile rank in Written Expression (59), the difference is not large enough to be meaningful, due to the margin of error (i.e., standard error of measurement) that accompanies the test. This is an apparent rather than a real difference (see Chapter 17). It does not necessarily indicate a decline in reading achievement or the need for tutoring. Both scores indicate that Thomas is slightly above the national average in Reading and Written Expression.

2. Illness is a student-related factor that bears consideration in interpreting standardized test scores. However, if Thomas was ill, his performance most likely would have been affected across all the tests rather than limited to the Science subtest. Thus we would have expected low scores across the board, and scores lower than Thomas has obtained in the past. The latter is not the case, according to his parents, and only in Science is his percentile rank below 50.

The press-on label is helpful in comparing a pupil's performance to that of others nationwide, and in comparing performance from year to year. However, it tells us nothing about specific skills. That is, we can't tell whether Thomas has mastered geometric operations, or capitalization and punctuation, or any other specific skill. The detailed skills analysis reports illustrated in Figure 18.11 and Figure 18.12 will enable us to make such determinations, however.

A Criterion-Referenced Skills Analysis or Mastery Report

Figure 18.11 is the criterion-referenced skills analysis report for Linda Adams. You can see the skills report is quite detailed. You may have felt a twinge of fear or concern due to the detail included. This is a fairly typical reaction to these types of reports, since they are often very confusing and intimidating to the casual test user (i.e., most parents and students and some teachers). This is unfortunate because much information relevant to sound educational decision making may be gleaned from such reports if they are approached in a systematic way. Let's see how this can be done.

Read the text adjacent to the large letters A, B, C, D, E, and F in Fig. 18.11 to orient yourself to the information being reported. (Note: OSS, referred to in B and E, is an Optical Scan Summary request form) The ITBS and other standardized tests have become increasingly flexible in recent years in allowing districts to request breakdowns like those indicated on this report in order to better match and assess local educational goals and objectives. While not a substitute for teacher-made tests, such custom score reports from standardized tests can now provide information relevant to classroom and local decision making as well as provide a basis for normative, national, and longitudinal comparisons. Where norm-referenced tests like the ITBS have been adopted for use in state high-stakes testing programs, detailed mastery reports like this are common, with state standards listed instead of publisher-determined skill or subskill areas.

Similar reports are increasingly being sent home to parents. Unfortunately, adequate interpretive guidelines may not be provided to parents and students (or even teachers). As a result, reports like these are often misinterpreted, ignored, or devalued by educators and parents alike. Our position, however, is that these reports can be useful in fine-tuning parent–teacher conferences and in helping you make better classroom decisions. As you did with the press-on label in Fig. 18.10, use Fig. 18.11 to respond to the following interpretive exercise before looking at the authors' responses.

Interpretive Exercise

1. Parent: "I can't believe it! It says right here that this test is for tenth-grade level students. How can you people give a tenth-grade test to a fourth grader and expect valid results?"

2. Parent: "Mrs. Cooper, I'm appalled at Linda's performance on the ITBS. She's never had a grade below C and yet she got two zeros, a 38, and several 50s and 60s on this test. I don't want her to be promoted if she doesn't know her basics. What do you suggest I do with her? Should we retain her?"

Authors' Responses

1. Looking at the section identified by the large "A" we can see how a parent might come to this conclusion. The third line from the bottom on the right of the box reads

"LVL/Form: 10/K." If read quickly, this may look like a tenth-grade test! Standardized tests typically have multiple levels, versions, and forms. Often these are indicated by numbers rather than letters or other symbols. The level and the grade can be confusing to the casual reader. In this case we would explain to the parent that her fourth grader took Level 10 of the test, but that this is the correct level for a fourth grader, pointing out that it does indicate "Grade: 4" just above the level information.

2. We would suggest that you explain to Linda's parent that it is not unusual for even top students to show some irregularity in skill achievement when such a detailed analysis is done. Point out that 71 separate skills were assessed. Be careful, however, not to minimize the fact that Linda did miss all the items on the Maps and Diagrams: Explain Relationships subtest, and the Reference Materials: Dictionary subtest. Point out that this finding, while significant, needs to be viewed in a larger context; 77% of the items in the Maps and Diagrams skills cluster and 80% of the items in the Reference Materials skills cluster were answered correctly. This indicates that her weaknesses are specific and not indicative of a broad-based skills deficit. Further reassurance that Linda does not suffer from broad deficits may be provided by referring to the national percentiles included at the top of the report. These indicate that Linda obtained national percentile ranks of 69 for Maps and Diagrams and 62 for Reference Materials. A similar approach could be taken to address the 38% correct score Linda obtained on the Usage and Expression: Verb Forms subtest and to address the other subtest where she obtained less than 70% correct. This should help minimize the parent's concerns and answer the question of retention.

An Individual Performance Profile

Detailed criterion-referenced skills cluster and mastery reports that also include norm-referenced information like the one in Fig. 18.11 are becoming increasingly common. Sometimes they are offered with subtest profiles like the report illustrated in Fig. 18.12. This report, also for the ITBS, is called an individual performance profile. The bar graph profile of subtests and skill scores can ease interpretation, especially for those who tend to be intimidated by numbers.

However, this report also provides less comparative detail regarding the various skill areas than the report illustrated in Fig. 18.11. Omitted are the "Number Correct This Student" and "Class Average Percent Correct" columns from the report in Fig. 18.11. Whether the omission of this information is offset by the added interpretive ease of the profiles illustrated by Fig. 18.12 is a decision you may need to make.

Decisions about the types of standardized test reports to purchase from test publishers are sometimes based on teacher input. Since it is usually teachers who are called on to make these interpretations, this seems to make good sense! If you have the opportunity to provide such input, be sure to study carefully the various score reports available from standardized test publishers. Remember, the reports you select should help you, your students, and their parents understand test performance, not confuse or frustrate. Only by investing adequate time up front, before reports are ordered, will this goal be realized.

Regardless of the type of feedback provided to parents by your district, you will be asked to interpret test scores for parents and students. When these questions come up, refer to Fig. 18.8 to help you consider the test- and student-related factors that may influence standardized test scores, and use whatever individualized score reports are available to fine-tune and personalize your interpretation. Once you have done this a few times, you will join the ranks of informed, intelligent test users.

Other Publisher Reports and Services

The three examples of score reports covered are only the tip of the score report iceberg. A host of other reports are readily available, for example, alphabetical lists with scores for classes, grade levels, schools, and the district; similar lists ranked by performance and indicating each student's percentile rank or percentage of items passed for subskills and content areas; and histograms and line graphs that include the standard error of measurement for each subtest to facilitate band interpretation. In the highly competitive standardized test market, publishers have had to become increasingly creative and flexible in meeting the needs of educators at the classroom, school, and district levels. Where norm-referenced standardized tests are employed for NCLB accountability and other high-stakes testing purposes, even more types of reports are available. Requests for custom scoring services are given serious consideration and support by test publishers today. Frequently, larger districts will enjoy not only telephone contact and support from test publishers, but personal visits, training, and consultation as well.

Performance-Based and Portfolio Assessment and Standardized Tests

Many, if not all, standardized test publishers are either involved in the development of standardized performance and portfolio assessments or are at least closely watching developments around the country related to such assessments. With the advent of DVD and CD-ROM multimedia applications for the personal computer, the development of standardized simulations for classroom performance assessment appears imminent. Will this prove to be the death knell for traditional standardized testing? While some would hope so, we doubt that this will happen.

More likely, in our opinion, performance-based and portfolio assessment will join standardized and teacher-made tests in educational evaluation. Should standardized performance-based and portfolio assessments become mandatory, standardized test publishers will be among the first to begin offering standardized performance-based and portfolio assessment systems. Fortunately, when this becomes a reality, your background in standardized test theory and practice will enable you to assimilate their systems with little difficulty. Just as we now use both teacher-made and publisher-constructed tests, we envision that both teacher-made and publisher-constructed performance and portfolio assessment procedures and systems will be employed increasingly in the future.

Chapters 8 and 9 have given you a head start on this movement, from the teacher-made end. If performance-based and portfolio assessment becomes mandatory in your district, you have the tools needed to begin implementing such measures. This chapter on standardized test theory, application, and practice will need only minimal modification to be applicable to standardized performance-based and portfolio assessment procedures and systems. By mastering the content and procedures covered in this chapter, you are learning how to properly use standardized tests, which will be a benefit to you as soon as you begin to teach; in addition, you are preparing yourself to properly use standardized performance-based and portfolio assessments in the future.

In this chapter we have described various aspects of standardized test construction, administration, and interpretation. In the next chapter we will discuss the various types of standardized tests and describe examples of each type of standardized test.

SUMMARY

This chapter introduced you to the use, administration, and interpretation of standardized tests. Its major points are as follows:

1. Standardized tests are carefully constructed by specialists, and they carry specific and uniform, or standardized, administration and scoring procedures; they may be both norm-referenced and criterion-referenced.

2. Standardized tests may be achievement, aptitude, interest, or personality tests.

3. Standardized norm-referenced achievement tests facilitate comparisons across districts, states, and regions because of uniformity of content, administration, and scoring and a common basis for comparison—the nationally representative norms table.

4. Standardized achievement tests are frequently used to make comparisons over time or across students, schools, or districts. IDEA–04 and NCLB now require that all children with disabilities participate in annual assessments but encourage accommodations and alternate assessments that will compromise comparisons IDEA–04 and NCLB intended to enable for children with disabilities.

5. Although standardized achievement tests are not as useful to the classroom teacher as teacher-made tests, NCLB accountability requirements and high-stakes testing have made it necessary for teachers to administer and interpret them. And, with participation of children with disabilities in annual assessments now required, classroom teachers may also have to interpret standardized test results to parents of children with disabilities.

6. When administering standardized tests, all administrators should uniformly follow instructions in order to minimize error in test administration.

7. Since standardized tests have become requirements under NCLB and state high-stakes testing programs, incidents of teachers and administrators violating standardized test administration procedures have increased.

8. Although grade-equivalent scores are commonly used, they have several limitations, including the following:
    a. They tend to be misinterpreted as indicative of skill levels, rather than relative degrees of performance.
    b. Equal differences in units do not reflect equal changes in achievement.
    c. They have limited applicability except where subjects are taught across all grade levels.
    d. They tend to be seen as standards rather than norms.
    e. Comparability across subjects is difficult.

9. Age equivalents are much less commonly used and suffer from limitations similar to those of grade equivalents.

10. Percentile scores compare a student's performance with that of his or her peers. Although percentiles are superior to grade and age equivalents, they suffer from the following two disadvantages:
    a. They are often confused with percentage correct.
    b. Equal differences in units do not reflect equal changes in achievement.

11. Standard scores also compare a student's performance with that of his or her peers. In addition, equal differences in units do reflect equal differences in achievement. Standard scores are superior to percentile ranks for test interpretation, but they tend to be not well understood by many educators and by much of the general public.

12. Percentiles are recommended for interpreting standardized test results to the public. However, their limitations must be kept in mind.

13. Both test-related and student-related factors should be considered in interpreting standardized test results.

14. Test-related factors require the teacher to assess the test's score reliability and validity evidence, the appropriateness of the norm group, and the extent to which standardized procedures were adhered.

15. When a class is considerably different in composition from the norm group, the appropriateness of comparison to the norm group becomes questionable. In such situations specialized norms tables now available from some test publishers may be used, or local norms may be established.

16. Differences in student-related factors require the teacher to consider the following in interpreting standardized test scores: the child's language proficiency and cultural background; age, gender, and development; motivation; emotional state on the test day; disabilities; and aptitude.

17. Students whose obtained achievement scores are lower than their obtained academic aptitude scores are said to be below expectancy.

18. Students whose obtained achievement scores are higher than their obtained academic aptitude scores are said to be above expectancy.

19. Students whose obtained achievement and academic aptitude scores are equivalent are said to be achieving at expectancy.

20. Students whose obtained achievement scores show "real" differences when compared with their obtained academic aptitude scores have aptitude–achievement discrepancies. Band interpretation using 95% levels is recommended for such comparisons.

21. Interpreting standardized test scores by comparing students to their individual potential or aptitude can lead to more effective educational decision making than comparing students to the norms.

22. Under IDEA–04, the previous requirement that a student must demonstrate a significant discrepancy between aptitude and achievement to be eligible for special education under the Specific Learning Disability category has been made optional.

23. Consider the various test- and student-related factors that can affect performance on standardized tests, along with other available information (e.g., grades, cumulative folders), in consulting with parents about important educational decisions. Considering all sources of data before making a decision decreases the likelihood that test results will be over- or underinterpreted.

24. Standardized test publishers provide a wide variety of score reports. Depending on district policy, students and parents may receive reports that are fairly straightforward or are complex and require careful scrutiny. In any case, the classroom teacher who is skilled in their interpretation will be the one most likely to use these reports in the best interests of the students.

25. As the push for performance and portfolio assessment gains momentum, standardized test publishers will likely begin marketing standardized performance and portfolio assessment systems. The teacher skilled in standardized test theory, application, and interpretation will have little difficulty incorporating performance and portfolio assessment tools into the decision-making process.

FOR PRACTICE

1. "Our principal is so insensitive," said Donna. "He knows Billy Brown has trouble reading, but he won't let me help him read the test questions when we give the California Achievement Test next week." Should the principal allow Donna to read the questions to Billy? Support your decision with arguments based on points made in this chapter.

2. "I'm so glad Congress passed NCLB," beamed Mr. A. D. Vocate. "Now we'll finally be able to see just how well the students in each of our special ed classes is learning because they will all have to take the annual standardized achievement tests, just like the regular ed kids do, although accommodations for their disabilities will be made." Will NCLB enable Mr. Vocate and others to compare scores for special ed kids with each other and regular ed kids. Why, or why not?

3. "Blanketiblank Public Schools Again Score Below National Average on CTBS—Mayor Calls for Freeze on Teacher Pay Until Scores Reach National Average." As a teacher in the Blanketiblank Public Schools, how would you respond to such a newspaper headline? In your response, critique the assumption underlying the headline and suggest an alternative way to measure student progress.

*4. Consider the following data obtained from the Wechsler Intelligence Scale for Children–IV (WISC–IV) and the Stanford Achievement Test at the end of fourth grade.

Student	Verbal IQ	Reading Vocabulary		Reading Comprehension	
		GE	SS	GE	SS
Bonnie	107	5.9	113	6.5	119
Chris	94	4.5	93	4.0	88
Jack	125	5.8	112	5.6	110
	$S_m = 3.0$	$S_m = 2.5$		$S_m = 3.5$	
	M = 100, SD = 15				

After inspecting the data, answer the following questions:

a. Is each student's achievement about what we would expect? If not, who is not achieving at expectancy?

b. Are there any aptitude–achievement discrepancies?

5. Check your work in Question 4 by constructing a table like Fig. 17.7 and subject the scores to band interpretation. Now answer the same questions again.

6. Mr. Simpson "simply can't understand" why his third-grade son can't skip fourth grade. "After all," he says, "your own test scores show he's reading and doing math at a fifth-grade level." Tactfully explain to Mr. Simpson why his son may not really be ready for fifth-grade reading and math.

7. Mr. Gregg, fresh out of college (and having taken a tests and measurements course), is constantly extolling the virtues of standard scores over other types of converted scores. Parent conferences are coming up and he is confident that the parents he meets with will "finally get a clear and precise interpretation of their children's test results" because he will interpret the tests using standard scores, not grade or age equivalents or percentiles. As a "seasoned veteran," what advice would you give to Mr. Gregg?

*8. Thomas, a fourth grader in your class, obtained the following raw scores on the CTBS. Using Table 18.2, convert his raw scores to Standard Scores.

Subtest	Raw Scores
Reading	12
Vocabulary	14
Language	7
Language Mechanics	4
Mathematics	35
Mathematics Computation	18
Science	20
Social Studies	6
Spelling	5
Word Analysis	5

*The answers for questions 4 and 8 appear in Appendix F.

CHAPTER 19

TYPES OF STANDARDIZED TESTS

IN THIS CHAPTER we will describe various types of standardized, typically norm-referenced, tests classroom teachers may come into contact with. We will consider achievement test survey batteries, single-subject achievement tests, and diagnostic tests. Next we will consider individual and group tests of academic aptitude. Finally, we will describe various personality tests that sometimes appear in student records. Our intention is *not* to evaluate or recommend any of these tests. Each of the tests we describe is simply an "accepted" test with satisfactory psychometric (mental measurement) properties. At the same time, we do not mean to imply that the tests we have selected are the only tests with acceptable psychometric properties. The question is how appropriate is a test for you, your school, or your district. The answer to that question depends on a variety of factors. Several of the test-related factors were discussed in Chapter 18. With the rapid spread of the high-stakes testing phenomenon to all 50 states, and the passage of the No Child Left Behind Act (NCLB) (described in detail in Chapter 2), teachers will also be certain to be exposed to their state's high-stakes test, which may be either norm-referenced or criterion-referenced. If you are interested in learning more about what these specific tests are like, most state education agencies now carry extensive information about their state's high-stakes tests on their Web pages.

STANDARDIZED ACHIEVEMENT TESTS

The first standardized tests came into existence around 1900. These tests were tests of a single achievement area, such as spelling. Single-subject achievement tests are still used today, although they are largely confined to the secondary grades.

A variation of the single-subject achievement test is the diagnostic achievement test. However, use of the diagnostic test is normally limited to those elementary and secondary school pupils who are experiencing academic difficulty. These tests are administered to "diagnose" or indicate the specific cause or causes of a problem (e.g., faulty letter identification) in some general academic area (e.g., reading recognition). Seldom are such tests administered to an entire class or grade. Students are typically selected for diagnostic testing after a single-subject test or an achievement battery has indicated a problem in some general academic area.

The most frequently used type of achievement test is the achievement test battery, or survey battery. Such batteries are widely used, often beginning in the first grade and administered each year thereafter. There are several reasons survey batteries are more popular than single-subject achievement tests. The major advantages of survey batteries over single-subject achievement tests are as follows:

1. Each subtest is coordinated with every other subtest, resulting in common administration and scoring procedures, common format, and minimal redundancy.

2. Batteries are less expensive and less time consuming to administer than several single-subject tests.

3. Each subtest is normed on the same sample (if it's a norm-referenced standardized test, of course!), making comparisons across subtests, both within and between individuals, easier and more valid.

This last point is probably the major reason batteries have had widespread use. Recall that we often use standardized tests to compare students, classes, or schools. It takes less time to make these comparisons when a single norm group is involved than when several are involved. Furthermore, the likelihood of clerical errors is minimized when single, comprehensive score reports from a battery are used to make comparisons, as opposed to several single-subject score reports.

Of course, batteries have their disadvantages, too:

1. The correspondence (content validity) of various subtests in the battery may not be uniformly high.

2. The battery, which emphasizes breadth of coverage, may not sample achievement areas in as much depth as a single-subject achievement test.

Nonetheless, many districts conclude that these limitations are offset by the advantages of an achievement battery. Indeed, as we mentioned in Chapter 2 several states have utilized standardized norm-referenced tests for their high-stakes testing programs and to meet NCLB accountability requirements. Next we will briefly describe some of the more popular achievement test batteries.

Achievement Test Batteries, or Survey Batteries

California Achievement Test, Fifth Edition (CAT/5) The CAT/5 battery is published by CTB/McGraw-Hill and is appropriate for students in grades K–12. It has 13 levels appropriate for various grades, and two alternate forms of the test are available. Scores are provided for Reading (vocabulary and comprehension); Language (mechanics, usage, structure, and spelling); and Mathematics (computation, concepts, and problems).

Iowa Tests of Basic Skills (ITBS), Form A The ITBS battery is published by the Riverside Publishing Company. It is appropriate for students in grades K–8. The ITBS was normed on the same sample as the Cognitive Abilities Test (CogAT), an academic aptitude test. Determination of aptitude–achievement discrepancies is facilitated when these two tests are used. Scores are provided for Listening; Word Analysis; Vocabulary; Reading; Comprehension; Language (spelling, capitalization, punctuation, and usage); Visual and Reference Materials; Mathematics (concepts, problem solving, computation); Social Studies; Science; Writing and Listening Supplements; and Basic and Total Battery.

Metropolitan Achievement Tests, Eighth Edition (MAT) Harcourt Inc. publishes the MAT battery, which is appropriate for students in grades K–12. Thirteen levels span the various grades, and two alternate forms are available. The Primer level includes scores for Listening for Sounds, Language, and Mathematics. The next level, Primary, includes scores for Sounds, Reading Vocabulary and Reading Comprehension, Mathematics Computation, and Mathematics Concepts, Language Spelling, Science and Social Studies. The remaining levels eliminate the Sounds subtest. The MAT-8 was normed with the Otis-Lennon School Abilities Test, 7th Edition, to facilitate identification of aptitude-achievement discrepancies.

SRA Achievement Series (SRA) The SRA battery is published by Science Research Associates and is appropriate for students in grades 1–9. Five levels cover the grade range, and no alternate forms are available. The two lowest levels include subtests for Reading (word–picture association, sentence–picture association, comprehension, vocabulary); Mathematics (concepts and computation); and Language Arts (alphabetization, capitalization, punctuation, spelling, and usage). The three highest levels include subtests for Reading (comprehension, vocabulary, total); Language Arts (usage, spelling, total); Mathematics (concepts, computation, total); Social Studies; Science; and Uses of Sources.

Stanford Achievement Test Series, Ninth Edition (SAT-9) Like the MAT, the SAT-9 battery is published by Harcourt Inc. It is appropriate for grades K through 13. Thirteen levels are provided for the various grades and two alternate forms are available. Subtests for Reading, Mathematics, Language Arts, Spelling, Study Skills, Listening, Science, and Social Science are available, with open-ended writing tests available for grades 3–13. The SAT-9 was normed with the Otis–Lennon School Abilities Test, Seventh Edition, to facilitate aptitude–achievement discrepancies.

Terra-Nova (CTBS) Multiple Assessments Editions Published by CTB/ McGraw-Hill, the Terra-Nova test was derived from the Comprehensive Tests of Basic Skills (CTBS). It is approapriate for grades K–12 and has 12 levels and two alternate forms. The Multiple Assessments feature allows for assesments of various combinations of Reading/Language Arts, Mathematics, Science, Social Studies, Language Mechanics, Spelling, and Mathematics Computation.

Tests of Achievement and Proficiency (TAP), Forms K, L and M The TAP is published by Riverside Publishing Company and is appropriate for students in grades 9–12. The TAP is designed to allow for continuity with the ITBS, and it has also been normed concurrently with the Cognitive Abilities Test (CogAT), an academic aptitude test. Thus identification of aptitude–achievement discrepancies is facilitated when these two tests are used. Scores are provided for Reading Comprehension, Mathematics, Written Expression, Using Sources of Information, Social Studies, and Science. Listening and Writing supplements are also available.

Single-Subject Achievement Tests

Gates–MacGinitie Reading Tests, Fourth Edition The Gates–MacGinitie Reading test is published by Riverside Publishing Company. It is appropriate for grades

K–12 and uses nine levels to cover these grades. Two alternate forms, S and T, are available for the six highest levels. The upper seven levels include subtests measuring Vocabulary and Comprehension. The formats vary across the levels, with stimuli ranging from pictorial at the lower levels to increasingly complex prose at the higher levels. Items measure recognition rather than recall.

Modern Math Understanding Test (MMUT) The MMUT test is published by Science Research Associates and is designed for grades 1–9. The three areas of mathematics measured at each level are Foundations, Operations and Geometry, and Measurement. Each of these areas is broken down further into the following: knowledge and computation, elementary understanding, problem solving and application, and structure and generalization.

Nelson–Denny Reading Test, Forms G and H The Nelson–Denny Reading tests are designed for high school, college, and adult populations and are published by Riverside Publishing. Forms G and H are appropriate for grades 9–16 and adults. A CD-ROM version of Forms G and H is appropriate for grades 9–14 and adults. Each form includes a Vocabulary and a Reading Comprehension subtest. Norms are available for high school and for two year and four year colleges. Special norms also are available for extended-time administrations and for law enforcement academies.

Diagnostic Achievement Tests

California Diagnostic Mathematics Test (CDMT) The CDMT is published by Harcourt Inc. and is designed for grades 1–12. The test can be completed on paper or on-line. Six levels span the grade range with scores available for Number Concepts, Computation, and Applications at all six levels and Life Skills at the highest level only.

Gates–McKillop-Horowitz Reading Diagnostic Test Published by Teachers College Press, the Gates–McKillop-Horowitz test is designed for use at all grade levels. Two forms of the test are available. It is administered individually, and the pupil responds orally. Scores are provided for Oral Reading, Word Perception, Phrase Perception, Blending Word Parts, Giving Letter Sounds, Naming Letters, Recognizing Visual Forms of Sounds of Nonsense Words, Initial Letters, Final Letters, Vowels, Auditory Blending, Spelling, Oral Vocabulary, Syllabication, and Auditory Discrimination. Like the Diagnostic Tests and Self-Helps in Arithmetic, cross-referencing subtests helps pinpoint weaknesses. However, no estimate of reading comprehension is available, and all scores depend on the pupil's oral reading level. At times a pupil's oral reading achievement may be significantly different from his or her silent reading achievement.

California Diagnostic Reading Test (CDRT) The CDRT is published by Harcourt Inc. and is designed for grades 1–12. Unlike the Gates–McKillop, this test can be group administered, with pupils responding on paper or on-line. Six levels are provided. The lower three levels provide scores for Word Analysis, Vocabulary, and Comprehension, with the higher levels adding an Applications subtest.

STANDARDIZED ACADEMIC APTITUDE TESTS

Thus far in this chapter we have discussed tests that are used to measure past achievement. The intent of these tests is to identify what students have learned. At times, however, we are also interested in measuring an individual's potential for learning or an individual's academic aptitude. Such information can be useful in making selection and placement decisions and to determine whether students are achieving up to their potential, that is, to indicate aptitude–achievement discrepancies. In short, aptitude tests are used to predict *future* learning. Achievement tests are used to measure *past* learning.

The History of Academic Aptitude Testing

The development of tests to predict school achievement began in France at the beginning of the 20th century. France had embarked on a program of compulsory education, and the minister of public instruction realized that not all French children had the cognitive or mental potential to be able to benefit from instruction in regular classes. "Special" classes were to be established for the instruction of such children. Admission to these classes was to be dependent on the results of a medical and psychological evaluation. However, at the time no tests were available that could be used to identify children who had the cognitive or mental potential to benefit from instruction in regular classes. In 1905 Alfred Binet and his assistant, Theo Simon, were commissioned to develop such a test. The aim of their test was to measure a trait that would predict school achievement.

They revised their test in 1908 and again in 1911. The concept of mental age (as opposed to chronological age) as an index of mental development was introduced with the first revision and refined with the second. Since Binet was commissioned to develop a test that would predict school achievement, he was concerned with the predictive validity of his scale and repeatedly studied its validity for use in the public schools.

By the time of his death in 1911, Binet's scale was widely used and heralded as an "intelligence" test. English translations of the 1908 and 1911 revisions were made, and in 1916 a Stanford University psychologist, Louis Terman, standardized the Binet test on American children and adults. That version of the test became known as the Stanford–Binet Intelligence Scale or IQ test, and it was revised and/or restandardized again in 1937, 1960, 1972, 1985, and 2003. What had begun as a test designed to predict *school achievement* evolved into a test of intelligence.

Since Binet's seminal work, several other intelligence or IQ tests have been developed. Some, like the Stanford–Binet, are designed to be administered individually (e.g., Wechsler Intelligence Scale for Children–IV, Wechsler Adult Intelligence Scale–III, Kaufman Assessment Battery for Children–II, Slosson Intelligence Test); others are designed for group administration (e.g., Cognitive Abilities Test, Otis–Lennon Mental Ability Test, Kuhlmann–Anderson Intelligence Tests). Although each of these tests is different from the Binet, each also has similarities and correlates strongly with the Binet. Recall that tests that correlate strongly measure much the same thing. Since Binet's test predicts school achievement, it is no surprise that both individually and group-administered intelligence tests also predict school achievement. In short, a test developed to predict school achievement has come to be considered as a test of intelligence.

But do we know that the tests *actually* measure intelligence? We *do* know they predict academic achievement. To answer the question, we first need to define intelligence and then determine whether people who score high on intelligence tests possess more of these elements than people who score low on intelligence tests. Unfortunately, we can't agree on what the "stuff" of intelligence is. For example, one of the recent conceptions of intelligence (Sternberg, 1989) is that it can be defined by its underlying components and altered through instruction. Thus traits previously thought inherited and unalterable could be taught. Theorists have been hypothesizing and arguing for decades about what intelligence is, and the debate will likely go on for decades more. Consequently, since we do not agree on what intelligence is, we cannot be sure we are measuring it. Discussions of definitions and theories of intelligence may be found in most graduate level measurement tests. For our purposes, we will conclude that the tests mentioned here, and others like them, do predict school achievement. We are not at all sure, however, that they are measuring intelligence. Since we are not sure they are measuring intelligence, we are reluctant to call them intelligence tests. We can use such tests intelligently, though, by restricting their application to what we know they can do— predict school achievement. Before we review some of the more common of these tests, we will consider two important aspects of the scores such tests yield, namely, their stability and other characteristics they predict.

Stability of IQ Scores

In general, IQ scores tend to increase in stability with increases in age. In other words, IQ scores for younger children are less reliable or more subject to error than are IQ scores for older children and adults. Furthermore, test–retest reliabilities tend to decline as the time interval between test and retest increases. Table 19.1 illustrates these relationships.

As Table 19.1 indicates, little is gained in terms of predicting later performance by administering IQ tests to children less than four years of age. Once children reach the age of about six, their IQ scores tend to remain fairly stable. An individual's obtained score can still change beyond this age, but changes are likely to be small and not greatly affect the individual's overall percentile rank in the general population.

What Do IQ Tests Predict?

Academic Achievement We have said that IQ tests, or tests of academic aptitude, predict school achievement. But just how well they do predict school achievement

TABLE 19.1 Approximate Correlations between Individual IQ Tests and Retests

Age at First Test	Age at Second Test	Approximate Correlation
2	14	.20
4	14	.55
6	14	.70
8	14	.85
10	14	.90

depends on what we use as an outcome measure. Correlations between IQ tests and standardized achievement tests generally range from .70 to .90. However, correlations between school IQ tests and grades generally range from .50 to .60. Standardized achievement tests tend to be carefully constructed and measure outcomes similar to those measured by academic aptitude tests. By keeping this in mind and realizing that grades tend to be considerably more subjective, it is no surprise that the correlation with grades is somewhat lower. As might be expected, IQ scores also correlate highly with the highest level of schooling completed.

Job Success   In any criterion-related validity study, the size of the obtained correlation will depend on the particular outcome measure or criterion measure employed. Gottfredson (1997) reported that when completion of a training program is considered as a criterion for job success, moderately strong correlations are found, especially if the job requires complex skills (i.e., r = .35 to .45). Several studies also have reported weaker to moderate correlations with self-help skills, independent living skills, driving ability, academic success, vocational skills, and employment status (Kubiszyn et al., 2000). In short, the predictive validity evidence for IQ test results is stronger for academic achievement than for job success. Part of the reason for this may be the often subjective nature of the criteria used to rate job success (e.g., supervisor's ratings). Just as subjectivity in teacher-assigned grades may lead to a lower correlation between IQ and school performance, subjectivity in determining job success may be responsible for the lower correlation between ratings of job success and IQ test scores.

Emotional Adjustment   No firm conclusion may be drawn about the relationship between IQ and emotional adjustment. At the beginning of the 20th century, it was commonly held that very high-IQ individuals tended to have more severe emotional and adjustment problems than did individuals with more "normal" IQs. However, a long-term follow-up (over several decades) of high-IQ individuals begun by Terman in 1921 did much to dispel this myth. Current thinking suggests that high-IQ individuals have emotional difficulties about as frequently as low- to moderate-IQ individuals.

Happiness   Perhaps in part because we do not have a suitable definition or measure of happiness, we do not really know the extent to which IQ scores may predict happiness. Since they do predict school achievement and to a lesser extent job success, we might infer there would be a positive correlation between IQ and happiness. However, such a position is not supported by research data and assumes that school and job success are themselves correlated with happiness.

In summary, the characteristic that IQ tests predict most strongly is school achievement. Recall that the first IQ test was developed to predict school achievement. Ninety years later, in spite of repeated attempts to modify and improve on the IQ test, we find that it still does best just what it was designed to do. Although it has been used in a variety of ways, the IQ test remains, first and foremost, a good predictor of school achievement. Whatever else it measures or predicts, it does so far less effectively and efficiently. Our recommendation is to recognize IQ tests for what they are—predictors of school achievement—and avoid the tendency to make them into something they are not.

In the next section we will briefly describe some of the commonly used group and individually administered IQ tests.

Individually Administered Academic Aptitude Tests

Stanford–Binet Intelligence Scale, Fifth Edition The Stanford–Binet test, published by Houghton Mifflin, is appropriate for ages 2 through adult. As mentioned, it was originally developed in France in 1905 and revised for American use in 1916. The Fifth Edition appeared in 2003 and represents a significant revision and renorming effort. It is a substantial improvement over previous editions. Stimuli are now more contemporary, and the test now has 15 subtests organized into five areas: Fluid Reasoning, Knowledge, Quantitative Reasoning, Visual–Spatial Processing, and Working Memory, which provides a more complete assessment of individual intelligence. Subtest scores are standard scores with a mean of 10 and a standard deviation of 3, and overall IQ scores have means of 100 and standard deviations of 15. The Fifth Edition has considerably more utility than the previous version, but it may take longer to administer than the Wechsler scales and other individually administered IQ tests.

Wechsler Intelligence Scale for Children–IV (WISC–IV) The WISC–IV test is published by the Psychological Corporation. It is appropriate for students between 6 and 16 years of age. Along with its companion tests, the Wechsler Preschool and Primary Scale of Intelligence–Revised (WPPSI–III), appropriate for ages 2–7, and the Wechsler Adult Intelligence Scale–III (WAIS–III), appropriate for ages 16–adult, the Wechsler scales are the most popular individually administered IQ tests.

The WISC–IV, published in 2003, contains a number of changes from previous versions of the WISC. While the WISC–III used a dual factor IQ that was composed of four statistically validated index scores, the WISC–IV changed its factor structure by doing away with the dual factor IQ and implementing a full scale IQ model based on four statistically validated indices. The WISC–IV is now more closely aligned with a recent advancement in intellectual theory known as the Cattell-Horn Caroll (CHC) theory. The WISC–IV eliminated three WISC–III subtests: object assembly, mazes, and picture arrangement. In addition, the WISC–IV added several new subtests, including word reasoning, matrix reasoning, picture concepts, letter–number sequencing, and cancellation. The subtests that make up the four factors are listed below.

Verbal Comprehension

Similarities
Verbal Comprehension
Comprehension
Information (optional)
Word Reasoning (optional)

Perceptual Reasoning

Block Design
Picture Concepts
Matrix Reasoning
Picture Completion (optional)

Working Memory

Digit Span
Letter–Number Sequencing
Arithmetic (optional)

Processing Speed

Coding
Symbol Search
Cancellation (optional)

Group Administered Academic Aptitude Tests

Cognitive Abilities Tests (CogAT), Form 6   The CogAT test is published by Riverside Publishing Company and has two forms. Levels K, 1, and 2 are appropriate for kindergarten through second grade and Levels A–H are appropriate for grades 3–12. It includes a nonreading test at the lowest two levels and eight multilevel tests that provide Verbal, Quantitative, and Nonverbal scores. This test was normed simultaneously with the Iowa Tests of Basic Skills and Tests of Achievement and Proficiency, facilitating aptitude–achievement comparisons. The nonreading test has four subtests: Oral Vocabulary, Relational Concepts, Multimental, and Quantitative. The Verbal test includes Vocabulary, Sentence Completion, Verbal Classification, and Verbal Analogies subtests. The Quantitative test measures Quantitative Comparisons, Number Series, and Equation Building. The Nonverbal subtests eliminate reliance on reading ability entirely. They consist of items to measure Figure Analogies, Figure Classification, and Figure Synthesis.

Otis–Lennon School Ability Tests, Seventh Edition (OLSAT-7)   The OLSAT-7 is published by Harcourt Inc. and is appropriate for grades K–12, with seven grade-based levels of materials available. Earlier versions of this test were called the Otis Quick-Scoring Mental Ability Test and the Otis–Lennon Mental Ability Test. The test requires 60 to 75 minutes to administer. The OLSAT-7 measures Verbal Comprehension and Verbal Reasoning, Pictorial Reasoning, Figural Reasoning, and Quantitative Reasoning and yields scores for Verbal, Nonverbal, and Total performance. The OLSAT-7 was normed with the Metropolitan Achievement Test, Eighth Edition, and the Stanford Achievement Test, Ninth Edition, to facilitate identification of aptitude–achievement discrepancies.

Test of Cognitive Skills, Second Edition (TCS/2)   Published by CTB/McGraw-Hill, the TCS/2 is appropriate for grades 2–12. Six levels of the test cover the grade range. A related test, the Primary Test of Cognitive Skills (PTCS), is available for grades 1 and 2. The TCS/2 has four subtests at each level: Sequences, Analogies, Memory and Verbal Reasoning.

STANDARDIZED PERSONALITY ASSESSMENT INSTRUMENTS

Of the types of standardized tests with which the classroom teacher comes in contact, personality tests are probably the least used and the least understood. Perhaps this is the way it should be, since teachers are mainly concerned with academic development and are not trained in personality development or assessment. Nonetheless, teachers cannot help but have some impact on and ideas about personality development, and results from such tests do show up in pupil folders. Interpretation of such tests is beyond the scope of this text and the training of classroom teachers. Thus we will limit ourselves to briefly considering what personality is, discussing the two major approaches to personality assessment, and briefly describing several examples of personality tests.

What Is Personality?

As in the case of intelligence, no one has arrived yet at a definitive, universally accepted definition of personality. We do know that people tend to behave in certain relatively fixed ways across various situations. One such pattern of typical and expected behavior may be considered to be a personality *trait*. For example, individuals who tend to become nervous or anxious when speaking in front of groups tend to become anxious in any public speaking situation, large or small. A personality trait for such individuals would be anxiety. All of an individual's traits or characteristics, taken together, make up an individual's personality. Thus perhaps we can define personality as the typical or characteristic ways individuals behave. This is a deceptively simple definition, however. Allport and Odbert (1936) estimated that the number of typical ways individuals behave is in the *thousands*. If we accept this definition, then, we must admit that the task of measuring these traits would be an enormous one. Nevertheless, the task has been approached with considerable success over the last 80 years. Essentially, the efforts to measure personality have moved in two directions: objective personality assessment and projective personality assessment. We will describe each of these and then some examples of each type of assessment instrument.

Objective Personality Assessment Objective personality assessment usually employs self-report questionnaires. Items are often based on questions used in psychiatric interviews. The first instrument of this type appeared during World War I. Since then, they have gained considerable popularity among psychologists, the military, and industry. This approach provides a lengthy list of statements, adjectives, or questions to which examinees respond. A variety of formats have been employed, including checklists, true–false, and multiple choice. Some items are obviously indicative of serious psychopathology; others are much more subtle. In most cases *individual* responses are not that meaningful in the interpretation. Instead, *patterns* of responses or a *profile of scores* is relied on for interpretation.

Objective personality instruments have the advantage of being economical to administer. They can be group administered and monitored by a clerk rather than requiring the time and training of a psychiatrist or psychologist for valid administration. Major disadvantages include their sometimes questionable validity, their dependence on reading comprehension, a tendency to mark answers in a safe or socially desirable fashion (thereby perhaps masking certain traits), or attempts to fake a normal or pathological response pattern. This latter point has received extensive attention by personality test developers, and validity scales have been built into some instruments to inform the examiner that responses have been faked, or that reading comprehension may be suspect.

Projective Personality Assessment Projective personality assessment involves requiring examinees to respond to unstructured or ambiguous stimuli (e.g., incomplete sentences, inkblots, abstract pictures). The basic theory underlying projective personality testing can be summarized as follows:

1. With the passage of time, response tendencies in various situations tend to become resistant to change and tend to reproduce themselves in the presence of various stimuli.

2. When presented with suggestive or ambiguous stimuli, examinees will respond to them in ways that relate to conscious or unconscious motives, beliefs, or experiences.

3. Projective tests will make individuals respond in ways that reflect their conscious or unconscious motives, beliefs, or experiences by presenting stimuli that are suggestive of various aspects of the individual's life (e.g., mother–father relationships, the need for achievement) or are ambiguous.

A major advantage of projective over objective tests is that the stimuli are often sufficiently abstract to allow scoring criteria to detect a variety of appropriate and inappropriate behaviors. Such techniques may uncover a broader range of psychopathology and allow for the use and interpretation of unique responses. Major disadvantages of projective techniques include questionable validity related to their often complex scoring rules and their expense. Projective personality tests always require administration and scoring by an appropriately trained psychologist or psychiatrist.

Objective Personality Tests

Adjective Checklist   Published by the Consulting Psychologists Press, the Adjective Checklist is appropriate for individuals in ninth grade through adults. It consists of an alphabetical list of adjectives and is usually completed in about 15 minutes. The subject checks those adjectives that are applicable. Scores can be obtained in 24 variables, including self-confidence, self-control, counseling readiness, and various needs and aspects of personal adjustment.

Edwards Personal Preference Schedule (EPPS)   The EPPS is published by the Psychological Corporation and is appropriate for college students and adults. It is normally completed in 45 to 50 minutes. Subjects respond by choosing one of a pair of statements that apply to them. Each statement represents a need, and each of these needs is assessed by nine pairs of statements.

Minnesota Multiphasic Personality Inventory–2 (MMPI–2)   The MMPI–2 is appropriate for individuals over 18 years of age and is published by National Computer Systems. It generally takes about one hour to complete. The MMPI–2 is the most widely used of the objective personality tests and has been in use for over 60 years. It requires individuals to respond to 567 statements presented in true–false format. Responses are scored on several scales, including validity scales and scales measuring concern for bodily functioning, depression, hysteria, psychopathological tendencies, paranoia, anxiety, schizophrenia, level of mental activity, and social comfort. The MMPI–2 is widely used as a screening instrument in psychiatric, educational, military, industrial, and government institutions. A modified version of the MMPI–2, called the MMPI–A, was published in 1992 and is appropriate for adolescents.

Myers–Briggs Type Indicator (MBTI)   The MBTI is published by the Educational Testing Service. It is appropriate for ninth grade through adult and requires about one hour to complete. The format is forced-choice, and scores are provided for introversion versus extroversion, sensation versus intuition, thinking versus feeling, and judgment versus perception. The MBTI has been in use for over 50 years and enjoys widespread popularity.

Projective Personality Tests

Rorschach Inkblot Technique   The Rorschach test is published by Hans Huber Medical Publisher, Berne, Switzerland. It consists of 10 cards or plates. Each card contains an inkblot, some black and white, some colored. Examinees are asked to describe what they "see" in the ambiguous blot. Responses are scored according to location, content, and a variety of other factors, including whether form or color was used to construct the image, whether movement is suggested, and whether shading or texture was considered. Scoring is complex, but acceptable validity is evident when properly trained scorers are used. The Rorschach has been one of the most popular projective tests used by clinical psychologists. In the hands of a skilled clinician it can yield a surprising variety of information.

Thematic Apperception Test (TAT)   The TAT is published by the Harvard University Press and is designed for individuals aged 10 through adult. Adaptations of the test for younger children (Children's Apperception Test) and senior citizens (Senior Apperception Test) are also available. The subject is presented with a series of pictures (usually 10 or 12 of the total of 30) and asked to make up a story to fit each picture. The pictures vary in degree of structure and ambiguity. The record of stories is then examined to determine the projection of the subject's personality, as indicated by recurrent behavioral themes, needs, perceived pressures, and so on. Interpretation is often complex and requires an appropriately trained psychologist or psychiatrist.

This concludes our discussion of the types of standardized tests. By no means all-inclusive, our presentation of various types of tests has focused on those tests that the average classroom teacher is most likely to come into contact with.

SUMMARY

This chapter has described various types of standardized tests and briefly reviewed examples of each type. Its major points are as follows:

1. The survey battery is the type of achievement test most frequently used today.

2. The main advantages of a survey battery over several single-subject tests are the following:
   a. Coordinated subtests are provided.
   b. Savings in time and expense are realized.
   c. A common norm group is used.

3. The disadvantages of a survey battery over single-subject tests are the following:
   a. Content validity may vary across subtests.
   b. Depth of coverage may be less than that obtained with a single-subject test.

4. Single-subject achievement tests are mainly used in the secondary grades.

5. Diagnostic achievement tests are usually administered only to selected students who have already exhibited difficulties in achievement.

6. Academic aptitude or IQ tests are used to predict future learning; achievement tests measure past learning.

7. Academic aptitude tests were initially developed over 100 years ago to predict school performance but came to be known as intelligence tests. Today, they still do a good job of predicting school performance and have moderate ability to predict a variety of other variables.

8. After about age six, IQ scores tend to be fairly stable for the remainder of an individual's life. Prior to age six, and especially during the first few years of life, they tend to be unstable.

9. One definition of personality is the typical and characteristic ways people behave.

10. The objective approach to personality assessment relies on self-report questionnaires that are economical but suffer from questionable validity, test takers' perception of the social desirability of answers, and faking.

11. Projective personality assessment is based on the theory that when individuals are presented with suggestive or ambiguous stimuli, these stimuli will elicit responses that are fairly rigid and reflective of conscious or unconscious motives, beliefs, or wishes.

12. Projective tests are more flexible than objective personality tests but suffer from questionable validity and greater expense.

FOR DISCUSSION

1. Identify two advantages and two disadvantages of standardized tests.

2. Discuss some of the ways IQ scores should be used and some of the ways they should not be used. Give specific examples.

3. Describe the advantages and disadvantages of objective versus projective personality tests. If your personality were being measured, which would you choose?

CHAPTER 20

ASSESSING CHILDREN WITH DISABILITIES IN THE REGULAR CLASSROOM: A GROWING NEED

AT FIRST GLANCE you may wonder why we have included two chapters about testing and assessing children with disabilities in a text primarily for regular education teachers. You might say, "That's the responsibility of the school psychologist." Or, "Children with disabilities are in special ed classrooms, not regular ed classrooms." Or, "I won't have to deal with children with disabilities if I'm going to be a regular ed teacher."

These statements were largely true in the past. Today, thanks to the passage of the 1997 Amendments to the Individuals with Disabilities Education Act (IDEA–97), the reauthorization of this act in 2004 (IDEA–04), and the No Child Left Behind (NCLB) Act in 2002, they no longer are valid. The days when children with disabilities received instruction only from special education staff in segregated (e.g., resource, self-contained) settings, received only annual progress reports, were assessed only by specialists, and were excluded from annual district-wide assessments are over. The intent of these three pieces of federal legislation is to better integrate regular and special education to raise expectations for students with disabilities, and to enable them to benefit from general education reforms.

The intention of the U.S. Congress and Presidents William Clinton and George W. Bush in signing IDEA–97, NCLB, and IDEA–04 and into law is clear: Children with disabilities will

- be integrated meaningfully into the general education curriculum and setting,
- be taught and assessed by both regular and special education staff,
- receive regular reports during the school year of progress toward their annual Individual Educational Plan (IEP) objectives,
- be included, like their general education peers, in annual state- and district-wide assessments, with state approved accommodations and alternate assessments when required by their IEPs, and
- scores for children with disabilities on the annual assessments will be separated from the scores for regular education students, with schools to be held accountable if students with disabilities do not demonstrate sufficient annual progress.

Unless they want to risk loss of needed federal funds and to be subject to potential civil rights suits and investigation by the U.S. Department of Justice, schools must now demonstrate that children with disabilities are integrated meaningfully into the general education setting, curriculum, and annual academic assessments, and that their educational outcomes are improving.

Before we discuss the specific ways recent federal legislation will affect classroom testing and assessment practice, consider the following dialogue, which identifies several important changes resulting from IDEA–97, NCLB, and IDEA–04 that will impact the regular and special education teacher:

> *"Hi Mr. Past, this is Ms. Future calling, you know, the school special education coordinator. Hard to believe the new school year is beginning already isn't it?"*
>
> *"Sure is," said Mr. Past. "I wish the vacation was about a month longer."*
>
> *"I've got to call all the regular ed teachers to let them know about the IEP meeting schedule for September so I'll get right to the point, Mr. Past," said Ms. Future.*
>
> *"Oh, don't bother," replied Mr. Past. "Like I told you last year, I just don't have time to attend those meetings. I need to get 28 kids ready for the state high-stakes test, you know, and that means I don't have the luxury of just teaching six or eight kids like the special ed teachers do. Thanks to NCLB, if my class doesn't do well the whole school will suffer, including the special ed staff and students. You wouldn't want that to happen would you? Each year now, the state raises the bar we have to reach to demonstrate Adequate Yearly Progress, or AYP, as they call it, so we just don't have time for special ed meetings anymore. Besides, I don't know anything about teaching special ed kids so I wouldn't have anything to contribute. I'd really like to help the kids out, but I wouldn't want to mess them up. Their learning and assessing their progress is best left to specialists like you, Ms. Future. It's what's best for the pupils, and that's what I'm about. Thanks for thinking of me though. Bye!"*
>
> *"Wait! Don't hang up, Mr. Past!" exclaimed Ms. Future. "Haven't you heard about how Nickel-B applies to the 1997 and 2004 Amendments to IDEA?"*
>
> *"Of course I've heard of Nickel-B, but we call it the No Child Left Behind Act or NCLB, not Nickel-B", said Mr. Past, haughtily. "Every year you keep bringing this IDEA thing up. Whose idea are you talking about anyway?" quipped Mr. Past.*
>
> *"Not whose idea, Mr. Past, the IDEA. That's I-D-E-A, the 1997 and 2004 amendments to the Individuals with Disabilities Education Act. The amendments were passed in 1997 and reauthorized in 2004, and the IEP portion, which requires a regular classroom teacher to attend all IEP meetings, was fully implemented with the beginning of the 1998–1999 school year," said Ms. Future. "You've had to attend these meetings for several years now. Remember?"*
>
> *"Of course I remember," said an irritated Mr. Past, "but since NCLB things are different here on the regular ed side. I am a regular, that's R-E-G-U-L-A-R, education teacher, Ms. Future. That means I teach and assess regular education kids. We have so much to keep up with now because of all the requirements of NCLB that I really don't have time for special ed stuff. Since NCLB was passed in 2002 we now have to see that our kids do well on multiple benchmark tests, because these predict how well they will do on the annual assessment in April. And you know how important that is, don't you? To be sure they are prepared we have to test these kids at least once per week using formal teacher-made or standardized measures. I guess simply checking their progress with benchmarks isn't enough for the people in the capitol. And, you know what happens if we don't reach the proficiency goals the legislators have established for us? Our school gets labeled as 'in need of improvement' and we have to work even*

harder to get our scores up the next year or we face serious consequences, including being labeled as 'in corrective action.' And we could be restructured if we don't make AYP for five years! To make matters worse, we have to report not just overall average scores, but we have to break them down, disaggregation of scores they call it, so that we are judged based on scores for different categories of students. These categories include students who are economically disadvantaged, who are limited English proficient, and for each of the major ethnic groups. Can you imagine that? They really expect us to have all students achieve at proficiency. And yet, you want us to get more involved with special ed kids too? Lots of luck! I think I'll mention our little conversation to the principal and see how she feels about your efforts to take away what little instructional time I have left, thanks to all the NCLB testing requirements, and give that valuable time to special ed students when I could be focusing on raising test scores for all of my regular ed kids instead. I don't think shell be too happy about that. Do you?", asked a frustrated Mr. Past.

"I agree, Mr. Past, she won't be pleased", fumed Ms. Future. "She won't be pleased because she is fully aware that IDEA–04 retained the IDEA–97 requirement that regular education teachers, whether they feel they are qualified or not, must be members of each student with a disability's Individual Educational Plan, or IEP, team. But I think she will really be unhappy to learn that you don't seem to realize that the NCLB provisions that apply to regular ed also apply to special ed. Students with disabilities must participate in the annual state assessments that are required for regular ed kids, with appropriate accommodations or alternate assessments, as needed. Furthermore, according to NCLB, it is the IEP team that determines whether a student with a disability may participate in the standard annual assessment or whether the student needs accommodations or an alternate assessment. When we determine the student can't meaningfully participate in the standard annual assessment we have to document why the standard assessment is not appropriate and describe how the student will be assessed using a state-approved accommodation or alternate assessment! And, in addition to the groups you mentioned, scores must also be disaggregated for students with disabilities, most of whom now receive the majority of their instruction in the regular ed classroom and curriculum! In fact, everything you mentioned about NCLB applies to special ed students. NCLB has put a lot of additional pressure on everyone in the system, but it's increased pressure on everybody, Mr. Past, not just regular ed teachers!" exclaimed a frustrated Ms. Future. Low scores for special ed kids also affect the whole school under NCLB!

"I ... I ... umm ... Are you sure about this," gasped Mr. Past, "I though it was just regular ed that was affected by NCLB."

"Positive," said Ms. Future. "It's all part of the movement away from providing segregated instruction for students with disabilities in resource and self-contained classrooms. It's called full inclusion, and it's happening because research has demonstrated that the old way of isolating children with disabilities has not been as effective as integrating children with disabilities into the regular education curriculum and raising expectations for their achievement. And, as you know, we have been discussing the integration of special and regular students at faculty meetings for the last several years." said Ms. Future. "Do you remember?" she asked.

"I know, I know. Now I remember, I just forgot," said Mr. Past with some hesitation. "But we've been integrating special ed kids and regular ed kids for years. The special ed kids can play with the regular ed kids on the playground and at lunch. And one of the special ed aides reads to a couple of them in my social studies class. Heck, I

encourage my own aide to read to them whenever she can too, even though she's paid out of regular ed funds. So, I'm supportive of the special ed program and of inclusion," said Mr. Past.

"I'm glad you are, Mr. Past, but what you are describing is not meaningful inclusion, and it is not enough! Providing socialization opportunities at lunch and recess and helping them read is not meaningful integration under IDEA–97 and IDEA–04, and it's not going to help our students with disabilities achieve at the annually increasing levels required by NCLB. If any group, the economically disadvantaged, the minorities, the limited English proficient, or the students with disabilities, fails to meet state proficiency goals for NCLB the whole school will be held accountable!" said Ms. Future. "That's why it's critical that regular education staff consult and coordinate actively with the special ed staff concerning instructional and behavior management strategies, and the testing and assessment of academic, social, emotional, and behavioral progress toward not only IEP objectives—objectives identified by you and the rest of us during the IEP team meetings you now are required to attend—but also the state proficiency standards required under NCLB."

"But the way we've been doing it has worked just fine. I'd like to keep it that way. Everyone knows the routine. Consulting and coordinating sounds great, but who has the time? If it ain't broke, don't fix it," exclaimed Mr. Past, becoming irritated again.

"But that's just it! It hasn't been working, at least not for children with disabilities. Congress has recognized that isolation in special classes and superficial inclusion deprived special ed kids of the benefits of education reform such as higher standards, an enriched curriculum, and annual assessment of their progress. By requiring more collaboration between special and general education teachers Congress intended to ensure that special education kids are meaningfully included in general education, from planning to implementation and evaluation of the annual objectives identified on their IEPs and in the state standards. In the past we often excluded children with disabilities from the annual statewide test program. Now, under NCLB, they all must be included, with only a small percentage of exceptions, and when their IEPs call for it we will need to make individualized state-approved accommodations or employ alternate assessments," explained Ms. Future.

"Are you telling me that in addition to trying to help my kids meet annual proficiency standards required by NCLB I am going to have to attend IEP meetings, include special ed kids in my classes and curriculum, teach them, help them socialize, raise academic expectations, test and assess them, and coordinate all this with the special ed staff? Is that what you're telling me?" asked a disbelieving Mr. Past.

"I'd say that about covers it. Basically, regular and special ed need to pull together to help all of our students meet NCLB and IDEA–04 requirements, or else we will all have to face uncomfortable consequences," replied Ms. Future.

"Umm, uhhh, well, you know I'm just trying to do my job, and I am a team player," said Mr. Past.

"I'm glad to hear that, Mr. Past. I am too, and I look forward to collaborating and coordinating with you and the other regular education teachers toward improved educational outcomes for our children with disabilities," said Ms. Future. "With the passage of NCLB and its accountability provisions we all need to pull together to ensure that all of our students make adequate yearly progress. Now, about the IEP meeting schedule. On Monday at 8:15 we are scheduled to meet with . . ."

Farfetched? Unbelievable? Overstated? An exaggeration? We don't think so. In fact, everything Ms. Future said in the dialogue is an accurate reflection of new requirements for general education teachers under NCLB, IDEA–97, and IDEA–04.

To help you understand why these changes were made, we will review briefly what we have learned has worked and has not worked in relation to the education of children with disabilities. Later in this chapter we will discuss how the testing and assessment skills of the regular classroom teacher will play an important role in the implementation of NCLB and IDEA with students with disabilities. More specifically, we hope to familiarize you with the ways in which the testing and assessment practices you have learned in this text can guide you in the identification, instruction, and evaluation of children with disabilities in your regular education class. We will also describe an important and very controversial change in the way special education eligibility is determined for students with the most common category of disability, specific learning disabilities (SLD). Under IDEA–04 school districts now have the option of continuing to use the discrepancy model that has been in place since 1977, or they may use a response to instruction /intervention model, called RTI, or some combination of both. We will discuss these approaches and their impact on the regular classroom teacher in more detail later in this chapter. In Chapter 21 we will describe a number of methods, procedures, and instruments that may be helpful to both regular and special education teachers in testing and assessing children with disabilities.

A BRIEF HISTORY OF SPECIAL EDUCATION

A variety of social, cultural, and legal developments subsequent to World War II contributed to the guarantee of a free and appropriate public education, or FAPE, enjoyed today by all children with disabilities. Critical court cases such as *Brown v. Board of Education of Topeka, Pennsylvania Association of Retarded Children v. Commonwealth of Pennsylvania*, and *Mills v. Board of Education* established the educational rights of children with disabilities in different states. These cases spurred Congress to pass legislation that established a coherent national legislative requirement to guarantee FAPE to all children with disabilities.

P.L. 94–142 and the Individuals with Disabilities Education Act (IDEA)

School-age children with disabilities were guaranteed FAPE in 1975 with the passage of Public Law 94–142, the Education for All the Handicapped (EAH) Act. In 1986, Public Law 99–457 was enacted to extend the guarantee of FAPE to preschool children with disabilities. In 1990, the law was reauthorized as Public Law 105–17 and the name of EAH was changed to the Individuals with Disabilities Education Act (IDEA). In 1997 Public Law 105–17 was reauthorized as the 1997 Amendments to IDEA (IDEA–97). In 2004 the law was amended again and was reauthorized as H.R. 1350, the Individuals with Disabilities Improvement Act of 2004 (IDEA–04).

Like previous versions of IDEA, the 2004 reauthorization reaffirms Congress' intent to ensure the rights of children with disabilities to receive FAPE. Like IDEA–97 before it, IDEA–04 acknowledges the successes of EAH and IDEA, while also requiring changes designed to address the shortcomings of EAH and IDEA. The accomplishments and shortfalls of EAH and IDEA will be discussed next.

Prior to the implementation of Public Law 94–142, about one million children with disabilities were denied a public education. Since its passage the number of children with developmental disabilities in state institutions has declined by almost 90%. The number of young adults with disabilities enrolled in post-secondary education has tripled and the unemployment rate for individuals with disabilities in their 20s is about half that of older individuals with disabilities.

Yet, not all children with disabilities have obtained equal or significant benefit from IDEA. Students with disabilities are failing courses and dropping out of school by an almost two to one ratio compared to students without disabilities. Advocates have also been concerned that children from economically disadvantaged and minority backgrounds and children with limited English proficiency have been too often inappropriately placed in special education. School officials, providers, parents, and others complained that under EAH and IDEA the focus was on paperwork and process rather than outcomes, and IDEA had not been adequately implemented in many areas. It was to remedy these and other shortcomings that IDEA–97 was passed, and IDEA–04 reinforces many of the reforms implemented under IDEA–97, although some feel that IDEA–04 compromised the rights of students with disabilities to provide schools with more flexibility.

IDEA–04 supports expanded opportunities for parents, special educators, related services providers, regular educators, and early intervention services providers and other personnel to develop new partnerships and work collaboratively at the state and local levels. Incentives are included to enhance the capacity of schools and other community-based providers and entities to work effectively with children with disabilities and their families by targeting funding for personnel training, research, media, technology, and dissemination of technical assistance and best practices. We have described only a few of the many facets of IDEA–04. A more comprehensive analysis of this complex piece of legislation is beyond the scope of this text (and probably beyond most of your interests!), but we will revisit relevant aspects of IDEA–04 as we discuss the role of the regular classroom teacher in the special education referral and evaluation process later in the chapter.

Section 504 of the Rehabilitation Act

A separate piece of legislation, Section 504 of the Rehabilitation Act of 1973, has come to play an increasingly important role in service delivery to children with disabilities since the late 1980s. Commonly referred to as "Section 504," it has expanded special services eligibility standards to students whose disabilities interfere with learning but who fail to qualify for special education services under IDEA's requirements (Hakola, 1992).

IDEA–97 and its predecessors required that a student's behavior or learning be seriously or severely affected by one of the 12 categories of disability it delineated before a student is eligible to receive special educational services. Section 504 established a broader standard of eligibility. It defined a person with a disability as anyone with a physical or mental impairment that substantially limits one or more major life activities. Students who qualify for assistance under Section 504, but not IDEA, have come to be referred to as "504 only" students and the services provided to them have come to be referred to as "504 only" services. This law also empowered the Office of Civil Rights to enforce Section 504 compliance.

In recent years Section 504 has generated considerable controversy, in part because of the "ambiguity and brevity of Section 504 in regard to requirements for elementary and secondary schools" (Gammel, 1992, p. 298). One example of the lack of clarity involves funding for services. When a child qualifies for special services under Section 504 (i.e., 504 only), but not under IDEA–04, the child is not eligible for funding through IDEA monies. This means that local or state funds must then be used to fund 504 only special services. Needless to say, such funds are scarce in most districts. Thus provision of special services for 504 only children are likely to be within the less expensive regular classroom setting. This also is in keeping with the intent of Section 504, which, like IDEA–04, is for services to be provided within the least restrictive environment. While the funding and eligibility issues of Section 504 will continue to be clarified in coming years through legal interpretation and/or legislation, it appears reasonable to conclude that the involvement of the regular education teacher with 504 only students and service providers may be expected to increase.

SPECIAL EDUCATION SERVICE DELIVERY: AN EVOLUTION

IDEA–04, with its requirements for full inclusion of children with disabilities in the general curriculum and setting, is the latest development in an evolution in special education services that began prior to the passage of P.L. 94–142 in 1975. This evolution has altered thinking regarding the appropriateness of the special education service delivery setting, eligibility criteria, and disability categories. We will describe this evolution next.

Service Delivery Setting

While P.L. 94–142 and IDEA required placement of children with disabilities in the least restrictive educational environment, many children with disabilities were routinely placed in educationally segregated resource or self-contained classrooms on the assumption that they could not benefit from regular class instruction. This was especially true for students who were viewed as more severely mentally, physically, emotionally, and behaviorally challenged. The common wisdom for decades was that it was not only in the best interests of such severely challenged children to be in segregated classrooms, but that this was also essential to protect the regular educational process from disruption due to the presence of such challenged students.

The traditional special education "pull-out" system, in which the special learner is taught in a self-contained classroom for at least part of the day, has been criticized as discriminatory, ineffective, and inefficient (Davis, 1989). Indeed, the National Council on

Disability (1989) clarified that the intent of the Education for All Handicapped Children Act (P.L. 94–142) never was to segregate children with disabilities, even those with multiple or severe disabilities.

Legal decisions in the 1990s increasingly required the inclusion of children with disabilities in the regular education classroom. A 1993 decision by the U.S. Court of Appeals found that a New Jersey school district failed to make a reasonable effort to meet a student's special learning needs when it excluded him from the regular classroom (Viadero, 1993). In the early 1990s, special education leaders and policy makers also advocated for greater inclusion of children with disabilities in the regular classroom (Cannon, Idol, West, 1992; Conte, 1994; Hale & Carlson, 1992). Nevertheless, not everyone believed that full inclusion is in the best interests of special and regular education students. This may have been especially true for more experienced teachers (Coker & Griffith, 1994). In the end, the prevailing view was that the regular classroom teacher should expect to increasingly collaborate and cooperate with the special educator in both teaching and assessing the special learner's academic, physical and behavioral progress (Bauwens, Hourcade, & Friend, 1989; Cannon et al., 1992; Friend & Cook, 1992).

This view prevailed, in part, because of an accumulating body of research attesting to the beneficial effects of inclusion of students with disabilities in the regular classroom and curriculum. Reviews of research in the 1980s and early 1990s (Halvorsen & Sailor, 1990; Stainback & Stainback, 1992) documented improved educational and social outcomes for children with disabilities, even those who were severely challenged, who were in integrated placements (i.e., placements that included contact with regular education students and curriculum as well as special education services) as compared to peers in segregated placements (i.e., self-contained special education only). These reviews led Sailor, Gee and Karasoff (1993) to conclude, "The body of research literature is sufficient to demonstrate that educators need no longer spend energy and resources debating the issue of whether or not to integrate or include students with severe disabilities in the learning environments of their non-disabled peers but can concentrate instead on how best to do it" (p. 2).

These findings led many special and regular educators to accept and adopt "full inclusion" as a goal for all children with disabilities. The passage of IDEA–97 codified and formalized this consensus, and IDEA–04 reinforces it. Sailor et al. (1993) identified the following key elements of full inclusion for children with disabilities:

- Full general education class membership.
- Full perception of "ownership" from both special and general education.
- Individual outcomes-based decision making.
- Student-based services with team curriculum design.
- Site-team coordination of services and educational support.

Yet, even before full inclusion came to be as accepted as it is today, it was clear that, in keeping with the nonsegregatory intent of P.L. 94–142, the trend was already toward increased mainstreaming of the challenged learner. For example, Fig. 20.1 illustrates that as far back as the 1987–1988 school year approximately 75% of all students with disabilities received their primary educational services in the regular classroom or in a combination of the regular classroom with one or more periods in a resource room.

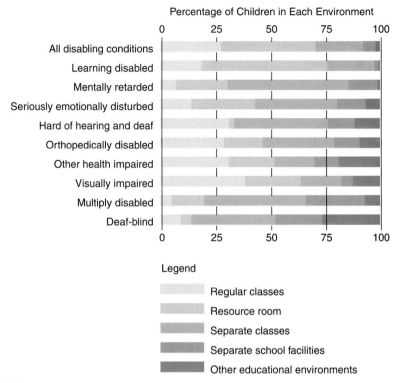

FIGURE 20.1   Environments in which 6- to 21-year-old disabled students were served during the 1987–88 school year.

Source: U.S. Department of Education, Office of Special Education and Rehabilitation Services, *Twelfth Annual Report to Congress on the Implementation of the Education of the Handicapped Act,* 1989.

More than a decade later, an annual report to Congress on the implementation of IDEA (U.S. Department of Education, 2001) indicated that 45% of students in the SLD category spent less than 20% of their instructional time in special education. Thus, more than 80% of the instruction for students with SLD was left to general education teachers. Because reading is a primary emphasis of the elementary, and especially the primary grades, these data indicate that there is no doubt that if you are an elementary school teacher you will be responsible for the majority of instruction for students with SLDs and especially SLDs in reading. Furthermore, because the performance of students with disabilities must be reported separately to meet NCLB requirements, regular testing and assessment of these students in the regular curriculum will be needed to ensure they are making adequate progress.

Determining Eligibility for Services

Under EAH and IDEA a number of categories of disability existed that could qualify a child to receive special education related services. However, students were unable to qualify to receive services until their disabilities were demonstrably severe or serious.

By requiring that a child first be identified and labeled as a child with disabilities before services could be provided, the old IDEA unintentionally impeded prevention and early intervention activities. The result was that a child's problems had to become chronic or intensify to crisis proportions in many cases before assistance under IDEA could be provided. By the time the problem escalated to this level only intense and expensive interventions had any hope of resolving the problem—a costly, ineffective utilization of limited resources.

One of the intentions of IDEA–97 was to encourage early identification and intervention within the regular class environment, a process sometimes referred to as pre-referral intervention (meaning before referral for a comprehensive special education evaluation). IDEA–97 also allowed special education related services to be delivered, at the discretion of state and local educational agencies, to children between the ages of 3 and 9 experiencing developmental delays, as defined by the state and as measured by appropriate diagnostic instruments and procedures, in physical, cognitive, communication, social or emotional, or adaptive development. By including developmental delays Congress signaled its intent to break from the categorical service delivery requirements of the old IDEA that discouraged early identification and intervention. IDEA–04 continues to support these changes.

In practice, prior to the passage of IDEA–97 and IDEA–04 many districts and related service providers developed mechanisms to deliver early identification and intervention services to students with suspected disabilities before students were referred to the costly special education eligibility process. Referred to by various names (e.g., pre-referral services, teacher or student assistance or study teams, intervention assistance programs), these programs were intended to provide immediate service to teachers and students in regular classrooms and to reduce the number of referrals to special education (Ross, 1995). However, because there was no provision for such services to be funded under the old IDEA, they instead were funded on a patchwork basis with funds from local, site-based managed schools, districts, state and regional service centers, the Office of Special Education Programs (OSEP), and private foundations.

Learning Disability Determination: Discrepancy or RTI?

To stimulate even more early intervention within the regular classroom, and to address difficulties with the existing method of eligibility determination, IDEA–04 implemented an optional, controversial change in the way eligibility for special education services is to be determined for the disability category of Specific Learning Disability (SLD), the most common disability category. Since 1977, under EAH, IDEA, and IDEA–97 a severe discrepancy between aptitude and achievement (see Chapter 18) was required for SLD eligibility. Under IDEA–04, to determine SLD eligibility school districts have the option of continuing to use the discrepancy model or using a response to instruction/intervention (RTI) model, or some combination of the discrepancy model and the RTI model. Heated debate has arisen between proponents of the RTI models and alternative models, and readers interested in the complexities and nuances of the debate are referred to articles by Fletcher and Reschly (2005) and Kavale, Kaufman, Naglieri, and Hale (2005). For our purposes, we will simply say that the issues are complex, and the jury is still out in terms of which approach is "better." Nevertheless, it is important for regular education teachers to have some familiarity with what discrepancy, RTI, and alternative approaches entail, because regular education teachers will contribute to all methods of SLD determination.

The Discrepancy Model Since 1977 eligibility for special education services as a child with a SLD hinged on whether a severe discrepancy was found between a child's predicted achievement, as measured by an aptitude or IQ test, and a child's actual achievement, as measured by an achievement test. Under this model, an appropriately trained psychologist had to perform an individual assessment, including at least an IQ and an achievement test, to determine whether the child's achievement was significantly discrepant (i.e., whether there was a large enough gap between between predicted and actual achievement that was not attributable to other factors, such as inconsistent schooling). The actual size of the discrepancy necessary for SLD eligibility varied, depending on state laws, from one to two standard deviations. Demonstrating this discrepancy was the purview of school psychologists and other qualified professionals, supported by assessment data provided by classroom teachers.

The discrepancy model has been criticized for a variety of reasons. These include

- It is a "wait to fail" model (e.g., if a child's discrepancy was not large enough to qualify as a learning disability in first grade, the gap would eventually widen if we wait long enough and the child would then qualify in later years, after achievement has suffered, perhaps irreparably).

- IQ–achievement discrepancies lack specificity in differentiating among low achievers (i.e., poor achievement may result from linguistic, cultural, attendance, motivation, teaching, emotional, or other factors than a learning disability).

- Different tests (IQ and achievement) yield different scores for the same student, so evaluators may select combinations that are more or less likely to yield a discrepancy (i.e., careful selection of IQ tests that "run high" and achievement tests than "run low" will increase the likelihood of finding a significant discrepancy).

- Similar factors can depress both IQ and achievement scores and eliminate mathematical discrepancies (e.g., poor vocabulary).

- The utilization of the discrepancy model has swelled SLD identification rates to 12% to 15% of the general education population in some states, taxing budgets and resources and generating an anti-special education backlash when general education funds have been tapped to fund services for learning disabled students

- The identification process has been lengthy and expensive, with an evaluation and report often requiring 6–8 hours or more of the psychologist's time for each referred child.

Response to Intervention/Instruction (RTI) RTI is an acronym that stands for response to intervention or instruction in some circles, or resistance to intervention in others. Regardless of the language used the key features of the RTI model for learning disability determination are similar:

- Early identification of learning (especially reading) difficulty and early intervention with evidence-based treatments (i.e., scientifically based). This is very similar to the pre-referral intervention process that we discussed earlier.

- Monitoring/graphing of the child's progress (using classroom curriculum-based tests and norm-referenced instruments). These assessments will often be completed by the regular classroom teacher.

- Intensive intervention with evidence-based programs when performance and rate of progress lag the norm for grade and educational setting (i.e., compared to local norms).

- If a strict RTI identification model is employed, failure to respond to the intensive intervention would make a student eligible for special education as a child with SLD.

- If a combination RTI and other models is employed, referral for comprehensive evaluation by a multidisciplinary team to determine special education eligibility occurs if the child fails to respond to intensive intervention.

Referral for a comprehensive special education evaluation is often the *first* step when SLD is suspected under the discrepancy model. The comprehensive evaluation will be *eliminated* completely (under strict RTI models) or will become the *last* step if a combination RTI and alternative models is adopted for SLD identification.

The RTI model has also been criticized for a number of reasons. Some of these follow:

- Development of RTI models is uneven with some states (e.g., Iowa, Minnesota) ready for broad implementation but with others in need of intensive technical training and support.

- Local norms for curriculum-linked assessments will need to be developed and it is unclear who will be responsible for this.

- There is disagreement about what constitutes scientific, evidence-based interventions.

- Methods and procedures for wide-scale data collection, graphing (necessary to show progress), analysis, and management await development.

- Special education eligibility for the gifted learning disabled child (i.e., the child with an above average IQ whose achievement is only average) will be eliminated.

What would a switch to the RTI model have to do with general education teachers? Plenty. Under the new language, the primary criterion for learning disability determination can be whether a child is resistant to scientifically based instruction. Guess who will be providing the brunt of this instruction? Yes, general education teachers. General education teachers, likely in consultation with the school psychologist, special education teacher, and other school staff, will now have to (a) document that the child is falling behind age or grade norms, using appropriate assessment tools, (b) implement evidence-based, scientifically validated interventions, and (c) track the child's progress after the interventions have been implemented, and (d) if the child fails to catch up, only then can a referral for a special education evaluation be made.

Sound like more work? Yes, it does. Fortunately, your work in this course has prepared you well to develop and administer the formal and informal tests and assessment that will be necessary to document deficits and then evaluate outcomes on an ongoing basis. At this point, with final IDEA–04 federal regulations still unavailable, we cannot say whether the RTI approach or an alternative approach will dominate SLD determination. In any case, at least you now have some background that will inform your input into any discussions that may emerge in your district or campus.

We have described a number of important changes initiated by both IDEA–97 and IDEA–04. The overall effect of these changes is clear. Whereas P.L. 94–142 and IDEA were focused on categorical procedure, identification, and eligibility, the intent of IDEA–97 and IDEA–04 is to support early identification and intervention, integrated best practices, and assessment of educational outcomes, all toward improved educational outcomes for children with disabilities and developmental delays.

Disability Categories to Developmental Delays

Over the past few decades challenged students have been classified and defined in a number of ways. New definitions of challenging conditions will continue to evolve as more and more becomes known about this subgroup of schoolchildren. A number of categories of challenging conditions have been identified under IDEA. These categories usually include children with physical disabilities, hearing impairments, visual impairments, mental retardation, behavior disorders, learning disabilities, communication disorders, autism, other health impaired and multiple disabilities, which are described in Fig. 20.2.

IDEA–04 continues these disability categories and the expanded special education services eligibility to children with developmental delays initiated by IDEA–97. At state and local district discretion, special education funds may now be used to provide services to children between the ages of 3 and 9 who experience state-defined developmental delays in five areas: physical, cognitive, communication, social and emotional, and adaptive development. States have been given considerable latitude in defining developmental delays. IDEA–04 only requires that the presence of a developmental delay be identified through the use of appropriate diagnostic instruments and procedures. Figure 20.3 identifies the new categories of developmental delay.

The purpose of the disability and developmental delay categories is not to label or stigmatize the child who needs help but may not be eligible for special education, but to identify learners in need of assistance. That is, these categories enable a short-hand way of communicating about those learners whose physical, emotional, and/or cognitive functions are already, or are at risk for becoming, so impaired from any cause that the individuals cannot be adequately or safely educated without the provision of special services. While these special services are the direct responsibility of the special education program within a school, under IDEA–04 the regular classroom teacher is expected to play an important, integrated role in both the provision and evaluation of services delivered to students with developmental delays as well as students with disabilities.

Physical Disabilities	Students whose body functions or members are impaired by congenital anomaly and diseases, or students with limited strength, vitality, or alertness owing to chronic or acute health problems
Hearing Impaired	Students who are hearing impaired (hard of hearing) or deaf.
Visually Impaired	Students who, after medical treatment and use of optical aids, remain legally blind or otherwise exhibit loss of critical sight functions.
Mental retardation	Students with significantly subaverage general intellectual functioning existing concurrent with deficiencies in adaptive behavior. Severity of retardation is sometimes indicated with the terms *mild*, *moderate*, *severe*, or *profound*.
Emotionally/ Behaviourally Disordered	Students who demonstrate an inability to build or maintain satisfactory interpersonal relationships, who develop physical symptoms or fears associated with personal or school problems, who exhibit a pervasive mood of unhappiness under normal circumstances, or who show inappropriate types of behavior under normal circumstances.
Learning Disabled	A disorder in one or more of the basic psychological processes involved in understanding or in using language, spoken or written. The disorder may manifest itself in the imperfect ability to listen, think, speak, read, write, spell, or do mathematical calculations. Learning disabilities include such conditions as perceptual disabilities, brain injury, minimal brain dysfunction, dyslexia, and developmental asphasia but do not include a learning problem that is primarily the result of visual, hearing, or motor disabilities, of mental retardation, of emotional disturbance, or of environmental, cultural, or economic disadvantage.
Communication Disordered	Students whose speech is impaired to the extent that it limits the communicative functions.
Autistic	Students with severe disturbances of speech and language, relatedness, perception, developmental rate, or motion.
Traumatic Brain Injury	Students with acquired brain injuries caused by an external force that adversely affect educational performance.
Multiple or Severe Disabilities	Students who have any two or more of the disabling conditions described above.

FIGURE 20.2   Categories of disabling conditions.

IDEA–04 AND THE CLASSROOM TEACHER

The acquisition, interpretation, and reporting of data pertaining to the performance of children with disabilities in the regular classroom and general curriculum will be an important function of the regular classroom teacher under IDEA–04. This may involve the use of a range of tests and assessments, including performance assessments and portfolios, checklists, structured observations, rating scales, and both teacher-made and standardized tests.

Developmental delays must be defined by the state and measured by appropriate diagnostic instruments in the following areas:

Physical development

Cognitive development

Communication development

Social or emotional development

Adaptive development

FIGURE 20.3   Categories of developmental delay for which students may be eligible for special education assistance under IDEA–04, at state or local discretion.

Testing or the Assessment Process?

Do you recall the distinction we made between testing and the assessment *process* in Chapter 1? We stated, "If important educational decisions are to be made, critically evaluated test results should be combined with results from a variety of other measurement procedures (e.g., performance and portfolio assessments, observations, checklists, rating scales—all covered later in the text), as appropriate, and integrated with relevant background and contextual information (e.g., reading level, language proficiency, cultural considerations—also covered later in the text), to ensure that the educational decisions are appropriate."

Educational decisions about children with disabilities certainly are important. They can have significant impact on the special learner's current and future life and have implications for school staff, related service providers, and always limited resources. Furthermore, parents and advocates for both children with disabilities and schools may monitor these decisions very closely, and may challenge decisions made and the data on which such decisions may be based. Obviously, the classroom teacher, and all others involved in the testing and assessment of children with disabilities, would be well advised to employ sound measurement practice in selecting, administering, scoring, and interpreting test results, and in incorporating these results into the assessment process.

Note that only some of the data we referred to in distinguishing between testing and the assessment process come from formal tests (i.e., teacher-made or standardized). This is intentional. Remember, because tests are fallible, many and varied forms of data should be collected to obtain as diverse and accurate a picture of the child's performance as is possible. Thus the classroom teacher's role in the identification and evaluation process should not be construed as only "testing," but more broadly as "contributing to the assessment process."

Ysseldyke and Algozzine (1990) have organized the many levels at which regular classroom teachers can be involved in the assessment process into a flowchart, shown in Fig. 20.4. Although predating the passage of IDEA–04, this flowchart remains relevant today. Figure 20.4 shows many of the functions that Mr. Past will need to "get up to speed on" if he is to truly contribute to the education of children with disabilities, as teachers are now required to do under IDEA–04. This flowchart illustrates how the testing and assessment skills of regular education teachers are instrumental in every step of the special education identification, instruction, and evaluation process. Clearly, with the passage of IDEA–04, the involvement of the regular education teacher with testing and assessment of children with disabilities can only increase.

FIGURE 20.4 Teacher participation throughout the special learner identification, instruction, and evaluation process.

Source: James E. Ysseldyke and Bob Algozzie, *Introduction to Special Education*, 2nd ed. (Boston: Houghton Mifflin, 1990), p. 312. Reprinted by permission.

Next we will consider in more depth the ways the classroom teacher's assessment skills are required to comply with IDEA–04 and, increasingly, Section 504. These data are all important in provision of the following services required by IDEA–04 and implied by Section 504: child identification, individual assessment, Individual Educational Plan (IEP) development, individualized instruction, and review of the IEP.

Child Identification

Child identification, or "child find," refers to a school's or a district's procedures for identifying challenged preschool and school-age children in need of early intervention or special education services as required by IDEA–04. It is in the identification of school-age students that you may be expected to play an important role as a K–12 teacher.

One stage of this identification is the referral. While referrals may be made by parents, physicians, community agencies, and school administrators as a result of district-wide testing or screening, students may also be recommended for special services by you as a teacher. For regular education students you will be the most likely individual to identify students with needs for special services. In such cases you will initially be a liaison between the child and the multidisciplinary special education eligibility team, or MDT[1]. Under IDEA–04, referrals are processed through the MDT, which usually includes

- the professional who recommends the child for special services,
- the child's parent,
- the building principal or designated representative,
- a special educator,
- a school psychologist or other assessment specialist, and
- the classroom teacher or any other individual who has special knowledge about the student.

The purpose of the eligibility committee is to reach a decision regarding the eligibility of the child for special education services and the educational alternatives appropriate for the child. It is important that you not only play a prominent role on this committee when you are recommending a child for special services, but that the data provided by you in support of your recommendation be valid, reliable, and accurate. This can only be accomplished by applying sound measurement principles and by selecting the test and assessment data that most accurately characterize the child's need for particular kinds of services. These may include data that accurately portray the following:

1. The student's current educational status, including attendance records, grades and achievement data (e.g., teacher-made and standardized tests, portfolios, and performance assessments).

2. The student's social, emotional, and attitudinal status, as documented through written accounts of classroom observations, or results from any teacher-made or standardized behavior and attitude rating scales or questionnaires, sociograms, checklists or other instruments that you may have administered to the child.

[1] These teams are known by a variety of names and acronyms in various states (e.g., ARD for admission, review, and dismissal and SST for student study team).

3. Previous instructional efforts and intervention strategies provided to the student and documentation of the result of those efforts (e.g., observation reports, behavior and attitude rating scales and questionnaires, sociograms, or checklists).

4. Data about the child reported or provided to the teacher by parents.

Individual Assessment

A second process to which you may be expected to contribute is individual child assessment. Individual assessment is the collecting and analyzing of information about a student in order to identify an educational need in terms of the following:

1. The presence or absence of a physical, mental, or emotional disability;

2. The presence or absence of a significant educational need;

3. The identification of the student's specific learning competencies together with specific instructional or related services that could improve and maintain the student's competencies.

Although the formal individual assessment of a child's capabilities falls within the responsibilities of certified professionals who have been specifically trained in assessing students with disabilities, you can and often will be expected to corroborate the findings of these professionals with achievement, social, behavioral, and other data from the classroom. The corroborative data you can be expected to provide fall into the following categories:

Achievement

Language

Physical

Intellectual

Emotional/behavioral

Sociocultural

Thus far in this text you have been exposed to measurement techniques that will enable you to present systematic, useful data about a referred child that address the first four of these six areas. In Chapter 21 we will provide you with additional measurement techniques that can be used to collect systematic classroom-based data regarding the emotional/behavioral and sociocultural areas. For illustrative purposes, several of these areas are included in the individual assessment report shown in Fig. 20.5. This figure is from a special education eligibility team, or MDT, whose composition was described in the previous section.

Language First and foremost among these data are formal and informal indications taken from performance assessments, portfolios, workbooks, homework assignments, weekly and unit tests, and classroom observation as to the student's primary language and proficiency in both the expressive and receptive domains. Often, your observation and recording of these data will suggest to special educators the validity of the standardized tests that may have been given to the student and whether they may have been given in a language other than that in which the child is proficient.

Admission, Review, and Dismissal (ARD) Committee Report
Page 3

Student *Miller, Jeremy*

ID# *072431*

II. INDIVIDUAL EDUCATIONAL PLAN
(as noted on page 1 of this report)

A. Present Levels of Competencies:
(Complete AREAS as appropriate)

*Specify name as appropriate, may include Norm-Referenced Tests, Curriculum/Performance-Based and Criterion-Referenced Tests, and Teacher Observation(s).

	Eval. Date	Eval. Method Data Source*	Grade/Age Level	Information on Current Functioning (include information on strength/weakness as appropriate)
MATHEMATICS CALCULATION				*Jeremy is functioning on grade level in math. He is currently learning subtraction of 2 digit numbers with borrowing. This is an area of strength for him.*
REASONING				
READING BASIC SKILLS	10/15/92	*Woodcock/Johnson Teacher Informal Inventory*	1.0	*Reading is a area of weakness for Jeremy. He is currently functioning below grade level in both comprehension and skills in reading*
COMPREHENSION	10/15/92	*Woodcock/Johnson Teacher Informal Inventory*	1.0	
SPELLING/WRITTEN EXPRESSION	10/15/92	*T.O.W.L Brigance*	ρ	*Jeremy has difficulty both orally and manually producing correct spelling. He is unable to write a complete sentence with correct capitalization and punctuation.*
OTHER				
PRE-VOC/ VOCATIONAL				Indicate skills which may be prerequisite to participation in vocational education.
PHYSICAL	10/16/92	*Health History Inventory O.T. Assessment*	*Below Age Level*	Indicate physical abilities/disabilities which would affect participation in instructional settings or in P.E. *Jeremy's fine motor coordination is not adequately developed for his age. It hinders his ability to learn writing skills.*
SPEECH/LANGUAGE	10/16/92	*Language Sample Speech Therapy Assessment*	*Below Age Level*	*Jeremy's language development is below average. He has a significant need for articulation instruction. This weakness currently impedes his performance in oral expression.*
INTELLECTUAL/ DEVELOPMENTAL	10/15/92	*WISC-R*	*Average Range*	*Jeremy's performance on the WISC-R indicates that he is of average intelligence for his age.*
SOCIAL/ BEHAVIORAL	10/15/92	*Informal Assessment Parent & Teacher Reports*		Indicate behaviors which would affect educational placement, programming or discipline. *Jeremy is a cooperative student. He gets along well with both peers and adults. This is a area of strength for him.*

FOR EMOTIONALLY DISTURBED STUDENTS ONLY—AS NOTED IN THE ASSESSMENT REPORT (Date:_____) one or more of the following chacteristics have been exhibited over a long period of time, have occurred to marked degree, have adversely affected his/her educational performance:

___an inability to learn which cannot be explained by intellectual, sensory or health factors;
___an inability to build or maintain satisfactory interpersonal relationships with his peers/teachers;
___inappropriate types of behavior or feelings under normal circumstances;
___a general pervasive mood of unhappiness or depression; or
___a tendency to develop physical symptoms or fears associated with personal school problems.

SE-605-83

Page 3 of ___

Date of meeting: _____

FIGURE 20.5 Individual assessment data from the admission, review, and dismissal committee Report.

Physical   Corroborative data pertaining to the physical attributes of the student can also be recorded. Only you may be in a position to observe on a daily basis the ability of the child to manipulate objects necessary for learning, to remain alert and attentive during instruction, and to control bodily functions in a manner conducive to instruction. In some instances you may provide the only data available to the MDT regarding the physical ability of the child to benefit from regular class instruction.

Intellectual   You may also be asked to provide data relevant to the student's intellectual functioning, as demonstrated by verbal and nonverbal performance and by the child's behavior. Although verbal and nonverbal behavior are usually assessed by professionals certified in special education, you may be asked to provide corroborating data pertaining to the child's adaptive behavior. Adaptive behavior is the degree to which the student meets standards of personal independence and social responsibility expected of his or her age and cultural group. Within the context of the classroom, you will have many opportunities to observe the social functioning of the child and to gain insights into the appropriateness of this functioning, given the age range and cultural milieu in which the child operates. In fact, you may be the only individual in a position to provide trustworthy data about this side of the special learner's social and interactive behavior.

Emotional/Behavioral   You can also provide useful data about the emotional behavior of the exceptional child. These data may be derived from standardized behavior checklists, in-class structured observations, adaptive behavior scales, sociograms, and student–teacher interactions that have been designed either to corroborate the need for special services or to monitor the progress of the child in the regular classroom. Several of these sources of data will be described in detail in Chapter 21.

Sociocultural   Another area in which you may be expected to provide data pertains to the sociological and environmental influences on the child that may, in part, influence the child's classroom behavior. Sociocultural data about a child often are obtained through communications with the family and knowledge of the circumstances leading up to and/ or contributing to the student's intellectual and emotional behavior. The extent to which the child's home life, culture, and out-of-school support and services contribute to the educative function can provide an important adjunct to in-school data. Methods and instruments that may be used to assess these behaviors will be described in Chapter 21.

Finally, if your district adopts the RTI model for SLD determination you may also expect to collect both norm- and criterion-referenced assessment data that will help determine whether a pupil is responding to instruction or is resistant to it. As we noted earlier in this chapter, at this point it is not known how widely the RTI method will be adopted, so this point may be moot.

Individual Educational Plan (IEP) Development

IDEA–04 requires that regular education teachers are included on each student with a disability's IEP team. The IEP team is responsible for developing, implementing, and evaluating the IEP after the eligibility team (i.e., the MDT) has determined that a child qualifies for special education assistance. The IEP team consists of at least the following required members, any of whom may also have been members of the eligibility team, or MDT:

- the child's regular education teacher,
- the child's parent, and the child, when appropriate,
- a special education teacher,
- a representative of the school who is knowledgeable about both the general and special education curricula, and who is qualified to provide or supervise the delivery of special education services,
- an individual who can interpret the results of the eligibility assessments, and
- at school or parent discretion, other individuals who have special knowledge about the child.

The IEP team's initial charge is to review the findings of the eligibility team and develop an IEP suitable to the child's needs, as identified by the eligibility team. Under IDEA–04 the IEP no longer requires short-term objectives. Instead the IEP is written to state annual objectives in the general curriculum and how these objectives will be measured. If the student with disabilities is unable to participate meaningfully in the annual academic assessment required by NCLB, the IEP team must identify whether the assessment may be taken with accommodation or whether a state-approved alternate assessment is needed. In either case the team must document the reasons why the standard assessment is not appropriate and why the accommodations or the alternate assessment are needed. The need for related services (e.g., psychological, speech and hearing, social work) to be delivered to the child is included, and the least restrictive environment in which the instruction is to take place is specified. A portion of an IEP is shown in Fig. 20.6.

The IEP developed for each student by the IEP team generally includes the following:

1. A statement of the student's present competencies taken from the overall assessment data, which generally includes
    a. The competencies of the student in academic content areas or his or her developmental skills level.
    b. The physical abilities and disabilities exhibited by the student that could affect his or her progress in the general curriculum.
    c. Social, emotional, or behavioral factors that may affect his or her progress in the general curriculum.
2. A statement of annual instructional objectives. The statement of these objectives generally is accompanied by a designation of the professional(s) or persons responsible for implementing the activities designed to help the student achieve the objective and may include a statement of special materials, resources, or methods used in achieving the objective.
3. A statement of the specific educational services to be provided the student within the least restrictive environment designated. These services should relate directly to the annual and short-term objectives for the student.

Individual Educational Plan: Educational Priorities Stated as Annual Goals
Page __ of __

Goal: *Jeremy will demonstrate reading comprehension and word attack skills at the 2.0 grade level.*

Objectives	Criteria	Evaluation Procedure	Date of Review	Code
Complete all reading skills assignments in the first grade text and workbooks. *Answer detail recall, sequence, and conclusion questions re: a 2.0 grade level selection*	*85% accuracy average of assignments* *95% accuracy*	*Record of completion and grades for text and workbook assignments* *Informal reading inventory* *Brigance Criterion referenced Inventory*	*6/2/92*	

Goal: *Jeremy will write complete sentences of at least 5 words with correct capitalization and punctuation.*

Objectives	Criteria	Evaluation Procedure	Date of Review	Code
Capitalize the beginning word of each sentence. *Capitalize proper nouns.* *Use period, question mark, or exclamation mark as end punctuation correctly.*	*Write 5 sample sentences without any punctuation or capitalization errors.*	*Written Sample:* *Informal text of written expression.*	*6/2/92*	

Goal: *Jeremy will spell words orally and in written form correctly at the 1.5 grade level.*

Objectives	Criteria	Evaluation Procedure	Date of Review	Code
Complete all spelling units with weekly spelling tests.	*80% accuracy average of test scores.* *1.5 grade level on inventories.*	*Informal spelling inventory based on the spelling test word list.* *Brigance Criterion-referenced Inventory Test of written spelling.*	*6/2/92*	

Related Service Goal: *Jeremy will correctly articulate "l" and "r" sounds and express himself in complete, descriptive sentences of at least 6 words in length.*

Objectives	Criteria	Evaluation Procedure	Date of Review	Code
Read orally a passage containing 10 words with beginning, medial, and final "r" and "l" sounds. Orally describe a current activity in complete, descriptive sentences of at least 6 words in length.	*100% accurate pronunciation* *Can perform this task upon request.*	*Language sample* *Informal assessment by the speech therapist.*	*6/2/92*	

Related Service Goal: *Jeremy will write legible capital and lowercase letters in word and sentence form upon request in manuscript.*

Objectives	Criteria	Evaluation Procedure	Date of Review	Code
Write all alphabet letters in uppercase form correctly in manuscript. *Write all alphabet letters in lowercase form correctly in manuscript*	*Legibility of writing of all manuscript letters, both upper and lowercase*	*Written sample* *Informal assessment by occupational therapist.*	*6/2/92*	

FIGURE 20.6 Portion of an Individual Educational Plan.

4. A statement of the dates for the initiation of the services, the approximate amount of time to be spent providing each service, and a justification for the services and settings in which they will be provided.

5. A statement of the criterion for and time of evaluating each annual objective.

6. When participation in annual state and district-wide assessments requires accommodation or alternate assessment techniques, these accommodations and alternatives must be specified, along with the reasons they are necessary.

As should now be obvious, writing the IEP is a complex and comprehensive process. Prior to the passage of IDEA–97 and IDEA–04, the involvement of a regular teacher in developing the IEP was optional, now it is a requirement. In other words, the IEP cannot be written without the assistance and cooperation of a regular classroom teacher.

It should be obvious that you will play a significant role in developing, monitoring, and reporting the progress the student is making toward fulfilling the general curriculum objectives of the IEP. Because parents must now receive regular progress reports, and because progress data must be reported back to the IEP team for decision-making purposes, the reliability, validity, and accuracy of the data you provide will be of significant importance. You may be the only link between the child and the team for relatively long periods of time. Thus your measurement skills to systematically observe, record, and monitor the performance of the challenged child become of paramount importance with respect to the effective implementation and evaluation of the student's IEP.

Individualized Instruction

A fourth stage in which you may become involved in the implementation of IDEA–04 is in providing individualized instruction in the general curriculum to the challenged student. Individualized special education instruction is the day-to-day instruction provided to the student based on the objectives set forth in the student's IEP. This program of individualized instruction should be consistent with the needs of the student with disabilities and the general curriculum. Your activities may include providing any or all of the following:

- Specific instructional objectives based on student needs as stated in the IEP.
- Learning activities appropriate to each student's learning style and presented as specifically and sequentially as needed for the student to progress toward attainment of each instructional objective.
- Instructional media and materials used for each learning activity selected on the basis of the student's learning style.
- An instructional setting that provides multiple arrangements for learning.
- A schedule of teaching time assuring the provision of instruction to each special learner in individual or group arrangements.
- A procedure by which the teacher measures, records, and reports each exceptional student's progress.

- Implementation of a behavior management plan when a special learner's behavior impedes progress in the general curriculum.

You may be responsible for documenting the provision of an individualized instructional program for each student with a disability in your classroom as well as for monitoring and recording the success of the individualized program. The writing of specific instructional objectives in accord with the student's IEP and the preparation and administration of teacher-made tests, or attitude or rating scales to assess student progress toward these objectives are tasks for which you also may be responsible.

Reviewing the IEP

In spite of the best efforts of all involved, some children with disabilities may not achieve in the regular education setting, or they may be unable to handle a modified general curriculum. On the other hand, some students will do very well under full inclusion and may be better served by dismissal from the special education system.

School districts must have an established set of procedures or a system for reviewing each special learner's progress based on the objectives stated in the student's IEP. The purpose of this review is not only to determine the student's progress toward the objectives of the plan but also to determine the need for modifying the plan and for further special services.

A recommendation for major changes in the IEP, including changes in the student's placement (e.g., to a more or less restrictive environment), is the responsibility of the IEP team. Many pieces of information must be gathered prior to a major change in a student's placement. They include the following:

- The number of instructional options that have been attempted, including those within the regular classroom.
- The appropriateness of the annual educational objectives, including those written by the regular classroom teacher.
- The reliability, validity, and accuracy of the testing that led or contributed to a review of the student's current placement, including testing completed within the regular classroom and results from annual district-wide achievement tests that all children with disabilities must participate in under IDEA–04 and NCLB.
- When a behavior plan has been in effect, evidence of the appropriateness of the plan's implementation and the effectiveness of the plan.

In each of these areas, data provided by the classroom teacher are often critical, since you may be in the most advantageous position to make assessments about the stability of, or change in, the behavior of the student. With the implementation of IDEA–04, the reliability, validity, and accuracy of the data you provide will be a direct reflection of the testing and measurement skills you have acquired. While the specific measurement and testing requirements of Section 504 continue to be determined, it appears reasonable to conclude that a similar set of expectations will emerge for the role of the classroom teacher in identifying and evaluating 504 only children.

AT THE OTHER END OF THE CURVE:
THE GIFTED AND TALENTED CHILD

As you have seen, much recent attention at the federal and state levels has been directed toward improving educational opportunity for children with disabilities, including those who are cognitively challenged. Recalling our discussion of the normal distribution, we recognize that roughly 2% of the population will fall into an area defined as two standard deviations below the mean, and this is typically the cutoff that is used for identifying children as having cognitive disabilities. But remember there are also children at the other end of the curve. They score in the upper 2% on IQ, aptitude, and achievement tests. Are there any school programs or special instructional techniques for them? Since these students are also two standard deviations away from (in this case, above) the mean, won't they be shortchanged by an educational system designed to educate children who are "only average"? Do these learners have special needs that also should be addressed? In this section we will expose you to some of the assessment approaches and instruments that currently exist to at least identify those children who are far above average in creative and intellectual ability.

Defining "Gifted and Talented"

Definitions of giftedness vary, just as philosophies about how we should teach the gifted vary. Generally speaking, the term "gifted" has given way to the term "gifted and talented" or some other descriptor. The definition of giftedness has been expanded to include not just those who score in the upper 2% on IQ tests, but also those who have achieved exceptionally on standardized assessments, those who are excelling in art or music, or those who exhibit exceptional creativity. Lest you think that the federal government has forgotten about the gifted and talented population, let's review the definition of gifted and talented children provided by the U.S. Office of Education:

> Gifted and talented children are those identified by professionally qualified persons who by virtue of outstanding abilities are capable of high performance. These are children who require differentiated educational programs and services beyond those normally provided by the regular program in order to realize their contribution to self and society. Children capable of high performance include those with demonstrated achievement and/or potential ability in any of the following areas: (1) general and intellectual ability, (2) specific academic aptitude, (3) creative or productive thinking, (4) leadership ability, (5) visual and performing arts, (6) psychomotor ability.
> [Marland, 1972, p. 10]

Except for the "tail" of the normal curve that one is referring to and the specific areas of giftedness, we see little difference between this definition and the one that provides the rationale for the provision of proper educational experiences to the disabled learner.

Assessment and Identification

Although perhaps the most commonly used method to identify a gifted student has been an individually administered IQ test, it is by no means the only method. As we have discussed, IQ tests are designed to measure theoretical models of intelligence, and no specific IQ test can claim that it actually does measure "intelligence," in large part because we fail to agree on just what intelligence is. Therefore to use only an IQ test to identify gifted children excludes those individuals whose particular gift or talent may lie outside the realm of the theories or concepts that define the IQ test. For that reason, it has become increasingly popular for several other criteria to be used in identifying potentially gifted and talented children. Let's look first at the role of IQ, then at some of these other characteristics that define giftedness.

Intelligence Most formulas for defining giftedness include general intelligence. This is particularly true in the elementary grades; it is believed that although school children are still developing their specialized intellectual capacities, their general intelligence is almost completely formed by the end of the critical preschool years. The emphasis on general intelligence for aiding identification of giftedness at the elementary level is also a function of the difficulty of measuring specific aptitudes at that age, when many of the words and concepts required for accurately testing specific aptitudes have yet to be taught.

At the junior high and secondary levels, measures of specific intelligence are more likely to be substituted for general intelligence. The most common are verbal and mathematical aptitude scores, which can be derived from most general IQ tests. For example, a sufficiently high score on verbal intelligence could qualify a learner for gifted English but not for gifted math, and vice versa; this gives greater flexibility to the definition of giftedness.

How high must a student score on tests of general or specific intelligence to be considered gifted? That depends on the school district's criteria. However, it is known how intelligence is distributed among individuals in the entire population. Recall that intelligence is distributed in a bell-shaped curve, with most individuals scoring around the middle of the curve, which represents an IQ score of 100. From the shape of this curve, we also know that less than 1% of the population scores 145 or higher, about 2 to 3% scores 130 or higher, and approximately 16% scores 115 or higher.

Although these percentages vary slightly depending on the test used, they are a useful guideline for selecting gifted learners. An IQ score of about 130 or higher generally makes one eligible for gifted instruction (Dembo, 1981). However, in practice, because giftedness almost always is defined in conjunction with at least several other behaviors, admission to gifted programs and classes usually is far less restrictive. It is not uncommon to accept scores below 130 as eligible for gifted instruction, but even this is highly variable among schools and states. Sometimes IQ is not considered at all in determining giftedness, in which case the learner must exhibit unusual ability in one or more other areas.

Because IQ tests rely greatly on standard language usage that predominates in the middle and upper class, a school district with a high concentration of students from lower socioeconomic strata may not require a high level of tested intelligence (at least not as measured by standardized tests). In most cases, general intelligence is only one of several behaviors that are defined as constituting giftedness. Rarely is general intelligence used as the only index of giftedness, nor should it be.

Although general intelligence is the most frequently used measure of ability, other components of intelligence have also been hypothesized. Gardner (2004, 2000; Gardner & Hatch, 1989) proposed eight different "intelligences," and has recently added a ninth intelligence, based on skills found in a modern technological society. Campbell, Campbell, and Dickinson (1996) and Lazear (1992) provide some practical applications of these to the classroom. These intelligences, along with some representative individuals who would be expected to possess high levels of these abilities, are identified in Table 20.1.

TABLE 20.1 Gardner's Multiple Intelligences

Dimension	Example	Things They Are Good At
Linguistic intelligence: Sensitivity to the meaning and order of words and the varied uses of language	Poet, journalist	Creative writing, humor/jokes, storytelling
Logical–mathematical intelligence: The ability to handle long chains of reasoning and to recognize patterns and order in the world	Scientist, mathematician	Outlining, graphic organizers, calculation
Musical intelligence: Sensitivity to pitch, melody, and tone	Composer, violinist	Rhythmic patterns, vocal sounds/tones, music performance
Spatial intelligence: The ability to perceive the visual world accurately, and to re-create, transform, or modify aspects of the world based on one's perceptions	Sculptor, navigator	Active imagination, patterns/designs, pictures
Bodily kinesthetic intelligence: A fine-tuned ability to use the body and to handle objects	Dancer, athlete	Folk/creative dance, physical gestures, sports/games
Interpersonal intelligence: The ability to notice and make distinctions among others	Therapist, salesperson	Intuiting others' feelings, person-to person communication, collaboration skills
Intrapersonal intelligence: Access to one's own strategies, inventing "feeling life"	Self-aware individual	Silent reflection, thinking
Naturalist intelligence: Observing, understanding, and organizing patterns in the natural environment	Molecular biologist, rock climber	Sensing, observing, nurturing
Existential intelligence: The ability and proclivity to pose (and ponder) questions about life, death, and ultimate realities	Philosopher, clergyman	Creating meanings, seeing wholes and relationships

Source: Adapted from Gardner (2004, 2000); Gardner and Hatch, 1989: Campbell, Campbell and Dickson, 1996; and Lazear, 1992.

Gardner and associates have developed instructional materials and modules to teach some of these abilities. Their theory derives from the observation that many individuals who are successful in life do not score high in traditional indicators of ability, such as verbal or mathematical reasoning. Gardner and his associates suggest that these individuals, to be successful, used other abilities, such as those in Table 20.1, to minimize their weaknesses and accentuate their strengths. Their theory may have particular relevance for teaching gifted learners, some of whom may not learn from school in the traditional classroom setting using the traditional curriculum. These researchers reason that alternative forms of learning could tap into other dimensions of intelligence that may go unnoticed or underutilized in the traditional classroom.

Achievement   Among other behaviors frequently used to determine giftedness is the learner's achievement, usually in the areas for which gifted instruction is being considered. Achievement is measured by annual standardized tests that cover areas such as math, social studies, reading comprehension, vocabulary, and science. Cutoff scores in the form of percentile ranks are determined in each subject area, with a percentile score of 90 to 95 representing a typical cutoff. Although cutoff percentiles differ among school districts, a cutoff percentile of 90 means that a learner is eligible for gifted instruction if his or her score on the appropriate subscale of a standardized achievement test is higher than the scores of 90% of all those who took the test.

Creativity   In addition to intelligence and achievement, indices of creativity often are considered in selecting gifted learners. Inclusion of this behavioral dimension has broadened the definition of this type of learner to include both the gifted and the talented. The significance of this addition is that not all gifted learners are talented, and not all talented learners are gifted. The phrase "gifted and talented," which is widely used, can mean talented but not gifted, gifted but not talented, mostly talented with some giftedness, mostly gifted with some talent, or both gifted and talented.

These alternative categorizations are made possible by inclusion of creativity indices in the eligibility standards. Because creative behaviors generally are considered in selecting gifted students, this type of learner more appropriately might be called "gifted and/or talented." Some observable signs of creativity in a learner include the following:

Applying abstract principles to the solution of problems.

Being curious and inquisitive.

Giving uncommon or unusual responses.

Showing imagination.

Posing original solutions to problems.

Discriminating between major and minor events.

Seeing relationships among dissimilar objects.

In identifying the gifted and talented learner, the creative component usually is composed of recommendations from teachers based on these and other signs of creativity from performance assessments and any observable creative products from portfolio assessments (e.g., sculpture, painting, musical score, science fair project, short story). It is interesting to note that studies have shown only a modest relationship between intelligence and creativity, indicating that creativity is fairly independent of both IQ and achievement.

Task Persistence   A fourth behavior sometimes used in selecting gifted and talented learners involves recommendations from teachers and other knowledgeable sources concerning a learner's task persistence. This behavior, although difficult to evaluate, is often considered indispensable for satisfactory achievement in a gifted and talented program, because both the quantity and quality of the work are likely to be considerably higher than what is expected in the regular classroom. This trait alone would not be sufficient for qualifying a learner for gifted instruction, but if such instruction is indeed geared to the extremely able student, students will need unusual levels of task persistence to succeed. Behaviors that teachers look for in determining task persistence include these:

> Ability to devise organized approaches to learning.
>
> Ability to concentrate on detail.
>
> Self-imposed high standards.
>
> Persistence in achieving personal goals.
>
> Willingness to evaluate own performance, and capability to do so.
>
> Sense of responsibility.
>
> High level of energy, particularly in academic tasks.

Implicit in these four characteristics of giftedness—intelligence, achievement, creativity, and task persistence—is the assumption that not all gifted children are equally gifted in every area of their functioning (intellectual ability, academic achievement, social skills, artistic accomplishment, etc.). Indeed, it would be no surprise to the average classroom teacher to find that he or she may have a child in the classroom who is gifted or talented in mathematics, or science, or music, but not necessarily in any other academic area. Furthermore, gifted children are not immune to physical, emotional, or neurological deficits that can reduce their capacity to demonstrate or express their gifts or talents consistently or frequently enough to obtain recognition and attention. Rather than assume that "gifted" always means the child is able to cope and excel, it is far better to keep in mind that the label usually applies to some specific subset of an individual's behavior rather than the entire person, and that a gifted and talented person is not immune to the frustrations and feelings that are evident in others.

Nonetheless, neither the federal nor state governments fund programs for the gifted and talented at levels comparable to funding for children with disabilities. This does not mean, however, that giftedness, happiness, success, and acceptance necessarily go hand in hand. The gifted child, if identified, may respond well to relatively inexpensive interventions that may provide you with unanticipated rewards for your efforts.

Current Trends in Teaching and Assessing the Gifted and Talented

Gifted and talented education has taken on added prominence in recent years as a result of the increase in alternatives by which the gifted learner can accelerate—or move through the traditional curriculum. There is little evidence to support the claim that homogeneously grouped—or tracked—classes increase overall school achievement relative to heterogeneously grouped classes (Slavin, 1990; Gamoran, 1992; Kerchoff, 1986). However, this research specifically excluded gifted learners who represent about the top 3–5% of the school population. Research tends to support programs and classes specifically targeted to the gifted and talented when they are allowed to pursue accelerated programs, where a grade can be skipped and/or advanced courses taken, such as Advanced Placement (AP) courses for college credit (Slavin, 1990). Other gifted and talented programs that simply enrich—or add to—the existing curriculum, by allowing students to pursue games and simulations to promote creativity and problem solving, conduct individual investigations, or simply use computers or other technology, tend to be less successful in increasing the achievement of these learners (Kulik & Kulik, 1984). Gifted and talented programs that are exclusively enrichment programs have been criticized for providing few activities that would not benefit all learners. Their primary advantage tends to be that they provide beneficial opportunities for learners who can master the regular curriculum rapidly enough to take advantage of them.

Lack of progress within enrichment programs has led to the increasing popularity of "magnet schools" whose primary purpose is to provide curriculum in specialized areas such as science, language arts, and the creative arts to a broad range of students whose interests and abilities qualify them. Some magnet schools are schools within a school, thereby promoting heterogeneous interactions among learners while providing advanced and accelerated course work leading to college credit and/or early high school graduation to those who can master the curriculum more quickly. The magnet school concept, as well as other alternatives, such as early graduation, that move the gifted learner more rapidly through the school curriculum are coming to define programs for the gifted and talented.

SUMMARY

This chapter has acquainted you with the field of children with disabilities and its relationship to the regular classroom teacher. Its major points are as follows:

1. The field of special education has undergone tremendous growth with respect to its programs and services as well as significant change with respect to the laws and policies governing the education of the disabled.

2. The most significant of these laws and policies have been P.L. 94–142 and its successors, IDEA and IDEA–97, IDEA–04, and the policies that have followed from them. These federal laws guaranteed the right of every child with disabilities and—at state and local discretion—developmental delays to receive free public education appropriate to his or her needs, including infants, toddlers, and preschoolers. Recent interpretations of Section 504 of the Rehabilitation Act have broadened the eligibility of students with disabilities for special instruction.

3. Under IDEA–04, a regular classroom teacher is now required to be a member of the IEP team. This expands the planning, instruction, and evaluation role of the regular education teacher with regard to children with disabilities.

4. IDEA–04 requires inclusion of children with disabilities into the general curriculum and setting, regular reports of progress to parents, and participation in annual state- and district-wide assessments, with accommodations and alternate assessments when stipulated in the child's IEP.

5. The role of the regular classroom teacher in implementing IDEA includes increased responsibilities in:
   a. child identification,
   b. individual assessment,
   c. Individual Educational Plan (IEP) development,
   d. individualized instruction, and
   e. review of the IEP.

   Similar responsibilities appear to be evolving as a result of legal interpretations of Section 504.

6. A traditional example of the measurement skills needed by the regular classroom teacher for child identification is initially distinguishing students who are potentially learning disabled from those who are "slow learners," although this may change where response to intervention (RTI) models are implemented.

7. Response to Intervention (RTI) is an optional, controversial method under IDEA–04 that states and districts may adopt to determine special education eligibility for children with suspected Specific Learning Disabilities (SLD).

8. An example of the measurement skills needed by the regular classroom teacher for individual assessment is collecting and analyzing information pertaining to the learning competencies of the student and the effects of specific instructional activities on these competencies.

9. An example of the measurement skills needed by the regular classroom teacher for IEP development is writing annual instructional objectives for the student, specifying both the outcomes to be reached and the instructional activities to be implemented.

10. An example of the measurement skills needed by the regular classroom teacher for individualized instruction is documenting the implementation of an individualized instructional program for each exceptional child and monitoring and recording the success of this program.

11. An example of the measurement skills needed by the regular classroom teacher to review the IEP is determining the reliability, validity, and accuracy of the measurement procedures used to indicate the need to change the child's placement to either a more or a less restrictive environment.

12. While the field of special education typically focuses on those individuals within the lower 2% of the normal curve, those individuals at the upper 2% of the normal curve, sometimes referred to as gifted and talented, may receive at least some federal, state, and local attention in terms of their particular needs.

13. Some learner characteristics that have been used to identify students as gifted and/or talented are intelligence, achievement, creativity, and task persistence.

14. Magnet schools, early graduation, and Advanced Placement courses for college credit are increasingly being used to meet the educational needs of the gifted and talented.

FOR DISCUSSION

1. List four implications of IDEA–04 for how you will construct tests and collect other data to assess the progress of children with disabilities in the general curriculum.

2. Describe at least two methods for determining whether a special learner's behavior is interfering with learning.

3. Assume you are asked by a multidisciplinary team to monitor and collect data on one of your students who may be mildly mentally retarded. What types of information would you collect, and in what form would you report these data to the multidisciplinary team?

4. IDEA–04 requires that infants, toddlers, and preschoolers be identified and, if needed, provided with special education services. Speculate about the role, if any, you may play in this effort as a K–12 classroom teacher.

5. Compare and contrast the traditional discrepancy model of learning disability determination to the new, optional response to intervention (RTI) method. Be sure to compare and contrast the eligibility procedures and the shortcomings of both approaches.

6. What effect will recent interpretations of Section 504 of the Rehabilitation Act have on you as a classroom teacher? What are the costs and benefits of these interpretations to teachers, students, and society?

*7. What four characteristics are typically used to identify a learner as gifted and/or talented? What kind of information would you try to obtain to assess a student in each of these areas?

*8. What has the research told us about the relative merits of homogeneous grouping, accelerated programs, enrichment programs, and magnet schools as they apply to the gifted and talented?

*Answers for questions 7 and 8 appear in Appendix F.

CHAPTER 21

METHODS TO ASSESS CHILDREN WITH DISABILITIES IN REGULAR EDUCATION CLASSROOMS

IN CHAPTER 20 we discussed the implications for general education teachers of the 2004 reauthorization of the Individuals with Disabilities Education Act (IDEA–04). It was IDEA–97 that first required general education teachers to be members of the Individual Educational Program (IEP) team of each child with a disability. Under IDEA–04, the IEP team is responsible for developing the child's IEP, which is to include the following:

- a statement of the child's *present* levels of educational performance
- a statement of measurable *annual* goals, and
- a statement of (I) *how* the child's progress toward annual goals will be measured and (II) how the child's parents will be *regularly informed* about the child's progress.

IDEA–04 relaxed certain requirements that were included in IDEA–97. The changes included elimination of two requirements, namely short-term objectives and informing parents of progress as often as parents of nondisabled students are informed. However, IDEA–04 reaffirmed that it is the IEP team that determines whether a student with a disability takes (a) the same annual academic assessment required by the No Child Left Behind Act (NCLB) as do nondisabled peers, (b) the assessment with accommodations, or (c) a state-approved alternate assessment. And, if the IEP team recommends accommodations or an alternate assessment, the IEP team must justify why this is necessary.

Congress's intent in passing IDEA–97, IDEA–04 and NCLB is clear: Children with disabilities must now be instructed within the general curriculum, their progress within the general curriculum must now be assessed regularly and, except where the IEP team can justify accommodations or an alternate assessment, all students with disabilities must participate in the same annual academic assessment required for their nondisabled peers. Because the general education teacher will be the professional on the IEP team most familiar with the general curriculum and the annual academic assessment, the general education teacher, in collaboration with the special education teacher, can expect to play an important role in IEP team meetings. And, because the progress of children with disabilities can often be hampered by behavioral, social, and attitudinal needs that result from the disability, these too will have to be assessed regularly to determine whether they impeded progress in the general curriculum, whenever called for in the IEP.

IDEA AND NCLB: ISSUES AND QUESTIONS

The IDEA and NCLB requirements we have described raise a number of important issues and questions. Several of these are listed here:

Who will be responsible for collecting the educational, behavioral, social, and attitudinal data that will be needed by the IEP team to determine the child's

- current educational performance,
- progress toward annual goals,
- needs that when filled will enable the child with a disability to profit from the general curriculum, and
- other needs that result from the child's disability?

Who will be responsible for determining how the child's progress toward annual goals will be measured?

How will the child's parents be notified about progress?

If general education teachers, as experts in the assessment of progress in the general curriculum (e.g., through teacher-made tests and performance and portfolio assessments) are to collect these data, how can the general education teacher find time to do so?

When a child's disability requires accommodations or an alternate assessment, what kind of data can the regular classroom teacher provide to support such a decision?

If behavioral, social, and attitudinal factors related to the disability impede the progress of a child with a disability in the general curriculum, how are general education teachers to assess these factors?

ASSISTANCE FOR TEACHERS

Congress was aware that many of these questions and issues relate to the classroom teacher's skill in the assessment of children with disabilities, and to the available time to do so. Congress recognized that general education teachers will need assistance if they are to comply with the additional requirements of IDEA. The legislation stipulates that additional resources are to be made available to general education teachers to facilitate adaptation to this expanded role. For example, special education staff and related service providers are to be increasingly available to consult with general education teachers to facilitate instruction and assessment of children with disabilities within the general curriculum. Additional funding is to be sought to support such efforts.

All this may sound promising to you as a general education teacher. However, there may be substantial obstacles to the actual provision of needed support services to general education teachers.

Most special educators and related service providers are not experts in the general curriculum, assessment of performance and progress in the general curriculum, or your state's annual academic assessment that is required under NCLB. Thus even well-intended efforts by special educators to assist general educators in the general curriculum may be less than adequate. In addition, funding of such additional activities and resources can be interpreted to be a local responsibility. This means that funding for additional support will have to be found in what often are financially strapped local budgets or other, unspecified local sources. In an era of heightened competition for limited financial resources, other priorities may be funded first, with efforts to help general teachers comply with IDEA and NCLB requirements left with little or no additional funding. In spite of Congress's recognition of the added burden IDEA places on general education teachers, expectations for significant, consistent assistance may be unrealistic. In any case, both IDEA and NCLB ensure that the regular teacher will play an expanded role in the assessment of the performance and progress of children with disabilities in the general curriculum.

CAN REGULAR TEACHERS ASSESS CHILDREN WITH DISABILITIES?

We believe regular teachers can assess children with disabilities, as long as expectations are appropriate. As a result of completing this course you will have learned many, if not most, of the skills, tools, and techniques needed to assess the current educational performance and progress of children with disabilities in the general curriculum, and to help determine whether they can participate appropriately in the annual academic assessment required by NCLB. These skills, techniques, and tools can be, sometimes with modification, those we have already covered in this text (e.g., teacher-made objective and essay tests, and performance and portfolio assessments).

Many of the skills, techniques, and tools that the teacher may use to collect data for the IEP team to consider in its evaluation of the behavioral, attitudinal, and other impediments to progress in the general curriculum are related to academic assessment techniques. For example, to develop and use tools to assess the behavior of a child with a disability will require skill in the specification of observable, relevant behaviors, something you learned to do when we covered instructional objectives in Chapter 5. Later in this chapter we will discuss tools used to assess attitudes. As you will see, tools to assess attitudes, which are not directly observable, are constructed in much the same way as are objective achievement test items, which we covered in Chapter 6. Because this groundwork has been laid, you may find that assessment of pupil behavior and attitude may be considerably less time-consuming and demanding than it would be if you were not already skilled in the construction and use of achievement tests and assessments.

SHOULD REGULAR TEACHERS ASSESS CHILDREN WITH DISABILITIES?

We believe regular teachers should assess children with disabilities, for two reasons. One is that IDEA now requires this involvement. You will not have a choice. The other is that the classroom teacher may be the only professional on the IEP team with general curriculum expertise and specific knowledge about your state's NCLB required academic assessment. To evaluate the academic performance and progress of a child with a disability in the general curriculum, the IEP team will rely largely on data gathered in the regular classroom, which is the domain of the classroom teacher. No other professional will be better positioned to collect and provide data on a day-to-day basis about the child with a disability's academic performance and progress.

Next, we will discuss more specifically the assessment of current educational performance and progress in the general curriculum. Then, we will discuss the assessment of behavioral and attitudinal factors that can interfere with progress in the general curriculum, with special attention given to the assessment of children with disabilities who take medications that can influence directly learning, behavior, and attitudes.

ASSESSING ACADEMIC PERFORMANCE AND PROGRESS

The educational performance and progress of the child with a disability in the general curriculum may be assessed with teacher-made and standardized tests and assessments. We will discuss each approach in turn.

Teacher-Made Tests and Assessments

Objective and essay tests and performance and portfolio assessments can all be used to assess the performance and progress of children with disabilities in the general curriculum. Depending on the learner's disability, some modifications in administration and scoring may be necessary to obtain accurate information about the learner. Some examples of possible modifications include providing additional time to complete tests and assessments, using stimuli with larger print or Braille, limiting distractions, or taking more frequent breaks. Because the case of each child with a disability may be unique, modifications appropriate for one learner may or may not be appropriate for others.

The objectives and content emphasis of teacher-made tests, including performance assessments and portfolios, can be customized to directly assess the performance and progress of children with disabilities in the regular curriculum. Instead of administering identical tests and assessments to children with disabilities and nondisabled pupils, teachers may tailor or customize the tests they develop to emphasize or address academic, behavioral, and other issues identified in the child with a disability's IEP. Use of teacher-made instruments for the educational assessment of children with disabilities offers the general education teacher needed flexibility to assess children with a wide range of disabilities. By utilizing a personal computer and the various software packages we described in the sidebar for Chapter 6 (see Box 6-1), teachers will be able to make accommodations in teacher-made tests and assessments appropriate to the needs of children with disabilities much more easily than could be done without this technology.

Teacher-made tests and assessments can be customized to meet the needs of children with disabilities far more easily and appropriately than can standardized tests and assessments. Indeed, modifying administration and scoring procedures for standardized tests and assessments undermines the reliability and comparability of the results. For this reason, we expect that much of the data that the IEP team will use to regularly evaluate the performance and progress of each child with a disability will come from teacher-made rather than standardized tests and assessments. In the next section we will detail the problems associated IDEA's requirements that standardized test accommodations and alternate assessments must be provided for children with disabilities who are not able to participate in the same way as their nondisabled peers in annual state- and district-wide standardized assessments required under NCLB. These requirements can seriously limit the usefulness of the results of annual state- and district-wide assessment for children with disabilities.

Standardized Tests and Assessments

IDEA–04 and NCLB require that all children with disabilities be included in state- and district-wide annual assessments, with accommodations and alternate assessments provided that are appropriate for their disabilities. NCLB also requires that the results from these assessments be made available to the public each year.

These requirements are the result of a well-intended effort to improve accountability for the progress of children with disabilities in the general curriculum, which in turn was intended to result in enhanced educational outcomes for children with disabilities. Prior to IDEA–97 and NCLB, most children with disabilities were excluded from annual state- and district-wide assessments. That made assessment of their progress from year to year and across different schools and programs difficult, and it made accountability for district-wide instructional programs and IEPs difficult.

By requiring the participation of all children with disabilities in annual state- and district-wide assessments, Congress hoped to enhance accountability by enabling comparisons to be more easily made among children with disabilities in different classes, schools, districts, and states, and over time. It was believed this would enable the progress of children with disabilities to be tracked over time and across settings in the same way that annual standardized assessments enable such comparisons for nondisabled students. What Congress may have failed to realize, however, is that there is an important difference between comparisons based on standardized tests and comparisons based on nonstandardized accommodated tests and alternate assessments.

Limitations of Accommodations and Alternate Assessments

In Chapter 18 we explained that standardized administration and scoring procedures were necessary to reduce error and thereby enhance reliability. Standardized administration and scoring also enable comparisons among different schools, districts, states, and learners by ensuring that all test takers are evaluated under the same uniform administration conditions and that scoring procedures were followed for the norm group. Yet, both IDEA and NCLB allow modification of the very standardized procedures that are necessary to enable such comparisons to be made. Does this seem contradictory? Can standardized assessments be standardized if they are customized rather than uniform? The answer, of course, is no. Making accommodations in administration or scoring on state- or district-wide assessments or administering alternate assessments will affect test reliability and validity in unknown ways and will compromise comparability of scores.

For some children with disabilities the effects of such accommodations or administering alternate assessments may be minimal, and for others they may be large. In the absence of systematic study of the actual effects of accommodations for disabilities it will be impossible for districts, schools, parents, and others to know whether the test results obtained by children with disabilities under modified administration or scoring conditions represent increased scores, decreased scores, or no effect. Without standardized accommodations across all settings, and without systematic study of the effects of these accommodations on scores, comparisons like those intended under IDEA and NCLB will be plagued by questionable reliability and validity.

Nevertheless, under IDEA and NCLB districts will have no choice but to participate in such programs. The classroom teacher on the IEP team may be called on to assist in the justification for and the interpretation of accommodated standardized or alternate assessments to children with disabilities. Keeping in mind that test reliability will be affected in unknown ways as a result of accommodations and alternate assessments will enable you to appropriately qualify the results of these annual assessments for the IEP team, parents, school staff, and others.

ASSESSING BEHAVIORAL AND ATTITUDINAL FACTORS

Assessment of behavior and attitude in the classroom has not been a formal or routine activity for teachers. Then why are we including this section in this text? There are two reasons. First, the classroom teacher who is able to expand his or her skills to include assessment of special and regular pupil behavior and attitudes may be better able to facilitate the transition to meaningful inclusion and provide important, otherwise unavailable data to the IEP team. Second, IDEA specifically requires that classroom teachers participate in the development and evaluation of behavioral intervention plans.

Assessment, Not Diagnosis

Are we suggesting that teachers should now diagnose behavior and emotional problems? Absolutely not! Diagnosis of behavior and emotional problems is best left to members of the multidisciplinary assessment team and related services providers (e.g., psychologists, psychiatrists, social workers). As we have said before, formal diagnosis, assessment, and treatment of emotional and behavioral disturbance and other disabilities is not the job of the classroom teacher.

Nevertheless, the classroom teacher can contribute importantly to the diagnoses made by other professionals because diagnoses will be dependent, in part, on data obtained in the regular classroom by the classroom teacher. The classroom teacher is also uniquely positioned to provide to the IEP team data regarding the behaviors and attitudes of both special and regular learners that may affect the child with a disability's progress in the general curriculum. Such data, if they are reliable and valid, may enable the classroom teacher, the IEP team, and other professionals to optimally assist the adaptation of the child with a disability and the class to one another. In turn, this should enhance the capacity of the child with a disability to progress in the general curriculum. Ideally, this will then be reflected in improved performance on the NCLB required annual assessment.

In the long run, these data also may save staff time by facilitating learning and adjustment and thereby reducing distractions and behaviors that interfere with learning.

Classroom Diversity, Behavior, and Attitudes

The diversity of students included in the regular classroom will only increase as a result of the spread of full inclusion. Both children with disabilities accustomed to learning in resource or self-contained settings and regular education students unaccustomed to the inclusion of children with disabilities in the classroom can be expected to go through a period of adjustment as more and more children with disabilities are included. As the process of adjustment continues, we may expect both special and regular learners to exhibit behavioral, emotional, and attitudinal reactions to these changes. This may be especially true when children with serious and multiple disabilities are included, particularly those with emotional and behavioral disturbances or serious disabilities that require various assistive technological devices if they are to progress in the general curriculum.

By assessing behavior and attitudes of special and nondisabled learners, the classroom teacher may be able to better monitor the adjustment process and its effects on the performance and progress of children with disabilities. By monitoring patterns and changes over time, the classroom teacher may be able to identify or develop potential strategies based on these data that may result in a facilitation of the adjustment process. Such an outcome would be beneficial to both special and regular learners and staff.

The classroom teacher also can assist the IEP team in determining whether children with disabilities are progressing in the general curriculum by collecting appropriate educational data. When children with disabilities are not progressing in the general curriculum, it will be the task of the IEP team to modify the IEP to enhance the chances that a child with a disability will progress. Such changes may involve nothing more than curricular or educational test and assessment modifications. In these cases the kinds of information provided by teacher-made and standardized achievement tests and measures may be sufficient for the IEP team.

In other cases more than achievement data will be needed. This may be particularly true in the case of children with severe and multiple disabilities, and especially for children with severe emotional and behavioral disturbances. Typically, with severely and multiply disabled children, more than curriculum and assessment changes may be needed. These changes may include referrals to related service providers in the community, a more or less restrictive educational environment, the development of positive behavior improvement plans, provision of counseling or other related services at the school, peer- or classroom-based counseling or interventions, or any one of a number of interventions designed to address the behavioral, emotional, and attitudinal issues that often accompany severe and multiple disabilities.

Behavior Plan Requirements under IDEA

As an IEP team member under IDEA, the regular education teacher is required to participate in the development and evaluation of behavioral intervention plans and the determination of the need for supplementary aids and services, program modifications, and support for school personnel. Earlier in this chapter we also mentioned that if behavioral, emotional, and attitudinal factors are believed to be interfering with performance or progress in the general curriculum, these too will need to be assessed and addressed.

Thus there may be multiple, important reasons for you to assess behavior and attitudes. To enhance your skills in assessing the behavior, social skills, and attitudes of children with disabilities, we will present a number of teacher-made and standardized assessment instruments in the remainder of this chapter. We will first review a variety of teacher-made behavior and attitude assessment instruments, because these teacher-made instruments offer the flexibility needed to assess children with disabilities whose behaviors, needs, disabilities, and issues may vary widely. Then we will provide you with examples of several standardized behavior checklists and rating scales that have demonstrated ability to assess behavior, and which also have proved useful in assessing the effects of medication on behavior and learning. Because many of the medications that children with disabilities and other students take may directly and indirectly affect learning or behavior; and because the number of students taking medication is on the rise, it will increasingly be important for teachers and the IEP team to assess the effects of these medications on learning and behavior.

TEACHER-MADE BEHAVIOR AND ATTITUDE ASSESSMENTS

Before discussing teacher-made tools to assess pupil behavior and attitude, it will be helpful to clarify the distinction between behavior and attitude.

Distinguishing Behavior from Attitude

What is the difference between a behavior and an attitude? If you are a bit unsure, you are in good company! Because these two terms are often confused it will be helpful for us to distinguish between them before we describe how the teacher can develop and use teacher-made measures to assess behavior and attitude. Consider the following:

> *"Just thinking about it makes me mad," said Bob. "I hate this class. The only reason I'm here is because I have to take it. Even though I like my other classes, this one ruins the whole day for me. The teacher is okay, but we always have to wait for the special ed kids. Besides, the materials are useless and the text is a waste of time. Sometimes I don't even attend class or do the readings. And when I am in class I can't think about anything except how frustrating those special ed kids are. I told the teacher about my feelings. I thought she would see that some changes were needed. You know, get the special ed kids out of the class, or get a better book. Anything! Guess what she said? She said that things wouldn't get better until my attitude changed! To top it off, she said she had suspected I had a bad attitude all along and listening to me just confirmed her suspicions. She said the special ed kids were not slowing things down because the aides give them extra help, and that they're here to stay. Then she told me that I have a bad attitude about including the special ed kids. But it's her attitude that's bad. If she had a good attitude she'd be doing something to help me. I think she's had a bad attitude about me all along and listening to her just proved I was right."*

In the situation just described, what do you think a behavior is? What do you think an attitude is? The teacher concluded Bob had a bad attitude from what she saw and heard. Bob came to the conclusion that the teacher's attitude was negative from what he saw and heard. Seeing, looking, hearing, saying—these are all behaviors, and these are what the teacher and Bob focused on to conclude that the other had a bad or negative attitude. But just what are attitudes? Attitudes are fairly consistent and stable ways that people think and feel, and are predisposed to think and feel in the presence of various stimuli. Attitudes describe how people typically think and feel about or react to other people, places, things, or ideas. Neither Bob nor the teacher was able to directly observe the attitude of the other. This is because attitudes themselves, a person's internal thoughts and feelings, never are directly observable! So, we always draw conclusions about unobservable attitudes based on observable behaviors—what someone does, writes, or says.

Does this notion of drawing conclusions about something unobservable sound familiar? It should, because in Chapter 5 we discussed the importance of specifying observable behaviors to draw conclusions about something that is unobservable, namely, learning. We can apply the same skill we learned in Chapter 5 to facilitate our ability to assess attitudes, to directly measure behaviors to assess the effects of behavior on progress in the general curriculum, and to assess the success of our efforts to change behaviors that impede learning.

Assessing Behavior

In this section we will discuss two teacher-made approaches to the direct assessment of student behavior that can also be used to make inferences about students' attitudes. These are observation and sociograms.

Observation   Observation can be classified into two categories, structured and unstructured. For our purposes, the difference between these two methods of assessing behavior lies in the extent of the preparation we go through to "plan" an observation and to record what we observe. Observations may be made over time to (a) assess changes in behavior targeted in a behavior improvement plan, (b) help the IEP team assess the degree to which a child with a disability's behaviors are impeding performance in the general curriculum, or (c) make inferences about a special or regular education pupil's underlying emotions or attitudes. Next we will describe unstructured and structured observations. Then we will consider the pros and cons of observation as a means of assessing pupil behavior.

Unstructured Observation   As the name implies, unstructured observation is open ended. Essentially all that is done to prepare for an observation session is that the teacher identifies the time and place for the observation and how long it will last. Very little preparation time is required. The teacher then observes the behavior of the pupils, recording as much as possible, or whatever appears to be useful, important, or unusual. The following illustrates data produced from an unstructured observation on the playground.

Class: Fourth grade
Date: March 26
Time: 10:25 a.m.
Place: Playground
Activity: Recess

Notes: Sunny, cool, lots of energy. Jim rides wheelchair around fringe of activity. Paul and Barb arguing, Mike running and yelling. Jim rides to the swings and talks to Dorothy and Mike but they ignore him. Jim leaves swings and rides to the school door by himself. Paul playing ball with Pat, Paula tells Mark about math assignment, much activity, but beginning to slow down, bell, time to line up, Paula is first, Jim is second, but Dorothy and Mike step in front of him.

Once the data are recorded, the teacher's task is to make some sense of it. From this record, what conclusions can be drawn? It seems that Jim, a child with a disability in a wheelchair, is not well integrated with the class, at least during recess, and that Dorothy and Mike in particular seem to be negative toward him. Beyond these conclusions, little else that is useful is available. Unfortunately, this is often the case when unstructured observation is employed. Why is this so? One major reason is that no specific purpose was identified for the observation. By attending to all behavior, important patterns or trends may have been overlooked. Was there something that Jim did to antagonize Dorothy and Mike? Were Dorothy and Mike antagonistic to others as well? If these questions were formulated in advance of the observation, specific and potentially more useful data may have been obtained. Identifying the purpose of the observation too often is overlooked in unstructured observation.

When we specify the purpose of the observation before doing the observation, the task of the observer is focused. Now, rather than trying to record everything or all of what seems important at the moment, the observer can zero in on specific approach and avoidance behaviors that indicate positive and negative feelings or attitudes toward whatever or whomever has been identified. Of course, focusing an observation like this incurs the risk of the observer overlooking potentially interesting events. Nevertheless, the benefits in terms of reliability and relevance of the data obtained are substantial. In reality, clearly identifying the purpose of the observation is the first step in conducting a structured observation. Our recommendation is that you refrain from unstructured observation sessions and focus instead on structured observations to help assess pupil behavior.

Structured Observation   A structured observation requires more preparation time, often substantially more than an informal or unstructured observation session. It is necessary to determine why you are observing, what you expect to see or think you might see, and how you will record what you see. The following steps are useful in preparing for a structured observation session:

1. Indicate why you are observing, for example:
   a. To determine how students feel about included children with disabilities.
   b. To see whether particular pairs or groups of students are helping or hindering the acceptance of included students.
   c. To determine whether students feel more positive about reading after your Fun-in-Reading program.

2. Assemble an outline of approach and avoidance behaviors appropriate to why you are observing. To develop an appropriate list of approach and avoidance behaviors, it is often helpful to simply watch what a student does who is turned on or turned off to the person, thing, or activity in question and note the behaviors exhibited. For example, if you want to assess attitude toward reading after the Fun-in-Reading program, the following might be appropriate for an observation during free time:

Approach	*Avoidance*
Looks at books on table	Moves away from books on table
Picks up books on table	Makes faces when looking at books
Reads book(s)	Tells others not to read
Tells others about a book recently read	Expresses dislike for reading

3. If possible, list behaviors in terms of likelihood of occurrence to save time scanning the list and recording the behavior. For example, "read books" would be further down the list than "looks at books on table" and "picks up books on table," since before you read a book you must first look at it and then pick it up.

4. Decide how to record the behaviors you observe. Two common methods are illustrated in Fig. 21.1.

   a. Counting approach: Place a check mark to the right of a behavior listed each time it occurs.

   b. Rating approach: Arrange five columns labeled "Always," "Often," "Sometimes," "Seldom," or "Never" to the right of the behavior, and then put a check in the appropriate column for each behavior to indicate the approximate frequency of occurrence.

   The rating checklist is most useful when the teacher is not able to devote sufficient attention to a student or students long enough to obtain valid frequency counts. Here, the teacher checks the appropriate column after observing for a while. Naturally, such an approach increases the chances of error. However, it is a substantial improvement over an unstructured observation.

Sociograms Before we describe how to measure social interaction, consider the following interchange between Mr. and Mrs. White, the parents of a child with an emotional disturbance, and their son's fifth-grade teacher, Mr. Kelley:

Mr. White: Thank you for taking time out to meet with us today.

Mr. Kelley: I'm pleased you both could make it.

Mrs. White: We're worried about our son, Johnny. He seems more depressed now that he is in the regular classroom. You know he was in the self-contained classroom for the last four years. He never had a lot of friends, but there always were a few kids he liked. But he says no one likes him in the regular class. We're afraid he is becoming a "loner" since he was included. Is he fitting in?

Mr. Kelley: Uh ... well ... Johnny always does his work—he's never been a behavior problem.

Mr. White: We're happy to hear that, but what about socially? Does he have a friend or group of friends he pals around with?

Checklist 1 *(Frequency Approach)*

Name _____   Date _____   Time _____

Behaviors	Frequency
1. Looks at books on table	_____
2. Picks up books on table	_____
3. Reads books	_____
4. Tells others about books read	_____
5. Moves away from books on table	_____
6. Makes faces when looking at books	_____
7. Tells others not to read	_____
8. Expresses dislike for reading	_____

Checklist 2 *(Rating Approach)*

Name _____   Date _____   Time _____

Behaviors	*Always*	*Often*	*Sometimes*	*Seldom*	*Never*
1. Looks at books on table					
2. Picks up books on table					
3. Reads books					
4. Tells others about books read					
5. Moves away from books on table					
6. Makes faces when looking at books					
7. Tells others not to read					
8. Expresses dislike for reading					

FIGURE 21.1 Two checklists for a structured observation to assess attitudes toward reading.

MR. KELLEY: Oh, I wouldn't know about that. Under IDEA–04 we have to be sure he progresses in the general curriculum so I'm focused on helping him that way. He's never gotten in trouble, though!

MRS. WHITE: Please. We're more worried about his emotional and social development. We know he is a good student and that he has good conduct. We can see that from his report cards we now get regularly. What we want to know is how well he fits in socially. Can you tell us that? Please?

MR. KELLEY: I'm a teacher, not a sociologist. I'm teaching him and he's progressing in the general curriculum. Not every one of these kids does, you know. I have 28 other kids to worry about and so much paperwork you wouldn't believe it. All I know is that he's progressing academically, he's not a troublemaker, and he gets good grades.

MRS. WHITE: But could we just get an idea of how Johnny is getting along with his class-mates?

MR. KELLEY: If you want, come by during recess and lunch and watch. You're welcome to!

MR. WHITE: But couldn't you find out some other way? Is observation the only way to tell whether kids are developing socially?

MR. KELLEY: (*Looking annoyed*) What else is there?

Although observation is one way to obtain information on social development or group behavior, a sociogram is another. A sociogram is one type of sociometric measure. Sociometry is the measurement of interaction patterns in groups. In the classroom, the following steps may be followed to develop a sociogram:

1. On a sheet of paper, ask each child to nominate two of his or her peers for a given activity (e.g., "With whom would you like to play at recess?").

2. Construct a table to record "choosers" and "chosens," and record the choices on it. Such a table is illustrated in Fig. 21.2. In this table, choosers are listed vertically and their two choices are indicated by X's under the names of the students they chose (e.g., Don chose Bob and Bill). By inspecting the row of totals, you discover the number of times each student was chosen—an index of popularity for the activity chosen.

3. Based on your table of choices, develop a sociogram, a graphical representation of the choice patterns in the group. A sociogram representing the choice pattern from Fig. 21.2 is illustrated in Fig. 21.3. The sociogram is constructed by drawing arrows among the circles to indicate the direction of the choices.

4. Interpret the sociogram, which is done by inspecting the choice patterns and looking for cliques, cleavages, stars, mutual choices, and isolates. These terms are defined as follows:

   a. Cliques: Pupils select only each other and avoid selecting others in the group. In our example, Don, Bill, and Bob represent a clique.

   b. Cleavage: Two or more groups in the class fail to nominate each other. In our example there is a cleavage, a split between Don, Bill, and Bob, and Pat, Joan, Maria, Mary, and Ted.

   c. Stars: Pupils most frequently selected. In our example there is no single star. Instead, both Maria and Mary may be considered stars, since each was chosen three times.

| | | Chosen | | | | | | | |
		Don	Maria	Pat	Joan	Bob	Bill	Mary	Ted
	Don					X	X		
	Maria			X	X				
	Pat		X					X	
	Joan			X				X	
Choosers	Bob	X					X		
	Bill	X				X			
	Mary		X		X				
	Ted		X					X	
Totals		2	3	2	2	2	2	3	0

FIGURE 21.2 Table illustrating first and second choices.

d. Mutual choices: Two individuals who select each other. Don and Bill, Don and Bob, Bob and Bill, Joan and Mary, and Pat and Maria all represent mutual choices.

e. Isolates: Individuals not selected by any other pupil. In our example, Ted would be the isolate.

After the sociogram has been interpreted, decisions can be made about possible interventions. For example, steps may be taken to get Ted more involved in the class, or an effort may be made to weaken the clique or bridge the cleavage. Care should be taken in interpreting sociograms, however. While they do have certain advantages, they also have their limitations. Some of the limitations of sociograms are as follows:

1. Only choices, not the reasons for the choices, are indicated.

2. Mutual choices and cliques do not necessarily indicate social acceptance or integration. For example, they may indicate common difficulties in being accepted or integrated into the class or some common advantage, depending on the situation. If the question "With whom would you like to sit during the math test?" were asked, the responses might indicate a hope to accidentally or intentionally "share" answers.

3. It is tempting to assume that isolates are actually rejected by the other pupils. Rather than being seen as undesirable, isolates may simply be new, shy, or not chosen for some other relatively minor reason. In general, however, isolates do tend to be less popular socially than nonisolates.

4. Popularity or isolation often depends on the situation. As mentioned before, choices may change depending on the kind of questions asked.

5. Finally, with a class of 25 to 30 pupils, a sociogram can be quite complicated and time consuming to construct. In general, use of a sociogram at the beginning and end of the school year, with perhaps one more administration at midyear, is about the extent to which the average teacher can use this method of measurement.

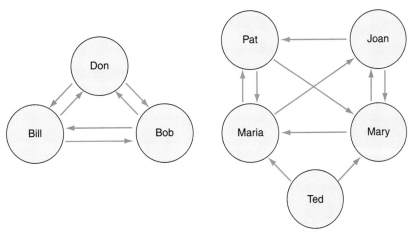

FIGURE 21.3 Sociogram representing choice pattern in Fig. 21.2.

Assessing Attitudes

Why bother measuring attitudes anyway? Under IDEA more and more children with disabilities will be seen in regular classrooms. Not all students will enjoy, or even be neutral about, the inclusion of a child with a disability in the classroom. No teacher will be fortunate enough to have only students who are supportive, sensitive, and welcoming toward included children with disabilities. Not everyone believes children with disabilities should be included, so we should expect that they will not always be welcome with open arms. Therefore some students are likely to already have, or will develop, negative attitudes about children with disabilities. If such attitudes can be assessed before children with disabilities actually appear in the classroom, or can be identified shortly after they have been included, the classroom teacher or other professional may be able to intervene to prevent or minimize negative attitudes and thereby enhance acceptance of the child with a disability. This, in turn, should enhance progress in the general curriculum and save the teacher considerable time in the future. Although inappropriate in the lower or primary grades, paper and pencil teacher-made attitude questionnaires can help assess attitudes in most other classroom settings. We will review three examples of attitude scales next: the Likert scale, two-point scales, and semantic differentials.

Likert Scales   One paper and pencil method of assessing attitudes was developed by and named after Rensis Likert (1932). The Likert scales have become one of the most widely used methods of attitude assessment. Likert scales consist of a series of attitude statements about some person, group, or thing. Respondents indicate the extent to which they agree or disagree with each statement, and the overall score then suggests whether the individual's attitude is favorable or unfavorable. Figure 21.4 illustrates a very brief Likert scale that might be used to assess attitudes toward a tests and measurement course.

Scoring Likert Scales   To complete this scale, students would simply circle the appropriate letter for each item. To score the scale, weights are assigned to each choice, depending on whether the item is worded positively or negatively.

Directions: Indicate the extent to which you agree or disagree with each statement by circling the appropriate letter to the right of each statement.

	Strongly Agree	Agree	Uncertain	Disagree	Strongly Disagree
1. I have a hard time keeping awake in class.	SA	A	U	D	SD
2. This course should be required for teachers.	SA	A	U	D	SD
3. I like learning to write objective test items.	SA	A	U	D	SD
4. I daydream a lot in class.	SA	A	U	D	SD
5. I often feel like coming to this class.	SA	A	U	D	SD

FIGURE 21.4   A five-item Likert scale to assess attitudes toward a tests and measurement course.

For example, the weights assigned to the options for item 1 in Fig. 21.4, which is worded negatively, would be

SA = 1

A = 2

U = 3

D = 4

SD = 5

The weights assigned to the options for item 2, which is worded positively, would be

SA = 5

A = 4

U = 3

D = 2

SD = 1

An individual's score for each item would be the value assigned to the choice selected. For example, if an individual circled SA for item 1 (negatively worded), his or her score for that item would be 1. If the same individual circled SA for item 2 (positively worded), his or her score for that item would be 5. Figure 21.5 illustrates the attitude scale depicted in Fig. 21.4 with items marked as either positive or negative, options circled, and weights assigned for the choices.

To score the scale, sum up the weights for the options selected and then divide the total by the number of items. This provides the student's mean attitude score. The mean attitude score for our hypothetical student is 2.0 because $(2 + 2 + 1 + 1 + 4)/5 = 2.0$. Next, we would have to conclude whether the student's responses reflected a positive or negative attitude toward the course. If the score is less than 3.0, as was the case for our hypothetical student in Fig. 21.5, a negative attitude exists.

Advantages and Disadvantages of Likert Scales   The following are some of the most salient advantages and disadvantages of Likert scales:

Advantages

1. They are quick and economical to administer and score.
2. They are easily adapted to most attitude measurement situations.
3. They provide direct and reliable assessment of attitudes when scales are well constructed.
4. They lend themselves well to item analysis procedures (see Chapter 10).

Disadvantages

1. Results are easily faked where individuals want to present a false impression of their attitudes (this can be offset somewhat by developing a good level of rapport with the respondents and convincing them that honest responses are in their best interests).

Directions: Indicate the extent to which you agree or disagree with each statement by circling the appropriate letter to the right of each statement.

	Strongly Agree	Agree	Uncertain	Disagree	Strongly Disagree
1. I have a hard time keeping awake in class. (Negative)	SA (1)	Ⓐ (2)	U (3)	D (4)	SD (5)
2. This course should be required for teachers. (Positive)	SA (5)	A (4)	U (3)	Ⓓ (2)	SD (1)
3. I like learning to write objective test items. (Positive)	SA (5)	A (4)	U (3)	D (2)	ⓈⒹ (1)
4. I daydream a lot in class. (Negative)	ⓈⒶ (1)	A (2)	U (3)	D (4)	SD (5)
5. I often feel like coming to this class. (Positive)	SA (5)	Ⓐ (4)	U (3)	D (2)	SD (1)

FIGURE 21.5 Sample Likert scale with items labeled as positive or negative, options circled, and weights assigned to choices.

2. Intervals between points on the scale do not represent equal changes in attitude for all individuals (i.e., the differences between SA and A may be slight for one individual and great for another).

3. Internal consistency of the scale may be difficult to achieve (care must be taken to have unidimensional items aimed at a single person, group, event, or method).

4. Good attitude statements take time to construct (it is usually best to begin by constructing several times as many attitude statements as you will actually need, then selecting only those that best assess the attitude in question).

The last point, that attitude statements are time-consuming to construct, bears elaboration. In Chapter 6 you learned how to avoid common errors in constructing objective test items. Fortunately, many of the same guidelines apply to the construction of attitude statements. Next we provide some suggestions for writing attitude statements.

Suggestions for Writing Attitude Statements While some of the following suggestions are straightforward, others are not. Examples of poorly written and well-written attitude statements are provided to clarify the suggestions. A five-choice scale (strongly agree to strongly disagree) would follow each statement.

1. Write simple, clear, and direct sentences. Keep in mind that your goal is to assess attitude in as valid and reliable a fashion as possible. You are not trying to assess another person's intellectual ability, vocabulary, or reading comprehension or to demonstrate your own!

Poor item: In any kind of choice situation, we are likely to discover that different individuals will think and express themselves in ways that are idiosyncratic to them, and we should be willing to tolerate different kinds of behavioral manifestations, which by inference are related to their unobservable cognition and affect.

Better item: We should be tolerant of different kinds of behavior.

2. Write short statements. A general rule is that attitude statements should rarely, if ever, exceed 20 words. The previous item is a good example of excessive wordiness. Another follows:

Poor item: When a person finds himself or herself in a situation in which he or she can take advantage of another person, he or she can usually be expected to do so.

Better item: Basically, people can't be trusted.

3. Avoid negatives, especially double negatives.

Poor item: There isn't a teacher in this school that does not respect student rights.

Better item: Teachers in this school respect student rights.

4. Avoid factual statements. Remember that you are attempting to assess affective responses, not cognitive responses.

Poor item: Career education programs require considerable developmental funds to begin.

Better item: The price tag for starting up career education programs is too high to be warranted.

5. Avoid reference to the past. Unless you are for some reason interested in retrospective accounts of past attitudes (which are likely to be less reliable than present-day attempts at attitude assessment), phrase your statements in the present tense.

Poor item: I have always gotten good grades when I wanted to.

Better item: I get good grades when I want to.

6. Avoid absolutes like *all, none, always,* and *never.* At best, such terms add little or nothing to the statement. At worst, they add either confusion or certainty.

Poor item: I never met a child with a disability I didn't like.

Better item: I like most children with disabilities.

7. Avoid nondistinguishing statements. Such statements fail to discriminate between various attitude positions. In other words, they are statements with which most people either agree or disagree.

Poor item: I would rather go to school than do anything else.

Better item: School is one of my favorite activities.

8. Avoid irrelevancies. Such statements fail to address the real issue in question.

Poor item: My morning walk to school is pleasant.

Better item: I look forward to walking to school in the morning.

9. Use *only, merely,* and *just* sparingly. Although such terms do not always introduce ambiguity, in many instances they do. It is usually better to avoid them.

   Poor item: Including children with disabilities is the only way we can ensure their success.

   Better item: Including children with disabilities is the best way to ensure their success.

10. Use one thought per statement. If double-barreled statements are written, respondents will not know which part of the statement to respond to.

    Poor item: A good teacher knows the subject matter and treats both special and regular students fairly.

    Better item: A good teacher treats both regular and special students fairly.

Now you have some suggestions for writing attitude statements. However, these suggestions will be ineffective unless you thoroughly sample the relevant aspects of the attitudes to be measured. In other words, it is useful to consider several different kinds of statements that will enable you to tap the attitude in question adequately and avoid tapping irrelevant aspects of attitudes. You do this by focusing your Likert scale.

Focusing the Likert Scale   Writing good attitude statements takes time. It makes sense to focus your writing on those aspects of the attitude in question that are relevant. What are they? The following suggestions should help you determine them:

1. List the attitudinal area in question (e.g., attitudes toward including children with disabilities that have serious medical conditions).

2. List relevant approach and avoidance behaviors, that is, behaviors that indicate a positive or negative attitude toward a person, subject, group, or object. The list would include behaviors that lead to

   a. increased or decreased contact with the person, object, or group in question, or
   b. exhibitions of support or disdain for the person, object, or group.

(For example, approach behaviors may include the following: talks about inviting the child with a disability to a birthday party, takes time to help a child with a disability without being asked to do so, reads books about serious medical conditions. Avoidance behaviors could include these: talks about avoiding a child with a disability outside of class, avoids contact with a child with a disability during class, tells other students they may "catch" the medical disorder.

3. Write your attitude statements. A good way to begin is to lump them into two categories, including those that someone might say to indicate approach or avoidance tendencies.

4. Write several such statements for each approach or avoidance behavior listed in Step 2.

5. Use the suggestions given for writing attitude statements to avoid common flaws.

You are now ready to begin constructing your own Likert scales. As with any skill, practice will be necessary if you want to be good at it. Two other commonly used attitude measures, the two-point scale and the bipolar adjective scale, will be described next.

Two-Point Scales   The two-point scale is a variation of the Likert scale. The only differences between this scale and the Likert scale lie in the response options and in the scoring of the scale. Rather than selecting from among five degrees of agreement or disagreement, the respondent must choose between two options: yes to agree, or no to disagree. For this reason, this type of scale is often referred to as a forced choice scale. In essence, the respondent is forced into an all or none indication of agreement or disagreement. Figure 21.6 is an example of a two-point scale measuring attitudes toward two-point scales.

Advantages and Disadvantages of Two-Point Scales   The two-point scale has several advantages. It is simpler and more straightforward than a Likert scale, responses are less likely to be inaccurately indicated, and many times a clearer indication of attitudinal preference is obtained than could be from the Likert scale. Its main disadvantage is that such a scale can rub people the wrong way. Most people do not have clear yes or no, black or white perceptions or attitudes, and they sometimes resent scales that suggest the world operates in such simplistic terms. Such individuals may purposely respond inaccurately in protest of such scales, damaging the validity of the attitude assessment. Problems like this can be defused somewhat by addressing the issues before administering the scale and giving individuals whose views differ the opportunity to voice their objections.

Scoring Two-Point Scales   Coming up with an attitude score for a two-point scale follows much the same process as was used in scoring a Likert scale. The difference is that weights of +1 and −1 are assigned to the options depending on whether the statement contains positive or negative wording. After summing and averaging the weights for the entire scale, decisions are made as to whether the score indicates a positive or negative attitude according to the following rule.

> Rule: If the average is greater than zero, a positive attitude is reflected. If the score is less than or equal to zero, a negative attitude is reflected.

Figure 21.7 illustrates the two-point scale presented in Fig. 21.6 with options circled and scoring completed. Adding up the weights of the options selected, we have

(1)	+1
(2)	−1
(3)	+1
(4)	+1
	+2

DIRECTIONS: Circle *yes* or *no* to indicate whether you agree or disagree with each statement.

1. Two-point scales are underutilized.	yes	no
2. I prefer Likert scales to two-point scales.	yes	no
3. When I teach, I will use two-point scales.	yes	no
4. Likert scales are easier to use than two-point scales.	yes	no

FIGURE 21.6   A two-point scale measuring attitudes toward two-point scales.

DIRECTIONS: Circle *yes* or *no* to indicate whether you agree or disagree with each statement.

1. Two-point scales are underutilized.	(yes) (+1)	no (−1)
2. I prefer Likert scales to two-point scales.	(yes) (−1)	no (+1)
3. When I teach, I will use two-point scales.	(yes) (+1)	no (−1)
4. Likert scales are easier to use than two-point scales.	yes (−1)	(no) (+1)

FIGURE 21.7   A scored two-point scale with weights assigned to options.

Dividing by the number of items, we have

$$2/4 = 0.5$$

According to our rule, since 0.5 is greater than zero, this respondent has a positive attitude toward two-point scales.

Bipolar Adjective Scales   The bipolar adjective scale differs from the previous two scales mainly because it does not use attitude statements. Instead, a word or phrase referring to the person, object, or group in question is presented, along with a list of adjectives that have opposite, or bipolar, meanings. By circling one of the seven points in the scale, respondents indicate the degree to which they feel the adjective represents their attitude. Figure 21.8 illustrates a bipolar adjective scale.

As you may have guessed, the major task in constructing a bipolar adjective scale is the selection of adjectives. A handy source of such adjectives is Osgood, Suci, and Tannenbaum (1957), which provides a lengthy list of bipolar adjectives. However, you are encouraged to think of adjectives that will be particularly relevant to what you want to measure. Many times this is better than borrowing from the lists of others.

Scoring the scale can be done in two ways. The first way is very similar to the procedures outlined for the Likert and two-point scales. Weights could be assigned, depending on whether the positive adjective was on the left (1 would get a weight of 7,

DIRECTIONS: Circle one of the numbers between each pair of adjectives to best indicate how closely one of the adjectives describes your attitude about essay questions.

			Essay	questions				
good	1	2	3	4	5	6	7	bad
unplesasant	1	2	3	4	5	6	7	pleasant
fair	1	2	3	4	5	6	7	unfair
ugly	1	2	3	4	5	6	7	beautiful
meaningful	1	2	3	4	5	6	7	meaningless
unimportant	1	2	3	4	5	6	7	important
positive	1	2	3	4	5	6	7	negative
painful	1	2	3	4	5	6	7	pleasurable

FIGURE 21.8   A bipolar adjective scale.

and 7 a weight of 1) or on the right (1 would get a weight of 1, and 7 a weight of 7). The weights would then be summed and averaged, and a score of 3.5 or more would be indicative of a positive attitude. However, there are so many numbers involved that such an approach may become cumbersome, and the likelihood of clerical errors is considerable. Consequently, we recommend an alternative procedure to score a bipolar adjective scale:

1. Assign weights of 7, 6, 5, 4, 3, 2, 1 to each option, regardless of whether the positive or negative adjective is on the left.

2. Sum all the scores (weights) for the pairs with the positive adjective on the left.

3. Sum all the scores (weights) for the pairs with the negative adjective on the left.

4. Subtract the score for the left-negative adjective pairs from the score for the left-positive adjective pairs.

5. Divide the score by the number of adjective pairs.

6. Make a decision as to the direction of the attitude according to the following rule: If the average is greater than zero, a positive attitude is reflected. If the average is equal to or less than zero, a negative attitude is reflected.

Figure 21.9 illustrates part of the bipolar adjective scale presented in Fig. 21.8, with choices circled and scoring completed. Adding up the weights for the left-positive adjectives we have $2 + 2 = 4$. Adding up the weights for the left-negative items we have $7 + 4 = 11$. Subtracting the left-negative sum from the left-positive sum, we have $4 - 11 = -7$. Dividing this score by the number of adjective pairs, we have $-7/4 = -1.75$. Since -1.75 is less than zero, according to our rule these responses indicate a negative attitude toward essay questions.

MONITORING CHILDREN WITH DISABILITIES WHO ARE TAKING MEDICATION

Next we will consider a growing category of special and regular learners, those who take prescription and nonprescription medications that may affect learning, behavior, emotions, and attitudes.

DIRECTIONS: Circle one of the numbers between each pair of adjectives to best indicate how closely one of the adjectives describes your attitude about essay questions.

				Essay questions				
good	1	2	3	4	5	6	7	bad
(*positive*)	(7)	(6)	(5)	(4)	(3)	(2)	(1)	
unplesasant	1	2	3	4	5	6	7	pleasant
(*negative*)	(7)	(6)	(5)	(4)	(3)	(2)	(1)	
fair	1	2	3	4	5	6	7	unfair
(*positive*)	(7)	(6)	(5)	(4)	(3)	(2)	(1)	
ugly	1	2	3	4	5	6	7	beautiful
(*negative*)	(7)	(6)	(5)	(4)	(3)	(2)	(1)	

FIGURE 21.9 A scored bipolar adjective scale (weights assigned to choices are in parentheses)

Medication Use Is Increasing

With full inclusion now being federal law, the regular classroom teacher may expect to see increased numbers of severely and multiply challenged students in the regular classroom. Many of these children with disabilities will have significant emotional, behavioral, and medical disorders that are managed with medication. Recent literature reviews are unanimous in concluding that the use of psychiatric (i.e., psychotropic or psychoactive) medications such as stimulants, antidepressants, antianxiety agents, and antipsychotics with children is rapidly increasing, with 5% of more of school-age children now taking psychiatric medications (Delate, Gelenberg, Simmons, & Motheral, 2004; Olfson, Marcus, Weissman, & Jensen, 2002; Zito et al., 2003). This is in spite of a relative lack of objective, empirical support for their safety and efficacy with children and adolescents, with the exception of stimulants for the child with attention deficit hyperactivity disorder, or ADHD (Brown & Sammons, 2002; Kubiszyn, Brown, & DeMers, 1997).

Side Effects Are Always Present

All medications prescribed for the management of emotional or behavioral problems (i.e., psychotropic or psychoactive medications) and many that are prescribed for other difficulties (e.g., anticonvulsants, antihypertensives) have potential for unexpected side effects, such as impairments in learning, concentration, memory, awareness, coordination, consciousness, respiration, heart rate and rhythm, and other vital functions (Birmaher & Brent, 2003; Labellarte & Ginsburg, 2003). Thus psychoactive and other powerful medications can interfere with the ability of children with disabilities to progress in the general curriculum. If collection of classroom-based data is required by the IEP team to assess the extent to which medication may be interfering with a special learner's progress in the general curriculum, the classroom teacher may again play a pivotal role in the collection of such data.

The Teacher's Role in Evaluating Medication and Psychosocial Interventions

Traditionally psychiatrists, pediatricians, and other physicians who prescribe the medications have relied on parent report or student self-report, typically in the practitioner's office, to make important decisions about initiating, adjusting, or terminating a child's medication. Since the reliability and validity of data obtained in this way may be questioned, school- and teacher-based data are increasingly being requested to help make these decisions (DuPaul & Carlson, 2005; Kubiszyn & Carlson, 1995). Practitioners are now asking teachers to complete one or more of a variety of medication-related and behavior rating scales and questionnaires. Completion of these instruments provides prescribers with needed real-world data about medication safety and efficacy. Thus the classroom teacher may expect to play a more and more active and important role in collecting and validating the data prescribers must have before making decisions about medication for children with disabilities. Similarly, the IEP team could benefit from this information to help it determine the degree to which medication may be affecting a special learner's progress and performance in the general curriculum.

In addition, psychologists and child and family therapists also are recognizing the importance of obtaining classroom data to help assess the efficacy of their psychosocial interventions with children with disabilities and their families. They, too, are increasingly asking, either directly or through parents of children with disabilities, for teachers to provide a variety of types of classroom data (e.g., from observations, sociograms, and questionnaires or rating scales). The bottom line is that both prescribers and mental health professionals are increasingly recognizing the importance of obtaining reliable and valid data from the classroom teacher to assess the safety and efficacy of their interventions.

With full inclusion of children with disabilities now mandated under IDEA, classroom teachers can expect more severely and multiply disabled learners in their classrooms who are under the ongoing care of prescribing and mental health professionals. Thus more requests for classroom data from nonschool professionals may be expected.

To familiarize you with some of the data collection tasks you may be asked to perform, we present some examples of several of the more commonly used medication and behavior rating scales. Our mention of these instruments does not represent an endorsement of them; these are simply some of a wide range of similar instruments that are in use.

Commonly Used Standardized Scales and Checklists

Probably the most commonly used questionnaire in schools is the teacher version of the Conners' Rating Scale–Revised (CRS-R) (Conners, 1997a). The Long Form has 59 items and the Short Form is 28 items long. There is also an accompanying Conners' Teacher Information Form (CTIF) (Conners, 1997b) that helps clinicians collect and organize information about the child based on information available to teachers. These forms are useful for children with a variety of emotional and behavioral problems including ADHD. The CRS-S Short Form will take about 5–10 minutes to complete. A similar rating scale for parents also exists. The CRS-R teacher version (short form) appears in Fig. 21.10.

The Child Behavior Checklist–Teacher Rating Form, or CBCL–TRF (Achenbach, 1991) is the teacher version of a similar questionnaire for parents. It is longer than the Conners questionnaires (118 items) and is useful in identifying a variety of emotional and behavioral symptoms. It is often used in conjunction with the parent version (CBCL-PRF) to compare teacher and parental perceptions of the same child for screening, diagnosis, and ongoing evaluation of both medication and psychosocial interventions. The CBCL–TRF will take 15–20 minutes to complete. Page three of the four-page TRF is reproduced in Fig. 21.11.

The Behavior Assessment System for Children–Teacher Rating Scales (BASC–TRS) (Reynolds & Kamphaus, 1992) is a slightly longer but perhaps more versatile rating scale in that it also has parent and self-report versions that the child completes. This enables comparison among teacher, parent, and child for screening, diagnosis, and ongoing evaluation of both medication and psychosocial interventions. It too is useful for identifying a variety of emotional and behavioral symptoms. The BASC–TRS 6 to 11-year-old version is 148 items long and the 12 to 18-year-old version is 138 items long. The BASC–TRS takes about 20 minutes to complete. A portion of the first page of the BASC–TRS is reproduced in Fig. 21.12.

Conners' Teacher Rating Scale-Revised (S)

by C. Keith Conners, Ph.D.

Child's name: _____ Gender: M   F

Birthdate: ____/ ____/ ____   Age: _____   School Grade: _____
          Month Day Year

Teacher's Name: _____ Today's Date: ____/ ____/ ____
                                                                    Month Day Year

Instructions: Below are a number of common problems that children have in school. Please rate each item according to how much of a problem it has been in the last month. For each item, ask yourself, "How much of a problem has this been in the last month?" and circle the best answer for each one. If none, not at all, seldom, or very infrequently, you would circle 0. if very much true, or it occurs very often or frequently, you would circle 3. You would circle 1 or 2 for ratings in between. Please respond to each item.

	NOT TRUE AT ALL (Never, Seldom)	JUST A LITTLE TRUE (Occasion-ally)	PRETTY MUCH TRUE (Often,Quite a Bit)	VERY MUCH TRUE (Very Often, Very Frequent)
1. Inattentive, easily distracted	0	1	2	3
2. Defiant	0	1	2	3
3. Restless in the "squirmy" sense	0	1	2	3
4. Forgets things he/she has already learned	0	1	2	3
5. Disturbs other children	0	1	2	3
6. Actively defies or refuses to comply with adults' requests	0	1	2	3
7. Is always "on the go" or acts as if driven by a motor	0	1	2	3
8. Poor in spelling	0	1	2	3
9. Cannot remain still	0	1	2	3
10. Spiteful or vindictive	0	1	2	3
11. Leaves seat in classroom or in other situations in which remaining seated is expected	0	1	2	3
12. Fidgets with hands or feet or squirms in seat	0	1	2	3
13. Not reading up to par	0	1	2	3
14. Short attention span	0	1	2	3
15. Argues with adults	0	1	2	3
16. Only pays attention to things he/she is really interested in	0	1	2	3
17. Has difficulty waiting for his/her turn	0	1	2	3
18. Lacks interest in schoolwork	0	1	2	3
19. Distractibility or attention span a problem	0	1	2	3
20. Temper outbursts; explosive, unpredictable behavior	0	1	2	3
21. Runs about or climbs excessively in situations where it is inappropriate	0	1	2	3
22. Poor in arithmetic	0	1	2	3
23. Interrupts or intrudes on others (e.g., butts into others' conversations or games)	0	1	2	3
24. Has difficulty playing or engaging in leisure activities quietly	0	1	2	3
25. Fails to finish things he/she starts	0	1	2	3
26. Does uctions and fails to finish schoolwork (not due to oppositional behavior or failure to understand instructions)	0	1	2	3
27. Excitable, impulsive	0	1	2	3
28. Restless, always up and on the go	0	1	2	3

FIGURE 21.10 The Conners Rating Scale–Revised, Teacher Version.

Below is a list of items that describe pupils. For each item that describes the pupil **now or within the past 2 months**, please circle the **2** if the item is **very true** or **often true** of the pupil. Circle the **1** if the item is **somewhat** or **sometimes true** of the pupil. If the item is **not true** of the pupil, circle the **0**. Please answer all items as well as you can, even if some do not seem to apply to this pupil.

0 = Not True (as far as you know)   1 = Somewhat or Sometimes True   2 = Very True or Often True

0 1 2	1. Acts too young for his/her age		0 1 2	31. Fears he/she might think or do something bad
0 1 2	2. Hums or makes other odd noises in class		0 1 2	32. Feels he/she has to be perfect
0 1 2	3. Argues a lot		0 1 2	33. Feels or complains that no one loves him/her
0 1 2	4. Fails to finish things he/she starts		0 1 2	34. Feels others are out to get him/her
0 1 2	5. Behaves like opposite sex		0 1 2	35. Feels worthless or inferior
0 1 2	6. Defiant, talks back to staff		0 1 2	36. Gets hurt a lot, accident-prone
0 1 2	7. Bragging, boasting		0 1 2	37. Gets in many fights
0 1 2	8. Can't concentrate, can't pay attention for long		0 1 2	38. Gets teased a lot
0 1 2	9. Can't get his/her mind off certain thoughts; obsessions (describe): _____		0 1 2	39. Hangs around with others who get in trouble
			0 1 2	40. Hears sounds or voices that aren't there (describe): _____
	_____			
			0 1 2	41. Impulsive or acts without thinking
0 1 2	10. Can't sit still, restless, or hyperactive		0 1 2	42. Would rather be alone than with others
0 1 2	11. Clings to adults or too dependent		0 1 2	43. Lying or cheating
			0 1 2	44. Bites fingernails
0 1 2	12. Complains of loneliness		0 1 2	45. Nervous, high-strung, or tense
0 1 2	13. Confused or seems to be in a fog		0 1 2	46. Nervous movements or twitching (describe): _____
0 1 2	14. Cries a lot			
0 1 2	15. Fidgets			_____
0 1 2	16. Cruelty, bullying, or meanness to others		0 1 2	47. Overconforms to rules
0 1 2	17. Daydreams or gets lost in his/her thoughts		0 1 2	48. Not liked by other pupils
0 1 2	18. Deliberately harms self or attempts suicide		0 1 2	49. Has difficulty learning
			0 1 2	50. Too fearful or anxious
0 1 2	19. Demands a lot of attention			
0 1 2	20. Destroys his/her own things		0 1 2	51. Feels dizzy
			0 1 2	52. Feels too guilty
0 1 2	21. Destroys property belonging to others			
0 1 2	22. Difficulty following directions		0 1 2	53. Talks out of turn
			0 1 2	54. Overtired
0 1 2	23. Disobedient at school			
0 1 2	24. Disturbs other pupils		0 1 2	55. Overweight
				56. Physical problems without known medical cause:
0 1 2	25. Doesn't get along with other pupils		0 1 2	a. Aches or pains (**not** headaches)
0 1 2	26. Doesn't seem to feel guilty after misbehaving		0 1 2	b. Headaches
			0 1 2	c. Nausea, feels sick
0 1 2	27. Easily jealous		0 1 2	d. Problems with eyes (describe): _____
0 1 2	28. Eats or drinks things that are not food — **don't** include sweets (describe): _____			
			0 1 2	e. Rashes or other skin problems
	_____		0 1 2	f. Stomachaches or cramps
			0 1 2	g. Vomiting, throwing up
0 1 2	29. Fears certain animals, situations, or places other than school (describe): _____		0 1 2	h. Other (describe): _____
				_____
	_____			
0 1 2	30. Fears going to school			_____

PAGE 3   *Please see other side*

FIGURE 21.11 The Child Behavior Checklist–Teacher's Rating Form, or CBCL–TRF.

Source: Achenbach, T. (1991). *Manual for the Teacher's Report Form.* Burlington: University of Vermont, Department of Psychiatry. Copyright © T.M. Achenbach. Reproduced by permission.

BASC

Teacher Rating Scales **TRS-C (6-11)**

Computer Entry Form

Cecil R. Reynolds and Randy W. Kamphaus

Child's name _____
First   Middle   Last

Date _____   Birth date _____   Age _____
Month Day Year   Month Day Year

School _____   Grade _____

Sex ☐ Female ☐ Male   Other data _____

Your name _____
First   Middle   Last

Position _____

What type of class do you teach? _____

How long have you known this child? _____

Instructions

On both sides of this form are phrases that describe how children may act. Please read each phrase and mark the response that describes how this child has acted over the last six months If the child has changed a great deal during this period, describe the child's recent behavior.

Please mark every item. If you don't know or are unsure, give your best estimate. A "Never" response does not mean that a child "never" engages in a behavior, only that you have not observed the child to behave that way.

Before starting, please provide the information requested in the box at the top of the page.

Circle **N** if the behavior **never occurs**.
Circle **S** if the behavior **sometimes occurs**.
Circle **O** if the behavior **often occurs**.
Circle **A** if the behavior **almost always occurs**.

How to Mark Your Responses

Be certain to circle completely the letter you choose, like this:

N Ⓢ O A

If you wish to change a response, mark an X through it and circle your new choice, like this: N Ⓧ Ⓞ A

1. Adjusts well to new teachers ....   N   S   O   A
2. Argues when denied own way ....   N   S   O   A

31. Cheats in school ....   N   S   O   A
32. Complains about being teased ....   N   S   O   A

FIGURE 21.12   The Behavior Assessment System for Children–Teacher Report Form (BASC–TRF).

Source: C. Reynolds and R. Kamphaus. *The Behavior Assessment System for Children (BASC).* Circle Pines, MN: American Guidance Systems, 1992. Reproduced by permission of American Guidance Systems.

The School Situations Questionnaire (SSQ) is a brief, 12-item questionnaire devised by Barkley (1997a). It is designed to identify situations in which children are manifesting various behaviors. It is used to aid in the diagnosis of ADHD and other behavior problems and is sensitive to the effects of stimulant medication. A similar version for parents called the Home Situations Questionnaire (Barkley, 1997b) is used to compare the child's behavior in home and school settings. The SSQ is shown in Fig. 21.13.

How often these or similar instruments come across your desk depends in large part on the practices of medical and mental health professionals in your area. Our perception is that it is increasingly likely that you will be asked to participate in these data collection efforts due to the effects of full inclusion and increased efforts to obtain classroom data to assess the efficacy of both pharmacological and nonpharmacological interventions.

Although the behavior and attitude assessment techniques presented in this chapter will certainly not be used as frequently as teacher-made tests, they clearly have a role in the classroom under IDEA. Use them to increase your understanding of all your pupils and to further the inclusion and development of special and regular learners, and you will have moved a step closer to educating the whole class and the whole child.

SCHOOL SITUATIONS QUESTIONNAIRE (FORM 7)

SCHOOL SITUATIONS QUESTIONNAIRE (FORM 7)

Child's name _____ **Date** _____

Name of person completing this form _____

Instructions: Does this child present any problems with compliance to instructions, commands, or rules for you in any of these situations? If so, please circle the word Yes and then circle a number beside that situation that describes how severe the problem is for you. If this child is not a problem in a situation, circle No and go on to the next situation on the form.

Situations	Yes/No		Mild			*If yes, how severe?*					Severe
When arriving at school	Yes No	1	2	3	4	5	6	7	8	9
During individual desk work	Yes No	1	2	3	4	5	6	7	8	9
During small group activities	Yes No	1	2	3	4	5	6	7	8	9
During free play time in class	Yes No	1	2	3	4	5	6	7	8	9
During lectures to the class	Yes No	1	2	3	4	5	6	7	8	9
At recess	Yes No	1	2	3	4	5	6	7	8	9
At lunch	Yes No	1	2	3	4	5	6	7	8	9
In the hallways	Yes No	1	2	3	4	5	6	7	8	9
In the bathroom	Yes No	1	2	3	4	5	6	7	8	9
On field trips	Yes No	1	2	3	4	5	6	7	8	9
During special assemblies	Yes No	1	2	3	4	5	6	7	8	9
On the bus	Yes No	1	2	3	4	5	6	7	8	9

· For Office Use Only ·

Total number of problem settings _____ Mean severity score _____

FIGURE 21.13 The School Situations Questionnaire, or SSQ.

Source: Barkley, R. A., The School Situations Questionnaire. *Defiant Children: A Clinician's Manual for Parent Training,* 2nd ed. New York: Guilford Press, 1997. Reproduced by permission of The Guilford Press.

SUMMARY

1. Under the 2004 reauthorizarion of the Individuals with Disabilities Education Act (IDEA), a regular classroom teacher is now a required member of the Individual Education Program (IEP) team for each child with a disability.

2. Added responsibilities under IDEA for classroom teachers may now include collecting information about the performance and progress of children with disabilities in the general curriculum to help the IEP team make decisions regarding the IEP as well as to make instructional decisions about children with disabilities.

3. When behavior interferes with learning, classroom teachers may also be required to collect behavior and attitudinal data to assist the IEP team in planning, implementing, and evaluating behavior improvement plans.

4. Although IDEA documents the need for additional resources for classroom teachers to meet the requirements of IDEA, budgetary and other local constraints may complicate resource allocation.

5. Many of the skills needed to develop teacher-made achievement tests for regular education students are directly applicable to the testing and assessment of children with disabilities, with accommodations as appropriate.

6. With some modification many of these same skills can be applied to the development of teacher-made behavior and attitude assessment scales and procedures.

7. IDEA and the No Child Left Behind Act (NCLB) now require all children with disabilities to participate in annual state- and district-wide assessments.

8. IDEA and NCLB allow accommodations (i.e., modification) of standardized test administration procedures and stimuli and the development of alternate assessments for children with disabilities, when justified by the IEP team, but accommodations and alternate assessments will limit comparability of scores and have unknown effects on test reliability and validity.

9. Attitudes, like learning, are unobservable. Therefore inferences about attitudes must be obtained from observable behaviors.

10. Both regular pupils and children with disabilities may be expected to have a variety of attitudes about full inclusion. Assessing these over time may assist with adjustment to full inclusion.

11. If a negative attitude toward the regular class, curriculum, or students is interfering with the ability of a child with a disability to progress in the general curriculum, the regular teacher may be called on to assess the learner's attitude for consideration by the IEP team.

12. The IEP team may also expect the teacher to provide behavioral observations or complete or develop behavior rating scales to assess the effectiveness of behavior plans when a child with a disability's behavior interferes with learning.

13. Both attitudes and behavior may be assessed by unstructured and structured observations, Likert scales, two-point scales, bipolar adjective scales, sociograms, and both teacher-made and standardized behavior rating scales, checklists, and questionnaires.

14. Likert scales consist of attitude statements to which respondents indicate the degree to which they agree or disagree with the statements, usually on a five-point scale.

15. Two-point scales are very similar to Likert scales, except that responses are made on a two-point scale. Respondents are "forced" to indicate their agreement or disagreement, and they cannot take a neutral position as they could with a Likert scale.

16. Attitude statements should be short and written simply and clearly. They should avoid negatives (and especially double negatives), factual statements, reference to the past, absolutes, nondistinguishing statements, and irrelevancies. They should use *only, merely, just,* etc., sparingly. They should have one thought per statement and equal numbers of positive and negative statements.

17. The bipolar adjective scale consists of a stimulus word or phrase and a list of several pairs of adjectives with opposite meanings. The respondent circles numbers from 1 to 7 to indicate the degree to which each adjective pair best represents his or her attitudes.

18. Social behavior or social interaction may be measured with a sociogram, a graphical representation of social patterns in a specific situation.

19. Sociograms only indicate choice patterns, not the reasons for the choices.

20. Use of medication to manage behavior and health of children is increasing, and many medications can affect learning and behavior.

21. Classroom teachers increasingly are being asked to collect information via observations, checklists, and rating scales to help assess the safety and effectiveness of medications, and the effectiveness of psychosocial interventions.

22. A variety of commercial instruments exist to complement teacher-made assessments of medication and psychosocial interventions.

FOR DISCUSSION

*1. Until recently classroom teachers had little responsibility for evaluating the performance and progress of children with disabilities. Explain why this is no longer the case, and identify four possible ways that data collected by the classroom teacher may be useful to a child's IEP team.

2. Imagine that you are a regular education teacher with no familiarity with children with disabilities. What kind of assistance do you think would be most welcome in helping you evaluate their progress in the general education curriculum? From whom do you think this assistance should come? How realistic do you think it is that such assistance will be available? What will you do to meet the requirements of IDEA if no such assistance is available?

3. What specific teacher-made test development skills will be helpful in evaluating the academic and behavioral progress of children with disabilities? Explain why.

*4. At lunch your principal tells you he is going to tell a newspaper reporter that children with disabilities at your school are actually doing better in the general curriculum than are the general education students. His conclusion is based on the finding that children with disabilities in your school obtained higher average percentages correct on a series of alternate assessments than the average percentile scores of regular students on their annual standardized scores. Would you support his conclusion? Why or why not?

5. Make a list of observable approach and avoidance behaviors for a subject you will be teaching to regular and special education pupils. Arrange these in either a checklist or rating scale format.

6. The principal of a certain junior high school schedules assemblies every Friday during the last period. For some time a few teachers have been telling him that the assemblies are not well received by the students or faculty. The principal asks for evidence that their opinion is shared by others. Develop an observation checklist. List eight behaviors that you might observe from which you could infer something about the students' attitude toward

assemblies. Include four approach and four avoidance behaviors.

7. Now develop a Likert scale for measuring student attitude toward the subject area discussed in Question 6.

8. Construct a bipolar adjective scale using 10 bipolar adjectives of your own choosing to measure student attitudes as referenced in Question 6. Try to make these adjectives as specific and meaningful as possible in regard to the attitude you are measuring.

9. Make up a sociometric table similar to Fig. 21.2 using fictitious names. Now randomly place X's throughout the table. Practice converting the resulting data into a sociogram similar to that shown in Fig. 21.3. Identify stars, mutual choices, and isolates.

*10. Compute this person's attitude score for the following scale measuring attitude toward your class.

a. I should have taken a different course.

SA   A   U   (D)   SD

b. I have a hard time keeping awake

SA   A   U   (D)   SD

c. Class time should be lengthened.

SA   A   (U)   D   SD

d. I like writing objectives.

SA   (A)   U   D   SD

e. I daydream a lot in class.

SA   A   U   D   (SD)

*11. You are interested in determining attitudes toward utility companies, and you have generated the following list of behaviors that you feel will be helpful in assessing these attitudes. Classify these behaviors as either approach or avoidance behaviors by placing AP (for approach) or AV (for avoidance) in the blank to the left of the behavior.

_____ **a.** Complaining about rising utility bills

_____ **b.** Volunteering to work for the utility company

_____ **c.** Picketing the central office

_____ **d.** Painting the glass on your electric meter black

_____ **e.** Paying utility bills the same day you are billed

_____ **f.** Including a $5 tip with each electric payment

_____ **g.** Writing a letter to your congressperson, supporting utility rate hikes

_____ **h.** Defending utility companies in a debate

_____ **i.** Paying your utility bill in pennies

*12. The following statements were written as part of an attitude scale. In one sentence, explain what is wrong with each statement.

*Answers for questions 1, 4, 10, 11, and 12 appear in Appendix F.

a. Mathematics in my school is fun to take, and my teacher teaches it well.

b. Classrooms in an open-education system are often without walls.

c. Last year I had some boring math assignments.

d. There is nothing I would rather do than make attitude scales.

e. I am often seized by an inexorable urge to engage in irrelevant rumination in math.

13. Imagine that you are asked to complete questionnaires like those presented in this chapter on two or three students taking medication in your class on several occasions over the school year. Do you think this is time well spent? If so, why? If not, why not?

CHAPTER 22

IN THE CLASSROOM: A SUMMARY DIALOGUE

THE FOLLOWING IS a dialogue between Ms. Wilson, a sixth-grade teacher, and some of the school staff with whom she works. Ms. Wilson is three months into her first teaching assignment at a middle school in a medium-sized metropolitan school district. We begin our dialogue with Ms. Wilson on a Friday afternoon as she wraps up the final class session before a quarterly testing period is to begin.

Ms. Wilson: I know you all feel we've covered a tremendous amount this year. Well, you're right. We have. And now it's time to find out how much you've learned. It's important for you to know how well you're doing in each subject so you can work harder in the areas where you might need improvement. It's also nice to know in what areas you might be smarter than almost everyone else. So, next week, I want you to be ready to take tests over all the material we have covered so far. (*A few students groan in unison.*) Remember, this will be your chance to show me how smart you are. I want you to get plenty of sleep Sunday night so you'll be fresh and alert Monday. (*As the bell rings, Ms. Wilson shouts over the commotion of students leaving the classroom.*) Don't forget, I'll be collecting homework on Monday! Oh yeah! Keep in mind that these tests will also help you prepare for the state PAG test (*NOTE: the PAG Test is the Promotion and Graduation Test—the state high-stakes test*) that you will have to pass to be promoted to the seventh grade.

(*As Ms. Wilson collapses into her chair, Ms. Palmer, an experienced teacher, walks in.*)

Ms. Palmer: Glad this grading period is just about over. Next week will be a nice break, don't you think? Just reviewing and giving tests. It'll sure be nice to have this weekend free without any preparations to worry about. Except of course we have to start getting the kids fired up for the PAG test. I'm on the pep rally committee this year. Are you on the tee-shirt committee?

Ms. Wilson: You mean you won't be making up tests this weekend!

Ms. Palmer: No. I have tests from the last three years that I've been refining and improving. With only a few modifications, they'll do fine.

Ms. Wilson: You're awfully lucky. I'm afraid I haven't had a chance to even think about how I'm going to test these kids. All these subjects to make tests for, and then all the scoring and grading to do by next Friday. I think I'm going to have an awful weekend. And I really hate even thinking about the PAG test committees right now. It seems that PAG testing is all we care about these days.

Ms. PALMER: Well it is important that kids get promoted and graduate, isn't it? I think it's good that we have the PAG. It helps keep everyone focused and our scores have gone up for several years in a row now. Back to your class though .... Will you be giving criterion-referenced or norm-referenced tests?

Ms. WILSON: Umm ... well ... I don't know. I remember hearing those terms in a tests and measurement class I once took, but I guess I just haven't had time to worry about those things until now. I suppose I'm going to have to get my old textbook out tonight and do some reviewing. Gosh! I hope I can find it.

Ms. PALMER: Well, if you use norm-referenced tests, there are some available in Ms. Cartwright's office. You know, she's the counselor who is always so helpful with discipline problems. In fact, she has a whole file full of tests.

Ms. WILSON: Will *you* be using norm-referenced tests next week?

Ms. PALMER: Not really. For these midsemester grades, I like to make my tests very specific to what I've been teaching. At this point in the year it seems to provide better feedback to the kids and parents—especially the parents of the fully included kids with disabilities. Anyway, the parents aren't really interested in where their kid scores in relation to other students until later in the semester, when I've covered more content and the kids have had a chance to get their feet on the ground. The norm-referenced tests also don't cover our state academic standards very well so they don't really identify the kids who need more attention to pass the PAG.

Ms. WILSON: You mean these norm-referenced tests don't cover specifically what you've taught?

Ms. PALMER: (*Trying to be tactful*) Well, no. Not exactly. I guess you have forgotten a few things since you took that tests and measurement course. If we're going to raise PAG scores we've got to teach to the state academic standards, otherwise we may be teaching things to the kids that the PAG doesn't measure.

Ms. WILSON: I guess so. I just thought that all tests were pretty much the same. You know, I thought we could use any test and get the same results.

Ms. PALMER: Well you *might* find a norm-referenced test that happens to measure the state standards, but I doubt it. Those tests are designed to measure broad national objectives, not the state standards. They're very specific you know! Why don't you make a test blueprint and then you can compare it to the test items in the norm-referenced tests in Ms. Cartwright's test file?

Ms. WILSON: A test *what* print?

Ms. PALMER: A test blueprint. You know, where you take the objectives from your lesson plans and construct a table that shows the content you've been teaching and the level of complexity—knowledge, comprehension, application—that you're shooting for. Then, see how Ms. Cartwright's tests match the test blueprint, making accommodations for the students with disabilities, of course.

Ms. WILSON: But what if I didn't write down all my objectives? I had objectives, of course, but I just didn't write them down all the time, or when I did, I usually didn't keep them for long. You know what I mean? (*No comment from Ms. Palmer.*) And I don't think I wrote them so they included levels of complexity according to that taxonomy of objectives thing I think you're referring to. And I haven't even thought about accommodations!

Ms. Palmer: But I'm afraid that without objectives, you don't know whether you're teaching to the state standards! And without objectives that are linked to the state standards you won't know if the items on Ms. Cartwright's tests match what you've taught. Would you believe that last year a teacher in this school flunked half his class using a test that didn't match what he taught? Boy, what a stir that caused! And now that the PAG is being used for promotion decisions you can bet there will be lots of people looking over our shoulders to be sure we're teaching what kids need to know to pass that test! And with IDEA and NCLB, you better be aware of accommodations and use them appropriately!

Ms. Wilson: (*Looking worried*) I guess I'll have to start from scratch, then. It looks like a very long weekend.

Ms. Palmer: Of course, you might consider giving some essay items.

Ms. Wilson: You mean long-answer, not multiple-choice questions?

Ms. Palmer: Yes, but you'll have to consider the time it will take to develop a scoring guide for each question and the time you'll spend grading all those answers. And, then, of course, only some of your objectives may be suited to an essay format and some children with disabilities may not be able to use them at all. Needless to say, since the PAG doesn't have any essay questions on it some parents may not feel like you're helping their kids prepare for the PAG.

Ms. Wilson: (*Trying to sort out all of what Ms. Palmer just said without sounding too stupid*) By scoring guide, do you mean the right answer?

Ms. Palmer: Well, not quite. As you know, essay items can have more than one right answer. So, first you will have to identify all the different elements that make an answer right and then decide how to weight or assign points to each of these elements, depending on what percentage of the right answer they represent.

Ms. Wilson: How do you decide that?

Ms. Palmer: (*Trying to be polite and being evasive for the sake of politeness*) Well … very carefully.

Ms. Wilson: I see. (*Long pause*) Well, maybe my old tests and measurement book will have something about scoring essays

Ms. Palmer: Well, I'm sure it will, but it probably won't have anything on high-stakes tests like the PAG. This is such a recent phenomena that high-stakes testing has only recently been addressed in testing textbooks. I mean … I hate to sound judgmental but it sounds like you don't really understand how the PAG fits in with your classroom tests, state standards and your instructional objectives.

Ms. Wilson: I … I … I guess you're right. It's just that this is all so new to me. It sounds as though I have my work cut out for me. I guess I'll just have to organize my time and start to work as soon as I get home.

(*Ms. Palmer and Ms. Wilson leave the classroom and meet Mr. Smith, another teacher.*)

Mr. Smith: You won't believe the meeting I just had with Johnny Haringer's parents!

MS. PALMER AND MS. WILSON: What happened?

MR. SMITH: Well, they came to see me after Johnny missed an A by two points on one of my weekly math tests. It was the first time that he had missed an A the entire semester.

MS. WILSON: Were they mad?

MR. SMITH: They were at first. But I stayed calm and explained very carefully why two points on the test really should make a difference between an A and a B.

MS. WILSON: What kinds of things did you tell them?

MR. SMITH: Well, luckily I keep student data from past years for all my tests. This allows me to calculate reliability and validity coefficients for my tests using one of the PCs in the math lab. I simply explained to Johnny's parents, in everyday, commonsense language, what reliability and validity of a test meant, and then gave them some statistical data to support my case. I also explained the care and deliberation I put into the construction of my tests—you know, all the steps you go through in writing test items and then checking their content validity and doing qualitative and quantitative item analyses. I think they got the idea of just how much work it takes to construct a good test.

MS. WILSON: And?

MR. SMITH: And after that they calmed down and were very responsive to my explanation. They even commented that they hadn't realized the science of statistics could be so helpful in determining the score reliability and validity evidence for a test. They even commended me for being so systematic and careful. Can you believe that?

MS. WILSON: Umm ... score reliability and validity? Do you mean we have to know the score reliability and validity for every test we use?

MR. SMITH: Ever since that lawsuit by the parents of some kid over at Central for unfair testing, the school board has made every teacher individually responsible for using reliable tests and for identifying evidence of the validity of the test for the specific purpose it's being used for. And don't forget, now that promotion as well as graduation decisions will be made based solely on PAG scores we need to ensure that our teacher-made tests measure the same state standards that the PAG does. It's just a matter of time before someone gets sued over that!

(*Looking surprised, Ms. Wilson turns to Ms. Palmer and Ms. Palmer slowly and painfully nods to indicate her agreement with what Mr. Smith has been saying.*)

MS. WILSON: Boy! I don't think I could explain reliability and validity that well—at least not to parents—and I know I wouldn't have the slightest idea of how to compute a reliability coefficient or identify validity evidence. And Ms. Palmer can tell you that I need to brush up on the PAG test and the state standards too.

MR. SMITH: Well, that I don't know about you but I'm sure glad we won't have any preparations to worry about this weekend ... nothing but review and testing next week. You have a nice weekend.

MS. PALMER: Well, it may not be all that bad. You've got that tests and measurement text at home, and next quarter, who knows? You may have time to plan for all this ahead of time. As for the PAG and state standards, if you go to the state education agency's website you can find a lot of helpful information there.

Ms. Wilson: (*Being purposely negative*) That's if I have any time left after I try to learn about reliability and validity, construct a test blueprint, learn the difference between norm-referenced and criterion-referenced tests, develop accommodations for special learners, make a scoring key for an essay test, and, of course, compute some test item statistics I probably can't even pronounce!

Ms. Palmer: Let's get to our cars before the roof falls in. (*To Ms. Wilson under her breath*) Speaking of the roof.

(*The principal approaches them.*)

Principal: Ah, Ms. Wilson. I'm glad I ran into you. How'd things go for you this quarter? Which PAG committee are you on? We really need to keep up the push to raise PAG test scores. Never can settle for what you have.

Ms. Wilson: Very well, thank you. I really like my classroom, and the parents I've met have been very nice. All my students—well, almost all—have made me feel at home. I'm on the PAG tee-shirt committee.

Principal: Good. I've had good reports about your teaching, and your classroom discipline and management seem to be improving. I suppose you're all set for the end of this grading period. It's only a week away, you know. (*The principal looks at Ms. Wilson for some kind of response.*)

Ms. Wilson: (*After a brief pause, she responds almost inaudibly*) Yes.

Principal: Well, that's excellent, because you know how much emphasis our parents place on grades. All of our teachers spend a lot of time on grading. We've never had a serious incident in this regard like they've had over at Central. I'd like to think it was because of my policy that every teacher be responsible for using reliable tests with adequate evidence of their validity, for making accommodations for special learners, and for interpreting test scores to parents. I only wish that all teachers in the state would have to prove themselves competent in tests and measurement to be certified, like they do in some other states. I'm sure there would be a lot fewer angry students and parents if this were the case. Well, Ms. Wilson, glad things are going so well. Of course, the final test will be whether scores go up for your class on the PAG. I am counting on you to make that happen. In fact, we are all counting on you to make the PAG scores go up. You wouldn't want to be the one responsible for the school losing its "exemplary" rating, would you? Gotta run . . . have a nice weekend. You too, Ms. Palmer.

Ms. Wilson: Thank you.

Ms. Palmer: You too.

Ms. Wilson: (*On the verge of tears*) I don't think I've had a more miserable Friday afternoon. I can only guess what the weekend will be like.

Ms. Palmer: Maybe I can help. (*Ms. Wilson looks directly at her.*) I have the new, eighth edition of a tests and measurement book called *Educational Testing and Measurement: Classroom Application and Practice*, which covers the kinds of things that might be helpful in preparing your tests for next week. It talks a lot about NCLB requirements and has an entire chapter devoted to high-stakes testing that can help you get up to speed on the PAG issues we've talked about. If you're not busy, why don't I bring it over and help you with those tests?

Ms. WILSON: (*Straining to be reserved and matter of fact*) I guess that would be . . . okay. (*Then, with a sigh of relief*) Yes, I think that would be fine.

You might think this scenario is a bit farfetched. It may come as a surprise, but we are willing to bet that something like this will happen to you long before the end of your first grading period. The incidents we have described repeat themselves thousands of times each school day in schools across the country. Unlike the preceding story, some have unhappy endings. Let's examine the testing issues that confronted Ms. Wilson.

HIGH-STAKES TESTING AND NCLB

The Promotion and Graduation (PAG) test that Ms. Wilson, Ms. Palmer, Mr. Smith, and the principal discussed is fictitious. The impact of high-stakes testing on public education is not! In only a few years high-stakes testing and standards-based educational reform have swept across the country, with important effects on students, teachers, administrators, schools, and property values. Although the use of these tests for promotion, graduation, and school accountability purposes is controversial, multiple polls have shown the majority of taxpayers support high-stakes testing.

Neither Ms. Wilson nor any other public school teacher can afford to ignore or minimize the importance placed on the results of high-stakes tests anymore. Although the quality of high-stakes testing programs varies from state to state, and in spite of recommendations from national measurement associations that such programs only be used as part of a broader system to evaluate student achievement, there appears to be no let up in the intensity of high-stakes testing programs across the country. Indeed, the January 2002 passage of the No Child Left Behind Act (NCLB) federal law now mandates annual academic assessments of all public school children. And, following the passage of NCLB, most states decided to use their own state high-stakes test to meet NCLB accountability requirements. This means the state high-stakes test results will also comprise the annual Adequate Yearly Progress (AYP) report that must describe overall performance and also break it down for students with disabilities, for the economically disadvantaged, for the limited English proficient (LEP), and for ethnic minorities.

Clearly NCLB and high-stakes testing will be with us for years to come. NCLB was discussed in detail in Chapters 1 and 2 and its far-reaching implications were described in many other chapters, with high-stakes testing being the primary topic of Chapter 2.

CRITERION-REFERENCED VERSUS NORM-REFERENCED TESTS

Ms. Wilson also had to deal with whether to use criterion-referenced or norm-referenced tests. Of course, she hardly knows the difference between them, so it should be no surprise later if there are misunderstandings between her, her pupils, and their parents over the meaning of her grades. Recall that criterion-referenced tests report test scores in relation to instructional objectives. That is, they are graded in terms of the number or percentage of items a student gets correct. Grades—A, B, C, etc.—are usually assigned indicating the level of knowledge or skill that was attained. These grades should reflect estimates of the level of performance necessary to do well according to certain criteria, for example, to divide and multiply four-digit numbers with decimals, to divide and multiply fractions, or to square whole numbers. It is these types of criteria that Mr. Smith is likely to have related to Johnny Haringer's parents in order to explain why the two-point difference in Johnny's test score should make a difference. In other words, Mr. Smith's grades were based on real performance skills that Johnny's parents could understand and appreciate. For most interim grades from which teachers are expected to diagnose learning difficulties and prepare remedial instruction, criterion-referenced tests are, generally, the most useful. Unfortunately, Ms. Wilson forgot or never knew that one of the first steps in preparing a test is to determine the purpose of the test.

If Ms. Wilson's purpose (and the school's) for this grading period was to determine where each student stood in reference to other students, an existing norm-referenced test might have been perfectly adequate. Needless to say, this testing purpose might have saved Ms. Wilson's weekend. Generally, however, interim grading periods are used for the purpose of providing feedback to students, their parents, and the teacher as to how well students have learned and teachers have taught specific skills. This objective usually calls for the use of a criterion-referenced test.

Even if Ms. Wilson had decided beforehand to use criterion-referenced tests, Ms. Palmer's suggestion of looking at Ms. Cartwright's norm-referenced tests was a good one. This is especially true in light of Ms. Palmer's suggestion that a test blueprint be used to determine which, if any, items from those tests matched the specific content that Ms. Wilson taught. As long as the norm-referenced tests were not to be given to the students at a later time, items from them might be effectively used in a criterion-referenced test, saving Ms. Wilson from preparing every item from scratch.

NEW RESPONSIBILITIES FOR TEACHERS UNDER IDEA

Assessing and making accommodations appropriate to the needs of special learners in her classroom came up several times during the dialogue, but with little comprehension of the scope of the law's requirements evident from Ms. Wilson. These requirements are the direct result of the passage of the Individuals with Disabilities Education Act (IDEA). This important legislation was discussed at length in Chapters 1, 18, 20, and 21. It requires that regular classroom teachers play greater roles than ever before in the instruction and evaluation of the progress of students with disabilities in the general education curriculum, and even participate in behavioral assessment and intervention when behavior interferes with progress in the general curriculum. In addition, the new law requires that results obtained from appropriate teacher-made and standardized tests (sometimes with accommodations appropriate for the student's disability) must now be provided to parents on a regular basis as well as to members of each special learner's Individual Educational Plan (IEP) team to enable the team to evaluate the special learner' progress. Finally, regular classroom teachers must now be part of each IEP team, and it is the IEP team that must determine whether a student with a disability will take the same annual academic assessment required under NCLB, take it with accommodations recommended by the IEP team, or take a state-approved alternate assessment.

INSTRUCTIONAL OBJECTIVES

Another issue raised in the course of this dialogue concerned the proper use of instructional objectives. One implication should be clear. Not only do instructional objectives help teachers organize their teaching, they help them write tests, too. However, Ms. Wilson took a careless approach to writing instructional objectives, so they could not be used to help construct her tests. It's likely that some objectives failed to specify the level of behavior or the conditions under which the behavior could be expected to be performed. This would prevent her from matching her instruction to the items in Ms. Cartwright's test files. It also means that Ms. Wilson must rely only on her memory as to what was and was not covered during the grading period. Let's hope Ms. Wilson's tests don't ask her students questions that were never formally taught or that were taught at a level different than that represented by her test items.

Lawsuits involving unfair testing stem from situations similar to that in which Ms. Wilson now finds herself. Settlements against teachers and districts can occur if it can be shown that some harm has come to the student as a result of the neglect of proper testing procedures. Ms. Wilson seems to be in such a precarious position on this issue that we can only hope her weekend makes up for the effort that was missing earlier in the semester. Given that this is an interim grading period in which formal decisions about a student's progress are not likely to be made, Ms. Wilson will probably avoid any serious problems—this time.

THE TEST BLUEPRINT

We've already discussed the use of the test blueprint, but a few more points about this important tool can be made. Recall from Chapter 5 that a test blueprint is simply a table that lists the important objectives to be taught and the levels of student behavior that can be expected from these objectives. In the cells of the table are placed the number or percentage of items that cover each topic at a particular level of behavior. The test blueprint can be an important device for planning a test. It is used in deciding the number of items that should be written for each major objective and, in evaluating an existing test, it is used to determine how well a test compares in types and numbers of items with what has been taught.

Ms. Wilson had the opportunity of using a test blueprint in both of these ways. Had a test blueprint been prepared, Ms. Wilson could have quickly sorted through Ms. Cartwright's test file to determine if the content of any test items matched the content of any of the cells in the test blueprint. This might have precluded the need for Ms. Wilson to personally write every test item needed. The key to preparing a test blueprint is the preparation of instructional objectives that include the level of behavior that is being taught.

Unfortunately, Ms. Wilson now must pay for failing to properly prepare instructional objectives with the more arduous task of constructing all new test items and the uncertainty of whether these test items accurately and fairly reflect the content she has taught.

ESSAY ITEMS AND THE ESSAY SCORING GUIDES

Recall that another suggestion given by Ms. Palmer was that some of the items Ms. Wilson needed could be essay items. Ms. Palmer's suggestion was probably based on the notion that a large block of content could be tested with one or a few essay items. While the implication here is that some time could be saved in the test preparation process for some content areas by writing essay items, Ms. Palmer was correct in suggesting that essay items will only be appropriate for some content areas and some teaching objectives (e.g., where rote recall and memorization of facts were not the primary objectives). Also, it should be recognized that the time needed to prepare scoring guides and to grade essay items might outweigh the fact that the initial essay question might be easy to write. Ms. Wilson seemed to be unaware of the need for scoring guides, presumably thinking that essay items are simply scored right or wrong as multiple-choice items are. But, as was seen in Chapter 7, this is not the case. Points are assigned to essay items in relation to the extent to which the student includes in his or her answer the elements of a good response. The scoring of essay items requires specifying these elements before the grading begins and identifying examples of the different alternatives that might adequately represent the elements of a good response. All this takes considerable time and effort, which Ms. Wilson did not expect.

Like many new teachers, Ms. Wilson probably saw the essay item as an easy way out of having to write many different test items. As Ms. Palmer pointed out, though, scoring essays reliably is time-consuming. Nevertheless, Ms. Wilson should have considered essay items. We say this because it is entirely likely, even probable, that some of the content Ms. Wilson has taught during the semester should be tested with essay items. Since Ms. Wilson will have to cram all of her test construction into a single weekend, it is unlikely that time can be spent in identifying which content is best tested with an essay format and in preparing scoring guides. Here again, an earlier start on a test blueprint might have paid rich dividends in time saved later.

RELIABILITY, VALIDITY EVIDENCE, AND TEST STATISTICS

Mr. Smith raised the important issues of reliability and validity. Nothing could be more fundamental to a good test than its score reliability and validity evidence—that is, its capacity to consistently give the same or a similar score over repeated testings and to measure what it is supposed to measure. These two terms have technical meanings, which were presented in Chapters 15 and 16, but they also have practical, commonsense meanings, and these should be second nature to any beginning teacher.

The practical or commonsense notions that lie behind the concepts of reliability and validity are present in our everyday lives far more than is frequently believed. These two words, reliability and validity, appear in all types of writing—from newspapers and weekly magazines to popular books— as well as in the language of businesspeople, engineers, nurses, social workers, and people from all walks of life. The significance of this fact for the teacher is that parents and even some of your students will be aware of these concepts and will not hesitate to confront you with them (albeit sometimes inaccurately) when they feel they may be used to their advantage. It is unfortunate that many parents have only a partial or limited knowledge of these concepts as they apply to testing. But it is even more unfortunate that some teachers are unable to correct the misunderstandings that parents sometimes have about these concepts. It is not that most teachers lack textbook definitions for these terms, but that they are unable to convert these definitions to the practical language that students and their parents are likely to understand. Of course, the main advantage for the teacher knowing practical ways to discuss the concepts of reliability and validity evidence is that they can be invaluable tools in communicating the meaning of test scores to parents and in justifying and defending decisions based on those test scores.

Mr. Smith's interaction with Johnny Haringer's parents provided some evidence of practical as well as technical knowledge of reliability and validity evidence. Mr. Smith was able to defuse a potentially difficult meeting with Johnny's parents essentially because he could talk their language. He described score reliability and validity evidence with words that they could relate to. This is how Mr. Smith was able to strike a responsive chord, to get beneath the emotional issue that brought him together with Johnny's parents, and to communicate a commonsense understanding of the characteristics of a good test. This commonsense understanding went a long way toward turning a potentially nasty confrontation into a useful and productive meeting about Johnny's progress.

Recall also that Mr. Smith went beyond the simple commonsense notions of reliability and validity to actually show Johnny's parents some statistics indicating his test's score reliability and validity evidence. While most standardized tests will have these statistics already calculated and displayed for the teacher in the test manual, the teacher will have to understand the test manual and give parents a faithful interpretation of what all the statistics mean, if the situation requires. Most of what was covered in Chapters 12 through 18 was intended to prepare the teacher for this task. On the other hand, Mr. Smith's test probably was not standardized, and, therefore, Mr. Smith needed to calculate the statistics. Here, the availability of a computer program for calculating test statistics and his knowledge of the uses of a PC made this easy.

Any first-year teacher, particularly in the first quarter of teaching, could not be expected to be prepared as well as Mr. Smith. But note that Mr. Smith made a point of saying that he always kept his test scores on file, probably on the PC's hard drive. When time permitted, he used the PC to calculate the necessary statistics to show a test's reliability and validity evidence. This foresight paid off handsomely in his meeting with Johnny's parents. It would have been impossible for Mr. Smith to have calculated these statistics on the spot and probably even unlikely that they could have been calculated between the time Johnny's parents called for an appointment and the actual time the meeting took place. Instead, Mr. Smith used the PC to calculate reliability. The computer program he used might have computed reliability using the odd–even or Kuder–Richardson method, and validity evidence could be obtained by correlating a test's scores with end-of-semester or end-of-year test scores as was described in Chapters 15 and 16.

Even though Mr. Smith's score reliability and validity statistics were not determined with student data from Johnny's test, they were calculated with student data from past semesters in which students similar to Johnny took the same test. As long as Mr. Smith's data were not too dated, they are acceptable evidence of the test's score reliability and validity. Mr. Smith's foresight is within the reach of every teacher, and, if we are to take seriously the principal's admonition that parents and teachers place a great deal of emphasis on testing in this school, we suspect Ms. Wilson should plan on having some of this same foresight.

GRADES AND MARKS

There is no better way in which to end this chapter, and indeed this book, than by reinforcing the critical role that grades and marks play in the testing process. As a visible sign of the testing and measurement process, grades and marks stand as the end products that can make or break a test. Since Ms. Wilson had not thought about whether a criterion-referenced or norm-referenced strategy was appropriate, it is unlikely that she had given much thought about what marks or grades would be used in reporting the results of her tests to parents and students. Would she simply have used the school's formal reporting system to convey all the pertinent facts about a student's performance, or would there be other marks that might make finer distinctions and interpretations of a student's strengths and weaknesses? Would Ms. Wilson even know the strengths and weaknesses of her students at the end of this testing? And, if so, how would they be communicated to students and parents?

It was apparent from Mr. Smith's discussion with Johnny's parents that information was available from his tests that separated students into more than simply A's, B's, C's, and so on. Specific differences between an A and a B presumably were recorded or at least could be retrieved from the test score data for the parent–teacher conference. Perhaps Mr. Smith's test was divided into a certain number of competencies, each of which could be marked "pass" or "fail." Then, maybe an A was based on a student achieving passes on all competencies, a B based on a student achieving passes on 9 out of 10 competencies, and so on.

By making further differentiations across letter grades, Mr. Smith armed himself with some powerful ammunition as to why Johnny deserved a B, even though he missed an A by only two points. Mr. Smith learned the important point that grades are meaningless to students and parents unless some criterion can be attached to them that is seen as being of value to parents and teachers. Telling Johnny's parents that Johnny does not know how to divide and multiply two-digit numbers that have decimals—such as those that occur on end-of-year examinations, balancing a checkbook, in homework assignments in the next grade, and in finding the best buy per ounce among competing products in a grocery store—goes a lot further to convince his parents that Johnny has a weakness that must be remedied than simply telling them that Johnny deserves a B, not an A.

These are only a hint of the many problems involved in choosing grades and marks, which were covered in Chapter 11. Even if a test is meticulously constructed, has high score reliability and validity evidence, and has been carefully administered and graded, it still can be considered a poor test, unless the grades that are based on it can be communicated meaningfully to parents and students. While Mr. Smith has obviously given some thought to this aspect of testing, Ms. Wilson still has this lesson to learn.

SOME FINAL THOUGHTS

In the previous discussion of issues related to our dialogue, we admittedly have been pretty hard on Ms. Wilson. Even in this seemingly small slice of classroom life, Ms. Wilson has been confronted with more problems than she can possibly deal with in the time available to her for constructing the following week's tests. But if you think this brief dialogue has been hard on Ms. Wilson, you will be surprised to learn that these are not all the problems that she would need to confront in the real world. We believe we have been kind to Ms. Wilson by limiting her distress and discomfort to one Friday afternoon and to only the few measurement concepts we chose to discuss in our dialogue.

The real world of the classroom is not so accommodating. It presents testing and measurement problems every day of the week and each week of the school year. Also, the cast of characters will be larger in the real world than the few who were included here. And we haven't even begun to characterize the different responses of students with disabilities and their parents, each of whom produce a unique challenge to the teacher who must explain and justify testing decisions.

After reading this book, you should have a better understanding of the practical side of testing and maybe even some insights into how to handle yourself should similar situations arise. But real life is not easily portrayed on the pages of a book. For you, the reader, and for us, the authors, it occurs only in classrooms, and this of course is why we have chosen to spend the better part of our lives in those classrooms. Our advice is to use this book to prepare for that real world. Review its contents often and keep this book close at hand for future reference. Combine the skills you have learned with your own good judgment and experience and you will be sure to continue to learn as you teach.

MATH SKILLS REVIEW

THIS **REVIEW** of math skills covers all operations necessary to complete the calculations in this text. The Self-Check Test and answer key that appear at the end of this appendix can help you determine which skills you may need to review.

ORDER OF TERMS

The order of terms in addition is irrelevant.

$$2 + 3 = 3 + 2 = 5$$

The order of terms in subtraction is important.

$$3 - 2 \neq 2 - 3$$

The order of terms in multiplication is irrelevant.

$$3(2) = 2(3) = 6$$

There are several ways to write "multiplied by."

$$3 \times 2 = 3(2) = 3 \cdot 2 = 6$$

The order of terms in division is important.

$$6/2 \neq 2/6$$

There are several ways to write "divided by."

$$4 \div 2 = 4/2 = 2\sqrt{4} = 2$$

ORDER OF OPERATIONS

When multiplying (or dividing) the sum (or difference) of several numbers by another number, you may either multiply (divide) or add (subtract) first.

$$2(3 + 4) = 2(7) = 14 \quad \text{or} \quad 2(3 + 4) = 6 + 8 = 14$$

$$3(5 - 1) = 3(4) = 12 \quad \text{or} \quad 3(5 - 1) = 15 - 3 = 12$$

$$\frac{6 + 4}{2} = \frac{10}{2} = 5 \quad \text{or} \quad \frac{6 + 4}{2} = \frac{6}{2} + \frac{4}{2} = 3 + 2 = 5$$

$$\frac{9-6}{3} = \frac{3}{3} = 1 \quad \text{or} \quad \frac{9-6}{3} = \frac{9}{3} - \frac{6}{3} = 3-2 = 1$$

The operations within parentheses are completed first. Within the parentheses, multiplication and division are completed *before* addition and subtraction. After math in the parentheses is finished, other multiplications and divisions are completed before additions and subtractions.

$$(3-2) - 4(6+1) + 8 = 1 - 4(7) + 8 = 1 - 28 + 8 = -19$$

$$(6+4) - 6(3-2) + 11 = 10 - 6(1) + 11 = 10 - 6 + 11 = 15$$

$$(4/2) + 3(2+6) - 3 = 2 + 3(8) - 3 = 2 + 24 - 3 = 23$$

FRACTIONS

For addition and subtraction, fractions must have the same denominator. If a common denominator is not obvious, multiply the two denominators to get a common denominator. In order to keep the value of the new fractions equal to that of the original fractions, multiply each numerator by the denominator of the other fraction (cross-multiply).

$$\frac{1}{2} + \frac{1}{4} = \frac{4}{8} + \frac{2}{8} = \frac{6}{8} = \frac{3}{4}$$

$$\frac{2}{3} - \frac{2}{5} = \frac{10}{15} - \frac{6}{15} = \frac{4}{15}$$

$$\frac{1}{5} + \frac{1}{2} = \frac{2}{10} + \frac{5}{10} = \frac{7}{10}$$

This could also be accomplished by multiplying both the numerator and the denominator of each fraction by the denominator of the other fraction.

$$\frac{1}{2} + \frac{1}{4}$$

$$\frac{1}{2} \times \frac{4}{4} = \frac{4}{8} \quad \text{and} \quad \frac{1}{4} \times \frac{2}{2} = \frac{2}{8} \quad \text{so} \quad \frac{4}{8} + \frac{2}{8} = \frac{6}{8} = \frac{3}{4}$$

$$\frac{2}{3} - \frac{2}{5}$$

$$\frac{2}{3} \times \frac{5}{5} = \frac{10}{15} \quad \text{and} \quad \frac{2}{5} \times \frac{3}{3} = \frac{6}{15} \quad \text{so} \quad \frac{10}{15} - \frac{6}{15} = \frac{4}{15}$$

$$\frac{1}{5} + \frac{1}{2}$$

$$\frac{1}{5} \times \frac{2}{2} = \frac{2}{10} \quad \text{and} \quad \frac{1}{2} \times \frac{5}{5} = \frac{5}{10} \quad \text{so} \quad \frac{2}{10} + \frac{5}{10} = \frac{7}{10}$$

To multiply two fractions, simply multiply across the numerators and across the denominators.

$$\frac{3}{4} \times \frac{1}{2} = \frac{3}{8} \qquad \frac{2}{7} \times \frac{1}{3} = \frac{2}{21} \qquad \frac{3}{6} \times \frac{1}{3} = \frac{3}{18} = \frac{1}{6}$$

To divide two fractions, invert the divisor and then multiply.

$$\frac{3}{8} \div \frac{1}{2} = \frac{3}{8} \times \frac{2}{1} = \frac{3}{4} \qquad \frac{2}{3} \div \frac{3}{4} = \frac{2}{3} \times \frac{4}{3} = \frac{8}{9}$$

$$\frac{1}{2} \div \frac{3}{5} = \frac{1}{2} \times \frac{5}{3} = \frac{5}{6} \qquad \frac{3}{4} \div \frac{4}{5} = \frac{3}{4} \times \frac{5}{4} = \frac{15}{16}$$

To simplify multiplication and division of fractions, you may cancel out equal amounts in the numerators and denominators.

$$\frac{1}{2} \times \frac{2}{3} \div \frac{1}{9} = \frac{1}{2} \times \frac{2}{3} \times \frac{9}{1} = \frac{1}{\cancel{2}_1} \times \frac{\cancel{2}^1}{\cancel{3}_1} \times \frac{\cancel{9}^3}{1} = \frac{3}{1} = 3$$

$$\frac{3}{24} \times \frac{8}{9} \div \frac{1}{2} = \frac{3}{24} \times \frac{8}{9} \times \frac{2}{1} = \frac{\cancel{3}^1}{\cancel{24}_3} \times \frac{\cancel{8}^1}{\cancel{9}_3} \times \frac{2}{1} = \frac{2}{9}$$

$$\frac{1}{32} \div \frac{1}{16} \times \frac{3}{4} = \frac{1}{32} \times \frac{16}{1} \times \frac{3}{4} = \frac{1}{\cancel{32}_2} \times \frac{\cancel{16}^1}{1} \times \frac{3}{4} = \frac{3}{8}$$

MIXED NUMBERS

In addition and subtraction, it is only necessary to have the denominators of the fractions the same.

$$2\frac{1}{4} + 3\frac{1}{3} = 2\frac{3}{12} + 3\frac{4}{12} = 5\frac{7}{12}$$

$$8\frac{2}{3} - 3\frac{2}{7} = 8\frac{14}{21} - 3\frac{6}{21} = 5\frac{8}{21}$$

$$6\frac{2}{3} + 4\frac{1}{4} = 6\frac{8}{12} + 4\frac{3}{12} = 10\frac{11}{12}$$

In subtraction it is sometimes necessary to "borrow" from the whole number in order to subtract the fractional part.

$$4\frac{1}{2} - 2\frac{2}{3} = 4\frac{3}{6} - 2\frac{4}{6}$$

You cannot subtract the fractions, but since $1 = \dfrac{6}{6}$ you can convert $4\dfrac{3}{6}$ to $3\dfrac{9}{6}$, so

$$3\dfrac{9}{6} - 2\dfrac{4}{6} = 1\dfrac{5}{6}$$

An easier way to convert mixed numbers is to multiply the whole number by the denominator of the fraction, then compute the numerator.

$$3\dfrac{1}{2} = \dfrac{(3 \times 2) + 1}{2} = \dfrac{6 + 1}{2} = \dfrac{7}{2}$$

$$2\dfrac{3}{4} = \dfrac{(2 \times 4) + 3}{4} = \dfrac{8 + 3}{4} = \dfrac{11}{4}$$

$$8\dfrac{1}{3} = \dfrac{(8 \times 3) + 1}{3} = \dfrac{24 + 1}{3} = \dfrac{25}{3}$$

DECIMALS

To convert a fraction to a decimal fraction, perform simple division.

$$\dfrac{3}{8} = 8\overline{)3.000} = 0.375 \qquad \dfrac{1}{2} = 2\overline{)1.0} = 0.5 \qquad \dfrac{3}{4} = 4\overline{)3.00} = 0.75$$

The number of decimal places is not changed by addition or subtraction.

0.2	0.68	0.374	0.949
+0.5	−0.32	−0.234	+0.055
0.7	0.36	0.140	1.004

In multiplication, the number of decimal places in the answer is equal to the total of the number of places in the numbers you are multiplying.

0.42	0.81	0.5	0.24
× 0.003	× 0.2	× 0.5	× 0.02
0.00126	0.162	0.25	0.0048

In division, the divisor is converted to a whole number by moving the decimal point to the right as many places as necessary. The decimal point in the number you are dividing into must be moved the same number of places to the right.

$$0.25\overline{)1.000} = \text{ becomes } \quad 25\overline{)100.0} = 4.0.$$

$$0.32\overline{)6.4} = \text{ becomes } \quad 32\overline{)640} = 20.$$

$$0.482\overline{)14.46} = \text{ becomes } \quad 482\overline{)14460} = 30.$$

SQUARES AND SQUARE ROOTS

Squaring a number is multiplying it by itself.

$$3^2 = 3(3) = 9 \qquad 4^2 = 4(4) = 16$$

Taking a square root is finding a number which, when multiplied by itself, equals the number from which you are taking the square root.

$$\sqrt{4} = +2 \text{ or } -2 \qquad \text{since} \qquad 2(2) = 4 \quad \text{and} \quad -2(-2) = 4$$

$$\sqrt{16} = +4 \text{ or } -4 \qquad \text{since} \qquad 4(4) = 16 \quad \text{and} \quad -4(-4) = 16$$

$$\sqrt{9} = +3 \text{ or } -3 \qquad \text{since} \qquad 3(3) = 9 \quad \text{or} \quad -3(-3) = 9$$

ALGEBRA

To solve equations, you must get the unknown (usually symbolized by x) on one side of the equation and all other numbers on the other side. This is done by adding, subtracting, multiplying, or dividing both sides of the equation by the same number.

$$2x = 4$$

Divide both sides by 2.

$$\frac{2x}{2} = \frac{4}{2}$$

$$x = 2$$

$$\frac{x}{6} = 3$$

Multiply both sides by 6.

$$\frac{6x}{6} = 3(6)$$

$$x = 18$$

$$x + 3 = 9$$

Subtract 3 from both sides.

$$(x + 3) - 3 = 9 - 3$$

$$x = 6$$

$$x - 4 = 6$$

Add 4 to both sides.

$$(x - 4) + 4 = 6 + 4$$

$$x = 10$$

This procedure can also be done in combinations of the above.

$$2x + 4 = 10$$

Subtract 4 from both sides.

$$(2x + 4) - 4 = 10 - 4$$
$$2x = 6$$

Divide both sides by 2.

$$\frac{2x}{2} = \frac{6}{2}$$
$$x = 3$$

$$3x + 15 = 75$$

Subtract 15 from both sides.

$$(3x + 15) - 15 = 75 - 15$$
$$3x = 60$$

Divide both sides by 3.

$$\frac{3x}{3} = \frac{60}{3}$$
$$x = 20$$

$$4x + 10 = 110$$

Subtract 10 from both sides.

$$(4x + 10) - 10 = 110 - 10$$
$$4x = 100$$

Divide both sides by 4.

$$\frac{4x}{4} = \frac{100}{4}$$
$$x = 25$$

SELF-CHECK TEST

Directions: Solve the following problems.

_____ **1.** $13^2 = $ _____

_____ **2.** Convert $\frac{1}{4}$ to a decimal. _____

_____ **3.** $\sqrt{144}$ = _____

_____ **4.** 24(380 + 20) = _____

_____ **5.** $\frac{2}{5} + \frac{3}{15}$ = _____

_____ **6.** 144 ÷ 0.048 = _____

_____ **7.** 16x + 10 = 330 = _____

_____ **8.** $\frac{2}{3} ÷ \frac{7}{10}$ = _____

_____ **9.** 1.32 × 0.07 = _____

_____ **10.** $2\frac{2}{3} + 6\frac{1}{12}$ = _____

_____ **11.** Convert $\frac{1}{5}$ to a decimal. _____

_____ **12.** $\frac{2}{3} ÷ \frac{14}{15} × \frac{2}{5}$ = _____

_____ **13.** (24 − 15) − 2(17 + 4) + 32 = _____

_____ **14.** 1.375 + 0.139 = _____

_____ **15.** 9x + 72 = 342 _____

Answers:

1. 13 × 13 = 169

2. 0.25

3. 12 or −12

4. 9600

5. $\frac{3}{5}$

6. 3000

7. $x = 20$

8. $\frac{20}{21}$

9. 0.0924

10. $8\frac{3}{4}$

11. 0.2

12. $\frac{2}{7}$

13. −1

14. 1.524

15. $x = 30$

PREPARING FOR THE PRAXIS II: PRINCIPLES OF LEARNING AND TEACHING ASSESSMENT

THE PRAXIS SERIES: Professional Assessments for Beginning Teachers is a set of validated assessments that provide information to colleges, state education agencies, and school districts for teacher graduation, licensing, and hiring decisions. The majority of states now use the Praxis for these purposes. Thus, passing the Praxis will likely be necessary for you to begin, or continue, your teaching career. In addition, colleges and universities may use the basic academic skills component of the Praxis Series to qualify individuals for entry into teacher education programs.

WHAT IS THE PRAXIS, AND WHAT IS THE PRAXIS II?

The three areas of assessment in the Praxis Series are

1. For entering a teacher training program, Praxis I: Academic Skills Assessments.
2. For licensure into the teaching profession, Praxis II: Subject and Pedagogy Assessments.
3. For the first year of teaching, Praxis III: Classroom Performance Assessments

The Praxis II: Subject and Pedagogy test contains two types of assessments:

- Principles of Learning and Teaching
- Multiple Subjects Assessments

Why Are We Focusing on the Praxis II?

Since you have already entered a teacher training program Praxis I is not applicable. And, since you have not started teaching yet Praxis III will not be applicable until sometime in the future. As you near completion of your teacher training program (soon, we hope!) the Praxis II will loom large on the horizon.

Specifically, the Praxis II: Principles of Learning and Teaching Assessment is the portion of the Praxis series that is most closely aligned with this text. The Principles of Learning and Teaching Assessment is designed to assess knowledge in evaluation and assessment as well as educational psychology, human growth and development, class-room management, instructional design, and delivery techniques. The assessments are divided into grades K–6, grades 5–9 and grades 7–12 to reflect areas of certification.

The Principles of Learning and Teaching Assessment includes four case histories followed by a short answer question related to the case history that is scored on a scale of 0 to 3 by two or more raters using question-specific scoring guides and model answers. This section is followed by 24 multiple-choice questions that test the student's general knowledge in the areas mentioned previously.

How Will This Exercise Help Me Prepare for the Praxis II?

We have designed this exercise to parallel the style and format of the Praxis II, although it is not as long as the Praxis II. While the content of the actual Praxis II items will differ, the format will not, so it should feel familiar to you when you take it after completing this exercise. Here's how to approach this exercise:

1. You will be given two case histories, and each case history is followed by a short answer question. Then we provide a series of multiple-choice items following the case histories. This is just like the Praxis II, except shorter. Read each case history and on a separate sheet of paper respond to the short answer questions as best you can. Then complete the multiple-choice answers. Rather than simply circling the correct multiple-choice option, also write a sentence that explains why you think the option you selected is correct. For maximum benefit, approach this exercise as though you are actually taking the Praxis. So

   - leave your text and notes alone,
   - set a reasonable time limit for yourself, and
   - DON'T peek at the sections titled Case Study Scoring Guide/Model Answers or Multiple-Choice Answers and Rationale!

2. After you have responded to the short answer and multiple-choice questions, look at the Case Study Scoring Guide/Model Answers and Multiple-Choice Answers and Rationale sections. Using the scoring guide and the model answers, assign a score to each of your short answer responses (just like you learned to do in Chapter 7), and then score your multiple-choice answers according to the Multiple-Choice Answers and Rationale section. If you do not understand any of the rationales, refer back to the appropriate sections in Chapters 6–9 to clarify any questions you may have. Good luck, both now and when you actually take Praxis II!

PRAXIS II PREPARATION: SAMPLE CASE HISTORY 1

Ms. Velchek had been pleased when she was hired for her current teaching job. The middle school was newly built and featured state-of-the-art facilities, including computer, language, and biology labs. When she looked at the standardized test scores of her sixth grade social studies class, she was pleased. Most of the class was functioning above grade level in the critical areas such as science, vocabulary, reading comprehension, and mathematics, as well as in her own area of social studies. On back to school night her classroom had been packed with parents who seemed concerned and supportive.

Now, just six weeks into the year, she was discouraged. She was having every bit as much trouble with this "ideal" class as she had had when she taught a crowded inner city class with at-risk learners. Even though her students excelled on their weekly quizzes and objective tests, she suspected that they earned their high grades with only cursory reading of the assignments. Most were earning A's and B's, yet none seemed really interested in class, and she doubted that much of the information they gave back to her on tests was remembered over the long run.

Reading their essays had been exhilarating at first. They wrote well-constructed sentences, their thoughts were fairly well organized, and spelling errors were at a minimum. Nevertheless, now Ms. Velchek wondered if their writing ability was disguising a rather superficial understanding of the concepts she was teaching.

Ms. Velchek thought that by changing her tests and maybe even her grading system she could help promote and test for higher levels of understanding. She decided to eliminate the true/false quizzes in which half of the items could be gotten correct by guessing. She would continue using multiple-choice items, but she would write them to elicit her students' skill at applying what they learned, not just memorizing.

The class had just finished a unit on world geography and her students expected an exam that would emphasize facts about climate and topography. As usual they would come prepared with freshly memorized facts—this time about annual rainfall, the proper names of bodies of water, mountain ranges, and desert regions.

Mark hoped that all the facts and figures he had crammed for while watching TV last night would last until mid morning. He had given the chapters a quick once over during breakfast, so he felt as well prepared as always. But his mouth dropped when he saw the first question.

All the memorized figures, the knowledge of rainfall, temperature, and terrain, were no help now. What lay before him was an invented country, complete with data on mineral deposits, vegetation, rainfall, temperature, and never seen before rivers, lakes, and mountains. The question stated:

> *Given your knowledge of geography and its influence on economics and population growth, answer the following questions concerning this hypothetical country. Here are four possible sketches showing population distributions. Using the data given, which of these populations do you believe these data best represent?*

Another question asked about economic development, showing four maps with different areas sketched in for livestock ranching, commercial grain, mining, and industry.

Mark swallowed hard and flipped to the last page, the essay question, usually one he could easily answer. Most of the time his paraphrasing of the textbook passages would be sufficient for a high score. He "had a way with words," and made up for forgotten details with well-chosen adjectives. But his narrative ability wouldn't be of much help today. This essay question asked:

> *Write a paragraph explaining in detail the reasoning behind each of your multiple choice map selections.*

It was close to the end of the period, and no one had finished early this time. The puzzled expressions of the students at the beginning of the test had been replaced by looks of determination and, on some faces, subtle satisfaction.

Short Answer Question

DIRECTIONS: Question 1 requires you to write a short answer. Base your answers on your knowledge of principles of learning and teaching. Be sure to answer all parts of the question.

1. Ms. Velchek made a major change in her test construction and intends to make some modifications in her grading policy as well. To what extent do you think these changes are fair? What might you suggest to make the transition more equitable and comfortable to students?

NOTE: Remember to write your response on a separate sheet of paper. After you have completed your response read the next sample case history.

PRAXIS II PREPARATION: SAMPLE CASE HISTORY 2

Mr. Tan's first-grade class was representative of the unique urban pocket that surrounded the old brick elementary school. Some of his students resided in once fashionable three-story structures that were no longer homes to single families but had been transformed into apartments. These students were mostly from immigrant families with parents who worked long hours and had great expectations for their children. Other students were the children of young professionals who lived in renovated townhouses. They looked on their choice of public school positively and took it for granted that their children would excel. At the edge of the district a small enclave of modest houses housed workers at a nearby candy factory. Those families expected their sons and daughters to get through 12 grades of school and take a secure job at the factory.

Mr. Tan couldn't help but notice that his students brought their parents' expectations with them to school. Van's brown eyes were fastened on the teacher, and she copied the printed letters from her workbook with painful accuracy. The red marks on her returned papers seemed like bloody daggers to Van.

Ian's parents told Mr. Tan at back to school night that they had already taught their son to read through one of those phonics programs available for purchase. He had already read some books. His boredom with the first-grade texts was obvious and he amused himself by rolling his eyes whenever someone made a mistake in class.

Raul already had an expression on his face that would eventually become a mask of indifference as he put in his time at something he knew would make no difference in his preprogrammed life. He expected to be in the slow reading group and thought it a mistake when Mr. Tan suggested otherwise.

Yet out on the playground it was a different story. Van ran with delight as she ascended the monkey bars—she couldn't get a wrong answer there. When Raul ran around the track he did so to win and usually did, and a competitive spark filled his no longer expressionless eyes. A determined rather than bored Ian tried hard to keep up with Raul, emerging breathless to re-enter the classroom.

Without pencils and papers in hand these were different children, much more themselves, Mr. Tan thought. If only he could bring that enthusiasm and confidence to the classroom.

That night the smog was so thick as he walked to the bus stop that Mr. Tan's eyes stung. Then an idea emerged: a unit on air pollution, but not one from a textbook. It would be like the playground experience—hands on.

The next day Mr. Tan arranged for his class to go on a short walk around the school neighborhood. He told them about his stinging eyes from the day before and asked them to look for things that made the air dirty sometimes. When they returned, he asked them to draw them. Raul produced several sketches with draftsman-like skill. Ian clearly had several ideas, but labored to get them into recognizable form, while Van's colorful images seemed to make even a billowing smokestack beautiful.

Mr. Tan decided that what he wanted to focus on was not so much knowledge or basic skills, but on developing higher forms of thinking like professionals use to solve problems in the real world. He also wanted his students to develop positive attitudes toward learning and to have respect for themselves and others.

The next day Mr. Tan told the class that they were going to be scientists trying to fix the problem of dirty air. He asked them what kinds of things scientists do to learn about problems. Some students responded.

"They do experiments, in dark basements with lots of tubes and machines around."

"Those are only the bad scientists. They work in hospitals and test blood."

"They go to Egypt and dig up mummies and broken pots."

Mr. Tan was quick to ask, "Then they might do some of their work outside a laboratory, in the outdoors?" The class agreed.

"And they're always measuring things."

"And writing everything down, too."

"When we went on our walk, looking for things that made the air dirty, and then when we came back and drew pictures of these things, were we acting like scientists?" Mr. Tan asked. Heads nodded as he continued. "If we want to continue to work like scientists, what things would we have to do that might be different from somebody who is, say, an artist or store clerk or bus driver?"

Mr. Tan looked at Raul, who was now excited and waving his hand eagerly. Van's brown eyes sparkled with enthusiasm instead of anxiety, and Ian for the first time all year seemed alert and engaged.

Short Answer Question

DIRECTIONS: Question 2 requires you to write a short answer. Base your answers on your knowledge of principles of learning and teaching. Be sure to answer all parts of the question.

2. Mr. Tan wants to try portfolios, another form of authentic assessment. It is suggested that parents, students, and teachers work together as a team to plan a portfolio. What suggestions would you give him to encourage parental involvement in portfolio planning? Explain your answer.

NOTE: Remember to write your response on a separate sheet of paper. After you have completed your response respond to the following multiple-choice items.

PRAXIS II PREPARATION: MULTIPLE-CHOICE ITEMS

DIRECTIONS: Base your answers to questions 3–10 on your knowledge of the principles of learning and teaching. In addition to indicating the correct option for each item, on a separate sheet of paper also write a sentence that explains why you believe the option you selected is correct.

3. Mr. Malone wants to learn to what extent his tenth-grade honors history class understands his unit on the complex causes of the Civil War. Which type of assessment would be most likely to give him the information he seeks?

   (A) A norm-referenced test
   (B) A true–false test
   (C) A matching test
   (D) An essay test

4. Recent criticism of this type of test has questioned its relevance to day-to-day classroom learning, its usefulness in making instructional decisions, and its fairness to students of diverse cultural and ethnic backgrounds. The subject of the above criticism is which of the following?

   (A) Standardized tests
   (B) Criterion-referenced tests
   (C) Objective tests
   (D) Essay tests

5. Mr. Acuna needs a test which he can score quickly and reliably, reduces the effects of guessing, and is capable of measuring higher level objectives. Which of the objective-item formats is *best* suited to this purpose?

   (A) True–false test
   (B) Matching test
   (C) Multiple-choice test
   (D) Completion test

6. An essay test is most appropriate when

   (A) A considerable number of test items need to be graded
   (B) Instructional objectives specify high level cognitive processes
   (C) Test security is not a problem
   (D) Class size is a consideration

7. When a teacher creates a performance test, he or she must decide in advance about such things as time allotted for testing, if any type of reference material is allowed, whether there can be any sort of collaboration with others, as well as the scoring criteria. These considerations are termed

   (A) Testing reliability
   (B) Testing conditions
   (C) Testing validity
   (D) Testing accuracy

8. Teachers often use scoring guides that provide pre-established criteria for evaluating student performances. These detailed guides, containing precise definitions by which the quality of a learner's performance is judged against specific criteria, are called

   (A) Rubrics

   (B) Assessment contexts

   (C) Habits of mind

   (D) Primary trait scoring

9. Which type of assessment tells the story of a learner's growth, long-term achievement, and significant accomplishments?

   (A) Test blueprint

   (B) Multimodal assessment

   (C) Performance test

   (D) Portfolio

10. Which of the following could be considered ways of assessing student behavior at the end of a lesson or unit?

    (A) Lab assignment

    (B) In-class workbook assignments

    (C) Portfolio submission

    (D) All of the above

CASE STUDY SCORING GUIDE/MODEL ANSWERS

This section presents an overall Case Study Scoring Guide, or rubric, and model answers for items 1 and 2. You should apply the Case Study Scoring Guide criteria to your own answers, using the Model Answers as a check of your ratings. When you read these sample answers, keep in mind that, like your own answers, they are less polished than if they had been developed at home, edited, and carefully presented. Examinees do not know what questions will be asked and must decide, on the spot, how to respond. Raters take these circumstances into account when scoring the responses.

Case Study Scoring Guide

Rating   Descriptors

2. Demonstrates a thorough understanding of the aspects of the case that are relevant to the question.

   Responds appropriately to all parts of the question.

   If an explanation is required, provides a strong explanation that is well supported by evidence.

   Demonstrates a strong knowledge of pedagogical concepts, theories, facts, procedures, or methodologies relevant to the question.

Rating	Descriptors

1   Demonstrates some understanding of the aspects of the case that are relevant to the question.

Responds appropriately to a portion of the question.

If an explanation is required, provides a partial explanation that is supported by evidence.

Demonstrates some knowledge of pedagogical concepts, theories, facts, procedures, or methodologies relevant to the question.

0   Demonstrates misunderstanding of the aspects of the case that are relevant to the question.

Fails to respond (blank) or fails to respond to the specific question.

If an explanation is required, provides none that is supported by evidence.

Fails to demonstrate any knowledge of pedagogical concepts, theories, facts, procedures, or methodologies relevant to the question.

Model Answers

Item 1, First Model Response

> *"Ms. Velchek's students had been taking shortcuts by memorizing facts and writing superficial essays. However, it was Ms. Velchek who had written tests that emphasized memorization. And, it was she who had accepted glib responses to her essays.*
>
> *She should have prepared the students for the change by mentioning that this test would be something different from those in the past, and that they should be expected to apply what they learned rather than merely recall and regurgitate it. As for the possible changes in grading, I think Ms. Velcheck should discuss the purpose and advantages of any new grading system and elicit input from her students before it is implemented so they know why a particular grading system would be used."*

Application of the scoring guide criteria to this response would result in a score of 2.

Item 1, Second Model Response

> *"It was fair for Ms. Velchek to make the test and questions harder. She is the teacher and has the right to write a test they way she wants. She doesn't need to tell her class exactly what to expect or else a lot of the class will get high scores. It's better to keep them alert by wondering what type of test they will get.*
>
> *The grades are different though. Those kids have been through five or six years of school with one system that everyone expects. It would be confusing and counterproductive to change at this point in the game."*

Application of the scoring guide criteria to this response would result in a score of 0.

Item 2, First Model Response

"Mr. Tan might be tempted to minimize parental involvement in portfolio planning due to parental expectations that could increase anxiety, boredom, and apathy in some of his students. However, by inviting parental involvement he could receive useful suggestions for improving his portfolio project and engage in candid discussions about ways to improve student attitudes.

Mr. Tan should begin by sending home a detailed explanation of his portfolio project with explanations of its goals and grading system. He might schedule individual conferences with parents at certain points during the year where they can see the work and progress of their son or daughter. After new, positive attitudes toward learning take root in his learners, Mr. Tan could continue the dialogue by inviting more input from parents on other projects."

Application of the scoring guide criteria to this response would result in a score of 2.

Item 2, Second Model Response

"Mr. Tan is better off keeping the parents out of the portfolio project. Some, like Ian's parents, are going to be overly controlling and might be upset if their kid doesn't get to do the project he wants. Raul's parents are likely to be as indifferent to school as he initially was. And, Van's parents might disagree with the fun of a performance task during regular school hours.

Another reason to keep parents out of it is because he needs to show his authority as teacher. He is the one who is trained in education and he knows the best ways to teach. They are only parents, and some of them have never gone to college."

Application of the scoring guide criteria to this response would result in a score of 0.

Multiple-Choice Answers and Rationale

The correct answers for items 3–10 follow. Each answer is followed by a brief rationale and explanation. Compare these with your own answers and your one-sentence explanations, and refer back to the text to resolve any confusion or to refresh your memory.

3. The correct answer is D. An essay test is the best option presented for Mr. Malone to assess his students' understanding of the complex causes of the American Civil War. A norm-referenced test would yield information that compares his class to others in the general area of history, but it would not be specific enough to tell him if his students have learned what was taught. Both the true–false and the matching tests would tend to emphasize rote memorization of knowledge rather than complex understanding.

4. The correct answer is A. Standardized tests are constructed by test experts to determine a student's performance level relative to others of similar age and grade.

Recent criticism has questioned their relevance to classroom learning, their usefulness in making instructional decisions, and their fairness to students of diverse cultural and ethnic backgrounds.

5. The correct answer is C. Of all the objective-item formats, the multiple-choice question is the only one that combines efficiency of construction and grading with versatility in measuring higher levels of cognitive complexity, for example, by using pictorial and tabular aids, using analogies, or requiring the application of procedures and principles. It also reduces the effects of guessing, which is an inherent weakness in true–false items.

6. The correct answer is B. Essay test items are most suited to measuring high levels of cognitive processing. Essay items should be considered cautiously when test security is a consideration and the number of test items to be graded and class size are large.

7. The correct answer is B. Testing conditions are the constraints imposed on learners during tests. In performance tests, the importance of testing constraints lies in their real-world nature. The teacher must consider which constraints replicate those of the real world, as well as which will enhance student performance.

8. The correct answer is A. Rubrics are scoring criteria that minimize the arbitrariness of teacher judgments of a performance while holding learners to a high standard of achievement. Ease of construction, scoring efficiency, reliability, defensibility, and quality of feedback should all be considered in choosing the appropriate rubric.

9. The correct answer is D. The portfolio, a planned collection of learner achievement, documents what a student has accomplished and the steps taken to get there. It is an ideal way to assess final mastery, effort, reflection, and growth in learning and provides a richer array and more complete portrait over time than do paper and pencil tests alone.

10. The correct answer is D. All of the alternatives are correct and equally valid means of assessing the extent to which the objectives of a lesson or unit have been met.

DETERMINING THE MEDIAN WHEN THERE ARE MULTIPLE TIED MIDDLE SCORES

THE **FOLLOWING** example illustrates how the methods we presented in Chapter 12 to determine the median can sometimes over- or underestimate the true value of the median. Specifically, this is most likely to occur when there are m*ore than two* tied scores in the middle of a distribution of scores. Let's begin with the example we presented in Chapter 12.

Students	*Scores*
Bo	110
Deanna	105
Julio	100
Janelle	100
Joe	100
Jill	100
Juanita	100
Thomas	95
Dara	95
Richard	90

Joe and Jill: Two middle scores: $\dfrac{100 + 100}{2} = \dfrac{200}{2} = 100 = \text{MDN}$.

As we said in Chapter 12 this method is generally close enough for most classroom purposes. However, it is a bit misleading. Notice that of the five tied scores of 100, three scores of 100 are present in the upper 50% of scores and only two scores of 100 are present in the lower 50% of scores—the distribution of tied scores in the middle of the distribution is not balanced. Thus, a truly accurate value for the median should be slightly *more* than 100 to reflect this imbalance.

To arrive at a more accurate value for this distribution we must first understand the difference between test scores and the underlying traits or characteristics they measure. Although test scores are typically reported as *discrete*, whole numbers, or integers (70, 71, 86, etc.), the scores are only estimates of underlying variables such as achievement or intellectual ability that are *continuously* increasing or decreasing. In other words, change in one's true, underlying achievement or intellectual ability does not occur in discrete, uniform one-point increments. Instead, those changes are *continuous* or fractional in nature. Thus an obtained score of 79 may reflect an underlying value of 78.7, 79.4, or some other value close to 79. How close? Statisticians have adopted the convention of using the obtained score plus or minus 0.5 to acknowledge that discrete test scores actually reflect a continuum of underlying values. Thus, a score of 79 would have a *lower limit* of 78.5 and an *upper limit* of 79.5.

We can apply this convention to arrive at the most accurate value for the median when tied scores in the middle of a distribution are disproportionately distributed between the upper and lower halves of a distribution, as is the case in our example. If we consider a score of 100 to actually represent continuous values from a lower limit of 99.5 to an upper limit of 100.5 (the convention), then we can use interpolation to arrive at the median. Here's how:

1. Divide the number of tied scores in the middle of the distribution into 1:

   $1/5 = 0.2$

2. Multiply this value times the number of tied, middle scores in the lower half of the distribution

   $0.2 \times 2 = 0.4$

3. Subtract this value from the upper limit

   $100.5 - 0.4 = 100.1$

This value, 100.1, more accurately represents the median because it reflects the fact that more of the tied middle scores fell in the upper half of the distribution. If more of the tied scores fell in the lower half, the value for the median would be slightly less than 100. For example, if only one of the tied scores of 100 was in the upper half and four scores of 100 were in the lower half, using this method of interpolation would yield a median of 99.7.

PEARSON PRODUCT–MOMENT CORRELATION

THE FOLLOWING example illustrates the raw score method for computing the Pearson product–moment correlation coefficient (r). Listed in the X and Y columns are pairs of raw scores for each student. The X^2 column lists the squares of each X score. The Y^2 column lists the squares of each Y score. The XY column lists the cross-products of the X and Y columns (X multiplied by Y).

Name	X	Y	X^2	Y^2	XY
Art	10	14	100	196	140
Ben	7	12	49	144	84
Cathy	5	7	25	49	35
Debbie	9	12	81	144	108
Eugene	6	9	36	81	54
Fred	11	15	121	225	165
Glenda	2	5	4	25	10
Henry	2	4	4	16	8
Mary	5	14	25	196	70
Sharon	4	7	16	49	28
	61	99	461	1125	702

To compute a Pearson product–moment correlation coefficient for this data, follow these steps:

1. Square each X score and each Y score.
2. Multiply each person's X score (not the squared X score) times the same person's Y score (again, not the squared Y score).
3. Sum the X, Y, X^2, Y^2, and XY columns.
4. Plug the values into the following formula:

$$r = \frac{\Sigma XY - \dfrac{(\Sigma X)(\Sigma Y)}{N}}{\sqrt{\Sigma X^2 - \dfrac{(\Sigma X)^2}{N}}\sqrt{\Sigma Y^2 - \dfrac{(\Sigma Y)^2}{N}}}$$

where

ΣXY is the sum of the XY column

ΣX is the sum of all X scores

ΣY is the sum of all Y scores

N is the number of persons observed

ΣX^2 is the sum of the X^2 column

ΣY^2 is the sum of the Y^2 column

Then, for the data given in this example we get

$$r = \frac{702 - \dfrac{(61)(99)}{10}}{\sqrt{461 - \dfrac{(61)^2}{10}}\sqrt{1125 - \dfrac{(99)^2}{10}}} = \frac{702 - 603.9}{\sqrt{461 - 372.1}\sqrt{1125 - 980.1}}$$

$$= \frac{98.1}{\sqrt{88.9}\sqrt{144.9}} = \frac{98.1}{(9.43)(12.04)} = \frac{98.1}{113.54} = .86$$

There is a strong positive relationship between X and Y.

STATISTICS AND MEASUREMENT TEXTS

Airasian, P. W. (1997). *Classroom Assessment* (3rd ed.). New York: McGraw-Hill.

Anastasi, A., and Urbina, S. (1997). *Psychological Testing* (7th ed.). Upper Saddle River, NJ: Prentice–Hall.

Bartz, A. E. (1999). *Basic Statistical Concepts* (4th ed.). Upper Saddle River, NJ: Prentice–Hall.

Gravetter, F. J., and Wallnau, L. B. (2000). *Statistics for the Behavioral Sciences* (5th ed.). Belmont, CA: Wadsworth/Thomson Learning.

Linn, R. L., and Gronlund, N. (2000). *Measurement and Assessment in Teaching* (8th ed.). Upper Saddle River, NJ: Prentice–Hall.

Popham, W. J. (2002). *Classroom Assessment: What Teachers Need to Know* (3rd ed.). Boston: Allyn & Bacon.

Spatz, C. (1997). *Basic Statistics: Tales of Distributions* (6th ed.). Pacific Grove, CA: Brookes–Cole.

Stiggins, R. J. (1997). *Student-Centered Classroom Assessment* (2nd ed.). Upper Saddle River, NJ: Prentice–Hall.

Thorndike, R. M., Cunningham, G., Thorndike, R. L., and Hagan, E. (1991). *Measurement and Evaluation in Psychology and Education*. New York: Macmillan.

Young, R. K., and Veldman, D. J. (1981). *Introductory Statistics for the Behavioral Sciences* (4th ed.). New York: Holt, Rinehart & Winston.

ANSWERS FOR PRACTICE QUESTIONS

CHAPTER 2

3. A state-developed test is more likely to be aligned than a national test when the state has established clear academic standards and the state's test is designed specifically to measure those standards, and when the national test measures more general objectives across many states.

4. Some states may have been pressured into utilizing a test before they had time to develop academic standards and/or a specific test to measure them.

CHAPTER 4

10. (a) B (b) E (c) B (d) E (e) B (f) B (g) E (h) B

12. (1) c (2) d (3) d (4) e

CHAPTER 5

4. (1) d (2) a (3) b (4) e (5) f

5. (a) 2 comprehension, 1 application (b) 30% multiplication, 30% division

CHAPTER 6

3. (a) The "a" should be "a/an."

(b) National origin of the names in the stem provides a clue to the answer.

(c) Contains an absolute; opinionated.

(d) Multiple defensible answers; lacks specificity.

(e) Begins with a blank; lacks specificity.

(f) Lists should be titled and arranged in some logical order; too wide a variety of concepts being measured, making some answers obvious (i.e., nonhomogeneous lists).

CHAPTER 8

1. Conventional tests are given to obtain data on which to base grades, indicate how much has been learned, make decisions about instructional placement, talk to parents about, and help others make employment decisions. Performance assessments are given to stimulate higher order thinking in the classroom and simulate real-world activities.

2. By refocusing the curriculum on thinking, problem solving, and student responsibility for learning.

3. An indirect measure, such as knowledge shown in a multiple-choice test, will only suggest that something has been learned. A direct measure, such as a problem-solving activity, requires that acquired knowledge can be applied and exhibited in the context of a real-world problem.

5. For example, the Darwin School records percentage of words read accurately during oral reading, number of sentences read with understanding, and number of story elements learners can talk about on their own. The West Orient School requires portfolios of poetry, essays, biographies, and self-reflections.

8. Scoring rubrics are model answers against which a learner's performance is compared. They can be a detailed list of what an acceptable answer must contain or a sample of typical responses that would be acceptable.

CHAPTER 10

1. (a) $p = 0.22$ (a difficult item)
(b) $p = 0.64$ (a moderately difficult item)

2. (a) $D = 0.40$ (an excellent discriminator)
(b) $D = -0.33$ (poor item, delete or modify)

3. (a) ambiguity (b) miskeyed (c) ambiguity (d) guessing (e) miskeyed

4. p = 0.25; D = 0.10, The key discriminates positively, but not all distractors discriminate negatively. Probably some guessing and/or ambiguity is involved

CHAPTER 11

5. Numerical mark = 74.7, letter grade = C; both approaches yield the same result because they differ only in the point at which the equating procedure is applied.

CHAPTER 12

1. Grade 1, positively skewed; grade 3, normal; grade 5, negatively skewed

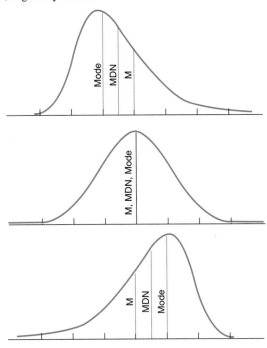

2. Group 1: (a) N = 10, (b) R = 13, (c) M = 93.3, (d) MDN = 94.0, (e) mode = 90, 94, and 97. Group 2: (a) N = 10, (b) R = 36, (c) M = 89.6, (d) MDN = 92.5, (e) mode = 97. (f) The difference in means is caused by the very low score of 61 in Group 2. (g) For Group 1 the mean would be the best measure of central tendency; for Group 2 the median would be the best measure of central tendency.

3. Use from 8 to 10 intervals. Choose the number that best demonstrates variations in the frequency of scores.

4. (1) c (2) c (3) a (4) b (5) b

5. $P_{25} = 93.5$; $P_{50} = 99$

6. (a) Normal; (b) negatively skewed; (c) positively skewed

7. (a) Simple frequency distribution; small number and small range of scores

(b) List; small number but large range

(c) Grouped frequency distribution; large number and large range of scores

CHAPTER 13

1. (a) N = 10; (b) mode = 5; (c) median = 4.5; (d) mean = 4.0; (e) standard deviation = 1.61; (f) variance = 2.6; (g) range = 5

2. (a) 2.0, 3.2, 4.0, 4.5

(b) 75, 106, 112.5, 121.5

(c) 125, 88, 85, 78

(d) About 15%; 82%; 34.13%; about 11%

3. (a) 1.33 (b) 74.5 (c) about 16%

4. 35

5. John, −1.0, 40; Mary, +2.0, 70; Jim, +0.5, 55; Claire, −1.5, 35

6. (a) 42.5, 121 (b) 700

CHAPTER 14

2. Curvilinear. Income goes up until age 60, then income decreases with age.

3. .84; positive and strong

4. 71%

5. (a) 4 (b) 7 (c) 1 (d) 2

6. Disagree. A third variable, yet unmeasured, could cause both big feet and large vocabularies in the same individuals, making the relationship only appear causal. More likely, however, since such a variable probably could not be identified, it would be appropriate to regard the high correlation as erroneously caused by insufficient N or sampling error.

7. Truncation restricts the variability of scores and, hence, cannot reveal the covariation of X and Y scores in the larger distribution of scores.

CHAPTER 15

1. The concurrent validity coefficient is −.97. The test has no concurrent validity evidence when compared with the old test.

2. Predictive validity evidence: Correlate the test scores with scores on a subsequent test in social studies, or with end-of-quarter grades in social studies. Construct validity evidence: Correlate the test scores with ratings on citizenship, scores on a test of social awareness, or any test that measures a part of what the new test measures to see that there is a positive correlation. Conversely, you would expect a negative correlation with the opposite of what the test measures.

3. Both Test A and Test C would be acceptable. Test C is unusual because predictive validity evidence is higher than concurrent. Normally the opposite is true.

4. Test C is most acceptable, followed by Test A and Test B.

5. (a) content

(b) predictive

(c) concurrent

(d) predictive

(e) concurrent

(f) content

6. A lower correlation is expected since your gifted group is homogeneous. Therefore the strength of the correlation is limited due to the truncated range of scores involved.

CHAPTER 16

1. Test C

2. $r_w = .75$

3. (a) internal consistency

(b) internal consistency

(c) test–retest

4. Test C

5. (a) test–retest

(b) alternate forms (long interval)

(c) split-half

(d) alternate forms

(e) test–retest

6. Test B

7. Use neither test, unless acceptable validity evidence can be established.

CHAPTER 17

In the problem at the end of Chapter 17, there is a real difference between John's Reading and Math scores, but not between his Writing and Science scores.

1. $S_m = 400$

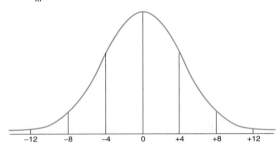

2. 95%, 8–24; 99%, 4–28; 68%, 12–20

3. Within student (illness); within test (poor items); within administration (timing); within scoring (miskeys)

4. (a) Most subject to administrative and scoring; least subject to within test

(b) Most subject to within student; least subject to within test

(c) Most subject to within test; least subject to within student

(d) Most subject to all sources

(e) Least subject to all sources

5. The following subtest profile shows bands for 68% certainty.

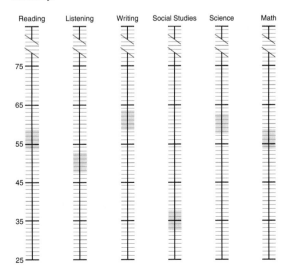

Subtest	Band	
Reading	53.6–58.4	$S_m = SD\sqrt{1 - r}$
Listening	47.6–52.4	$= 8\sqrt{1 - .91}$
Writing	58.6–63.4	$= 8\sqrt{.09}$
Social Studies	32.6–37.4	$= 8(.3)$
Science	57.6–62.4	$= 2.4$
Math	53.6–58.4	

Interpretation: Social Studies is significantly lower than all others. Listening is significantly lower than all but Social Studies. Writing is significantly higher than all but Science. Other differences are due to chance.

6. None shows real differences.

7. Differences of this size and direction are expected since each method is affected by different sources of error.

8. S_m for A equals 6 and S_m for B equals 5; scores from A would fluctuate most.

CHAPTER 18

4. (a) Jack is achieving below expectancy, Bonnie is above, and Chris is at expectancy.

(b) There is an aptitude–achievement discrepancy between Jack's Verbal IQ and his Vocabulary and Comprehension achievement.

8.

Subtest	Standard Score
Reading	552
Vocabulary	604
Language	458
Language Mechanics	466
Mathematics	565
Mathematics Computation	579
Science	585
Social Studies	491
Spelling	455
Word Analysis	507

CHAPTER 20

7. Intelligence, achievement, creativity, and task persistence.

Intelligence: standardized intelligence test, observations

Achievement: standardized achievement tests (norm- and criterion-referenced), teacher-made tests, observations, work samples

Creativity: standardized test of creativity, observations, work samples

Task persistence: observations, work samples

8. Homogeneous grouping has little research support, except when homogeneously grouped gifted and talented students are able to pursue accelerated programs. Enrichment programs alone have not been demonstrated to be successful for gifted students. Magnet schools, because they emphasize acceleration, seem to be helpful for the gifted and talented.

CHAPTER 21

1. Under IDEA–97 and IDEA–04 regular education teachers are now required to be members of IEP teams for special learners. Teachers may be required to collect information needed by the IEP team to (a) establish annual goals, (b) measure progress in the general curriculum during reporting periods, (c) identify behaviors that interfere with learning, or (d) identify other needs that may be a result of the child's disability or that may interfere with learning.

4. The principal's conclusion should not be supported. First, percentages and percentiles are not directly comparable. Second, because the special learners were evaluated with alternative assessments they cannot be compared to students evaluated with standardized tests, and they cannot be accurately compared with one another, unless the alternative assessments were administered and scored uniformly (i.e., in a standardized way).

10. 4.0

11. (a) AV (b) AP (c) AV (d) AV (e) AP (f) AP (g) AP (h) AP (i) AV

12. (a) Too many thoughts (double-barreled)

(b) Uses a negative; factual

(c) References the past

(d) Uses an absolute

(e) Not direct or clearly written

SUGGESTED READINGS

CHAPTER 1

American Educational Research Association, American Psychological Association, National Council on Measurement in Education. (1999). *Standards for Educational and Psychological Testing* (3rd ed.). Washington, DC: Author.

Cosden, M., Zimmer, J., and Tuss, P. (1993). The impact of age, sex, and ethnicity on kindergarten entry and retention decisions. *Educational Evaluations and Policy Analysis*, 15: 209–222.

Gardner, H. (1990). Assessment in context: The alternative to standardized testing. In B. R. Gifford and M. C. O'Connor (Eds.), *Future Assessments: Changing Views of Aptitude, Achievement and Instruction.* Boston: Kluwer Academic Publishers.

Haladyna, T. M. (2002). *Essentials of Standardized Achievement Testing.* Boston: Allyn & Bacon.

Holmes Group. (1986). *Tomorrow's Teachers.* East Lansing, MI: The Holmes Group, Michigan State University.

Individuals with Disabilities Education Act Amendments of 1997, 20 U.S. Code, Sec. 101.

Lissitz, R. W., and Schafer, W. D. (2002). *Assessment in Educational Reform.* Boston: Allyn & Bacon.

National Commission on Excellence in Education. (1983). *A Nation at Risk: The Imperative for Educational Reform.* Washington, DC: National Commission on Excellence in Education.

Resnick, L., and Resnick, D. (1989). Assessing the Thinking Curriculum: New Tools for Educational Reform. Pittsburgh: Learning Research and Development Center, University of Pittsburgh.

Spitzer, S., Cupp, R., and Parke, R. D. (1995). School entrance, age, social competence and self-perception in kindergarten and first grade. *Early Childhood Research Quarterly*, 10: 433–450.

CHAPTER 2

American Psychological Association. (2001). *Test User Qualifications: A Data-Based Approach to Promoting Good Test Use.* Washington, DC: American Psychological Association.

Haladyna, T. M. (2002). *Essentials of Standardized Achievement Testing.* Boston: Allyn & Bacon.

Lissitz, R. W., and Schafer, W. D. (2002). *Assessment in Educational Reform.* Boston: Allyn & Bacon.

National Research Council. (2000). *Tests and Teaching Quality: Interim Report.* Washington, DC: National Academy Press.

RAND Corporation. (2000). What Do Test Scores Tell Us? October 24, Santa Monica: RAND Corporation.

CHAPTER 3

Collier, M. (1986). A specific investigation of relative performance of examination markers. *Assessment and Evaluation in Higher Education*, 11(2): 130–137.

Cronbach, L. J. (1990). *Essentials of Psychological Testing* (5th ed.), Chapter 2. New York: HarperCollins.

Gullickson, A. R., and Ellwein, M. C. (1985). Post hoc analysis of teacher-made tests: The goodness-of-fit between prescription and practice. *Educational Measurement: Issues and Practice*, 4(1): 15–18.

Hall, B. W., et al. (1985). How beginning teachers use test results in critical education decisions. *Educational Research Quarterly*, 9(3): 12–18.

National Research Council (2000). *Tests and Teaching Quality: Interim Report.* Washington, DC: National Academy Press.

Smith, C. W. (1987). 100 ways to improve and use teacher-made tests. *Illinois Schools Journal*, 66(3): 20–26.

Stiggins, R. J. (1985). Improving assessment where it means the most: In the classroom. *Educational Leadership*, 43(2): 69–74.

CHAPTER 4

Green, K. E., and Stager, S. F. (1987). Differences in teacher test and item use with subject, grade level taught, and measurement coursework. *Teacher Education & Practice*, 4(1): 55–61.

Hall, B. W., et al. (1985). How beginning teachers use test results in critical education decisions. *Educational Research Quarterly*, 9(3): 12–18.

Mehrens, W. A., and Lehmann, I. J. (1987). Using teacher-made measurement devices. *NASSP Bulletin*, 71(496): 36, 38–44.

Neeb, K. E., et al. (1984). Empirical evaluation of different procedures for the construction of criterion-referenced items and instructional tasks. *Studies in Educational Evaluation*, 10(2): 191–197.

Stiggins, R. J. (1988). Make sure your teachers understand student assessment. *Executive Educator*, 10(8): 26–30.

CHAPTER 5

Ball, D. W., et al. (1986). Level of teacher objectives and their classroom tests: Match or mismatch. *Journal of Social Studies Research*, 10(2): 27–31.

Green, K. E., and Stager, S. F. (1987). Differences in teacher test and item use with subject, grade level taught, and measurement coursework. *Teacher Education & Practice*, 4(1): 55–61.

Gronlund, N. E. (2000). *How to Write and Use Instructional Objectives*. Upper Saddle River, NJ: Merrill, Prentice–Hall.

Gullickson, A. R., and Ellwein, M. C. (1985). Post hoc analysis of teacher-made tests: The goodness-of-fit between prescription and practice. *Educational Measurement: Issues and Practice*, 4(1): 15–18.

Mager, R. (1975). *Preparing Instructional Objectives* (2nd ed.). Palo Alto, CA: Fearon.

Neeb, K. E., et al. (1984). Empirical evaluation of different procedures for the construction of criterion-referenced items and instructional tasks. *Studies in Education Evaluation*, 10(2): 191–197.

White, J. D. (1988). Who writes these questions, anyway? *College Composition and Communication*, 39(2): 230–235.

Wiggins, G. (1998). *Educative Assessment: A Practical Guide for Designing Assessment Instruments*. San Francisco: Jossey-Bass.

Zeidner, M. (1987). Essay versus multiple-choice type classroom exams: The student's perspective. *Journal of Educational Research*, 80(6): 352–358.

CHAPTER 6

Frary, R. B. (1985). Multiple-choice versus free-response: A simulation study. *Journal of Educational Measurement*, 22(1): 21–31.

Frisbie, D. A. (1988). Instructional module on reliability of scores from teacher-made tests. *Educational Measurement: Issues and Practice*, 7(1): 25–33.

Gronlund, N. E. (1998). *Assessment of Student Achievement* (6th ed.). Boston: Allyn & Bacon.

Karras, R. (1985). A realistic approach to thinking skills: Reform multiple-choice questions. *Social Science Record*, 22(2): 38–43.

Royer, J. M., et al. (1987). The sentence verification technique: A practical procedure for testing comprehension. *Journal of Reading*, 30(5): 414–422.

White, J. D. (1988). Who writes these questions, anyway? *College Composition and Communication*, 39(2): 230–235.

Zeidner, M. (1987). Essay versus multiple-choice type classroom exams: The student's perspective. *Journal of Educational Research*, 80(6): 352–358.

CHAPTER 7

Baker, S., and Hubbard, D. (1995). Best practices in the assessment of written expression. In A. Thomas and J. Grimes (eds.), *Best Practices in School Psychology—III*. Bethesda, MD: National Association of School Psychologists.

Blok, H. (1985). Estimating the reliability, validity and invalidity of essay ratings. *Journal of Educational Measurement*, 22(1): 41–52.

Braun, H. I. (1988). Understanding scoring reliability: Experiments in calibrating essay readers. *Journal of Educational Statistics*, 13(1): 1–18.

Dansereau, D. F. (1988). Cooperative learning strategies. In C. E. Weinstein, E. T. Goetz, and P. A. Alexander (Eds.), *Learning and Study Strategies: Issues in Assessment, Instruction, and Evaluation* (pp. 103–120). San Diego: Academic Press.

Gronlund, N. E. (1998). *Assessment of Student Achievement* (6th ed.). Boston: Allyn & Bacon.

Kemerer, R., and Wahlstrom, M. (1985). An alternative to essay examinations: The interpretive exercise, how to minimize test time and save dollars. *Performance and Instruction*, 24(8): 9–12.

Smith, C. W. (1987). 100 ways to improve and use teacher-made tests. *Illinois Schools Journal*, 66(3): 20–26.

Zeidner, M. (1987). Essay versus multiple-choice type classroom exams: The student's perspective. *Journal of Educational Research*, 80(6): 352–358.

CHAPTER 8

Bransford, J. D., and Vye, N. J. (1989). A perspective on cognitive research and its implications for instruction. In L. B. Resnick and L. E. Klopfer (Eds.), *Toward the Thinking Curriculum: Current Cognitive Research* (pp. 173–205). 1989 ASCD Yearbook. Alexandria, VA: Association for Supervision and Curriculum Development.

Fuhrman, S. (1988). Educational indicators: An overview. *Phi Delta Kappan*, 2: 486–487.

Gardner, H. (1990). Assessment in context: The alternative to standardized testing. In B. R. Gifford and M. C. O'Connor (eds.), *Future Assessments: Changing Views of Aptitude, Achievement and Instruction.* Boston: Kluwer Academic Publishers.

Resnick, L., and Resnick, D. (1990). Assessing the thinking curriculum: New tools for educational reform. In B. R. Gifford and M. C. O'Connor (Eds.). *Future Assessments: Changing Views of Aptitude, Achievement and Instruction.* Boston: Kluwer Academic Publishers.

Shepard, L. A. (1989). Why we need better assessments. *Educational Leadership*, 46: 4–9.

CHAPTER 9

Borich, G. (2000). *Effective Teaching Methods* (4th ed.), Chapter 13. Upper Saddle River, NJ.: Prentice–Hall/Merrill.

Borich, G., and Tombari, M. (1997). *Educational Psychology: A Contemporary Approach* (2nd ed.), Chapter 13. New York: Addison-Wesley Longman.

Marzano, R. J., Pickering, D., and McTighe, J. (1993). *Assessing Student Outcomes.* Alexandria, VA: ASCD.

Nolet, V. (1992). Classroom-based measurement and portfolio assessment. *Diagnostique*, 18: 5–26.

Shavelson, R. J., and Baxter, G. (1992). What we've learned about assessing hands-on science. *Educational Leadership*, 49(8): 20–25.

Swicegood, P. (1994). Portfolio-based assessment practices: The uses of portfolio assessments for students with behavioral disorders or learning disabilities. *Intervention in School and Clinic*, 30: 6–15.

Tombari, M., and Borich, G. (1999). *Authentic Assessment in the Classroom: Applications and Practice.* Upper Saddle River, NJ: Prentice–Hall/Merrill.

CHAPTER 10

Anastasi, A., and Urbina, S. (1997). *Psychological Testing* (7th ed.), Chapter 8. Upper Saddle River, NJ: Prentice–Hall.

Kolstad, R., et al. (1984). The application of item analysis to classroom achievement tests. *Education*, 105(1): 70–72.

Nimmer, D. N. (1984). Measures of validity, reliability, and item analysis for classroom tests. *Clearing House*, 58(3): 138–140.

Secolsky, C. (1983). Using examinee judgments for detecting invalid items on teacher-made criterion-referenced tests. *Journal of Educational Measurement*, 20(1): 51–63.

Smith, C. W. (1987). 100 ways to improve and use teacher-made tests. *Illinois Schools Journal*, 66(3): 20–26.

CHAPTER 11

Millman, J., et al. (1983). Does grade inflation affect the reliability of grades? *Research in Higher Education*, 19(4): 423–429.

Nottingham, M. (1988). Grading practices—Watching out for land mines. *NASSP Bulletin*, 72(507): 24–28.

Ornstein, A. C. (1994). Grading practices and policies: An overview and some suggestions. *NASSP Bulletin*, 78: 55–64.

Polloway, E. A., Epstein, M. H., Bursuck, W. D., Roderique, T. W., McConeghy, J. L., and Jayanthi, M. (1994). Classroom grading: A national survey of policies. *Remedial and Special Education*, 15: 162–170.

Strein, W. (1997). Grades and grading practices. In G. Bear, K. Minke, and A. Thomas (Eds.), *Children's Needs—II*. Bethesda, MD: National Association of School Psychologists.

CHAPTERS 12–14

See Appendix E

CHAPTER 15

Anastasi, A., and Urbina, S. (1997). *Psychological Testing* (7th ed.), Chapter 6. Upper Saddle River, NJ: Prentice–Hall.

Frisbie, D. A. (1973). Multiple-choice versus true–false: A comparison of reliabilities and concurrent validities. *Journal of Educational Measurement*, 10: 297–304.

Nimmer, D. N. (1984). Measures of validity, reliability and item analysis for classroom tests. *Clearing House*, 58(3): 138–140.

CHAPTER 16

Anastasi, A., and Urbina, S. (1997). Psychological Testing (7th ed.), Chapter 5. Upper Saddle River, NJ: Prentice–Hall.

Braun, H. I. (1988). Understanding scoring reliability: Experiments in calibrating essay readers. *Journal of Educational Statistics*, 13(1): 1–18.

Costin, F. (1972). Three-choice versus four-choice items: Implications for reliability and validity of objective achievement tests. *Educational and Psychological Measurement*, 32: 1035–1038.

Frisbie, D. A. (1988). Instructional module on reliability of scores from teacher-made tests. *Educational Measurement: Issues and Practice*, 7(1): 25–33.

Nimmer, D. N. (1984). Measures of validity, reliability, and item analysis for classroom tests. *Clearing House*, 58(3): 138–140.

Oosterhof, A. C., and Glasnapp, D. R. (1974). Comparative reliability and difficulties of the multiple-choice and true–false formats. *Journal of Experimental Education*, 42: 62–64.

CHAPTER 17

Anastasi, A., and Urbina, S. (1997). Psychological Testing (7th ed.), Chapter 5. Upper Saddle River, NJ: Prentice–Hall.

Nimmer, D. N. (1984). Measures of validity, reliability, and item analysis for classroom tests. *Clearing House*, 58(3): 138–140.

Rudner, L. M. (1983). Individual assessment accuracy. *Journal of Educational Measurement*, 20(3): 207–219.

CHAPTER 18

Anastasi, A., and Urbina, S. (1997). Psychological Testing (7th ed.), Chapter 4. Upper Saddle River, NJ: Prentice–Hall.

Dreher, M. J., and Singer, H. (1984). Making standardized tests work for you. *Principal*, 63(4): 20–24.

Hadebank, L. (1995). Developing local norms for problem solving in schools. In A. Thomas and J. Grimes (Eds.). *Best Practices in School Psychology—III*. Bethesda, MD: National Association of School Psychologists.

Hills, J. R. (1983). Interpreting stanine scores. *Educational Measurement: Issues and Practice*, 2(3): 18–27.

Lopez, E. C. (1995). Working with bilingual children. In A. Thomas and J. Grimes (Eds.). *Best Practices in School Psychology—III*. Bethesda, MD: National Association of School Psychologists.

Lopez, E. C., and Gopaul-McNicol, S. (1997). English as a second language. In G. Bear, K. Minke, and A. Thomas (Eds.). *Children's Needs—II*. Bethesda, MD: National Association of School Psychologists.

Stone, B. J. (1995). Use of standardized assessments. In A. Thomas and J. Grimes (Eds.). *Best Practices in School Psychology—III*. Bethesda, MD: National Association of School Psychologists.

CHAPTER 19

Anastasi, A., and Urbina, S. (1997). *Psychological Testing* (7th ed.), Chapter 14. Upper Saddle River, NJ: Prentice–Hall.

Cronbach, L. J. (1990). *Essentials of Psychological Testing* (5th ed.), Chapter 7. New York: HarperCollins.

Knoff, H. (1995). Personalty assessment. In A. Thomas and J. Grimes (Eds.). *Best Practices in School Psychology—III*. Bethesda, MD: National Association of School Psychologists.

Mehrens, W. A., and Lehmann, I. J. (1991). *Measurement and Evaluation in Education and Psychology* (4th ed.), Chapter 3. New York: Holt, Rinehart and Winston.

Reschly, D., and Grimes, J. (1995). Intellectual assessment. In A. Thomas and J. Grimes (Eds.), *Best Practices in School Psychology—III*. Bethesda, MD: National Association of School Psychologists.

Sternberg, R. (1989). *The Triarchic Mind*. New York: Viking Penguin.

CHAPTER 20

Ash, C., and Huebner, F. S. (1998). Life satisfaction reports of gifted middle-school children. *School Psychology Quarterly*, 13: 265–280.

Boatman, T. A., Davis, K. G., and Benbow, C. P. (1997). Gifted education. In A. Thomas and J. Grimes (Eds.). *Best Practices in School Psychology—III*. Bethesda, MD; National Association of School Psychologists.

Bricker, D., and Gumerlock, S. (1988). Application of a three-level evaluation plan for monitoring child progress and program effects. *Journal of Special Education*, 22(1): 66–81.

Davis, G., and Rimm, S. (1989). *Education of the Gifted and Talented*. Englewood Cliffs, NJ: Prentice–Hall.

Gresham, F., MacMillan, D., and Bocian, K. (1998). Agreement between school study team decisions and authoritative definitions in classification of students at-risk for mild disabilities. *School Psychology Quarterly*, 13: 181–191.

Pianta, R. C., and Walsh, D. J. (1996). *High-Risk Children in Schools: Constructing Sustaining Relationships*. New York: Routledge.

Schwartz, L. L. (1994) *Why Give "Gifts" to the Gifted? Investing in a National Resource*. Thousand Oaks, CA: Corwin Press.

Woodrich, D. L., Stobo, N., and Trca, M. (1998). Three ways to consider educational performance when determining serious emotional disturbance. *School Psychology Quarterly*, 13: 241–264.

CHAPTER 21

Anastasi, A., and Urbina, S. (1997). *Psychological Testing* (7th ed.), Chapter 17. Upper Saddle River, NJ: Prentice–Hall.

Cronbach, L. J. (1990). *Essentials of Psychological Testing* (5th ed.), Chapter 17. New York: HarperCollins.

Individuals with Disabilities Education Act Amendments of 1997, 20 U.S. Code, Sec. 101.

Markus, E. J. (1980). Mapping the social structure of a class: A practical instrument for assessing some effects of mainstreaming. *Journal of Special Education*, 14(3): 311–324.

McConaughy, S. H., and Ritter, D. R. (1995). Multidimensional assessment of emotional and behavioral disorders. In A. Thomas and J. Grimes (Eds.), *Best Practices in School Psychology—III*. Bethesda, MD: National Association of School Psychologists.

Rehabilitation Act of 1973, 20 U.S. Code, Sec. 794 (1973).

Schibeci, R. A. (1982). Measuring student attitudes: Semantic differential or Likert instruments? *Science Education*, 66(4): 565–570.

REFERENCES

Achenbach, T. (1991). *Manual for the Teacher's Report Form.* Burlington: University of Vermont, Department of Psychiatry.

Allport, G. W., and Odbert, H. S. (1936). Trait-names: A psycho-lexical study. *Psychological Monographs,* 47: 1–171.

American Educational Research Association. (July, 2000). *High-Stakes Testing in PreK–12 Education.* Available at http:///www.aera.net/policyandprograms/?id=378.

American Educational Research Association, American Psychological Association, and National Council on Measurement in Education (1999). *Standards for Educational and Psychological Testing* (3rd ed.). Washington, DC: Author.

American Federation of Teachers. (2001). *Making Standards Matter 2001, the Annual Report of the American Federation of Teachers.* Available at http://www.aft.org/pubs-reports/downloads/teachers/msm2001.pdf.

American Psychological Association. (2001). *Test User Qualifications: A Data-Based Approach to Promoting Good Test Use.* Washington, DC: American Psychological Association.

American Psychological Association. (2004). *Publication Manual of the American Psychological Association* (5th ed.). Washington, DC: American Psychological Association.

Americans for Better Education, (2004). *Support for No Child Left Behind Is Growing Stronger, New National Survey Shows.* October 18, 2004, press release available at http://www.bettered.org/1081/.

Amrein, A. L., & Berliner, D. C. (2002). High-stakes testing, uncertainty, and student learning. *Education Policy Analysis Archives,* 10 (18). Retrieved May 29, 2002, from http://epaa.asu.edu/epaa/v10n18/.

Archer, J. (2005, April). Connecticut pledges first state legal challenge to NCLB law. *Education Week on the Web.* Retrieved June 2, 2005, from http://www.edweek.org/ew/articles/2005/04/13/31conn.h24.html.

Axtman, K. (2005). When tests' cheaters are the teachers. *Christian Science Monitor.* Retreived May 11, 2005, from http://www.csmonitor.com/2005/0111/p01s03-ussc.html.

Bauwens, J., Hourcade, J., and Friend, M. (1989). Cooperative teaching: A model for general and special education integration. *Remedial and Special Education,* 10, 2: 17–22.

Barkley, R. A. (1997a). The school situations questionnaire. In: *Defiant Children: A Clinician's Manual for Parent Training* (2nd ed.). New York: Guilford Press.

Barkley, R. A. (1997b). The home situations questionnaire. In: *Defiant Children: A Clinician's Manual for Parent Training* (2nd ed.). New York: Guilford Press.

Birmaher B., and Brent, D. A. (2003). Depressive disorders. In Martin, A., Scahill, L., Charney, D. S., and Leckman, J. F. (Eds.), *Pediatric Psychopharmacology: Principles and Practice.* New York: Oxford University Press.

Blair, J. (2001). Teacher tests criticized as single gauge. *Education Week on the Web.* Available at http://www.edweek.org/ew/articles/2001/04/04/29teach.h20.html.

Bloom, B., Englehart, M., Hill, W., Furst, E. and Kratwohl, D. (1956). *Taxonomy of Educational Objectives: The Classification of Educational Goals. Handbook I: Cognitive Domain.* New York: Longmans, Green.

Brown, R.T., and Sammons, M. T. (2002). Pediatric psychopharmacology: A review of new developments and recent research. *Professional Psychology: Research and Practice,* 33, 135-147.

Campbell, B., Campbell, L., and Dickinson, D. (1996). *Teaching and learning through multiple intelligences.* Boston: Allyn & Bacon.

Cannon, G. S., Idol, L., and West, F. J. (1992). Educating students with mild handicaps in general classooms: Essential teaching practices for general and special education. *Journal of Learning Disabilities,* 25(5): 314.

Cavanagh, S. (2004, December). U.S. gets better on latest international math and science exam: TIMSS shows improvement for U.S. minorities, but standing of 4th graders declines. *Education Week on the Web.* Retrieved February 28, 2005, from http://www.edweek.org/ew/articles/2004/12/14/16timss_web.h24.html.

Cavanagh, S. and Robelen, E. (2004). U.S. students fare poorly in international math comparison. *Education Week on the Web.* Retrieved February 28, 2005, from http://www.edweek.org/ew/articles/2004/12/07/15pisa_web.h24.html.

Cizek, G. J. (1998). *Filling in the Blanks: Putting Standardized Testing to the Test.* Washington, DC: Thomas B. Fordham Foundation.

Coffman, W. E. (1972). Essay examinations. In R. J. Thorndike (ed.), *Educational Measurement* (2nd ed.). Washington, DC: American Council on Education.

Coker, D. R. and Griffith, P. (1994). Collaboration in the classroom: Joint responsibilities for teachers for specified instruction. *Journal of Instructional Psychology,* 21(1): 3–7.

Conners, K. (1997a). *Conners' Rating Scales-Revised (CRS-R).* North Tonawanda, NY: Multi-Health Systems, Inc.

Conners, K. (1997b). *Conners Teacher Information Form.* North Tonawanda, NY: Multi-Health Systems, Inc.

Conte, A. E. (1994). Blurring the line between regular and special education. *Journal of Instructional Psychology,* 21(2): 103–113.

Dansereau, D. F. (1988). Cooperative learning strategies. In C. E. Weinstein, E. T. Goetz, and P. A. Alexander (Eds.), *Learning and Study Strategies: Issues in Assessment, Instruction, and Evaluation* (pp. 103–120). San Diego: Academic Press.

Davis, W. (1989). The regular education initiative debate: Its promises and problems. *Exceptional Children,* 55(5): 440–446.

Delate T., Gelenberg, A. J., Simmons, V. A., and Motheral, B. R. (2004). Trends in the use of antidepressant medications in a nationwide sample of commercially insured pediatric patients, 1998–2002. *Psychiatric Services,* 55: 387–391.

Dembo, M. H. (1981). *Teaching. for Learning: Applying Educational Psychology in the Classroom* (2nd ed.). Santa Monica, CA: Goodyear.

Doherty, K. M. (2002, February 27). Assessment. *Education Week on the Web.* Available at http://www.edweek.org/rc/issues/assessment/.

Driesler, S. D. (2001, September). Whiplash from backlash? The truth about public school testing. *National Council on Measurement in Education Newsletter,* (9): 3.

Duffy, E. (1972). Activation. In N. S. Greenfield and R. A. Sternbach (Eds.), *Handbook of Psychophysiology.* New York: Holt, Rinehart and Winston.

DuPaul, G. J., and Carlson, J. C. (2005). Child psychopharmacology: How school psychologists can contribute to effective outcomes. *School Psychology Quarterly,* 20(2): 172–187.

Education of All Handicapped Children Act of 1975, 20 U.S. Code, Sec. 401 (1975).

Ehrenfeld, J. (2001, October 24) The trouble with testing. *Education Week on the Web.* Available at http://www.edweek.org/ew/articles/2001/10/24/08ehrenfeld.h21.html.

FairTest (2002, January 7). *Statement of Fair Test: National Center for Fair & Open Testing in Reaction to President Bush Signing "No Child Left Behind Act.".* Available at http://www.fairtest.org/pr/ESEA%20press%20release.html.

Fletcher, J. M., and Reschly, D. J. (2005). Changing procedures for identifying learning disabilities: The danger of perpetuating old ideas. *The School Psychologist,* 59: 10–15.

Friend, M., and Cook, L. (1992). The new mainstreaming. *Instructor,* 30–36.

Gammel, D. L. (1992). Comments on the legal rights of students with Attention Deficit Disorder. *School Psychology Quarterly,* 7(4): 298–301.

Gamoran, A. (1992). Synthesis of research: Is ability grouping equitable? *Educational Leadership,* 50(2): 11–13.

Gardner, H. (2004). The Theory of Multiple Intelligences Revisited. Invited Address presented to the International Conference on Multiple Intelligences, Beijing, China, May 21, 2004.

Gardner, H. (2000). Intelligence Reframed: Multiple Intelligence for the 21st Century. New York: Basic Books.

Gardner, H., and Hatch, H. (1989). Multiple intelligences go to school. *Educational Researcher,* 18(8): 4–10.

Goetz, E.T., Alexander, P.A., and Ash, M.J. (1992). *Educational Psychology: A Classroom Perspective.* Upper Saddle River, NJ: Merrill/Prentice–Hall.

Goldstein, L. (2004). Harvard analysis is critical of "No Child" law. *Education Week on the Web.* Available at http://www.edweek.org/ew/articles/2004/02/18/23harvard.h23.html.

Gottfredson, L. S. (1997). Why *g* matters: The complexity of everyday life. *Intelligence,* 24: 79–132.

Gulliksen, H. (1987). *Theory of Mental Tests.* Hillsdale, NJ: Erlbaum.

Hakola, S. R. (1992). Legal rights of students with Attention Deficit Disorder. *School Psychology Quarterly,* 7(4): 285–297.

Hale, R. M., and Carlson, L. B. (1992). *Issues and Trends in Special Education.* Lexington, KY: Federal Resource Center for Special Education.

Halvorsen, A., and Sailor, W. (1990). Integration of students with severe and profound disabilities: A review of research. In R. Gaylord-Ross (Ed.), *Issues and Research in Special Education* (Vol. 1, pp. 110–172). New York: Teachers College Press.

Harrow, A. J. (1972). *A Taxonomy of the Psychomotor Domain*. New York: David McKay.

Hoff, D. (2005). Education department fines Texas for missing NCLP transfer deadline. *Education Week on the Web*. Available at http://www.edweek.org/ew/articles/2005/04/25/34texas_web.h24.html.

Holmes Group. (1986). *Tomorrow's Teachers*. East Lansing, MI: The Holmes Group, Michigan State University.

Individiuals with Disabilities Education Act Amendments of 1997, 20 U.S. Code, Sec. 101.

Individuals with Disabilities Education Improvement Act of 2004, 20 U.S. Code 1400 et. seq., Sec. 101.

Katzman, J., and Hodas, S. (2001). A proctor for the testers? *Education Week on the Web*. Available at http://www.edweek.org/ew/articles/2001/09/12/02katzman.h21.html..

Kavale, K., Kaufman, A. S., Naglieri, J. A., and Hale, J. B. (2005). Changing procedures for identifying learning disabilities; The danger of poorly supported ideas. *The School Psychologist*, 59, 16–25.

Keillor, G. (1985). *Lake Wobegon Days*. New York: Penguin.

Kerchoff, A. C. (1986). Effects of ability grouping in British secondary schools. *American Sociological Review*, 51: 842–858.

Koppel, T. (2000, June 6). Cheating teachers. *Nightline*. New York: American Broadcasting Company.

Krathwohl, D. R., Bloom, B. S., and Masia, B. B. (1964). *Taxonomy of Educational Objectives. Handbook II: Affective Domain*. New York: David McKay.

Kubiszyn, T., Brown, R. T. and DeMers, S. (1997). Pediatric psychopharmacology. In G. G. Bear, K. M. Minke, and A. Thomas (Eds.), *Children's Needs—II* (pp. 925–934). Bethesda, MD: National Association of School Psychologists.

Kubiszyn, T., and Carlson, C. I. (1995). School psychologists' attitudes toward an expanded health care role: Psychopharmacology and prescription privileges. *School Psychology Quarterly*, 10: 247–270.

Kubiszyn, T., Meyer, G .J., Finn, S. E., Eyde, L. D., Kay, G. G., Moreland, K. L., Dies, R. R., and Eisman, E .J. (2000) . Empirical support for psychological assessment in clinical health care settings. *Professional Psychology: Research and Practice*, 31(2): 119–130.

Kulick, J. A., and Kulik, C. C. (1984). Effects of accelerated instruction on students. *Review of Educational Research*, 54: 409–425.

Labellarte, M. J., and Ginsburg, G. S. (2003). Anxiety disorders. In A. Martin, L. Scahill, D. S. Charney, and J. F. Leckman (Eds.), *Pediatric Psychopharmacology: Principles and Practice* (pp. 497–510). New York: Oxford University Press.

Laitsch, D. (October, 2003). Reflections on implementation: Two years and counting. *Infobrief*, Issue 35. Association for Supervision and Curriculum Development. Available at http://www.shop.ascd.org/productdisplay.dfm?productid=107139.

Lazear, D. G. (1992). *Teaching for Multiple Intelligences*. Bloomington, IN: Phi Delta Kappan Foundation.

Likert, R. (1932). A technique for the measurement of attitudes. *Archives of Psychology*, 140.

Linn, R. L. and Gronlund, N. (2000). *Measurement and Assessment in Teaching* (8th ed.). Upper Saddle River, NJ: Prentice–Hall.

Loucks-Horsley, S., Kapiton, R., Carlson, M. D., Kuerbis, P. J., Clark, P. C., Melle, G. M., Sachse, T. P., and Wolten, E. (1990). *Elementary School Science for the '90s*. Alexandria, VA: Association for Supervision and Curriculum Development.

Marland, S. P., Jr. (1972). *Education of the Gifted and Talented: Report to the Congress of the United States by the Commissioner of Education*. Washington, DC: U.S. Government Printing Office.

Martinez, M. (2002, January 9). District fined for altering test data: Austin school district pleads no contest to tampering with TAAS reports, fined $5,000. *Austin American-Statesman*, p. A1.

Miller, G. A. (1956). The magic number seven, plus or minus two: Some limits on our capacity for processing information. *Psychological Review*, 63: 81–97.

Miller, M. J. (1992). *Model standards for beginning teacher licensing and development: A resource for state dialogue*. Available at http://www.ccsso.org/Publications/Download.cfm?Filename=corestrd.pdf.

National Commission on Excellence in Education. (1983). *A Nation at Risk: The Imperative for Educational Reform*. Washington, DC: National Commission on Excellence in Education.

National Council on Disability. (1989). *The Education of Students with Disabilities: Where Do We Stand?* Washington, DC: National Council on Disability.

National Council of Teachers of Mathematics, 1993, *Assessment standards for school mathematics*, Working Draft, October 1993, Reston, VA: NCTM.

National Research Council. (1999). *High-stakes Testing for Tracking, Promotion and Graduation.* National Academy Press: Washington, DC.

National Research Council. (2000). *Tests and Teaching Quality: Interim Report.* National Academy Press: Washington, DC.

News from the Committee on Education and the Workforce. (2004). *New National Survey Shows Public Support Rock-Solid for "No Child Left Behind" at Two-Year Mark.* Available at http://edworkforce.house.gov/press/press108/second/01jan/nclbsurvey010704.htm.

No Child Left Behind Act (2002). Public Law 107–110.

Olfson, M., Marcus, S. C., Weissman, M. M., and Jensen, P. S. (2002). National trends in the use of psychotropic medications by children. *Journal of the American Academy of Child and Adolescent Psychiatry,* 41: 514–521.

Olson, J. (2001, February 21). Usefulness of annual testing varies by state. *Education Week on the Web.* Available at http://www.edweek.org/ew/articles/2001/02/21/23annual.h20.html..

Osgood, C. E., Suci, G. J., and Tannenbaum, P. H. (1957). *The Measurement of Meaning.* Urbana: University of Illinois Press.

Parker, W. C. (1991). *Renewing the Social Studies Curriculum.* Alexandria, VA: Association for Supervision and Curriculum Development.

Pollock, J. (1992). Blueprints for social studies. *Educational Leadership,* 49(8): 52–53.

Popham, J. (2000). *Educational Mismeasurement: How High-Stakes Testing Can Harm Our Children (And What We Might Do About It).* Paper presented at a joint session of the National Staff Association for the Improvement of Instruction (NSAII) and the National Staff Association of Legislative and Political Specialists for Education (NALPSE), the National Education Association, Sanibel Island, Florida, November 19, 2000.

Quellmalz, E. S. (1991). Developing criteria for performance assessments: The missing link. *Applied Measurement in Education,* 4(4), 319–332.

Redding, N. (1992). Assessing the big outcomes. *Educational Leadership,* 49(8), 49–53.

Rehabilitation Act of 1973, 20 U.S. Code, Sec. 794 (1973).

Resnick, L., and Resnick, D. (1989). *Assessing the Thinking Curriculum: New Tools for Educational Reform.* Pittsburgh: Learning Research and Development Center, University of Pittsburgh.

Reynolds, C., and Kamphaus, R. (1992). *Behavior Assessment System for Children (BASC).* Circle Pines, MN: American Guidance Systems.

Robelen, E. W. (2001). Appellate court rejects challenge to Louisiana high-stakes testing. *Education Week on the Web.* Available at http://www.edweek.org/ew/articles/2001/09/26/04suit.h21.html.

Robelen, E. W. (2004a). Opposition to school law growing, poll says. *Education Week on the Web.* Available at http://www.edweek.org/ew/articles/2004/04/07/30pen.h23.html.

Robelen, E.W. (2004b). School law's story: Read all about it. *Education Week on the Web.* Available at http://www.edweek.org/ew/articles/2004/06/23/41media.h22.html.

Ross, R. P. (1995). Best practices in implementing intervention assistance programs. *Best Practices in School Psychology—III.* Bethesda, MD: National Association of School Psychologists.

Sacks, P. (2000). *Standardized Minds: The High Price Of America's Testing Culture And What We Can Do To Change It.* Cambridge, Mass.: Perseus Books.

Sailor, W., Gee, K., and Karasoff, P. (1993). Full inclusion and school restructuring. In M. Snell (Ed.), *Instruction of Students with Severe Disabilities* (4th ed.). Macmillan: New York.

Samuels, C. A. (2005). Suit says NCLB's demands conflict with those of IDEA. *Education Week on the Web.* Available at http://www.edweek.org/ew/articles/2005/02/16/23suit.h24.html.

Sax, G. (1989). *Principles of Educational and Psychological Measurement and Evaluation* (3rd ed.). Belmont, CA: Wadsworth.

Schrag, P. (2000, August). High-stakes tests are for tomatoes. *The Atlantic Monthly,* 286(2): 19–21.

Shavelson, R. and Baxter, G. (1992). What we've learned about assessing hands-on science. *Educational Leadership,* 49(8): 20–25.

Shavelson, R., Gao, X., and Baxter, G. (1991). *Design Theory and Psychometrics for Complex Performance Assessment.* Los Angeles: UCLA.

Slavin, R. (1990). Achievement effects of ability grouping in secondary schools: A best evidence synthesis. *Review of Educational Research,* 60: 471–499.

Stainback, S., and Stainback, W. (Eds.) (1992). *Curriculum Considerations in Inclusive Classrooms: Facilitating Learning for All Students.* Baltimore, MD: Brookes.

Steinberg, L. (2002). *Adolescence* (6th ed.). Boston: McGraw–Hill.

Sternberg, R. (1989). *Intelligence Applied.* New York: Harcourt Brace Jovanovich.

Szetela, W., and Nicol, C. (1992). Evaluating problem-solving in mathematics. *Educational Leadership*, 49(8): 42–45.

The states of NCLB. (2004, October). *Teacher Magazine*, 16(2), 32–33. Available at http://www.edweek.org/tm/articles/2004/10/01/02nclb.h16.html.

The Waco Experiment. (1998, June 12). *The Austin American-Statesman*, p. A14.

Thomas B. Fordham Foundation. (2005). *State standards fail to meet NCLB challenge*. January 5, 2005 press release. Available at http://www.edexcellence.net/foundation/about/press_release.cfm?id=14.

Thorndike, R. M., Cunningham, G., Thorndike, R. L., and Hagen, E. (1991). *Measurement and Evaluation in Psychology and Education*. New York: Macmillan.

Tombari, M., and Borich, G. (1999). *Authentic Assessment in the Classroom: Applications and Practice*. Upper Saddle River, NJ: Prentice–Hall/Merrill.

Tuckman, B. W. (1975). *Measuring Educational Outcomes*. New York: Harcourt Brace Jovanovich.

U.S. Department of Education. (2001). *Twenty-third Annual Report to Congress on the Implementation of the Individuals with Disabilities Education Act*, Washington, D.C.

Viadero, D. (1993). Disabled New Jersey boy must be placed in regular classroom, court rules. *Education Week*, 13(37): 12.

Wiggins, G. (1992). Creating tests worth taking. *Educational Leadership*, 49(8): 26–34.

Willoughby, S. S. (1990). *Mathematics Education for a Changing World*. Alexandria, VA: Association for Supervision and Curriculum Development.

Ysseldyke, J. E., and Algozzine, B. (1990). *Introduction to Special Education* (2nd ed.). Boston: Houghton Mifflin.

Zito, J. M., Safer, D. J., dos Reis, S., Gardner, J. F., Magder, L., Soeken, K., Boles, M., Lynch, F., and Riddle, M. (2003). Psychotropic practice patterns for youth. *Archives of Pediatrics and Adolescent Medicine*, 157: 17–25.

CREDITS

FIGURE 9.1: "An Example Performance Activity and Assessment" from R. J. Shavelson and G. Baxter, "What We've Learned About Assessing Hands-On Science" from *Educational Leadership*, 49 (8). Copyright © 1992 by the Association for Supervision and Curriculum Development. Reprinted with the permission of the publishers.

FIGURE 9.4: "Example Habits of Mind in Performance Assessment" from S. Loucks-Horsley, et al., *Elementary School Science for the '90's*; Parker, Renewing the Social Studies Curriculum; and Willoughby, *Mathematics Education for a Changing World*. Copyright ©1990 by the Association for Supervision and Curriculum Development. Reprinted with the permission of the publishers.

FIGURE 18.1: "Directions to Read Aloud to Students Taking the Comprehensive Tests of Basic Skills" from CTB/McGraw–Hill, TerraNova. Copyright © 1996 by CTB/McGraw–Hill. Reprinted with the permission of The McGraw–Hill Companies.

TABLE 18.1: "A Comparison of Standardized and Teacher-Made Achievement Tests" from Norman E. Gronlund and Robert L. Linn, *Measurement and Evaluation in Teaching*, Seventh Edition. Copyright © 1985 by Norman E. Gronlund and Robert L. Linn. Reprinted with the permission of Prentice–Hall, Inc., Upper Saddle River, NJ.

TABLE 18.2: "Raw Score to Scale Score with SEM for Raw Score and Pattern (IRT) Scoring Methods: Complete Battery, Form A, Level 12" from CTB/McGraw–Hill, TerraNova. Copyright © 1996 by CTB/McGraw–Hill. Reprinted with the permission of The McGraw–Hill Companies.

FIGURE 18.4: "Norm Group Description from the Tests of Achievement and Proficiency" from *Riverside 95* Catalog. Copyright © 1995. Reprinted with the permission of the publisher, The Riverside Publishing Company, 8420 West Bryn Mawr Avenue, Chicago, Illinois 60631. All rights reserved.

FIGURE 18.10: "A Press-On Label for the Tests of Achievement and Proficiency" from *Riverside 95* Catalog. Copyright © 1995. Reprinted with the permission of the publisher, The Riverside Publishing Company, 8420 West Bryn Mawr Avenue, Chicago, Illinois 60631. All rights reserved.

FIGURE 18.11: "A Criterion-Referenced Skill Analysis for a Fourth-Grader for the Iowa Test of Basic Skills (ITBS)" from *Riverside 95* Catalog. Copyright © 1995. Reprinted with the permission of the publisher, The Riverside Publishing Company, 8420 West Bryn Mawr Avenue, Chicago, Illinois 60631. All rights reserved.

FIGURE 18.12: "An Individual Performance Profile for a Fourth-Grader for the Iowa Test of Basic Skills (ITBS)" from *Riverside 95* Catalog. Copyright © 1995. Reprinted with the permission of the publisher, The Riverside Publishing Company, 8420 West Bryn Mawr Avenue, Chicago, Illinois 60631. All rights reserved.

TABLE 20.1: "Gardner's Multiple Intelligences" from H. Gardner and T. Hatch, "Adaptation of Multiple Intelligences Go to School: Educational Implications of the Theory of Multiple Intelligences" from *Educational Researcher*, 18, no. 8 (November 1989). Copyright © 1989 by the American Educational Research Association. Reprinted with the permission of the publisher.

FIGURE 20.4: "Teacher Participation throughout the Special Learner Identification, Instruction and Evaluation Process" from James E. Ysseldyke and Robert Algozzine, *Introduction to Special Education*, Second Edition. Copyright © 1990 by Houghton Mifflin Company. Reprinted with permission.

FIGURE 21.10: "The Conners' Teacher Rating Scale-Revised, Short Form." Copyright © 1997, by Multi-Health Systems, Inc. Reprinted with the permission of Multi-Health Systems, Inc.

FIGURE 21.11: "The Child Behavior Checklist-Teacher Report Form, or CBCL-TRF" from T. Achenbach, *Manual for the Teacher's Report Form.* Copyright © 1991 by Thomas M. Achenbach. Reprinted with permission.

FIGURE 21.12: "The Behavior Assessment System for Children Teacher Rating Form, or BASC-TRF, by American Guidance Systems, Inc. Reprinted with the permission of American Guidance Systems, Inc.

FIGURE 21.13: "The School Situations Questionnaire, or SSQ" from R. A. Barkley, *Defiant Children: A Clinician's Manual for Parent Training* (2nd ed.). Copyright © 1997 by Guilford Press. Reprinted with the permission of The Guilford Press.

INDEX